Falcon and Crow . . . took some of the earth brought up by Duck from the mud beneath the primeval floodwaters. . . . The Water was so deep that the trip down to the bottom and back to the surface had taken Duck a day and a half. Carrying some of the earth, Falcon flew west and Crow flew east, and as they flew they scattered grains of soil and told them to become mountains. Falcon and Crow met in the south at Tehachapi Pass. Crow, who had built the Sierras, asked Falcon, "Why didn't you put up bigger hills?" Falcon answered, "Because you had more dirt than I!"

—*Yokuts story of the making of the Sierra Nevada and the Coast Range*

CONTENTS

ILLUSTRATIONS

The Sierra Nevada—John Muir called it the "Range of Light, the most divinely beautiful of all the mountain chains I have ever seen." For those of us who come after him to write about it, that creates a problem. We are forever seeking to find a name that can trump the Scottish-born mountaineer and writer. We strive to come up with a descriptive word or phrase of our own that carries the same power and economy as his. Try the "Mighty Sierra." John of the mountains has staked that out as well. The same goes if you try to move from the shining granite of the range's core to its other components. Whether it is the "torrid" foothills, the "grandest and most beautiful" mixed-conifer forests, the range's meadows that he compared to "landscape gardens," its "glacial-sculptured" granite valleys, or even the lower but still inspiring volcanic summits of its northern end "covered with floods of lava," Muir has powerfully described them all.[1]

I had to put the powerful presence of Mr. Muir aside if I was going to succeed in my endeavor to write an environmental history of the Sierra Nevada. He was immensely important in shaping our image of the Sierra and in beginning the struggle to preserve some of its wonders from overdevelopment or destruction. But his contributions to its environmental history form only a piece of its nearly 10,000-year human story. We have, for better or worse, been making our marks on the range for a very long time. The interaction of humans with the Sierra over some ten millennia is the subject of this book. In it I offer a comprehensive summary of the ways in which people have contributed to changing the Sierra over the whole period of its human occupation. To symbolize this long relationship, I have based the book's title on a Yokuts creation story.[2] They were the people whose homeland was the area below Yosemite before the gold rush. Their account of the birth of the Sierra Nevada is both charming and evocative. In it, Crow triumphs over Falcon in a contest to see who could build the highest mountains in California. Crow won because he had more dirt than Falcon. We are dealing with Crow's range here.

The Sierra Nevada is one of the most unique geomorphic features in the world. It is the largest unbroken mountain range in the contiguous United States, stretching north to south for more than four hundred miles. It is not a series of mountain systems such as the Rockies or the Cascades and is best understood as a single ecosystem. It is the Sierra Nevada, singular, not the "Sierras."

It is my basic assumption that all human cultures that have lived in the range have changed it through their actions. There are clear cultural, economic, technological, and ideological differences in how successive generations of humans have gone about this changing. My narrative reflects how different times and people left their distinct impressions on the Sierra.

For most of its human history, native people used Sierran resources, occupied well-defined homelands, and began the shaping of its environment to suit their daily needs. The lower-elevation chaparral and oak woodlands and the higher-elevation forests evolved in part through their intelligent interaction with natural process at work in the range.

Since 1848, when commercial development of Sierran rivers and forests began, the Sierra has provided water, timber, minerals, grazing land, and recreational opportunities for a developing nation and region. Eight national forests are either wholly or partly located in the Sierra—Plumas, Tahoe, Eldorado, Stanislaus, Sierra, Sequoia, Toiyabe, and Inyo. Because of special environmental issues, the Lake Tahoe Basin Management Unit was carved out of two adjoining national forests as well following the Second World War. The privately owned lower-elevation Sierra Nevada commercial forestlands were completely cut over by the 1930s. Now that they have become productive of timber again, debate over their future is of key interest to foothill communities no longer dependent on extractive industries as they were in the past. The role of fire in these forests is the focus of intense national and state public interest as well. The Sierra's forested watersheds provide the lifeblood for California's and northern Nevada's urban and farming communities. The fate of the Sierra's public and private forestlands and its water is at the center of a national debate today.

Lake Tahoe, Yosemite, Sequoia, and Kings Canyon are also the subject of national and international interest and wonder. Early on they were recognized as worthy of protection from private exploitation, even as the rest of the range was being ravaged by uncontrolled development in the aftermath of the gold rush. Although Tahoe was not saved for public use, the movement to preserve the other scenic marvels for that purpose marks the beginning of conservation in America. Concern about these national wonders is part of a national and international debate over the use of natural spaces that continues to make headlines.

Throughout the range's human history, it also has been changing in response to nonhuman actions. The range is constantly evolving through the forces of uplifting and downthrusting, rockfall, erosion, climate change, and fire. Humans entered the range as another shaping force—glaciation—was declining in immediate importance. The onset of a massive human invasion since 1850 with the gold rush came when the Sierra was entering a warmer and wetter phase of its existence. All of our assumptions about how to live in the Sierra are based at best on a weather pattern that is only 150 years old. Drought cycles of many decades' length were common in earlier California weather history.[3] Modern California—including such cities as San Francisco and Los Angeles—has staked its future on being able to get water from the Sierra. Earthquake and climate shift could call all that into question.

The Sierra Nevada is home to countless forms of native plants and animals. Some of these are found naturally only in the Sierra. Some of its threatened nonhuman inhabitants, such as the California spotted owl and similar rare and endangered species, carry the same weight in development of forest policy as the California owl's cousin did in the Northwest. The Sierra's giant sequoia trees are so unique that a national park was created to protect them. One of the nation's newest national monuments provides even more protection for some of those giants left out in 1890 when the park was created.

Because of its significance, I believe the Sierra Nevada deserves a comprehensive environmental history. This work is a synthesis of primary and secondary sources. The Sierra is huge. Its human record is long and complex, and materials relating to it are widely dispersed. While it is generally recognized to be a single ecoregion, the great variety of geographic subregions it encompasses requires hard labor to bring the subject together into some coherent whole. To make it even more daunting, the rate of development of many of its heavily used regions today and the intense struggle over recent policy issues affecting the range are accelerating. For many years I devoted time to researching and writing about aspects of the range's environmental history. But it was only after retiring from a heavy teaching load that I finally decided that now was the time to act. The worst that could happen was that I would fail. And no one else I tried to talk into sharing the burden was willing to take it on with me.

My approach to the writing of this book is that of a teacher. But this is not a textbook. For over twenty-five years I taught California history to college undergraduates. My special area of interest and research during that time was the Sierra Nevada. It was easy to make the Sierra my life's work. I came to California predisposed to seek out the range as a rock climber and mountaineer even before I began to take study of its environmental history seriously.

Over the years I had begun to integrate physical knowledge of the range with the historical study of the human actions that contributed to changes in its natural spaces. This firsthand and direct experience with large portions of the Sierra helped me to better understand the range, especially when it came to appreciating the long struggles of individuals to protect some of its natural marvels, such as Mono Lake, Hetch Hetchy, and Mineral King. And that is true whether the preservation struggle was successful or not. Standing on a stump of a sequoia in Converse Basin or overlooking Hetch Hetchy Reservoir is a humbling experience. Once you see these places, it is easy to understand why people would give much of their life and time in a fight to preserve them.

Also, I found that taking students to places where human actions changed the landscape, and explaining how the changes occurred, led me to a deeper understanding of what environmental history in the Sierra is all about. It is one thing to write about an event or place, and quite another to integrate the physical setting with the human action that took place there. Consider, for example, the massive impact hydraulic mining had on the once-forested hillsides of a tributary of the Yuba River. All I have to do, literally, is look out my studio window to see Sailor Flat and the North Columbia Diggings. To the east of them is Malakoff Diggings, now a California state park. While standing there underneath a wall of compacted sand and gravel exposed to view by the actions of the hydraulic monitors or water cannons, I have explained to students that behind the immediate altered terrain lay a whole supportive series of industries. Capturing Sierran water was the key. I had to explain the logging of the area's forests to build dams and flumes from the cut timber, and the transportation and coordination of water delivery necessary to make the whole process work. Mercury was mined elsewhere in California, and tons of it was used to capture the fine gold that was washed into giant wooden sluices. It is not just the scarred hillsides of the immediate hydraulic mine or even the still-existing mercury deposited into the streams. The process involved the use of whole drainages and many industrial operations. The immense scale of the industry became clearer to me as I explained how it all worked.

The experience of understanding a Sierra-wide industry can also be achieved on a smaller and more intimate scale. You can sit in an aspen grove on Pole Creek in the Truckee River drainage, for example. It was there that I chose to explain how carvings on the white bark of the grove's trees documented the time that Basque sheepherders spent as part of a Sierran grazing industry over many decades.[4] I would ask the students to apply the experience of these herders and the thousands of sheep they tended at that one spot to nearly every river drainage or alpine meadow on both sides of the range. Whatever this did for the students, I know that it made the scale of impact clearer for me. I hope that this combination of understanding the terrain and having explained the effects of human actions in the Sierra will enliven and inform my narrative and analysis of Sierran environmental history.

My narrative describes how at different times people left distinct impressions on the Sierra, creating ecological baselines that reflect the dominant cultural perspectives that guided their actions. The key factors in each successive stage include technology, population size, and that elusive factor called "world view," which at times in the historic period I equate with formal government policies.

It has taken a quarter of a century for me to create this environmental history of the Sierra. Research for the work was conducted in the traditional ways of examining printed and manuscript sources, but it was also enriched by years of climbing, hiking, and "sauntering," as John Muir would say, throughout the Sierra. Francis Farquhar's *History of the Sierra Nevada*, Douglas Strong's *Tahoe*, Lary Dilsaver and William Tweed's *Challenge of the Big Trees*, Alfred Runte's *Yosemite*, Tim Palmer's *The Sierra Nevada: A Mountain Journey*, and John Walton's *Western Times and Water Wars* provided models for what I was trying to do: that is, to think of the range in broader historical and environmental terms.[5]

In 1995 and 1996, I was fortunate to participate in the Sierra Nevada Ecosystem Project (SNEP). My role in this monumental study of the Sierra was small when compared to the scope of the project. My job was to provide a summary of Sierra Nevada environmental history from 1820 to 1960. I was asked to put together all the pieces of the range's history that I had worked at, as well as using material given me by a number of other scholars working on SNEP. This activity forced me for the first time to "see" the range as a whole, including both of its flanks, and from top to bottom.

The book is primarily intended for the general public—to provide a comprehensive view of the Sierra's environmental history both for those who already know and love the range, as well as those who will come to know it over time. It can also serve professional historians by providing a comprehensive survey of the significant, but often widely dispersed, primary and secondary historical materials that pertain to the range. I hope that it will contribute to the creation of what historian Dan Flores refers to as "bioregional history"—specifically, a history that tries, as Flores suggests (using Fernand Braudel's idea of *longue durée*), to investigate the "'big view,' not through wide geographic generalizations in shallow time, but through analyzing deep time in a single place."[6] I have tried to create a comprehensive look at 10,000 years of how humans have changed the Sierra Nevada by their actions.

The Sierra Nevada is not just the subject of this book. It is also the key player. The range has always been a dynamic and active force to be reckoned with by individuals and societies that lived in it. Many have acted in its name, or fought tenaciously to use its resources for their own benefit. The beauty of its natural features has compelled political action and fierce loyalty far beyond its actual boundaries. I have chosen to organize this narrative in a generally chronological order that reflects what I believe are the major periods in the range's long environmental history. I modify this approach by applying a technique that I developed while teaching the hundreds of not completely dedicated students I have worked with over the years. I found it useful to draw students into a historic subject by relating a current example that reflected the spirit or substance of a past historical event. Obviously, this technique involved the use of analogy to stimulate students' interest. But it had another purpose. History as I see it is alive, and it has consequences. Past actions shape the present. Our forests today are the result of choices made in the past. And native people still live in the Sierra, although their influence has been reduced. Hopefully my mixing of past and present will act to illuminate my re-creation of the Sierran past.

As a final word, I want to make clear to readers that this book was not begun solely out of scholarly interest in a unique mountain range. That is part of the reason, of course. But there is something else at work on me. I feel a kinship with mountain environments. I grew up near the Wasatch Range in Utah and have climbed and hiked there and in the Tetons, Cascades, Sierra, Castle Crags, and the Swiss Alps. I am drawn to mountains just as other writers have been attracted to deserts, grasslands, red-rock canyons, seashores, giant forests, or lakes. But it is the Sierra Nevada where I have chosen to live, and I feel a strong commitment to tell its story. I hope that for others who care about the Sierra, this book can give them information and perspective they can use. I hope that it can aid in the ongoing debate concerning the fate of the Sierra Nevada, just as John Muir hoped his writing would. So there it is, caught in the long shadow cast by John Muir, even though I said I was going to try to break free. Oh well, being in Muir's shadow is not only deserved on my part, but it's not such a bad place to be.

ACKNOWLEDGMENTS

A good many people have played a role in the making of this book over a great number of years. Closest to hand are the supportive people at the University of Nevada Press. Margaret Dalrymple initially expressed interest in my work as editor-in-chief of the press in 1999, when it was a much longer manuscript, and she continued to provide guidance as project editor until its publication. Joanne O'Hare as editor shepherded it in the crucial period of presentation to the Editorial Advisory Board of the press and through the production process. And although Sandy Crooms is no longer with the Press, her cheerful support and advice as assistant director helped in getting the manuscript reviewed and accepted. I owe gratitude as well to William D. Rowley and two anonymous readers of the manuscript for their suggestions for its improvement. I would also like to thank Sara Vélez Mallea and Gerry Anders for their help on the manuscript.

Others have read parts of the manuscript and have given advice. They include Tim Duane, Tim Palmer, and Malcolm Margolin. Of special note here is my colleague of many years Michael P. Claytor, whose advice and extensive knowledge of California Native Americans made chapter 1 easier to write. He and I also walked together over most of the drainage systems of the northeastern and northwestern Sierra. As part of those adventures, he pointed out unerringly where native people had worked or lived and why they did so, giving me a sense of the long and close ties of these first inhabitants to the Sierra. Our main purpose in these jaunts was to search out Basque tree carvings in aspen groves and to study and compare how this interesting ethnic group blended their culture into Sierran use patterns. Gracias, Miguel.

Many others gave advice, help, and information, including Steve Nicola, Susan Lindstrom, Dana Supernowicz, Pamela Conners, Stephenie Tungate, William Tweed, Lary Dilsaver, James Johnson, Norman Wilson, William Laudenslayer, Linda Lux, Kevin McKelvey, Hank Meals, Douglas H. Strong, and Len Berardi. Special assistance came from Richard Markley, Carmel Meisenbach, and William Baker and other support staff at the Tahoe National Forest who gave me their help and information while I was using the archives there. Richard and Carmel also helped with summaries of information about Tahoe National Forest history while I was working on the Sierra Nevada Ecosystem Project.

Through good fortune I had the honor to be chosen to contribute a chapter to the monumental Sierra Nevada Ecosystem Project. I would like to thank Don C. Erman for placing his confidence in me to carry out my charge, and to Michael Barbour for giving sound editorial direction. I wish to thank Sierra College for approving my request for support for time off to work with SNEP, and for an earlier sabbatical leave to begin serious work on the Sierra. In another project, for the Forest Service Employees for Environmental Ethics, Bob Dale worked closely with me to see that my chapter on Sierra Nevada forest history was well integrated into that group's study of Sierran forests.

Research librarians and staff at the California Historical Society Library, the California State Library, the Huntington Library, the Bancroft Library, the Searls Historical Library, the Yosemite and Sequoia National Park Libraries, and the Library of Congress were generous with their assistance. I would also like to say thank you to Charlene Sims for her hard work in keeping my research files organized.

I would especially like to thank Phillip Sturges of the University of Utah for first inspiring me to want to become a teacher and professional historian, and for providing guidance as I learned the craft.

Finally I would like to express my gratitude to my wife, Louise, for her support. The book almost killed me, and without her love and confidence that I could do it, I am not sure that I would have persevered.

CROW'S RANGE

Introduction: Major Forces That Have Shaped the Sierra Nevada

Here are some environmental basics about the Sierra to get to a common starting point. Another historian might favor a different set, but I chose these because they figure significantly in the range's human history and at the same time provide a good introduction to what makes the Sierra Nevada unique.

By most accounts, the Sierra Nevada has been forming for at least 600 million years, and it has taken many shapes during its complex geological history. In its current form—the product of a massive uplift on a fault along its eastern flank—many geologists say that the Sierra is likely to be from 1 to 3 million years old. That makes it a relatively young mountain range when compared with such hoary counterparts as the Appalachians on the other side of the North American continent. Even so, the range's human environmental history, which began only some 10,000 years ago, represents a brief fraction of the Sierra's life span. During this phase, geology, climate, natural history, and fire have interacted with human activity, technology, and worldview to produce recognizable patterns in its landscape and resource use.[1]

An Ever-Changing Mountain Giant

The Sierra Nevada is always changing, making and remaking itself under the influence of powerful natural forces. Poet and Sierra Nevada resident Gary Snyder, referring to such mountain creating forces, put it this way:

Erosion always wearing down;
shearing, thrusting, deep plates crumpling,
still uplifting—ice-carved cirques
dendritic endless fractal streambed riffs on hillsides

. . . Streams and mountains never stay the same.[2]

When humans first entered the Sierra, a long ice age was temporarily releasing the range from its frozen grip. But the ice would return later in what has been called a mini–ice age, a last gasp that produced some small glaciers that have managed to hold on into the historical present.[3]

It is troubling to consider that what is referred to as "settlement" by European Americans began about 1850 to 1870, at the end of that mini–ice age.

All the development and planning of the reservoirs that keep California and northern Nevada alive today occurred late in the last brief century and a half when the current warmer and wetter climate pattern emerged. For many of the years of the range's life before that time, very long cycles of drought or cooling produced very different climate patterns. How many years of drought could California's or Nevada's urban centers and commercial agriculturists survive if old patterns reemerge?[4]

The shape-shifting nature of the range has affected its human inhabitants in different ways. Tectonic changes, often of interest only to geologists and geomorphologists, have also impinged upon the human history of the Sierra.

Consider an example from the eastern side of the range. Thousands of earthquakes have rattled the eastern Sierran community of Mammoth Lakes, California, since 1979. In that year a magnitude 5.8 quake occurred. It was followed the next year by four magnitude 6 temblors in a one three-day period. In the fall of 1997, quakes came with such frequency that they attracted national attention. Eight thousand quakes above 1.2 magnitude occurred between October and December. Thirty small quakes occurred in just four days the following April. Such periods of intense earthquake activity are called "quake swarms" by the United States Geological Survey scientists monitoring them, almost as if the tremors were a cloud of bothersome stinging insects.

But some of the quakes of this swarm were substantial, reaching magnitude 5. Responding to the increased activity, the USGS prepared a notice of possible volcanic hazard to heighten public awareness of potential risk. Merchants in the area promptly complained that the notice could frighten away fainthearted tourists and skiers, the lifeblood of the community.[5] Clearly, this was a classic case of conflict between Mammon and science in a mountain enclave.

In March of 1990, the subsurface volcanic activity triggering these earthquakes nearly turned deadly. A United States Forest Service supervisor seeking shelter in a March snowstorm entered a snowbound cabin near Mammoth and nearly died from breathing carbon dioxide. The odorless gas had been accumulating inside the structure, released from a volcano directly underneath. Both the cabin and Mammoth are located within the Long Valley Caldera. This valley was created 760,000 years ago in a previous eruption. Below the surface at Long Valley a new mass of molten magma was forming, pushing up a dome. One of the forces that created the Sierra Nevada was still very much at work.[6]

For residents of the Mammoth area, the trembling in Long Valley was a troubling reminder. Natural forces have a way of disrupting everyday life for those who have chosen this mountain environment. The veneer of civilization that modern technologies have built there is no guarantee of security. Can you imagine how you would feel in an earthquake swarm? How many earthquakes would it take to make you concerned? The imposition of urban patterns on a natural landscape such as the Sierra Nevada brings potential risks. The geological forces that molded the Sierra Nevada—faulting, uplifting, earthquakes, erosion, volcanism, and glaciation—shouldn't be spoken of in the past tense. These influences have varied in intensity over the millions of years it has taken to shape the range, but they remain with us.[7]

Mammoth stands as a useful metaphor for human contact with the Sierra Nevada. For over 10,000 years, people have had to cope with all the complex environmental and climatic variety that the range has imposed. This relationship of humans with the Sierra has been not only long, but dynamic. People have been involved in an intense and conscious shaping of the Sierran landscape and the use of its resources from the beginnings of human settlement. Collectively they have greatly altered the Sierra Nevada's "natural" systems. For thousands of years, waves of human occupation have left their imprint: native, Spanish Mexican, European American. But in the end, the Sierra Nevada still remains a force to be reckoned with in the lives of its occupants.[8]

Similar geological forces create different responses and actions in different cultural contexts. Prehistoric Northern Paiute people and suburban Mammoth Lake residents alike have coped with Sierran geology in their own ways. Obsidian was a by-product of volcanism. In prehistoric times the Paiutes used it to fashion projectile points for hunting, and also traded it with other Sierran natives who lacked this valuable mineral resource. But because the Paiutes did not build permanent structures and lived there only seasonally, the effects of quake activity would have had limited physical significance to them. For example, Paoha Island rose in nearby Mono Lake from a huge volcanic eruption sometime in the 1700s. The Mono Paiute oral tradition was undoubtedly enriched with the explanations that the event inspired. But my guess is that volcanic activity is far more troublesome to current Mammoth residents and commercial interests than to their prehistoric predecessors, what with the millions of dollars invested in urban infrastructure in that recreation community today.[9]

The Range That Crow Built

The Sierra is best seen as a whole—a single mountain range.[10] But as with anything as huge and complex as the Sierra Nevada, it is hard to take it all in with a brief, though accurate, descriptive phrase. It would help to consider some of its aspects from several angles, especially its physical characteristics and life zones. Putting the two together will help in understanding how its human history has developed.

The Sierra Nevada that the Yokuts attribute to the master builder Crow is both majestic and unique. Most often recognized for its splendid peaks, it is also distinguished by its forest-covered ridges, river and glacial valleys, lake basins, deep midrange western canyons filled with magnificent mixed-conifer forests, and of course its alpine meadows. It rises from its base on its eastern side some 11,000 feet from the Owens Valley floor to the summit of Mount Whitney at 14,495 feet. This is a far greater rise in elevation than the Rocky Mountains, which lift up only 9,000 feet above the Great Plains. One of the elements that makes the Sierra Nevada so unique is its granitic core, pushed up as a single block. Because this great granite mass sparkled and shone in the sun, John Muir called the Sierra Nevada the "Range of Light."[11]

The Sierra is massive, stretching some 430 miles along its north to south axis. It begins where the earliest rock formations of the range are overlaid by the Cascades' volcanic flows. From there it stretches far to the south to Tehachapi Pass. From the beginnings of its western foothills to the bottom edge of its steep eastern escarpment the range is around eighty miles wide. It is one of the three most dominant geomorphic features within California, along with the Central Valley and the Coast Range. And though mostly in California, the range flanks roughly a third of Nevada's long western border.[12]

Its existence shapes climate and life forms on both of its flanks. Pity poor Nevada, because the Sierra cuts off most of the Pacific storms that water the range. The Sierra Nevada can generate massive amounts of snow and rain seasonally. This water, when trapped by dams, is distributed within a complex, modern hydraulic system. It provides the basis of life for the farms of the Central Valley in California and northern Nevada. The largest cities of California and northern Nevada could not exist without it.[13]

If it were possible to cut the Sierra Nevada in half and observe it in profile on some gigantic laboratory table, another characteristic of the range would be revealed—the asymmetrical shape that resulted from the creative forces of upthrust and tilting. The eastern half of the range is marked by a steep escarpment along a prominent fault line. Observed from Owens Valley at its southeastern end, the jagged 14,000-foot peaks of that part of the range appear to rise almost straight out of the level valley floor. This escarpment is one of the most impressive in the world. Extending nearly the whole length of the range, it has acted as a barrier to weather as well as making human entry difficult. The western slope of the range, rising more gradually from

California's Central Valley, appears tame by comparison, although many of the middle and southern peaks viewed from their western crest lines are impressive.[14]

If we were still observing the Sierra Nevada on that imaginary laboratory table, but now viewing it in a north-to-south perspective, another aspect of the range would become apparent. The Sierra Nevada rises steadily in elevation from around 6,000 to 7,000 feet at its northern end to 13,000 feet in its center around Yosemite, then reaches heights of over 14,000 feet in the south before finally descending to around 6,500 feet at its southern terminus.[15]

There is a rough continuity in the single crest line of the northern two-thirds of the Sierra Nevada. It lies well to the east of the center of the range because of the long and gently rising western slope. The area immediately around Lake Tahoe is an exception to this general pattern. There a graben or subsidence occurred, causing a deep depression to form along a prominent fault line. This created not only the lake that is nearly 1,600 feet deep,[16] but also a dual crest that soon rejoins to the south. The area surrounding the lake remains geologically active.[17]

Continuing down into the southern one-third of the range, another transformation in the crest line becomes apparent. In the area south of the Kings River, the Sierra Nevada forms a prominent double crest. The highest peaks of the main ridge remain to the east, but a second or parallel crest referred to as the "Great Western Divide" rises to its west. Within this complex geological area lies Kings Canyon. It is the deepest river canyon in the United States at 8,240 feet—yes, even deeper than the Grand Canyon—and contains the longest river in the Sierra Nevada.[18]

This description of attributes of the range should make clear that no single human response to it is possible. Ways of life that might work in the western foothills are not possible on its eastern fringe. Population densities from pre-European settlement times to the present, for example, have always been greater on the western California flank.[19]

Life Zones and Forests

The Sierra Nevada is immense. It extends between 36 degrees to 40 degrees north latitude and by its sheer length encompasses several climatic or life zones. Other factors that contribute to shaping these zones and their floral inhabitants are elevation, latitude, rain shadow, soil composition, and slope effect. The distribution of vegetation in the Sierra Nevada generally follows these climate zones in clear patterns. John Muir, in describing these zonal differences on the western flank, went beyond the bare scientific terminology to describe four horizontal, colored bands, blending from one into the next. From an imaginary prospect on the crest of the Coast Range facing east, he saw the "torrid foothills" as belonging to the "rose-purple" spectrum, followed by a transition to the "dark purple" of the lower montane, then the "blue" of the upper montane, and finally the "pearl-white" of the subalpine and alpine zones.[20]

Elevation has a major influence on Sierran vegetation. For every gain in elevation of 1,000 feet, it is as if you had moved 300 miles in a northerly direction. Elevation gains generally bring with them lower temperatures, increasing precipitation, shallower soils, less oxygen, and higher winds, all of which have an effect on the plant communities within them. The areas that mark the transition from one zone to the next, referred to as "ecotones," are not distinct, but instead flow into each other as vegetation mixes. These transition zones are generally richer in species number and variety as a result of this mingling.[21]

The vegetation zones of the range include not only forests, but also a great diversity of other forms, among them meadows, chaparral shrubs, woodlands, savannas, canyons, and alpine habitats. The greatest diversity in Sierran plants occurs on the western side at the foothill elevation.[22]

Before the onset of European settlement, the Sierra Nevada was richer and more diverse in its vascular plant life. The vegetation of the montane regions was arrayed in a complex mixture shaped by such disturbances as fire (natural and human-caused), storms, insects, disease, avalanches, and flooding. This interplay of forces created a mosaic that has no modern counterpart. In the forested zones, trees developed in a succession, affected by the constant disturbances, until they achieved a stage known as "late successional," or more popularly, "old growth." Each of the forested stands had its own complex history.[23]

John Muir, in *The Mountains of California,* captured the beauty and diversity of the lower west-side montane forests in 1894:

> In many places, especially in the middle region of the western flank of the range, the main cañons widen into spacious valleys or parks, diversified like artificial landscape-gardens, with charming groves and meadows, and thickets of blooming bushes, while lofty, retiring walls, infinitely varied in form and sculpture, are fringed with ferns, flowering-plants of many species, oaks, and evergreens, which find anchorage on a thousand narrow steps and benches. . . .
>
> Here, too, in the middle region of deepest cañons are the grandest forest-trees, the Sequoia, king of conifers, the noble Sugar and Yellow

Pines, Douglas Spruce, Libocedrus, and the Silver Firs, each a giant of its kind, assembled together in one and the same forest, surpassing all other coniferous forests in the world, both in the size and beauty of its trees.[24]

Once the crest is reached, the prospect to the east is very different from what ecologist Elna Bakker called the "Great Green Wall," her memorable term for the western coniferous forests.[25] From the north-central portion of the summit, a view to the east takes in the Lahontan Basin, named after a Pleistocene-epoch lake that long ago disappeared. The forested areas of the eastern side were never as dense or complex as on the west, even before they were cut over to serve Nevada mining and urban development.[26]

The forests of the Sierra Nevada have been a center of concern for California and Nevada political officials and conservationists from at least the 1860s. Today these forests, on both public and private lands, continue to generate controversy and are the subject of major initiatives to manage them in an environmentally sustainable manner.[27]

Sierran Water

To respected geologist François Matthes, Yosemite was the "Incomparable Valley." As he made clear, though, its beauty came not just from the massive granite walls and glaciated domes, but also from the "splendor and variety of its falling waters."[28] Mark Twain expressed a similar view of the beauty of Sierran water when he first saw Lake Tahoe: "As it lay there with the shadows of the mountains brilliantly photographed upon its still surface I thought it must surely be the finest picture the whole world affords."[29] Both Matthes and Twain, separated though they are by time, place, and perspective, provide us with an understanding of what makes the Sierra Nevada unique amongst mountain ranges. The synergy created when its waterfalls, rivers, and lakes combine with its rock formations, forests, and meadows may not be found anywhere else in the world.

Sierran rivers and streams are renowned for their beauty. But Sierran waters have also been put to many practical uses since human occupation of the range began. Native use, while longer in duration than that which followed European American settlement, had less impact upon the Sierran water systems. Fishing weirs and some irrigation diversions amounted to ephemeral modifications that were often swept away in times of spring runoff.[30] Mining, grazing, and logging in the nineteenth century led to more permanent alteration. The development of dams to generate electricity or impound water for urban and agricultural uses has exponentially expanded human influence. About 60 percent of the water used by Californians today comes from the Sierra Nevada.[31]

The rivers and streams of the Sierra Nevada are included in five of the nine major hydrologic systems of California. Three of these, the Sacramento, San Joaquin, and Tulare Lake systems, capture all of the stream flow of the western Sierra Nevada. These systems are heavily influenced by the orographic, or rain shadow, effect of the range, which causes the warm and moist Pacific winds to shed their moisture content in the form of rain and snow as the wind currents sweep up the western side of the range. The combined runoff from snowpack, rain, and the base flow from the Sierra's vegetated watersheds creates many streams that run year round. The two major hydrologic systems of the eastern Sierra Nevada reflect the arid conditions engendered by the rain shadow. They are the North and South Lahontan (the latter sometimes referred to as the northernmost part of the Death Valley system).[32]

Because of the orographic effect, most streams of the range are found on its western slope. There are fourteen major rivers. Most of these have numerous tributaries and forks higher upslope. All of the major rivers and many of their tributaries have been significantly altered in historic times by mining and the construction of dams. The rivers of the northern and west-central Sierra Nevada include tributaries of the Sacramento, the Feather, Yuba, Bear, American, Consumnes, Mokelumne, Stanislaus, Tuolumne, and Merced. The southern Sierran rivers are the San Joaquin, Kings, Kaweah, and the Kern. The rivers of the north and central-west slope of the Sierra eventually all join the Sacramento and flow into the Delta. The rivers of the south, with the exception of the Kern, which in prehistoric and early historic times flowed into Lake Buena Vista, all join into the San Joaquin. It then merges in the Delta with the Sacramento, which in turn empties into San Francisco Bay.[33]

The rivers and drainage systems of the eastern slope of the Sierra Nevada are fewer, generally do not have as many large tributaries, and contain less water. Even though there is less water, some of the drainage systems, such as that of Lake Tahoe, are very complex. Tahoe's system contains sixty-three creeks. All of the eastern Sierran rivers flow into separate Great Basin lakes that have no outlets to the Pacific Ocean. Because of this condition, several of these lakes are extremely saline, Mono Lake being the most extreme example. The rivers of the eastern side include the Truckee, which originates in Lake Tahoe; the Carson, Walker, and the Mono drainage that includes Lee Vining and Rush Creeks; and the Owens.[34]

The Sierra Nevada contains thousands of lakes. Many originate in cirques created by melting glaciers. Other lakes and ponds result from rain and melting snow. These lakes vary in size from surface areas of 300 square miles to very small glacial tarns. As with its rivers, the western Sierra Nevada has the more numerous natural lakes. In Yosemite National Park alone, for example, there are 429 small lakes. While numerous, these western lakes are generally small. There are fewer lakes on the eastern flank because of the steepness of the escarpment and because precipitation is limited by the rain shadow. The lakes of the arid eastern side, ironically, are generally larger than their western counterparts. Of these eastern lakes, the most magnificent is Tahoe. It is one of the largest and deepest mountain lakes in the world, twenty-two miles long, twelve miles across, and nearly 1,600 feet deep.[35]

Fire and the Sierra Nevada

Since the time when the modern or so-called Mediterranean climate pattern of dry summers and winter rains became the norm in California, fire has been a constant factor in the shaping of the Sierra Nevada.[36] The summer always brings thunderstorms, and these create lightning strikes and fires wherever vegetation and weather conditions allow. While many observers of the range have noted this truth, naturalist Verna Johnston perhaps said it best of all: "Lightning fires are thus a natural climatic feature of the Sierran environmental scene, and rate as an important landscape architect of the past—as far back as similar climate prevailed, throughout the eons of time when fire suppression and control measures of today were totally lacking in the summer-dry forests."[37]

Well before humans entered the Sierra, fires were frequent. Their frequency varied according to such factors as weather conditions and climate, elevation, topography, and vegetation type. Before the arrival of humans, Sierran landscapes experienced fire once or several times during the lifetime of the dominant plant species, and these species' survival and reproduction were often dependent upon fire. Fire in the Sierra Nevada was not a problem—it was a necessity.[38]

A few examples can demonstrate fire's complex function in the Sierra. Fire stimulates seed germination in several plant species, such as deer brush. It promotes rapid growth in other plants, so that their life cycles can be completed before the next fire cycle begins. It prompted the evolution of fire-resistant buds, twigs, and bark in certain conifers. Other species, such as oaks, developed adventitious or ancillary buds to replace those that might become fire-damaged. Fire stimulates seed release in various pines and the giant sequoia, and flowering in plants such as soaproot. It regulates accumulation of forest debris, thus allowing certain seeds to take hold in relatively clear ground. In general, it has helped shape the pattern or mosaic of vegetation, promoting uneven-aged stands, varied vegetation types, and gaps in forest cover, reducing the danger of crown fires.[39]

With the advent of humans, culture added new dimensions to fire's role in shaping the range's environment. Cultural perspective is all-important. As with the other powerful shaping forces in the Sierra Nevada, fire can be viewed as either destructive or creative. For those generations of Americans raised on Smokey Bear's warning that only you can prevent forest fires, wildfire is seen as the enemy. For over a century, conservationists and forest managers have stressed the need to exclude or suppress it if possible. Consider the novel *Fire* by California writer George Stewart. Personified as a character, "Spitfire," the wildfire that drives the action of the novel is treated as a wily adversary from its infancy to its death as firefighters, consumed fuel, and changing weather conditions prevail to end its rampage of destruction. Stewart treats it as a natural, living force:

> Like a man, a fire exists in time. First as a tiny spark, it lives faintly. A breath of wind might blow it out; some drops of water quench it. But if born in happy circumstances, it feeds lustily and grows. It takes shape and develops structure, growing in fresh air along the ground, throwing off smoke and consumed air skywards. Where once it scarcely crept, now suddenly it walks and runs. The vigor and power of youth rises within it. It grows adult, and casts out sparks to kindle new fires.
>
> Yet, even as it sweeps ahead in power and glory, the shadow lies over it. . . . Failing to find food, rained upon, blown by contrary winds, fire loses vigor. Grown weaker, it searches less strongly for food, and so grows weaker still. It lies in the quiet of old age. At last, quickly or slowly, it dies.[40]

For Sierran Native Americans, fire in the forest and woodlands they occupied was seen very differently than by their fire-hating successors. Fire was a natural force to be respected and used effectively, not suppressed. Sierran natives preferred open conditions that fire helped sustain in forests. Fire made travel easier, gave them better protection from ambush, promoted the growth of food-producing plants and trees such as oaks, encouraged the growth of basketry materials, and enhanced the growth of deer browse—the list of things natives used fire to promote is long.[41]

In the decades that followed the coming of miners, stockmen, and lumbermen to the Sierra, fire continued to play a role in shaping the range. Large blocs of forestland were cut. Fires were caused through loggers' carelessness or planned by the sheepherders to open more ground for grazing. The forests remained open, as in the native period. But in the century that came after, the goal of the new managers and conservationists was to exclude wildfire where possible. And they were to prove to be remarkably effective.[42]

Between the 1880s and the 1960s, the U.S. Forest Service, National Park Service, and California Division of Forestry developed the skills and organization necessary to effectively suppress most wildfires. But if fire could be controlled in many cases, the resulting addition of fuel in the form of denser forest and brush cover created conditions that allowed huge, forest-destroying fires that lay beyond the best abilities of the federal and state agencies to suppress. In the 1950s and 1960s, experiments using "prescribed burning" to reduce understory thickets of small trees and the duff and needles that collected proved that fire had a place in the Sierra Nevada's forests. Not only could forests be returned to a more "fireproof " condition, but trees such as white firs that had grown in the wake of fire suppression and were in some instances crowding out the reproduction of sequoias and oaks could be controlled as well. In a draft of a plan to manage the forests of the Sierra Nevada, the Forest Service advocated prescribed burning as one method of reducing overly dense forest cover that had resulted from earlier fire-suppression policies. Fire again, as in prehuman and native times, was accepted as a necessary force in shaping healthy forests.[43]

The Other Shaping Force: Human Influence

The people who have interacted with the Sierra Nevada have molded it in distinct patterns. These people include the native inhabitants who originally occupied and changed the range, early Hispanic American interlopers whose contact first brought European influences and catastrophic disease to the foothills, and the later European American and other occupiers who began the systematic exploitation of its resources and ushered in successive waves of changing uses.

Environmental history involves analysis of the interaction of human beings with the natural environment over time. The patterns of change in the Sierran environment reflected the worldview, technology and economy, and population size of successive human groups. Effects of these three elements have in turn brought changes in the geography, hydrology, and biology of the Sierra.

For an aging white male professional historian living in a postmodern culture, it was difficult to fully understand the native worldview in what has aptly been called the "Natural World of the California Indians."[44] I have relied not only upon professional anthropologists and geographers, but also on accounts from descendants of Sierran Native Americans to help give me insight into the lives of those early residents of the Sierra Nevada and their role in shaping the range.

Writing about the worldview of the non-native successors who shaped the Sierra following the displacement of native control was also difficult. But a unifying theme emerged from study of the data. The key lies in understanding how attitudes toward the range clearly changed during its human history and how these perceptions actually contributed to alterations in the landscape. They evolved from the defensive and tentative approaches of the Californios and early European American immigrants through the more aggressive actions of the gold miners and resource developers and onward to the successive stages of conservationists, public agency managers, and environmentalists into the twenty-first century.

Public attitudes and the public policies they produced interacted to play an important part in shaping the Sierra. The interaction of attitudes shaped by land-use laws with actions that encouraged rapid and unregulated resource development lay behind the opening of the Sierra during the time from 1848 to the 1880s. Concern about this unregulated use led to the rise of conservation in California and the nation, defining a new view of natural spaces even if no one knew how to go about protecting them. Since the turn of the twentieth century, most of the Sierra Nevada's land has come to be managed by public entities, ranging from the National Forest and Park Services to municipal water agencies and local irrigation districts. These agencies' views also evolved over time, influenced by changes in public attitudes toward the range.

This book is not a public policy history, however. Changing public policies need to be considered because they underlay how successive generations thought about the range, and in turn influenced how the Sierra Nevada would be used. They will be integrated into a broader account of how human influences have acted along with uplift, glaciation, climate, natural history, and fire in the Sierra Nevada's environmental history.

Chapter 1 focuses on the Sierra Nevada's native people and the changes that came with the invasion by Hispanic and other European Americans. It introduces the native world and the environmental effects these first inhabitants had on the Sierra Nevada. The disruption and near destruction of the native populations had not only tragic consequences for these earliest inhabitants, but environmental effects as well. The Sierra Nevada that its native people had helped to shape was subjected to powerful influences created by invading cultures that nearly obliterated the native use of the range.

Chapter 2 covers the effects of the discovery of gold and the uncontrolled use of Sierra Nevada resources that came with it. The chapter deals with the development of gold mining and its rapid transformation into an industry that exerted tremendous influence on the range as a whole. The direct effects of gold mining on Sierran stream environments, wildlife, and forestlands are discussed, as well as the effects of the supporting industries that the gold rush spawned. These included logging, grazing, water resource development, market hunting, urbanization, and transportation.

Chapter 3 focuses on the beginnings of conservation as a movement in the Sierra Nevada. That new way of looking at the Sierra and its resources grew in response to concerns about the environmental effects of unregulated use of the Sierra during the gold rush period. The chapter places the Sierra Nevada experience in the context of a larger national movement. It discusses the origins of conservation and the beginnings of state and national parks in the Sierra as Yosemite Valley, the adjoining high country, and sequoia groves were given a new status. The consideration of Lake Tahoe at this time for inclusion in a state park, and the reason it was not given park status, is also discussed. The forests of the Sierra during this period also became the concern of state and national forestry conservation advocates, leading to the creation of Sierra Nevada forest reserves in the higher-elevation forests of the range.

Chapter 4 discusses the growing recognition that national regulation of the uses of reserved lands in the Sierra and elsewhere required the creation of regulatory agencies such as the U.S. Forest Service and the National Park Service. The tragic role of Hetch Hetchy's transformation into a reservoir and the diversion of Owens Lake water into the Los Angeles Aqueduct are related as examples of municipal agency actions affecting the range's waters at that time. The policies and actions of two new federal resource agencies (the Forest Service as "caretaker" and the Park Service as "popularizer") in the Sierra Nevada before World War II are included here. The fateful commitment to total wildfire suppression in Sierran forests was one of the most important policy decisions of the era. Thus, agency management of the Sierra became another agent of environmental change.

The next chapter covers the period after the Second World War, when tremendous demand for timber, water, and recreational opportunities led to increased use of public lands, parks, and lakes such as Tahoe in the Sierra Nevada. In its effects, the postwar growth phase matched or exceeded the use of Sierran resources that occurred during the gold rush period. The difference was that the federal agencies, through "intensive management" in the national forests and meeting the goals of "Mission 66" for the Park Service, accomplished increased use (and therefore an intensified environmental alteration of the Sierra) as part of expanded agency planning.

Chapter 6 details the rise, from the 1960s to the 1980s, of a new environmental movement in response to the energetic promotion of resource use. Through political organization, the passage of environmental legislation, and federal and state court action, all public agencies operating in the Sierra were forced to consider and act upon the effects of their growth- and use-oriented policies. Wilderness and Wild and Scenic River designations under federal law and the reconsideration of policies in the national forests and parks are considered, along with numerous environmental struggles in the range. Environmentalism, like conservation before it, became a new shaping force in the Sierra.

Chapter 7 takes the reader to the post-1990 and post–California spotted owl world. All public agencies with responsibilities for the range's forests and wildlife were forced to come to grips with the environmentally destructive effects of management decisions that had placed commodity or service supply as their primary purpose. The 1990s began with a startling recognition by the public that the whole of the Sierra Nevada was in peril from overuse and agency actions. The response of the state of California and federal agencies to this public awakening was to shift to the concept of ecosystem or bioregional management, with long-term sustainability and survival of the "resources" of the Sierra as a goal. The uneven response of the agencies operating in the Sierra to this new bioregional management paradigm is considered in this last chapter.

1: A Sierra Shaped by Native People

For the Ahwahnichi of the south-central Sierra Nevada, Yosemite Valley was an everyday place. It was loved, to be sure, and the people who considered it part of their home territory have struggled to maintain their ties to it regardless of the efforts of military conquerors and federal authorities to deny their rights of ownership and occupation.[1] This devotion to the Valley is clearly expressed in the following Miwok creation story:

> The Great Spirit gathered a band of his favorite children and led them on a long and wearisome journey until they reached the Valley now known as Yosemite. Here the Great Spirit made them rest and make their home. Here they found food in abundance for all. The streams were swarming with fish. The meadows were thick in clover. The trees and bushes gave them acorns, pine-nuts, fruits and berries, while in the forests were herds of deer and other animals which gave them meat and skins for food and clothing. Here they multiplied and grew prosperous and built their villages.[2]

The Valley is at about 4,000-foot elevation and snowy in winter. So this group of Mountain Miwok spent part of their year in villages lower down, on the Merced River at El Portal, Bull Creek, Hite's Cave, or at other sites nearby on the Tuolumne River. This was more typical and warmer western Sierra foothill country, and it was here that permanent villages were located. But when the snow receded, many Ahwahnichi reclaimed their Valley camps, accepted other Miwok and Yokuts visitors from adjacent areas, and made the long trek over the Sierra to renew trade and other social contacts with their Mono Paiute neighbors to the east.[3]

Yosemite was a place where people lived, where they raised families, and where they obtained food, fibers, and construction and ceremonial materials that made their life possible. They also burned unwanted shrubs and trees and thus helped maintain the Valley in an open and more usable condition.[4] The same was true for other native groups whose homelands were in the range. As with the Ahwahnichi, these other native groups have made attempts to assert their claims to traditional areas.[5]

Sierran Natives: The Mountain Miwok As Icons

For thousands of years Sierran natives made the range their home. In areas they inhabited or used frequently, they may have played a role in influencing the local geography, landscapes, and hydrological systems. Some anthropologists now call their actions a form of environmental management. The choices they made in their relationship with plants of their home regions may have affected local forest composition, as well as shaping nearby meadows, river system environments, and grasslands. Their hunting activities may have influenced population numbers and diversity of the mammals that they regularly killed. Most significant of all their effects on Sierra landscapes was their intelligent use of fire. Through their actions they worked within natural fire conditions to make those portions of the Sierra they inhabited relatively fireproof, useful, and productive of diverse floral resources.[6]

The native period provides a constructive example in how people can imagine a sustainable relationship with the Sierra, one that left all of its natural systems basically intact even though modified by human occupation. It is the only period in the Sierra Nevada's environmental history when such a relationship of humans with the range has existed.

As a result of the great diversity in subregions, elevations, latitudes, and vegetation types, and because of the differences between the east and west slopes of the Sierra, generalizations about Sierran natives' use of the range are not simple to make. Also, the fact that much of the native way of life in the Sierra was rapidly destroyed in the nineteenth century makes reconstruction of their lives difficult. But by focusing on the Mountain Miwok and the Awahnichi, we can piece together a tentative picture of the native environmental world. This account of their life-ways sets the stage for a more comprehensive consideration of Sierra Nevada native environmental history later in the chapter—one that will introduce other native groups and their interaction with the range.

Collectively, the Mountain Miwok occupied a very large portion of the central-western slope of the Sierra. They shared many cultural traits with their neighbors because all occupied similar environmental zones stretching north to south. The Miwok also traded and had contact with eastern Sierran groups including the Washoe and the Mono Paiute, thus bringing a blending of eastern with western Sierran cultural patterns.[7] Fortunately for historians, the Mountain Miwok and Ahwahnichi have been widely studied by anthropologists. They were also the focus of early observations by the first Europeans and European Americans to enter the range.[8]

In modern aesthetic terms, the Miwok people were certainly among the most fortunate of California natives. The territory they occupied included some of the most beautiful landscapes of the range, encompassing the drainages of four major Sierran river systems, the Mokelumne, Stanislaus, Tuolumne, and Merced, as well as numerous tributaries of these rivers. The nearly twin and spectacularly beautiful Yosemite and Hetch Hetchy Valleys were within tribal boundaries, as was the sequoia grove at Mariposa. The three major geographic groups that made up the Mountain Miwok (Northern, Central, and Southern) utilized all the territory from the eastern edge of the San Joaquin Valley up to the snowy regions along the Sierran crest.[9]

The Miwok inhabited all the life zones of the central Sierra, ranging from the lower Sonoran through the upper Sonoran and on into the transition zone higher up. Most permanent village sites were located below the 4,000-foot level. Like other California Indian groups, the Miwok used higher-elevation areas seasonally—archeologists have discovered numerous village sites that were reoccupied after the snow disappeared. Yosemite Valley was also a travel route for trade.[10]

The Sierra Miwok were not numerous compared with their related Plains Miwok neighbors. But for a mountain people their population was relatively large—somewhere between 2,000 and 2,700.[11] Some village sites were quite large and long occupied, as witnessed by recent discoveries near Sonora, California. In 2001 a California Department of Transportation roadbuilding project unearthed an Indian site of at least twenty acres. Dated artifacts show that the Miwok and their predecessors used the area for at least 8,000 years. A CalTrans archeologist said that because of its off-and-on habitation for thousands of years by so many people, "we're probably looking at the equivalent of a town."[12]

Dependence on natural food sources tied the Miwok closely to their environment. The lower reaches of their territory connected them to the freshwater marshes associated with the San Joaquin River. Adjacent to this and moving up the major river systems they encountered broadleaf deciduous forests growing along the riverbanks and in the rich bottomlands. The lower and upper Sonoran areas of Miwok territory contained slower-moving streams with riparian vegetation such as willow and other plant species associated with meadowlands. Live oak, gray pine, and blue oak mixed with dry grassland above this.

Rocky slopes marked a further gain in elevation. In the transition or lower montane zone the streams became swifter and boulder talus and rocky cliffs appeared. Two types of chaparral could be found there. Black and golden oak, yellow pine, and Douglas fir were the dominant tree species. In the upper montane, subalpine, and alpine zones, even swifter streams occurred.

Riparian vegetation included aspen at this higher elevation. Lodgepole and Jeffrey pine and red fir also became evident. Granite outcroppings and cliffs and deep river canyons were part of this mountain environment as well.[13]

In their quest for food, the natives incorporated nearly all mammals, birds, reptiles, fish, and mollusks into their larder. Only one bird, according to pioneer ethnologist Ralph Beals, lay outside the category of what was defined as food: the turkey vulture. Its feathers did find ceremonial uses, however. A Miwok creation story even said that the legendary Coyote made native chiefs from turkey vulture feathers, whereas crow feathers sufficed for making common people.[14]

The overall Miwok territory was very large, but most Miwok lived in small communities and occupied only a relatively small portion of it. Within this tribal area they utilized all the life-zones that the village "owned." Their knowledge of these places was intimate and included names and oral stories for all the local features and various plants and animals they encountered. Within the village's sphere, they carefully categorized their resources and visited productive sites on regular seasonal cycles. They applied appropriate technologies not only to gain the resource but also to ensure its long-term availability. Proper ceremonial observances were part of this process. Some areas supplied food. Others were regularly visited to provide materials for shelter or cordage, or for minerals.[15]

Plants were extremely important in the Miwok resource inventory. Acquiring knowledge through observation and practice was key to native survival, and the plants they interacted with evolved through natives' intervention and manipulation.[16] A classic study of Miwok culture by Samuel Barrett and Edward Gifford illustrates the depth and breadth of native knowledge of the natural bounty in their territory. Available resources provided all the necessities of life, but it was food resources that tied the Miwok most closely to the natural environment. Although animals, birds, fish, and insects were all important parts of their diet, the plant world served as the most important and most reliable source of seasonal and storable food and medicines. Barrett and Gifford take thirty-six pages of their "Miwok Material Culture" to list and discuss various plants used by those living near Yosemite. Sixty-seven plants are noted for medicinal purposes alone.[17]

Miwok use and management of plant resources was intended to encourage abundance. Ethnographic accounts given by surviving native elders point to a spiritual connection with plants that they believed ensured continuing bounty. Proper attention and ritual were needed to show that humans cared for plants and animals. Human-caused disturbances, as well, may have helped shape certain plant species. Pruning of dead or old branches helped restore productivity in useful plants. Fire was probably the natives' major land-use tool. Controlled fire eliminated unwanted plants or trees and promoted new growth that was more useful than older woody stems and branches. It kept areas open to encourage desirable plants to spread and at the same time produced browse that attracted deer.[18] The Miwok credited the mythical figure Coyote with bringing fire to them and their neighbors, the Yokuts people. He was said to have stolen it from its guardian, Turtle, thus allowing humans to keep warm and to benefit in countless other ways.[19]

Of special interest to resource managers in the Sierra today is how intervention by the Miwok in the sequoia/mixed-conifer forests of what is now Yosemite National Park possibly acted to sustain sequoia health. The Mariposa Grove, as we call it today, was a long-occupied Miwok village site. Its native owners relied on it for food and for materials for making weapons, fiber, and baskets. By burning on a regular basis, the Miwok villagers possibly shaped the structure, composition, and vegetation patterns of the grove and the surrounding forestland. Their fires helped sequoia seed germinate. Along with the natural force of lightning, they may have played a role in maintaining the grove and controlling undergrowth that could have fueled life-threatening or resource-destroying large fires.[20]

The Sierra Nevada, as illustrated by this account of Miwok life, was shaped in part by Sierran natives long before European contact. The geography, hydrological systems, forest structure, plant and animal species, and other important natural elements of the range were modified to suit people who called it home.

Introducing Sierran Native Cultures and Their Homelands

Native Sierrans have had a long and dynamic relationship with the range. This bond imposed restrictions—seasonality and mountainous terrain set limits even today—on the use of its resources. In return, native people used burning and proto-horticultural practices to increase the productive capacity of the land. From this relationship emerged a native perception of the Sierra Nevada and its natural systems—what could be called a landscape of the mind. At the same time, the landscape itself was formed in part by this mindset.[21]

Who were the people who lived in and shaped the Sierra for so many thousands of years? How did these original Sierrans interact with the range and shape it to their needs?

Just as the last glaciers that helped shape the primeval Sierra Nevada began to subside, human beings entered the range. Exactly when these Native Americans first occupied California, Nevada, and the Sierra Nevada is hotly debated by archeologists, but it was probably between 11,000 and 8,000 years ago in the early Holocene, as the region's weather stabilized and grew warmer at the end of the Ice Age. Evidence for this Sierra Nevada occupation is fragmentary, but tantalizing to consider.[22]

The earliest Sierran habitation may have occurred along the northeastern escarpment and the adjacent high country. These first Sierrans are likely to have come from the nearby Great Basin. There the unstable climate— associated with the transition away from Pleistocene patterns—may have forced them to seek refuge in the eastern Sierra to escape drying conditions in the basin. A series of related cultures, called "Tahoe Reach," "Spooner," "Martis," and "Kings Beach" by archeologists, developed over an 8,000-year-long sequence. It is generally assumed that the late Kings Beach group is ancestral to the present-day Washoe. Occupation farther south, in the Owens Valley area, has been dated to 8,000 years ago as well.[23]

Entrance into the western flank of the Sierra Nevada came later. Evidence has been found in the southern and central areas adjacent to the Sierra Nevada for human activity around 7,000 to 8,000 years ago. Native Californians may have visited and crossed over the Sierra Nevada at this time but chose to settle permanently elsewhere. Settlement may have been delayed because of low population pressures in other California areas. Those places—plains, valley marshlands, and riparian woodlands—simply offered an abundance of food and material resources. The Sierra Nevada did provide lithic materials, and therefore higher-elevation camps were periodically occupied in very early times. Information gathered at lower foothill sites established nearly 3,000 years ago gives some idea of where their residents lived and camped. It is clear that they relied on their hunting and collecting skills to feed their relatively small populations, thus giving archeologists some idea of their social organization as well. They used Sierran lithic resources, often crossing even the more rugged southern part of the range to acquire them.[24] The technology for acorn use, developed around 1,400 to 1,500 years ago, promoted permanent settlement of the southern and central Sierran foothills.[25]

From a rangewide and ecological perspective, the native people of the Sierra Nevada in the late prehistoric period fall into two main groups. First, there were those who lived in the warmer and moister western flank of the range. These natives relied on hunting, gathering, fishing, and what some anthropologists call "prehorticultural" activities—pruning, tending, and fire management—to provide for their material needs. Then there were those who collected, hunted, pruned, tended, and burned—or, in one notable case, practiced a form of irrigation horticulture—in the arid eastern regions of the range. Both of these groups traded widely and used the higher elevations in the range seasonally.[26]

The population of Sierran native people is estimated to have been about 90,000 to 100,000 at its highest point, just before European contact. Most of this population was concentrated on the western slope where resources were greatest.[27]

Ethnographers and surviving descendants of these Sierran natives tell how prehistoric occupants of the range went about their daily lives and interacted with the environment. Their names and territorial homelands are well known for the period when historic contact occurred.[28]

Often the major drainages of Sierra Nevada rivers and their tributaries marked well-defined group boundaries for west-side dwellers. Although there were some exceptions, complete watersheds of Sierran streams were generally included within these territories. The Maidu lived in the area from Lassen Peak south to the Sierra Buttes, including portions of the northern Feather River system. The Konkow claimed the territory from the lower part of the Feather River drainage southward into the American River basin. The Nisenan homeland included the drainages of the Yuba, Bear, and American Rivers from the foothills to the Sierra Nevada crest. The Miwok of the central Sierra Nevada lived in the very large area stretching from the northern reaches of the Mokelumne River drainage south to the Fresno River. The southern part of the range was home to four groups. The Yokuts established themselves in the foothills south of Miwok territory. The Monache or Western Mono occupied the upper San Joaquin and Middle Fork of the Kaweah River to the south of the Yokuts. The Tubatulabl people had a homeland in the mountainous areas drained by the Kern River system. Below this, the Kawaiisu established their villages at the southern end of the range.[29]

On the eastern side of the Sierra Nevada, except for the Owens Valley, seasonal occupation, rather than settled homelands, was the rule. Harsher weather and diminished resources in this generally arid and higher-elevation region set limits on permanent occupation. The Washoe claimed the northeastern part of the range from the Great Basin to the Sierra crest, moving beyond it at times for trade or other purposes. Lake Tahoe, included in their territory, was not only a place to catch fish in great numbers during springtime spawning but also represented the center of the Washoe spiritual world.[30] The Northern or Mono Paiute seasonally utilized the area below the Washoe down to Mono Lake, ranging widely in their collecting and hunting rounds. The Owens Valley Paiute occupied the well-watered valley of the Owens River. They lived year round in permanent villages and outnumbered their east-flank neighbors.' This territorial stability came from their development of specialized irrigation systems, which included dams and canals that utilized Bishop Creek and other runoff sources in the drainage. The water collected and controlled by them was used to encourage natural seed-grass growth. The Panamint or Western Shoshone—classified by some as marginally involved at the extreme southern end the Sierra Nevada—utilized the area south of the Owens Valley.[31]

Natural World, Economy, and Environmental Influences

Imagine a life tied directly with the natural world. The leap of consciousness from our postindustrial times to that of the Sierra Nevada natives takes us not very far back in years—only about two hundred. But the leap to their world, where the forces of nature were at the center of their existence, is much greater. Anthropologists have tried to help those of us with an interest in that native worldview to bridge the gap. Consider this reconstruction by Robert Heizer and Albert Elsasser of what they call "The Natural World of the California Indians":

> Thus it can be seen that the Indian lived in two worlds at the same time. One was the practical everyday world where you were hungry, your wife was sulky, you stubbed your toe on a rock, and you got in a quarrel with your neighbor who had thrown a sharp deer bone out his door, which you stepped on. The other was the very real supernatural world where trees, animals, springs, caves, and mountains contained souls, or spirits, which had to be treated with respect. For this reason, taking a part of any tree, killing an animal, using a spring, or entering a cave was prefaced by some kind of ritual, however simple, in the form of a request or an acknowledgment.[32]

The world inhabited by Sierran natives was not "pristine"; that kind of world only existed before the Holocene and the earliest human arrivals. But as Gary Snyder has noted, the natural world of the native was one where most ecosystems were "fully functioning," even if they had been changed by human actions. All of the plant and animal communities that survived or reestablished themselves after post–Ice Age climate stabilization were still there.[33]

Native Sierrans in the time before the arrival of Europeans established a sustainable economy, gave tribute and respect to the nonhuman forces around them, and helped shape the landscapes they occupied. Their population size was certainly a factor in how this relationship developed. Whether they could have maintained such a relative balance into future times, had Europeans not arrived, cannot be known.

Key to this balancing act was a thorough understanding of what the environment could provide. This knowledge came through observation, experimentation, and classification. Learning what was useful, edible, and adaptable was the work of both women and men. Though activities such as hunting and basketmaking were usually determined by gender, the community was a productive whole. Sierra Nevada Native Americans utilized all of the life zones in the range, moving as seasons changed and different natural foods matured or ripened.[34]

The food economy of Sierra Nevada natives on both western and eastern sides was based on a mixture of hunting, fishing, and gathering. An impressive array of wild animal, fish, insect, and plant resources awaited them. Prehorticultural activities also shaped landscapes and plant species to the needs of the mountain people, enhancing this balanced food culture. All required a highly developed system of effective management of wild food sources. The Sierra Nevada, with its many biotic zones and seasonally available resources, provided a rich supply base.[35]

Seasonal variation in availability of food sources meant that the settled villagers of the western side and the more nomadic groups from the Great Basin both moved from lower to higher Sierran elevations on seasonal cycles. Although the Sierra Nevada has a moderate climate because of its latitude, late fall was a time for most to move down to less snowy areas, where they gathered into permanent villages. Stored foods such as acorns in the western foothills or pinyon or grass seeds in the Carson and Owens Valleys to the east sustained life during the winter. Streams and lakes, especially in spawning season, supplemented other food sources on both flanks.[36]

It is impossible for a person with modern sensibilities to enter fully into the natural world of Sierran natives. But some understanding of its dimensions comes to us from ethnographic sources and the memories of native elders. California's first people lived very close to nature. It is generally conceded that they believed themselves to be part of this world. This relationship was shaped by a basic belief in a shared existence—plants, animals, and humans were part of a larger whole, and all had souls and spirits. Anthropologists refer to such a belief system as animism. Humans were responsible for their actions because they affected the balance of this natural system. Ceremonial activities were intended to ensure a continued supply of the plants, fish, and animals upon which the natives depended. Hence the common thread of native creation stories, in which animals such as Crow, Falcon, or Coyote are often the creators of the world they would share with humans.[37]

In this pre-European world, environment greatly influenced where Sierra Nevada native people settled, as well as their population densities. For the natives of the western Sierra, most permanent living sites were located in the areas from the lower to upper Sonoran and lower transition zones. They were situated below the snow line and generally had southern exposures for warmth. Today we would call such foresight good passive solar planning. Other environmental factors influencing settlement included view, aspect, slope, drainage, isolation, vegetative cover, wind protection, bedrock proximity for mills, and flood or fire hazard. Village sites were chosen for their access to water and resources such as acorn-bearing oak trees. The communities with the greatest population densities were located near ecotones—areas of overlapping biotic communities—where a greater variety of resources existed. These life zones, which ran along north to south lines in the foothills, were important in determining cultural similarities among the western-slope inhabitants.[38]

Sierran natives on both sides of the range actively used the higher-elevation montane, subalpine, and alpine zones when weather permitted. They traveled in regular annual cycles, moving from the lower-elevation camps or villages on both sides to the summit and often beyond to secure plant, animal, fish, and mineral resources during the spring, summer, and fall. Seasonal occupation produced campsites that were often revisited annually. As a consequence of contact between western and eastern Sierran natives, the trading of acorns, lithics, and other resources was common.[39]

Environmental Impact of Sierran Natives

What impact did California natives have on the Sierra Nevada in the centuries before European settlement? How did they influence or shape the range's natural systems? According to some anthropologists, native Sierrans took an active role in shaping the range in the areas they used or occupied, and these ecosystems could have evolved in part through their actions. This view of Sierran natives as active shapers of the range is not universally accepted, however.[40]

Sierran natives were likely to have had environmental impacts ranging from lower foothill grass and woodlands zones through the chaparral and mixed-conifer areas and into the higher-elevation red fir and subalpine environments. Their worldview played a role. So did their population size, neolithic technology, resourceful and thoughtful land-use practices, and the long duration of their occupation. The reliance of California natives on natural sources of food and other materials required them to engage in systematic management practices that affected the environment at many levels. Native Sierrans were more than hunters and gatherers acting within limits set by environment and technology. Their activities came to include effects on individual organisms as well as on larger plant and animal communities. These influences may have reached all the way up to landscapewide levels.[41]

In this sense, the Sierra Nevada was not a "wilderness" during the time of native occupation. The term *wilderness* in its modern Western European and American usage generally connotes a place lightly touched, sparsely occupied, and separate from humans. This commonly held perspective does not describe the Sierra Nevada during pre-European times. Most parts of the range were utilized and many of its spaces were occupied the year round for centuries, even if the population density was small compared with today's. The hope of conservationists such as John Muir and modern wilderness advocates to set aside areas essentially free from human intervention, whatever its merits in an industrial and urban society, would not have been understood by Sierran natives. It should also be noted that modern land-use ideas concerning the Sierra Nevada have until recently excluded consideration of the practices of prehistoric natives and, in this sense, have contributed to long-term detrimental effects on the range.[42]

The most current view has it that there were three broad ways in which Sierra natives acted as "agents of environmental change." They acted as dispersal agents through their activities, whether planned or unplanned. They actively modified the environment. And they may have changed the genetic characteristics of the plant communities they used most intensively.[43]

Sierran natives sustained themselves in the range for thousands of years by hunting, fishing, gathering, lithic quarrying, prehorticultural activities, and trading. Changes in native technology, notably the acquisition of the bow and arrow approximately 1,500 years ago, may have led to more intensive exploitation of both large and small mammals, contributing to impacts on population sizes in the immediate precontact phase of Sierran history.[44] Other actions had ecological and possibly evolutionary effects on the distribution, structure, composition, and extent of plants that were utilized. This influence came from sowing seeds, pruning, weeding, tilling, irrigating (in the case of the Owens Valley Paiute), and harvesting.[45]

Native collection of firewood for numerous domestic uses had an important influence in occupied areas. Firewood consumption by hundreds of villages is estimated to have totaled in the range of hundreds of thousands of pounds daily over thousands of years. This activity helped to keep inhabited areas free of accumulated fuels that might have fed wildfires that could endanger those settlements. Heavy use of firewood may also have led to depletion of easily obtainable fuel locally, forcing natives to relocate village sites periodically.[46]

The term *gathering* has often been used to describe California native techniques of obtaining plant foods. Gathering implies a more passive response to food production than farming. Though respect is accorded to the observational and cataloging skills of the natives, the implication is that agriculture as practiced by other—and especially European—groups marks a degree of sophistication that California's natives did not achieve. But what if California and Sierra Nevada Indians developed far more active prehorticultural responses in their relationship to plants? What if they actively shaped them to suit human needs, creating effects that influenced the evolution and distribution of plant species in the Sierra Nevada? This possibility is exactly what many anthropologists and plant specialists are now suggesting.[47]

Simple prehorticultural techniques were employed in the daily lives of all Sierra Nevada natives. The old saying that straight lines do not occur often in nature is especially true in California native plants. They more often have lateral branches that make them useless in construction of woven articles. Pruning of useful plants was necessary to encourage the growth of straight sticks for making cradle boards and baskets. Weeding discouraged plants that competed with preferred ones. Tilling of the soil, sowing seeds on prepared land, and harvesting the seeds of tended plants such as tobacco occurred. One of the most significant and sophisticated examples of careful prehorticultural activity arose from the work of native Sierran women involved in basketmaking. For the mobile Sierra Nevada natives, baskets were needed to store, transport, cook, and collect valuable food resources. The making of baskets, according to plant expert Kat Anderson, "constituted an industry-size operation, requiring large-scale effort to manage, harvest, size, cure, and weave plant materials into baskets for each village."[48]

Far and away the most significant effect of natives on the Sierra Nevada environment resulted from their use of fire as a "management" tool. Early historical figures and anthropologists have written about fire use by California and Sierra Nevada Native Americans for years. In 1902, USGS scientist John B. Leiberg completed a systematic study of forests in the northern Sierra. He noted that the "most potent factor in shaping the forest of the region has been, and still is, fire." As he wrote disapprovingly, "Fires ravaged the forest long before the American occupation of California. The aboriginal inhabitants undoubtedly started them at periodic intervals to keep down the young growth and the underbrush."[49]

But as anthropologist Henry Lewis has noted, observations by Leiberg and numerous others, including anthropologists such as A. L. Kroeber, did not effectively explain exactly why and how the native Californians went about this business of burning. Were they just pyromaniacs, he asked? Or was something far more important at work? What significance did Indian burning have in California landscapes? Lewis acknowledged reports by many observers that California natives did burn over the environments they occupied. These early observers even offered simple reasons for the burning of local landscapes—for example, to drive game or to increase seed production in grasslands. But as late as the 1970s, no really effective analysis of native burning existed. By using an ecologically oriented analysis of all sources that commented on Indian burning, and by applying the perspectives of fire ecologists, Lewis arrived at a new view of native burning practices.[50]

Lewis concluded that the key question was not whether California natives used or set fires—he accepted that they did. But more important, he said, was whether fire was a factor in a "system of environmental relationships" for California natives. The accounts of Indian burning he examined did not effectively tell where burning occurred, what were its specific characteristics, and what was the timing involved. By placing the information he had in an ecosystem context, he was able to answer those three questions.[51]

His answers led Lewis to a larger issue: namely, what were the effects of Indian burning in an ecological context for the Sierra Nevada? As he saw it, this burning was purposeful and conducted across all three of the major vegetation zones that natives occupied or used. In sum, he said, "the single most important organism in the interchange which occurred between different belts, or zones, was of course the Indian." Lewis stated the consequence of living and using all three of these zones and modifying them by fire:

Like men everywhere—the pioneer who clears the forest or the farmer who plants trees on the prairies—the Indian did not simply take the habitat as he found it. Even though the overall environment already provided two and often more natural ecotones, the Indian was able to create a variety of local ecotones within vegetational zones. At the same time, even where natural ecotones already existed—e.g., between woodland-grass and chaparral zones—aboriginal burning pushed back the upper zones of brush or trees to favor a more productive cover of mixed trees, grass and shrubs.[52]

Lewis noted that even though the California native population, including the Sierra Nevada groups, was relatively large by aboriginal standards, they could not have burned all or even most of the California and Sierra Nevada landscape.[53] But because they could be considered an "edge species" in ecological terms, their burning helped create "a much more complex overall ecosystemic pattern than would have been the case with only natural fires."[54]

Much of Lewis's analysis was based on non-Indian sources. Recently, systematic use of information provided by native Sierran elders has expanded the new perspective that Lewis provided. In an important study carried out for the Sierra Nevada Ecosystem Project of 1996, Kat Anderson and Michael Moratto relied significantly on native informants to answer six key questions about the environmental influence of native burning and other activities in the Sierra. Their first question asked if Sierran Native technologies were capable of creating widespread ecological change in the range. The answer was yes. Their second question was whether the settlement and land-use patterns of the natives were capable of causing permanent effects on vegetation. The answer was yes. The third dealt with whether the population of precontact natives was large enough to cause widespread ecological impacts. Their answer was probably. The fourth question was which land-use activities required the highest quality of plant resources from areas the natives actively managed. That activity was basketry. The fifth question was what land-use activity had the greatest impact on Sierran Nevada plant communities. The answer was fire. The sixth question was how selected plant species were affected by their use. Their answer was that Sierran natives selected plant species that thrived under repeated disturbance, especially those that provided "plant parts" used for "construction, firewood, basketry, cordage, and foods."[55] By continually selecting the same plant species, the native users shaped, to a high degree, the evolution of the species they preferred.

The information that underlay Anderson and Moratto's report was based on Anderson's earlier exhaustive study of native fire-based management of plant resources and landscapes in the central and southern Sierra Nevada.[56] Anderson relied heavily on numerous interviews with native elders. Consider, for example, this comment on the use of fire by Rosalie Bethel, a North Fork Mono tribal member:

I'm going by what the elders told me happened in the 1800's. Burning was in the fall of the year when the plants were all dried up when it was going to rain. They'd burn areas when they would see it's in need. If the brush was too high and too brushy it gets out of control. If the shrubs got two to four feet in height it would be time to burn. They'd burn every two years. Both men and women would set the fires. The flames wouldn't get very high. It wouldn't burn the trees, only the shrubs.

They burned around the camping grounds where they lived and around where they gathered. They also cleared pathways between camps. Burning brush helped to save water. They burned in the valley and foothills. I never heard of the Indians setting fires in the higher mountains, but don't take my word for it.[57]

Indians often burned areas that they utilized frequently and in seasonal cycles, thus introducing disturbances that gave them a measure of control over these areas. Lightning-caused fires were also common. The forests of the range were generally less crowded with densely packed smaller trees, and therefore less prone to stand-destroying fires than today. Fire-return intervals averaged less than twenty years, reflecting the reduction of fuel accumulations that could produce large fires. Natural and native-caused fires stimulated flowering, sprouting, seed release, and germination. According to scientists associated with the Sierra Nevada Ecosystem Project of 1996, those precontact fires affected the "dynamics of biomass accumulation and nutrient cycling, and generated vegetation mosaics at a variety of spatial scales."[58]

Areas that Sierran natives regularly managed (as well as other parts of the pre-European-period forests) have often been described as open and park-like. The most frequently quoted description of Sierra Nevada forests in the nineteenth century is from John Muir:

> The inviting openness of the Sierra woods is one of their most distinguishing characteristics. The trees of all the species stand more or less apart in groves, or in small, irregular groups, enabling one to find a way nearly everywhere, along sunny colonnades and through openings that have a smooth, park-like surface, strewn with brown needles and burs. . . .
>
> One would experience but little difficulty in riding on horseback through the successive belts all the way up to the storm-beaten fringes of the icy peaks. The deep cañons, however, that extend from the axis of the range, cut the belts more or less completely into sections, and prevent the mounted traveler from tracing them lengthwise.[59]

Few young trees were to be found around native camps. Ridgelines were often kept free of trees. Favored oak-production areas were controlled by fire to reduce competing species such as cedars, which tended to grow faster than oaks. Thickets of unmanaged trees and brush were more likely to be found in canyons or damp areas, or in places the natives did not use. The landscapes Sierran natives burned included the mixed grass-and-oak woodlands of the western foothills, mixed-conifer and sequoia forests higher up, red fir and lodgepole pine forests, meadows (for example, Yosemite Valley), and the riparian systems that they frequented.[60]

There are many reasons for such frequent burning by Sierran natives. Open areas encouraged browse for deer—which in turn increased the number of deer. Burning facilitated travel. It made it easier to collect acorns, pine nuts, and other food resources and to clear land for sowing tobacco seed. Burning enhanced the production of basketry and cordage materials. It was employed to modify understory forest composition and reduce fuel accumulation. It helped to decrease diseases of acorn and oaks and to eliminate acorn pests. The list goes on. Fire was used to spur growth of mushrooms, seed-bearing grasses, and herbaceous plants, to provide cleared vistas for security reasons, and to improve stream flow. Fire helped maintain meadow openings as food-production areas, preventing the colonization of these areas by less useful plants or brush. Deliberate burning for any of these reasons may have caused larger forest fires at times, but in the foothills where permanent villages were located and frequent small-scale burning had reduced chaparral, this would not have been a serious problem.[61]

Lightning strikes and a Mediterranean climate can explain many of the frequent fires of the past in the Sierra Nevada. But for a significant number of the prehistoric fires that have been recorded by scientists, especially at the foothill and montane forest levels, native initiative must also be considered. In their use of fire, the native inhabitants of the Sierra were important participants in the shaping of the range. Conversely, modern fire scientists regard the destruction and removal of California natives from the Sierra as a major factor in changes that have made the range more prone to serious fire damage.[62]

For the current-day "suburban pioneers" in the Sierra Nevada foothills, encroaching rapidly into the chaparral areas that grew after logging and large-scale fire-suppression policies were adopted, a cautionary word is necessary. Sierra Nevada natives would not have risked their lives in the now densely packed chaparral and montane forests that have replaced pre-European settlement. Fire will come! The forests of the Sierra Nevada are fire-adapted. If not "Indian burning," some other methods to reduce the current fuel levels of these areas are necessary for safety.[63]

Environmental Change Follows Invasion

Between 1769 and the 1850s, Spanish, Mexicans, and Americans conquered California. Monumental political and social changes followed, as well as significant effects on the Sierra Nevada environment. The contrast between native uses of the range and those of their successors is of a magnitude that defies any simple comparison.

One of the best explanations of that transformation comes from geographer William Preston. In describing the changes that followed the end of native control of the California landscape, he borrowed a concept from conservation biology and aptly termed California Indians the "keystone species" in pre-European times. Preston observed that the varied environments of California—forest, plain, river basin, and Sierra—had evolved because of human intervention as well as natural processes. Native Californians did not passively reside in their homelands. Instead, they shaped the environment to their human needs. Remove them, the "keystone" in the arch of their natural world, and the Sierran and other ecosystems in the state may have evolved very differently.[64]

This alteration of the native-occupied environment began with Spanish and Mexican influences on Sierra Nevada Indian populations in the 1790s. It accelerated after the American invasion in 1848. The displacement of the natives and their way of life had important environmental consequences, some of which continue today. Rapid and wide-ranging changes in the landscape followed native removal. Reduction in plant and animal densities and variety occurred. Foothill plant communities, riparian systems, meadows, oak stands, and forest composition were forever changed. New animals and plants were introduced. The end of native control and management of the Sierra Nevada created a "disequilibrium" that some wildland managers believe should be reexamined today.[65]

In that century that followed European occupation of California, successive waves of Spanish colonials, Mexican Californios, and immigrants from the United States and Europe met and conflicted with California and Sierran natives. This contact forced change upon the indigenous population at a rate and with an intensity that had no parallel in the native experience. California and Sierra Nevada Indians resisted the intruders when they could, and adapted to elements of the new cultures under duress. In the end, their way of life and their ownership of their homelands were terminated. The near annihilation of Sierran natives was a tragedy of great human significance. The replacement of their land use and the ethic that guided it marks a profound change in the environmental history of the Sierra Nevada.[66]

Conquest began with the establishment of an extended Spanish foothold along the California coast, with indirect influences from those colonial outposts reaching into the Coast Range and Central Valley between 1769 and 1821. Next came the transition of California to the status of a territory in the new Republic of Mexico between 1821 and 1846. Hispanic influence extended into the Central Valley and Sierra Nevada foothills. With it came the entrance of American fur trappers, military reconnaissance expeditions, and the beginnings of overland immigration through the Sierra Nevada from the United States. The years from 1846 to 1853 saw the invasion and political annexation of Mexican California and interior Indian lands by the United States, and the rush of gold seekers into the mountains.[67]

Until the last of these three period, California Native Americans remained in control of much of their territory across the Coast Range and into the Sierra. They actively contested Spanish and Mexican penetration, especially in the San Joaquin Valley and adjacent foothills.[68]

While the Spanish generally kept to the coast, in some instances they traveled east into the Central Valley and the Sierra Nevada foothills. There is an account of a Spanish conflict with Western Mono people south of Yosemite in the 1780s. In 1806 and 1811, Lieutenant Gabriel Moraga led expeditions out of the Mission San Juan de Bautista into areas close to Yosemite as well. Other forays in the years that followed may have contacted foothill Indians.[69]

Recruitment of natives for the missions from the numerous coastal groups reached its peak in the late 1790s but continued for several years afterward. Conditions in the missions caused very high Indian death rates. The spread of European diseases to the mission natives, who had no effective immunity to them, and a diet that did not sustain native health contributed to this population collapse. Thus, raids for replacements across the Coast Range were deemed necessary. In addition, a steady increase in escapes by the partially christianized "neophytes," as the natives were called, further reduced the mission Indian populations. The Franciscans and their military allies began to recruit from native groups across the Coast Range and into the interior zone of the Sacramento and San Joaquin Valleys. They also carried out raids to capture and return mission fugitives.[70]

As a result of these ever-lengthening forays, natives in the foothills of the Sierra Nevada were affected, and changes in their population size, culture, economy, and worldview resulted. Spanish Mexican influences included the introduction of new technologies, plants, and animals. Both valley and Sierra Nevada natives became familiar with horses, and diet and mobility changes followed. Unexplained diseases such as smallpox, scarlet fever, measles, and influenza, along with escalating violence, accompanied this contact, causing the decline of the interior native population. In response, some natives relocated farther into the valley interior and the foothills of the Sierra Nevada, taking with them new perspectives that would change Sierran native economies and outlook.[71]

In 1821 Mexico won independence from Spain. The missions continued to operate, but with less effective support from territorial officials. Coerced neophytes ran away more frequently. The missions were finally dissolved and secularized by the Mexican government in the mid-1830s. Most mission land was granted to powerfully connected Californios, as the newly independent ex-colonials called themselves. New lands were granted outside the immediate mission zone to a new class of rancheros such as Mariano Vallejo or to favored American immigrants such as John Sutter.[72]

The new rancheros competed for labor from the same pool of former mission neophytes and valley and foothill natives. Not surprisingly, most neophytes elected not to accept unpaid work on the ranchos and instead left for old homes in the valley and Sierra Nevada foothills. Some former mission Indians who could not return to their old groups affiliated with interior groups that would accept them. They thereby brought new numbers to groups reduced by disease, and in addition brought knowledge of the Spanish language, food, clothing, and technology, including an interest in horses. Conflict between Mexican soldiers and rancheros and the natives of the valley and Sierra Nevada foothills increased between the mid-1820s and 1840s.[73]

Valley and Sierra Nevada foothill Indians, now in possession of the horse and culturally transformed by their contact with Spaniards and Mexicans, began to counterattack the Mexican intruders. Escaped mission neophytes such as Estanislaus staged fierce organized resistance to Mexican authority and used the tule swamps and foothill thickets as defensive strongholds when needed. Other contacts changed the native world. Trade developed among Indians, New Mexican traders, and American fur trappers such as Jedediah Smith, Zenas Leonard, and Joseph Walker. This led to exchanges of manufactured products for domesticated horses stolen by valley and foothill natives from the Californio ranchers.[74]

In 1830, conflict between foothill Miwok and fur trappers Ewing Young and Kit Carson resulted in horse raids by the natives, with a retaliatory raid that took Carson into the Sierra Nevada to regain his stolen animals. In the Sacramento Valley, John Sutter maintained a tentative hold on his claims through a mixture of diplomacy, bribery, and selective use of force against his Nisenan neighbors. Herds of wild horses descended from original Spanish stock roamed freely in the Central Valley and Sierra Nevada foothills and were hunted by mounted Central Valley and foothill natives, primarily for food. Long-established trans-Sierran trade between the Monache and the

Mono Paiute in the Great Basin now included horses and European-made goods.[75]

An example of the growing reliance on horses stolen by southern Sierran natives for food is recounted by John Bidwell, a member of a packing train of American immigrants who crossed the Sierra in the Stanislaus drainage in 1841. After having lost some horses to a group of Indians, probably Miwok, he tracked the raiders to the main gorge of the Stanislaus. There he observed the Indians cutting up "our poor horses." He saw a "great quantity of horse bones" and figured that the natives must have been stealing horses by the hundreds from the Californios.[76]

Disease transmitted by contact in the Mexican California period ravaged foothill groups. Malaria, probably brought by French Canadian fur trappers from the Hudson's Bay Company who were working in the valley, decimated valley natives and possibly affected lower foothill tribes in the early 1830s. Some natives fled their home villages because of the disease, moving farther into the Sierra Nevada foothills. An oral account of the Ahwahnichi inhabitants of Yosemite Valley illustrates one Sierran group's response. They were struck with an epidemic possibly spread from contact with escaped neophytes. Frightened by the severity of the contagion, survivors fled across the Sierra Nevada and took refuge with the Mono Paiute, with whom they had well-established trade and other contacts. Several years later, Tenaya, the leader of a mixed group of Paiute and Miwok, returned to the deserted Yosemite Valley. There, former mission Indians and Monache or Miwok from areas south of the Yosemite area joined him. From this isolated haven, his band joined other foothill natives in launching raids into the valley in the 1840s.[77]

In 1846 the United States declared war on Mexico and by 1848 had compelled the Mexican republic to surrender its borderland territories, including California, to American ownership. Even before the formal treaty was operative, conflict began between the American army and valley and foothill natives. The Americans simply took over where the Mexican authorities had left off in their continuing struggle with mounted interior bands. The valley and Sierran natives probably considered the new challengers in the same context as the Spanish and Mexicans before them. Except for Sutter's holdings, the natives still remained in control of most of their territory and continued to try to protect it and to make interlopers pay tribute. The balance of power, however, soon shifted against them in favor of the Americans.[78]

Between 1841 and 1857, more than 165,000 people and perhaps a million animals traveled the immigrant and gold rush trails to California.[79] The immigrants used various routes that crossed the Sierra Nevada. The impact of their passage affected native people and the Sierra Nevada environment. This migration of humans and their domesticated stock, while transitory, began the process of the opening of the Sierra Nevada to a very different land-use pattern. Most important would be the commercial exploitation of its resources. This economic development did more to alter the Sierra Nevada landscape in three decades than what had occurred in the previous thousands of years of native use.[80]

Gold Rush Displacement of Sierran Natives

American fur trappers, western immigrants, and Sierra Nevada natives had little contact before the gold rush. Native groups in the Great Basin and the Sierra Nevada felt the effects of the immigrants' passage, but the disruption of their lives was limited. Most of the newcomers were hurrying across what they perceived as a dangerous and formidable mountain barrier. They had no intentions of staying. The discovery of gold in 1848 changed that. Instead of a dreaded barrier, the Sierra Nevada was now seen as a treasure trove, and Sierran natives stood in the path of an onslaught of miners intent on occupying their territory.[81]

The collision with Sierra Nevada Indians during the gold rush created a new period of United States Indian policy. Before the war with Mexico and the conquest of California, many eastern Native Americans had been forcibly removed from the Ohio and Mississippi Valleys to areas west of the Mississippi River, leaving the valuable valley lands for white farmers. Once relocated, the Indians were supposed to be guaranteed permanent landholdings out of the way of American expansion—"Indian Territory," if you please. The conquest of California required the creation a new policy. For the most part, this approach was defined on the ground, with Indian agents acting beyond any formal instructions from the Bureau of Indian Affairs. After 1849 the policy was to extinguish Indian land titles first, try to remove the natives to temporary holding centers, and then figure out what to do with them later. Given the sheer force and violence of the onrushing miners and settlers, the policy had disastrous effects.[82]

J. Ross Browne, appointed by federal authorities to observe and report on the conditions of West Coast natives in 1857, reported later his view of what had resulted: "The wild Indians inhabiting the Coast Range, the valleys of the Sacramento and San Joaquin, and the western slope of the Sierra Nevada, became troublesome at a very early period after the discovery of the gold mines. It was found convenient to take possession of their country without recompense, rob them of their wives and children, kill them in every cowardly and barbarous manner that could be devised, and when that was impracticable, drive them as far as possible out of the way."[83]

Between 1848 and 1860, the gold rush massively transformed the environment of the Sierra Nevada and devastated its native occupants. In place of the few Spanish Mexican priests, soldiers, and rancheros to contend with at the periphery of their holdings, Sierran natives now were overwhelmed by thousands of heavily armed miners crowding into their territory. When the natives resisted, fighting back to protect their lands and lives, they were crushed by irregularly constituted armed groups, organized California state "militias," and federal troops. By the 1850s and the early 1860s, treaties imposed upon Sierran Indians stripped them of their lands and forced most of the survivors to move to areas outside their Sierra Nevada homelands. Those few natives left behind, or those who escaped the roundups and returned to their homelands, had to occupy the lowest rungs in the new Anglo-American economy and society. Their old ways were largely obliterated. The history of this conquest has been told by others and will not be recounted here.[84]

What is necessary, though, is to understand what this conquest and removal meant in environmental terms. Several important questions arise at this point. What effect on Sierran native populations did this onslaught have? How did environmental changes set in motion by the gold rush affect native economies and the systems they were based on? What were the regional differences in Sierran native responses to intruders during the gold rush time? What natural systems of the range that natives depended heavily upon were most affected? How did natives adapt to changes in their resource base? What did it mean for the Sierra Nevada environment as Sierra natives and their way of life were displaced by alien intruders?

The full environmental impacts on the Sierra Nevada caused by the gold rush will be examined later. Here only a few changes, and their immediate effects on Sierran natives and the landscapes they relied upon, will be considered. Placer mining fouled streams with millions of cubic yards of mud and debris. Oaks and pines were cut down, damaged, or made infertile by mining and settlement activities. Grazing animals and hogs competed for plant resources. Settlements excluded natives from traditional food-gathering activities. Indian burning was suppressed.[85]

The most significant effects of mining operations were to disturb the ecology of the native food technology. The available stores of native plant, fish, animal, and insect food sources were depleted or destroyed by miners and their livestock. Communal hunting and gathering activities nearly ceased. Because much of the natives' natural food was gathered seasonally and immediately eaten or stored, destruction or denial of access to it meant starvation. Damage to streams, groves, and meadows imposed long-term hardships on native economies. Native burning was significantly reduced as Indian land tenure ended.[86]

The decline of Sierran native populations during the gold rush was catastrophic. Precontact population figures for Sierra Nevada natives are inexact, but estimates range from as low as 50,000 to a more likely figure of 100,000 before contact with Europeans. Many official or unofficial accounts by contemporary Anglo-Americans note the immediate collapse of native population resulting from the ferocity of the conquest. Death from disease, including various venereal types contracted from coerced prostitution, was greater than from violence. The ten most active years of the gold rush and the development that followed reduced Sierra Nevada Indian populations by two-thirds. Forced removal of natives from mining and foothill areas adjacent to the Sacramento and San Joaquin Valleys completed this ghastly picture.[87]

Indian groups living in the north and central western-slope foothills and montane areas were hardest hit, although all were to suffer. It was in that region that most mining and most Anglo-American settlement concentrated. Nisenan and Miwok territories, the river systems of the American, Yuba, Stanislaus, Mokelumne, Merced, and Tuolumne, were inundated first. Mining soon developed in Maidu and Konkow homelands in the upper drainages of the American and the Feather Rivers. The spread of mining and ranching into the areas from the Stanislaus to the San Joaquin drainages caused conflict as well. The Yokuts, Mono, Tubatulabl, and Kawaiisu at the extreme southern part of the range in the San Joaquin drainage did not face the same large numbers of armed miners that their northern counterparts did, but the conquest of the southern Sierrans would be just as complete and as devastating.[88]

By 1900, over 90 percent of the population was dead. Of the survivors, many had been relocated, although some few escaped and returned to old areas where they adjusted as best they could, joining with others to form new settlements where possible. Their material culture, their diet, and much of their old way of life were radically changed. They found ways to work with whites and in some cases tried to supplement meager food supplies in the old ways, by hunting, fishing, and gathering on the reduced land base open to them.[89]

The Washoe, Northern Paiute, and Owens Valley Paiute of the eastern Sierra lost their territory, as did all Sierran Indians. But the pattern was different than in the western Sierra. The variations had to do with differences in native traditions and with divergent pressures and demands from the Anglo-American intruders. Mining was less of a direct factor in this region, although it had significant indirect influences in areas to the east in the Comstock region and other parts of western Nevada.[90]

If we consider the case of the Washoe, the immensity of the change can be understood. The Washoe population was always small, and physical resistance to challengers from the outside was not an option for them. They often hid or limited contact with explorers and encroaching wagon trains in the 1830s and 1840s. After the gold rush they gave up their extended journeys over the Sierra Nevada that had brought trade goods such as seashells and acorns. It had become too hazardous. The Washoe generally abandoned their territories as land was fenced, pinyon trees cut, and stock occupied their old grasslands. Their beloved Lake Tahoe was relinquished because of pressure from whites. They did continue fishing for trade with settlers until commercial fishermen drove them from this activity by the 1880s. Whites also usurped hunting territories. The Washoe in numerous ways adapted to survival at the lower economic level of the occupying white society's economy. Some even remained at Tahoe as laborers at the growing number of resorts.[91]

The Northern Paiute had always been highly mobile. Those utilizing the Sierra Nevada did not occupy permanent village sites. European contact with Northern Paiute in the vicinity of western Nevada and the Truckee River began with trappers such as Joseph R. Walker and explorers such as John C. Frémont in the 1830s and 1840s. Although Walker attacked the Paiute, contact was generally transitory and limited. In the 1840s and 1850s, wagon trains and gold seekers created devastating environmental effects on native subsistence economies as animal and plant resources were consumed. Acquisition of horses in the 1840s gave Northern Paiutes the mobility to retaliate with raids on the intruders' stock. Gold and silver discoveries in the nearby Virginia Mountains in western Nevada in 1859 led to further conflict and a tremendous increase in European American population. U.S. military forces eventually forced most Northern Paiute bands onto reservations. The two closest to the Sierra Nevada were the Pyramid Lake and the Walker River Reservations.[92]

The Owens Valley Paiute story is slightly different from that of their eastern Sierra Nevada neighbors. From the 1830s into the 1850s, contact had occurred as trappers and prospectors entered the area, but because of the climate and lack of gold, few had lingered. A California boundary survey in the 1850s pointed out that some settlement potential existed, but no one responded. In 1859, a U.S. military expedition entered the area in pursuit of suspected stock thieves. The army suggested a reservation site be established, but no action followed. In 1861, cattle ranchers from Nevada and California claimed lands there, especially those irrigated by the Indians. Hostilities began immediately. By 1863, the Owens Valley Paiute had been forcibly removed to a reservation near Fort Tejon, outside the Sierra. As with other groups, some of the Owens Valley natives escaped and returned to their old homelands. There they were forced to work on the lands they had first developed for irrigation of native grasses, forming a valuable labor source for the conquering white farmers.[93]

Thus, between 1848 and 1860, the native-held areas of the Sierra Nevada were massively affected by immigration, mining, and other activities. The richest and most fertile production areas, such as river systems and bottomlands, grasslands, meadows, and oak groves, were quickly and, for the long term, effectively destroyed or denied to west-slope natives. Eastern groups, in a more fragile ecosystem, faced exclusion and destruction of their resources through grazing or increased hunting by immigrants and settlers.[94]

Jack Forbes, an anthropologist specializing in the study of contact between Native Americans and European Americans, wrote about the legacy of the conquest of California and Nevada Indian peoples. Two sentences effectively summarize the first thirty years of contact: "To be conquered at all is a very sad fate, but to be conquered by those who hate and despise you is the worst of all possible situations. The Native Californians were unfortunate in that they were overcome by a people whose view of them was so filled with hostility that it easily supported genocide."[95]

The conquest of Sierra Nevada natives had environmental consequences as great as the demographic and cultural ones. Mining and other economic activities destroyed the ecosystems that native people had depended upon.[96]

Indians living on both sides of the Sierra Nevada had relied to varying degrees on five basic staples for much of their food supply: acorns, seeds, fish, game, and insects. Miners and settlers cut down, damaged, or fenced off oak trees, and hogs ate acorns, thus depriving west-slope Indians of this food source. Seed grasses were grazed, uprooted, and trampled by cattle, sheep, and hogs, and exotic weeds were introduced by this foreign stock. These actions eventually changed the composition of Sierra Nevada ranges. Miners turned Sierran streams into veritable mudflows, killing fish and preventing spawning. Natives who had depended heavily on spawning runs were also driven out of areas not affected by mining, such as Lake Tahoe and the Truckee River. Game became scarcer and more skittish as a result of increased white hunting. Some whites turned to market hunting of the larger Sierran mammals, further reducing available game supplies. Even access to insects—included in most Sierran native seasonal diets—was affected by white settlement. In some cases native groups were forced to negotiate agreements among themselves to ration the diminishing insect supply.[97]

An account by Special Indian Agent E. A. Stevenson to Indian Superintendent Thomas J. Henley in 1853 illustrated the effects of gold rush intruders on natives in foothills of the central Sierra Nevada. He described the Indians in his district as having no place to live, hurt by the vices of the mining camps, and subject to brutal treatment. He saw no hope for them except removal to a reservation out of harm's way, as they were unable to subsist as in the past:

> They formerly subsisted on game, fish, acorns, etc., but it is now impossible for them to make a living by hunting or fishing, for nearly all the game has been driven from the mining region or has been killed by the thousands of our people who now occupy the once quiet home of the children of the forest. The rivers or tributaries of the Sacramento were as clear as crystal and abounded with the finest salmon and other fish. . . . But the miners have turned the streams from their beds and conveyed the water to dry diggings and after being used until it is so thick with mud that it will scarcely run it returns to its natural channel and with it the soils from a thousand hills, which has driven almost every kind of fish to seek new places of resort where they can enjoy a purer and more natural element.[98]

Sierra Nevada Native Americans adapted to this onslaught in different ways, depending on where they were located and how directly they were confronted. Native subsistence patterns in the Sierra Nevada had already undergone some change in the time from the early 1800s to the gold rush, largely as a result of their acquiring horses and having contact with ex-mission Indians. Horse and cattle flesh had been added to the traditional diet. Some trade in the southern Sierra Nevada with Hispanic traders and American fur trappers had provided European goods such as blankets and cloth to the natives. As part of the wars of conquest after 1848, most attacks on native bands by federal troops or state militias included destruction of native food stores and other supplies so as to force them to negotiate and leave traditional lands.

The perpetrators of this scorched-earth policy left a record of the native goods they wasted or burned, allowing us to observe the transition that was occurring. Consider the conquest of the Ahwahnichi by the so-called Mariposa Battalion. The militiamen burned the natives' food and possessions, but not before a member of the battalion made an inventory. It included traditional food staples such as acorns, seeds, berries, larvae, and grasshoppers, demonstrating a continuance of old ways as long as access to them was assured. Baskets and rabbit-skin robes went into the flames. Various trade items or goods obtained in raids, such as knives, blankets, lariats, cloth, and dried beef and horsemeat, were also noted.[99]

The gold rush rapidly extinguished most independent activities by the natives. Some Indians responded with aggressive raids and counterraids at first, a few using guns that had been acquired by trade. But the sheer numbers of whites and their superior armament and organization placed native fighters at a severe disadvantage. Resistance was crushed. Many natives were coerced to leave and assemble at hastily constructed reservations after treaty negotiations were conducted in the early 1850s. Although some eighteen treaties were negotiated with California Indians at the time, none was ever confirmed by the United States Senate. This effectively left the natives landless.[100]

Some California Indians adapted to the loss of their resource base by trying gold mining. In 1848, in fact, the majority of miners were Indians working either for themselves or for powerful patrons. By 1849, however, increasing numbers of white prospectors had forced them from the diggings. Some women were coerced into prostitution in order to survive; moving accounts exist, some from Indian agents, of their pitiful conditions and disease-ridden bodies. Some Indians worked for whites as agricultural laborers or in other menial pursuits. Some, such as the Washoe, continued to fish in a commercial capacity until European American competition and state-imposed game laws by the turn of the century ended that activity. Death, relocation, and forced acculturation summarizes the native condition, 1848–1860.[101]

A Sierra Nevada Without Indians?

A rapid transformation of Sierra Nevada landscapes accompanied the tragic destruction of its native people. For thousands of years, from the early Holocene to the early nineteenth century, the areas occupied or used by natives had evolved with this human presence. Those Indian-influenced landscapes, as we understand them today, contained a greater variety of life forms than at any time since. The range's waterscapes of the native period also were far different from those that remained after gold mining, timber cutting, grazing, and water development. Native management produced a diversity and abundance in the Sierra Nevada that may never exist again.

In 1989 Jim Rust, a Southern Sierra Miwok, described his view of what had resulted after whites took control of Sierran lands from his people:

The white man sure ruined this country. It's turned back to wilderness. In the old days there used to be lots more game—deer, quail, grey squirrels, rabbits. They burned to keep down the brush. The fires wouldn't take all the timber like it would now. Burns were started in October, November, or December . . . from the bottom of the slope. They burned every year. The fires wouldn't get up in the trees. There wasn't enough vegetation to get up into the trees. The plants were widely spaced. . . . They burned to keep the brush down, as they were leaving. . . . In those times the creeks ran all year around. You could fish all season. Now you can't because there's no water. The timber and brush now take all the water.[102]

In the time after removal of native control of the range, concerted efforts to exclude wide-scale burning of Sierran landscapes brought environmental changes of great significance. The introduction of public agency–based fire suppression, specifically rejecting what the Forest Service called "Indian Burning," has contributed to an ongoing alteration of the Sierra's forests, resulting in more crowded, fire-prone conditions. This policy of suppressing all human-caused and wildfires also ironically made larger and more deadly fires more likely. It is impossible to return to the worldview, population size, settlement patterns, and fire practices of the precontact native period that shaped Sierra Nevada forests. But it is possible to learn from and adapt native practices and modify current policies to achieve healthy forests. Public agency managers have become more open to such ideas in recent years.[103]

There is another interesting possibility to consider: involving native communities in planning for land use in the Sierra. The Ahwahnichi and many other Indian peoples in the range have never given up their claims to their old territories. This is true even if the United States, state agencies, or private claims have usurped the use of these homelands. Until after the 1950s and 60s with the rise of the civil rights and native rights movements, Indian claimants had little success in pressing their requests to use or regain territories. But their enduring presence and changes in policies concerning recognition of tribal or community rights have brought some significant changes in actions of the dominant federal and state agencies that control native lands and resources.[104]

In the Sierra, inclusion of natives in agency decisions has matured well beyond the paternalistic "Indian Field Days" and Yosemite Museum and Village displays of earlier times. They now involve substantial participation in planning for a return of a native policy-making presence. And this entails more than just imposing limits on highway or housing developments through environmental-impact review processes.[105] For some time now, the state of California has had an ongoing involvement with natives in such projects as the Indian Grinding Rock State Historical Park at Chaw'se, an area once inhabited by the foothill Miwok near Volcano. It serves as a park and cultural center for all California native peoples. The Forest Service also included native participants from the beginning of public participation in the creation of its Sierra Nevada Ecosystem Project. And the Miwok-Mono people took part in the creation of the management plan for Yosemite Valley in 2000 that included a native-managed cultural center in the Valley and actions to enhance environmental conditions there for native plant-resource gathering.[106]

Other examples of agency interaction with natives from the Sierra include cooperating with the Washoe on management of portions of Lake Tahoe's shoreline and meadows, working with members of several Sierra Nevada native communities in collecting traditional plant materials by basketweavers and for medicinal uses, and even joining with native people to clean up toxic mine-waste in tribal homelands. The U.S. Forest Service in the late 1990s initiated "Participatory Research" and "Stewardship" programs that involved Native Americans in shaping forestry practices. While intended to have regional and national impact, the most promising outcomes centered on local communities that, according to one advocate of the idea, "live and work under the forest canopy."[107]

Return of the native? Perhaps it is possible to a limited degree. As national and state land-use planning continues to expand its active promotion of native participation in ongoing decisions and management plan revisions, the possibility is real.

2: The Sierra Gold Made

From the South Fork of the Yuba River at Edwards Crossing, you can look upstream from the aging metal-and-wood bridge to the North Bloomfield–Graniteville Road as it continues its winding progress toward the old hydraulic-mining town of North Bloomfield. North Bloomfield is now incorporated into a California state park. It is late spring and the water is running high. The beauty of the river takes your breath away. Growing on the steep hillsides are yellow pine, manzanita, and deer brush, blending together and spreading up from the edge of the water. California poppy and lupine stand out in exposed sunny areas.

The river here crashes among granite boulders that shape the changing currents in its channel. River runners in brightly colored kayaks maneuver in the rapids. They practice running down these rapids and then return upstream by skillfully using their paddles in the slack water at the edge of the current. What could be more beautiful or natural?

But the rivers of the north and central part of the Sierra are only partially the product of the rushing runoff from winter rains that constantly reshapes them. The Yuba and all the other rivers of the region are actually artifacts. The other force that created their present channels is human. Placer and hydraulic miners between 1848 and the 1880s shaped them on a massive scale. They diverted the flowing water into wooden flumes, wrenched boulders out of the channels and piled them on the banks, blasted tunnels to deflect water and expose the riverbeds, and filled them anew with rock and debris washed from the river hillsides by powerful hydraulic-mining "monitors." In addition, the water that courses through the South Fork of the Yuba is controlled. Far above Edwards Crossing are three modern dams, themselves successors to earlier dams built in the historic days of hydraulic mining.[1]

Numerous examples of this reshaping of the Sierra Nevada's river systems by the gold seekers of the nineteenth century appear in the diaries and memoirs they left behind. Consider the remarks of James Delavan about his experience at Big Bar on the Middle Fork of the American River:

> The good fortune of this company induced other adventurers to imitate them, and forty of them organized themselves, choosing an old Californian miner as president, with a treasurer and secretary of expe-

rience, and four directors. This company had begun their work systematically, and a splendid race cut through the Rocky Bar opposite the Big Bar, had been partly completed, fourteen feet wide, of sufficient depth to carry off the water, and which would be about two hundred and thirty yards long. The whole structure would be a creditable specimen of workmanship in any country. A dam of adequate length, compact and tight, diverts the water from the bed of the river, leaving it free to the operations of the miners. . . .

Immense rocks required to be removed by main force, and much blasting has been done. . . . By this important movement, a small portion of the bar, and the bed of the river adjacent to it, had been uncovered, and the labor of several years could hardly suffice to exhaust the metal it contained.[2]

Eleven major rivers in pre–gold rush times flowed westward from the Sierra Nevada and, with but one exception, joined into two large rivers—the Sacramento and the San Joaquin. Together they created the Bay-Delta system.[3] Ten of these rivers, most with several tributaries, were rich in the eroded or placer gold they carried. The four northernmost rivers, with the greatest volume of water, were the Feather, Yuba, Bear, and American. South of these were the Consumnes, Mokelumne, Stanislaus, Tuolumne, Merced, and the Mariposa. It was on these rivers that development of the Sierra Nevada focused in the gold rush decade from 1848 to 1858. In a widening ripple effect, this development stimulated other economic and environmental changes, stretching on into the 1880s.[4] The discovery of gold changed the Sierra Nevada forever, at least in the time frame in which humans operate.

On January 24, 1848, James Marshall found gold on the South Fork of the American River. Word of the discovery spread from the immediate area around Marshall's sawmill to Sacramento and San Francisco. The news reached the eastern United States, Mexico, South America, Europe, Australia, and China within the year. Because of the discovery, 300,000 people came to California between 1849 and 1854, most seeking out the mining areas in the western Sierra. Around $300 million in gold was taken from the streams of the range. The gold rush was an event of national and worldwide significance. It had profound impact on the states of California and Nevada, and the United States.[5]

By the early 1850s, the surface gold of the western foothill streams had been skimmed off. Miners moved on to explore the river systems of the northeastern Sierra Nevada and discovered gold and silver in what became western Nevada at the Comstock Lode as well.[6] These mining operations changed Sierran stream systems and adjoining forests and meadows directly.[7] The gold rush and subsequent developments can almost be compared to glaciation and uplift in the alterations they initiated in the Sierra.

The geology and climate of the Sierra Nevada were prime contributors to the rush for gold. At first, the mining of placer gold in the form of dust, flakes, and nuggets that had been freed by millennia of erosive forces from veins embedded in quartz, required little skill, capital, or knowledge. Luck and being first in line determined success. A primer in Sierran geology explains why.[8]

The gold in Sierran streams was created over 40 million years ago in the Eocene—the earliest of the geological epochs of the Tertiary Period of the Cenozoic Era. Following deposition, massive uplift and downfaulting of the Sierra Nevada occurred. Uplift created a mountain barrier. Immense runoff from snowmelt and rain (caused by the orographic effect of the mountains upon Pacific wind currents) wore it down. Subsequent uplift and glacial action during the Pleistocene, coupled with more runoff in the newly configured mountains, created the modern river canyons of the range.

These new and incredibly forceful young streams carved directly into the Eocene deposits, strewing huge amounts of auriferous materials in or alongside the streams. They exposed the older alluvial deposits on the sides of the river canyons as well. The gold was not exactly for the taking, but much of the hard work of freeing it from its quartz matrix had been done for the forty-eighters, forty-niners, and others who followed.[9]

The northern rivers, where the discovery of gold occurred, illustrate the opportunity presented to the acquisitive miners. The major drainage basins that formed there in the great uplift are complex. They include the North, Middle, and South Forks of the Feather River; the North, Middle, and South Forks of the Yuba; the Bear; and the North, Middle, and South Forks of the American. All are of significant size, have numerous tributaries, and carry the melt that resulted from the heaviest snowfall the range received.[10]

Their canyons are steep, some having a fall of 2,000 feet per mile. Most contain gorges with precipitous or perpendicular walls that often rise over a thousand feet above the water on both sides. The most notable of these spectacular canyons is the American River's Royal Gorge, whose north wall rises 3,750 feet above the stream course. Many of these rivers' walls are composed of hard-packed Eocene deposits, now exposed to view. All major tributaries of these rivers contain sections that are boulder-strewn. The river courses made natural sluices that trapped the gold they freed from the auriferous gravel formations that they incised.[11]

It was this gold that drew the placer miners and their successors to the Sierra. They in turn began a new phase in the range's environmental history.

Mining promoted economic development in the range. It stimulated the growth of logging, grazing, market hunting, water development, and transportation. Urbanization of the range also came with industrialization.[12]

As with the native people before them, the miners' population size, worldview, and technology combined to produce changes in the geography, hydrology, and environment of the Sierra Nevada. But the populations of the European Americans and other miners and developers were immensely larger than those of their native predecessors. The worldview of this new group of occupiers promoted economic development that was not restrained by any sense of responsibility for maintaining balance or sustainability. And the technologies that they applied were capable of producing changes in the range that were permanent and massive in scale.

Gold Mining and Environmental Change

Mining in the Sierra Nevada developed in three overlapping phases. These represent a transition from an adventure of many footloose individuals to a mature industry organized by capitalists in a remarkably short length of time. During the first period, from 1848 to the early 1850s, essentially amateur miners exploited surface deposits of placer gold. With experience and by necessity, these neophytes soon expanded beyond simple technology that included spoons, knives, pans, "rockers," and short sluices to more sophisticated and larger-scale operations. Every river and tributary in the northern and central Sierra Nevada drew large numbers of gold seekers.[13]

In the second phase, miners who had exhausted the surface deposits turned more and more to the exploitation of riverbeds, veins of gold embedded in quartz, and deeper deposits of alluvial gravel. This change required more capital, new techniques (such as wing dams, drift mining, and ground sluicing), and larger supplies of water. As "companies" of cooperating miners formed to work larger volumes of gravel, individual mining declined. In the third period, from 1858 to the late 1880s, Sierran mining became a capital-intensive industry employing wage-earning miners and better-trained engineers in gigantic hydraulic and quartz operations.[14]

The early placer-mining frenzy radically altered the Sierra's riparian systems, causing erosion and depositing mud and sand in the once clear streams. Fish and riverside vegetation were killed. In 1853, federal Indian agent E. A. Stevenson, concerned about the catastrophic impact he observed on California native food supplies, also vividly described the effects of mining. The once crystal-clear water that miners diverted out of the Sacramento River was returned to it "so thick with mud" that it could "scarcely run."[15]

Hillsides and level river floodplains became pockmarked from mining explorations and operations. Channels and tunnels were cut to divert water so that streambeds could be mined. The building of wooden flumes, also to divert river water, necessitated the cutting of adjoining forests. For proof, look at any of the numerous contemporary daguerreotypes of mining camps and towns—few had any standing timber left after mining began. Boulders moved out of streambeds to expose the placer gold were placed elsewhere, creating new riverine environments.[16]

Erosion was massive and ubiquitous, as might be expected with so many men working placer deposits in so many different locations. All miners depended on water to process the gravel they dug. Flumes and dams built by amateurs often leaked or collapsed. A letter by Englishman John Wallace provides an illustration. On July 18, 1853, he told how six weeks earlier one of "the largest reservoirs" burst, causing a "rush of water mixed with mud, stones, logs, trees" to crash into the town of Columbia. He noted problems from leaks that caused the flume to settle, creating spills that produced flooding, gullies, and erosion.[17]

Mercury was used by the miners to assist in recovery of fine gold particles in placer, hydraulic, and quartz mining. Much of it escaped back into the environment. The impact of this use of mercury has not been fully measured, and much of the metal still remains in Sierran streams and soils, causing concern for modern municipalities. Its use expanded exponentially in the later industrial phases of hydraulic and quartz mining.[18]

By 1850, placer miners realized that individuals stood little chance of success. The easy gold in exposed bars or on the river's edge had been picked up. Cooperation and pooling of resources was necessary to reach the riverbed by forcing the river to change its course—the beginnings of river mining. James Delavan in 1850 described the rapid transition to group action in placer mining and indirectly chronicled the growing environmental effects that came with this change:

> The bed of the river at Rector's Bar is rocky, and in the process of collecting the deposits is attended with severe labor. There are small bars above, but the gold diminishes as you advance upwards. There had been an attempt to obviate the difficulty by turning the river from its course, but having been undertaken by inexperienced persons, the dam was not properly constructed, and failed to produce the desired effect. But there can be little doubt that a better erection, and more extensive excavation, would have crowned the labors of the adventurers with success.

I now formed the resolution of sending my horse to a carral, on the road to Culloma, and to proceed down the river on a tour of observation. I had not advanced far when I came to a remarkable curve in the course of the stream, which, after a sweep of nearly two miles, forms what is called a *teton* on the Mississippi. The narrowest part of this peninsula is but sixty or eighty feet across, and the place is known by the very appropriate name of "Horseshoe Bend." Here is a most admirable place which to divert the channel of the river. A short dam, of no great elevation, would arrest the course of the water, and force it through a straight cut across the heel of the bend. This cut could easily be made to carry off the water, and to leave a large extent of the river bottom entirely bare. No place could be better adapted for improvement at small expense, and none presents so great opportunity for a Joint Stock Company to enrich themselves for the purpose.[19]

Delavan was always optimistic—it came with the territory. The task of constructing a dam on the South Fork of the American was not as easily done as he envisioned. Temporary diversion dams were tried and just as swiftly washed away at the oxbow or horseshoe bend that he described. Eventually larger amounts of capital were raised, and a diversion tunnel was cut through solid rock across the neck of the bend. The river took the straight path through the tunnel, as it still does today, leaving the horseshoe bend dry and exposed to placer mining techniques after the rocks in the bed were removed. Rafters and kayakers still race through the tunnel in one of the most exciting runs on this section of the river.[20]

It is hard to imagine the impact placer mining had on the Sierra Nevada. Many of the scars have healed with regeneration of forest and chaparral, and the return of streamside vegetation sometimes screens from view the piles of river rock moved by the miners. One way of envisioning the overall environmental change that occurred in the placer mining areas is to focus on just one of the miners at work. By examining the efforts of this one individual, multiplying those by the actions of several hundred thousand miners, and projecting these across the northern and central western flank of the range, a fuller picture of the impact emerges.

Adolphus Windeler was a German sailor who tried mining between 1849 and 1853. His diary provides a valuable record of the activities and accumulating environmental effects of mining on the Feather River. At first he tried small-scale placering as an individual. Like many miners, he eventually joined other men to pool labor and assets to engage in mining directly in the riverbed. This complex placer mining involved the application of many interrelated techniques to process more gravel. It also entailed the acquisition of numerous locally obtained resources, including wildlife for food and timber for construction.[21]

Endless hours of hard physical labor formed much of Windeler's and the other miners' needed "capital." River mining required the diversion of water away from its bed by constructing dams that isolated portions of the river. Next followed the removal of rocks or huge boulders from the exposed bed and the use of pumps driven by water-powered wheels to get water out of the pockets where gold would most likely collect. Before they could begin work on their claim area, the men had to wait until the high water of the river subsided, surviving as best they could off the land or by taking work when available. High water usually occurred by June or July. In the meantime, the river miner had to be resourceful to keep body and soul together.[22]

In slack times when not working directly on his river claim, Windeler tried some individual placering, "coyote"-style shaft digging, and drift mining into hillsides. He hunted deer and ducks, fished, cut firewood, and at times worked for wages for other miners. He even accepted a job that required sailoring skills in scaling a tall pine tree to capture a grizzly bear cub for another man who wished to put the animal on commercial display. All these activities had environmental effects.[23]

From the end of May 1852, Windeler and his partners worked at constructing their river dam and mining race. They cut oak and pine trees (especially the highly desirable sugar pines, which would split evenly) and shaped them for specialized functions. Next came digging and removal of boulders in the race. Windeler's group purchased sawed lumber for the race and dam from an enterprising mill operator nearby. Then came the building and testing of the water wheel and pumps made from locally harvested trees, and rebuilding the dam completely when it leaked badly.

Constant delays and problems led Windeler to write on August 24, "So it goes, botheration again & fall coming along, hand over fist." By November, when rain began to fall, Windeler and his partners abandoned their operation with very little to show for their work and investment. In September he noted: "All the gold we do get is rather fine than coarse, so at present it looks as though we won't make anything of any account this year. But that is nothing new . . . better luck next time."[24]

J. D. Borthwick, a miner who also happened to be an artist, turned his discerning eyes on several mining camps that he encountered beginning in 1851. He left behind a vivid description of the collective devastation that the placer miners created. Borthwick's earliest observation was of Placerville. Although the camp appeared deserted when he first arrived—with a number of unoccupied cabins and abandoned mining claims visible—the area revealed great amounts of hard work expended earlier:

> The beds of the numerous ravines which wrinkle the faces of the hills, the bed of the creek, and all the little flats along side of it, were a confused mass of heaps of dirt and piles of stones lying around the innumerable holes, about six feet square and five or six feet deep, from which they had been thrown out. The original course of the creek was completely obliterated, its waters being distributed into numberless ditches, and from them conducted into the "long toms" of the miners through canvas hoses, looking like immensely long slimy sea-serpents.[25]

Farther north, at Nevada City, he encountered a comparable scene where placering and some early quartz mining was going on:

> [The city] is beautifully situated on the hills bordering a small creek and has once been surrounded by a forest of magnificent pine-trees, which, however, had been made to become useful instead of ornamental, and nothing now remained to show that they existed but the numbers of stumps all over the hill-sides. The bed of the creek, which had once flowed past the town, was now choked up with heaps of "trailings"—the washed dirt from which the gold has been extracted—the white colour of the dirt rendering it, still more unsightly. All the water in the creek was distributed among a number of small troughs, carried along the steep banks on either side at different elevations, for the purpose of supplying various quartz-mills and long toms.[26]

So what were the effects of such endeavors? All aspects of the Sierran environment—rivers, forests, and wildlife—were used, transformed, and degraded. The collective impact of the placer miners was astonishing. As stream expert Jeffrey Mount noted, "No longer would the rivers operate in blithe disregard for the organisms dependent on them. In a geologic blink of an eye, a billion years of California river processes were transformed."[27]

Drift and "coyote" mining were other forms of complex placer mining that developed in the early 1850s and required pooling of assets and labor. The normal practice was to cut tunnels or drifts into hillsides or dig down into the hard-packed Tertiary deposits. The resulting "gravel" was then processed through sluices treated with mercury to separate the gold from the unwanted material. The drift method was often a highly risky enterprise, with paydirt being more often hoped for than actually reached. This form of mining was generally abandoned when more efficient hydraulic processes were developed after the mid-1850s.[28]

But between the early and middle fifties, hundreds of such shafts were cut and many companies were at work. For example, in the Iowa Hill district in Placer County in 1856 alone, nearly ninety such tunnels were driven into the Tertiary deposits. Of these it was reported that thirty-four were soon abandoned, work continued on twenty-three without any sign of success, and only thirty-two had produced some income.[29] Clearly this was an extremely inefficient way of going about mining. No wonder it was abandoned for the hydraulic method.

As to environmental effects of placer mining, one of the most obvious was the impact it had on the stream systems themselves. Streams and adjacent areas were radically transformed. Riparian vegetation was destroyed. Rivers were turned out of their beds. Fish and aquatic life were affected by extraordinary amounts of silt, mud, and mining debris that had no natural parallel. Seasonal flooding and silt loads had always been a natural part of Sierran stream processes, but the watercourses were unable to clean themselves as greater and greater burdens were placed on them.[30]

As a result, fish populations, including trout, steelhead, spring and winter salmon runs were decimated. Salmon, once reported in the headwaters of most of the streams of the Sacramento and San Joaquin River systems, rapidly declined. Gill-net fishermen outside the Sierra Nevada contributed to the decline in population in these years, but habitat destruction in the mountains played a major part in the collapse of the fishery.[31]

A reliable estimate of direct effects of placer mining comes from G. K. Gilbert, one of the pioneers of California earth science. He estimated that placer mining produced 60 million cubic yards of debris deposited into Sierran streams from the Feather River in the north to the Tuolumne River in the south. Drift mining was credited with producing an additional 30 million cubic yards. The combined placer and drift mining total was 90 million cubic yards. That is a lot of debris, although it would be dwarfed in comparison with the amount deposited by the hydraulic mining companies.[32]

Hydraulic mining occurred in thirteen counties in the Sierra, but the largest operations were located in the northern parts of the range because of the availability of water in the Feather, Yuba, Bear, and American Rivers. Hydraulic mining in the Yuba tributaries where the largest alluvial deposits were located formed the heart of the industry.[33]

Originally, hydraulic mining involved the focusing of water flow under pressure through canvas hoses over surface alluvial deposits. It was a cheap way to wash surface gravels and generally was more economical and less dangerous than drift mining. Early success led to technological improvements steadily through the 1860s.[34]

Water for hydraulic mining was stored in high mountain dams or lakes, transported through thousands of miles of flumes and ditches, forced under great pressure through iron nozzles called "monitors," and directed against Sierran hillsides. The mud and debris washed loose were channeled into long sluices coated with immense amounts of mercury, where some of the freed gold was collected.[35]

Hydraulic mining was relatively efficient in processing the small amounts of fine gold locked up in Eocene/Tertiary gravel deposits. Millions of cubic yards of mud and debris washed into sluice boxes produced large profits. Smaller mining operations were absorbed by large American and English water and mining companies. San Francisco became the investment-capital center for the mountain operations.[36] By 1862, these companies were producing vast amounts of debris from their operations. Larger dams and more extensive water-distribution systems were developed, necessitating the expenditure of millions of dollars for labor and construction materials.[37]

Soon the amount of debris generated by hydraulic mining exceeded the ability of upland creeks to absorb all the mud and rocks discharged into them. At that point, the huge mining and water companies drove drainage tunnels through the granite and let the accumulating debris spill into the larger river canyons. There it accumulated in vast quantities, waiting for the spring runoff to carry it away. A report submitted to the state of California in 1880 estimated that more than 680 million cubic yards of debris had been washed into northern Sierra Nevada stream systems by hydraulic operations. A federal report published in 1917 by Gilbert estimated that the total volume of mining debris from hydraulic mining, most of it produced between 1860 and 1884, was 1.5 billion cubic yards. That is eight times the amount of earth moved in the making of the Panama Canal.[38]

Hydraulic mining was indeed efficient, and the effects were immense where the operations were concentrated. Some contemporary observers feared that the areas affected, stripped as they were of trees, all other vegetation, topsoil, and animal life, could never expect to recover. Government scientist John B. Leiberg, who surveyed the basins of four major northern Sierra Nevada rivers in 1902, noted the effects of earlier hydraulic mining: "Every acre of forested ground torn up by the hydraulic giants and covered by tailings, or converted into a dumping ground for the debris, is an acre of forest land irretrievably lost. Centuries will pass before the mounds of debris and crumbling bluffs of sand and gravel left by this class of miners will possess much forest cover."[39]

On present-day Interstate 80 near the town of Dutch Flat, and in the area of Malakoff Diggings near the ghost town of North Bloomfield, examples of the scarred landscape are still evident as Leiberg predicted. They have the appearance of mini–Grand Canyons if you employ a positive perspective— or a barren moonscape if you are less upbeat.

If the mud and debris generated by hydraulic mining had remained in place, the damage might have been localized in the Sierra Nevada. But from the 1860s to the 1880s, winter and spring floods carried the increasing amount of debris, mud, and rocks to foothill and valley communities lower down. The effect on those communities was disastrous. Foothill orchards were buried, river corridors were filled with the tailings, and floods devastated the farms in the valley. Marysville, Yuba City, and Sacramento had been imperiled since 1862 whenever severe winter storms occurred. Attempts were made to channel the rivers. This actually increased the speed and power of the storm-swollen rivers and caused more damage when the poorly built levees failed. The debris spread into the Delta and eventually into San Francisco Bay, raising and filling them with mud, sand, gravel, and rock as the force of the water subsided in the flat areas.[40]

Eventually valley farmers, townspeople, and navigation interests turned to political and legal actions. In 1884, a federal court injunction in what is called the "Sawyer decision" (after the name of the judge, Lorenzo Sawyer) effectively stopped hydraulic mining. It prohibited mining operations from allowing debris to escape into the navigable rivers and San Francisco Bay. Attempts to revive the industry with federal legislation and money to create debris-collection basins and dams in the 1890s failed to save it.[41]

The action of the farmers against the miners is hailed as the beginning of environmental regulation in California.[42] It is significant for that reason but must also be seen in the context as the beginnings of regulation of industries in the public interest, an emerging element in the rise of federal and state regulatory powers. In this regard it was mountain mining corporations and their financiers in San Francisco versus farmers and cities in the valley and those dependent on the river and bay for transportation uses. The concern was for the valley and Bay-Delta interests. No one was standing up for the mountains or the forests, however. The hydraulic miners were not being prevented from destroying hillsides, forests, or mountain river systems because these things had value of their own. It would take later sensibilities to begin the process of true conservation or preservation.[43]

Hydraulic mining in the Sierra Nevada extended the general impact caused by placer and drift mining.[44] But the degree of environmental alteration is more than just a mathematical increase in the amount of debris that hydraulic operations created. The impacts on the Sierra Nevada are gigantic.

The most detailed analysis of hydraulic mining's impact on Sierra Nevada streams is Gilbert's 1917 report. It was part of a USGS survey carried out in the decades after hydraulic mining was halted. Gilbert's conclusion that over one and a half billion cubic yards of debris was deposited in the river basins from the Feather to the Mokelumne is still useful. He focused primarily on the Yuba River basin for his detailed studies. He noted that the amounts of debris and eroded materials that originated in placer and lode mining, farming, road use and construction, trail development, and overgrazing in the basin were very small in comparison with hydraulic mining's effects.[45]

Gilbert wrote that since hydraulic mining had been stopped, and if no large-scale mining resumed, normal stream processes would clear riverbeds in about fifty years. This stream action would have moved hydraulic materials—depending on their size and consistency—down into the foothills, the lower river systems, the Delta, and even San Francisco Bay. As he said: "It is possible that none of the gravel now in transit will reach the bays as gravel, but it may be assumed that as the pre-mining slopes of the river channel are approached the character of the pre-mining channel bed will also be approached."[46]

There is some question about Gilbert's prediction that Sierran stream processes and sediment loads would return to normal.[47] There is evidence that much of the material washed out by hydraulic mining, contained at present in various streams, terraces, floodplains, and sediment reservoirs, is still making its way into Sierran streams and the reservoirs that have been built after Gilbert's time.[48] One current estimate of hydraulic-mining debris deposited in the Bear River claims that removal of hydraulic deposits will continue into the next millennium, clearing around the year 3000.[49] The construction of dams such as Englebright, on the Yuba River just as it leaves the foothills of the Sierra Nevada, has also disrupted the natural stream processes. It and other dams built on tributaries of the Yuba and American have acted as collectors of debris, something beyond Gilbert's predictions.[50]

The direct impact of hydraulic mining can be measured in another way, by looking at its effect on the forested lands washed away by the hydraulic monitors. In 1902, John B. Leiberg conducted a detailed study of the conditions and composition of forests in the forest reserve that later became Tahoe National Forest. His remark that hydraulic mining created "forest land irretrievably lost" was part of his summary of the four major "Destructive Agencies" contributing to forest degradation. Listed in order of importance, these four horsemen of the environmental apocalypse were cutting, fire, grazing, and mining, with hydraulic mining being of much grater significance than the earlier placer forms.[51]

Leiberg surveyed the tributaries of the Feather, Yuba, Bear, and American. In each he applied the same research report design, including a section on the forces of forest destruction that had been unleashed in the aftermath of the gold rush. His remarks about hydraulic mining's effects were consistent for all the tributaries he visited where such mining had occurred.

Of the North Fork of the Feather, Leiberg noted that "enormous holes have been torn in the Pleistocene or glacial gravel ridges." He added: "Reproduction on worked out placer grounds [placer as he used the word in these examples referred to areas damaged by hydraulic mining] is poor. In such places the soil and humus have been washed away and only coarse gravel, bowlders, and bare bed rock remain." In the North Fork of the Yuba, the "hills and flats have been torn in all directions by hydraulic mining." As to reproduction of the forest there, "The logged areas in the western portion of the basin are restocking abundantly, except where the ground has been turned up by the placer miners and the soil washed away from underlying sharp, unproductive gravel and bowlder drift." On the South Fork of the Yuba he found that the hillsides "have been torn up in all directions by the hydraulic giants. Vast masses of debris have resulted." As to reproduction, "The gravel heaps which mark the placer mines are practically without mold, or humus, and cannot produce much forest for hundreds of years to come." Similar remarks occur in descriptions of the Bear and American systems.[52]

Hydraulic mining in Sierran streams affected fish populations. Although these populations declined somewhat in the early years of the gold rush, miners still continued to note large numbers of fish. Spring-run salmon were reported in the headwaters of all the major river systems that fed into the Central Valley well into the 1850s. Steelhead and salmon were seen all the way up to Downieville on a tributary of the Yuba until the later 1850s.[53]

Hydraulic mining went well beyond simple placer mining in dealing a devastating blow to local trout and to the anadromous salmon and steelhead that used Sierran streams. Debris silted over the spawning beds. Dams constructed to impound water for the industry interrupted natural runs. Hydraulic mining (before the construction of large dams on the lower reaches of the rivers) is generally charged with being the chief culprit in the decline of salmon and steelhead populations, although logging and overfishing had impact as well.[54]

Another major environmental legacy of hydraulic mining is mercury deposited in the streams of the Sierra Nevada. Placer mining began the process.

Hydraulic mining magnified the effect a thousandfold. In order to trap fine gold released by the hydraulic monitors, sluices—sometimes hundreds or thousands of feet long—were coated or charged with mercury. Fine eroded gold amalgamated with the mercury. The amalgam was then heated, driving off the mercury and leaving the gold behind to be further purified. Thousands of kilograms of mercury were used in this process in the 1870s and 1880s, the peak time of the industry.[55] For example, one English-owned mining corporation on the Yuba River used two tons of mercury in 1873 alone.

Much of the mercury and the finest surface amalgam were swept away into the streams. It was not the intent of the companies to have this happen, but it was unavoidable. Loss of mercury was considered part of doing business. One calculation put the losses at about 12.5 to 15 percent of the total mercury used. The North Bloomfield Mine, on a Yuba River tributary, lost a total of 21,512 pounds from 1876 through 1881.[56]

Widespread accumulation of mercury occurred in the rivers of the northern Sierra Nevada. The Yuba and Bear, especially, contain very large quantities. The Sacramento Regional County Sanitation District has noted "hot spots" where mercury deposits are especially concentrated on these rivers. The bioaccumulation of methylmercury in the flesh of fish in some areas of the Yuba exceeds the amount accepted as safe for human consumption by the National Academy of Sciences. The greatest accumulations are found behind dams such as Englebright on the Yuba. Dams accelerate concentrations in fish in the reservoir by preventing the dispersal of mercury that would occur if the dams were not present.[57]

Another environmental effect of hydraulic mining in the Sierra Nevada came from impounding and transporting huge quantities of water. By the late 1860s, when the industry was in its takeoff phase, there were 231 identifiable ditch systems with a combined length of over 3,390 miles serving operations in thirteen Sierran counties. These systems were fed by numerous dams and significantly altered the waterscapes of the range. Thousands of miles of main pipelines and branch ditches brought millions of gallons of water to the mining areas into the 1880s. Flumes bridged canyons and snaked along steep slopes or cliffs, funneling water to the powerful hydraulic monitors that were washing away Sierran hillsides.[58]

Dams on streams and at the outlets of natural lakes stored snowmelt or rain from higher elevations. Connected to the ditches and flumes, they supplied a reliable source of water to the hydraulic monitors, reducing problems caused by the Mediterranean climate. The dams ranged from small to very large, the latter with heights from 60 to 130 feet. The smaller ones were typically constructed of rubble, sand, and clay, but the largest were constructed of cedar or sugar pine with supporting wooden ribs and plank skins. Among the largest dams were the English and the Bowman, feeding the operations at North Bloomfield.[59]

Within a few years after the 1884 Sawyer decision halted unregulated hydraulic mining in the Sierra Nevada,[60] some of the water-delivery systems began to decay and fall apart because they were not maintained. Some ditches were destroyed later by logging operations. In an important transition, some of the hydraulic delivery systems were taken over by hydroelectric companies such as Pacific Gas and Electric in the 1890s, or in some instances by irrigation districts that used the former mining ditches to deliver water to foothill orchards. These now also serve the expanding urban populations of the northern foothills with domestic water. Some of the converted ditches and water systems have become part of a permanent alteration of Sierran waterscapes.[61]

In 1849 another gold-mining industry—quartz or hard-rock mining— was born. At Mariposa in the south-central western foothills, the discovery of veins of gold embedded in quartz formations created great excitement. Similar discoveries to the north in the Grass Valley area fueled another boom. Soon investors from California, elsewhere in the United States, and even Europe joined the feeding frenzy. As with most Sierran gold schemes, the excitement quickly peaked and then crashed—in this case because of the difficulties and expense of getting the gold out of its quartz matrix. By 1852, quartz mining was in disrepute, its failed investors turning to other endeavors. In placer mining and even the earliest forms of hydraulic mining, amateurs with few skills could sometimes get lucky. Quartz mining required patience, scientific knowledge, and large quantities of capital to sustain operations that did not usually produce quick profits. From the beginning, quartz mining needed industrial organization.[62]

From 1852 to 1860, a few hardy quartz operations managed to hang on and carry out limited mining. Techniques for extracting the ore, crushing it, and separating gold particles were painstakingly experimented with and improved. Existing knowledge from Mexico and the American Southeast was applied and allowed shallow operations to continue in areas where the concentration of gold in the quartz veins was high enough—especially in Grass Valley. Mercury, mined elsewhere in California, had first been used in placer and hydraulic mining to increase the capturing of fine gold. In quartz mining it allowed for capture of about 20 to 30 percent of the gold freed by crushing the ore.[63]

In 1860 the discovery of incredibly rich deposits of silver mixed with gold and other minerals in the Comstock area in western Nevada brought about a rush of miners that stripped much of California's population. This discovery quickly moved into the industrial phase because of the complexity of the operations. The Comstock required professional miners to dig the ore. Timber from the Sierra was needed to shore up the deepening mineshafts and excavated ore bodies. Special pumps adapted from those used in Cornish tin mines raised water out of the deep shafts. Iron machinery was a necessity, and transportation improvements across the Sierra Nevada quickly developed. Complex chemistry and industrial organization were needed to extract gold and silver from the ore. But what kept the industry alive was huge amounts of capital, most of it coming from San Francisco.[64] Until the late 1870s when the Comstock played out, it dominated the California and Sierran economies.[65]

With the demise of the Comstock, miners and capitalists returned to Grass Valley, Nevada City, and other areas in the western Sierra Nevada, such as the Sierra Buttes and Amador County, where quartz deposits were rich. Discoveries of silver and gold on the eastern side of the Sierra at Cerro Gordo, Panamint, and Bodie also generated industrial mining development. Advances in skill, technology, and organization aided the industry's rebirth. California industry inside and outside these areas responded with even more investment in manufacturing. Urban population soared in the Sierra where the mines developed. In the eastern Sierra, communities such as Bishop gained new life. The mining development promised continued growth and possible rail connections. The new hard-rock industry acted as a catalyst for further economic growth.[66]

The increased industrialization also enlarged the effects of quartz mining on the Sierra Nevada environment. In the Grass Valley area, for example, where the gold veins were narrow, huge amounts of the rock surrounding them had to be cut away to reach the gold.[67] G. K. Gilbert reported on the amount of debris that came from quartz mining in the northwestern area of the Sierra Nevada from 1849 to 1909. He estimated that 50 million cubic yards—only 10 million less than that generated by placer mining—ended up in Sierran streams.[68]

Mercury, employed to amalgamate with fine gold particles, found its way into Sierran streams, as did chemical residuals from the newly applied industrial chlorination process that supplemented mercury in the larger and more efficient mines.[69] To this day mercury released from quartz and hydraulic gold mining seeps into Sierran systems. Large amounts can be found in the Central Valley, threatening current water quality and poisoning fish and wildlife.[70] Acid runoff from many abandoned gold mines is also a long-term legacy of the heyday of quartz mining in the northern and central Sierra Nevada today.[71]

Unlike placer and hydraulic mining, hard-rock mining of gold did not stop in the nineteenth century. It continued to be significant in the economies of the northern and central Sierra until after the Second World War. Labor troubles in the Grass Valley area, a wartime mine-closure order in the 1940s, and declining prices for gold generally halted operations in most of the larger mines by the 1950s.[72]

Logging and Environmental Change, 1848–1890

Logging in the Sierra Nevada developed in support of local mining activities. Sierran lumber was used to build miners' rockers, long toms, and sluices. It was used for lining millraces, building dams, and constructing water wheels and pumps. Wooden flumes transported water, especially in the more arid west-central foothills where rich deposits were distant from water sources. Firewood and lumber for cabins and other buildings in the numerous mining camps was locally obtained.[73]

By the early 1850s, all communities in the placers had small sawmills cutting ponderosa pine. As mining locations shifted and ponderosa stands dwindled, lumbermen moved their mills higher to utilize sugar pine and white and red fir. Power for the mills generally came from water or steam engines. (In one rare exception in 1850, a sawmill on the Middle Fork of the American River experimented with using galloping horses for power.) Many diaries of miners and others in the mines comment on the operation of mills and the high prices for lumber.[74]

For many enterprising individuals, selling lumber to miners was a much better investment than mining itself. All nineteenth-century Sierra Nevada county histories feature the early lumbermen in their pages. One estimate of the number of early sawmills in the gold rush era was that 320 were operating in the state. For the counties of the Sierra Nevada north of Sacramento from 1849 to 1900, nearly 150 mills were estimated to have been in operation. There may have been many more, for in Nevada County alone in 1858 there were 42 mills producing 40 million board feet of lumber. Most of these mills were small and had single operators or perhaps two or three men acting as partners. As the mining became more industrialized, larger mills supported by railroads or complex flume systems came to dominate.[75]

High lumber prices encouraged many to log rather than mine. H. G. Livermore, who had been a lumberman in Maine before coming to California, reported sawing 4,000 board feet of lumber a day and selling it to fluming companies at $50 to $75 per thousand board feet. Some mill owners cut 8,000 to 12,000 board feet a day. Mill operators also sold water from their flume systems. High profits justified investment in building water systems or, in areas where water could not be counted on, the purchase of woodburning steam engines. John Wallace in 1852 to 1853 reported that his mill on the headwaters of the Stanislaus River was highly profitable. He quickly reduced his debt of $75,000 incurred in building the mill and flume system to $50,000 through the sale of lumber and water to miners. William Higby, operating a mill at Mokelumne Hill in the central Sierra Nevada, wrote to a relative that his sales of lumber and water to miners would net him a $100,000 a year.[76]

The lumber industry of the Sierra Nevada expanded after 1860. The building of the Central Pacific Railroad across the range required ties, timbers, and planking. In turn, as railroads expanded, Sierran timber could be sold into the Great Basin and distributed to places as far away as Salt Lake City or the mining areas in Arizona. Sierran lumber was used to build the Virginia and Truckee Railroad, which then transported millions of board feet of timbers and cordwood to the deep mines and smelters of the Comstock and other mining areas in the eastern Sierra Nevada. Sierran wood supported the rails of the Nevada County Narrow Gauge, serving Nevada City and Grass Valley. Markets for Sierran timber soon developed in valley and coastal cities, and eventually in southern California.[77]

Massive cutting of sequoia occurred in the central and southern Sierra Nevada. In the Calaveras Grove one of the largest trees was cut in 1853 and its stump used as a dance floor. In the same grove a tree over three hundred feet high was stripped of a portion of its bark. The bark was exhibited in the eastern U.S. and London. The tree died, of course. John Muir, on a tour of the Kaweah area in the 1870s, observed a mill in its third year of operation. It cut two million board feet of sequoia in one year alone. He was especially troubled that 25 to 50 percent of the cut wood was wasted. When the giants fell, he said, "the sequoia breaks like glass," often making it unfit for the mill to process. In 1891 Muir noted accelerated cutting in southern groves, where millmen often resorted to blasting the felled logs to reduce them to manageable sizes. While only a fraction of the generally inaccessible giant forest had been cut by the late 1880s, in areas around Grant Grove and the North Fork of the Tule River the cutting was intense.[78]

The amount of timber cut between 1849 and the turn of the century is incalculable. Few accurate records exist. One useful estimate comes from the California Forestry Board, established in 1885. Its first biennial report, in 1886, stated that twenty years of cutting had "consumed and destroyed" one-third of the Sierra Nevada's timber. It predicted that at the same rate of consumption, all marketable timber in the Sierra would soon be gone.[79]

Two U.S. Geological Survey reports from the turn of the century detailed the impact of unregulated cutting in the west-central and most of the northern Sierra Nevada (including all the river systems of the Sacramento River drainage and the Tahoe-Truckee Basin). In certain areas of the western foothills close to mining activities, 90 percent or more of the merchantable timber was stripped and reduced. Brush and other nonmarketable species of plants had replaced trees in those areas. A clear pattern of cutting was noted. Around lumbermill sites, everything of value in a two-and-a-half to three-mile circle was cut. The mill site was then abandoned and the machinery moved to another stand of timber, where the process was repeated. The reproduction of certain species such as sugar pine was imperiled by the wasteful "high-grading" practices of shake makers. They took only the best parts of the large trees, leaving the rest as waste. This added to fire danger. No large seed trees remained.[80]

Cutover lands were prone to flooding. Miners' accounts note with awe the effects of flooding in the American and Feather River drainages. Trees, debris, and all manner of manmade construction such as flumes were swept away by water rushing off the denuded hillsides. Elsewhere, silt and waste filtering into Lake Tahoe from the stripped hills around it produced an algal bloom by the late nineteenth century.[81]

Cutover lands were so damaged by logging operations and by fires in the waste or slash left behind that regeneration of forests was delayed for years. Fires caused by logging operations at the mills or as part of general operations were frequent and swept away mills, trees, and cut lumber in huge amounts. Ignition sources varied, but often sparks from steam engines or locomotives used to transport timber were to blame.[82]

It is difficult to imagine the extent of the cutting in the Sierra Nevada before the 1880s. No one was keeping accurate records across the accessible forested lands in the region. But if we examine in detail the Tahoe-Truckee Basin, where good estimates of the amount cut exist, a clearer picture of the overall environmental effects from unregulated logging in the range emerges. The basin includes the northeastern Sierra Nevada adjacent to the Comstock mining district in western Nevada, the forested hillsides surrounding Lake Tahoe, and the drainages of the Truckee River that extend from Lake Tahoe to Pyramid Lake in Nevada. The forested areas in the basin were included in the eastern parts of the California counties of Sierra, Nevada, Placer, El Dorado, and a small portion of Alpine. The forestland on the eastern side of the Sierra adjacent to Tahoe Basin includes portions of the Nevada counties of Washoe and Douglass.

The *Reno Gazette* in 1881 estimated that 7 billion board feet of saw timber and 10 million cords of fuel wood had existed before cutting began. The reporter for the *Gazette* subtracted all the timber cut for the Comstock, the railroad, and Great Basin cities such as Salt Lake City. In his estimate, nearly 2 billion board feet had been cut by 1881. He maintained that perhaps 5 billion board feet remained in the rest of the basin. ("Such vast figures as are given above afford little significance to the ordinary reader," the reporter admitted. "A city like San Francisco could be built out of such a body of timber and it would never be noticed.") Most of the remaining accessible timber was cut by the turn of the century, although logging in some of the smaller drainages of the Truckee continued until the 1930s, when nearly all the virgin forest had been consumed.[83]

Major environmental effects grew from this massive cutting. For a starting point, the timber industry was a consumer of its own product. Steam-driven "donkey" engines, locomotives, and tractors burned some of the mining slash and cordwood. Complex log chutes and V-shaped flumes built to transport logs and lumber stretched for miles throughout the basin drainages and required 135,000 board feet per mile for their construction. The planks for the flumes had to be of the highest quality, knotholes obviously being a problem for a water-delivery system. Much of the timber used in such construction was simply abandoned to rot after cutting in an area was finished.[84]

The Truckee River and its tributary the Little Truckee were used directly to transport logs to mills. Sierran rivers, however, especially on the arid eastern side, rarely have enough flow in summer to move logs. Loggers on the Truckee created "splash dams" to overcome this problem. At key points on the river below the dam constructed at Tahoe, they built log dams that temporarily raised the water level enough to float large logs. When water levels pushed logs against the dam, the loggers removed the top section, and the resulting torrent carried the logs along to the next splash dam. The method was ingenious, but also environmentally destructive. The flooding created by this technique damaged the stream banks, scoured the streambed, and killed fish. Logs not pushed all the way to the next splash dam littered the riverbanks. In some instances, the gates of the dam constructed at the mouth of the river at Lake Tahoe had to be opened to flush suspended logs downstream. Complaints and lawsuits over damages caused to streamside property owners led to the ending of the practice even before the area's forests were cut over.[85]

Lumbermills in the Tahoe-Truckee Basin produced massive amounts of sawdust. Circular saws claimed a significant percentage of every log as sawdust, some 40,000 board feet annually being consumed in this way. Mills found disposal a problem. Fire danger was very high already, and mill operators decided to rid themselves of this bothersome byproduct by dumping it into the Truckee River or its tributaries. Sawdust fouled the streams, destroyed fisheries, and threatened the downstream water supply for Reno.[86]

In cutover areas, fires, caused in part by logging operations, damaged possibilities for a healthy regeneration of the forest. The successor forest was dominated by a single species, white fir, which was less fire-resistant and drought-resistant than the pines it replaced. Fir predominates in the fire-prone forests that surround Lake Tahoe today.[87]

In the Comstock, logging directly supported mining and smelter operations. Because of the area's unique geological configuration, the mines required large timber-support cubes, called "square sets," constructed from clear lumber. An imaginative person could envision a very large part of the finest-quality lumber cut from the basin's forests silently rotting away under Virginia City and Silver City in the now-abandoned mine stopes.[88] During the latter days of the Comstock boom, 70 million board feet were cut annually to support mining operations. Vast quantities of wood literally went up in smoke: Comstock furnaces (used for smeltering and for powering mine pumps) consumed 1,087,180 cords between 1873 and 1879.[89]

The Central Pacific used timber cut from its own right-of-way or elsewhere in the basin to provide crossties, build snow sheds to facilitate winter operation, support tunnels, and of course burn for locomotive fuel. From the late 1860s to 1880, nine large logging corporations dominated the industry at Tahoe. They hired hundreds of loggers who cut 300 million board feet to build the Central Pacific's western-slope snow sheds and another 20 million board feet annually to repair them. In 1868, mills in Truckee shipped fifty carloads of ties daily for railroad use. The Truckee area mills in the decade from 1867 to 1877 produced 376 million board feet of lumber. The Central Pacific used 75,000 cords in 1877 to power its locomotives.[90]

What does this all add up to? No one knows for certain. One can choose to accept the estimates of the *Reno Gazette* reporter who placed the total of cut timber at around 2 billion board feet by 1881. Or one can accept the estimate by U.S. government scientist John Leiberg, who in 1902 claimed that 1,450,000 board feet had been cut in the accessible formerly forested areas of the basin he surveyed, an area that was limited to a portion of Truckee River drainage.[91]

Logged-clean or cutover areas by the 1880s comprised 170,000 acres, or nearly 59 percent of forestland in the Tahoe-Truckee Basin. Nearly all healthy commercial yellow pine and sugar pine in the immediate lake basin and the Truckee River Canyon to the town of Truckee had been cut. The only areas left uncut were steep, inaccessible tracts, private estate holdings, and lands in the eastern Truckee and Little Truckee drainages (these two drainage areas were cut over from 1900 to the 1930s).[92]

Grazing and Environmental Change, 1850–1890

In the Sierra Nevada, the livestock industry grew alongside mining and lumbering. The grazing of sheep and cattle to supply meat and dairy products to miners, timber camps, and towns began with the gold rush, though some damage from immigrants' stock already existed along wagon trails. The use of Sierran pastures was important in the ongoing transformation of the range.[93]

Sierran meadows were heavily grazed before 1900. Most beef cattle and dairy cows used lower-elevation and higher-quality fenced ranges. But livestock grazing also involved seasonal transhumance—animals were grazed on low-elevation winter grasslands in the Central Valley or foothills and then driven to alpine areas for summer range.[94] Cattle, sheep, horses, goats, and even pigs were involved in the industry. (While cattle drives inspired songs and much western lore, it is hard to imagine that anyone sang "Get along little sooey" or called himself a "pigboy.") Meat, butter, and cheese were supplied to railroad workers, lumberjacks, miners, and town or camp dwellers in the Sierra Nevada.[95]

Cattle grazing in the higher elevations occurred in the mid-1860s when drought in the Central Valley drove cattlemen to seek range in the Sierra. Clarence King, a member of Josiah Whitney's California Geological Survey, noted large numbers of cattle using the higher-elevation areas in Kings Canyon. He saw one herd that he estimated at 4,000.[96] Meat and dairy cattle, pigs, and goats were grazed in the Truckee Basin to serve railroad and timber markets. Sheep grazed on all other rangeland. Most of the Sierra Nevada was affected by grazing. Foothills, middle-elevation forests, and subalpine areas such as the upper Kern Basin were heavily impacted. Only alpine fell fields escaped impact because they had little vegetation and were located in difficult terrain.[97]

John Muir had the ability to create unforgettable images in defense of western wild spaces. "Hoofed locusts," his name for the sheep he herded one summer and later condemned for their damage to Sierran meadows, ranks high in a long list of memorable phrases. Long after Muir publicized damage to what he called the Sierra's "gardens," concern is still expressed over grazing in the ranges and riparian systems in the Sierra and other areas in the west. The sheep industry deserves attention here.[98]

Before the advent of domestic livestock, Sierran rangelands evolved in part from the actions of numerous large wild grazing mammals. These were quickly displaced in the early settlement period by domestic livestock.[99] Sheep grazing in the Sierra Nevada developed in two distinct periods before 1900. The first, 1848–1860, involved the driving of animals from New Mexico and southern California to mining camps and towns in the western foothills. This did not result in much actual grazing in the Sierra Nevada. After 1860, herders depended on Sierran pastures directly. Itinerant, or so-called gypsy, sheep bands were driven into both sides of the Sierra Nevada from southern and central California, where drought and competition for land had made free range in the mountains desirable.[100]

The number of sheep that foraged on Sierran meadows before Forest Service regulation can only be guessed at. There was no limit to the size or number of bands that entered the Sierra Nevada before 1900, or on how long herders could utilize a specific area. But certainly millions of sheep grazed meadows in the Sierra during this time. One result of this unregulated sheep grazing was the reduction of some native perennial plants and their replacement by more aggressive imported annual species, especially in the higher elevations in the southern Sierra Nevada, where some areas were left completely denuded of native plants.[101]

Sheep grazing in the Sierra Nevada before 1900 was condemned by many contemporary observers. It was judged to be more destructive than cattle grazing. Muir's "hoofed locusts" were, in his view, more effective than fires or glaciers in destroying vegetation.[102]

Complaints were raised by many, including professionals from the state of California and the U.S. Geological Survey. All said that too many animals were grazing for too long on Sierran pastures. The *First Biennial Report of the California State Board of Forestry for the Years 1885–1886,* reflecting this anti-sheep view, recommended that all sheep be excluded from the Sierra Nevada because of the damage they caused to soils and vegetation. In a report to Board of Forestry chairman Abbott Kinney, field investigator Luther Wagoner wrote: "The high Sierra is composed of rocky soil generally quite thin and easily dislodged. The sheep make numerous nearly horizontal trails, and dislodge the soil and humus, and kill young trees by trampling and dislodging soil. I think there is no doubt that the damage done by sheep is greater than their value, and if they could be shut out entirely the State would be the gainer by doing so."[103]

Sheepherders were also blamed for setting fires to improve future range or to remove barriers to sheep movement—fires that destroyed valuable timber when they burned out of control. It is doubtful that most of the fire damage in the Sierra Nevada at this time could be blamed on the Basque or other "tramp herders." Anti-foreign bias and a general dislike of the sheep industry colored the understanding of contemporary critics. Fires caused by careless logging operations (sparks from their steam engines and woodburning locomotives), the clearing of land by settlers, and of course lightning-caused conflagrations were also at work.[104] Some present-day Park Service personnel have even suggested that burning by the herders may have continued the pattern of low-level burning by Native Americans and therefore may have had a positive effect in reducing overall fire danger.[105]

Wildlife: Habitat Loss, Market Hunting, and Fishing

In 1996 the U.S. Forest Service issued the Sierra Nevada Ecosystem Project's *Final Report to Congress*. The product of a three-year study of environmental conditions in the range, its most poignant concern was expressed for the nonhuman inhabitants of the range—especially its terrestrial vertebrates. Three of these (the grizzly bear, the California condor, and a bird named Bell's vireo) had once been "well distributed in the range." They were now extinct there. The grizzly fell quickly in the invasion by European Americans. The condor's decline took longer and came about from more-complex reasons: the displacement of the larger natural grazing animals and the shooting of the big birds by protective livestock owners. Bell's vireo lost its riparian habitat over the years following Sierran development.[106]

Besides these extinctions, the SNEP report noted that 69 terrestrial vertebrate species (some 17 percent of the total of such species found in the range) were at risk, with such labels as "endangered," "threatened," "special concern," or "sensitive" attached to them. They belonged to "perilously declining or dangerously low populations" that were now "rare when compared to their presence in historical records." The fundamental cause of the declining fortunes of these Sierran inhabitants was loss of habitat—especially in the range's western foothills, old-growth forests, and riparian zones.

SNEP's scientists were concerned with the loss of genetic diversity represented in these declines. They indicated a break in "the chain of natural selection and adaptation," and thus in the genetic integrity, of the Sierran ecosystem. They noted: "Human-caused activities threatening genetic integrity include severe wildfire, habitat degradation and conversion, landscape fragmentation, introduction of non-native fish, improperly conducted reintroduction of native plants and animal species in ecological restoration, habitat improvement, fire reclamation, and unregulated harvest of special forest products."[107]

This disruption of presettlement Sierran wildlife habitat began even before the gold rush.[108] The use of dray animals by the early immigrant wagon trains prepared the way for a significant transformation of the floral and faunal landscape—overgrazing opened land for new "weeds" to take hold, and game animals were reduced in number by hunting along the most used routes. Mining activities followed, muddying, polluting, or otherwise dramatically altering riparian systems across the full length of the western slope. Logging and grazing changed habitat from forest to open areas, transformed meadows to pasture, drove some animals to the point of extinction, and replaced native animal life with domesticated sheep and cattle. Towns and camps created urbanscapes. Market hunting and fishing developed as other extractive industries in the gold rush.[109]

Predators were the first animals to be especially affected by the intrusion of humans and their domestic animals during the period before 1890. Wildcats, mountain lions, and coyotes were killed to prevent loss of sheep. Grizzly bears were shot to protect cattle or to be used for meat or for their hides. The reduction of deer by heavy hunting also affected mountain lions by reducing their normal prey. Adolphus Windeler, the German miner spoken of earlier, noted the howling of mountain lions around his camp on the Feather River; as their accustomed food declined, the big cats were being lured close to the miners by "Butchers offal."[110]

The attitudes of early gold rush miners toward wildcats and mountain lions are instructive.[111] Apparently both these animals inspired a combination of fear and curiosity, and they were often simply shot without much thought whenever seen. One of the finest accounts of experiences in the Sierra Nevada during the gold rush is that of the Belgian miner Jean-Nicolas Perlot. Along with a well-written telling of his experiences as a miner, he described two encounters with predators—one with a large wildcat, and another with a mountain lion. His account provides interesting insight into the mindset of the Euro-American miners in the Sierra at that time.[112]

Perlot's search for gold took him into the central Sierra in the Yosemite area. He often traveled alone, having replaced his original fear of Indians with a genuine respect for the natives he encountered. He was often out and about with only his dog, Miraud, for company. On one such occasion the dog ran ahead barking excitedly, refusing to come when called:

Rather puzzled, I advanced with my gun at the ready; hardly had I taken a hundred steps from the path, when I saw Miraud, who was running around a tree: from the ardor of his pursuit, I immediately conjectured that he had business with a hereditary enemy of his race. In fact, on raising my eyes, I saw perched in the tree, an enormous feline, something like an ocelot. I shot, the animal fell to the foot of the tree, writhed some seconds more before dying; I prudently stayed fifteen paces away, ready to fire my second shot, if it was needed. When it no longer moved, I at last hazarded an approach: it was enormous, it was a good three feet from the nose to the base of the tail, which was cylindrical and comparatively short. All that I could do with this game was to take its coat, which was superb, then roast a quarter for my supper; it was edible without being very good, but not at all to Miraud's taste, who did not want to touch it.[113]

Perlot spent a restive night fearing that the mate of the cat—which had been a female—might come and attack him in revenge. The next day he met up with some other miners. One of them admired the newly acquired skin and offered twenty-five francs for it. Perlot accepted, offered in turn to pay for drinks, and after several such friendly exchanges with the other men in the camp, drank the evening away. As he said, "In the morning, after having breakfasted with these gentleman and paid for a farewell round, I had nothing left of my catskin."[114]

Perlot later encountered an animal that caused him even more concern:

One day I came upon the track of a wild beast in which I thought I recognized a near relative of the terrible cat which had caused me so much disquiet.

However, the print was much too big to be that of a wildcat! It could as well be a panther or a California lion, that lion without a mane and of medium size, which though less redoubtable than its African cousin, is none the less provided with claws and teeth. The print was fairly recent, for it was not covered though it had snowed the night before.[115]

Perlot tracked the animal to its "enormous nest," where he hesitated to take it on. Later he returned with a miner named Carter, "the cleverest rifle shot I had ever seen." He, Carter, and another man tracked the mountain lion and eventually found and shot it:

It was not as big as it seemed to me when alive; however it was almost four feet from the eye to the base of the tail, which was almost three feet long and the same thickness from one end to the other. The pelt, of a uniform reddish tawney color, was not beautiful: Carter skinned it on the spot. It was a female, pregnant with three little ones.

These gentleman insisted that I return with them to camp, in order to celebrate the victory. We arrived at Bull Creek drenched to the bone; after having dried ourselves as best we could, and having had a proper spree, we presented Carter with the skin, on condition that he pay the score.[116]

In addition to predators, the Sierra was rich in deer and other game animals, and these became part of a mixed food economy for the Sierran miners, loggers, camp residents, and city dwellers. In the early period, transportation limitations meant that packers could bring in only such staples as meat on the hoof and flour from lower-elevation supply centers. In some instances where there was good soil and year-round water available, local production of fresh vegetables was possible.[117]

Local game was hunted not only by miners diverting time from work, but frequently by professional hunters who found killing animals more profitable than placer mining. Most market hunting occurred in the northern and central Sierra, where mining was concentrated. But William Brewer, while working on the California Geological Survey in the Sequoia and Kings Canyon area, reported buying venison from a market hunter in 1864. Survey team member Clarence King reported meeting two market hunters in Kings Canyon who had accumulated a very large number of deer hides.[118] The most common game animals hunted besides deer were quail, rabbits, and squirrels.[119]

Deer in the western foothill gold regions were especially hard hit by market hunting. In pre–gold rush times they were common in the foothills, but generally scarcer at higher elevations. Gold mining and the importation of domestic cattle and sheep drastically reduced available range at the lower elevations. Unlimited hunting was carried on between 1848 and 1903, with established commercial camps located in many areas in the Sierra or nearby. Besides serving local markets, with improved transportation jerky, meat, and hides were shipped to San Francisco. The scientist John Woodhouse Audubon, the wildlife artist and portrait painter, reported that miners had killed thousands of the animals in 1851. One commercial hunter reported making $500 in eighteen months selling deer meat to miners. A hunter in the Kaweah River area sold 120 of the animals in 1873. Another in the Mineral King area killed 300 in the 1880s. Deer hides were reported as being carted off by the wagonload. One Redding firm, perhaps drawing from northern Sierran, Klamath, or Trinity sources, shipped some 35,000 hides to San Francisco in 1880. As a consequence, by the turn of the century, deer were becoming scarce in the Sierra Nevada.[120]

While deer persisted once hunting controls were initiated near the turn of the century, pronghorn antelope, mountain sheep, wolverines, fishers, and martens were almost exterminated by hunting or trapping. The decline of mountain sheep in the alpine areas of the Sierra Nevada was chiefly due to hunting. Antelope in the lower foothills and the valley were hunted but were also affected by the transformation of their range to pasture for domestic cattle.[121]

Development also decimated native trout populations. Besides pollution and alteration of river habitat by mining and lumbering activities, commercial fishing by natives or European Americans drove species such as Lahontan trout to near extinction. On the east side, heavy fishing served local markets in the Comstock and Tahoe at first. Markets developed in San Francisco when the railroad was completed. Depletion of the Lahontan cutthroat led to introduction of other trout to replace the natives. In 1880, commercial fishermen using boats took 70,000 pounds of trout from Lake Tahoe. Between 1871 and 1881, a commercial fish hatchery at Donner Lake bred non-native trout, producing an estimated half a million in the decade it operated. Early explorers and settlers by the 1860s had carried non-native trout to high mountain lakes in the Sierra that formerly had no fish in them, possibly affecting native Sierran amphibians.[122]

As noted, grizzly bears were the first extinction. Once common throughout the lower elevations of the western Sierra Nevada, they immediately became targets for exploitation and extermination by miners, grazers, and settlers. Humans killed grizzly for self-protection or to protect livestock in the Sierra and across the bears' range.[123]

The bears were also captured for exhibition—James Capen "Grizzly" Adams, mountaineer and showman, gained local fame by showing the grizzly he named Ben Franklin—or were pitted against bulls in commercially produced fights. The artist-miner J. D. Borthwick described and illustrated a particularly graphic struggle between a chained grizzly and two bulls in a contest staged at Mokelumne Hill. The fight left the bulls maimed and bloody, and they were shot to end their suffering. The bear survived but shortly afterward was gored and died in another battle. Grizzlies were also hunted for flesh, oil, and hide for use as blankets. In 1876, the California legislature established a bounty for killing grizzly bears in a limited number of counties. It was repealed the next year, however, because the grizzly population, in dramatic decline, was no longer perceived as a danger.[124]

Besides bringing in domestic cattle, sheep, and pigs, the miners also introduced domestic pets such as cats and dogs. Inadvertently, they also brought in rats that became a scourge in their camps, adding further discomforts to the miners' lives. J. D. Borthwick noted the ubiquitous existence of these vermin: "Hardly was a cabin built in the most out-of-the-way part of the mountains, before a large family of rats made themselves at home in it, imparting a humanized and inhabited air to the place. They are not supposed to be indigenous to the country. They are a large black species, which I believe those who are learned in rats call the Hamburg breed." Borthwick mentioned an advertisement by a French physician that, besides touting medical services to miners, offered "Destruction to Rats." In addition to being a nuisance to the miners, the introduced rodents played a part in the larger and significant faunal change underway in the range.[125]

Effects of Unregulated Development, 1848–1880

Any environmental historian should walk with care when challenging the opinion of Raymond Dasmann, the dean of California environmental studies. His perspective on the gold rush differs from mine, however.[126] Consider his recent assessment:

> It is tempting to blame the Gold Rush for starting the process of severe environmental damage in California, in what had previously been a place where nature thrived, little disturbed by humans. Unfortunately this simplistic view would not be correct. California in 1849 had already experienced serious environmental changes resulting from human activity. Extensive open-range livestock grazing introduced by Spaniards and Mexicans had resulted in modification of native grasslands. . . . Russian, Aleut, and American poachers had also hunted populations of sea otters and other marine animals to near extinction. . . . Certainly the Gold Rush directly caused even more severe damage to streams, rivers, their watersheds, and flood plains, and undoubtedly it accelerated the damage to grasslands, wildlife, forests, and other natural communities. But the damaging processes were already in place and those states that experienced no gold rush, such as Oregon, were to experience similar changes, although at a slower rate.[127]

Even though it is true that Oregon and undoubtedly all other western states experienced large-scale environmental change following settlement by European Americans, the environmental impact on California's Sierra Nevada was unique. Nowhere else in the American West did change come with such a dramatic and rapid effect. And the gold rush was also only the beginning of what would become a four-decade-long period of unregulated development.

It should be emphasized that within a decade, every area in the Sierra Nevada that could be reached, and that offered something that could be made into a commodity, had been brought into some state of economic production. All environments in the range, except those of its most isolated alpine regions, had been significantly altered. In this regard, the contrast with the native world that preceded the European American occupation is stark.

This transformation of the range was carried out from a fundamentally different worldview than that of the native. It is probably wrong to label this new way of using and living in the Sierra as "Euro-American." It is true that most of those who came were citizens of the United States or were British, Irish, Western European, Australian, or Basque immigrants. But there were also a small number of African Americans and a significant contingent from Mexico and various countries in South America. Also important in this mix were those who came from China. Certainly, as James Holliday has pointed out, it was the whole world that rushed in, and those who came shared an acquisitive perspective that was international.[128]

The economic development of the Sierra by these wealth seekers was carried out within a national context to be sure—the land was mostly "public domain" of the United States, and certain "rules" regarding land claims were hammered out on the spot. For the most part, the concept of regulation of uses for land or resources as they are understood today was not yet an idea whose time had come in the Sierra Nevada—or, for that matter, anywhere else in the United States.[129]

The combination of an acquisitive and no-holds-barred economic perspective, an ever more effective set of technologies and industrial-scale production techniques, and a significantly larger population lay at the base of this rapid and thorough exploitation of Sierra Nevada resources. But even as free-for-all development went on, concern over this unbridled activity was also beginning to take shape. This anxiety about the Sierra came from several different economic interests in California and Nevada. It focused on the destructive effects of mining, lumbering, and grazing on the range's watersheds and forests. In addition, a new perspective about natural landscape wonders, several of them located in the Sierra Nevada, was being born. It is well to remember that during the Civil War, and only sixteen years after the discovery of gold, a number of California politicians persuaded a congressional majority and President Lincoln to set aside Yosemite Valley in perpetuity for the public to enjoy. Conservation and preservation were being born in the Sierra Nevada even as the gold rush was in progress.[130]

3: Conservation Shapes the Sierra Nevada, 1864–1900

What a people or an individual says about a place is a reflection of the cultural values that guide their thinking. Thus the Ahwahnichi account of their arrival into Yosemite Valley tells us today what these natives valued in the natural world they inhabited. In the same way, gold miner and gold-rush publicist James Delavan made it clear that the abundant food potential of the black oaks in a mountain valley or the fish that swarmed in Sierran rivers was not what he most esteemed. No, his concerns were directed to how, through ingenuity, a river could be turned out of its normal bed so that the gold trapped in the natural riffles of its bottom could be reached.[1]

Consider for its cultural context a quotation from James M. Hutchings about the Yosemite Valley:

> But little seems to have been said, and that very casually, about *the marvelous grandeur* of the Yo Semite, at least but little found its way, impressibly, to the public through the press of that day. It is therefore only a historical verity to confess that, but for the contemplated publication of an illustrated California monthly—afterwards issued for a number of years in San Francisco—its merely fortuitous mention would probably have escaped the attention of the writer altogether as it seemed to have the public. As the account given, however, mentioned the existence of "a water-fall nearly a thousand feet high," it was sufficient to suggest a series of ruminating queries. A water-fall a thousand feet in height, and that in California? A thousand feet? Why, Niagara is only one hundred and sixty-four feet high! A *thou-sand* feet!! The Scrap containing this startling and valuable statement, meager though it was, was carefully treasured.[2]

It is a description of the impact Hutchings had in promoting the fame of Yosemite Valley. The purpose behind his remarks is not exactly that of James Delavan. Hutchings did care about the beauty of Yosemite Valley. But there is also a commercial edge to his remark. He is touting Yosemite in order to lure people to the Valley so that he can profit from their presence. His perspective is commercial. It is that of the developer of Sierran resources.[3]

During the early years of the opening of the Sierra Nevada, outlooks such as Delavan's and Hutchings's were dominant. But there were other views of the Sierra as well. It is useful to consider some of these different nineteenth-century perspectives.

For example, it is hard now to imagine the Sierra Nevada as a place of fear on a clear late-spring day. But project your imagination back into the early nineteenth century, before roads, cars, and state agencies made a Sierran crossing relatively easy. Listen to the voice of legendary fur trapper Jedediah Smith describing his attempt to cross the Sierra in a snowstorm in May of 1827:

> The storm still continued with unabated violence. I was obliged to stay in camp. It was one of the most disagreeable days I ever passed. We were uncertain how far the Mountain extended to the East. The wind was continually changing and the snow drifting and flying in every direction. It was with great difficulty that we could get wood and were just able to keep our fire. Our poor animals felt a full share of the storm and 2 horses and one mule froze to death before our eyes. . . . Night came and shut out the bleak desolation from our view but it did not still the howling winds that yet bellowed through the mountains bearing before them clouds of snow and beating against us cold and furious. It seemed that we were marked out for destruction and that the sun of another day might never rise to us. . . . I shall never forget the 26th of May 1827. Its incidents are graven on my mind.[4]

Similarly, fur trappers Zenas Leonard and Joseph Walker and the military exploring expedition led by John C. Frémont reinforce this fearsome image. Their crossings of the Sierra Nevada brought them a similar fate—namely, a close brush with death. The same was true of many other overland immigrants. The Sierra Nevada—John Muir's glorious sun-bathed "Range of Light" and David Brower's "Gentle Wilderness"—could also be a killer when spring storms or winter's full fury struck. It was this frightening aspect of the range that dominated many accounts of contact with the Sierra Nevada until after the 1850s.[5]

Thus Franklin Langworthy, who followed the Carson River route across the Sierra Nevada, noted in his diary that after a rough, two-mile, uphill climb, he had finally reached the point "which is most dreaded by emigrants of any upon the entire land route to California." Vincent Geiger and Wakeman Bryarly, crossing on the Truckee River route in 1849, referred to the Sierra Nevada as the "*Great Bugaboo.*" They noted that as they passed Donner Lake, the scene of the "lamentable Donner Party," they found human and animal bones, one nearly whole human skeleton, and trees cut at the height of ten feet—the depth of the snow in the winter of 1846–1847.[6]

Reflections on hard work and bone-wearying labor were as common as accounts of fear. It was necessary to unload wagons, haul them over steep outcroppings, load them again, ford and reford the Truckee or Carson Rivers, feed tired and hungry animals with limited supplies of local wild grasses, and deal with the odd and not always helpful assortment of individuals who comprised the immigrant parties. A comment of one diarist, Dr. John Wayman, who was anxious to get across the Sierra Nevada but frustrated at delays caused by people in his party, recorded a view of his crossing that makes it hard to romanticize the pioneer spirit: "Shit, Hell and Granny with a cock and bollocks Damnation and Hellfire Camphire Fox Fier and all else that is low, mean and shitting. May the Good Lord ever deliver me from such asses for all coming time, and I will thank him kindly, and return the compliment the first practical opportunity."[7]

But amidst fear and hardship, some early immigrants took time to record their astonishment at the beauty of the Sierra Nevada.[8] One entry by the diarists Geiger and Bryarly stated that the "scenery around us last night would put at defiance the artist's pencil." Donner Lake they said was "one of the most beautiful on record," surrounded by a pleasant sandy beach. Numerous other immigrant diaries and journals provide similar accounts of the beauty of the range's lakes, peaks, forests, and valleys. They contain such phrases as "wondrous works of nature," "beautiful sheet of water," "majestic grandeur," "high towering peaks surrounding a beautiful lake," and "scenery today has been truly sublime."[9]

One of the earliest comments on the beauty of Sierra Nevada trees is that of the trapper Zenas Leonard. After crossing the crest and peering into Yosemite Valley without fully understanding what he had seen, Leonard remarked at the end of October 1833 that the foothill soil must be "very productive—the timber is immensely large and plenty"; in fact, he added, "the timber stands as thick as it could grow." But what really astonished him were trees of a different type: "In the last two days traveling we have found some trees of the Red-wood species, incredibly large—some of which would measure from 16 to 18 fathoms round the trunk at the height of a man's head from the ground."[10]

Scenery and amazing forests—almost from the beginning of contact, this image of the Sierra Nevada emerges. But with this new view of Sierran splendor also came concern. The effects of the dominant acquisitive urges stimulated by the discovery of gold, as well as the chaotic private economic development of other Sierran resources, deeply worried some early observers. At what cost to the range's unique natural features or to its forests would such unrestricted development come? These advocates of what came to be called conservation were early on joined by powerful political and economic interests that favored reform in resource policies for their own reasons. Both agreed on the need for a more orderly development of the range's resources and the protection of some of its more significant landscape features.[11]

Whether considered in their California context alone or as part of larger national movement, these ideas are certainly among the most important contributions to the intellectual history of the United States in late nineteenth and early twentieth centuries. Many prominent American writers, publicists, artists, and scientists of that era sought through action and words to change the American public's perception of wildlands and forests—and by doing so, to change how these wild spaces and their resources were to be used.[12]

In California this new cultural perspective had significant connections to a growing national crusade. And although the other mountain ranges of the state were included in this emerging shift in public interest, most actions focused primarily on the Sierra Nevada because it was the state's most prominent mountain feature. This new vision would exert a powerful shaping force on the range's forests, rivers, wildlife, and natural wonders. An increasingly important role for public policy in the environmental history of the Sierra Nevada emerged clearly at this time.[13]

Of all the periods in the environmental and resource history of the Sierra Nevada, this crucial era when conservation began has probably received the most attention from historians. Alfred Runte's work on Yosemite Valley, Douglas Strong's study of Lake Tahoe, Lary Dilsaver and William Tweed's coverage of the southern Sierra Big Trees, and C. Raymond Clar's study of California state forestry policies are of immense value to anyone wishing to understand how conservation and preservation in the Sierra began. Yet as well as they cover their pieces of the range's history, these studies remain fragmentary.[14]

A comprehensive synthesis of the Sierra Nevada's environmental history is needed at this crucial juncture. And this is true both for professional historians and for those coming to the subject for the first time. The struggles over conservation in California and the Sierra Nevada did not arise as discrete events. Environmental histories of the range have generally dealt only with individual areas or features. But the range's broader environmental history arose out of a common pool of ideas and concerns.

Many individuals, politicians, and economic interests in nineteenth-century California were at work. None were following a clear blueprint; they were making it up as they went along. Yet in trying to cope with their often separate concerns about uses and ownership of the public lands in the range, collectively they developed larger public policy changes that affected the entire Sierra Nevada environment.

Most land in California and the Sierra Nevada at this time belonged to the federal government, which often had to be dealt with as a seemingly uncaring absentee landlord. In the case of hydraulic mining, however, the federal courts proved to be helpful to state interests by halting destructive actions. But it was control over Sierran lands that became the major goal of the state of California. Those who became known as conservation advocates—writers, scientists, publicists, and irrigation interests—worked closely with the state at first. Some limited cooperation between California and Nevada also occurred concerning the Tahoe Basin. It is at the state level that conservation begins in the Sierra Nevada. And it was with state conservation actions that continuing environmental change in the Sierra would also come.

Eventually it became clear to many in the conservation community that the state of California was ineffective in protecting scenic features and other forested lands in the Sierra. At that point, conservation advocates in the state joined with other national reform proponents in the hope of compelling the national government to change its standoffish policies concerning the range, its forests, and its special scenic wonders. This change in direction by the conservation movement in the Sierra, and its effects on the range's environment, will be covered later in the chapter.

Yosemite, Mariposa, and Science, 1850–1890

In the Sierra Nevada, conservation began with actions taken by the state of California. These actions arose out of public concern over unrestricted private development in the range. Special scenic areas such as Yosemite or Tahoe and the magnificent redwood forests of both the coast and the Sierra Nevada were being privately developed or cut over to serve only a few of the state's most acquisitive citizens. Sierran forests, judged by some influential observers to be limited in size at best, were seen as being plundered, overcut, or wastefully burned by logging and grazing interests.[15]

These industries' actions also reduced the Sierra's water-storage capacity and thus threatened the development of irrigated agriculture and of the state's growing cities, and therefore the future of California. In addition, Sacramento Valley farmers and residents of Marysville, Yuba City, and Sacramento found themselves at the mercy of flooding caused by hydraulic-mining activities in the Feather, Bear, and Yuba River systems.[16]

Beginning as early as 1850 and continuing into the 1860s, the California legislature considered initiatives aimed at surveying public lands within the state's boundaries and bringing them under state control, including the forests and scenic wonders of the Sierra. The first initiatives were relatively simple, focusing on reducing fire damage in the forests through various methods, including fines for those who carelessly set the fires. Other legislation tried to bring lands given to the state by the federal government—swamp or overflow lands and so-called public school land grants—under effective management. A special office of state surveyor general was created. Its functions included carrying out surveys, creating maps, and identifying valuable forestlands. Eventually the legislature supported a broader scientific study of the Sierra Nevada.[17]

As an example of early state interest, Assemblyman Henry A. Crabb of San Joaquin County introduced legislation in 1852 that would secure the transfer of title for all redwood lands to the state of California. Crabb intended to include both the Sierran redwoods and the coastal redwoods. It is not clear whether he knew the botanical difference between them. But his intent is interesting. He would have made the trees common property of all the state's "citizens," and none of these trees apparently were to be the "subject of trade and traffic." His measure did not pass. Crabb was far out in front of anyone at a time when the gold rush was still the dominant force in the state. But it appears from the language of his resolution that he did not necessarily look at the redwoods as just another timber resource.[18]

Protection of forest areas—for example, by preventing fire or illegal trespass—was a common theme of the many early attempts to gain some measure of state control over Sierran and other forestlands. These attempts generally foundered because actual title to the lands lay in the hands of the federal government. And the federal government seemed unwilling to control or regulate uses of the western lands.[19]

The "general government," as it was commonly called, was willing to consider granting title only to settlers and farmers who could file under the Preemption and Homestead Acts passed between the 1840s and 1860s. Federal legislation that followed in the 1870s focused on timber and stone resources. But these measures were vague, and therefore encouraged fraudulent filing. They did little to protect Sierran forestlands from trespass by grazers and timbermen, and complaints of destructive illegal use mounted. In 1865, California senator John Conness tried to secure federal legislation that would at least allow for regulated sales of timber on federal lands in the western states. But this and all other measures concerning federal forestlands failed to win passage until the 1890s.[20]

California initiatives to gain control of forested and scenic areas were part of the broad pattern of state interest in Sierran scenic features and resources. Ultimately most of these initiatives either failed or had only partial success. The failure arose because of the limits of state power. But importantly, the fact that a state such as California would seriously consider such ambitious programs reveals that the federal government at the time was either unable or certainly unwilling to take on the task itself. It was the state that pushed the general government to act.

The uncoordinated and halting steps by the state of California reflect the beginnings of conservation and preservation in the Sierra Nevada. They were the first public policy actions taken to shape the range. For the first time, alongside the natural forces of uplifting, erosion, glaciation, and fire, and the human force of unregulated commercial development of the gold rush, government made conscious choices to attempt to protect certain areas or limit certain actions in the range.

The designation by Congress in 1864 of Yosemite Valley and the nearby Mariposa Big Trees as scenic reserves to be held in trust by the state of California was one of the first practical achievements of the American conservation movement. The legislation transferring ownership of these areas to the state was authored by Senator Conness, a veteran in California's long campaign to gain control over its forests and picturesque wonders. The two scenic sites mentioned in the legislation were to be managed by the state of California. They were to "be held for public use, resort, and recreation" and were to "be inalienable for all time."[21]

At the time of Conness's legislation, Yosemite Valley was already well known, as witnessed by the words of one of its early eastern visitors, Samuel Bowles: "The Yosemite! As well interpret God in thirty-nine articles as portray it to you by word of mouth or pen. . . . The overpowering sense of the sublime of awful desolation of transcending marvelousness and unexpectedness that swept over us as we reined our horses sharply out of the green forests and stood upon high jutting rock. . . . It was Niagara magnified."[22]

The desire for public control of these two monumental scenic wonders represented the attitudes of an influential minority of Californians who formed the core of the conservation movement in the state. At the same time, state actions involving the Valley and the Big Trees illustrated the problems that came with management of public spaces by people not used to such activities. Rather than just selling them off as other lands in the United States had been in the past, state officials were responsible for managing them in the public interest. A new idea about land use was taking shape, and the Sierra Nevada was one of its birthplaces.[23]

The "discovery" of Yosemite Valley and the nearby Mariposa Grove of Big

Trees initiated a different approach by Americans to natural spaces. Instead of damming the Valley to provide irrigation water for John C. Frémont's nearby Mariposa ranch or cutting all the trees down for utilitarian uses, the two sites received a measure of protection from private commercial development. (Thank heavens there was no gold of significance in the Merced.) From the beginning of contact with these wonders, they were considered special.[24]

Lafayette Bunnell was a member of the Mariposa Battalion (a semi-organized militia band) that had followed Tenaya and his band of Ahwah-nichis into the Valley in 1851. He was one of the first non-Indians to be struck by the incomparable beauty of Yosemite. As he noted in an account of his experience: "It has been said that 'it is not easy to describe in words the precise impressions which great objects make upon us.' I cannot describe how completely I realized this truth. None but those who have visited this most wonderful valley can even imagine the feelings with which I looked upon the view that was there presented."[25]

Bunnell and the many others who followed him to gaze upon the Valley—saying they were unable to describe it in words—promptly set about describing it to as many people as they could, without any sense of contradiction.[26]

Gold prospectors first came to the Mariposa region in the "southern mines" in 1850. In 1851 the Mariposa Battalion entered Yosemite Valley as part of an attempt to suppress Indian resistance in the central Sierra Nevada foothills. The Mariposa Big Trees Grove was seen in 1852 by a group of prospectors. In the next two years other prospectors and James Capen Adams (in search of grizzly bears to capture and train) entered the Valley. The area remained isolated, however, and some Ahwahnichis continued to try to reclaim their old territory.[27]

Yosemite and the Mariposa trees became more widely known through the promotional work of James M. Hutchings, who visited the Valley with artist Thomas Ayres in 1855. Hutchings's purpose was to reveal the area's beauty to the world (and, if possible, to profit from it). In the same year that Hutchings led his first tourists to the Valley, Galen Clark surveyed it to see if water could be exported to irrigate Frémont's Mariposa property nearby. Clark eventually shifted his focus to development of tourist facilities near the Mariposa Big Trees. Later still, he became guardian of Yosemite when it was designated a state park. In 1856, the first structure intended for tourist use was built in the Valley.[28]

From these humble beginnings, tourist interest in Yosemite rapidly grew. It was stimulated at first by Hutchings's information and Ayres's sketches reaching eastern readers.[29] Soon many easterners—including New York City newspaper editor Horace Greeley and New England lecturer and minister Thomas Starr King—visited Yosemite and the Big Trees. Greeley and King published accounts of their visits. Writing within a romantic literary context well understood by their educated and affluent contemporaries, they were part of a near industry of nineteenth-century travel literature that focused on western scenery. To Greeley, "no single wonder of nature on earth" could match Yosemite. King, standing above the Valley as many who followed him would, struggled to describe the size and splendor of what was before him: "How can I express the awe and joy that were blended and continually strug-gling with each other, during the half hour in the hot noon that we remained on the edge of the abyss where the grandeurs of the Yo-Semite were first revealed to us."[30]

Commercialization and building of new facilities by James Lamon and James Hutchings in the Valley, and by Galen Clark at Wawona and Mari-posa Grove, expanded between 1856 and 1864. Photographers C. L. Weed and C. E. Watkins and well-known nature artists such as Albert Bierstadt added to the visual knowledge of Yosemite Valley and the Mariposa Grove for Americans in the East. The image of Yosemite became as familiar a natu-ral wonder to affluent Americans as Niagara Falls. Access to the Valley and Wawona remained difficult and tourist facilities remained crude, however. Eastern writers praised the Valley's beauty even as they complained of the hardships of visiting it.[31]

Travel to the Valley was especially difficult before 1856. Eventually inves-tors provided more convenient connections. The first commercial trail from Coulterville to Yosemite was constructed in 1856 and 1857. In succeeding years, trails opened from other locations and improvements converted the Coulterville trail to a road. Lafayette Bunnell, who invested in the Coulter-ville operations, contemplated a narrow-gauge railroad with tunnels, trestles, and bridges across the Merced River as early as 1855, anticipating actual rail connections by many years. By the mid-1860s, although the Valley was still uncomfortable to visit, the door to more-ambitious commercial development was open.[32]

Yosemite area developers such as Lamon and Hutchings continued to operate their facilities and expand their holdings. Hutchings promoted the Valley in his *Hutchings' California Magazine* and with a book entitled *Scenes of Wonder and Curiosity in California*. In person, he extolled the beauties of Yosemite to his captive hotel clients, making comparisons to Swiss alpine landscapes. A growing number of easterners and Californians took up the challenge to visit the Valley and the Big Trees. Easterners were fulfilling a need to escape urban areas and get "back to nature." Californians saw this natural wonder as a defining element of the new state's identity.[33]

But the commercialization and private ownership of the two scenic wonders did not sit well with everyone. By 1864, powerful and well-known business leaders such as Israel Ward Raymond, as California representative of the Central American Steamship Transit Company of New York, contacted Senator Conness to request that Yosemite Valley and the Mariposa Big Trees be protected by federal action. As Alfred Runte has shown, this legislation led to the first federal protection of a natural wonder, marking the beginnings of America's national parks.[34]

The Yosemite grant—signed into law by Abraham Lincoln—was accepted by California in 1865. The state created a commission consisting of eight members to oversee its new charge. Frederick Law Olmsted, the noted landscape architect, acted as first head of the commission.[35] Isolation of the Valley soon ended with the completion of the Central Pacific across the Sierra Nevada and an extension of the rail line to Merced. The carving out of the Great Oak Flat Road and the extension of the Coulterville Road and the Wawona Road from the Mariposa Grove to the Valley between 1869 and 1875 also encouraged tourism, which expanded rapidly following each improvement. From 1864 to 1870 around 5,000 people visited the Valley. Between 1870 and 1880 nearly 20,000 tourists arrived.[36]

The completion of America's first transcontinental railroad allowed an affluent and newly mobile American and European middle class to visit western landscape wonders in relative comfort—Yosemite and the Big Trees among them. The railroad advertised a circuit that included northern Sierra Nevada lakes such as Tahoe on the way to Yosemite and Mariposa.[37] This increasing tourist use had direct environmental effects on the Valley. These changes came from the ending of Indian land-use practices, alterations made by private developers or state and federal managers, and unintended results that grew from these actions. These effects were noted by concerned visitors to the new California state park.[38]

Those who stayed in the Valley and at Mariposa required lodging, food, and other comforts. Private developers built the earliest structures. The California legislature authorized new construction of tourist facilities in the 1860s and 1870s. These included Leidig's Hotel, the Cosmopolitan Bath House and Saloon, and the Sentinel Hotel, all in the Valley, and tourist accommodations above Vernal Falls, at Glacier Point, and along the Yosemite-Wawona trail. Facilities were also constructed near the Mariposa Grove at Wawona. Most of these early tourist facilities were crude by national and European standards. Under pressure, the Yosemite Commission secured state funding in 1885–1886 to build a first-class hotel called the Stoneman House.[39]

Not all visitors stayed at the new hotels. Before 1856, camping had been a necessity because no commercial housing existed. After facilities were built, some people still chose to camp out for free wherever they found level terrain that was unoccupied. The first established commercial campground was built in 1878. In 1898 the state rented campsites for the first time. In 1899 the Curry Camping Company was created, and in 1901 it moved to a site below Lost Arrow. Most camping was done on the meadows east of the major hotels. By the 1880s and 1890s, the number of campers and the size of the parties had ballooned. One group numbered three hundred. By this time cost was becoming less important to campers. Many sought outdoor experiences and hiking trails rather than being hauled around in carriages or wagons as the hotel crowd was.[40]

The new facilities affected the environment even while they were being built, as all construction materials and firewood were obtained locally. It should be remembered that John Muir's first job in Yosemite was as operator of a sawmill for Hutchings. Muir did not cut down live trees but did cut up downed trees. Removal and use of this material did have environmental effects, of course. But the direct construction of facilities was just the beginning and ultimately had limited impact when compared with other effects of tourist activities.[41]

Some visitors expressed concern about the effects of growing commercialization. While commenting favorably that Yosemite Valley and the Big Trees had been protected, travelers expressed doubt that these areas would be spared the overcommercialized fate of Niagara Falls. This vision of a spoiled Niagara was frequently mentioned. One visitor who later wrote about her experiences in the park, Sara Jane Lippincott, deserves to have her remarks quoted. Regarding the protection of Yosemite, of which she approved, she noted: "But it may be a comedy after all,—horse-railroads and trotting tracks, hacks and hand organs, Saratoga trunks and croquet parties, elevators running up the face of El Capitan, the domes plastered with circus bills and advertisements of 'Plantation Bitters.'"

As for the state commissioners' administration of the Valley and their expenditures for "improvements," Lippincott wrote with disdain:

> But whether the fund be large or small, the commissioners—certain magnificent and mysterious gentlemen of whom you hear much but see nothing in the valley—should look to it that the money be judiciously expended. I was told that the sum of five hundred dollars has

been or was to be allowed to a certain "cute" Yankee, in payment for the extraordinary enterprise of cutting off the pretty little side cascade of the Nevada [Falls], by means of a dam, and turning all the water into the great cataract. "Fixing the falls," he calls the job of tinkering one of God's masterpieces. There is a pun on "the deep damnation of that cutting off," but I forbear.[42]

Alterations of the Valley and the Big Trees from tourist activities were the outgrowth of both planned and unplanned actions by Valley occupants and the state park commissioners. To understand these changes, a baseline for the Valley's condition at the time of occupation by European Americans is needed. Before the outsiders' first arrival in 1851, Valley natives had used fire and other techniques to maintain open meadows and stands of oak to facilitate the collecting of acorns and other wild food and materials. The open landscape encouraged wildlife, provided security, and reduced fire danger. Between 1851 and 1854, the native inhabitants were removed, and although some returned as laborers, by 1854 native use patterns were generally ended.[43]

Two accounts by early visitors help to establish the condition of Yosemite Valley at that time. One comes from Lafayette Bunnell, who first saw the Valley in 1851, and the other from prospector Gustavus Pierson, who arrived in 1855. Bunnell reported that his expedition found only a few trails and a limited number of native villages—which the invading whites burned. He noted that while approaches from Mariposa had dense stands of undergrowth such as manzanita, the Valley itself was clear: "The whole valley had the appearance of park-like grounds, with trees, shrubbery, flowers, and lawns." Black oak was abundant. Gustavus Pierson, trying to stake a mining claim in the Valley, remembered that there were "no signs of a white man" having been there before his party. He observed "not a log or tree being cut, no mark of a hatchet" before he blazed a mark on a tree to establish his claim. Occupation of the Valley by whites began in 1856 with construction of the first rude tourist facilities.[44]

The effects of occupation (in both the period of private claims to 1864 and the time of state management afterward) were a direct result of making the Valley serve the interests of the tourists who began to arrive after 1856. From 1860 to 1868, before state title to the Valley and Mariposa was reconfirmed by congressional action, several tourist lodgings were constructed in different Valley locations and on the way to the Big Trees. In places, especially at Lamon's and Hutchings's, the Valley was planted with orchards and berry bushes and the meadows were fenced and grazed. The meadows were also plowed and planted with non-native grasses when demand for pasturage and fodder exceeded the natural supply. Even though the commission from the start prohibited the cutting of live timber, trees were removed at times to improve views. Tourist-related construction and services included a Wells Fargo office, a post office, photography studios, saloons, a sawmill, workers' and guides' housing, and livery and saddle works.[45]

Commercial ferries crossed the Merced and trails and ladders were built to Vernal and Nevada Falls. As Sara Jane Lippincott noted, Nevada Falls was "fixed" to provide more water into the main cataract channel for late-summer visual pleasure. Mirror Lake, with its early-morning reflection of Mount Watkins considered as required viewing, had a summer house, dance floor, and saloon built by it, and a platform extended out into the water. Growing siltation, although primarily from development outside the Valley, was already raising concern for the lake's future. Under early state control, ten-year leases to private individuals—only loosely supervised—ensured private management in actuality. In addition to such obvious changes, the building of wooden structures required fire suppression, which led to the growth of brush. This resulted in the closing in of meadow areas. In 1878 and again in 1881, tunnels were cut through sequoia trees at Tuolumne and Mariposa Groves. The board of commissioners banned Indians from burning. The board also arranged to have rocks and foliage removed from the Merced River in order to reduce flooding. These actions only hastened native vegetation loss and encouraged encroachment of brush onto the meadow floor.[46]

Even as this alteration went forward with the idea of "improving" the Valley to make it into a "pleasuring ground" for tourists, voices were raised in protest. Park commissioner Frederick Law Olmsted proposed that nothing be done to undermine the chief goal of maintaining the park in as natural a state as possible. He believed that tourist comfort should be secondary to preservation. He proposed a good road so that lumber, hay, and supplies for tourists could be brought in, rather than using the Valley's own meadows and trees. Olmsted predicted that too much accommodation of tourists' demands would hasten environmental change in the interest of a few, at the expense of future generations.[47] His words echo to the present day, as the struggle of "natural park" versus "mountain resort" still goes on.[48]

Olmsted's preliminary report as commissioner also warned of changes at Yosemite resulting from its increased use. As he noted in August of 1865:

Many of the finer specimens of the most important tree in the scenery of the Yosemite have been already destroyed and the proclamation of the Governor, issued after the passage of the Act of Congress, forbidding the destruction of trees in the district, alone prevented the establishment of a saw mill within it. Notwithstanding the proclamation many fine trees have been felled and others girdled within the year. Indians and others have set fire to the forests and herbage and numbers of trees have been killed by these fires; the giant tree before referred to as probably the noblest tree now standing on the earth has been burned completely through the bark near the ground for a distance of more than one hundred feet of its circumference; not only have trees been cut, hacked, barked, and fired in prominent positions, but rocks in the midst of the most picturesque natural scenery have been broken, painted and discolored, by fires built against them. In travelling to the Yosemite and within a few miles of the nearest point at which it can be approached by a wheeled vehicle, the commissioners saw other picturesque rocks stenciled over with the advertisements of patent medicines.[49]

The policy of the other park commissioners, however, was to oblige tourists. Then as today, pleasing tourists and concession operators received priority over keeping the park natural. An article in the *Overland Monthly* in 1874 noted that conflict and litigation between 1864 and 1868 had prevented commissioners from developing the park in the public interest, but that nothing stood in their way now. Instead of managing the Valley as a revenue source and allowing commercial development to hold sway, the author called for a change in policy that would encourage more natural values. The unnamed writer added: "We speak for the future, and every lover of nature will say amen."[50]

In 1880, mounting criticism of the commission led to state legislation that empowered the governor to make changes in personnel on the board. Amid controversy, the old board refused to resign, but after U.S. Supreme Court action, the newly appointed commission was confirmed. Over the next few years, the commission and state engineer tried to come to grips with the problems facing the park. Their concern was over the fencing of open land, encroaching brush, the need for new trails, siltation of the Merced River and Mirror Lake from logging and grazing outside the Valley, and demands for improving tourist facilities and access.[51]

The park commissioners' and state engineer's recommendations resulted in construction of the Stoneman House for first-class tourists, elimination of charges for use of some trails and roads, removal of some of the fences that cut up the meadow, the pruning and cutting of some trees, the razing of some second-rate tourist facilities, and dredging and damming Mirror Lake in order to preserve its reflective qualities. In all, the results were not spectacular and did not come close to achieving the natural goals that Olmsted had proposed. Grazing and the rapid encroachment of brush continued to be problems. But the call of those who wanted to accommodate tourists and the animals they brought with them remained the dominant force governing state park administration.[52]

Continued concern over the effects of development, grazing, and timber cutting in the drainages above Yosemite Valley eventually led to a political campaign by Muir and editor Robert Underwood Johnson of *Century* magazine to gain federal protection for the area. Support for such guardianship also came from the Southern Pacific Railroad, in part because of its interest in promoting tourism. In 1890, Yosemite National Park, including much of the Merced and Tuolumne River drainages, was created by federal legislation. The Valley and the Mariposa Big Trees remained in state control, awaiting a new campaign to bring these two areas back into federal hands after 1900.[53] These actions will be discussed later in the chapter.

The changes in Yosemite Valley that came with tourism and state park status illustrate that public ownership did not stop what many of that day, and certainly today, would see as negative effects. Yosemite had been created as a public park, but it was not protected from damaging effects to its precontact state. Those who were involved with the park saw that earlier state as "natural," although of course it was not. It was an Indian-managed landscape. But the open landscapes that were taken under state management were soon altered significantly, that much is certain.[54]

This new force of change grew directly from four main sources. Two involved early practices of uncontrolled development. First came private promoters such as Hutchings and others whose venture led to logging, building construction, fences, grazing, and vegetation alteration. Second came the time of weak state commission control. Because the state refused to provide adequate funding to operate the park, private concessionaires did pretty much as they pleased, continuing the early chaotic development.

A third major factor was philosophical and concerned the definition of what the park was to be. The natural view that Olmsted and the writer from the *Overland Monthly* advocated was clearly ignored, and the idea that Yosemite was to be a "pleasuring ground" for tourists prevailed. This philosophical conflict arose from the contradictory language of the legislation that created Yosemite—and this remained true even after the first park commission was ousted and more effective planning occurred.

A fourth factor was simply the haphazard way people went about their business throughout this period—altering landscape features, suppressing fires, building structures and fences, ignoring problems such as encroaching trees and brush, dredging Mirror Lake, and a whole rash of heedless activities that had significant environmental effects. Except perhaps for Olmsted, few people had any idea of what they were about. There was no plan.

But perhaps the early state park advocates should not be so harshly criticized. They were, after all, doing something that no one else even tried to do until the 1870s when Yellowstone was taken under weak federal protection. At least the frightening vision that Sara Jane Lippincott had of patent medicine signs on the domes, or elevators running up the face of El Capitan, did not come to pass. But the concern for the new park was real, and the Valley had been spoiled. As John Muir noted in 1874: "The plow is busy among the gardens, the axe among its groves, and the whole valley wears a weary, dusty aspect, as if it were a traveler new-arrived from a wasting journey. Lovers of clean mountain wilderness must therefore go higher, into more inaccessible retreats among the summits of the range."[55]

As part of California's growing official interest in its land and resources, the need for proper surveys in the state was recognized very early. The beginnings of such survey work in California and the Sierra Nevada were practical. The question most asked at first was how to get over the Sierra Nevada. Thus the first surveys by the state and federal governments related to transportation routes. Another practical issue was where, exactly, the boundary between Nevada Territory and California lay. Legislation to create a state surveyor in the early 1850s also represented a practical attempt to gain information on valuable timberland. Purely scientific studies of the state's geology had to wait. Isolated from the rest of the nation's scientific community, those California scientists interested in broader issues than wagon roads, boundaries, or timberland also eventually turned to state government for financial support.[56]

In 1853 the newly formed California Academy of Natural Sciences (later the California Academy of Sciences) sought public support for a survey "of every portion of the state and the collection of a cabinet of her rare and rich productions." The legislature became interested, and between 1853 and 1860 momentum grew for the creation of a state geological survey. The legislature may have been motivated less by pure science than by a desire to identify gold-bearing ground. Whatever the reasons, the need for a complete geological survey was widely conceded.[57]

The surface mining activity of the 1850s had come up against the fact that the easy pickings of the early gold rush days were over. Better geological information was needed. In addition, the legislature sought development of resources such as timber, pasture, and agricultural land. But it was the interest of the state's scientists that ultimately won significant support for a full-scale survey. They were backed with strong lobbying by the very influential chief justice of the California supreme court, Stephen J. Field. His contacts with a very active promoter of resource legislation, John Conness (at that time still in the California legislature), led to funding to create a state geological survey in 1860. The distinguished scientist Josiah Whitney, a close friend of Field's, was appointed state geologist and empowered to head the survey.[58]

Whitney's most important scientific colleagues in the survey included William Brewer, Charles Hoffman, William Ashburner, and Clarence King. Fieldwork in various locations in the state began in 1860, but not until 1863 did the survey enter the Sierra Nevada. In the first year of the Sierran part of the survey, lower elevations, including Walker Pass, Hornitos, Calaveras, Yosemite, Tenaya Lake, Tuolumne Meadows, Mono Pass, and Mono Lake, were mapped and explored. The section of the report published in 1864 detailed the survey of the gold-mining belt from Mariposa County in the south to Plumas County in the north. The report provided a review of the gold-mining districts of the west-central side of the range. Mammon, along with science, was thus served in this portion of the Sierran survey.[59]

The geological survey entered the southern or high Sierra Nevada in the summer of 1864, exploring and mapping the Kern, Kings, and San Joaquin drainages. Often setting aside scientific language, the report revealed the authors' wonder at the high country and alpine beauty they encountered. Referring to the range itself, the report at one point gushed that "it is here that it rises to its highest elevation, forming as far as we know, the grandest mountain mass in the North American continent." William Brewer exclaimed: "Such a landscape! A hundred peaks in sight over thirteen thousand feet—many very sharp—deep canyons, cliffs in every direction almost rivaling Yosemite, sharp ridges almost inaccessible to man, on which human foot has never trod—all combined to produce a view the sublimity of which is rarely equaled, one which few are privileged to behold."[60] From the alpine regions, the team turned to investigate the headwaters of the Merced and Tuolumne Rivers, Sonora Pass, and the head of the Mokelumne River.[61]

In environmental terms, the California Geological Survey is very important. It added careful scientific observations and some mapping of well-known areas such as Yosemite and Lake Tahoe. Whitney and Ashburner were later appointed as commissioners overseeing the Yosemite Valley and Mariposa Big Trees along with Frederick Law Olmsted. Whitney later published a popular guide to Yosemite that promoted the new state park.[62]

There is some evidence, however, that Whitney and Ashburner may have hurt the new park when, as commissioners, they actively worked to suppress the dissemination of Olmsted's report of 1865. The two men apparently feared that Olmsted's appeal for some $37,000 to administer and manage the park might threaten funding for the California Geological Survey itself. Apparently Whitney and Ashburner saw any funding for the new park as competition for their survey work.[63]

The survey's scientific evaluation of the western foothills of the Sierra Nevada furnished important data. It described the auriferous gravels in the range and carefully mapped their locations. It provided a broad description of the western side of the range, clearly defining the difference between the metamorphic part of the western Sierra and the granite that dominated the southern portion.[64] It is the southern part of the Sierra Nevada, however—the land of high peaks and shining granite—that has drawn most attention from historians of the survey. One of the best descriptions of the 1864 expedition to the southern Sierra and its contributions, is that of James G. Moore, himself a geologist. Moore lists several major achievements of the survey: identifying and mapping the highest peak in the lower United States, exploring the Kern River and Great Western Divide, locating the main crest of the Sierra in the southern part of the range, and providing proof of the fairly recent glacial activity in this portion of the range. As Moore said, these were "extraordinary accomplishments." They were even greater if the expedition's "short duration and low budget," use of several unpaid volunteers, and essentially "reconnaissance nature" are considered.[65]

But this marked the high point of the survey. Disputes with the legislature and governor over funding grew. It seemed that the scientist in Whitney was out of step with their more pecuniary interests. Whitney was not anticommerce, but his idea of the task at hand did not square with the immediate profit-oriented motives of the state's politicians. The remainder of the survey relied on subsidies from Whitney himself. Its last major efforts included work in the southern Sierra that resulted in better maps, drawn by Whitney's associate Hoffman. In 1874 the legislature and governor ceased funding and the survey's life ended.[66]

An interesting by-product of this scientific interest by the state in the Sierra Nevada was the role that scientists such as Whitney and Joseph and John Le Conte played in promoting public visitation to the range through their scientific as well as more promotional writings. Whitney did so through his role as park commissioner and via his popular guidebook to the Yosemite Valley and surrounding area. The book was intended to promote public visiting, a far different type of activity than his fellow commissioner Olmsted had in mind in his very different report on the Valley.[67]

The Le Conte brothers as scientists also acted as promoters of Sierran features, including Yosemite and Lake Tahoe. Joseph's account of his 1870 field trip with several students to the Valley is certainly charming but, in his awe-struck descriptions of its scenic features, strays far from scientific objec-tivity.[68] The Le Contes were more prosaic in their scientific observations about Lake Tahoe, but even so, these writings contributed to public interest in the lake in the 1880s and thereby stimulated visitation at a time when logging there was beginning to decline and a tourist future lay just ahead.[69]

The better-known of the brothers, geologist Joseph Le Conte, contrib-uted to the knowledge of ancient glaciers in the Tahoe Basin in an article written in 1875 for the *American Journal of Science*. He described several areas of glacial activity—the lake valley itself, Truckee Canyon, Fallen Leaf Lake, Cascade Lake, and Emerald Bay. He noted several glacial moraines as well. He dismissed glacial action as the force that created the lake, opting instead for a mere sculpting role in the basin after creation. He cited the Whitney survey's volume 1 in his observations on glacial ice levels at Tahoe and at Mono Lake to the south.[70]

In three articles published in the *Overland Monthly* in 1883 and 1884, John Le Conte described the lake's depth and other physical characteristics. He speculated as to why the lake did not freeze in winter. He also reported the grisly fact that bodies drowned in the lake—fourteen people were reported as drowning between 1860 and 1874—did not rise to the surface if death happened in deep water (he dismissed certain notions on the lessened den-sity of the lake's water and gave great cold as the scientific reason for such permanent sinkings). He commented on the great purity and transparency of the water in the center of the lake, if not near "the fouling influences of the sediment-bearing effluents, and the washings of the shores."[71]

Protecting Lake Tahoe and the Truckee River, 1883–1889

Yosemite and the Mariposa Big Trees very early were the focus of tourist and conservation interest by the state of California in the central Sierra. Lake Tahoe and the forested basin around it at the northern end of the range drew similar attention. Some of the earliest explorers and immigrants began extol-ling Tahoe even as they struggled to get over the range.[72] Mark Twain in 1871, as noted earlier, expressed this wonder at the lake's beauty when he described the sense of awe he and his party felt when first seeing it after a hard climb:

> We plodded on, two or three hours more, and at last the lake burst upon us—a noble sheet of blue water lifted six thousand three hun-dred feet above the level of the sea, and walled in by a rim of snow-clad mountain peaks that towered aloft full three thousand feet higher still! It was a vast oval, and one would have to use up eighty or a hundred

good miles in traveling around it. As it lay there in the shadows of the mountains brilliantly photographed upon its still surface I thought it must surely be the fairest picture the whole earth affords.[73]

From the late 1850s to the 1860s, efforts were made to build better roads across the northern Sierra. One of these was supported by Placer County and crossed near Squaw Valley. Another was built through the Henness Pass. A third ran from Placerville over the Sierra. A California state-funded road used Johnson and Luther Passes. All these routes crossed the southern part of the Tahoe Basin. The discovery of the Comstock Lode in the late 1850s, in what would become the state of Nevada, made travel to the Lake Tahoe area more common.[74] With the completion of the Central Pacific, the northern Sierra Nevada lakes, including Tahoe, Donner, Webber, and Independence, attracted tourist interest. Numerous tourist manuals, guides, and descriptive accounts of the Sierra referred to Lake Tahoe as well as Yosemite. Many visitors to the Comstock encountered the lakes on their way to Virginia City or escaped to them as respite from the far less interesting terrain surrounding the silver-mining areas.[75]

Before development, the basin was surrounded by a lush, east-side mixed-conifer forest, consisting primarily of Jeffrey pine, ponderosa pine, incense cedar, white fir, and a limited amount of sugar pine. Before white occupation, fire was a persistent process that influenced the forests of the basin. These fires came from the actions of the Washoe or were natural in origin. White occupation that came with mining brought massive logging on the Nevada side first. Soon, further cutting denuded lower-elevation areas within Tahoe Basin itself. From there logging extended down into the Truckee drainage as the Central Pacific became both a market and a creator of markets for Tahoe Basin lumber. Because of fire suppression begun with white occupation, and because of the rapid regrowth of white fir, the forest composition radically changed. Jeffrey and ponderosa and sugar pines were greatly diminished in number, and a predominantly fir forest developed.[76]

In the basin itself, timber dominated the economy as long as the silver mines were operating and the building of the railroad continued. The tourist trade, although secondary, nonetheless drew many visitors. Steamships served tourists on Lake Tahoe by the late 1870s. Roads ringed the lake, and stage connections with Truckee brought a hundred people a day to Tahoe. By the 1880s a narrow-gauge railroad, originally built for logging purposes along the Truckee River, connected to the city of Truckee and the Central Pacific as well, swelling tourist numbers.[77]

Tourism eventually supplanted lumbering in the Tahoe Basin. The environmental changes that came with this use included urbanization and resort construction. Logging had produced three urban centers—Tahoe City, Glenbrook, and Incline, the first two of which survived to supply tourist needs. In addition, by the first decade of the twentieth century, nineteen well-developed resorts or camps were constructed around the lakeshore. Dairying and some small-scale agriculture developed to supplement the supplies brought in to these resorts from outside the basin. Fish hatcheries were constructed, and eastern brook trout and other fish were released into the Tahoe Basin streams and the lake by the thousands to supplement the diminishing numbers of native fish. Automobiles, too, entered the basin in the century's first decade.[78]

As a consequence of this development, pressure for privatization of land along the shores of the lake increased, raising public concerns. An interesting example of such interest comes from a Placer County historian, W. B. Lardner. He first visited Lake Tahoe in 1873 by stagecoach, touring its shoreline on the steamer *Governor Stanford*. Lardner became an advocate of public access to the lake. He joined in lawsuits and lobbying for legislation to ensure public ownership of the shoreline—including a campaign to have California keep title to the fish hatchery land at Tahoe City after the state took over from private owners at the turn of the century.[79] Lardner's comments regarding encroachment on what he called the "Commons" at Tahoe City illustrate his distress:

> From the earliest settlement on the lake there has been manifest, it seems to the writer, a disposition of a few to "grab" and monopolize the lake shore. From the date of entry of Tahoe City townsite in 1868, back to 1863, when the first townsite survey was made, there have always been public Commons, or public grounds, for the citizens, clear down to the shore line; but for the past twenty years the Commons have been occupied by the lines of a railroad, car barns, a private dwelling, and other obstructive nuisances. The courts have decided that the public Commons belong to the people and not to any corporation, notwithstanding the fact that the people themselves, and their officers, have been negligent and allowed a trespassing railroad company to crowd upon and occupy the public property.[80]

This issue of public versus private control of lands around Lake Tahoe, of course, continues to the present.

Not only land disputes, but claims for Tahoe Basin water brought environmental consequences and controversy among competing users. The first involved the damming of the lake where it exited into the Truckee River.

Lumber interests had built a log-crib dam there by 1870, hoping to use the relatively shallow river for "log driving" in order to supply mills at Truckee. Splash dams built to help in this effort caused erosion and scouring in the riverbed. The more effectively regulated flow of water also allowed for other industries to develop on the Truckee, including hydroelectric production and a pulp mill downstream at Floriston. The paper mill there used fir from the surrounding hills. The fir was chipped and mixed with acids to produce paper pulp, releasing pollution into the river.[81]

In 1900 an engineer and promoter, A. W. Von Schmidt, as president of the Lake Tahoe and San Francisco Water Works, holding a contested claim on the outlet dam site—and therefore for water rights at Lake Tahoe—offered to sell the rights to San Francisco. The potential diversion of Tahoe and downstream Truckee water united many river and shoreline interests against Von Schmidt. The list of protestors was long and showed how complex the water usage on the river and lake had become. The protestors included farmers living along the Truckee, flour mills using water power, a smelting and reduction works, an electric light plant and water works at Reno, several other electrical generators, numerous sawmills, a box factory, a furniture factory, several ice-plants, and the paper mill at Floriston. Their position was that there was no surplus water for Von Schmidt and San Francisco to use. San Francisco never seriously considered joining with Von Schmidt, given the flimsy nature of his claims and the strong resistance from so many sources.[82]

A second issue involved diversion of water from Marlette Lake, on the eastern side of the basin. Early logging operations in the basin had built flumes to transport Marlette Lake water. But a more significant development included the damming of the lake and diversion of its water through a flume, tunnel, and pipe to the Comstock mills and to Carson City.[83] The diversion continues to serve the Carson Valley to the present.

A third environmental problem involved fluctuations of the shoreline once Tahoe in effect became a storage reservoir as a result of constructing the dam. This issue was complex because of the numerous shoreline landowners and downstream users affected and because it concerned not only private interests, but also the California and Nevada governments. The most extreme possibility involved early efforts to promote the boring of a tunnel through the lake rim at a point on its eastern shore, draining the lake for the advantage of Nevada's Carson Valley. Needless to say, everyone except the Carson promoters opposed this action.[84]

More realistic arguments concerning fluctuating lake levels centered on uses of the several feet of stored water that came from the building of the original dam. The potential existed that Tahoe would be treated as if it were a mere reservoir, its level allowed to rise or fall as needed to deliver water on demand to downstream interests. Eventually a sort of "gentlemen's agreement" staved off open warfare among the competing users until the federal government stepped in to settle things later in the twentieth century.[85]

Even though most business interests and the public in the basin supported logging and many developments around Lake Tahoe, some concerns were raised. John Muir, visiting between 1873 and 1875, commented on the beauty of the lake but noted the rapid denuding of its shores. The Wheeler survey, one of several federal geographical surveys conducted in the West, recommended in 1876 that the lake basin be protected "as a permanent pleasure ground." Some locals also worried about the damage caused by heavy logging, as evidenced by this comment of the *Truckee Tribune* in 1878: "If in some old cathedral there was a picture painted and framed by an angel. . . . the world would be shocked were some man to take off and sell the marvelous frame. But Tahoe is a picture rarer than ever glittered on cathedral walls. . . . and yet they are cutting away her frame and bearing it away. Have we no state pride to stop the work?"[86]

Pressure to change forest use in the Tahoe Basin, coupled with protection of the lake for tourist use, came from two sources. One was national, the other from the state of California. The first arose as a result of changing attitudes toward the profligate cutting of America's forests. At a meeting of the American Association for the Advancement of Science in 1873, members heard Dr. Franklin B. Hough demand a larger role for the federal government in managing its forested lands. An AAAS committee, which included California state geologist J. D. Whitney, lobbied the federal government to this end. The Division of Forestry in the Department of Agriculture was soon established, with Hough as its first director. Between 1877 and 1882, he issued several important reports that stressed the need for forest protection.[87]

Whitney's presence at the AAAS meeting illustrates that there was growing pressure in California to address forest problems. The strongest support for changes in forest use came from irrigation agriculture interests. In the days before large-scale dams and irrigation projects, they wanted protection of forested watersheds. The national pattern of depletion of forests was clearly seen to be at work in California. Specific interests at Tahoe also had influence, as wealthy landowners and tourists alike expressed concern at unrestricted logging in the lake basin. By the early 1880s, mining in Nevada was dead and logging was declining in relative value. Tourism was rapidly becoming the most important economic activity. Tourists flocked to the new first-class hotels and cruised on the growing number of steamships on the lake, and newspapers in the San Francisco Bay area joined in an increasing demand for protection of the lake.[88]

In 1883 the California legislature passed a resolution that, when supported by the governor, resulted in the creation of the Lake Bigler (the unfortunate "official" name for Tahoe at the time) Forestry Commission. The author of the original Assembly resolution called for the proposed state commission to consider the preservation of the lake and "the most noted, attractive features of its natural scenery . . . for the health, pleasure and recreation of its citizens and tourists." Acting on the model of a state park like Yosemite Valley, the commission in its report stated three major objectives: "The preservation of this lovely gem in California's coronet is urged, first as a fitting beginning in the direction of forestry legislation; second, because it is the duty of the state to keep for its people's enjoyment this perfect resort; and third, because such an attraction as Lake Bigler brings thousands of desirable visitors within the State for the State's profit and renown."[89] In addition to the preservation of the lake, the commission called on the legislature to create a forestry com-mission to provide protection for other forested lands in the state.[90]

To implement the commission's plan, the state had to get Congress to pass legislation to acquire land owned by the Central Pacific Railroad in the Tahoe Basin.[91] Railroad holdings were to be exchanged for land owned else-where by the federal government. California would then request ownership or trusteeship of the basin land for a state park or forest, much as it had acquired control of Yosemite Valley. It was hoped that with basin lands un-der state management, timber companies would lose interest in investing in logging. It was also assumed that wealthy private interests at the lake would provide support for the proposed park plans.[92]

Unfortunately, Congress rebuffed the proposal, and it quietly died. Con-gressional resistance arose for three probable reasons. First, California's man-agement of Yosemite and the Big Trees had been thoroughly discredited, and therefore many believed that the state was not to be trusted with another scenic area. Second, some in Congress were wary of any more land transfers in general because of fraudulent practices involved in earlier legislation such as the Timber Culture and Desert Land Acts. Third, the exchange of railroad lands in the basin was controversial. Some of it was already cut over, and the transfer was opposed vigorously by newspapers and other opponents of the Central Pacific. Thus, the saving of Tahoe Basin as a park was not to be.[93]

Although the park proposal did not succeed, concern about the basin continued. Conflict between California and Nevada interests over control of the eastern Sierra drainages, including the Truckee, Carson, and Walker Rivers, had been going on since the 1860s. The issue was complicated by the fact that the state boundary was itself in dispute. Another contentious bi-state issue involved the way logging operations in the Truckee Basin disposed of their chief by-product, sawdust. As noted earlier, they simply dumped it in the Truckee River and its tributaries. Observers reported piles of sawdust four feet high in the streams, and noxious smells rising from them after seasonal runoff declined.[94]

In the 1870s and 1880s, when cutting in the basin was at its peak, protests mounted. Fishing interests that included native Paiute claimed that dumping was causing fish populations to decline. Downstream, Reno had to deal with pollution of its municipal water source. Attempts to draft legislation in both California and Nevada to halt the practice failed. Defenders of dumping included the *Truckee Republican* newspaper, which attacked any idea that threatened logging. This faction claimed that there was no proof that sawdust harmed fish. They argued that declining fish populations could be blamed on heavy commercial fishing. The *Truckee Republican* said that even if fish were killed, the value of logging far exceeded the value of commercial fishing. Reno residents' claims that decomposing sawdust caused pollution and contributed to the spread of disease were also disputed. Powerful timber interests effectively blocked any controlling legislation in California during the early 1880s.[95]

In 1887 the political climate changed. California created the California Fish Commission. The commission persuaded some of the larger mills to voluntarily reduce their dumping in the river. In the 1890s the decline of logging in the area reduced the influence of large timber interests. A growing determination among California and Nevada lawmakers to bring the polluting of the Truckee under control and to settle the continuing boundary dispute led both state legislatures to cooperate and pass bills to prohibit dumping in 1889. The threat of revoking company charters compelled the last of the giant companies in California to go along. Dumping of sawdust into the Truckee River was halted by 1894. Growing state regulation had made its way into the Tahoe Basin even if the park proposal had failed.[96]

California State Forestry Legislation, 1869–1890

The rise of the national forest conservation movement had direct influence in California. The members of the Lake Bigler Forestry Commission were familiar with its ideas. As mentioned earlier, besides calling for protected status for Lake Tahoe's forests and the California land surrounding it, the commission recommended that the legislature create a forestry board to protect state forests, most of which were in the Sierra Nevada.[97]

The fact that the state and federal government did nothing to stop the wasting of the state's forests, especially damage from human-caused fires, troubled many Californians. The remarks of E. W. Masling, a fruit farmer who spoke out at a fruit growers convention about a fire he saw in the Sierra Nevada, are typical: "Nobody seemed to care; the land belonged to the Government, and what is everybody's business is nobody's business. In a few weeks a forest 10 miles long and a mile wide was burnt, never to be reclaimed in our lifetime."[98]

Public-spirited conservationists and valley irrigation interests combined forces and pressed the legislature, which finally created the California Board of Forestry in 1885.The Forestry Board idea was based on earlier, piecemeal attempts to increase state influence over its forests. (The creation of such an agency had been raised as early as 1869.) The new board was the first of its kind outside of the federal government. Because most of the state's forested lands were in federal or private control, however, the board's power was limited primarily to studying problems and recommending actions.[99]

As part of the educational role of the new state agency, the board's first chairman, Abbott Kinney, wrote an article for the *Overland Monthly* that explained the group's plans. Its first action would be to prepare a map of the state's forests, and then it would draft proposed legislation intended to reduce forest fires and prevent theft of timber on the public domain. Kinney argued that the state's forests were in need of protection. Much of his concern related to water issues. Forest destruction placed the state's water supply in danger, he maintained, and lack of protection also led to serious flooding damage. Further, the public's long-term needs for lumber and firewood necessitated state control. In short, Kinney was basically paraphrasing the arguments of the national conservationists and the state's irrigationists.[100]

The board published four biennial reports before it was abolished by the state after the federal Forest Reserve Act was passed under President Benjamin Harrison in 1891. The first report included Luther Wagoner's observations on the cutting of forests in the Sierra Nevada. His remarks provide a clear ecological baseline describing the effects of mining and logging in the range. He concluded that in the lower foothills, the former forests—heavily exploited to support mining activities—had been replaced by dense brush. No part of the forest had escaped being "ravaged by fires." Some of this damage was the result of lumbering operations and shake cutters, but Wagoner singled out grazers of cattle and sheep as being much more destructive because they purposely started fires to clear brush to promote the growth of browse. Much of the damage by sheep grazing occurred in the higher elevations of the range. Wagoner called on the state to exclude all sheep from the Sierra Nevada.[101]

The second report included comments from the state botanist and state engineer. In a literary vein, the botanist referred to the range and its forests as "King Sierra and His Royal Robe," giving an account of the great diversity of trees in Sierran forests. In another section of the report, and in more prosaic terms, the engineer condemned the damage from fires caused primarily by grazers of sheep in the high alpine regions. In order to control their activities, he called for the division of the range into districts with a forester or guard posted in each. He also criticized the illegal cutting of trees on federal lands by shake makers, calling them "forest pirates." As a solution, he suggested that Sierran and other forests be placed under the control of the state of California so that proper management could be established.[102]

The third biennial report gave up on gaining state control and asked the "general government" to establish proper management of the Sierran forests. The report noted that the board had drafted a memorial to Congress stressing the urgency of its request. The board stated its grievances concerning waste and mismanagement and called for more stringent federal regulation. The report noted the need for more state and federal coordination in related forest-management activities. It commended the federal government for protection of the Big Trees and for establishing two new national parks—Yosemite and Sequoia. These actions contributed to the increase of tourism in the state. The report pointed out that this park protection meant nothing unless federal actions were taken to control forest fires. It also praised the state for beginning to provide some protection for fish and game animals, in part at the prompting of "field" sportsmen, a new class of users of the forests and streams. But the board said that it would be of no use to limit the taking of too many fish or deer if their forest and stream habitats were not protected from fire damage.[103]

Controlling Hydraulic Mining, 1860–1884

The struggle over Yosemite and the Mariposa Big Trees was the first major environmental battle in the Sierra Nevada. It was followed by the struggles over the Tahoe Basin and the forested lands of the range. In the 1860s and 1870s, another conflict took shape, this time over the effects of hydraulic mining in the northern and central Sierra Nevada. It began as an intrastate issue but eventually drew in the federal courts and ultimately Congress as California found itself unable to resolve the key issues.

Unlike the Yosemite, Tahoe, and Sierra forest fights, which were centered in the range itself, the hydraulic mining struggle focused less on the environmental effects of mining on the Sierra Nevada (although these effects of course were huge) than on the debris that washed out of the mountains and caused damage in the valley below. The issue primarily pitted two competing economic interests—mining corporations in San Francisco and elsewhere and their allies in the mountains, and farmers and their economic and political allies in the Central Valley. The Sierra Nevada and the valley and the Bay-Delta system were permanently affected by the mass of debris unleashed by the hydraulic mining corporations. Actions to stop the damage led eventually to regulation of hydraulic mining in the Sierra.[104]

As noted in the previous chapter, the most immediate impact of hydraulic mining in the Sierra was in the drainages of the northern and central rivers, including the upper Feather, Yuba, Bear, American, and portions of the Mokelumne. Earth scientist G. K. Gilbert's estimate of a billion and a half cubic yards of debris displaced by hydraulic mining was made in 1917. Most of the deposits Gilbert examined had been produced between 1853 and 1884.[105]

Steady improvement of techniques had made hydraulic mining highly efficient by the 1870s. In essence, it involved impounding water in dams high in the mountain drainages, transporting it via some 6,000 miles of canals, flumes, and ditches to mining areas. There the water was forced into metal pipes by gravity and then into water cannons, usually called "hydraulic monitors" or "hydraulic giants." These monitors unleashed powerful streams of water that washed away whole hillsides and drainages as "overburden" to expose auriferous gravel beds.[106]

Hubert H. Bancroft's *History of California,* published in 1890, provides a nearly contemporary picture of the effects such activity had on Sierran streams. In the Bear River between Dutch Flat and Little York in 1879, the riverbed was 97 feet higher than it had been in 1870. In the same period, Steep Hollow between Little York and You Bet had risen 136 feet. The author of the volume noted: "In 1880 Bear River was filled to a depth of 120 feet, Steep Hollow 250, and the Greenhorn at the crossing of the Nevada and Dutch Flat Road 200 feet." The pattern of erosion left the largest "bowlders or cobble stones" farthest up in the drainage, with the sand and finer debris washed on down. The extent of the deposits was noted: "The Yuba spreads out its sand and gravel over 15,000 to 16,000 acres, rising above the level of the adjoining country." The amount of debris in the North Fork of the American River was estimated at 20 million cubic yards.[107]

The descriptions of hydraulic mining effects in John B. Leiberg's survey of Sierran forest reserves, already cited, are worth reemphasizing. In one case: "Since the introduction of hydraulic methods the auriferous gravel beds west of a line drawn north and south through Maybert to a junction with the Middle Fork of the Yuba have been torn up in all directions by the hydraulic giants. Vast masses of debris have resulted. . . . Much stands up in huge bluffs

50 to 150 feet in height, slowly caving out in the process of acquiring a permanent slope, while the smaller streams are choked with a finer debris gradually sliding into the main river."[108]

The debris accumulated in the higher tributaries of the large river systems soon overwhelmed these smaller watercourses. In 1862 a heavy winter rain produced flooding. It swept away the dams and water delivery systems of the hydraulic companies, sending mountains of mud, rock, and processed crushed material (referred to as "slickens") down into the valley. Marysville, Yuba City, and Sacramento were heavily damaged. With the smaller streams becoming choked by debris again in the 1870s, the mining corporations punched new drainage tunnels into the main river channels. A yearly cycle of flooding, levee building by the valley cities, and growing legislative and legal wrangling continued into the 1880s. Finally, in 1884, ruling in *Woodruff v. North Bloomfield Gravel Mining Company,* federal judge Lorenzo Sawyer issued a permanent injunction against the release of mining debris. The Sawyer decision ended most hydraulic mining, although the effects of the mining continue in the range to the present.[109]

Following the injunction, mining interests faced ruin unless a political compromise could be fashioned. That took nearly a decade to accomplish and required the federal government to resolve the issues involved. The Caminetti Act of 1893 allowed mining to resume, but only if mining companies constructed restraining dams to control all debris. The act also created a California Debris Commission with power to regulate mining activities. The commission could force mining operators to prepare plans, subject to its review, for the building of dams on or near claims to capture debris, and it used the courts to order compliance with its requirements.[110]

The Debris Commission was generally effective, but not all debris from hydraulic mining operations was blocked from entry into Sierran streams. Sometimes poorly built dams failed, as when the Omega Mine's dam on Scotchman's Creek in Nevada County collapsed, releasing 100,000 cubic yards of debris. This and other "burstings" led the commission to stiffen its regulation and, in some cases, deny licenses for mining. Sometimes small operations tried to escape regulation by operating in winter to avoid the telltale mud that was easy for commission agents to spot during times of clear water. Notable among the clandestine miners were Chinese immigrants, assisted sometimes in their noncompliance by American lawyers.[111]

Although most hydraulic mining stopped for the big companies, creating depression and social dislocation in the communities associated with them, the effects of the hydraulic era did not suddenly disappear. As we have seen, debris still exists in the foothill tributary systems. Scarred hillsides stripped of vegetation and topsoil are still a major feature of river canyons of the northern Sierra. Mercury remains in rivers in great quantities. Seasonal flooding of the terraces and floodplains of the Sierran river tributaries produces continued working of the old materials, adding new sediment to the mountain river systems. It continues to collect in dams on the major northern Sierra rivers such as the Bear and Yuba. In the opinion of California stream expert Jeffrey Mount, "No single industry in the history of the state of California has generated more long-term environmental damage for such a meager economic return."[112]

Beginning Federal Conservation in the Sierra Nevada, 1890–1905

By the 1880s, California had made serious attempts to address problems of unregulated and destructive forest use in the Sierra Nevada and to gain control over its two best-known scenic areas—Yosemite and Tahoe. But it could not claim much success in its goal of placing these forest and monumental scenic reserves under effective state authority. Yosemite in particular proved to many that the state was incapable of providing even minimum good management over its new park. California's poor record there unfortunately had led many to oppose its gaining control over the forested slopes of Lake Tahoe.

The state achieved some limited success cooperating with Nevada to prevent dumping of sawdust in the Truckee River basin, but it clearly failed at preventing the washing of mining debris from Sierran hillsides and the consequent severe damage to valley interests. For many Californians, and for their contacts among a small but growing number of conservationists elsewhere in the nation, hope of relief at the state level had faded. By the late 1880s, these advocates of reform in resource policies turned to the federal government for help.

Federal Surveys and Forest Reserves, 1870–1900

Advocates of scenic conservation and forestry reform in the Sierra Nevada hoped to compel the federal government to expand its powers to provide protection where California could not. With the failures or disappointments of Yosemite, Tahoe, and the State Forestry Board behind them, they looked elsewhere for help.[113]

Meanwhile, most of the higher-elevation forestland on both sides of the range remained subject to unregulated cutting and grazing. The High Sierra scenic areas containing the drainages of the Tuolumne and Merced Rivers above Yosemite and the Big Trees state parks were likewise unprotected from these activities. The condition of southern sequoia groves also drew criticism. The cutting of young as well as ancient redwoods had very early caused complaints from a number of sources. Between 1890 and 1900, national legislation led to the creation of two new national parks in the Sierra Nevada, and three forest reserves. More-effective conservation came to California with the action of a newly committed federal government.[114]

In California and the Sierra, the conservation idea was supported by a wide range of interests. Agriculturists wanted to protect Sierran watersheds to ensure water for the dry months of late July and August. Urban residents near the central and southern Sierra wanted scenic meadows and sequoia forests preserved to draw tourists. The Central Pacific Railroad joined in to promote tourism and because irrigation would increase the value of its landholdings.[115]

Although support from utilitarian interests was important in bringing protective legislation, the actions of two individuals committed to the preservation of scenic resources deserve special mention. John Muir and George Stewart contributed vision, inspired writing, and political acumen to the gathering movement to provide national park status for the Yosemite high country and the southern Sierran forests. Their commitment began in the 1870s and continued long after the passage of the legislation that created Yosemite and Sequoia National Parks.[116]

Collectively, the proponents of federal conservation in the Sierra Nevada in the 1880s and 1890s proved to be more successful than California had. They created and led a well-organized political movement and promoted new federal land policies that would effectively change how the Sierra was perceived. Their work also changed the environment of the range by helping to establish government controls over how Sierran lands would be used. Because at first they had no clear plan beyond taking forested lands and scenic resources out of the path of unrestricted development, new issues affecting how these lands would be used in the future remained unsolved. But that is another story. First, these early halting steps toward federal management of forest lands must be examined.

The majority of unclaimed or uncut Sierra forests remained open to unregulated exploitation for most of the nineteenth century. The national government was unwilling either to transfer such lands to California or to assume responsibility for protecting them itself. Forested areas were therefore open to being filed upon under several federal laws passed from the 1840s to the 1870s.[117]

The federal government seemed committed to letting the western forest lands slip away from its control by default, as it had in the middle states. But even as it did so, it made an effort to increase its knowledge of the area through more precise mapping. The general government acted to gain information about the Sierra as part of a broader survey of lands of the far western United States. Between the 1870s and 1890s, several efforts were mounted, including the U.S. Coast and Geodetic Survey, the Geological Surveys West of the Hundredth Meridian, and the U.S. Geological Survey. All involved triangulation of Sierran peaks.[118]

Most notable of these federal mapping efforts as they affected the Sierra were those of an Army Corps of Engineers officer, George M. Wheeler, in the late 1870s. Working under Wheeler's direction, Lieutenant M. M. Macomb carried out three years of field study between 1876 and 1879 in the Sierra. The expeditions covered portions of the range from around Castle Peak and Tahoe in the north to the area between the Carson and Stanislaus Rivers farther south, stretching down to include triangulation studies in the Yosemite high country. These studies provide a picture of environmental changes underway in those areas.[119]

Macomb noted urbanization and the development of four sawmills and a planing mill at Glenbrook in 1876, and a narrow-gauge railroad and flume that allowed the shipment of lumber from there into the Carson Valley. He also observed the area around Castle Peak, with Central Pacific Railroad activities nearby.[120]

In the Carson-Stanislaus survey, Macomb provided a clear picture of the effects of overgrazing and a severe drought in 1877 on the central and southern parts of the range:

Another misfortune was the scarcity of feed in the mountains. This was due to the fact that the country was completely overrun with vast herds of sheep, which utterly denuded the mountain valleys of grass, and in fact of nearly every green thing within their reach. This unusual influx of sheep was caused by the drought throughout Central and Southern California, the water-supply having failed on account of the light rain and snow fall of the previous season, the average being one of the smallest on record for years. . . . There is no doubt that if the sheep continue to be driven up into these mountains in such vast numbers the grasses will eventually be killed out and great injury inflicted on the country.[121]

In addition to the scientific surveys at the end of the century, momentum for proper management for federal forests was slowly building. Between 1870 and 1890, more than two hundred separate bills to establish some type of federal role in forest management were proposed. One of these in 1881 produced a poorly funded agency in the Department of Agriculture called the Division of Forestry. By the late 1880s, the Division of Forestry and the American Forestry Association were active in pushing for the creation of permanent forest reserves and were working to create a public consensus to support the idea. In 1889 the American Forestry Association pressured President Harrison to take action on federal protection of the unclaimed forests. When he did not respond, the association memorialized Congress instead.[122]

By September of 1890, a bill to repeal the Timber Culture Act, one of the laws that had encouraged massive timber fraud, emerged from Congress. A conference committee took the measure under consideration and, without any discussion, attached a rider that came to be called the "Forest Reserve Act." The origin of the rider remains clouded in obscurity, as probably was intended. It allowed the president of the United States to "set apart and reserve" federally owned forested lands in any state or territory as "public reservations." The revised form of the bill passed both houses, and President Harrison signed it into law. One of the most important laws governing America's forests—the beginnings of its national forest system—was thus passed without any public discussion.[123]

In 1897 Congress passed revised forest reserve legislation, called the Forest Management Act—also known as the Organic Act—as an amendment to an appropriation bill. The rider defined timber production as one of the uses for the reserves, thereby quelling objections to reserve designation by western politicians who believed that the early reserves had "locked up" these forests. While this provision obviously conflicted with another defined goal—protection of watersheds—it was the price exacted for western support.[124]

The rider also required the USGS to inventory the forests of the newly established reserves. This legislation formed the basis for federal forest policy until the passage of the Multiple Use–Sustained Yield Act of 1960. As noted, the forest reserve provision was not subjected to full congressional review. And while it called for management of the new reserves, it did not provide for effective regulation of them. Under the leadership of Bernhard Fernow, the Division of Forestry in the late 1880s and early 1890s studied forest conditions in the U.S. and tried to apply scientific principles to forest management. In 1898 Gifford Pinchot was appointed head of the Division of Forestry, intent on strengthening the agency's control over federal forest land.[125]

All told, three presidents—Harrison, Cleveland, and McKinley—placed millions of acres of western forestland in forest reserves by the turn of the century. Between 1893 and 1899, three forest reserves were created in the Sierra Nevada. The southern reserve was called Sierra, and it made up most of the current Inyo and Sequoia National Forests. The drainages of the central Sierra Nevada rivers, the Mokelumne, Merced, Stanislaus, and Tuolumne, were in-

cluded in the central reserve, which eventually became Stanislaus National
Forest. Reserved lands in the northern part of the range included elements of
the future Tahoe and Eldorado National Forests. Scientific knowledge about
these reserves was scanty at best at the time they were set aside.[126]

The U.S. Geological Survey was authorized to investigate the new reserves and provide information on the conditions of the forested land in
them. A small study of the Yosemite and Sonora quadrangles by C. H. Fitch
and a larger survey by George B. Sudworth in the Stanislaus and Lake Tahoe
Forest Reserves were both reported on in 1900 by the USGS. A large survey by
John B. Leiberg, covering the north-central portions of the Sierra Nevada,
was reported on in 1902. The two major reports by Sudworth and Leiberg
gave a detailed breakdown of the conditions and composition of those forests, providing an important "snapshot" of these two Sierran reserves in the
time before actual resource management began.[127]

The 1900 USGS report, effectively introduced by division head Henry
Gannett, reinforces a picture of relatively open forests in the western-slope,
mixed-conifer zones of the Sierra Nevada, heavily altered in those areas
where mining had occurred. Summarizing Fitch's report on the forested belt in
the Yosemite and Sonora quadrangles, Gannett noted that yellow pine
"quickly becomes the dominant vegetation, covering the country with an open
forest." As for the mixed-conifer zone above this level and up to 8,000-foot
elevation, "The stand of timber in this belt ranges from 10,000 to 50,000 feet
per acre. Nearly all the timber is of merchantable size and quality. There is little
young growth, and the forest is everywhere open, with little underbrush."[128]

In an additional review of the report of George Sudworth, Gannett stated
that a similar type of mixed-conifer forest existed to the north in the Tahoe
and Stanislaus forests (the exception being the larger groves of *Sequoia
gigantea* that were reported on by Fitch). Speaking of the mixed-conifer forests above three thousand feet, Gannett noted: "This forest is open, with
little underbrush; indeed, at present there is little vegetation of any sort
other than trees." But a major exception was made for areas where heavy
mining had gone on between 1850 and 1860. In Gannett's words: "In the
early mining days, between 1850 and 1860, much of this timber was cut away,
and great areas are now covered with a young growth, mainly of yellow pine,
which is the principle tree to reproduce. Mining is still carried out on this
region, but on a much more limited scale, and the destruction of timber for
the supply of mines is not great."[129]

John Leiberg's 1902 report covered the drainages of the Feather, Yuba,
Bear, and American Rivers. His observations also reached across the Sierra in
the same latitude. Leiberg's findings on forest composition were similar to

those of Fitch and Sudworth farther south, except for differences between
the east and west slope. He included several types of conifers in what he
called the "yellow-pine type of forest" that ranged from 2,500 to 6,500 feet in
elevation on the two flanks of the range.[130] As he described these forests:

> The most conspicuous and important tree of the type is the yellow
> pine. It occurs abundantly between elevations of 3,000 and 4,500 feet
> in the central area, while in the eastern and trans-Sierran districts it is
> most common between altitudes of 4,500 and 5,800 feet. In past times,
> before logging operations commenced, it may have been the domi-
> nant species as regards the number of trees, but owing to the vast
> amount of cutting it is no longer. It has been more exhaustively logged
> than any other species in the type except the sugar pine, and restocking
> has not kept pace with the cutting.[131]

Leiberg also commented on the density of the forest areas he observed:

> In the eastern and trans-Sierran districts of the region the old-growth
> forests of the type are generally open on all slopes except the northern
> and on tracts with much seepage. In such localities the white fir is
> present in large quantities and gives density to the stands. In the cen-
> tral district, outside the canyon areas, the forest is of moderate density
> and is rarely what might be called open, except in stands of very old
> growth. Elsewhere, large quantities of white and red fir with oak com-
> bine to form thickset stands. On the rocky slopes of canyons and in the
> great gorges of the rivers the forest is always very open and scattered.[132]

Besides giving an inventory of tree species in the reserves, the USGS reports included descriptions of the destructive forces brought by historic
settlement. Both listed four major negative factors: the cutting of the forests
by lumbermen, fires caused by human use, grazing, and mining. Sudworth
and Leiberg especially condemned sheep grazing and fires associated with
the sheepherders, citing both as important reasons for establishing more
effective regulation of these forested lands. Their appeal reflected the concern
of both state and federal authorities and scientists about the need for an
effective forest policy as the century turned.[133]

Trespass, unauthorized grazing, and timber theft continued after the Sierra reserves were created. Forest reserve legislation may actually have stimulated timber speculators to file claims on forested, lower-elevation land with
the Government Land Office before these forests could be placed in reserves.

Railroads relied on another federal law, called the Lieu Land Act of 1897, to trade some of their lands (often cutover) in the reserves for forested lands not in the reserves. In addition, although in theory the reserve law called for effective management of the reserves, in practice it was quite different. A key problem was that actual physical control of the reserves remained in the hands of the Government Land Office in the Department of the Interior, while responsibility for policy formation and study of the reserves lay in the Division of Forestry in the Department of Agriculture. The separation created bureaucratic infighting and inefficiency.[134]

In the Sierra this issue of confused and inefficient management can be illustrated by following the career of a dedicated and talented federal employee, George B. Sudworth. Sudworth was enthusiastically hired in 1886 by the head of the Division of Forestry, Bernhard E. Fernow. Sudworth contributed to scientific studies of the forests of the Pacific area for many years. He was also asked to conduct the USGS survey of the Sierra Forest Reserve under Fernow's rival in the Division of Geography and Forestry, Henry Gannett. After completion of this USGS study of the southern Sierra, Sudworth was asked to inspect conditions in the Sierra Forest Reserve in 1900. The request reflected interest in how the reserves in general were faring after their designation. Notes taken by Sudworth on his inspection showed that control by the federal government in that reserve, even after the passage of the 1897 reserve act, was practically nonexistent.[135]

Summarizing Sudworth's notes, one can find the several concerns expressed. There was confusion on boundaries, with private parties sometimes using what Sudworth believed to be government land. This meant that trees and pastureland were being taken or used without permission. Cutting of sequoia in the sections he observed was often illegal and in any case led to between 50 and 80 percent of the cut tree being shattered and therefore of no commercial use. Fires routinely set by sheepmen or cattlemen to make movement of their animals easier damaged standing trees or even completely destroyed all regrowth. Large areas were denuded by grazing, turning the soil to barren ground or to dust. To top it all off, although the reserve had been assigned rangers to supervise it and assure compliance with regulations, the rangers were either corrupt or inefficient.[136]

This concern about ranger reliability is illustrated by the following excerpts from Sudworth's diary:

> Harry Quinn is said to own several thousand acres in "Dry Meadow" (Mouth Dry Creek) and ranged 2,800 sheep there this season; also a band on Peppermint Meadow (on creek immediately south of Free-

man Valley and Creek). There is evidence that most of the grazing was done on the forest-covered watersheds above the meadows, the latter not much reduced. Ranger Nelson states sheep kept within lines of deeded land, but this is not borne out by the appearance of forest land above. . . .

. . . . Bands of sheep found grazing on mid headwaters of Middle Tule; probably 1,000 sheep. . . . Said to be property of Clint Brown, near Porterville, Calif. Ranger in this district said to be in collusion with Brown, allowing sheep to remain. . . . No forest fire warnings posted in this canyon down to the point where trail forks for Dillon's Mill and head of Alpine Creek. . . .

. . . . Sheep camp 2–3 miles up the valley [head of basin of North Fork of Kings River] of the branch of river camped on Sept. 17. . . . Two herders in charge of 3000–5000 sheep. Evidence of having been in this region since June. Said to be property of Bosili (Bros.) Fresno. Said to have entered this valley via Russell camp and thence northeastward over headwaters of North Fork. No evidence on any of the No. Fk. sheds of forest rangers having covered the ground. Herder said "Too cold for ranger. No come here. No save."[137]

With such results apparently being common, it is no surprise that after the turn of the century, reform-minded conservationists would call for strengthening regulation in the Sierra and the nation's forests.

Sequoia, General Grant, and Yosemite National Parks, 1878–1890

By the 1870s, lumbermen had entered the Kings and Kaweah River watersheds, cutting pine, fir, and some sequoia for local and larger markets after the coming of the railroad. In 1875 two men cut down the so-called Mark Twain Tree, one of the oldest and largest in the southern forest, in order to ship sections of it east for display. John Muir visited the area in the 1878 and, while praising the sequoia, expressed concern about the logging.[138]

By the 1880s, log flumes extended cutting into the Converse Basin, considered by many to be one of the most impressive groves in the sequoia belt. Sheepmen were also using the southern drainages, and their overgrazing and fires were considered by many, including Muir and Clarence King, to be worse than logging. In 1878, *Visalia Delta* newspaperman George Stewart published his first complaint about sequoia cutting, demanding that protection be instituted.[139]

Stewart turned his early vision of protecting the sequoia into a mission. Others aided him. In 1880, the U.S. surveyor general for California acted on the request of some local citizens and California scientists to withdraw the Grant Grove from filing under the prevailing federal land laws. Stewart, seeing the potential to expand this isolated action into the creation of a southern Sierra Nevada national park, worked with California senator John Miller to introduce such legislation in 1880. The legislative action failed. In 1883, under prompting from some weather scientists, the Army Signal Corps set aside a military reservation around Mount Whitney for weather observations (although this action was reversed when Mount Whitney was placed within the Sierra Forest Reserve in the 1890s). All these measures demonstrated to Stewart that the wind was blowing in the direction of effective federal protection.[140]

Stewart was aware that a state preserve such as Yosemite was not a useful model to follow. He saw the federal protection of Yellowstone, set aside in 1872 and guarded after 1883 by the U.S. Army, as a more effective way to preserve the sequoias. But as he was plotting his next moves, a group of California socialists in 1885 formed a joint stock company called the Kaweah Cooperative Commonwealth. They filed under the federal Timber and Stone Act to claim much of the area know as the Giant Forest—the heart of the sequoia, pine, and fir stands in the southern Sierra Nevada.[141]

Spurred to action, Stewart used the *Visalia Delta* to demand a Government Land Office investigation of potentially fraudulent claims by the group. Though no proof of fraud was found, eventually the socialists' claims were rejected. Support for protection against the Kaweah group came also from San Joaquin Valley farmers fearing loss of valuable watershed. But even as the Kaweah Colony claims were being challenged, President Garfield's secretary of the interior opened much of the area around General Grant and elsewhere to filing. Many timber speculators promptly filed for the lands.[142]

At this juncture Stewart turned to a California congressman for help. William Vandever had strong connections with the Southern Pacific Railroad that made it possible for him to carry legislation successfully to the floor of Congress. With backing from the California governor, certain New York newspapers, and John Muir's friend Robert Underwood Johnson, the measure cleared its last hurdles and became law in September of 1890. The reserved area included seventy-six square miles of Sierran forest containing sequoias and some mountain meadow areas. The new reserve was not specifically designated as a national park, but the law ordered the secretary of the interior to protect timber, mineral deposits, and fish and game included in the grant and to open the area to accommodation of tourists.[143]

Just as the effective creation of Sequoia National Park involved the action of a dedicated preservationist, assistance from the railroad and its friends in high political places, and the influence of valley irrigationists, so also did the creation of a sister park to the north at Yosemite. John Muir provided the leadership and the writing, just as Stewart had done for Sequoia. The Southern Pacific, often working closely with Muir and *Century* magazine editor Robert Underwood Johnson, provided political muscle at key points.[144] Irrigationists and Valley urban interests, expecting to gain from increased farm revenues and tourism, gave steady support to the project as well. Just as Stewart and his allies had opted for federal protection for the sequoia, so also did Muir and his supporters see federal legislation to create a national park as the only way to provide effective guardianship for the country surrounding Yosemite Valley.[145]

Muir did not originate the idea of seeking national park status for the drainages of the Merced and Tuolumne Rivers. Observations of the effects of overgrazing and logging on the rivers, including siltation of Mirror Lake caused by runoff, had brought calls for protection in the 1870s. In 1881 even the beleaguered Yosemite Valley Commission had supported the idea. In a report on considering changes in management for the valley, State Geologist William H. Hall recommended protection of the upper Merced watershed as a way to give the Valley a measure of protection from mining, timber cutting, and sheep grazing above it. Local opposition blocked any action.[146]

Between 1881 and 1890, thousands of acres in the drainage of the Tuolumne and Merced had been filed on by private individuals. If any complaint was heard, it was mostly aimed at the park commissioners for actions degrading the Valley. Only Muir and Johnson consistently showed any broader concern for the problems outside the state park's boundaries. In 1889, one of the Yosemite commissioners, William H. Mills, resigned in protest of the policies being followed by the commission. In addition to being a commissioner, he was part owner of the *Sacramento Record Union* and a land agent for the Southern Pacific Railroad. He editorialized against the actions of his former colleagues on the Yosemite commission and reached out to Muir and Johnson with support.[147]

At this time, Muir and Johnson wanted to see the Valley taken back from the state and included in their proposed larger national park. But they decided to focus on the surrounding higher-elevation lands rather than trigger opposition from proud Californians opposed to a Valley retrocession. With aid from the same helpful Congressman Vandever, a bill was introduced into Congress to create a small Yosemite national park that would include the high country above and around the valley. To Muir's bitter disappointment, large parts of the Tuolumne drainage and Tenaya Lake were not included.[148]

All historians who have written on the subject admit that they do not understand what happened next. Vandever's "little Yosemite" measure was suddenly replaced with a new one that expanded the proposed park by including the lost drainages of the Tuolumne and Merced, and added acreage to the new Sequoia National Reserve as well. The measure also created a new park: General Grant, set aside originally in 1880, was incorporated in a separate national park to protect the giants left out of Sequoia a few weeks earlier.[149]

The changes in the bill coincided with the arrival in Washington of Southern Pacific land agent Daniel Zumwalt. His secret influence led to the legislation that would expand Yosemite National Park by five times and double Sequoia as well. At that point E. H. Harriman, head of the Southern Pacific Railroad, joined Muir and Johnson in pushing for passage of the bill. In October, President Benjamin Harrison signed the measure into law.[150]

The Sierra Club and the New Federal Holdings

The 1880s and 1890s were seminal decades for forest and park designations. Some scientists and foresters in government service had fledgling ideas about management of this new federal land, and activists like Muir, Johnson, and Stewart believed passionately in preservation of the new parks. But no one had a clear concept of what these new creations really were, or what to do with them. In the 1890s, advocates of increased federal protection for reserves and parks struggled to come up with workable answers to the questions these lands presented to the nation.[151]

The Sierra Club was founded to influence decisions being made about the parks and reserves. In 1889, Muir and artist William Keith had discussed creating such a club. In 1892, Muir joined with a number of University of California and Stanford University professors in chartering the organization. They were strongly influenced by Robert Johnson, who stressed the need for a group devoted to defending the new parks, the Sierra Nevada, and other Pacific Coast mountains against further destruction. The articles of incorporation defined three major purposes for the club: promoting enjoyment and accessibility of the Pacific Coast mountains, providing accurate information about them, and encouraging public and governmental support for the preservation of the Sierra Nevada's natural features. Muir was elected the club's first president.[152]

The new organization mixed scientific, educational, and recreational goals into a broad-based but loosely defined program. Muir was troubled by the fact that in order to gain public support for the new parks, he had to promote tourism, which would detract from the natural experience as it had done in Yosemite Valley. As no single agency effectively controlled the range's parks, serious problems developed.[153]

Yosemite and Sequoia National Parks were nominally under the control of the Department of the Interior. But no formal procedures or specific agency existed to prevent continued trespass by any number of illegal users, especially sheepherders and loggers. Between 1890 and 1916, the U.S. Cavalry patrolled the parks in the months when they were accessible, trying valiantly to exclude unauthorized interlopers. Even so, trespassing went on. Typically, sheepherders would wait until the troopers left in the fall and then drive their flocks in to graze until Indian summer ended. Poachers also operated in the parks. The cavalry did keep most trespassers out, but the Sierra Club favored the creation of a park service as a more effective regulatory approach.[154]

The three newly created Sierran forest reserves also concerned the club's members. Between 1892 and 1898, the club and its leader, Muir, struggled to get effective protection for the reserves. In an address to the club's annual meeting in 1895, Muir praised the army for helping exclude sheepherders from the new Sierra parks, noting that flowers were again blooming in the "highlands" thanks to the cavalry. As to the newly created Sierra Forest Reserve, however, he had to report that "the grand Sierra Forest Reservation, extending from the south boundary of the Yosemite Park to the Kern River, is not yet protected. Many government notices were nailed on trees along the trails as warnings to trespassers; but as there was no one on the ground to enforce obedience to the rules, cattle and sheep owners have paid little attention to them."[155]

Reporting on an expedition to the southern Sierra Forest Reserve in the club's bulletin of January 1896, Professor William Russell Dudley expressed concern about unauthorized uses he had witnessed. Yet, he said, the hunters, ranchers, and valley fruit farmers he had encountered generally accepted the necessity of the reserves and recognized the negative effects that came from unregulated sheep grazing and logging. He also noted a general consensus among forest scientists for a new federal role in forest protection, including the creation of professional forestry schools in universities, and perhaps at West Point, to train foresters. He advocated the addition of local assistant foresters to work with local populations on timber-use issues.[156]

In addition, Dudley suggested uses for protected forest reserves that anticipated policies of the next century. For instance, he pointed out that "game is decreasing, and there are scores of streams in the Sierra entirely devoid of fish. The stocking of the woods and streams throughout the reservations, and the establishment in certain sections of an open season for the sportsman, would greatly increase the popularity and usefulness of scientific forest administration."[157]

A final example of consensus by the Sierra Club was that of Marsden Manson, writing in the club's bulletin in 1899. Even though the Forest Reserve Act of 1897 had proposed the creation of effective management of the reserves, Manson believed that he had the solution for myriad problems still associated with them. He noted that wasteful forestry practices around the world and in the Rocky Mountains had long ago convinced most thoughtful persons of the need for better methods. He said conditions in the Sierra were worse than in many other areas of deforestation he had studied. The denuding of Tahoe's shores and the destruction of fish in the Carson River caused by logging and fires were proof that California's forests needed more effective policies. His solution was to have federal legislation drafted to place all forested lands in the state under the control of the regents of the University of California. They could then raise revenue through carefully supervised timber sales on these lands, using the resulting funds to create a school of forestry to train foresters. Manson's specific idea, while never seriously considered, nevertheless reflected the consensus of the club for a more effective reserve policy.[158]

Many of the club's general ideas for management of the Sierran reserves became part of the policies established by Gifford Pinchot after the reserves' transfer into the newly created national forests in 1905–1906. Many of the club's leaders, especially Muir, however, did not forgive Pinchot for allowing sheep to continue to graze in these forested lands.[159]

Conservation in the Sierra Nevada was an important accomplishment in the waning decades of the nineteenth century. The American public, acting through Congress or relying on the courts as in the hydraulic-mining issue, established a new way to approach the range, its forests and rivers, and its monumental wonders. The beginnings of conservation in the range came from motivations that mixed utilitarian, self-serving, and genuinely noble actions all together. (The image of saintly John Muir in bed with officials of the Southern Pacific Railroad comes to mind.) And as with all beginnings, the pathway ahead was uncharted.

Many Americans knew that the old ways of using land and resources could not continue, and so large blocks of Sierran forests were placed in forest reserves. But in some ways this was a minimal accomplishment. Sheepmen, hunters, and loggers continued trespassing, although at a lesser level. (The cavalry did mostly stop invasion of the new Sierran parks, but the Department of the Interior did not understand that the army was ill prepared to do more than perform a negative, if useful, function.) A very hard job lay ahead. How were these new reserves and parks to be protected from further encroachment? Could they be expanded and added to? Or should they be used in a new way that the original creators had not envisioned? Establishing management of these lands would prove to be as controversial as the actions that created them in the first place.

California Native American family in Yosemite Valley (n.d.). Courtesy Yosemite
National Park Research Library

California Native standing by cedar-slab structure typical of Sierra tribal peoples (n.d.). Courtesy California History Room, California State Library, Sacramento

Native grinding rock, Amador County. Courtesy California History Room, California State Library, Sacramento

(*opposite*) Young Paiute men visiting Yosemite Valley (n.d.). Courtesy Yosemite National Park Research Library

James W. Marshall at Sutter's Mill, Coloma, where gold was first discovered in California (ca. 1848). Courtesy California History Room, California State Library, Sacramento

Euro-American and Chinese placer miners employing simple "rocker" and short-sluice technology. Placer miners effectively opened the Sierra Nevada to development that clogged streams with mud and debris and damaged forests, fisheries, and wildlife. Courtesy Searls Historical Library, Nevada City, CA

English Dam on the Yuba River, an impound dam intended to provide water for hydraulic mining downriver. Courtesy Searls Historical Library, Nevada City, CA

River mining in the Sierra Nevada. Miners are working the riverbed after the stream has been redirected into a flume. Courtesy Searls Historical Library, Nevada City, CA

Hydraulic flume in Nevada County. Wood for the flume was provided by a local mill. The impact on local forests is evident, especially at the upper right of the photograph. Courtesy Searls Historical Library, Nevada City, CA

Monitors at work in a Nevada County hydraulic mine. Courtesy Searls Historical Library, Nevada City, CA

Hydraulic mine and flume, Nevada County, CA. Courtesy Searls Historical Library, Nevada City, CA

Trees regenerating a heavily hydraulic-mined hillside, Nevada County, CA. Courtesy Searls Historical Library, Nevada City, CA

Log dam at Blue Lakes, Alpine County, CA. Courtesy California History Room, California State Library, Sacramento

The gold rush encouraged the construction of roads across and through the Sierra. Here we see the Dutch Flat Toll Road at Donner Summit, with Donner Lake in the background. Lithograph by Edward Vischer, from *Vischer's Pictorial of California*. Courtesy California History Room, California State Library, Sacramento

BROCKLISS BRIDGE.
OLD EMIGRANT ROAD and BRIDGE, OVER THE NORTH FORK OF THE AMERICAN RIVER,
22 MILES FROM PLACERVILLE.

Brockliss Bridge over the North Fork of the American River, on the Old Emigrant Road east
of Placerville. This road was a major thoroughfare over the Sierra until the completion of the
Central Pacific Railroad. It connected the southern Sierra mines, via Carson Pass, with Nevada
and the Comstock silver mines. Today's Highway 50 follows much the same route. Lithograph
by Edward Vischer, from *Vischer's Pictorial of California.* Courtesy California History Room,
California State Library, Sacramento

Ox team hauling logs at Lake Tahoe in the 1860s or 1870s. Heavy logging led to erosion, thus beginning the reduction of the lake's clarity. Reproduced by permission of The Huntington Library, San Marino, CA

Loading a log wagon, Lake Tahoe, 1880s. Most of the Tahoe Basin had been logged by the end of the 1880s. The forest that returned was less diverse, less able to deal with prolonged drought, and more susceptible to fire. Reproduced by permission of The Huntington Library, San Marino, CA

A small Sierra lumber mill, typical of operations in the northern and central Sierra. Oxen were commonly used to drag logs to the mill. Oxen and lumber crews had to be fed, which led to the development of agriculture in many areas. Courtesy Searls Historical Library, Nevada City, CA

Pray's mill and wharf, Glenbrook, Nevada, on Lake Tahoe ca. 1870. Logging in the Tahoe Basin was stimulated by the discovery of the Comstock silver lode in western Nevada and the construction of the Central Pacific Railroad. Reproduced by permission of The Huntington Library, San Marino, CA

Glenbrook, Nevada, 1884. The effects of heavy logging are evident on the denuded hillsides. Courtesy Searls Historical Library, Nevada City, CA

"Steam donkey" used to pull cut logs to milling sites. Dragging logs damaged young trees, contributing to the slow regeneration of the forest in many parts of the logged-over Sierra. Courtesy Searls Historical Library, Nevada City, CA

(*opposite*) Cutting segments of the General Noble Tree for exhibition at the Chicago World's Fair. C. C. Curtis photograph. Courtesy California History Room, California State Library, Sacramento

Hobart Mills was typical of the large-scale railroad-supported lumber operations in the northern and central Sierra Nevada. Courtesy Searls Historical Library, Nevada City, CA

Loggers and felled sequoia, 1880s. Courtesy National Park Service Archives of Sequoia and Kings Canyon National Parks

Skeleton of the Mother of the Forest Tree, Calaveras County, after the bark had been stripped for exhibition. The metal frame indicates the tree's former girth. From Edward Vischer, *Vischer's Pictorial of California*. Courtesy California History Room, California State Library, Sacramento

Cutting down the Mark Twain Tree, Tulare County. C. C. Curtis photograph. Courtesy California History Room, California State Library, Sacramento

(*opposite, top*) A sequoia being cut by park officials near the Grant Forest facilities. It was leaning and considered a threat to the lodge and public visiting the park. Courtesy National Park Service Archives of Sequoia and Kings Canyon National Parks

(*opposite, bottom*) Ponderosa pine forest, Kern Canyon, seven miles south of Soda Springs. The openness of the forest reflects the effects of heavy grazing. Photograph by Mary Austin. Reproduced by permission

A band of sheep grazing in Tuolumne Meadows. Courtesy Yosemite National Park Research Library

Mountain lions shot as part of the predator-control efforts in Sequoia National Park. Courtesy National Park Service Archives of Sequoia and Kings Canyon National Parks

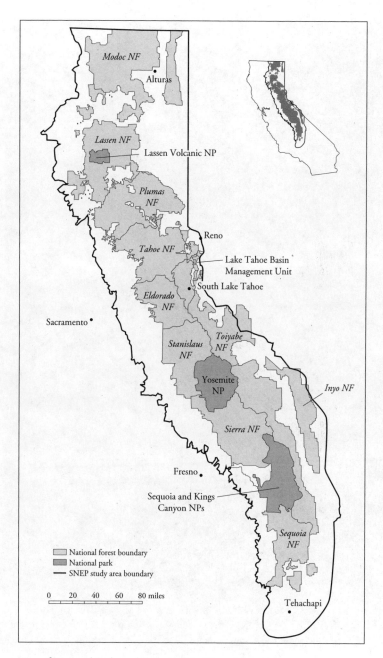

Map of National Parks and Forests of the Sierra Nevada

The author inspects a carving of "Jani" at Perazzo Meadows near Truckee. For many years, hundreds of Basque herders oversaw millions of sheep grazing throughout the Sierra Nevada and the Great Basin. Some of them recorded their presence and experiences in tree carvings like the ones in this photograph. "Jani" was apparently an itinerant prostitute known to many herders during the late 1920s and 1930s. The herder who carved this portrait left similar portraits of her in several aspen groves in the northern Sierra. Photo courtesy Michael P. Claytor

4: Establishing Resource Management, 1905–1945

The role of the federal government as manager of public lands is an established idea today, even if the details of how those lands are managed remain subject to conflict. There is no one living who remembers the time when something called the Government Land Office parceled out federal land in the West under the provisions of the Homestead, Timber Culture, or Desert Land Acts. "Doing a land office business" is a phrase from the past that some still use, but its meaning has become separated from the practices that led to its coining.

That era's version of "corporate welfare" is over. Railroads no longer get gargantuan land grants for free. Timber companies and ranchers cannot use fraudulent filings under swamplands or flooded lands acts to enrich themselves at the public expense and acquire landed empires. At the beginning of the last decade of the nineteenth century, federal law created Yosemite, Sequoia, and General Grant National Parks. The passage of the Forest Reserve and Forest Management Acts of the 1890s started a national forest policy that included Sierran forestlands. Even though conflicts over these public lands in the Sierra continued in the years that followed, the nation generally remained on a path of public management in the Sierra Nevada that has stood the test of time.[1]

Many historians have written about the politics of public land use during those years, and certainly the creation of the United States Forest and Park Services and the roles played by California and municipal agencies established after 1900 are important topics. But there is something missing from many of those past accounts. Few examine how new public policy that came with those agencies altered the Sierran environment and affected its wildlife and forests. Public management left behind a record of activities and contemporary ideas about the uses of Sierran lands. Unintentionally, the new agencies provided successive baselines or inventories of species as part of their activities, even as new policies reshaped public lands. They also interacted with some private interests, such as railroad logging companies, in cutting most of the range's most ancient trees in the Tahoe Basin and in lower-elevation west-side areas.

New public agencies interacted with the Sierra Nevada just as glaciers, fire, and past human generations did.

John Muir unfortunately was right in 1895 when, in an address to the

Sierra Club, he said: "The battle we have fought, and are still fighting, for the forests is a part of the eternal conflict between right and wrong, and we cannot expect to see the end of it."[2] For Muir and many Sierra Club members and other conservationists, it soon become clear that it would not be easy to sort out the good from the evil when competing conservation interests grappled over how the new public lands were to be used. Soon these conservationists, including Sierra Club members themselves, would be at war over who were the bad guys. The issue after 1900 was not if the public lands were to be managed, but how they were to be managed.[3]

In the early years of conservation and preservation of forests and parks, many alliances were forged that came apart as the strain over how the new lands were to be managed grew. One example suffices here. Consider the friendship and alliance of John Muir and Gifford Pinchot. Both agreed that forests needed protection from wanton destruction. But once reserves were established and Pinchot became the head of the Division of Forestry, differences grew. Muir wanted sheep out of the forests. Pinchot said they should be allowed in and could be managed to reduce damage. Muir wanted Hetch Hetchy Valley in Yosemite National Park protected from being dammed. Pinchot sided with the utilitarian conservationists who said it should be used for San Francisco's water needs.[4]

The forty-year struggle after 1900 over the management of the federal lands in the Sierra constitutes another clear period in the range's environmental history.

National Forests in the Sierra Nevada, 1905–1940s

Congress created forest reserves in 1891 as an important first step in limiting overcutting of western forests. It took another six years before scientists, foresters, and conservationists convinced a reluctant Congress to establish a management system for those reserves.[5] The Organic Act of 1897 that began management of those forests contained several provisions that affected Sierra Nevada public lands. Of most immediate influence was a provision requiring the U.S. Geological Survey to prepare reports on the nation's existing forest reserves.[6] In the Sierra Nevada, the reports of Sudworth and Leiberg, referred to earlier, began the process by inventorying the reserves as a first step in that management.

But even as a better picture of the conditions in the large, ungainly early reserves in the Sierra emerged, effective national control over forested lands remained elusive. Development of forest policies was eventually assigned to the Division of Forestry in the Department of Agriculture under Gifford

Pinchot in 1898. But authority over the reserves themselves remained in the Department of the Interior. The irony of a chief forester without any actual forests to control was obvious to many in Congress, the scientific community, and of course Pinchot.[7]

Theodore Roosevelt was elevated to the presidency with the assassination of McKinley in 1901. In 1905, Pinchot persuaded him and Congress that the forest reserves belonged in the Department of Agriculture. Pinchot next succeeded in getting the reserves redesignated as national forests. He then labored to create a professional agency that employed modern forestry practices. Science was a key component of his thinking in these founding years. His policies directly shaped the new national forests in the Sierra Nevada and across the West.[8]

Pinchot's philosophy was based on the idea that national forests and their resources were to be used by the American public, not locked up or preserved. Much of his time in the early years of his tenure as chief forester was spent educating the public as to what these new federal holdings were. As he said in one popular explanation of his policies, "Many people do not know what National Forests are. Others may have heard about them, but have no idea of their true purpose and use. A little misunderstanding may cause a great deal of dissatisfaction. The National Forests very closely concern all the people of the west and, indeed, of the whole country. They affect, directly or indirectly, many great business interests. It is the object of this publication to explain just what they mean, what they are for, and how to use them."[9]

Pinchot followed the direction of his immediate predecessor at the Division of Forestry, Bernhard E. Fernow, who said use "was not contrary to conservation." Another of Pinchot's key principles was that local industrial and economic needs were to be served first in the national forests—a policy that reduced local resistance to Forest Service management.[10]

Pinchot's principles were quickly put to work in the Sierra Nevada. To simplify the task of managing the huge, sprawling early reserves, the Tahoe, Yuba, and Sierra Forest Reserves were reorganized into eight more-manageable national forests. After some boundary shifts and renaming, these Sierran forests became the Plumas, Tahoe, Eldorado, Stanislaus, Sierra, and Sequoia, and parts of the Inyo and Toiyabe.[11]

Before World War II, most activities of the Forest Service were "custodial." They entailed establishing forest boundaries, creating ranger districts, building infrastructure such as fire watchtowers and ranger stations, and recruiting and training personnel. Forest Service employees marked and supervised timber sales but also promoted forest, range, and stream-system health and cooperated with state agencies to sustain fish and wildlife in the forests.[12]

Forest management also involved applying scientific silvicultural practices to the new national forests—the goal being to grow more trees and systematically cut, when possible, the older trees that were uniformly referred to as "decadent." Most actual timber cutting in the Sierra at this time occurred on private holdings as it had in the past, until those lands were cut over by the 1940s. Timber sales were an important part of a broader policy, but not the chief activity of national forest supervisors.[13]

Forest Service fire practices are of great concern to public land managers today. Through practical actions, scientific study, and decisions made by the Forest Service during the period from 1900 to 1945, wildfire suppression came to dominate the agency's policy. The hope of excluding fire in Sierran forests had been one of the key elements in the campaign to establish control over federal lands during the early conservation period from 1870 to 1890. Forest Service decisions and actions in turn influenced the fire policies of the National Park Service and the California Board of Forestry.[14]

In this custodial period, federal forest scientists helped create a very different kind of Sierran forest than had existed in previous times. After 1905, the Forest Service for the first time seriously tried to apply what forest scientists called "silvics." Its purpose was to grow more trees in the forests of the Pacific Coast. Hand in hand with growing more trees came scientific study to help create policies aimed at suppressing wildfire. Fire was defined as an unnatural and deadly force that limited the number and variety of trees that could be produced. It had to go.[15]

The beginnings of professional forestry and serious scientific study in public forests of the United States had been firmly established by the time of Bernhard Fernow in the 1890s. One of Fernow's most effective assistants, George B. Sudworth, combined significant experience in the field and serious scientific study of forest trees, as illustrated by his *Forest Atlas: Geographic Distribution of North American Trees*.[16] In another study, *Forest Trees of the Pacific Slope,* published in 1908, Sudworth wrote of an ideal he envisioned for scientific study of Pacific Coast forests. He promoted the use of "dendrology," which he defined as the "botany of trees." In this work he acknowledged the assistance of C. Hart Merriam, through being able to consult that pioneer ecologist's notes on "the distribution and occurrence of California trees."[17] Sudworth suggested a direction that Forest Service science could take in its future actions. Relying on Merriam, he spoke of Pacific Coast trees as living within a context—a "more or less definite habitat." They were not to be studied merely as isolated species. The Forest Service, he believed, must take a broader ecological view as well as engaging in specific practical silvicultural actions. He stated this ideal clearly:

Silvics, as the basis for all practical silvicultural operations, deals with the factors which influence the life and growth of trees in their natural or adopted habitat. In recent years the new science of ecology, a study of plant associations, has included, in so far as life habits of trees are concerned, a part of dendrology as one of its natural subdivisions. It appears logical, however, to consider dendrology as still including the study of tree associations. This leaves forest ecology in its proper place as a department of general ecology, and at the same time preserves the identity of an essential part of dendrology, a distinct division of general botany. However this may be, the serious student of tree life—dendrology—can make no mistake in taking the broadest view of the field and in striving to familiarize himself with all that pertains to trees, from a study of their distinguishing characteristics to their modes of life and associations.[18]

But the direction that Forest Service science took in the years that followed Sudworth's suggestion of broader associations and ecological approaches to forest management was to be quite different in practice. Forest science came simply to direct its energy to the question of how to increase the number of trees in public forests. To do so, Forest Service scientists ignored the issue of "modes of life and associations" and focused primarily on one thing that reduced the number and variety of trees in Sierran forests—fire. Forest Service science in the Sierra Nevada came to concentrate on the effects of fire in the range, whether it was possible to exclude it, and how new forests could be protected against it.[19]

Forest Service scientists helped launch the United States on a path to the creation of a new type of Sierra forest—a "totally stocked" forest protected by a well-organized fire-protection service. Leading this crusade were three forest scientists, Coert Du Bois, S. B. Show, and E. I. Kotok.[20] Their influence produced not only more fully stocked forests, but forests that tragically were subject to larger and more-destructive fires than had ever occurred in the past.

The scientists of the Forest Service in the Sierra Nevada did not question how Sierran trees lived and grew in complex natural systems. They were not interested, as some other Sierran scientists were, in the role of birds such as Clark's nutcracker in propagating pine forests in their typically high-elevation habitats. They did not consider the role of fire in the life cycle of certain forest trees or publicize the general studies of the effects of brush burning in California forests.[21] The Forest Service was interested in showing through scientific study that fire in the Sierra Nevada was a destructive force that should be discouraged. The service was also interested in proving that through cooperative measures with private and state agencies, efficient and cost-effective fire protection of Sierran forests was possible.[22]

In studying fires for these purposes, two prominent agency supporters of fire exclusion, Forest Examiners S. B. Show and E. I. Kotok unwittingly provided information that is of use for later generations. Their work of summary and analysis offers a view of past fire frequency in the range and a description of what the range's forests were like in the 1920s. They also reveal the mindset of the agency's fire scientists and serve as a guide as to how this thinking shaped a new type of Sierran forest.

As to the role of fire over time in the Sierra and other similar California forests, Show and Kotok wrote: "Physical conditions in the pine forests of California have led to the frequent recurrence of fires for centuries, but the fact that magnificent forests still cover large areas and give the appearance of well-stocked, vigorous stands has blinded the public to the harm that fires have done and are steadily working throughout the whole region."[23] They based their view of the role of fire in what they called the "virgin forests" of California on examination of the scars left on surviving trees by the "periodically recurring" fires of the pine region for a two-century period from 1685 to 1889.[24] The evidence covered a portion of the time of native occupation, as well as the period of unregulated European American use. It showed twenty-five clearly marked fire years, meaning that significant fires had occurred every eight years on average (in actual occurrence, from three to eleven years apart).[25]

The two scientists also said that studies of the sequoia region could take the data on fire frequency and effects even farther back than what could be gained from the "relatively short-lived pines, firs, and cedars." As they stated: "Although the fire history depicted by the big trees is fragmentary indeed, it is shown that as far back as A.D. 245 fires occurred in the pine region in restricted localities in which the big tree is found."[26]

Thus it appeared that fire had been a normal feature of the forests of the Sierra for a significant part of the range's human history. Fires had caused injury to all the trees in the study areas, as the scars attested. These fires were laid to three major causes: lightning, Native American burning, and European American activities such as mining, logging, grazing, and railroading. Fire had been especially prevalent in the lower-elevation yellow-pine belt of the "Mother Lode," included in the study. Cultural differences in fire use or causes reflected little concern either by natives or the "white man," the authors said, for timber as a "growing crop."[27]

Beyond information about the range's fire history, Show and Kotok revealed something about what the forests were like in the early 1920s. Their studies depicted several major types of landscapes in the north-central, lower-western Sierran areas on which they focused. Existing vegetation in these areas included a very small amount ("rare patches") of mature and relatively dense forestland, as well as larger mature and open ("patchy") forested areas not located near sites of major development. Show and Kotok noted that both of these two "virgin" forest types were relatively immune to crown or stand-destroying fires but had been degraded by past fires and were not as productive of timber as they hoped. Next came second-growth lands that had been cut over but were reforesting successfully and were more desirable as future timberland. Finally, where past cutting had been heaviest and fire had successively recurred, there were areas of chaparral and brush with few young trees, or simply pure brush.[28]

It was this last category that most concerned the two scientists, because they feared that it might become the public forest of the Sierra's future. They provided a chart demonstrating that nearly 12 percent of the Plumas, nearly 9 percent of the Tahoe, 7 percent of the Eldorado, around 16 percent of the Stanislaus, and slightly more than 11 percent of the Sierra National Forests had been converted to useless and unproductive brush. This process was labeled as "site retrogression," and Show and Kotok said that it resulted from frequently recurring fires in cutover forests. They also noted that in some forests where yellow pine had been cut, fire determined tree-type succession, with fir and cedar growing more rapidly than yellow pine.[29]

Show and Kotok hoped that their analysis would bring about increased fire protection in the cutover but reforesting lower-elevation lands of the national forests of the Sierra. They wanted to make fire suppression a key component of future forest management. In this they succeeded.

Because of the emphasis placed on fire suppression as a way of producing more lumber, by the mid-1920s all national forests in the Sierra Nevada and elsewhere in the West had fully developed fire-prevention policies, procedures, and organization in their jurisdictions. These measures took into account season, topography, and past fire histories for their special areas. Forest Service regulations for timber sales required that fire-control equipment be readily available, enforced brush and vegetation piling, and even established where loggers could smoke. All national forests in the Sierra Nevada developed infrastructure that included lookouts and phone systems.[30]

Some observers claimed that such policies did reduce fire frequency into the late 1920s. However, others said that historically low fuel levels dating from earlier forest conditions created by Native American burning, heavy logging, and grazing were actually the reason for fewer fires.[31] Either way, the

forests of that period, like the forests that have succeeded them, were artifacts of the fire practices that reigned at that time in their history.[32]

The decision to exclude fire from public lands came about after debate
between the Forest Service and other resource interests. At issue was whether
to permit "light" or "Indian" burning or to use systematic fire protection
instead. The Sierra Nevada was a perfect place to consider the problem because its extensive forests were prone to burning and because proponents of
the two major positions were well organized in the state. Studies conducted
between 1911 and 1923 in the Stanislaus Forest and elsewhere in California by
Coert Du Bois, Show, and Kotok strongly influenced the Forest Service to
opt for complete protection. Logging and grazing interests and the popular
nature writer Stewart Edward White opposed this view. They held that light
fires reduced fuel, thereby creating more-open forests and lessening the danger of destructive crown fires.[33]

Show and Kotok were especially influential in this struggle. They published two major studies, in 1923 and 1924, on fire in the national forests of
California. The first, *Forest Fires in California, 1911–1920,* used statistical analysis based on the study of 10,499 fires on four designated groups of California
federal forestlands. The Northern Group included the Klamath, Trinity, and
Shasta forests. The East Side Group included the Modoc and Lassen forests.
The Northern Sierra Group included the Plumas, Tahoe, and Eldorado forests. And the Southern Sierra Group consisted of the Stanislaus, Sierra, and
Sequoia forests.[34]

After reviewing the history of the development of effective fire-protection
infrastructure and organization between 1911 and 1914, Show and Kotok
evaluated contrasting theories of fire protection and the complex variables
that determined successful protection outcomes. They ranked fire causes according to frequency (lightning, camper-caused, incendiary, and industrial).
And finally, they stated their conclusions regarding major problems of fire
protection in California. Those problems were defined in terms of keeping
the cost of fire prevention and suppression to an effective minimum, being
consistent in how service personnel responded to emergency conditions, developing methods to predict emergencies, and instituting critical local studies to determine the best fire-protection strategies for specific areas. This
study identified fire as the chief problem facing the Forest Service in California but claimed that the agency was gaining in its ability to respond to wildfires in the state's highly combustible forests.[35]

Show and Kotok's second study of fire in the national forests was *The Role
of Fire in the California Pine Forests.* The effect of this and their earlier work
was to bring about the adoption of a policy calling for total exclusion of

wildfire in the national forests and other public lands in the West. Fire was identified as an enemy that must be excluded where possible. In their view, any policy that allowed fire in California's national forests was detrimental to forest health and productivity. They described California's forests as "broken, patchy, understocked stands, worn down by the attrition of repeated light fires." If these forests were ever to become fully stocked and achieve their full productive potential, fires that destroyed young seedlings must be prevented.[36]

Show and Kotok used their selective version of forest science to lead the fight against light burning, which they defined as "intentional burning of the forest at intervals" so as to reduce fuel hazard and damage to merchantable timber. They noted that two types of light burning existed: controlled burns to protect forests, and general or promiscuous burning to improve grazing, aid prospecting, or make forests more accessible. The latter type had been historically used in the days before regulation of public lands and had been generally condemned in the years before the creation of national forests or forest reserves. Controlled burning usually took place in the fall or spring, when only the top layer of litter was dry enough to burn. Generally such fires were set at the ridges so that the burn would go downhill, reducing heat and the danger of losing control.[37]

After extensive testing of the two procedures—with many of the tests being conducted in locations in the Sierra Nevada—Show and Kotok condemned light burning altogether. They said that it did not keep forests safe from extensive and long-term fire damage because fire-prone brush quickly grew back in the burned areas. Light burning also prevented regeneration of fully stocked forests. By this they meant regenerating forests with more than just the oldest and most fire-resistant species present in them.[38]

Show and Kotok were fully committed to the policy of fire prevention. They believed that without effective fire control, California's pine forests were unnatural as well as unhealthy products of a particular history. The forests of the time before the introduction of fire protection were often described as open and were the product of repeated fires from lightning, Native American, and historic American sources. The two scientists claimed that fire protection, by increasing the quantity of young trees (and thus the potential for more fires), had led to increased light burning and to political support for the practice.[39] In sum, "in the early years of protection of the national forests, the forests were still open as a result of the repeated fires of the past. The great outbreak of incendiarism and agitation for light burning did not come until later. As fire protection became an established fact and the young growth began to fill up the more open forest, the amount of inflammable material in the forests increased greatly. Thereupon renewed efforts were made to return to the unrestricted use of fire."[40]

To these forest scientists, a "natural" forest was one in which fire protection was a reality. That marked a radical change from the spotty, unprotected, and "understocked" forests of the past:

> This remarkable change [the appearance of more young forest trees] is in itself proof that the virgin forest as we find it does not represent the productive capacity of the land, for if an area of ground is fully occupied by a mature crop of timber the young individuals can not obtain a foothold because the available moisture and light are already fully utilized. That this alteration is due solely to fire protection is clearly evident from the descriptions of the virgin forest of a half century ago by historians and early settlers. In this picture the dominant note is the openness of the forest, emphasized in the oft-repeated statement that one could ride anywhere or could see for long distances through the timber. The general occurrence of young growth or advance reproduction of the virgin forest today is the effect of nature in response to fire protection, to utilize the full growing power of the land, and to restore the broken and understocked forest to a more normal condition.[41]

Show and Kotok maintained that light burning benefitted only lumbermen desiring mature open forests, or grazers and miners desiring clear land. When it became clear to timber interests and other forest users that the Forest Service was tilting toward this view, the conflict intensified. The debate between the two groups became so rancorous that the Society of American Foresters offered to arbitrate the differences. The California Board of Forestry finally convened a California Forestry Commission review to try to settle the issue. In 1924 the commission published its unanimous opinion that fire protection was superior to light burning. The commissioners generally accepted the position of Show and Kotok that all fire was destructive and must be controlled where possible.[42]

The commission reported that sustainable forestry could be ensured only by practicing systematic fire protection. Later in 1924 the California Board of Forestry concurred. That same year, Congress passed the Clarke-McNary Act promoting state and federal cooperation in implementing fire-suppression policies on public lands. The policy of aggressive fire protection, shaped in part in the Sierra Nevada forests, thus became the general pattern in all other public lands until questioned in the 1960s.[43]

Show and Kotok believed forest composition to be the product of human decisions—to burn or not to burn was the controlling question. They wanted more heavily stocked forests. Fire had to be excluded if reforestation was to be successful. Their influence launched the United States in the Sierra and elsewhere in the West on an untested proposition. Policy eventually became dogma.[44] How ironic that state and federal agencies today are trying to cope with the conditions to which fire suppression contributed. Human decisions about natural spaces ought to be made, it would seem, with great humility. Be careful what you wish for, the proverb warns.

This important policy debate can be effectively illustrated and humanized by examining the career of one of the dedicated forest supervisors at work at that time in the Sierra Nevada. The diary kept by Tahoe National Forest supervisor Richard L. P. Bigelow, who served from 1908 to 1936, illustrates the broad custodial emphasis of the Forest Service in these founding years. His activities for those three decades fall into three broad categories. The first involved getting the Tahoe National Forest started in an area where no lines or limits had existed before. This meant establishing clear jurisdiction and boundaries, sometimes requiring court challenges to those occupying federal land illegally. Regulating special uses such as grazing was part of this start-up activity and was worked out fairly easily with local ranchers, who came to appreciate Bigelow's willingness to provide them exclusive use of Tahoe rangelands. Mining interests were more troublesome, causing the greatest number of problems with trespass issues.[45]

A second activity that took much of Bigelow's time involved forestry and Forest Service logistical issues: preparing timber sales and supervising proper slash piling and burning, building ranger stations and fire lookouts, establishing roads and telephone communications to aid in fire suppression, and recruiting and training personnel. The third main facet of Bigelow's work involved service to a new class of forest users—namely, those seeking recreational facilities and services, including trails and campgrounds. Timber sales in the Tahoe and other national forests, so important in the period after the Second World War, were part of his job but did not dominate his time.[46]

Two entries from Bigelow's meticulously kept diary indicate the broad nature of his activities:

July 17 [1926]—Left at 7:30 A.M. and went to Sierraville to meet Dooley. Broke a hind spring. Sent for a new one and with Dooley went to Verdi sale and looked over sale in Sect. 18. Returned to Sierraville and found several calls from Truckee about the closing of the C.W. Paper Mill. Worked on my machine until 4 P.M. . . . . Got word of bad fire west of Nevada City.

July 18—Ranger Nelson and I left at 8 A.M. for the lake in his machine to meet Mr. Cheny from District 3-Chief of Lands and took him
from McKinneys to Tahoe Camp and went over camp grounds and
then around the Lake to Tahoe Vista and ate lunch. Saw Barriean and
told him we would consider the road they built across south line of
Sec. 12 as a public road. Went to Incline and saw Dean and looked over
Incline Camp Ground. . . . Returned to Truckee at 5 P.M. and found
that a big fire was burning near Washington on both sides of the river.
Gracey reported that he had sent about 75 or 80 men and that the
airplane would take Larsen over at 6 P.M. and that axes were coming
from Sacramento on it.[47]

In the 1920s and 1930s, access to the Tahoe and the other national forests
became easier with the creation of better state highways on both sides of the
range, and Bigelow spent more time supervising the construction of improved campsites to serve the new class of tourists using automobiles. In the
1930s he took advantage of a new labor source by employing Civilian Conservation Corps "boys" to assist in trail, camp, and fire-service duties. He
spent his last few days in office lobbying in Sacramento to get state support
for the creation of special "scenic road" funding. This emphasis on tourism
clearly reflected new public expectations about national forest uses.[48]

For Sierra Nevada forest supervisors such as Bigelow, the issue that occupied much of their time in the summer was fire. From the beginning of his
tenure, the entries in his diary—especially for August—record numerous
attempts to fight wildfires. Bigelow's records illustrate the growing technical
abilities of his staff, the development of lookouts, roads, and telephone communication networks, and the organizational emphasis on fire control and
suppression. He cooperated with private timber interests, irrigation districts,
and utilities in preventing wildfire damage. In later years he noted the addition
of bulldozers and spotter planes as part of his technical fire-control arsenal.[49]

In the Sierra Nevada, Show and Kotok's views became part of an educational message that forest supervisors carried to their communities. In April
of 1926, for example, Bigelow launched a Forestry Week campaign (based on
a presidential proclamation) that included meeting with Boy Scouts, minis-
ters, and high school students. On April 19 he told his diary that he had
placed "Kotok and Show's bulletin" at "every plate" at a Rotary Club luncheon. On June 5, 1926, he noted:

Left at 8 A.M. with Mr Tibbey of the Mountain Messenger [newspa-
per] of Downieville, went over Henness Pass Road to Bowman to see

what work on this road had to be done and to see if I could show Mr. Tibby [*sic*] what protection of brush areas meant to forestry. He is a great advocate of light burning. Returned at 5:30 P.M. to Downieville and stayed all night. Showed Tibby [*sic*] work we were doing and brush field coming into young timber and destruction by fire of young stuff in fires of 1924. Think I impressed him but don't know.[50]

National Park Management and Environmental Change

Just as had occurred in the new public forests, federal policy toward national parks brought environmental changes. Yosemite, Sequoia, and General Grant were set aside in 1890, but nowhere in the legislation creating them were the words *national parks* used. And nothing ensured that they would be safe from continued private exploitation.

Poaching, grazing of meadows and grasslands, and stealing or vandalizing of trees continued. The legislation creating these Sierran parks did not provide for any enforcement or protection measures. Ultimately, consensus emerged among conservationists, railroad companies and other business leaders, civic interests, and scientists who led the early national park movement. All agreed that some central, responsible agency had to administer these diverse parks and monuments. Otherwise they would deteriorate, as had all other national lands before them.[51]

The leaders of this national park movement included J. Horace McFarland, Frederick Law Olmsted Jr., Stephen T. Mather, Horace Albright, Robert Underwood Johnson, and John Muir, blending eastern and western perspectives. In a series of meetings, one of them held at Yosemite, three general principles emerged as rallying points for a national park political campaign: first, that the prime focus of the national parks was to provide effective protection of their spectacular scenery and natural features; second, that in order to generate broader public support, more visitors needed to be attracted to the parks, which in turn required better facilities and easier access; and third, that an effective national park administration must be created.[52]

Resistance to the idea of a centralized park agency soon appeared. Of no surprise were those who opposed extension of any government agencies or services in general. Also, western livestock interests opposed more federal authority that might further limit access to rangeland. Resistance came from Gifford Pinchot as well. Besides fearing "turf" encroachment from a new federal agency, Pinchot believed that many of the functions of parks and national forests were similar. A new federal service would result in duplication and waste. After all, he pointed out, some grazing went on in national parks, and utility right-of-ways were common to both forests and some parks. Horace Albright contested Pinchot's claims. He noted that there was a clear difference between the "woodlot" approach of the Forest Service and the "playground" goal of the proposed new park service.[53]

Key to the success of the park political campaign was establishing a principle of park purpose that could draw a broad base of support. A blending of the aesthetic and utilitarian perspectives of the conservation movement of the late nineteenth and early twentieth century resulted.[54] This blending was clearly enunciated in the Park Service's so-called Organic Act, passed in 1916. The purpose of national parks was to "conserve the scenery and the natural and historic objects and the wild life therein and to provide for the enjoyment of the same in such manner and by such means as will leave them unimpaired for the enjoyment of future generations."[55]

This dual purpose, and the allowance of some grazing in national parks (Yellowstone excepted), was the price for legislative success. The "enjoyment" emphasis clearly reflected that age's consensus on what parks were for.[56]

The Sierra Nevada and its three national parks played a role in the formulation of the national park idea. It was in part because of what was happening in these Sierran parks that the national park advocates were spurred to political action. Resource abuse, vandalizing and cutting of trees, lack of amenities for visitors, and difficulty of access to the Sierran parks were all noted by critics of the Department of the Interior, the agency nominally charged with protecting them.[57] Recognizing the problem, the various secretaries of the interior moved to extend a policy developed earlier to protect Yellowstone. They turned to the U.S. Cavalry to patrol the three California parks and placed army officers in charge as superintendent from 1891 to 1912.[58]

Sheep grazers, long the target of conservationists' ire, were the principle offenders trespassing in the new Sierran parks. The acting superintendent of Yosemite National Park in 1891 had noted that while cattlemen generally accepted limits on access to the new park, sheepmen ignored them. Another report from that same year stated: "The last days of May the sheep commenced their annual migrations to the mountain grazing grounds, and by the 10th of June there were fully 60,000 of them close to the southern and at least 30,000 near the western boundaries of the park." The military men assigned to patrol the parks did not have power to arrest or prosecute the herders, but with various harassing methods they generally succeeded in convincing the sheepmen to stay away—at least while the army was actually in place.[59]

As noted earlier, however, the cavalry's time in the park was limited to good weather, ending by the fall. Savvy herders simply waited until the troopers departed and then set sheep loose into the rangelands. This reversed the gains in grassland and meadow protection that had accrued in the spring and summer. Problems associated with rotation of experienced troopers and lack of familiarity with the terrain also reduced the efficiency of these armed guardians.[60]

Another factor that reduced the effectiveness of the cavalry was bribery by wily herders. Richard L. P. Bigelow reported on the problem in 1904. His first job as a ranger in the Sierra Forest Reserve put him into contact with the troopers and what he called the "sheep situation." His job required cooperation with the cavalry in excluding sheep grazing in the reserves and the parks where possible. In one instance he contacted a Major Bigelow (no relative), who was in charge of the "Negro Calvary [sic] Company," about sheepherders trespassing. The next day, August 9, 1904, he contacted a patrol under a Corporal Hipshaw and reported the following incident: "That day at Reds Meadows a Basque sheepman came into the soldier camp packing a demijon. When he saw us he hid the demi-jon. We had heard of the sheepmen buying their way into the park with liquor. I informed the corporal of my suspicions and he said he would handle it."[61]

No fire planning or organization existed for the Sierran parks at that time either. Fortunately, the problem was not as bad for the parks as for the national forests that were contiguous to them. Heavy grazing and earlier fires in the Sequoia National Park had reduced fire dangers there. Not until many years later would the problem become serious. The fact that Yosemite National Park included only the high country around the Valley, some of it also heavily grazed, reduced fire risk there as well.[62]

But increased use by campers—sometimes including Sierra Club members—meant new sources of fire. In one instance in Yosemite, a group of students from the University of California fought a fire started by careless campers, that they spotted near the Hazel Green area. No park response existed, and so volunteer action was the only other possibility. It was not until the 1920s, after the Forest Service policy on fires was adopted by the Park Service, that fire suppression became routine.[63]

One of the most significant problems facing the Sierran parks in their formative years came from competing claims and private in-holdings. As with the national forests, at first boundaries were unclear, competing claims existed, and private interests still demanded resources such as timber or mining ground in or near the parks.[64] The most serious conflicts of this kind occurred in Yosemite, though Sequoia had its share of difficulties at its beginnings.[65]

Private claims to valuable timberlands within the southern and western parts of Yosemite, and to potentially valuable timber and mining lands elsewhere in the park, were a source of concern to park officials in 1903 and 1904. In 1903 the Yosemite Lumber Company began cutting timber on its holdings in the southwestern area of the park. The resulting clear-cuts led the secretary of the interior to create a commission to study how the government should react. The commission recommended that because of the government's inability to effectively manage the lands surrounding these in-holdings, government control of adjacent lands should be terminated, thus eliminating conflict. This deletion included any timberland in the southwest and west, and the mineral lands in the Chowchilla Range, a very large area on that side of the public park. As a way of simplifying boundaries, the park was extended to the crest of the Sierra Nevada, including the headwaters of the Tuolumne River. Legislation to accomplish this reduction, known officially as the Yosemite National Park Act, was passed by Congress in 1905.[66]

It is ironic that this commission actually stated that its purpose was to protect Yosemite. Perhaps this view arose from the language of the act creating the commission in the first place: It ordered the commissioners to recommend what parts of the park could be returned to private use. The portions decided upon totaled more than 540 square miles. Devil's Post Pile and the Mount Banner and Ritter areas were removed from the park to suit the interests of miners. The nearby Minarets were surrendered for the same reason. Other reductions followed. In 1906, sixteen square miles were given away along the sides of the Wawona Road, ostensibly to allow for the building of a railroad to bring visitors to the park. In actuality, the area was logged and the only railroad built was for logging purposes. Thus, rather than fighting what they considered to be a losing battle, the government gave in consistently in these years.[67]

Though it might seem that all was dark at the beginning, not everything was being given up. In 1905 and 1906, the long campaign to wrest control of Yosemite Valley from the state came to a successful conclusion. Under pressure from such notables as John Muir and the railroad magnate E. H. Harriman, California gave up its claim to the Valley. In 1906, federal legislation returned the Yosemite Valley to national control.[68]

Sheep grazing was generally excluded from the Sierran parks by 1904. Seemingly inevitable conflict over rich timber and mineral land in the parks ended with government surrender shortly thereafter. But other destructive invasions were not so readily resolved. One of these involved the opening of the parks to dams and hydroelectric power generation. In the battles to decide what areas within the Sierra Nevada parks were to be given over to hydroelectric generation, the conservation community became divided. Two perspectives clashed. There were those who believed that parks could also be used for reservoir development and power generation, and those who believed use should be restricted to tourism and recreation. Making possible the invasion of the Sierran national parks was the passage in 1901 of the so-called Right of Way Act allowing utility corridors in all public lands in the West. These "corridors" could include aqueducts, tunnels, power lines, and power poles.[69]

Technological discoveries in the 1880s and 1890s contributed to the conflict by making it practical to generate hydroelectric power and transmit it over long distances. The Sierra Nevada and its rivers were now more valuable than before, as "white coal" replaced yellow gold in importance. The range's location near the expanding valley and coastal cities increased the stakes. By 1900, twenty-five hydroelectric plants had been built in the state, and five of them utilized streams that originated in national forests of the Sierra. Several surveys of Sierran rivers for hydroelectric potential were carried out. Demand rapidly mounted for the utilization of all Sierran streams with feasible power-generating sources. It was not long before streams in the Sierra's national parks were added to the list of potential electrical power sources.[70]

The first attempt to gain access to Sierran parks occurred in the Sequoia National Park. The Mount Whitney Power Company constructed power-generating facilities on the Kaweah River between 1898 and 1905, with a powerhouse that straddled the park boundary. In the years that followed, the company extended its operations. By 1913 it had secured permission from the Department of the Interior to construct flumes, dams, and a power-generation plant in the park itself. A proposal to build even larger production facilities, including a 100-foot dam on private land within the park boundaries, finally foundered because the base of the dam was sited on unsuitable terrain. The net result of the company's activities was road construction in the park, dams on park rivers, and clear-cutting of park timber in support of construction.[71]

But it was the damming of the Hetch Hetchy Valley, located within Yosemite National Park, that constituted the most egregious and perhaps most significant invasion of national park land in the history of the parks (although the damming of Glen Canyon following the political struggles of the 1950s and 1960s ranks high in destructive impact as well). The dam was built to give San Francisco water and hydroelectric power. Utilitarian resource use in the parks trumped recreational use, scenery was valued less than electrical power, and urban property values prevailed over natural beauty.[72]

John Muir, in *The Yosemite,* has left a description of Hetch Hetchy before the dam:

After my first visit to it in the autumn of 1871, I have always called it the "Tuolumne Yosemite," for it is a wonderfully exact counterpart of the Merced Yosemite, not only in its sublime rocks and waterfalls but in the gardens, groves and meadows of its flowery park-like floor. . . . The walls of both are gray granite, rise abruptly from the floor, are sculptured in the same style and in both every rock is a glacier monument.

On the opposite side of the Valley . . . there is a counterpart of the El Capitan that rises sheer and plain to a height of 1800 feet, and over its massive brow flows a stream which makes the most graceful fall [Tueeulala] I have ever seen. From the edge of the cliff to the top of an earthquake talus it is perfectly free in the air for a thousand feet before it is broken into cascades among talus boulders. . . . The only fall I know with which it may be compared is the Yosemite Bridal Veil; but it excels even that favorite both in height and airy-fairy beauty and behavior. . . .

So fine a fall might well seem sufficient to glorify any valley; but here as in Yosemite, Nature seems in nowise moderate, for a short distance to the eastward of Tueeulala booms and thunders the great Hetch Hetchy Fall, Wapama, so near that you have both of them in full view from the same standpoint. It is the counterpart of the Yosemite Fall, but has a much greater volume of water, is about 1700 feet in height, and appears nearly vertical, though considerably inclined, and is dashed into huge outbounding bosses of foam on projecting shelves and knobs. . . . Besides this glorious pair there is a broad, massive fall on the river a short distance above the head of the Valley. Its position is something like that of the Vernal in Yosemite, and its roar as it plunges into a surging trout-pool may be heard a long way, though it is only about twenty feet high. On Rancheria Creek, a large stream, corresponding in position with the Yosemite Tenaya Creek, there is a chain of cascades joined here and there with swift flashing flumes like the one between Vernal and Nevada Falls, making magnificent shows as they go their glacier-sculptured way. . . .

The floor of the Valley is about three and a half miles long, and from a fourth to half a mile wide. The lower portion is mostly a level meadow about a mile long, with trees restricted to the sides and the river banks, and partially separated from the main, upper, forested portion by a low bar of glacier-polished granite across which the river breaks in rapids.[73]

There is no way that we of the "future generations" who were supposed to be able, according to the Park Service Organic Act passed in the aftermath of Hetch Hetchy's destruction, to enjoy its "scenery" and "natural . . . objects" can do so unimpaired. The only way we can "see" that valley today is in old black-and-white photographs.[74]

The invasion of Yosemite National Park differed only in scale from those that occurred in Sequoia. The principle was the same, involving the question of what type of development was allowable in the parks. No clear policy existed to provide direction. It was in the realm of politics that the answer was given.

The struggle began in 1901 when San Francisco, after a survey of possible reservoir sites in the Sierra, asked the secretary of the interior for permission to dam Hetch Hetchy. After opposition arose from John Muir and others in the conservation community who felt the valley should be preserved, San Francisco was refused. The fight continued under various secretaries of the interior. The division over Hetch Hetchy's fate split the Sierra Club as well, weakening the impact of its efforts. William Colby, assisting Muir in the fight, formed a new group—the Society for the Preservation of National Parks—to spread the issue nationally.[75]

The city continued over the years to push its claims in Congress. The struggle pitted those in the conservation community who favored practical uses for the valley that would clearly benefit all the citizens of San Francisco against Muir and his band of preservationists.[76]

The actual odds against the preservationists were immense. All of the California delegation in the House of Representatives and one of its senators actively supported the bill. So did many of the state's mayors, chambers of commerce, boards of trade, business leaders, and major newspapers. President Woodrow Wilson and his secretary of the interior, Franklin Lane (who had been city attorney for San Francisco), endorsed it as well. Many Sierra Club members from San Francisco favored the measure. In addition, the two irrigation districts in the valley that had claims on the Tuolumne River, those from Modesto and Turlock, had their support "purchased" by San Francisco with promises of plentiful water once the dam was built. The preservationists included Muir, Robert Underwood Johnson, and many prominent scientists, naturalists, and progressive magazine editors from outside the state. In truth, they had very little influence in the actual debates in Congress.[77]

San Francisco did a thorough job of preparing for this political battle. Its field investigations and reports on the need for Hetch Hetchy water stand out in their appeal to what they saw as the "high road" of applied science and public interest versus the demands of what they characterized as a few selfish preservationists. Respected professional engineers were selected to conduct the city's surveys. One 1912 report focused on the Spring Valley Water Company, the private company that supplied the city with water. Written by H. M. Chittenden, it not only described the company's inadequacies in meeting the needs of the expanding city, but also praised Hetch Hetchy as a better source. Besides that utilitarian fact, Chittenden added his opinion that "utilization of that valley is perfectly possible" without detracting from the natural beauty and actually could add "materially thereto." Chittenden had served on the commission that in 1905 had recommended the reduction in size of Yosemite and the transfer of timber and mineral resources on parklands to private parties.[78]

The most effective report backing Hetch Hetchy as San Francisco's "best" answer to its water problem was written by John R. Freeman and published by the San Francisco Board of Supervisors. Its rambling title was *On the Proposed Use of a Portion of the Hetch Hetchy, Eleanor, and Cherry Valleys within and near to the Boundaries of the Stanislaus U.S. National Forest Reserve and the Yosemite National Park as Reservoirs for Impounding Tuolumne River Flood Waters.* Its approach was both utilitarian and aesthetic.[79]

The practical side of the report dismissed a number of suggested alternatives to Hetch Hetchy. These had included the McCloud, Eel, Stanislaus, American, Consumes, Feather, Yuba, and Mokelumne Rivers. All of these suffered one or several deficiencies from the city's perspective. They did not supply enough water, cost too much, or had competing claims for their water and hydroelectric potential.[80]

What was really ingenious about the report was its turning of the tables on the preservationists. A reservoir was sold as being far more beautiful than a mere valley floor. The "lake" to be created had much more potential for public use and enjoyment. Artists' sketches of a nearly full reservoir reflecting the walls of the canyon were compared to high mountain lakes in Norway. Descriptions of successful tourist developments around public water sources in New York and Glasgow, Scotland, were cited. A scenic roadway was proposed to bring in many thousands more tourists than had ever visited the valley before. Attractive drawings depicted the road. A hotel was envisioned for a meadow above the valley. Listen to how Freeman sums up his points for a public that had never seen the valley and probably never would. His comment is also a thinly veiled attack on Muir and other dam opponents:

Not far from the entrance to the Hetch Hetchy is a broad meadow, high above the proposed level of the lake, on the borders of which camp space can be found for ten-fold the number that have ever yet visited this upper Tuolumne valley at one time, save on a certain Sierra Club excursion, unless they happen to be of the type of man who needs an entire valley to himself in order to enjoy it.

Should the cities of Greater San Francisco be compelled to spend some ten million or twenty million dollars extra for another less desirable source of domestic water, simply in order that ten or twenty solitude lovers may have this beautiful valley to themselves?[81]

Never mind the fact that San Francisco did not make any effort to build the roads or hotels it promised the public. (As it was, eventually the Park Service itself would discourage a good road into the reservoir.) Regardless of promises kept or not, the outcome of the greater issue was that Muir and the preservationists lost. In 1913 the Raker Act was passed, authorizing construction of a dam and hydroelectric power plant. Horace McFarland, the veteran of many battles to protect the national parks, summed up the effect of the legislation: "Flooding the Hetch Hetchy will make a valley of unmatched beauty simply a pond, a reservoir, and nothing else." In 1934, long after the passage of the Raker Act, water from Hetch Hetchy reached San Francisco for the first time.[82]

The outrage that followed the Hetch Hetchy struggle fueled the legislation that created the National Park Service in 1916.[83] Horace Albright, second head of the Park Service and a participant in the Hetch Hetchy battle, claimed that his boss, Secretary of the Interior Lane, pushed for creation of the service because of the guilt and embarrassment he felt over the conflict's outcome.[84]

Secretary Lane quickly reached out to the conservation community. He needed an effective leader for the new Park Service. He had recently received a letter of protest from Stephen T. Mather, a fellow Californian and a major player in the group of distinguished businessmen and naturalists who had supported the creation of a park service. Mather had also opposed the damming of Hetch Hetchy. In his letter to Lane, Mather decried the conditions he had seen in Sequoia and Yosemite on a recent camping trip. His complaints included poorly maintained trails, cattle trespass in the parks, and the fraudulent use of the federal Swamp Land Act by lumbermen to acquire sequoia groves nearby. Lane knew Mather and his abilities and offered him the job of running the agency. Mather accepted a position as an assistant secretary of the interior and set to work promoting the park service idea.[85]

In 1915 Mather took several national political leaders, prominent Califor-nia officials, and writers and publishers into the high country of the southern Sierra Nevada. How better to demonstrate the need to protect this and other Sierran regions than to show the beauty of the country and the careless de-struction wrought by stockmen and other users? Mather stressed the need for a central agency. One member of the party, Gilbert Grosvenor, director of the National Geographic Society, promised to use his publication to pro-mote this idea before an influential public. A special edition of the *National Geographic* followed. Thus the High Sierra played a direct role in stimulating public support for the National Park Act.[86]

Stephen Mather served as head of the National Park Service from 1916 to 1929. Horace Albright, his assistant, was chosen to replace him and served until 1933. These appointments guaranteed a continuous policy over nearly three decades.[87] Mather and Albright emphasized access and enjoyment, working diligently to draw visitors to the parks, figuring that public use would protect the parklands from further assaults.[88]

This emphasis on increased use affected thinking about the new parks even in individuals not closely involved with park visitor promotion, such as scientists who hoped that the parks could become refuges for native plant and animal species. Consider the case of Joseph Grinnell of the Museum of Vertebrate Zoology at the University of California, Berkeley. He lobbied Mather for support for a thorough study of all vertebrate species living in Yosemite National Park even before Mather became director. He did so not in the name of science itself—although he was clearly dedicated to that—but on the grounds that knowledge of vertebrate life would boost park visita-tion. The park's animals, he said, were an "asset"; coming into the natural setting to see them provided not only aesthetic enjoyment but also pro-moted the health of visitors.[89]

Animal Life in the Yosemite, written by Grinnell and Tracy Irwin Storer (one of Grinnell's students and later a well-known naturalist in his own right) was published in 1924, is certainly more than just an example of park promotion. The study provides another important environmental baseline in the Sierra Nevada's environmental history. Based on the authors' careful scientific observations from 1915 to 1920 (with an interruption for Storer's military service) in a strip of land eighty-nine miles long and seventeen miles wide that stretched completely across the park from its western to its eastern boundary and ranged from 250 to 13,000 feet in elevation, it relied heavily on the ecological perspectives of C. Hart Merriam, stressing his theories on vegetation and vertebrate species zonation, temperature gradations, and plant and animal species associations.[90]

Grinnell and Storer, with several assistants, gained permission to shoot and trap species across this band of territory, and of course observed the behavior of countless animals they did not kill. They also conducted interviews with locals in key areas near the park concerning species that were no longer present, such as grizzly, bighorn sheep, tule elk, and pronghorn antelope. They counted a total of 231 bird species, 97 kinds of mammals, 22 different lizards, and 12 varieties of toads, frogs, and salamanders. They described the relationship of each species to specific areas and elevations and to other plants and animals, and noted the frequency or scarcity for each one "authentically known" as of 1920.[91]

As an ideal, Grinnell and Storer stressed that Yosemite should be an area where natural conditions and relationships of the resident species had top priority. They provided an important view on the relationship of carnivores and herbivores, maintaining that "if the Yosemite Park is administered as a true 'refuge' for its animals as well as plant life, then primitive conditions should be maintained absolutely, to the end that all constituent species persist in the same relative numbers as they did in early times. The maximum numbers of any and all herbivores which can exist will be determined by the amount of plant food available in the season of least supply; and the number of carnivores which can exist will be determined by the amount of animal food available to them at the season of scantiest supply."[92]

Two such animals they discussed were mountain lions and mule deer. Both were relatively abundant, though under stress. Associated with each other very closely as predator and prey, they illustrated the two scientists' point about animal associations. Both were targets of determined efforts to kill them. Mountain lions were killed in areas outside the park in large numbers—one report to Grinnell and Storer told of a private trapper who killed thirty-one in three winter seasons (1915–1918) near Wawona. Heavily reliant on deer for food, the predators followed them to winter range outside the park—where the lions were shot or trapped.[93]

As long as deer remained in relatively large numbers in the park, their chief predator also remained relatively abundant. But the deer population had fallen significantly. The problem was that although they were protected in the park, in winter they went to lower elevations outside park boundaries in search of browse. There they competed with cattle and goats for food and were shot by legal hunters or poachers, both in and out of season.[94]

The ecological perspective on animal associations that Grinnell and Storer applied to the park is well illustrated in their discussion of deer and lion. Humans were cited as being the greatest danger that both faced. The animals were safe in the park but could not survive on such a limited land base. Grinnell and Storer suggested temporarily closing land outside the park to hunting and rigorously enforcing game laws to allow deer numbers to recover. That would allow the balance between the two species to return to a stable and healthy level. Lions were described as being of no danger to humans, but instead were seen as being valuable in helping maintain healthy populations of prey (as, Grinnell and Storer argued, were all other predator species in the park).[95]

But applying balanced, natural management principles to park vertebrates was not the direction park officials took after 1916. Their focus was on human visitors. During the tenure of Mather and Albright, tourist facilities and trails were improved and expanded in both Sequoia and Yosemite. Tourist attractions, such as a golf course, zoo, and even a racetrack for the "Indian Field Days" at Yosemite, were added to draw visitors. In cooperation with the Sierra Club, the Park Service constructed the John Muir and High Sierra Trails into the Sequoia backcountry. New or improved roads also increased public use. A park-to-park highway plan backed by California automobile associations brought needed political support and appropriations. In Sequoia, this initiative included the "Generals Highway" connecting the valley towns to the General Sherman and General Grant trees. A misguided attempt to build a "Sierra Highway" completely across the Sierra Nevada high country in Sequoia, however, was resisted strenuously by Mather as inappropriate.[96]

Automobiles had been coming into the Yosemite Valley since 1900. They were not necessarily welcomed there. Secretary of the Interior Walter L. Fisher fulminated against them at a national park conference held in the Valley in 1912 to address problems they were causing. But he might as well have ordered ocean waves not to crash against the shore. In 1916, some 14,527 people entered the park by car, more than by rail. In 1926, Highway 140, the all-year highway to Yosemite, was completed. Mather used his own money to purchase the Tioga Road connecting Tuolumne Meadows with Yosemite Valley. Hoping that the road would draw people away from the crowded Valley into new park areas, he encouraged state automobile associations to pay for its improvement.[97]

The Park Service also promoted winter sports activities at Yosemite, hoping to make the park popular in winter as well as summer. Attempts were made to lure the Winter Olympics of 1932 to Yosemite, although there was considerable outcry about the potential for overdevelopment that would result. Yosemite officials worked closely with commercial concessionaires (the Curry and Yosemite Park Companies) to promote winter carnivals and sporting contests, ice skating (an ice rink was installed), snowshoeing, and other snow activities. Badger Pass Ski Lodge opened in 1935 for touring and downhill skiing.[98]

Other significant environmental effects reflected administrative policies on grazing and wildlife. The reduction in size of Yosemite National Park in 1905 had hurt park wildlife. By removing a significant amount of parkland below 5,000-foot elevation, much of it forested, park officials actually turned the winter range of park deer over to hunters. When cold drove the deer down to the now privately held lower-elevation areas, hunters ravaged the semitame animals. The slaughter contributed to an ever-decreasing deer population in the park.[99]

Grazing of dairy cattle was allowed to continue to serve tourists in Yosemite Valley until 1933. Wildlife policies in the new park system included killing predators so as to raise the numbers of species such as deer that were appealing to visitors. In 1919, more than fifty cougars were killed in or near Yosemite to "protect" the deer population. Elk were imported into Yosemite Valley and displayed behind fences. Bear feeding was allowed to continue. Non-native fish were stocked in some Yosemite streams. Eventually, criticism from the American Society of Mammalogists and the Ecological Society of America forced the Park Service to reconsider its wildlife policies.[100]

As part of this reevaluation, new studies were conducted. In 1932 a survey on national park fauna and problems resulting from management practices was completed. George M. Wright and two other scientists stationed at Yosemite recommended a broader-based scientific research program for all the nation's national parks. The parks, they said, contained the last vestiges of what had been a wild America, and thus made perfect laboratories.[101]

The Wright report provides another baseline for animal numbers in the Yosemite region, as well as for Sequoia to the south. As to Yosemite, Wright focused on the declining numbers of predators, especially those that in their quest for prey crossed park boundaries into private land. Grinnell and Storer had noted in *Animal Life in the Yosemite* that all predators in the park, large and small alike (with the exception of the scarce wolverine), could be counted in moderate numbers. But in slightly more than a decade, that pattern had changed—their numbers were declining rapidly. Martens, fishers, wolverines, and cougars were being heavily trapped and killed outside the park boundaries. As an example, Wright cited the case of a state of California professional hunter who reported that by himself he had killed thirty-one mountain lions since 1915, never having to encroach into the nearby national park.[102]

Wright and his coauthors relied on the observations of Judge Walter Fry for information on animal life in Sequoia National Park, based on Fry's surveys conducted between 1906 and 1931. Wright and his associates included an extensive quote from Fry to illustrate faunal changes in Sequoia:

> Bear and deer have increased by at least 60 per cent. Mountain and valley coyotes, skunks, weasels, porcupines, pikas, rats, gophers, moles, shrews, mountain beavers, and bats have held their own. Mountain lions, lynxes, fishers, martens, minks, foxes, racoons, ring-tailed cats, marmots, squirrels, chipmunks, hares and rabbits (other than the California jack rabbit) have decreased about 40 per cent. Mountain sheep, wolverines, and badgers are verging on extinction. . . .
>
> Of the 63 known species that inhabited the park in 1906, 2 have increased, 35 have held their own, 21 have been greatly reduced, 3 are verging on extinction, and 2 have disappeared [gray wolf and California jack rabbit]. One [non-native] animal has been added, the opossum.[103]

For a brief period Horace Albright, now head of the Park Service, saw to it that park scientists received more funding. Up until then, science was not a serious concern for the service. Albright also promoted the idea of scientific research in the parks to the public. In an article in the *Scientific Monthly* in 1933, he said that scientific research provided means of protecting "natural features in the Parks" and could bring positive results in both Yosemite and Sequoia. For example, concern for the declining health of sequoias in both parks had led park scientists to recommend protection of the trees' root areas from trampling and compaction. The rebuilding of soil and planting of native shrubs around them had promoted their recovery. Albright's comments, however, masked some less pleasant realities. Although briefly receiving some needed support, park scientists and wildlife programs did not fare well in the long run. In 1933 the head of the Wildlife Division reported to a new secretary of the interior that Yosemite had lost all of its bighorns and grizzlies and nearly all of its cougars. In 1940, in a reorganization of Department of the Interior personnel, park biologists were transferred to the Bureau of Biological Survey. Sierran parks generally reverted to the more tourist-oriented policies that had prevailed earlier.[104]

In these years of establishing management in Sierran parks, the battles had generally ended with what could be called equivocal success. Boundaries had been firmed up, but the parks as created in 1890 had been reduced in size or invaded with hydroelectric developments. The emphasis on tourist accommodation and access had led to a downplaying of science and natural wildlife policies. There were some small exceptions. In 1933 Yosemite National Park worked with ecologist Frederick Clements to bring about re-planting of native grasses and other plants alongside the newly improved Wawona Road.[105]

There were also some internal arguments between national park land-scape architects and park superintendents over how best to balance develop-ment and protection in "sacred areas" such as Glacier Point. The disagree-ments included faunal issues such as removal of fish hatcheries at Happy Isles and stocking fish in park "wilderness"-area streams.[106] But the development side was always the more influential in park policy through these years.

After fighting wearying battles against reduction and promotion, Sierran park advocates might have been expected to hunker down and play a defen-sive game. Instead, they launched yet another campaign to gain national park status for part of the Sierra Nevada, Kings Canyon. Between 1891 and 1935, over a dozen bills had been introduced in Congress to achieve that goal. John Muir and Robert Johnson led the way, as they had in the Yosemite struggle. Muir went so far as to proclaim that Kings Canyon featured an even "grander valley of the same kind" as its northern counterpart.[107] If Hetch Hetchy was lost, Tehipite Valley and the South Fork of Kings Can-yon—valleys of nearly comparable quality—could be set aside as part of a wilderness park north of Sequoia.[108]

The opposition to park status for Kings Canyon was strong and had turned back all attempts to achieve it for the first third of the century. Oppo-nents included the thirsty metropolis of Los Angeles, craving more water and hydroelectric sites. Local opposition included farmers in the San Joaquin who also wanted Kings Canyon's water, business interests who hoped to develop its tourist potential, and cattlemen and timber companies who desired to exploit its resources. The Forest Service was part of this oppo-sition. It had its own plans for tourist development.[109]

Successful for many years in thwarting the Park Service and park advo-cates, in the mid-1930s the opposition became divided. Under the leadership of Secretary of the Interior Harold Ickes, advocates pursued a winning cam-paign to build public support for a new park. Los Angeles dropped out of opposition, temporarily sated after having gained access to water from the Colorado River. San Joaquin farmers were bought off with the promise of a new dam outside the proposed park. Park Service officials convinced local businesspeople that road improvements and a new park would provide tour-ist dollars. Unfortunately, to placate those who still imagined dams at Tehipite Valley and in portions of Kings Canyon, these areas were kept out-side the proposed park's boundaries. In 1939 and early 1940, bills passed both houses of Congress creating Kings Canyon National Park. Fortunately, a quarter of a century later, Tehipite and the remainder of Kings Canyon were incorporated into the park.[110]

California State Forestry and Environmental Effects

After early failures, California took renewed interest in establishing a state forestry policy between 1905 and the 1920s. First came the creation of a new state Board of Forestry. Biennial reports from 1906 through 1920 provide a clear view of state concerns. The need for an effective state role in fire protection topped the list. Next came the strong desire to purchase or otherwise obtain and reforest cutover private land—of which there was now a substantial amount in the Sierra—as the beginning of a state forest system. A third concern was the need to establish regulations for timber cutting on the state's private forestlands, which continued to be rapidly cut. A fourth goal was cooperation with the U.S. Forest Service on fire issues. A fifth major emphasis was watershed protection and water conservation measures for the state's growing cities and farm industry. In 1927 the legislature and governor succeeded in creating a state Department of Natural Resources, setting the stage for a more effective forestry policy.[111]

State forestry interests had good results in their goal of cooperation with the U.S. Forest Service in creating an effective fire policy. The state Board of Forestry sided with the Forest Service on the issue of light burning. The controversy over such burning, as already noted, intensified in the mid-1920s. Powerful private timber interests generally supported light burning, while the Forest Service, under the influence of Du Bois, Show, and Kotok, opposed it. In 1924 the issue came to a head.[112]

Between 1919 and 1923 the American Society of Foresters facilitated a discussion of the issue, and both sides' contentions underwent review by a committee headed by Professor Donald Bruce of the University of California. In the ensuing report of 1923, Bruce summarized the two major positions. The three main points of the light burning advocates were "(1) that under favorable circumstances fire will run through the forest, consuming dead needles or branches, but with little or no damage to living trees (2) that the intensity of [a] given fire depends largely on the amount of inflammable debris which has accumulated on the ground since the preceding fire in the same area (3) that complete prevention of fire is impracticable." The three main points of Forest Service opponents of light burning were that "(1) even light fires do some damage to mature trees and much damage to young growth (2) after five or six years the debris in the forest begins to decay at least as fast as it accumulates and thick tree production is a natural essential to the continuation of a forest (3) the U.S. Forest Service had proved by experience that reasonable fire protection was practicable."[113]

In 1924, after studying the report, the state Board of Forestry interpreted it as a condemnation of light burning and accepted exclusion of fire on forested and watershed lands. In the same year, state forestry officials hailed the passage of the federal Clarke-McNary Act as a practical way of ensuring state and federal cooperation on fire protection. California forestry had thus established a clear direction in fire policy and close ties with the Forest Service in implementing it.[114]

Cutting of privately owned forested lands, by contrast, remained beyond the state's ability to regulate or limit it. As a result, most of the state's lower-elevation virgin forests, especially those in the Sierra Nevada not under the control of the U.S. Forest Service, were ravaged by so-called railroad logging interests. They had been filed on before 1890, in the days just before legislation was passed creating the forest reserves. Some were lands that the 1910 reduction of Yosemite had put back into circulation.

The rapid cutting of the private forestlands was fueled by the use of railroads to support industrial-scale logging. The railroad lumber industry of the Sierra Nevada grew fastest between 1890 and the 1920s, with the creation of more than eighty railroad logging companies. Areas that had formerly been inaccessible were opened to intensive cutting until the 1930s, when the depression and lack of remaining timber brought the industry to its knees. Privately owned rail-logging systems encouraged the Forest Service to open timber sales in lands close to rail systems, thereby aiding industrialists and the Forest Service in meeting their separately defined goals.[115]

On the western flank of the Sierra, railroad logging was concentrated in the northern and central parts of the range (much of the southern range remained in Forest Service or Park Service hands, though a few operations existed there). The areas that were most affected included portions of the South Yuba River drainage close to or in the Tahoe National Forest. The heaviest concentration was in or near the Eldorado and Stanislaus National Forests. In the Stanislaus area, the largest rail loggers included the California Peach Growers, the Hetch Hetchy (run by the city of San Francisco), the McKay, Pickering, Sierra, West Side, Yosemite, and Yosemite Sugar Pine operations. As an example of their output, the West Side Lumber Company cut more than 90 million board feet in the two-year span of 1915–1916.[116]

On the east side, railroad logging companies such as the Boca and Loyalton, Verdi, Sierra Nevada, and Hobart continued the heavy cutting in the Tahoe-Truckee Basin. For example, the Hobart Mills operation owned timberland in three counties in the northern Sierra. It cut 105 million board feet in Sierra County alone between 1916 and 1919.[117] This logging left many acres denuded, and because of its location on the arid eastern flank, some of this land never effectively reforested.

The railroad logging companies continued to use flumes, steam donkeys, and chutes to move timber or lumber to rail landings. The Forest Service judged these old-fashioned methods to be both wasteful and destructive. They often were employed on steep terrain and caused more erosion than the forest officials found acceptable. At times, such as when rail loggers cut on supervised Forest Service timber sales, the imposition of federal standards reduced fire danger and forest damage. But still, a report by S. B. Show of the Forest Service in 1926 warned that if the pine forestland in California, 80 percent of which was in private hands, continued to be cut at current rates, most of the companies involved would soon find themselves in the "cut-over land business."[118]

Rail connections reduced transportation costs. Until the late 1920s, these companies could maintain logging operations even though they continued to utilize old and wasteful methods. During the Great Depression, many companies operating on private lands went bankrupt or adopted even more-aggressive logging practices in order to maximize profits. The most significant effect of logging by private companies before 1940 was the removal of the largest yellow and sugar pines.[119]

Replacing these trees were smaller but more densely packed pines in some areas, more fir and cedar in other areas, and more shrubs than had existed in earlier forests. Many private timber holders turned to light burning of this new growth to reduce danger of larger fires. By 1934, more than half of the mixed-conifer forestland in the north-central Sierra Nevada had been entered for harvesting by railroad loggers. Their cutting focused primarily on ponderosa, Jeffrey, and sugar pines. Fir was less affected, although pulp operations in the Truckee River area cut fir extensively. Toxic chemicals were released into the river during pulp processing. The southern part of the range, where logging did not develop as fully, still served primarily local markets.[120]

Environmental Change and Managing Water in the Sierra

Water from the Sierra Nevada provides the lifeblood for modern urban California and northern Nevada. The multibillion-dollar California agriculture industry is heavily dependent on the Sierra and its streams. Early in both states' history, it became clear to urban developers and irrigation farmers that conservation of water and protection of watersheds was key to their future successes. Likewise, private investors and urban politicians foresaw the potential of Sierran rivers for hydroelectric generation. During the first four decades of the twentieth century, rivers on both sides of the Sierra Nevada came under extreme scrutiny. Some of the most significant environmental struggles in the West developed over Sierran water use.[121]

California water conservation policy began in 1911 when a new Republican Progressive majority in the state legislature voted to create a state Conservation Commission. During its lifetime, this commission faced various forestry issues, such as fire protection, but its greatest concern was for a state water conservation policy. Instructions to it from the legislature emphasized the need to study and recommend legislation on issues of water, land reclamation, and hydroelectric generation. Included in the Conservation Commission Act was the creation of a state Water Resources Control Board. In 1913 the Conservation Commission submitted a report to the governor on water rights and resources in the state. In 1917 both houses of the legislature passed a resolution asking the U.S. Forest Service to sell its "ripe" timber and apply the money raised by that to building dams in the national forests to impound water.[122]

The state of Nevada, normally opposed to any exertion of federal power in its boundaries, changed its tune when it came to water. The Truckee and Carson Rivers were vital to the northern part of the state, and by the turn of the century the legislature and Nevada's congressman, Francis Newlands, urged cooperation with the national government. The state's population decline in the aftermath of the Comstock collapse meant that resources would be inadequate for Nevada to establish its own water initiatives—hence the need to turn to Washington.[123]

Continuing shortages of water led California to try to develop its own state water project in the 1920s and 1930s, with a major dam proposed at Shasta, on the Sacramento River north of the Sierra. The Great Depression forced the state to abandon the project, opening the way for the federal government to step in and appropriate it. In the years following World War II, returning prosperity led to a revival of state water plans, centering on the Sierra Nevada's Feather River. From the start, Nevada was forced to rely on the federal government.[124]

In 1902, as part of the national conservation movement, Congress and President Theodore Roosevelt had supported the creation of the Bureau of Reclamation. One of its earliest projects was designed to carry water from the Truckee River into the Carson Sink area in Nevada. Called the Truckee-Carson Irrigation Project, it utilized water from the two closest Sierran rivers to fill the Derby and Lahontan Dams by 1915. Carson Sink farmers and those in the Fernley/Fallon area had high hopes that Sierran water would transform the Nevada desert into an agricultural paradise. But conflicting claims of the Paiute and other users on the Truckee and Carson River drainages reduced their dreams to a more realistic level.[125]

After years of bitter wrangling over water issues on Lake Tahoe, including control over the dam at the mouth of the river, a compromise was worked out. In 1934 an agreement was created to establish a steady source of water for the Nevada farmers. This led to the building of a dam at Boca, in the Sierra on the Little Truckee River. Federal control of the Tahoe dam was affirmed, but the Truckee-Carson Irrigation District was licensed to act as an agent for the national government in regulating flows out of the dam and maintaining minimum levels for the lakeshore. In 1944 a federal court upheld the agreement.[126]

With the help of the federal government, the growing cities of San Francisco and Los Angeles had moved aggressively ahead with water and hydroelectric developments in the Sierra Nevada in the early twentieth century. The East Bay cities followed in their wake. While the state had considered the Sacramento River, outside the Sierra, the cities directly focused on Sierran watersheds. San Francisco's seizure of Hetch Hetchy has already been discussed. Los Angeles turned much farther away, to the eastern side of the range and the watershed of the Owens River. Later it took control over the Mono drainage as well. In the Owens Valley, a political struggle with the farmers of the area generated a bitter conflict.[127]

The issue in the Los Angeles–Owens Valley fight was which economic interest was going to develop the project and therefore reap the benefits of the water and power it would generate. Early plans of the federal Irrigation Service focused on giving valley farmers the water. Los Angeles convinced President Roosevelt and forester Gifford Pinchot to dedicate the watershed of the Owens River to the city instead. Even though disappointed, valley irrigation supporters still hoped to be able to use surplus water from the project. When the city committed that water to the development of the San Fernando Valley, annexing it to the city, the Owens faction reacted with anger and violence.[128]

The story of the "Owens Valley War" between the southern metropolis and the beleaguered farmers has been told many times. Norris Hundley Jr. in *The Great Thirst* and William Kahrl in *Water and Power* point out that many writers and even a popular Hollywood movie of 1974, *Chinatown,* have created a legendary conspiracy story about the war. The legend involves the machinations of city officials and greedy land developers in league against the virtuous farmers of Owens Valley. The reality involved a straightforward power struggle over how the water of the Owens River was to be used. Unlike the Hetch Hetchy issue (should a beautiful valley be flooded within a National Park?), all parties to the Owens fight—farmers, city water managers, or land developers—wanted the Owens River water for their exclusive use. There were few who cared about a valley that had its own beauty.[129]

Important to consider here is what effect diverting the Owens River to Los Angeles, and the extension of the aqueduct to the Mono drainage to the north, had upon the Sierra Nevada environment. A brief chronology will help. In 1905, Los Angeles announced its intention to turn to the Owens River for water and electrical power. This occurred with the help of the U.S. Forest Service, through its protection of the forest watershed in the Owens drainage. Between 1905 and 1907, two bond elections were held authorizing funds to purchase water rights in Owens Valley and to build an aqueduct to transfer water to Los Angeles. The aqueduct was completed in 1913, and water flowed from the Owens River to the city. Drought problems in the 1920s led the city to pump groundwater and purchase water rights throughout the valley. Disgruntled valley residents turned to dynamite to show their anger, causing limited damage to the aqueduct. By 1933, most of the private land in the valley was held by the city and heavy pumping had reduced groundwater significantly. Between 1930 and 1940, the city purchased water rights in the Mono Basin. By 1940, an extension of the aqueduct began to strip away water from the tributaries of Mono Lake and lake level decline accelerated.[130]

One result of the water diversion was that Owens Lake dried into an alkali flat that sent whirling dust throughout the valley when the wind blew. Rabbitbrush and other weeds that could survive the loss of the valley's moisture spread widely. All this cannot be blamed solely on Los Angeles. Change had begun with the displacement of the area's Paiute inhabitants in the wake of the gold rush. Mining nearby opened markets for agricultural produce, and the valley lands were heavily grazed to meet mining community demands. But certainly the most important cause of the growing aridity in the Owens area was the diversion of valley water to its thirsty neighbor, Los Angeles.[131]

Before development, the central feature of the valley's ecosystem was the river that bisected it before entering Owens Lake. The borders of the main river and its tributary creeks were lined with willows of several varieties. Farther up the hillsides and canyons, ponderosa and Jeffrey pines grew. The meadow floor was covered with a varied profusion of flowering plants, all adapted to the alkaline soils. But the most striking visual impact came from the expanses of saltgrass meadows that changed color as the seasons progressed. The river ecosystem also contained numerous oxbows, sloughs, and depressions that were filled with water most times, offering a rich habitat for wildfowl. Even the banks of the alkaline Owens Lake and surrounding areas had a great variety of flowering plants and brush dependent on high ground-water levels.[132]

Writer and local resident Mary Austin described the valley and its river lovingly:

> The middle Sierras fall off abruptly eastward toward the high valleys. Peaks of the fourteen thousand class, belted with sombre [*sic*] swathes of pine, rise almost directly from the bench land with no foothill approaches. At the lower edge of the bench or mesa the land falls away, often by a fault, to the river hollows, and along the drop one looks for springs or intermittent swampy swales. Here the plant world resembles a little the lake gardens, modified by altitude and the use the town folk put it for pasture. Here are cress, blue violets, potentilla, and, in the damp of the willow fence-rows, false asphodels. . . . Native to the mesa meadows is a pale iris, gardens of it acres wide, that in the spring season of full bloom make an airy fluttering of azure wings. Single flowers are too thin and sketchy of outline to affect the imagination, but the full fields have the misty blue of mirage waters rolled across the desert sand, and quicken the senses to the anticipation of things ethereal.[133]

The diversion of the river and pumping of groundwater changed all that. Rabbitbrush and sagebrush spread as the water table dropped. Alkali pink, sand spurry, stinkweed, arrowscale, and greasewood died out around what had been Owens Lake. It became an alkali basin. Sloughs and water basins dried, displacing native and visiting waterfowl. The saltgrass meadows disappeared. To the north, the creeks that had fed Mono Lake were diverted into the aqueduct, killing most of the riparian forests and plant communities that lived on their banks. The economy of the area changed. Grazing on land leased from the city increased. Tourism and camping grew as a result of a road that now connected the valley to the urban metropolis to the south. This pattern continued to intensify until after the 1960s when environmental challenges would reverse some of the effects of water diversion.[134]

Elsewhere in the range at this time, private hydroelectric and water developments, while less politically explosive than the Hetch Hetchy or Owens Valley fights, had more significant environmental effect. In sheer numbers, if not in size, private corporate electrical-power-generating dams left their mark over the whole of the range on both sides.[135]

Industrial gold mining in the Sierra Nevada in the nineteenth century bequeathed many environmental effects to the range. One was the development of hydroelectric generation. The search for a cheap means of powering the hoists, mills, drills, and pumps of the deep mines and illuminating the hydraulic operations at night to maximize investments led to the first use of hydroelectric power. The so-called Pelton water wheel was easily adapted to power generation in many mining areas by the 1880s. Transmitting hydroelectric power over copper lines soon followed. Electric power that had been useful locally could now be produced in the Sierra Nevada and transmitted to urban markets hundreds of miles away. The hydraulic miners' complex ditch networks and the Sierra Nevada's streams could also be put to work to illuminate urban California.[136]

Numerous small corporations founded in the 1890s and the early twentieth century utilized Sierra streams to generate electrical power. These companies were at work in the northeastern and southeastern part of the range and all along the western side. The more numerous tributaries of the larger rivers of the west slope, from the Feather to the San Joaquin, were harnessed to supply cities such as Sacramento, San Francisco, Fresno, and even Los Angeles. The general pattern of industrial consolidation, so characteristic of this period in the nation's economic history, quickly asserted itself. By 1909, two giant monopolies dominated the field in California—Pacific Gas and Electric in the northern part of the state and Southern California Edison in the south.[137]

Unlike the damming of the Owens and the Tuolumne, the dams of the private power companies generated little complaint. Streams and valleys were flooded in what was sold as being in the best interests of the larger urban public. For example, the flooding of Big Meadows, creating Lake Almanor on the Feather River by 1911, met only limited local protest.[138]

The environmental effects of hydroelectric development in the Sierra Nevada were huge. The earliest of these involved the transformation and enlargement of the ditches, flumes, and dams of the hydraulic-mining companies into permanent alterations of Sierran water systems.[139] Meadows were transformed into reservoirs and ranching economies replaced.[140] Construction for electrical generation created new dams, ditches, flumes, and tunnels. Transmission lines required erecting steel towers along hillsides and cutting the forest on the towers' right-of-ways. When small dams proved vulnerable to California's summer drought conditions, companies such as PG&E built larger dams to store more water.[141]

An example of this policy change and its environmental effect can be found in the Spaulding-Drum project, or what PG&E proudly called "The

Big Job." It involved building a 305-foot-high concrete dam to replace a smaller hydraulic dam high up on the South Fork of the Yuba River. A tunnel and canal system was constructed to connect to a powerhouse nine miles away on the Bear River, thus effectively sending much of the flow of the South Yuba into a completely different drainage. Two large generators there produced 33,000 horsepower of electrical energy that was transported over a 110-mile stretch of steel-tower line to connect in with PG&E's power grid.[142]

The manager of PG&E's publicity department proudly described the effect of the Spaulding Dam in 1913 from a vantage point downstream on the South Fork of the Yuba, just before the dam's completion: "I remembered that when I had visited there in June I had found men paddling around in loose rock and water, and now there stood before my gaze a huge monolithic structure that made the little trickling stream below that stands for the South Yuba at the present time look puny indeed."[143]

The Effects of Establishing Sierran Management, 1900–1940s

In the first four decades of the twentieth century, many hopes of the leaders of the American conservation movement were realized. Federal and state agencies such as the U.S. Forest Service, the National Park Service, the U.S. Reclamation Service, the California Division of Forestry, and several municipal water agencies were created.[144]

These public agencies imposed limits on private use of much of the Sierra Nevada. Numerous conflicts erupted between those who favored utilitarian uses of the range's resources and those seeking to preserve certain of its natural wonders from development. The most notable was the fight over Hetch Hetchy Valley. Recreation on both public and private land also emerged as a significant new environmental force, largely because of automobiles and the construction of better roads. The Sierra Nevada continued to change in response to human actions, but patterns were very different from its opening phase in the nineteenth century. Management by federal, state, and municipal agencies replaced the unregulated free-for-all of the earlier period.[145]

The course of history in the Sierra Nevada has always shown that successive generations impose their distinctive marks upon the range. Constant change is the pattern of human use. The first forty years of the twentieth century produced a political movement that established agency control over much of the range, and in doing so changed the Sierra.

In the decades that followed, from the Second World War until the 1960s, agency policies continued this trend. But instead of the custodial emphasis of the Forest Service and the largely defensive posture of the Park Service in the years before the war, new societal demands pushed the agencies to adopt a far more aggressive stance toward the management of their resources. Population expansion and homebuilding in urban California and Nevada led to strong demand for lumber from public lands in the Sierra. Greater mobility and affluence led to increased use of Sierran national parks and national forests and the expansion of roads into the range. And urban growth on both flanks of the Sierra and far to the south in Los Angeles, meant that Sierra Nevada's greatest treasure—its waters—would also face new development pressures.

Federal and state agencies in this postwar period adopted new policies, or continued to apply successful older ones, that took resource development and use of the Sierra to a level that may have exceeded the gold rush in its environmental effects. That expanded development is the subject of the next chapter.

5: The Philosophy of "More," 1940–1970

Social and economic values change with time. What is sought by one generation is often rejected by its successors. The time following the end of World War II was a watershed in Sierra Nevada, California, and national resource history. After a decade of economic collapse, the war and postwar years saw the state's and the nation's natural resources and labor power put back to work. A surge of migration into California ushered in a new period of growth and development. By 1962 California had become the most populous state in the union. Issues of housing, transportation, education, and water supply became major public service concerns. Nevada, after losing population for decades following the collapse of the nineteenth-century mining boom, grew rapidly with the relegalization of gambling.[1]

Sierra Nevada resources figured importantly in this surge of construction and growth. Newly affluent urban dwellers also demanded access, improved facilities, and good roads into the national forests and national parks of the Sierra for recreation. Federal, state, and local public agencies actively supported attempts to provide more services and resources to meet these demands. It was their belief that the Sierra Nevada could provide an inexhaustible supply of resources with effective management. This optimistic viewpoint would be called into question in the 1960s.[2]

The G.I. Bill, Federal Housing Administration loans, and Cold War–supported military industries that created well-paying jobs promoted a boom in suburban tract home development.[3] Demand for lumber alone from national forest lands rose by more than 200 percent compared with prewar levels. The percentage of the nation's timber supply that came from Forest Service lands increased from 5 percent of the total to 10 percent by the 1950s and continued to rise. In the Sierra Nevada, contrast with the prewar years was even greater. The privately owned forestlands in the Sierra Nevada, with the exception of the Tahoe Basin, had been at low elevations and easily accessible. They had been almost totally cut over, as we saw in the last chapter. The construction boom in California and Nevada led to a turn to the range's national forests for lumber to a degree never experienced before.[4]

If timber from Sierran forests helped fuel the boom in home construction, the rapid urbanization of the state created a counterforce—the demand for open spaces where newly affluent and mobile families could find recreation outlets. The Sierra Nevada on both sides of the range experienced a substantially increased demand for access and improved services in both the national parks and the national forests. Most of the new visitors came from California, although many came from outside the state and even outside the nation. The previously built infrastructure that served tourism in the forests and parks sufficed only briefly in the immediate years after the war. Increasing demands rapidly exerted pressure for expansion. Soon federal and state agencies instituted ambitious plans to meet the public's needs.[5]

National forests and parks were not the only public entities that faced expanded demand. The Bureau of Land Management, the Bureau of Reclamation, and the Army Corps of Engineers were forced to reconsider their role as providers of water and recreation. The California state parks, Department of Fish and Game, Department of Water Resources, and State Lands Commission also joined in the task of meeting tourist demands in the Sierra. Utility companies such as PG&E supplied services in the campground facilities they owned for automobile tourists during this postwar surge, as did private tourist-camp operators. Tourist communities on both side of the range were affected. On the western side, El Portal, Groveland, and Three Rivers experienced a boom in building of motels and restaurants. On the eastside, Lake Tahoe, Truckee, Mammoth Lakes, Lee Vining, and Lone Pine faced similar expansion pressures.[6]

New highways and improvement of older state roads facilitated the tourist influx. The construction of Interstate 80 and the selection of Squaw Valley for the 1960 Winter Olympics fueled a dramatic expansion of a Sierra Nevada skiing industry and promoted growth in nearby Reno. And improved Highway 50 drew tourists, skiers, and gamblers to Lake Tahoe, Highways 49 and 20, improved and expanded, brought tourists into the older mining communities that now provided "history" rather than gold to spur new economic growth. Highways 70 into the Feather River Canyon, 41, 120, and 140 to Yosemite, and 180, 198, and 245 connecting with Kings Canyon and Sequoia were other state roads improved to meet the new tourist demands. Highway 395 was reworked to open access from cities along the eastern flank of the range, especially to Mammoth and June Lakes for skiing and summer uses.[7]

The most important fuel to growth in the central and southern parts of California and the Reno area came from water impounded by huge federal and state projects that relied on Sierra Nevada rivers. The federal Central Valley Project was approved during the 1930s but constructed mostly after the war. California followed suit between 1960 and 1968 with the creation of the State Water Plan utilizing water from the Feather River impounded at Oroville in a huge dam. From there it was distributed to the Central Valley and southern California through a complex hydraulic system. Water from the Sierra was the lifeblood of population and agribusiness growth. In 1955, California and Nevada, with federal help, took most of the remaining Truckee River water not used by the Truckee-Carson Irrigation Project and built new dams to aid Nevada and California growth.[8]

The period from 1945 to the late 1960s is another distinct phase of Sierra Nevada environmental history. Its effects marked the range just as past periods of human activity had. Responding to the new generation's increased demand for timber, water, and recreation, public agencies and private interests operating in the Sierra Nevada placed burdens upon the range that compare in their effects with the gold rush period. Eventually, environmental impacts from this expansion raised public concerns. And just as the unregulated development of the gold rush years created the early conservation movement, development in the postwar years generated a new environmental and conservation activism in the 1960s.

"Getting Out the Cut" and Rising Recreation Use

The Forest Service, the private timber industry, and nonpartisan forestry organizations in the wartime and postwar period strongly supported increased cutting on private and public forestlands in the Sierra: as they put it, "getting out the cut." National forests that had remained in reserve as the private forestlands were cut over by the 1930s were now expected to increase their share of the nation's wood supply. Wartime needs and postwar demand for expanded construction of homes necessitated the rapid and continuous production of forestry products. Cooperation between federal and state governments, the Forest Service, and private industry was seen as necessary if the new demands were to be met.[9]

Logging on public lands for the war and postwar period dramatically increased when compared with the earlier decades of "custodial management." Harold Steen's history of the Forest Service provides a useful summary to illustrate this point. In 1941 the national forests yielded 1.5 billion board feet. In 1951 that figure rose to 4.4 billion. By 1961 the amount was 8.3 billion board feet. In 1970 it was 11.5 billion.[10] Historian Paul Hirt, using various annual reports of the chief of the Forest Service, came up with slightly different figures (based on timber sales rather than actual cut), but they illustrate the same trend. Between 1935 and 1945 timber sales on the national forests rose 230 percent, from 1.3 billion board feet annually to 3.1 billion board feet, reflecting wartime demand. In 1946 timber sales of 2.7 billion board feet were reported. For the following years, 1951 produced 4.6

billion, in 1953 it was 5.1 billion, 1955 saw 6.3 billion, and 1960 came in at 9.6 billion board feet. This surge of production steadily pushed the percentage of Forest Service–supplied timber to 10 percent of the national total in the 1950s. By 1962 the figure rose to 16 percent, and it continued at that level until the 1980s.[11]

This increased output by the Forest Service was achieved through the use of new timber-management practices. The term *intensive management* was coined to describe a new set of forestry practices in the business-oriented years of the 1950s. There was pressure to increase cutting of what today the public calls "old-growth" stands in the national forests. These large, old trees were clearly more commercially profitable. Industry and Forest Service representatives called them "overmature" or "decadent." To leave them standing was considered wasteful. Clear-cutting (especially in the Pacific Northwest and the Rocky Mountains) was frequently defined by the Forest Service as the preferred method in these years. It replaced the older selective cutting of the custodial period. In the clear-cut areas, immediate replanting or seeding of preferred species in "plantations" followed, promising a future "crop" of more commercially desirable trees. Traps and poison were used to control rodents and other mammals that might damage the newly seeded or planted trees. Herbicides were deployed to discourage competing plants, including brush and noncommercial tree species.[12]

Expansion of access roads into virgin timberlands lay at the base of intensive management. Throughout the postwar period, private industry and the Forest Service lobbied Congress for increased appropriations for such roads. The cost of building and maintaining roads exceeded the revenue that came from timber sales. The difference could be only partially offset by "stumpage" allowances that compensated private companies for building roads into Forest Service lands by giving them timber. The service justified its calls for increased congressional funding by pointing to the need to remove older, diseased, or insect-infested trees quickly, while they still had economic value. It also argued that the roads would aid fire prevention and potentially serve other uses, such as providing the public access for recreation. The arguments and lobbying worked. Between 1940 and 1960, the amount of roads on U.S. Forest Service lands, most built for timber purposes, doubled to 160,000 miles. And, of course, more roads fueled more timber cutting.[13]

Increases in cutting and roadbuilding had immense environmental effects. Because Forest Service funding focused primarily on cutting, other areas— such as supervision of timber sales, fire management, insect-infestation treatment, reforestation, reduction of soil erosion, and wildlife management— were all neglected or underfunded in relation to timber management. Damage to watersheds, streams, and wildlife habitat increased and in some cases was irreversible. The emphasis on "even-age management" (as clear-cutting was called) also had very obvious visual effects. Clear-cutting startled a public raised on the view that the Forest Service existed to protect forests. Just when the pressure to "get out the cut" was propelling new timber cutting, the public demand for more national forest recreational opportunities created an inevitable clash of values.[14]

Forest Service intensive management in the postwar years was accompanied by increased emphasis on saving valuable timber from fire. A tree saved from fire was one more that could be added to the yield. According to the fire historian Stephen J. Pyne, the postwar years saw continued dedication to fire prevention and suppression, including rapid response to fire outbreak. This philosophy was especially evident in the area of public education, as manifested by the creation of Smokey Bear as an anti–forest fire icon. New techniques to deal with wildfire, including expanded use of firebreaks, and new fire-suppression tools such as chainsaws, tractor-plows, air tankers, and helicopters added to the Forest Service's firefighting ability after 1945. Suppression at all costs remained the operative policy until scientific information, federal legislation, and public pressure compelled the agency to reexamine its doctrines after 1967.[15]

The Forest Service had other functions than supplying timber, including watershed protection, wildlife management, forest health promotion, and recreation development. Some professionals within the service, as well as wildlife scientists in other agencies, registered their concern about being underfunded relative to the emphasis on serving timber interests. But they did not have organized constituencies to back them. Recreation, however, did develop an active and organized opposition to timber-dominant agency policies. Between 1945 and 1953, annual visits to national forests rose from just under 10 million to over 35 million. In 1960 the figure reached 81.5 million. Several new advocacy groups such as the Conservation Foundation, the Sport Fishing Institute, the Nature Conservancy, and Trout Unlimited lobbied Congress for more recreation funding. Ski interests demanded new areas for use. The Sierra Club, under the new leadership of David Brower, added to the growing wish list of nontimber forest uses by pressing for expanded wilderness designation.[16]

Population and economic growth in California after 1945 led the nation. The forests of the state played a significant role in providing the wood, water, hydroelectricity, grazing land, and recreational opportunities for California and neighboring northern Nevada. The northern coastal forests provided the majority of timber produced in the region. But timber cutting in the Sierra Nevada on public and private land on both sides of the range also increased greatly as part of the general expansion.[17] Demand for forest products rose, and the Forest Service and timber industry responded. Consider a statement by the American Forestry Association in 1958 as it promoted increased output: "California's zooming population will soon top that of any other state—with no end in sight. To meet the needs of the people for living room, food, water, and raw materials, and recreation it has 100 million acres of land—a fifth barren and desert, only a sixth suitable for cultivation. Since the area is fixed, production can be increased only by more intensive management."[18]

The quotation, from an AFA-sponsored publication concerning California forestland use, illustrates the similarity between national and state patterns. The AFA, a national organization for professional foresters and others in university forestry programs, issued a series of state studies focusing on forest policy issues. The group saw a coming emergency in California. Explosive population growth had placed great stress on public resources. The limited supply of timber, water, and recreation areas in California had to be effectively managed in order to avoid economic and social strain. The AFA wanted to encourage cooperation between public and private forest interests to meet the state's forest-resource needs.[19]

The organization clearly stated its vision of modern forest uses: water for many purposes, timber, forage, wildlife habitat, recreation, and some wilderness. (The "wilderness" category was tightly defined as a few mostly inaccessible rock and ice areas.) The AFA saw the vague and generally accepted view of "multiple uses" of forestlands as a source of potential conflict. Not all uses, after all, were compatible. Better information to guide public and private uses of the Sierra's forests was called for. As the organization summed it up: "Three things are certain—(1) That far more intensive resource management by all classes of owners will be essential to close the prospective gap between needs and supplies (2) that such management is dependent on increased and continuous study, and (3) that the results must find practical application."[20]

To promote the cooperation needed to meet the rising burden on forest resources in California, the AFA suggested the creation of a state natural resources council that would include representatives from industry, public agencies, and the general public. The council was expected to provide guidance for forest-resource policies.[21]

As we have seen, one element in intensified use of California and Sierran forestlands was the building of timber access roads. The authors of the 1958 AFA study, Samuel Dana and Myron Krueger, called for increased road-building to promote all uses of the forest. Most prime Sierra forestlands were located outside of the railroad and road systems of the earlier custodial period and were thus inaccessible to supply the accelerated demand of the postwar years. Dana and Krueger stated that all forest users would benefit from road creation, including timber producers, livestock grazers, hunters, fishermen, and other recreation interests. They advocated building complete networks of roads, either by direct public funding or through "stumpage" policies that subsidized private feeder-road construction.[22]

The AFA's appeal for increased timber production in California's public and private forests was heeded by the Forest Service and the state's timber corporations. The Sierra played its part in the surge of timber production. Wartime and postwar output generally matched the national pattern. Between 1945 and 1956, from 1.6 to 1.9 billion board feet were cut annually in Sierra forests. Production peaked in 1959 at 6 billion board feet. Between 1957 and 1978, with some steep declines or rises that reflected economic fluctuations in the state, the average was between 1.3 and 1.6 billion board feet annually.[23]

Examples from two forests, the Eldorado and the Tahoe, illustrate this Sierra-wide trend. Between 1909 and 1940, in the custodial period of the Forest Service, the Eldorado National Forest produced 138.3 million board feet of timber, or about 4.4 million board feet annually. During the four years of World War II, the Eldorado produced 175.4 million board feet, or more than the total production of the previous three decades. Between 1946 and 1979, the combined total was 3.85 billion board feet, with the majority of that coming after 1960.[24] The Tahoe National Forest from 1921 to 1949 supplied 345 million board feet, averaging 12.3 million annually. The Tahoe National Forest Timber Management Plan for 1949 projected a cutting level of 80 million board feet annually to meet the demands it foresaw.[25]

Another way to measure the acceleration of cutting of Sierran mixed-conifer forests in the postwar period comes from analyzing the revenue obtained by Sierra Nevada counties as a result of the "25 percent law." That law, passed in 1908, directed that 25 percent of all revenues collected in national forests be paid to the counties in which the forests were located. The revenue was typically used for funding county roads and public schools. The proceeds generated in the forests provided compensation to counties to make up for the fact that national forest lands were not on county tax rolls. The measure was originally intended to gain local support for national forests in their founding years.[26] Although this statute gave some needed revenue to rural counties in national forest areas during the custodial years, it did not generate large amounts of revenue until after the Second World War. (Most Sierran timber in that earlier period came from private timber holdings that were taxed in different ways.) But between 1947 and 1956, timber-sale revenue collected under the law increased by 500 percent.[27]

Twenty-six counties in California and Nevada are wholly or partially located in the Sierra Nevada.[28] Of these, ten counties in California produced most of the proceeds under the law. Plumas and El Dorado Counties in the northern Sierra, home to the Plumas and Eldorado National Forests, ranked first in revenues. These highly productive northern Sierra forests generated revenues of just under $4 million for Plumas County and just over $1 million for El Dorado County between 1950 and 1956. Nevada and Placer Counties, home to the Tahoe National Forest, gained revenue of just under $1 million during the same time. Tiny Sierra County generated nearly $800,000. The reliance of these counties on the revenue, mostly obtained from timber sales rather than other national forest uses, provided strong political support for continued high cutting levels in the period after 1945.[29]

Road expenditures during the postwar expansion generally show significant increases in cutting—the two were dependent on each other for obvious reasons. The prime timberlands of the Sierra by this time were generally in rougher terrain and at higher elevations. Between 1947 and 1956, forest road-construction expenditures in California rose steadily from $4 million annually to about $9 million.[30]

What makes the increased cut level of this period of Sierran logging most interesting is that before the 1960s, clear-cutting on national forests was not commonly used as a method or "prescription" for harvesting in the Sierra Nevada. The amounts of timber cut in the Sierra came primarily from very heavy selective cutting of the largest and oldest trees, particularly sugar, ponderosa, and Jeffrey pines and, to a lesser extent, Douglas, white, and red fir. By the 1950s the Forest Service had recognized that the Sierra Nevada's mixed-conifer forests consisted of a complex mosaic of different age classes of trees and varied forest structure. It determined that each of these areas required different silvicultural treatment. Sierran forests were not similar to the forests of the Pacific Northwest and therefore had to be dealt with differently. Regeneration practices the agency prescribed likewise had to recognize these differences to vary reseeding, defense against rodent predation of seeds, and brush control as needed. At this time, clear-cutting was not usually seen as productive.[31]

The older trees that the Forest Service and its timber-industry allies desired lay beyond the limits of the private lands that had been cut over by the 1930s or cut earlier, during the gold rush. Elevation or other factors had kept them off the commercial grid. Many were hundreds of years old, remnants of the forests known to the range's native inhabitants. Poet and essayist Gary

Snyder gives us a picture of such trees in an account of a ramble he took into an area above the North Fork of the American River:

> Then we headed southwest over rolls of forested stony formations and eventually more gentle slopes into a world of greater and greater trees. For hours we were in the company of elders.
>
> Sugar pines dominate. They are properly mature symmetrical trees a hundred and fifty feet high that hold themselves upright and keep their branches neatly arranged. But then *beyond* them, *above* them, loom the *ancient* trees: huge, loopy, trashy, and irregular. Their bark is redder and the plates more spread, they have fewer branches, and those surviving branches are great in girth and curve wildly. Each one is unique and goofy. Mature incense Cedar. Some large Red Fir. An odd Douglas Fir. A few Jeffrey Pine.[32]

A history of the cutting practices of one Sierra Nevada national forest illustrates how the Forest Service went about increasing output during the war and postwar years. An analysis of timber harvest plans from 1940 to the 1960s for the Tahoe National Forest (TNF) reveals three major phases in the accelerated cutting. The first period, between 1940 and 1947, saw TNF plans for timber cutting focusing on older and larger trees on public lands that had not been logged during the custodial phase. Three areas illustrate the pattern: Foresthill, Brandy City, and Camptonville. Access to local mills, whether large or small, was one criterion for the "sustained yield" cutting adhered to in these areas in the 1940s. The trees were generally located on higher elevation and had not been considered in earlier years. But they were still relatively close to either old timber railroad grades or public roads, or could be easily reached by using "cats." Easy access to very large trees was the key during this early phase of postwar cutting. These trees were sometimes referred to as "virgin," and invariably as "overmature," "deteriorating," or as "salvage" trees because of their age and nearing mortality. While selective cutting was the normal prescription for all timber sales, orderly planning was set aside to reach the "overmature" trees as rapidly as possible. It was by cutting these large trees at an accelerated rate that increased timber output was to be achieved.[33]

A second phase of increased cutting on the Tahoe developed by 1949. A policy statement of that year indicates a changing emphasis toward timber as a primary focus for the forest. The preface of the document included a number of objectives that reflected the older thinking of the agency. An initial premise for the timber management plan called for maintaining established practices of cutting in the working circle. The preface also stressed the need for proper soil management and the importance of water for irrigation, hydroelectric production, and domestic use. But following these initial statements, the bulk of the new plan stressed increased timber output. Under Section III, "Silviculture Objective," it stated that the TNF was to "manage lands to provide the highest possible sustained yield of timber on every acre that [would] grow timber." To do this, it noted, multiple-use objectives would require modification in many cases. The biggest problem facing the TNF, the plan said, was in "bringing its lands into the production of which they [were] capable." The planners cited two historical reasons as lying behind this problem. First, large areas of cutover lands were currently understocked and needed regeneration. Second, very large areas of second-growth and virgin-growth timber were inaccessible.[34]

The plan stressed the goal of cutting 80 million board feet annually by increasing efforts to reach "decadent" trees and shortening the cutting return cycle. New roads were given priority, both to provide the necessary access and to make possible a mixing of the "decadent" or mature trees with trees of lesser quality so as to improve sales profitability. Roads would also enhance fire prevention. To open more timberland, it was suggested that areas formerly used for grazing be reduced in size. The areas around campgrounds and along Highway 40 were to see more logging, leaving only screens to mask the effects of cutting from public view.[35]

Because much of the lower-elevation land in the forest was cut over and otherwise understocked, emphasis on improving stand productivity provided a second way to generate more timber—albeit from future plantation-style stands. Although the phrases "intensive management" and "even-age management" were not used, they clearly express the intent of this phase of the timber plan. It was proposed that pine was the preferred species and its production should be stressed, requiring cutting of some other young trees and the removal of fir, cedar, and of course brush, where necessary. The plan stated that if a stand was "not sufficiently well stocked with a good growing stock of acceptable species composition, establishment of reproduction will be the primary objective." The age of "plantation" forestry was beginning in the Sierra and the TNF.[36]

The third phase of increased cutting in the TNF is revealed in two timber management plans for the Auburn and North Yuba timber circles for 1959–1968 and 1960–1969, respectively.[37] Two things are immediately apparent. The first is the clearly stated goal of increasing timber output that came with the national leadership of Chief Forester Richard E. McArdle and his assistant, Edward P. Cliff, whose names were attached to the letters of approval of these two plans. No previous timber management plans that I consulted, going back to the founding years of the TNF, carried such direct endorsement by the agency's top leaders. Second, it is significant that the larger of the plans, the North Yuba Working Circle, had specific instructions that tied production increases to the initiative known as the Timber Resources Review (TRR), the Forest Service program that promoted the concept of "intensive management."[38]

The cutting instructions of the Auburn plan describe the cutting area—containing "over 60 percent of the area and 75 percent of the volume" that was in virgin condition. The uncut stands were typically labeled as "overmature" old growth, with about 45 percent of the volume (991.6 million board feet) classified as "poor risk trees." These were to be completely cut to create open areas to allow for "artificial regeneration." The cutting instructions also stated: "Uneven-aged management using individual tree selection may be retained" in areas along "roadside scenic strips, streamside strips, and in the immediate vicinity of campgrounds or meadows." The plan stressed that the sales should be targeted to remove "the most decadent stand conditions first." Intensive management was now clearly part of the TNF planning.[39]

The North Yuba Working Circle timber plan was the most complex plan developed on the TNF up to that time. The allowable cut was revised upward as required by a Forest Service Directive, # 5, February 17, 1962. The rotation period was also shortened from previous plans. The chief and assistant chief ordered the forest to adjust its growth figures upward so as to get an increase of 2.5 percent. And, marking a significant change from the past definition of sustained yield that tied cutting to markets provided by local mills, the new cutting levels were to include timber for which no firm market yet existed.[40]

The objective of the timber management plan was to harvest "all" of the allowable annual cut and to prepare the forest to meet the TRR goal. As part of intensive management, three elements were uppermost: achieving the full maximum allowable cut levels in target areas, building access roads for production and fire reasons, and maximizing planting or regeneration for future full productivity. The North Yuba plan contained all three of these ideas in its "Action Program." Specifically, it mandated increasing the annual rate of cut for the last five-year average from 21.9 to 39.0 million board feet, called for constructing an average of eight miles of access road annually during the first cutting cycle, and set a goal of reducing the area of poorly stocked noncommercial forestland by planting 600 acres per year.[41]

The "Timber Resource Management" section of the plan noted some potential problems in reaching all goals. For one, projections exceeded available identified saw timber supply. This discrepancy obviously would require some adjustments: "Consequently," the plan stated, "with certain other working circles hard pressed to meet TRR goals, no effort will be spared to reforest or stimulate growth to the maximum extent possible on the North Yuba Working Circle." A related problem was that efforts planned earlier for reforesting certain brush field sites were falling behind because of shortages in funding. This admission that intensive-management goals in reforestation were lagging suggests that in this working circle in the Sierra, the strain was beginning to show.[42]

The difficulty of meeting the Forest Service's self-imposed goal of maximum timber production was beginning to bedevil agency leaders and planning staffs. Meanwhile, another problem was becoming obvious to a recreation-oriented public. Demand for national forest use was not just for timber, but for new campgrounds, lake and meadow access, and the designation of new wilderness areas. As the 1949 policy statement and the 1959–1968 Auburn Working Circle plan revealed, meeting timber demand on the Tahoe National Forest required cutting closer and closer to campgrounds, scenic roads, and meadows. A "screen" left to mask the effects of increased logging could not long put off the inevitable discovery by the public that increased cutting was running head on into other forest values.[43] In addition, the "wilderness" issue brought Sierra Club resistance to the Forest Service's emphasis on timber. The Sierra Nevada became an important battleground in this mounting controversy.

The wilderness struggle in the Sierra Nevada in the 1950s escalated in a unique forested area called Deadman Creek, near Mammoth Lakes and the Mono Craters on the eastern side of the range. The disagreement between the Sierra Club and the Forest Service over how the area was to be used brought an end to the cooperation that had prevailed between the two on forest and wilderness issues for nearly a half century.

It is important to envision the Deadman Creek drainage because of the role it played in the ensuing battle. It is located on a plateau near the Sierra ridgeline close to Mammoth and Highway 395. Although the southern Sierra is generally high enough to block much of the moist Pacific Ocean air, between Mammoth Lakes and the Mono Craters the ridge dips. This anomalous feature allows moist air to cross and deposit rain and snow to a much greater degree than in most eastern-slope areas. The snow supported the development of an important ski resort on the east flank; the total moisture allowed a stand of very old Jeffrey pines and red fir to establish itself over several hundred years. The Deadman Creek forest was open, with trees spaced evenly, creating what advocates of its protection described as a natural parklike setting. It was the fate of this unique stand of trees that started the wilderness war in the Sierra.[44]

Within the context of McArdle's intensive-management initiative, the Inyo National Forest announced that it would begin logging in the Dry, Glass, and Deadman Creek watersheds, all included in its Owens Cutting Circle. Glass Creek was logged in 1952. Protest immediately arose about careless logging in this drainage and the potential for damage to recreation and scenic values in the other two areas. One local man appealed to have Deadman Creek placed under Park Service protection. He hoped that transferring it into the nearby Inyo Craters National Monument would protect it from logging. The Forest Service, as always, feared Park Service control in its jurisdictions. It was also unwilling to give up on the logging potential of the area. The agency countered the Inyo Craters transfer by claiming it intended only to salvage dead, dying, or insect-infested trees. As it had done for several decades on wilderness and primitive-area policy, the Forest Service solicited help from the Sierra Club to assist its campaign to discredit the protest. Based on past cooperation, the service had every reason to believe that it could convince the club's leaders that the local protest was unfounded. It stressed that the cutting in the contested areas would be limited and would actually improve forest health.[45]

The agency had not envisioned that the club's new executive director, David Brower, would actually conduct an investigation independent of the usual Forest Service–sponsored visitation. After consulting with the local protester, visiting the Glass Creek logging site, and joining a service-sponsored trip to Deadman Creek, Brower reported to the Sierra Club board that he recommended against the proposed timber cut. He had also learned that the Forest Service was proposing heavy cutting near the Devil's Post Pile National Monument in Reds Meadow. Brower said that the Deadman Creek area, while small, was a forest-and-recreation jewel. It was also located close to a major highway, thus providing easy access to the public. He said it should be saved. The site, especially its Jeffrey pine stand, had already been singled out by the American Museum of Natural History as the finest of its type on the Pacific Coast. Brower concluded that a cut comparable to the one at Glass Creek would destroy the stand and forever ruin its recreational value.[46]

Faced with Sierra Club opposition, McArdle ordered a study of the problem area by Forest Service employees. The ensuing report reaffirmed the need to cut the stands in question, citing forest health, hazards to the public from the "overmature and decadent" trees on the site, and a local mill's need for timber. Some disagreement ensued between Brower and a minority of the Sierra Club board as the issue heated up, but eventually a majority of the board voted to oppose the cutting. In the face of the club's resistance, the Forest Service distanced itself from further cooperation and forged ahead, intent on meeting its intensive logging goals. By 1956, Deadman Creek had been logged. In the same decade, further conflict between the club and the agency ensued over other western forest areas, such as the Kern Plateau in the southern Sierra. These early Sierra-based conflicts set the stage for further conflict by the club over the passage of the Multiple Use–Sustained Yield Act in 1960 and support for the Wilderness Act in 1964. The end of cooperation set the stage for the Sierra Club's and other environmental groups' activism in the decades that followed.[47]

In addition to recreation of the type envisioned by the Sierra Club, others saw potential after the war for development of mechanical, lift-supported alpine skiing. American commercial downhill skiing began in the East, but developers were not far behind in promoting it in western states and California's Sierra. Noncommercial skiing had existed since the 1850s in the mining areas of the Sierra Nevada; what the Far West needed was a way to get people to pay for it. But because of weather and terrain, the quality of Sierran skiing was irresistible, and the area soon surpassed the East in number of commercial ski developments. The Sierra Nevada ski areas that surged ahead in both noncommercial and commercial growth stood along the Sierra crest connected by Highways 40 and 50. Cooperation between the Forest Service and private developers was important in stimulating ski activities before 1940 in areas such as Rainbow Tavern along Highway 40 and Soda Springs near Norden. By 1941 as many as 12,000 skiers, arriving either by car or from special ski trains provided by the Southern Pacific, used the areas on a busy weekend day.[48]

The national forests in the Sierra Nevada promoted the commercial development of skiing. Informal help to stimulate winter use began in the 1920s. The Tahoe National Forest established formal policy assisting skiers in 1932 and worked with the Sierra Club to create ski trails along the northern Sierra crest shortly before the war. The TNF developed a promotional folder advertising the location of all winter sports areas within its boundaries and distributed it to other areas in the state in the late 1930s. Regional Forester S. B. Show in 1941 accompanied an official from Forest Service headquarters on a two-week survey of some of the major winter sports areas in California. Show claimed that 600,000 snow sports fans used national forest land in California each winter. More than fifty snow sports areas served them, with the Donner Summit area leading the way in popularity.[49]

After World War II the Forest Service continued cooperating with private developers in promoting commercial skiing. Most of the ski resorts built in the Sierra Nevada tended to serve California skiers. The Tahoe Basin and Donner Summit resorts drew heavily from San Francisco. The resort at Mammoth drew primarily from Los Angeles. This pattern continued into the 1990s. In the northern Sierra, resorts at Donner Summit, around Tahoe City, at Big Bend on Highway 40, Squaw Valley, Alpine Meadows, Sugar Bowl, and Mount Lincoln all benefitted from land and resource sharing by the Forest Service. Slide Mountain Resort on Mount Rose farther to the east was also created with Forest Service help. To the south, the resort area at Mammoth received the same kind of assistance.[50] Without the direct aid of the Forest Service, skiing as a major industry with a worldwide reputation could not have developed in the Sierra.

Los Angeles's population growth and skiers' demands led to development of skiing at Angeles Crest–Lake Arrowhead.[51] But because it was inadequate to meet the demands of southern Californians, developers searched in the 1940s for different and more challenging terrain. One prime candidate was Mineral King Valley in the southern Sierra. It was located in a Forest Service game preserve, tucked into an area surrounded by Sequoia National Park. Development there required both federal agencies to cooperate because of the location of access roads. The Forest Service was fully committed to the project. Between 1949 and the early 1960s, it sought out developers who could come up with the capital needed for a major ski resort. Early in the 1960s, Walt Disney, who had helped develop Sugar Bowl and contributed to the planning for the 1960 Winter Olympics, began to study Mineral King as a potential investment. But unlike the other areas that had been developed with Forest Service assistance and with no objections from the public, Mineral King became the center of controversy. The Sierra Club led a successful battle that eventually forced the Forest Service and the Disney Corporation to back down. In 1978, Mineral King was added to Sequoia National Park.[52] This issue will be explored further in the next chapter.

The environmental effects of the skiing industry in the Sierra Nevada have yet to be told in detail. But important changes came with the new ski resorts. The most obvious was the seasonal population increase. In 1967–1968, the number of "recreational visitor days" for skiers on Forest Service land (Eldorado, Inyo, Sequoia, Sierra, Stanislaus, and Tahoe National Forests and the Lake Tahoe Basin Management Unit) was estimated to be 970,000. Most of these skiers went to the resorts in the Tahoe and Mammoth Lakes regions.[53]

All developments brought construction of facilities, roads, and parking lots to areas that had not been developed before. Trees and other foliage were cut to make or improve runs. Runoff from this construction was followed by increased sewage and garbage output from the facilities in season as well as in slack times. Cars were the major means of reaching ski destinations, the days of special ski trains being a relic of prewar times, and water and air pollution resulted. Ski resorts promoted urbanization. The two most notable examples of transformation and environmental change occurred around Lake Tahoe and at Mammoth. The pattern of seasonal closure and light populations in the winter months at Tahoe was replaced by heavy winter usage. Both areas saw a increases in permanent population that transformed them into significant urban centers.

Sierran National Parks and Postwar Expansion

From 1940 to the early 1960s, two directors, Newton Drury and Conrad Wirth, shaped the policies of the National Park Service. The men were very different in their approaches to park management, as were the conditions under which they served. Drury faced devastating funding problems during his tenure, and his philosophy of park management stressed preservation of resources over commercialization. Wirth was blessed with more economic support from Congress and stressed access and building of park infrastructure.[54]

Drury had to grapple with a reduction of personnel and funding that amounted to being placed on a starvation diet. As historian Lary Dilsaver has noted, the period from 1940 to 1956 can be referred to as the "poverty years" for the Park Service.[55] During the war, Sequoia lost half of its administrative, ranger, and maintenance staff. The two Sierran parks also faced the threat of inappropriate uses based on claimed wartime needs. Pressure from mining interests to mine tungsten at Yosemite succeeded to a limited degree. Grazers demanded access to pasturelands in the parks, but Drury succeeded in resisting their claims. On the positive side, the war years did allow Drury and his limited staff to do some planning for future improvements in the parks. It was hoped that after the war increased funding would allow for execution of these plans.[56]

It was after the war, however, that Drury's most serious problems arose. Instead of a return to normality and a reasonable level of funding, Congress continued to starve the Park Service—even as the American public, with new affluence and mobility, flocked to the nation's parks in numbers far greater than ever before. As the years passed, there was no relief.[57] Historian and writer Bernard DeVoto tried to reach the sleeping Congress about the impending collapse of the National Park system. In an article published in

Harper's magazine in October 1953, he described the decay and distressing condition of facilities in the major national parks. Maintaining that there were "true slum districts in Yellowstone, Rocky Mountain, Yosemite, Mesa Verde, [and] various other parks," he offered a radical solution intended to shock the public: "The national park system must be temporarily reduced to a size for which Congress is willing to pay. Let us, as a beginning, close Yellowstone, Yosemite, Rocky Mountain, and Grand Canyon National Parks—close and seal them, assign the Army to patrol them, and hold them secure till they can be reopened."[58]

When Conrad Wirth assumed leadership of the agency, he proposed an ambitious policy called "Mission 66." The Park Service sought outside political support for this proposed plan of construction of park facilities and roads. In 1956, Wirth announced the opening of his campaign with the assistance of the American Automobile Association. In a presentation to President Eisenhower and his cabinet, Wirth noted:

> The areas of the National Park System are among the most important vacation lands of the American people. Today, people flock to the parks in such numbers that it is increasingly difficult for them to get the benefits which parks ought to provide, or for us to preserve these benefits for Americans of tomorrow.
>
> This is why the Department of the Interior and the National Park Service have surveyed the parks and their problems, and propose to embark upon MISSION 66—a program designed to place the national parks in condition to serve America and Americans, today and in the future.[59]

He said that Mission 66 would serve the millions of auto visitors expected to be using the parks in 1966, the fiftieth anniversary of the founding of the Park Service.[60]

In that same presentation to the president and his cabinet, Wirth proposed a Park Service commitment to infrastructure development. The agency focused on roadbuilding and improvement, campground construction and expansion, and the construction of new public buildings, ranger stations, fire lookouts, and other repair and storage areas. He stressed the need to provide adequate employee housing as well.[61] Congress, with public and presidential prompting, responded by providing more than a billion dollars for the ten-year program.[62]

Mission 66 succeeded beyond Wirth's dreams. Congressional appropriations rose sharply. From 1955 to 1974, visitation to the national parks tripled, from about 14 million to 46 million. Park buildings, roads, and personnel expanded greatly to serve these new visitors. But with increasing access, new problems also arose. As more money was spent and more people came, the environmental impacts were significant and brought complaints from groups such as the Sierra Club and the Wilderness Society. The scientific community joined this expression of concern. Anxiety was especially strong regarding increased use of backcountry areas in the parks—more roads meant more hikers and greater impact on natural areas.[63]

In 1963 two scientific reports critical of the Park Service appeared, one by the National Academy of Sciences, the other by the renowned National Park Service scientist A. Starker Leopold. Both reports were commissioned by Secretary of the Interior Stewart Udall in response to growing criticism of the Park Service's wildlife management practices. Park historian Richard Sellars has described the reports as "threshold documents," the "first studies of their kind," bringing to the Park Service effective outside reviews of its natural-resource management policies. The Leopold Report was widely distributed, used Sierra Nevada parks as examples, and was quoted and commented upon by the Sierra Club in its *Bulletin*.[64] The report of the National Academy was virtually hidden from sight by a nervous Park Service and not widely distributed.[65] Nevertheless, the two reports began slowly to erode support for the agency's growth-oriented policies. That story will be told in more detail in the next chapter.

The environmental history of Sequoia, Kings Canyon, and Yosemite during the postwar expansion period parallels that of the park system as a whole. People flooded into the parks because prosperity and mobility allowed them to. They were also drawn by active promotion of park use by the California Automobile Association. The concessionaires—the Yosemite Park and Curry Company at Yosemite and the Sequoia and Kings Canyon National Parks Company at Sequoia and Kings Canyon—encouraged mass commercial activities and development that drew auto visitors. This explosion of use came despite inadequate funding from a stingy Congress in the forties and early fifties. Mission 66 promoted roadbuilding in all three parks, with expansion of campground space, parking, and most facilities following suit. What ensued as well was environmental degradation, whether from lack of effective management, from increased use, or from both. Park Service leaders and Sierran park superintendents alike showed little interest in scientific research to guide the decisions that were being made. Staff at both parks made some valiant attempts to cope with increasing backcountry use and wildlife problems, but they were hampered by inadequate funding.[66]

The postwar demand on the national parks of the Sierra Nevada was most critical at Yosemite. From December 1953 to the next Christmas, the visitation count was 1,008,031. By 1961 the visitor level on peak days stood at nearly 70,000. As Alfred Runte noted, had they been spread out evenly across all of the park's territory, there would have been fewer problems. But most visitors went to Yosemite Valley. On an average day 33,000 could visit the park, with 15,000 staying overnight. By 1970 the annual visitation reached 2,000,000—again, mostly in the Valley—topping all U.S. national parks.[67]

At the very beginning of this onslaught, in 1945, Director Drury tried strong action to relieve pressure on Yosemite Valley. He was committed to removing unnatural features there as well. Drury recommended that the Yosemite National Advisory Board and the concessionaire consider moving several of the government buildings out of the crowded and overused Valley. As part of this "decongestion" strategy he proposed removing Yosemite Lodge, as it only encouraged visitor concentration. He called for limiting some of the more commercial activities at Camp Curry that encouraged a resortlike atmosphere and further crowding. And he recommended shifting some camping and visitor-support services to Wawona and Big Meadow outside the Valley. His preservationist and crowding-control measures were ignored by the advisory board and actively resisted by the Yosemite Park and Curry Company through forceful political lobbying. Expansion of uses and commercialization continued without respite.[68]

A basic factor contributing to overcrowding in Yosemite was pressure from the now united Yosemite Park and Curry Company to expand use of the high country. Hoping to draw more visitors to the High Sierra camp at Merced Lake, for example, the concessionaire's manager, Hilmer Oehlmann, urged the park superintendent to adopt an aggressive bear-removal policy. Bears at the site were becoming troublesome, he asserted, and discouraged some visitors. While he indicated that he did not propose "indiscriminate" killing of the animals because of the criticism it might bring, he stressed that the comfort and safety of the human visitors came first. In 1956 and 1957 he contacted U.S. senator Thomas Kuchel of California, asking him to oppose the Wilderness Preservation Bill of 1956, one of the precursors of the 1964 law. With the "country growing at its present rate and with the need for optimum use of our material and recreational resources," Oehlmann argued, the "principle of 'the greater good,' . . . should govern here as elsewhere." Development, not protection of resources, prevailed in his thinking and actions.[69]

Economic pressure also came from numerous commercial interests on the eastern side of the range. Chambers of commerce and individual business owners from the east-side communities had an agenda for economic growth that required Park Service assistance. Their hopes were twofold. One consistent demand was to plow the Tioga Pass Road early in the spring to increase tourist visitation. A second, and far more environmentally significant request, was to improve, pave, and straighten the road. The decision to complete the paving and improvement of the Tioga Road came as part of Mission 66. Resistance from the Sierra Club was fierce but failed. In 1964 the road was completed. It did not have a single switchback, and transit of the area from Lee Vining to the other side could be speedily accomplished.[70]

For those accustomed to the convenience of the Tioga Road in its developed form, no sense of what was lost by its construction is possible. Crossing the park on this new road was no longer an adventure that took people into what all knew then as a wilderness. The paving of the twenty-one-mile stretch that ran below Tuolumne Meadows and alongside Tenaya Lake changed the nature of the experience that visitors have of this area of the park. Elizabeth S. O'Neill, who wrote lovingly of the area around Tuolumne Meadows, described the transformation:

> Now indeed all was different. Although commercial trucking was prohibited through the park, all manner of thirty-foot trailers and motor homes could easily get to the meadows. Many of these new visitors saw the mountains as a park in the conventional sense, a recreation area, rather than a wilderness. The meadows sprouted with such hitherto unfamiliar gear as volley and beach balls, baseball bats, air mattresses to float on the river and rafts to run it, and frisbees. The staccato barking of motor scooters as well as the blaring of radios, electric generators, and tapes often drowned out chattering chickarees and hammering woodpeckers.[71]

The environmental changes and damage were both immediate and long-term. The immediate impact came from the construction itself. The blasting of the granite escarpment near Tenaya Lake permanently altered the rock formation. Nearer Tuolumne Meadows, road crews shoveled sand out of the Tuolumne River bed for construction purposes, changing the stream's configuration and damaging the meadow alongside. The newly aligned and improved road had long-term impacts as well. Its paving created a dike effect at the meadow, preventing water seepage from the north-facing slopes from reaching the meadow on the other side. This dried the meadow and encouraged invasion of trees, which then had to be cut to retain views. Increased use of the meadow led to heightened use throughout the meadow area from expanded camping and day visits.[72]

Environmental impact from Mission 66 showed itself most obviously in the overuse at Yosemite Valley. The continued tendency to consider it as a resort, supplying more and more urban-style services, was the chief reason for this overcrowding. Rather than limiting the number of visitors and services as Drury and preservationists had suggested, the Yosemite Park and Curry Company constantly expanded tourist facilities and commercialized events. Daily high attendance took its toll in increased automobile exhaust, trampling of meadows, and damage to other vegetation. An example of the highly commercialized activities that drew such crowding was the YPCC-staged "Firefall." Originating as a tourist-pleasing event in the nineteenth century, it was reestablished early in the twentieth by David Curry. His corporate successor kept it going. The Firefall was achieved by pushing burning debris off Glacier Point. The cascading flaming material fell 1,500 feet to the ledges at the base of the cliff. Its occurrences during the summer drew crowds who jammed the Valley with cars and trampled the meadows and areas adjacent to Curry Village.[73]

Postwar development at Yosemite generally did not proceed with any guidance from scientific research, leaving issues regarding flora or fauna outside of park consideration. The control of insect infestation reveals this lack of concern and knowledge. Between 1949 and 1963, for example, Yosemite Park officials funded the application of DDT from the air and by hand to control various infestations of needle-miner moths in lodgepole pine formations at several higher-elevation locations in the park. Protest arose from Sierra Club and University of California scientists about this activity, but the park did not respond with scientific study. No serious investigation of the possible effects on fish or wildlife was attempted. Scientific research would have shown that the infestations were part of an apparently natural cycle that contributed to the death of mature trees, encouraging the growth of young and more vital replacement stands. It would take the Leopold Report and Rachel Carson's *Silent Spring*, both appearing at about the same time, to bring about recognition of the need to establish a science program for the park.[74]

One exception to the unwillingness of Yosemite Park officials to consider science for some guidance in these years occurred in 1954. Concern over the heavy use of the Mariposa and Tuolumne Groves of sequoia led the superintendent to assign a committee of experts to study the effects on the giant trees. The resulting "Yosemite Report" unequivocally stated that most development—roads, buildings, sewage and power lines, and compaction of soil through heavy use—harmed the root systems of the big trees. The committee gave no solution for the problem short of removal of all the development. The Park Service was not ready to face up to such a radical proposal just yet, however.[75]

Another of the park's growing problems arose in the backcountry or wilderness areas. These were being used with greater frequency, but with little serious commitment of resources to planning. Most attention to the parks came in the form of more ordinary tourist roads and services.[76] Elizabeth S. O'Neill, historian of Tuolumne Meadows, spoke of mounting problems in the Yosemite high country by the 1950s and 1960s: "Yet as hikers returned from far and wide, they began to report that the back country was strewn with garbage dumps. Here was a painful meeting of old freedom and new reality. In the past hikers and more especially packers (who could bring in more stuff) habitually tossed cans, bottles, and old shoes into a dump near camp, serene in the thought that nature would rust it all back into the earth. Now there were many more people with much more trash, and there was plastic and aluminum."[77]

Mission 66 accomplished its purpose at Yosemite. Campgrounds were upgraded, park roads modernized, the visitor center improved, and accommodations increased in capacity. Support for these changes and the Tioga Road improvement drew applause from both east-side and west-side commercial and political sources. And as could be expected, preservationists felt that park values had been sacrificed for economic gain. They charged that not only were the park's natural features being defaced and degraded, but overuse of the Valley campgrounds had turned them into rural slums. This expansion and increased automobile access eventually forced the National Park Service to reconsider the effects of all its growth-inducing policies. In 1968 the service began work on a new Yosemite plan. That same year, the Camp Curry Firefall was stopped because of its contribution to too many visitors, too many cars, and the piles of litter that came with them. In 1970, Yosemite Park officials for the first time closed portions of the park to automobiles, shunting visitors into trams. A new era of questioning growth—based on new attitudes shaped by the Leopold Report—had begun. This change will be considered more fully in the next chapter.[78]

Use of Sequoia and Kings Canyon also increased after World War II. Although these parks did not receive as many visitors as Yosemite, the impact was still significant. One indirect influence was the extremely heavy logging that occurred primarily on Forest Service lands around these southern Sierra Nevada parks. This massive cutting of mixed conifers left the parks as biological islands, isolated from the heavily logged lands adjacent to them. Tourist traffic increased steadily in the immediate postwar period on roads that had been created in the parks' early years. As the influx continued to grow, park officials expressed a need to replace and upgrade facilities and roads. Mission 66 funding led to upgrading of most facilities. As with Yosemite, strict fire suppression remained park dogma. Wildlife and backcountry policies were consistent with those at other national parks, although some staff members were questioning these policies by the 1950s. Only after 1963 and publication of the Leopold Report, however, did the changes begin that would eventually place science on a par with visitor use in the southern parks. Even at that, effective action on Leopold's ideas had to wait until after park planning in the 1970s.[79]

John White, a dedicated preservationist and first superintendent of the combined Sequoia and Kings Canyon parks, compared the rush of new visitors in the immediate postwar years to a surge of floodwaters. Perhaps they could be diverted, but not controlled. He and Wirth also had to face demands to develop dams that would have affected Sequoia and other national parks and monuments. The two valiantly beat back these proposals, which would have inundated some Sierran parklands.[80] But they could do little about the parks' inundation by the public.

Annual visitation at Sequoia and Kings Canyon from 1940 to 1955 rose from 483,743 to 1,074,134—a 120 percent increase. The embattled Superintendent White complained that as a result, campgrounds had become run-down and natural areas were inadequately protected from overuse. As with other parks in this period before Mission 66, funding could not keep up with the new public demands.[81]

Had some of these park users been dispersed away from congested areas through effective planning, things might have been different. But most of the new visitors simply crowded into the limited areas at Giant Forest that they could reach by car. From the mid-1940s to the early 1950s, the pre–Mission 66 years, concessionaire interests prevailed in their attempts to increase use of the Giant Forest. Halfhearted proposals by park officials to disperse visitors to Cedar Grove or to remove concession buildings and services at Giant Forest were ignored. Park superintendent Eivind Scoyen, who replaced John White in 1947, even reversed some of White's decisions. He ordered the widening of the Generals Highway near four sequoias called the "Four Guardians" rather than protecting the trees as White had done. Scoyen also favored allowing most concession facilities to remain at Giant Forest. Concessionaires remained in the congested area through effective resistance and lobbying. In 1952 a new contract issued to the two concession owners, George Mauger and Howard Hays, threw out any mention of removing or dispersing tourist facilities. Conditions in the Giant Forest area continued to worsen. The concessionaires at that point controlled more than 400 structures to serve visitors and employees. As park historians Lary Dilsaver and William Tweed noted, "on crowded weekends and holidays, long lines of cars waiting at Sequoia's only gas station in the Village spilled onto the road.

Driving to the peaceful and edifying serenity of Giant Forest often became a chaotic and frustrating experience. Within the Village, pedestrian traffic at the post office, village market, and gift shops became equally disturbing. To any park administrator these alarming conditions begged for solution. To park resource managers and visiting scientists, such conditions boded poorly for the future of the grove itself."[82]

Mission 66 came as a relief to park officials and staff faced with such overcrowding. But the ten-year plan showed little or no concern about effects of expansion of facilities on environmental conditions in the park. High on the list of proposals was development at Cedar Grove to alleviate the Giant Forest congestion. Rerouting of the Generals Highway, redesign of old park structures and building of new ones, and funding to study the removal of concession holdings in the Giant Forest were also on the agenda. Some significant improvements did occur. Smaller projects such as upgrading campgrounds, repairing or providing new comfort stations, and doing needed work on amphitheaters went forward. But ultimately, resistance from concessionaires, who did not want to invest anywhere but in the Giant Forest area, prevented new development at Cedar Grove. The Generals Highway was not relocated either, nor was a new visitors' center near the Village built—but in these cases the resistance came from a different source: scientists outside the Park Service who predicted that such development could only hasten the decline of the big trees.[83]

Scientific research by Emilio Meinecke in 1926 and again in the 1940s had shown the negative effects of human activity on the sequoia. Superintendent White was strongly influenced by these studies. But White left the Park Service, and his prescriptions to limit human activity in the Giant Forest went unheeded. The 1954 "Yosemite Report," mentioned earlier, influenced some Sequoia and Kings Canyon staff with its expert panel's conclusions about damage to sequoia root systems. Then again, in 1959, a new study by Richard Hartesveldt resulted in pressure on the park superintendent to limit expansion. Hartesveldt's research, based on studies of sequoia in Yosemite, Sequoia, and Kings Canyon, reaffirmed what the other scientists had shown. Park officials were compelled to return to the position that development at the Giant Forest area had to be stopped. This would obviously affect the Generals Highway realignment and the building of a new visitors' center at the grove.[84]

In response, a high-level meeting of Sequoia and Kings Canyon personnel and officials from both the regional and national offices was held in 1960 to consider the immediate issue of the visitors' center and, more important, the condition of the sequoia in the two parks. The resulting report cited the scientific work of Meinecke, the "Yosemite Report," and Hartesveldt's conclusions. The siting of the visitor center was complicated by the fact that important decisions about realignment of the Generals Highway had not been made. If the highway was going to be realigned, the center would have to be built at Giant Forest. If not, it could be built at the Lodgepole area. All paved walkways and parking areas affecting the sequoia were considered for removal. The larger issue of commercial activity at Giant Forest pointed inescapably to relocation of the concession services and buildings "ultimately" to Lodgepole in order to allow the Giant Forest to recover its "natural aspects." How to do this remained the $64 question. A staged or phased removal was proposed, with the gas station and post office to go first. Removing overnight accommodations and campgrounds required further study.[85]

But if the staff had reluctantly cobbled together a position on relocation, Director Wirth would not commit to a policy so obviously non–Mission 66. He ordered studies to consider bypass highway routes as means of avoiding the removal option. All bypass routes suggested in these studies required cutting of sequoia to complete them, and all necessitated vast expenditures of money to construct them. Delays followed. Eventually, another study in 1969 reaffirmed that, for both ecological and traffic reasons, road realignment was not the solution to overuse and damage to the big trees. Thus removal of commercial and Park Service structures remained the only way to stop any more damage.[86]

The science was unquestioned, but the politics of removal was a different reality. Between 1962 and 1971, when a new plan for the park was considered, the Park Service did remove most of its own structures from the Giant Forest area. It also deferred building the Giant Forest visitors' center and focused instead on building a new center at Lodgepole, where new services were being developed. One small campground at Giant Forest was closed, and over a period of a few years camp facilities elsewhere were developed so that the remaining three could be closed as well. But if the Park Service was taking action on its own facilities, the concessionaire Mauger (replaced eventually by the Fred Harvey Company) held on to its Giant Forest holdings with passion. The concessionaire was compelled to remove the gas station (relocated to Lodgepole) and the old post office. But in return it was allowed to build a gift shop where the post office had been, increase its "pillow count" for overnight visitors, and expand its lodge dining facilities. Not until after 1971 was relocation seriously considered. Thus, throughout this period, protection of resources was secondary to commercial activity.[87]

Probably the most egregious examples of the policies of these expansion years occurred in 1950 and again in 1967. Two sequoias were cut down—only the first and second in the history of the park to suffer this fate—because they were deemed to be a threat to concession housing and therefore potentially to visitors. The first was near the Giant Forest Lodge, the second near concession buildings at Camp Kaweah. One was noted to be increasingly leaning, and the other was developing cracks near its base. How long they would have remained standing can only be guessed. Rather than move buildings, the Park Service chose to cut down the trees.[88]

At Yosemite, except for the studies on damage to the sequoia, little evidence of concerns about scientific research and the effects of human use on backcountry resources was openly expressed before 1960. But in 1960, Sequoia and Kings Canyon staff issued a recommendation for managing the increasing use of the backcountry that anticipated the views of the Leopold Report. In 1960 the staff had prepared a report that members entitled "A Back Country Management Plan for Sequoia and Kings Canyon National Parks." It was not released, however, until 1963. The document's first part addressed the general issue of human use of wilderness. The staff chose park official Howard Stagner's definition of wilderness as a large undeveloped wild area beyond mechanical transportation where natural forces largely prevailed. Wilderness areas were "islands of nature" where scientists could study human impact on natural processes. The staff reported the obvious fact that increased use of such areas was a direct result of the prosperity and leisure time of the new society.[89]

The report further noted the need to address overuse in the backcountry wilderness of the two Sierran parks.[90] Because of increasing visitation, the back country was rapidly becoming what they called "front country." The problem was part of a larger phenomenon: "Visitor use of the wilderness areas of Sequoia and Kings Canyon National Parks has doubled since 1950. The current and anticipated population growth of the State of California over the next 20 years precludes any thought that there will be a slackening off in the numbers of persons who visit the National Park wilderness of the Sierra."[91]

Several effects of overuse were apparent. Deterioration of the backcountry meadows, a phenomenon noted as early as 1940, continued apace. Fish populations in the high-country lakes and streams were another problem. Habitat for fish was limited, and with increasing use arising from easy access from adjacent lands on the park boundaries, fish populations were threatened along virtually the "entire length of the fertile zone of fish habitat." Another growing concern was litter. In 1958 three tons of litter was removed from one popular backcountry area. In 1960 a concerted effort to bring out and carry away litter from the park areas produced twenty tons.[92]

The report's authors proposed various solutions to the increasing problems of overuse. The most obvious was to begin planning to establish a carrying capacity for the areas. Carrying capacity was an idea clearly respected in scientific circles, the report stated. Natural limits had to be understood and established. The major problem foreseen in adopting this course of action was that some members of the public might feel that their freedom to use wilderness was being taken away by a federal bureaucracy. The report concluded that while it regretted having to consider setting limits, there was no other way to protect the natural spaces from further degradation. Actions that had been permissible when visitation was low could no longer be allowed. "The Committee recognizes a major responsibility to preserve all possible freedom of wilderness," the report concluded, "but feels that the answer to complaints over present day restrictions is not 'bureaucracy,' but 'Born too late.'"[93]

Impact of the Leopold Report

From 1945 to 1971, conditions and actions in Sequoia and Kings Canyon generally reflected the pattern that prevailed at Yosemite and in the Park Service as a whole. Increased use was not matched by funding to protect the resources. Excited response to Mission 66 possibilities did not include scientific study of effects on the parks' resources.[94]

If any one event acted as a catalyst to get the Park Service to reconsider the growth-oriented actions stimulated by Mission 66, it was the 1963 publication of A. Starker Leopold's report on the conditions in the national parks. As an example of growing problems in the parks, Leopold referred to past and present in the Sierra Nevada:

When the forty-niners poured over the Sierra Nevada into California, those that kept diaries spoke almost to a man of the wide-spaced columns of mature trees that grew on the lower western slope in gigantic magnificence. The ground was a grass parkland, in springtime carpeted with wildflowers. Deer and bears were abundant. Today much of the west slope is a dog-hair thicket of young pines, white fir, incense cedar, and mature brush—a direct function of overprotection from natural ground fires. Within the four national parks—Lassen, Yosemite, Sequoia, and Kings Canyon—the thickets are even more impenetrable than elsewhere. Not only is this accumulation of fuel dangerous to the giant sequoias and other mature trees but the animal life is meager, wildflowers are sparse, and to some at least the vegetative tangle is depressing, not uplifting. Is it possible that the primitive open forest could be restored, at least on a local scale? And if so, how? We cannot offer an answer. But we are posing a question to which there should be an answer of immense concern to the National Park Service.[95]

The Leopold Report envisioned a forest primeval, free of the destructive influences that came with European American contact and use. The forests of the Sierra Nevada had of course been shaped to a significant degree already by native use long before modern settlement. The open forests, where they existed, were the result of both human and natural fire actions. Leopold and the other scientists who worked on the report intended to reestablish a pre–gold rush Sierra. They were aware that past actions including mining, grazing, logging, market hunting, and fire suppression had created national parks that were, as they put it, "artifacts, pure and simple."[96]

The Leopold Report called for changes in park wildlife-management policies. This appeal was not new—after all, Grinnell and Storer and George Wright had said similar things earlier. But Leopold's words came forth in more receptive times. The report asked the agency to recognize the "enormous complexity of ecological communities" in park areas. These communities could be restored to a healthy condition, perhaps, through scientifically based wildlife management. To suggest what could be done to create such a policy, the report used examples taken from several national park areas, including those in the Sierra.[97] Two examples illustrate the new ideas Leopold's committee introduced to park officials. They also tell us something about the condition of the Sierran parks' backcountry and their wild inhabitants at the time, continuing the baselines revealed by earlier studies.

One example cited by the Leopold group was the failure of the Park Service to restore bighorn sheep populations on the eastern side of the range on the borders of Sequoia and Kings Canyon National Parks. The animals had been protected from hunting for nearly a half century, yet their numbers remained small, a little under four hundred. The question was, why? Leopold said that the damaged condition of their range, a product of early historic overgrazing of the high country, was obviously partly to blame. This snapshot of the high country attests to the long-term effects of unregulated sheep grazing from the previous century. But the scientists of the advisory board on wildlife saw other problems as well. Because the range of the bighorn included U.S. Forest Service as well as National Park Service lands, competition from domestic livestock as well as mule deer meant that the bighorns' range access remained less than optimum—unless, that is, the two often competing agencies could be induced to change their ways. Scientific study on the carrying capacity of bighorn habitat was needed. Establishment of common goals, requiring interagency cooperation on bighorn restoration, was necessary. Control of grazing and reduction of the deer population were possibilities. The Leopold Report stated that if such measures could be refined by cooperative research and applied in this one area, they might then be extended to Yosemite and Lassen National Parks, where similar problems existed.[98]

Another example taken from the Sierra involved not too few of a species, but the opposite. The committee report noted that in some instances, wildlife such as elk in Yellowstone and deer in some areas at Sequoia were destroying natural rangelands by overgrazing. So what should be done? Leopold again suggested that scientific study on the carrying capacity of Sierran and other ranges in the park system was needed. When Park Service scientists determined that too many deer were using a given area, then the service must use its own personnel to reduce their numbers by hunting. The result would be a more stable and healthy deer population and improvement in the ranges they used.[99]

Leopold mentioned in the report that Park Service policies in the past had encouraged predator reduction. Naturalist Verna Johnston has shown the direct connection between killing of grizzly bears, mountain lions, and coyotes and the problem of overpopulation of deer in the Sierra. Grinnell and Storer had also written of the relationship among these animals. By 1930, Johnston said, population growth in the summer months was only partially offset by starvation in the winter. Obviously, the fact that there were too many deer for the available range was contributing to the problem Leopold described. While it would be impossible to reintroduce grizzly, predator policies needed reexamination. New approaches that allowed coyotes to increase and reduce weakened winter deer numbers, or that encouraged mountain lion predation of healthy deer at other times, could aid in more natural population controls.[100]

Leopold's ideas did not bring immediate results, but within a decade they would stimulate changes in Park Service thinking and planning. These changes will be considered in more detail in the next chapter.

Lake Tahoe: Postwar Expansion

Following 1945, growth and urbanization occurred at such a rapid rate in the Tahoe Basin that, according to Douglas Strong, those experiencing it had no idea of what it would mean in their lives. Old patterns of locally oriented agriculture and summer recreation services were swept away in a boom of development. This population and construction growth overwhelmed all attempts to deal with its impact on Lake Tahoe and the adjoining areas. Not until the late 1950s would anyone start to ask hard questions about the problems generated by mushrooming growth. And effective regional action would not begin until the 1960s.[101]

The onslaught of new visitors to the lake basin in the postwar years was traceable to three causes. The most basic of these was development of reliable transportation. Before the war, roads closed with the onset of heavy snow. In the 1940s, business leaders in the basin, concerned by its isolation and near abandonment during the war, developed winter programs to draw in more tourists. Local booster agencies and governments cooperated in staging these winter events. They also worked to improve automobile access. The Placerville to Lake Tahoe Resort Owners Association exerted political pressure to make Highway 50 an all-weather road to the south shore of Tahoe (although the route, as many who have faced snow closures and mudslides on it could attest, may not have earned that title of "all-weather" even yet). Highway 89 was paved to connect Truckee on Highway 40 to Tahoe City. By 1960, Interstate 80 replaced the old Highway 40 that had used portions of the Donner Summit route. In 1946, the Tahoe Sky Harbor Airport opened to large airplanes. Access transformed the Tahoe Basin and adjoining areas.[102]

A second major factor affecting Tahoe growth was the metamorphosis of skiing from a noncommercial sport to a mechanized, commercially driven industry. As already noted, minor ski developments and private sports-club activities had been established along Highways 40 and 50 before the war. But with transportation improvements, these small-scale endeavors were transformed into an industry of significant proportions. By the 1950s, some nineteen resorts had been developed in or around the area. The basin had begun to deserve a reputation as a major ski destination. In the 1950s, two promoters, Wayne Poulson and Alex Cushing, transformed Squaw Valley from an enclave of dairying in the little valley and sheepherding in the meadows above into a small ski resort. In 1955 they were awarded the bid by the International Olympic Committee to develop facilities for the 1960 Winter Olympics. As a result, skiing in the area took a quantum leap forward. The immediate years after the Olympic Games saw development of skiing, urban services, winter traffic jams, and housing on both shores of Tahoe.[103]

The third cause of Tahoe Basin growth began with the relegalization of gambling in Nevada in 1931. Limited development followed in the 1930s. After the war, investment in casinos and hotels skyrocketed. By the 1950s, gambling was big business on the north shore, the south shore, and at the California-Nevada border. With it came all sorts of commercialized businesses to serve those visiting the casinos or traveling through the basin. Permanent housing and services along the lake's shores also grew, especially on the California side, for casino employees and others who chose now to live there year-round.[104]

Development profoundly changed Tahoe. Population swelled in the California counties and the various towns in the basin. El Dorado County alone, based on its 1959 general plan, projected a mix of permanent and visiting residents of 200,000 by 1984. Urban woes such as increasing crime and school crowding came with the new people. Uniform building codes did not exist in the basin's communities. Building lots were often created through inconsistent zoning processes with no regard to the population density that might result. Septic tanks were installed on the same principle, and soon sewage became both a human and a lake-purity problem.[105]

The environmental effects on Lake Tahoe of this growth manifested themselves in many ways. The new community of Incline Village, built on about 9,000 acres by a large commercial developer, brought permanent housing, condominiums, winter rentals, and service businesses, as well as skiing. Another new community on the south end of the lake was called Tahoe Keys. Some 5 million cubic yards of the marshland at the lake's edge was dredged and shaped into a marina resort for summer usage, with storage for some 2,000 boats in the winter. Tahoe Keys consisted of several 150-foot-wide lagoons, with around 2,000 luxury homesites proposed on the reclaimed marshland. It did not take long for this disturbed area to contribute to a new growth of algae. It apparently also contributed to the sprouting of water-rooted weeds. According to Douglas Strong, by building Tahoe Keys, the developer "destroyed a significant part of the largest marsh habitat in the basin, a natural filtering system for sediments and nutrients carried into the lake."[106]

A primarily local approach to zoning caused larger problems. Local interests and groups shaped each community in a different manner. They had one thing in common, though: Whenever they flushed their toilets or in other ways provided nutrients from human activities such as earth grading, the product of their activity stayed within the basin. Eventually much of it found its way to the lake. And with Tahoe's limited ability to clear itself by natural processes because of its depth and water-circulation patterns, the result was increasing loss of water clarity and purity.[107]

Both Nevada and California showed some awareness of the problem as early as 1949, but bi-state cooperation did not result. Nothing was done. Some communities such as Tahoe City, and north and south Tahoe, treated their sewage, but spreading of the effluent was still carried out in the basin. The issue changed in scope as some observers became concerned not only about the health effects of this haphazard sewage control, but also about its environmental effects on Lake Tahoe. In the middle 1960s, recognition that the problem had to be solved regionally stimulated efforts that finally addressed it on a basinwide scale.[108] Douglas Strong effectively summarizes the environmental effects of postwar development on the basin: "By the 1960s the Tahoe Basin was affected by runaway growth. The scattered cabins and summer resorts of the early decades of the century had given way to high-rise casino-hotels, year-round tourism, and urban sprawl in certain parts of the basin."[109] The regional responses to Tahoe's problems will be discussed in the following chapter.

The Sierra Nevada and Postwar Water Development

Water is modern California's and Nevada's greatest need and problem. Samuel Dana and Myron Krueger's 1958 study *California Lands* asserted what everyone at that time already knew about California water. Roughly 70 percent of the state's stream flows were north of Sacramento, while most potential users, whether agricultural or urban, lived south of that line. The Sierra Nevada and its streams became the focus of postwar water development.[110] From an economic standpoint, the exploitation of streams and rivers in the Sierra Nevada, either in its foothills or higher in the mountains, was the engine of urban and agricultural growth in the state after 1945.[111]

On the Nevada side of the range, Carson City, Carson Valley, and Reno depend on water from Lake Tahoe, the Truckee River, and the Carson and Walker Rivers. These are part of the Lahontan hydrologic system, named after a Pleistocene lake that left its mark in old lake terraces. Battles over use of the Tahoe and the Truckee began at the turn of the twentieth century and accelerated after World War II as gambling stimulated urban growth.[112]

The population of urban California and northern Nevada burgeoned after the war. Sierran water made it possible. The Sierra Nevada had already been put to use to supply water for two of California's largest cities. San Francisco relied on Hetch Hetchy, and Los Angeles obtained nearly 80 percent of its water from the Owens Valley and the Mono Basin. Los Angeles, even though it had already tapped the Colorado River to supplement its eastern Sierra water, was still thirsty. To the north, population growth throughout the Bay Area, in Sacramento, and in the Tahoe Basin and Reno-Sparks led to pressure for further Sierran water development. Besides supplying the cities of California and Nevada, Sierra Nevada water was demanded by Central Valley corporate farmers for irrigation. The watersheds of the Sierra Nevada were expected to do their part in promoting growth, just as its forests and national parks were meeting other postwar needs.[113]

The economic collapse of the depression forced California to give up on developing a state-controlled Central Valley plan. The Roosevelt administration succeeded in taking it over and set the U.S. Army Corps of Engineers to work building a complex hydraulic system. On its completion, the Bureau of Reclamation assumed the regulation of a significant portion of northern California's flow of stream water. Included were the Sacramento (much of it outside the Sierra), American, Stanislaus, and San Joaquin Rivers as part of the now federalized Central Valley Project. Initiated in the 1930s, the project was mostly constructed and completed after the war. By the 1950s, the Shasta, Keswick, Folsom, and Friant Dams had been built and a complex system of canals distributed more than 3 million acre-feet of water to California farmers and other state interests. These dams also generated electricity and provided recreation for thousands of users.[114]

After the depression and the war, California returned to its hope to build its own water project: there were still water shortages in parts of the Central Valley, and increasing urban demands in southern California. But by the time the state could afford to begin planning for such a huge project, it had lost control over the Sacramento and several Sierran rivers to the federal government. Many of the valley's agribusiness interests, aware that the federal project had set a 160-acre limit on subsidized water use, longed for a less restrictive water project run by the state. The recovery of the state's prosperity after the war opened the way for a state-controlled system. The focus of the state's water planners was on the Feather River. Flooding in nearby areas the 1950s added to the justification for a dam on the river in the eyes of many voters. Because of the high cost of the project, it was planned not only that Central Valley farmers would use the water, but that much of it could be shipped south over the Tehachapi Range into the Los Angeles basin. Governor Edmund "Pat" Brown secured passage of the legislation to authorize funding in 1959. By 1962, Sierra Nevada water began flowing south. Through technological and political legerdemain, California got the water to flow uphill over the mountains in 1971.[115]

California and federal projects of the postwar years relied on dams constructed at the extreme western fringe of the Sierra Nevada. Many big rivers were available, filled by wet Pacific Ocean storms—when it did rain in "Mediterranean" California, that is. Water needs in the Tahoe Basin were a variation on the California theme, but on the more arid eastern side and with fewer and smaller rivers to give up their bounty to human users. The need for water to meet urban growth in the basin and nearby Reno exceeded supply during the postwar boom. Nevada irrigation interests also demanded a share. As early as the 1930s, Lake Tahoe property owners and businesses were contesting with irrigators and nearby power suppliers over Tahoe and Truckee River water. The dispute was complicated because two states, several county governments on both sides of the state boundaries, and several federal agencies had conflicting jurisdictions. In 1934 a temporary solution, called the "Truckee River Agreement," was cobbled together to try to resolve the issues. It prohibited tunneling into Tahoe or cutting its rim as some Nevada interests had proposed. Minimum and maximum lake levels were established. A reservoir was to be built by federal water agencies at the former townsite of Boca on the Little Truckee River to store water for Nevada use. After the war, another dam was built on Prosser Creek near the town of Truckee. Shortly after this, Sierra Pacific Power and Light was allowed to build a small dam for power generation nearby.[116]

Accelerated postwar growth in the basin and in Nevada soon made the earlier compromises unworkable. Local, county, state, and national interests began to work at cross purposes. California and Nevada came to realize that, to achieve their different goals, they would have to cooperate and compromise. The other option was a lengthy court battle that promised to be expensive and unpredictable. Both states also realized that similar struggles over the other eastern Sierra rivers, the Carson and Walker, were just as problematic. In 1955 the two states created the California-Nevada Interstate Compact Commission. It took until 1963 for that group to formulate a report that apportioned water in the basin between the states. Not until 1971 did both state legislatures ratify the agreement. After implementation, Pyramid Lake levels continued to decline, seriously threatening the economic survival of the Paiute who were dependent on it. The water diversions also nearly drove the already imperiled Lahontan cutthroat trout to the verge of extinction.[117]

In California, demand for Sierra Nevada water after 1945 was strong, and political discourse was rancorous. This was true on both sides of the range, and if a consistent trans-Sierran "villain" could be named in these postwar water battles, it would have to be Los Angeles. The long reach of the southern metropolis had already fastened on the Owens Valley early in the twentieth century, and by the 1930s it had projected its power into the Mono drainage to the north. In addition, Los Angeles laid claims to water in the drainage of the Kings River. There the issue became very complicated, with the Bureau of Reclamation, National Park Service, PG&E, local irrigation interests, and Los Angeles vying for the river's water. The role of the thirsty and never-satisfied city needs to be examined.

In the 1930s, as part of an effort to gain more water, the Los Angeles Department of Water and Power proposed to extend its Owens Valley aqueduct northward into the Mono drainage. The project was completed in

1940. Water from this new source helped fuel the suburban housing growth of the San Fernando Valley and lessened the city's need to rely on expensive Colorado River water. The effect on Mono Lake, a 500,000-year-old saline sink that collected the water of several small creeks in the drainage, was immediate. The lake level declined at the rate of one foot per year until 1970, when a second aqueduct was completed by the city to capture more water in the area. The lake then accelerated its decline to one and a half feet annually. The environmental effects were catastrophic for the lake, especially for the gulls and other migratory birds that relied on its brine shrimp and flies for food. Negit Island in the lake became connected to the shoreline, opening up a land bridge that allowed coyotes to raid the nests of the gulls. Lowering water also exposed and weakened the tufa columns in the lake. In 1978, a small environmental group, calling itself the Mono Lake Committee, began a challenge to the city that would shape environmental law and eventually bring some added water to the lake.[118]

On the western side of the range, although the power of Los Angeles was feared, its influence was not as overwhelming as in the Mono-Owens drainage. The struggle to gain access to water from the tributaries of the Kings River was more even. At various times from 1940 to 1963, a weird coalition of interests beat back and eventually denied any claim by Los Angeles to water from the Kings. The victorious strange bedfellows of this union included the National Park Service, Pacific Gas and Electric, Fresno city functionaries, powerful San Joaquin Valley irrigation interests, state Water Resources Control Board representatives, and Sierra Club activists. Through various compromises among coalition members, three dams were built—Pine Flat, Courtwright, and Wishon—that essentially gave local interests control of the water outside of any sensitive areas desired by Kings Canyon National Park. In return, portions of the scenic Cedar Grove and Tehipite Valley areas and their watersheds were added into Kings Canyon National Park.[119]

In assessing the environmental impact of this water development in the Sierra Nevada, a study by William Stewart for the Sierra Nevada Ecosystem Project is useful. He points out that by the 1990s, there were some 490 dams in the Sierra Nevada large enough to be monitored by the California Department of Water Resources. These reservoirs fall into two major categories. The first are also the oldest—upstream dams that were built by municipalities and power companies from the 1920s to 1960s. The second are very large dams built in sites below the 3,000-foot elevation. They were constructed after 1950 and were funded by federal, state, or urban governments and agencies. Both types of dam sites provided a mixture of uses: recreation, power generation, flood control, or for agricultural or urban drinking water.[120]

The ecological effects of both types of reservoirs are enormous. As Stewart writes: "The main ecological impacts of foothill reservoirs within the region are that they stop nearly all salmon migration upstream, flood large areas of what was foothill riparian vegetation, and break the continuity of terrestrial riparian vegetation and habitats. Upstream reservoirs are more numerous, smaller, and not on every tributary. Overall, they withhold a much smaller fraction of the total runoff than the foothill reservoirs. Their ecological impacts within the region show up both in the reduced and seasonally altered downstream flows, and in site specific flooding of upstream areas." He also notes about the uphill reservoirs: "In addition to flooding areas behind the dams, impeding fish and amphibian movement up the water course, they also drastically modify in-stream flows within the Sierra Nevada itself."[121]

The Second Gold Rush in the Sierra, 1945–1960s

Public land-use agencies in the postwar era labored to supply resources and services: timber for houses, recreation for an affluent public, and water for farmers and urban consumers. The actions of the Forest Service, National Park Service, California State Department of Water Resources, and various metropolitan water agencies were taken with little regard to their environmental effects upon the Sierra Nevada.

With historical perspective, this postwar period in the Sierra Nevada's environmental history assumes clear form. It was through government action that a second gold rush of development after 1945 occurred. The cutting of Sierran forests and the application of intensive management, Mission 66, ski-resort promotion, and development of huge water systems using Sierran water were the work of public agencies acting in their definition of the public interest. In all instances, private profit-making was joined with these public actions in altering the Sierra Nevada's environment. But at the same time, the public began to show concern over these policies and a stirring of revolt arose. As historian Paul Hirt observes in his study of the Forest Service in the postwar period:

Conservation organizations that had been allies of the Forest Service before World War Two grew increasingly alarmed over the changes in national forest management after the war. Some of them, like the American Forestry Association, took the same path as the Forest Service in promoting maximum timber production, but most others became critics decrying the effects of intensive logging on other resources and forest values. These groups would become the Forest Service's alter ego. An outdoor recreation boom after 1945 led to spectacular growth in the memberships of the National Wildlife Federation, Sierra Club, Wilderness Society, Federation of Western Outdoor Clubs, and others. The consequent increase in public visibility and financial resources of these groups enhanced their effectiveness in lobbying for greater attention from the federal government for recreation and wildlife habitat protection.[122]

The National Park Service was also strongly committed to expanding tourist-related activities and services in the postwar years. Mission 66, growing out of the development values of Stephen Mather and Horace Albright, was effectively implemented by Conrad Wirth. The agency's dual mission preserving park resources and at the same time making them accessible to the public had almost always leaned toward the use side. Faced with challenges to its policies after the war, the Park Service, like the Forest Service, resisted change. As Richard Sellars has noted, "Before passage of the Wilderness Act in 1964, the Park Service was the only federal agency with a mandate specifically encouraging preservation of natural conditions on public lands; thus it might have been expected to assume a leadership role in the emerging environmental movement. Instead, entangled in its own history and the momentum of its tourism and park development, the Service had to be awakened to ecological management principles by outside critics."[123]

Conflict over land-use policies has always been a part of the Sierra's environmental history. In the period following 1945, agency activity focused on promoting economic growth and use. And many in the public were pleased. Staff resources in the national forests and parks were committed to silviculture, logging, and public access and comfort. But as we have seen, conservation groups, natural-resource scientists, and wildlife biologists were joined by many in the general public in beginning to question the growth-oriented activities of these agencies. There was growing resentment at forest policies that promised stewardship and multiple uses while delivering more cut trees and narrowing buffers between logged land and campgrounds. The Sierra Club protested the cutting of remarkable and irreplaceable east-side groves such as Deadman Creek. Scientists, most notably in the Leopold Report, criticized the lack of commitment by Park Service officials to scientific research in their natural holdings. There was anger at the cutting of sequoia trees by the Park Service in order to protect the buildings of Sequoia National Park concessionaires. There was resentment at the transformation of

Tenaya Lake and Tuolumne Meadows from wilderness areas into easy-access play fields through the straightening of Tioga Road. This protest in the growth years eventually coalesced into a reawakened conservationism and a potent environmental movement in the 1960s and 1970s.

The Bear Pit on "Bear Hill," Giant Forest, Sequoia National Park, in the 1940s. Exhibitions like this were common throughout Sierra parks until conservation efforts discouraged them. Courtesy National Park Service Archives of Sequoia and Kings Canyon National Parks

The Stoneman House, a first-class hotel built in Yosemite Valley with state funding in 1885–86 as part of an early effort to respond to growing tourism in the area. Courtesy Yosemite National Park Research Library

Storekeeper and dairyman John Degnan's dairy herd grazing in Yosemite Valley. Courtesy Yosemite National Park Research Library

U.S. Cavalry troops guarding Yosemite, 1909. Courtesy Yosemite National Park Research Library

John Muir, whose conservation efforts helped to preserve some of the scenic wonders of the Sierra Nevada. Courtesy Library of Congress

Although this photo of the Webber Lake Resort was taken in the 1930s, the resort was originally developed in the 1860s to serve visitors on their way to the Comstock. Similar resorts existed at Independence and Donner Lakes before 1900. Courtesy Searls Historical Library, Nevada City, CA

Steamer at Lake Tahoe. By the 1880s, tourism had exceeded lumber as the most important industry in the area. Courtesy Searls Historical Library, Nevada City, CA

Dam at the outlet of Lake Tahoe into the Truckee River, 1899. Regulating the flow of water allowed industries to develop on the Truckee, including hydroelectric production and a pulp mill downstream at Floriston. Courtesy Bancroft Library, University of California, Berkeley

Narrow-gauge railroad owned by the Lake Tahoe Railway and Transportation Company passing a fly fisherman along the Truckee River below Lake Tahoe. The railway was originally built for logging purposes along the Truckee River, but by the 1880s it carried tourists to visit the lake, connecting the town of Truckee and the Central Pacific Railroad to the Tahoe Basin. Courtesy Library of Congress

Theodore Roosevelt and John Muir, along with other notables, discuss Yosemite and the Mariposa Big Trees, 1903. Courtesy Yosemite National Park Research Library

Women hikers from a Sierra Club group explore the High Sierra ca. 1895 to 1910. Courtesy Bancroft Library, University of California, Berkeley

John Muir's last Sierra Club outing, 1912. Courtesy Bancroft Library, University of California, Berkeley

Railroad logging in the northeastern Sierra Nevada. Courtesy Library of Congress

Conflicting logging styles in the Sierra. Forest Service logging in the foreground reflects cutting practices during the custodial period. In the distance, the mountainside has been denuded by the Yosemite Lumber Company. Courtesy Yosemite National Park Research Library

The Yosemite Lumber Company logging on a 50-percent grade. This is an example of railroad logging practices. Photo courtesy Yosemite National Park Research Library

Abandoned construction project of the Mount Whitney Power Company. Trees were cut and a foundation was built, but the work was then abandoned. The area later became part of Sequoia National Park. Courtesy National Park Service Archives of Sequoia and Kings Canyon National Parks

Stand of mature Sierra pines. This photo was part of the campaign to promote passage of the Clarke-McNary Act of 1924. Courtesy Library of Congress

A forest fire in the Truckee River area, 1899. The openness of the forest at that time kept fires low, causing less damage to mature trees and keeping the forests more open. Reproduced by permission of The Huntington Library, San Marino, CA

Turkey Hill Power House under construction in El Dorado County, 1900. Courtesy Bancroft Library, University of California, Berkeley

Senator Charles McNary visits the Sierra Nevada pine region to promote cooperative fire suppression, 1923. Courtesy Library of Congress

The Hetch Hetchy Valley before construction of the dam. Courtesy Yosemite National Park Research Library

COMMENTS OF THE UNITED STATES PRESS
ON THE
INVASION OF THE YOSEMITE NATIONAL PARK
AS PROPOSED IN THE HETCH-HETCHY BILL, WHICH HAS PASSED THE HOUSE OF REPRESENTATIVES AND COMES BEFORE THE SENATE DECEMBER 1st TO 6th.

These Editorial Comments Are Entirely Spontaneous Expressions of National Opinion on a Thoroughly Dishonest Bill. They Are Inspired Also by a Strong and Almost Universal Sentiment as to the Danger of Invading Our National Parks.

WAPAMA FALLS, ONE OF THE HETCH-HETCHY CASCADES

Bulletin of the National Committee for the Preservation of the Yosemite National Park, part of the campaign to oppose damming of the Hetch Hetchy Valley. Courtesy Yosemite National Park Research Library

Construction of the O'Shaughnessy Dam, Hetch Hetchy Valley. Courtesy Yosemite National Park Research Library

Unregulated automobile camping in Yosemite Valley. Courtesy Yosemite National Park Research Library

Pack team of nearly twenty horses supporting a Sierra Club outing at Hutchinson Meadow, 1938. Courtesy Bancroft Library, University of California, Berkeley

(*opposite*) Hetch Hetchy Dam and tower, looking upstream. Courtesy California Historical Society, FN-13967

Hairpin curves on the Tioga Road before improvements, 1920s. Courtesy Yosemite National Park Research Library

Tenaya Lake as "wilderness" before construction of the new Tioga Road. Courtesy Yosemite National Park Research Library

Photograph of Owens Lake, the Alabama Hills, and Mount Whitney, taken by writer Mary Austin, defender of the valley. The Los Angeles Aqueduct would eventually dry up the lake, transforming the lakebed into a dust bowl. Reproduced by permission of The Huntington Library, San Marino, CA

A postcard view of the Los Angeles Aqueduct shortly after its completion. The card was sent to Mary Austin. The postcard note says, "This is a fairly good symbol of the valley." Reproduced by permission of The Huntington Library, San Marino, CA

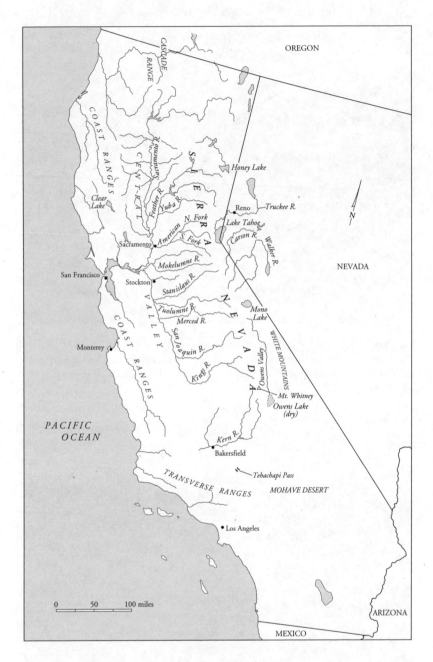

Map of River and Lake Systems of the Sierra Nevada

Mount Whitney Fish Hatchery, Independence, Inyo County. Courtesy California History Room, California State Library, Sacramento

Mineral King. This photo was part of the Sierra Club campaign to halt Disney Corporation's proposed development of the area into a major ski resort. Courtesy National Park Service Archives of Sequoia and Kings Canyon National Parks

Giant Forest/Grant Grove after World War II. Such overcrowding prompted Park Service calls for "Mission 66." Courtesy National Park Service Archives of Sequoia and Kings Canyon National Parks

The Firefall staged by the Yosemite Park and Curry Company was one of the highly commer-cialized activities in the park that contributed to traffic jams and air pollution. Courtesy Yosemite National Park Research Library

Prescribed burning
in Yosemite Valley.
Courtesy Yosemite
National Park
Research Library

MAJESTY AND TRAGEDY:

THE
SIERRA
IN
PERIL

We are wont to whittle away at our giants. I fear the Sierra awaits a sim

"The Sierra in Peril,"
June 9, 1991, evid-
ence of growing
public awareness of
the environmental
crisis in the Sierra
Nevada. Reporter
Tom Knudson and
the *Sacramento Bee*
received a Pulitzer
Prize for the series.
Photo by *Bee* staff
photographer Jay
Mather. Courtesy
Sacramento Bee

The disastrous Yosemite flood of 1997 forced the closing of the park for several months. The monetary effect of the flood was estimated by park officials to be nearly $180 million. Widespread damage—and its perceived causes—prompted a new plan for the use and administration of Yosemite Valley. Courtesy Yosemite National Park Research Library

City street in Truckee. Photo by the author

The "new" dam at the outlet to the Truckee River at Tahoe. Water levels at Tahoe continue to play a role in the debate over growth in the Tahoe Basin. Photo by the author

The view from Martis Valley Rock Shelter. Photo by the author.

Expanding uses of Lake Tahoe. Even dogs have their own facilities. Photo by the author

Continuing development in Squaw Valley, one of the expanding ski developments in the Sierra. Photo by the author

6: The Environmental Challenge, 1960–1999

Environmental activism helped reshape postwar American politics and culture. It was born along with other protest and liberation movements, and shared their spirit. The environmental impulse, as historian Samuel Hays has called it, cannot be divorced from this historical context.[1]

The complex social and political responses to environmental concerns after 1960 had their own dynamic. They took a distinct turn away from earlier conservation activities. Older ideals of resource husbanding and saving beautiful areas for public recreation were supplanted in the decades from 1960 to the 1980s by a broader environmental perspective.[2]

As an example of how this new viewpoint would infuse many aspects of the public's outlook, consider a dissenting opinion statement from U.S. Supreme Court justice William O. Douglas about what to do with the Mineral King Valley in the southern Sierra Nevada in 1972:

> I do not know Mineral King. I have never seen it or traveled it, though I have seen articles describing its proposed "development." . . . The Sierra Club in its complaint alleges that "One of the principal purposes of the Sierra Club is to protect and conserve the national resources of the Sierra Nevada Mountains." The District Court held that this uncontested allegation made the Sierra Club "sufficiently aggrieved" to have "standing" to sue on behalf of Mineral King.
>
> Mineral King is doubtless like other wonders of the Sierra Nevada such as Tuolumne Meadows and the John Muir Trail. Those who hike it, fish it, camp in it, or frequent it, or visit it merely to sit in solitude and wonderment are legitimate spokesmen for it, whether they may be few or many. Those who have that intimate relation with the inanimate object to be injured, polluted, or otherwise despoiled are its legitimate spokesmen. . . .
>
> The voice of the inanimate object, therefore, should not be stilled. That does not mean that the judiciary takes over the managerial functions from the federal agency. It merely means that before these priceless bits of Americana (such as a valley, an alpine meadow, a river, or a lake) are forever lost or are so transformed as to be reduced to the

eventual rubble of our urban environment, the voice of the existing beneficiaries of these environmental wonders should be heard.[3]

As historian Michael Cohen has noted, the Sierra Club had every reason to believe that its position as a defender of Mineral King and representative of environmentalists in general would have great power in the federal courts: "The courts were anxious to make environmental law, and over the years the Club would win three-fourths of its cases because the federal agencies had not complied with legal requirements or were asleep. Court cases offered good chances for publicity. A lawsuit gave citizen groups parity with developers or federal agencies."[4]

No brief introduction can capture the full flavor or analyze the complexities of the environmental movement. But a national context is needed to understand the relationship of the Sierra Nevada to the changes that unfolded in these tumultuous years. Four elements will be mentioned here.

First came heightened public awareness of a growing environmental crisis. Economic growth produced air and water pollution. Scientist-activist Rachel Carson, in her powerful book *Silent Spring,* brought home to the public an understanding of their vulnerability in the new petrochemical age. Television news brought troubling visions to millions of viewers: a massive oil spill off the coast of Santa Barbara, the Cuyahoga River near Cleveland burning, the announcement of the imminent death of Lake Erie from industrial pollution. The cumulative effects of these and other events revealed to a disturbed citizenry the threats created by their industrial way of life and were a powerful force in changing perspectives.[5]

Next came heightened activism on the part of the Sierra Club, Wilderness Society, and Audubon Society. They modified their older conservation ethic to stay in tune with new public expectations. They became more militant, recruited widely for new members, and turned often to litigation to accomplish their goals after 1970, when the organizing of the first Earth Day brought environmental concerns to a broad and diverse public audience. As a result of this new militancy, they lobbied a more receptive Congress for legislation. New groups emerged to organize even more-militant campaigns: the Environmental Defense Fund, the Natural Resources Defense Council, Friends of the Earth, Greenpeace, and uncountable local activists challenged the political status quo.[6]

This public awareness and political organization produced an impressive legislative outpouring. Politicians realized that environmental concerns could not or should not be ignored. The first legislation that resulted from growing public concerns focused on air and water pollution between 1963 and 1972. In addition, between 1970 and 1980, more than a dozen other environmental laws were passed by Congress and signed by such diverse presidents as Richard Nixon, Gerald Ford, and Jimmy Carter. Nixon also created the Environmental Protection Agency in 1970 by executive action.[7]

Conflict over forest, park, rangeland, river, and wildlife policy was intense during these years. Major statutes were passed that the new environmental activists hoped would compel the Forest Service to increase nontimber uses of the national forests: the Multiple Use–Sustained Yield Act (MUSY) of 1960, the National Environmental Policy Act (NEPA) in 1969, and the National Forest Management Act (NFMA) in 1976.[8] The Sierra Club and the Wilderness Society campaigned to create a separate wilderness system with the passage of the Wilderness Act of 1964.[9] Further, dissatisfaction with the Forest Service's Roadless Area Review and Evaluation (RARE I and RARE II) studies required under that law led to the passage of twenty state wilderness acts, including one for California that included more of the Sierra in 1984.[10] Endangered species legislation was passed in 1966, 1969, and 1973.[11] In 1968, passage of the Wild and Scenic Rivers Act elevated recreation and river health over the commodity values of water use on some public lands and created a separate system of management for designated rivers.[12]

As environmental legislation was passed, conservation and other groups turned to federal and state courts to compel reluctant agencies to change their practices.[13] Three important examples out of many cases illustrate this important tactic. The first was the Monongahela decision of 1975. It questioned the legality of the Forest Service's use of clear-cutting, striking at the very heart of intensive management.[14] A second case involved a challenge to the Forest Service's definition of *wilderness*. The issue arose over the actions of the service during RARE I in the 1970s. A court challenge, based on a claimed violation of NEPA, resulted. The Forest Service decided to settle the case out of court and was forced to conduct more-stringent environmental reviews of wilderness actions in the future.[15] A third case involved the northern spotted owl. After years of concern about the status of the bird, environmentalists sued, using provisions of the Endangered Species Act of 1973. A federal judge issued a permanent injunction in 1991 to stop logging in a critical area of the bird's habitat until adequate owl protection was assured. That litigation and its outcome got everyone's attention and, as we will see, led to significant changes in Forest Service policy.[16]

The Sierra Nevada played a key role in this environmental impulse. The national parks and national forests of the range, and especially its wilderness areas, lakes, rivers, and wildlife, had much to do with shaping the direction the movement took.

Environmentalism and Sierran National Parks, 1960–1990

Yosemite led the way as a battleground where the new environmental impulse would be tested against older Park Service pro-use policies. Two major influences brought change to the management of Yosemite in the environmental era. The first came from scientists, with the Leopold and National Academy of Science Reports exerting steady pressure within the agency and at individual parks such as Yosemite. The Leopold Report, especially, was widely publicized with the assistance of the Sierra Club. The second influence, one that worked together with the scientists, was public pressure for more-natural conditions in the park.[17]

In Yosemite, mounting public pressure and the Leopold Report compelled park officials to take scientific research more seriously, even if they acted slowly and cautiously. The most significant result was the study of the role of fire in the sequoia grove at Mariposa. Until the 1970s, all fires had routinely been suppressed. As a result, denser thickets of understory trees and greater accumulations of fuel threatened sequoia survival. In 1970 prescribed burning began, and in 1972 some naturally caused fires were allowed to burn.[18]

In the area of wildlife policies, Yosemite officials had uneven success. They reintroduced bighorn sheep in isolated areas of the park, even if the animals' survival became problematic. In the case of bears, park policies created a major scandal, as historian Alfred Runte has shown. In 1973 Yosemite Park officials admitted that they had killed more than two hundred so-called "garbage" bears since 1960 and revealed that they had little funding to pursue scientific studies of the issue. In the ensuing controversy, defenders of bears pointed out that killing animals hardly amounted to a wildlife policy. Under public pressure, the park agreed to increase scientific study, place more emphasis on educating visitors about dealing with bears, and provide better enforcement of park regulations concerning wildlife.[19]

Overuse and continuing promotion of carnival-like activities in the Valley generated problems as well. The ideal of "enjoying" was, as so often in the past, prevailing over the "preserving unchanged" part of the park mandate. Historian Stanford Demars called the Yosemite Valley of the 1950s and 60s an "outdoor slum," replete with ever-increasing crowds, traffic jams, drugs, and prostitution. Demars quoted a ranger at Yosemite to demonstrate his point that there was nothing "wild" about the visitor experience:

The roar of giant waterfalls is drowned out by the roar of motorcycles and hot rods echoing off the cliffs; . . . four thousand campfires morning and evening produce a pall of smoke which, combined with the automobile and stove fumes, hangs in the upper valley making eyes smart and clothes take on a charred odor. The huge garbage machines clang great iron trash cans into their mechanical maws with a hideous sound that is easily heard at Glacier Point 3000 feet above. At Firefall time (9:30 nightly) there is a two mile traffic jam reminiscent of the commuter rush out of any city—but with more dangerous obsolete roads and traffic patterns. This burgeoning metropolis has changed the center of Yosemite National Park into the Yosemite City Recreation Area, at its worst only slightly less crowded, commercial and honkeytonk than Coney Island or Disneyland.[20]

Crowded conditions in the Valley and overuse and abuse of the backcountry wilderness areas resulted from park policies that, with concessionaire backing, encouraged people to do just about anything they wanted—even including, for a while, hang gliding and parachute jumping. Rafting in huge numbers down the Merced River was another addition to the Valley "experience." By 1968, park officials finally began to consider changes. The Firefall was discontinued that year, and new park management planning was initiated. In 1970, what has been called the "Fourth of July Riot" occurred. Although apparently no pictures of this event exist in park archives, descriptions of it sound like what happens when too many rats are crowded into a small cage. In simplest terms, hundreds of angry youths clashed with park rangers—some, in Stoneman Meadow, mounted on horses—in what Alfred Runte called both an "ugly" and "prophetic" view of what the future of the park promised to be if restrictions on entry were not created.[21]

Under mounting pressure, park officials in 1974 produced a draft management plan, which was given to the MCA Corporation (the purchaser of Yosemite Park and Curry Company) for comment. The draft plan, when revealed to the public, brought howls of protest not only because of allegations that it had been changed to meet corporate demands for more development, but because it failed to address serious issues of crowding and overuse. The park officials withdrew it and began planning again. The new planning process produced, befitting the age of environmentalism and public comment, a very different document. It reflected the general agreement that the Valley was being overused and that wilderness values needed greater emphasis in the park.[22]

The final plan, approved in 1980, did address—on paper at least—some important issues. Some park services were to be removed from the crowded Valley. Campgrounds were reorganized and camping sites were to be restricted in number. Mass transportation was increased, and removal of all automobiles was envisioned. Plans put forward by the concessionaire to build a tram to Glacier Point were rejected. Golf courses, tennis courts, and some other unnatural visitor services were to be discontinued. But although this ideal existed on paper, failure of will and funding issues in the years that followed left many parts of the plan uncompleted. Criticism of the park bureaucracy focused on its lack of real commitment to bringing about the changes envisioned in the 1980 plan.[23]

In the meantime, MCA was accused of trying to influence guests to lobby to have parts of the 1980 plan put aside. After years of secrecy about how much it paid the park annually for its services monopoly, revelations that the corporation actually paid very little ($590,000 while receiving $78,000,000 in sales in the park in 1990) shocked the public. Attempts by MCA to sell its interests in the park in that year to the Japanese-owned Matsushita Corporation raised a firestorm of protest as well.[24]

At Sequoia and Kings Canyon, the pattern of gradually increasing scientific influence and public desire for more-natural conditions paralleled the history of Yosemite in the environmental decades. The heavy use of the southern parks, although never as serious as the problems at Yosemite Valley, was nevertheless an issue for park management. As with Yosemite, because of the confusion and lack of effective control over concessionaires, overuse in Giant Forest and Grant Grove continued. At the same time, pressure to use the backcountry increased. According to park historians Lary Dilsaver and William Tweed, from 1960 to the late 1980s park officials moved slowly, but with some success, to deal with these issues.[25]

As with Yosemite, coercion to expand and not limit or control visitation and commercial activities by the concessionaire was strong in Sequoia National Park. But as with Yosemite, counterpressure to make the park less crowded and less unnatural pushed park planners and managers to produce a product that could stand public as well as NEPA scrutiny. A plan for park management was produced in 1971 that identified visitor congestion in developed areas as a major problem, but little action was taken to relocate commercial facilities.[26]

Public pressure and NEPA-influenced staff changes eventually led to renewed efforts to improve the crowded Giant Forest area. The park's staff developed a new management plan. Public comment at hearings supported relocation and removal of overnight accommodations and the use of buses to reduce crowding and congestion. The required NEPA hearings forever changed the planning process, forcing concessionaires to face up to the imminent removal of some of their commercial facilities—something that earlier planning had never been able to accomplish. In 1980 the new management plan was accepted. Just as it appeared that real change was coming, however, Ronald Reagan was elected president. His administration cut funding for the park, and the removal process was delayed.[27] By the year 2000, however, much more removal and restructuring had been accomplished.

If unnatural development was a problem in parts of Sequoia, in neighboring Kings Canyon it was less of an issue. Created in 1940, the park was expected by many to be a wilderness park. Perhaps this was one reason that when a development and management plan was produced in the mid-1970s, it faced less commercial opposition. Another factor was that because of NEPA, the public was invited in at the start of the planning process. As a result, the development plan limited construction to a small lodge and a small camping area. In 1976 the draft plan and Environmental Impact Statement (EIS) reflected this public concern. In 1978 the facilities envisioned by the plan were built.[28]

Another problem area, the backcountry, also was subjected to more environmentally sensitive actions. By 1960, as we saw in the last chapter, Sequoia had begun to reconsider its backcountry policy due to damage from increasing use. Use continued to grow through the environmental era. Leopold's influence was at work in encouraging new planning by the staff, as was the passage of the Wilderness Act in 1964. Park officials, however, were slow to take up proposed changes of policy. But with Sierra Club pressure through the 1970s to expand designated wilderness areas of the park eventually the bureaucracy had to respond. The passage of the California Wilderness Act in 1984 saw most of the areas in question given wilderness designation. Policies to regulate uses and restrict numbers followed.[29]

Before 1960, scientific research in Sequoia and Kings Canyon was limited. Its emergence in the environmental era followed a pattern established throughout the Park Service. After publication of the Leopold Report, science staff at the two southern Sierra parks began to increase in number and slowly built up their research capabilities. Studies on grazing impact on the parks, wilderness problems, and air quality produced useful data.[30] This gradual growth of scientific research capability and resolve at Sequoia and Kings Canyon also led to notable successes involving wildlife. Golden trout and bighorn sheep were reintroduced to the parks, and scientific study of bears, as well as proactive public education about the animals, went forward.[31]

Without a doubt, however, the most significant scientific management commitment had to do with fire. Sequoia had, along with the Everglades, pioneered studies on the role of fire in the national parks. After the Leopold Report, investigations of fire in the mixed-conifer forests in the southern Sierra Nevada continued with even more vigor. Richard Hartesveldt's studies of sequoias and fire were influential, as were the research and fire-use demonstrations by Harold Biswell of the University of California.[32]

By 1968, park scientists allowed fires above 8,000 feet in elevation to burn naturally and studied their effects. Similar experiments were tried in less fire-prone red fir communities in the parks, and soon afterward in lower-elevation oak-chaparral woodlands. Between 1970 and 1972, fire was also used and studied at Cedar Grove and Redwood Mountain, and prescribed burning became part of a broader park policy.[33] Eventually, coming full cycle, scientists at Yosemite, Sequoia, and Kings Canyon supported a study by Kat Anderson of the effects of Native American burning in sequoia/mixed-conifer forests. Anderson's work provided recognition of the important role that natives had played in managing these fire-sensitive and important forests.[34]

Sierran Forests and Rivers in the Environmental Era

The environmental movement was deeply involved with the policies of the Forest Service in the Sierra Nevada. A large part of the national membership of the newly energized environmental organizations lived in California. The Sierra Club expanded its focus to include new issues concerning forest policy in the Sierra. Debates within the club over the direction it should take were resolved in favor of the broad ideal of environmental survival. The club also supported the passage of NEPA, recognizing its practical importance in shaping future forest policy in the Sierra.[35]

The passage of MUSY in 1960 committed the Forest Service to a more balanced planning process. But in practice, as Congress continued to favor the service's timber-harvest budget with increasing appropriations, the agency expanded its silviculture staff and cutting activities. As a result, environmentalist criticism grew. Many in the Sierra Club had grown to distrust the Forest Service—especially its wilderness policies. The club sought to influence Congress to compel change. The result was a string of laws that reflected broad public support for new policies.[36]

First came the Wilderness Act of 1964. Passed over Forest Service objections, it created a Wilderness System intended to protect some areas of scenic beauty, including several in the Sierra. Before passage of the act, only the Desolation area alongside Highway 50 had received formal recognition as a "primitive area," the early Forest Service category for land not to be developed for resource use. In 1969, Desolation was finally placed into the Wilderness System. Other Sierra Nevada locales given wilderness status under the new act included the Mokelumne, Hoover, John Muir, and Dome Land areas. The Mokelumne was created out of parts of the Eldorado, Stanislaus, and Toiyabe National Forests. The Hoover came from portions of the Toiyabe and the Inyo. The John Muir was carved from the Inyo and Sierra. Dome Land had been part of the Sequoia. These areas were primarily in alpine or subalpine zones, and in some cases, mining, grazing, or water development were allowed to continue in them.[37]

The new law required the Forest Service to research areas that might be included in the Wilderness System. Between 1967 and 1977, a number of Roadless Area Review and Evaluation studies were begun. Many of the potential wilderness acres were in Sierran forests. The Sierra Club became dissatisfied with the very restrictive or "purist" response of the Forest Service, which generally ruled out lands that had any sign of development in them, fearing that those lands might win wilderness designation and hence be ineligible for logging. Many of the acres thus rejected for wilderness were also heavily forested. The Sierra Club filed suit in a case called *Sierra Club v. Butz* (1972), alleging deficient EIS practices by the Forest Service. Facing a potential court loss, the agency backed down. An out-of-court settlement was eventually agreed upon that prohibited logging on the RARE lands until site-specific EIS studies were conducted.[38]

After further disagreement in Congress over what lands were to be designated in a newly proposed comprehensive wilderness statute, it was agreed to pursue wilderness legislation on a state-by-state basis. Proposed in 1979, the California Wilderness Bill was finally enacted in 1984. Sierran areas designated as wilderness in that law included Bucks Lake, Granite Chief, Carson-Iceberg, Yosemite, Ansel Adams, and Dinkey Lakes. They were all carved from adjoining national forests as the earlier wilderness areas were. Thus, between 1964 and 1984, wilderness actions created an almost contiguous belt of land stretching over much of the Sierran crest, with most human intervention (except visitation and fire suppression) excluded.[39]

The law also affected nearby national park lands. These were often adjacent to newly designated wilderness areas. For example, in Sequoia National Park and Sequoia National Forest, the lands were often separated only by some arbitrary agency category. The two services had to cooperate across agency lines. The newly defined wilderness lands in the Sequoia and Kings Canyon National Parks totaled nearly 740,000 thousand acres—the largest wilderness area in California. The issue of interagency cooperation in the environmental era would grow in importance.[40]

The popularity of the new wilderness areas soon produced overuse, causing concern among wilderness advocates. The Forest Service was supposed to provide effective management plans, but a new generation of wilderness hikers and backpackers rushed to the parks in great numbers, overwhelming them in some cases. In 1972, after considering how its own outings contributed to the problem, the Sierra Club published a study by Richard Hartesveldt (of sequoia science fame) and other San Jose State University scientists that touched on numerous specific issues, among them the effects of human foot traffic in mountain meadows, firewood use and availability, and waste disposal and water quality. The report made thirty-six concrete suggestions for addressing these problems, and of course called for more study of wilderness use.[41]

Obviously the issue did not go away. Planning and access limitation followed. An instructive example comes from Desolation Wilderness. It is one of the most extreme problem areas, located next to a major east-west highway. During the last decades of the twentieth century, use accelerated. By 1992, the problem had become acute. Both overnight and day visitors, many returning from visits to casinos in nearby Tahoe, overwhelmed the small area, making Desolation the most heavily used site in the Wilderness System. Group-size limits and day-use quotas were established to try to lessen the impact.[42]

The struggle to save wilderness in the Sierra Nevada also contributed to the passage of the National Wild and Scenic River Act of 1968. Many acres included in Sierran wilderness attained this status because a river named in the National River System flowed through them. The struggle to create the river system shared many of the same well-organized activists as the wilderness cause and arose from the same heightened public awareness of environmental values. According to river historian Tim Palmer, America's three greatest political battles to save rivers from development were over Hetch Hetchy, Glen Canyon, and the Stanislaus; two of the three occurred in the Sierra Nevada.[43]

Conflict over three rivers in the Sierra illustrates the development of the wild and scenic issue. All three cases involved river systems highly valued for their beauty and recreational use. All three were important in establishing precedents to protect other rivers in the Sierra Nevada and elsewhere.

The first struggle was the largest and exerted great influence on the battles that followed. Between 1944 and 1962 various proposals to build New Melones Dam on the Stanislaus River surfaced. Developers advanced propositions for irrigation, hydroelectric development, recreation, and protection of fish and wildlife in defense of their demands. Flood fears in 1964 finally created the impetus to build a dam that had heretofore been seen as too expensive for the benefits it offered. But by the time of its authorization, recreational use of the river had also increased.[44]

The fight against the dam now began in earnest. Friends of the River organized to take on the formidable coalition of interests that backed its construction. Passage of the Wild and Scenic Rivers Act in 1968 gave hope to the dam's opponents. In 1974 a statewide initiative to save the river lost narrowly in a hotly contested election. The dam was built. But before it was filled, one activist, Mark Dubois, chained himself in a secret place in the river canyon, vowing to drown if the filling was not stopped. Governor Jerry Brown influenced President Carter to stop the flooding. But later, when President Reagan ordered the filling to continue, the river valley was drowned. The significance of this struggle cannot be underestimated. River activists learned from their defeat. Because of it, river-protection interests organized more effectively and actually gained in influence and numbers. As a result, no other large dam has since been built in the Sierra.[45]

The Auburn Dam proposal attests to this point. Conceived as part of the Central Valley Project, it had been postponed because of its projected costs. At over 600 feet, it would have been the fifth-highest dam in North America. With growing political support from powerful backers in Congress in the 1960s, it was finally funded. Construction on its foundations began before a small citizens' group, Protect the American River Canyons, or PARC, organized against it. The New Melones struggle gave them hope. In 1974 the Natural Resources Defense Council joined the fight and delayed construction because the Bureau of Reclamation had failed to produce an adequate EIS.[46] At the same time, local supporters of the dam organized and loudly condemned its critics, especially as national support for the project declined. The head of the Auburn Dam Committee said: "This horseshit about protect the American River Canyons, as far as I'm concerned, is pure horseshit."[47]

Then an earthquake struck the nearby Oroville area, site of the state water project's largest dam, and heightened public awareness of flood danger should the dam fail. If a similar quake hit the slender, high-arch concrete dam proposed for Auburn, the effects on the Sacramento area would have been devastating. Further study revealed fairly recent earthquake activity at the site. Costs to redesign the dam—already the most expensive ever proposed in the United States—escalated. Both Presidents Carter and Reagan removed their support for the project, and for all intents and purposes it died.[48]

In 2001 the Bureau of Reclamation and the state of California agreed to block a diversion tunnel, built to facilitate construction of the dam, that had effectively drained all water out of the original stream channel. Closing the tunnel would allow the river to return to its natural course. Environmentalists hailed the action as the final nail in the Auburn Dam coffin. But remember, Dracula has often been killed, only to rise again—supporters of the Auburn project continue to refuse to admit defeat.[49]

The third case involved the twenty-seven-mile-long wild portion of the Tuolumne River between O'Shaughnessy Dam at Hetch Hetchy and the New Don Pedro Reservoir below it. The outcome of the struggle supports the general view that the time of big dam building in the Sierra was over unless significant change in public opinion occurred. The battle began in the 1970s when San Francisco and two local irrigation districts proposed a series of multipurpose dams for the lower river canyon and a diversion of water from its upper portions. They tried this even though local voters signaled their opposition to the project. In 1981 the Tuolumne River Preservation League formed and organized a broad base of support against the project—something learned from the Stanislaus fight. As a result, the river portion included in the proposed dam projects was protected in the 1984 California Wilderness Act and development was stopped.[50]

With passage of the National Wild and Scenic Rivers Act, the position of rivers designated as part of this system seems secure. California has sixteen rivers included, most of them in the Sierra Nevada. Segments of the Feather, American, Tuolumne, Merced, Kings, and Kern are part of this group. Numerous other portions of Sierran rivers are also eligible and are being studied for inclusion.[51]

Mineral King and Walt Disney

In the 1960s and 1970s, the Forest Service promoted large-scale commercial development of Sierran forests for skiing and year-round recreation. In doing so it demonstrated its commitment to projects heavily dependent on private corporate investment, automobile connections, and very little consideration of environmental effects. In recreational development as in timber harvesting, there was "intensive management," although of a different sort. Instead of clear-cutting and pine plantations, it was to be parking lots and recreation "villages."

The more important of the two major Forest Service mass-recreation initiatives concerned the fate of Mineral King Valley in the southern Sierra. Until the political struggle over its status began in the 1960s, it existed as a game refuge. It was a poor and forgotten stepchild, as it were, loosely managed by the Sequoia National Forest. Decisions to turn it into a massive year-round ski-and-destination resort in the 1960s brought the Sierra Club into contention with one of America's largest corporations. The fight involved the Forest Service and the National Park Service as well, demonstrating that cross-jurisdictional issues were becoming more important in the Sierra.[52]

A condensed history of Mineral King is useful here. In the 1870s and 1880s, the valley was opened for mining but quickly proved unprofitable. A long and tortuous road was carved into it for the mining boom. Some cabins were built, and limited recreational use developed in the almost pristine alpine valley. In the 1920s it was rejected for inclusion in Sequoia National Park because of this development, and it was designated a wildlife refuge by Sequoia National Forest instead. Postwar skiing interest led Los Angeles developers to search for likely sites near that urban center. The Sierra Club suggested a small ski center at Mineral King to divert this interest away from San Gorgonio, one of the few undeveloped alpine areas in southern California that could be converted to such use. In the 1964 Wilderness Act, San Gorgonio was included in the new Wilderness System, and Sequoia National Forest and the Walt Disney Corporation decided to develop Mineral King instead. Governor "Pat" Brown signaled his support for the project as well.[53]

In 1966, Disney signed a development contract with Sequoia National Forest and began planning. After some internal disagreement, the Sierra Club came out in opposition once the Forest Service and Disney's massive project was fully revealed. At various stages, some fourteen ski lifts, two hotels, several restaurants, specialty shops, a large parking garage and automobile service center, employee housing, an equestrian center, picnic and other use areas, skating rinks, and several other facilities were planned for the small (16,000-acre) valley. It was to be literally a "village," and an all-year "destination" resort. In 1969, after the Forest Service resisted public hearings on the project, the Sierra Club filed suit. It claimed that both the Park Service and the Forest Service had violated federal laws in going forward with the project. A federal court issued an injunction, halting all work until the issue was resolved.[54]

In the decade-long legal struggle that ensued, several important things happened. After passage of NFMA, continuing pressure from environmentalists forced the Forest Service to draft several environmental impact statements that systematically reduced the scale of development the original permit had envisioned. Each time the agency submitted a new draft, public rebuke forced the planners to back off and scale down the project still further. This scaling down not only made the Forest Service look pathetic, but it also made Disney nervous. The Disney company, faced with mounting costs and delays, quietly began looking elsewhere.

The Sierra Club attracted national attention to the issue, even though it lost its appeal to block the project in the Supreme Court in 1972. The club lost on the narrow grounds of whether it had legal standing in the matter. The Court practically begged it to submit an amended appeal. The club quickly did so and once more entered the legal battle. The Disney group now faced even more years of delay in their development activities.[55]

Another issue that brought grief to Disney and the Forest Service concerned access to Mineral King. The substandard state road that connected the valley to the outside world would not serve the thousands of car visitors expected in the summer or winter. And any new road would have to be built across Sequoia National Park land. Study began on a proposal for an enormously expensive new state road—the estimates ran to well over $20 million dollars, or about $1 million per mile. This amount would seriously strain a state highway fund already hard-pressed to meet statewide needs. Eventually the California legislature voted to drop the highway from its plans, dealing a body blow to Disney and the Forest Service. Alternative monorail or cog railway proposals increased costs and changed the nature of the project entirely, as far as the beleaguered corporation was concerned. The access problem was compounded by Park Service unwillingness to grant right-of-way to the proposed road where it crossed parklands because it required cutting sequoia.[56]

The Disney Corporation eventually decided to abandon its plans for Mineral King. The death knell for the proposed development, as far as the Forest Service was concerned, sounded in 1978. The Sierra Club had pursued two paths in their Mineral King strategy—litigate and, at the same time, lobby to get the valley included as part of Sequoia National Park. In 1978 it finally persuaded Congress to add Mineral King to the park.[57]

During the long Mineral King fight, Disney began to investigate another proposed ski development at Independence Lake, in the northern Sierra Nevada. Independence Lake was a glacial lake located near Donner Lake, close to the summit and with an easy connection to I-80. The site had been utilized for recreation since the nineteenth century and included a small tourist facility. The lake itself had also been used for commercial icemaking and water sales after having been dammed to raise its level. At first, Disney claimed that although it was considering the area, it was not contemplating abandoning Mineral King. It said that Independence Lake promised to be a good, family-oriented, year-round resort in its own right. This development and Mineral King would have placed a huge commercial recreational development at each end of the range.[58]

The Sierra Club remained neutral in this issue after its Mineral King success but still kept a watchful eye on the northern project. Discussions went forward between Disney representatives, county supervisors in Nevada and Sierra Counties, and representatives of the Southern Pacific Railroad and

Sierra Pacific Power and Light, which both owned land in the area. Having been accused of antibusiness attitudes on another issue, Governor Jerry Brown created a special task force to expedite the permit process for Disney. Negotiations began with Tahoe National Forest, which controlled Mount Lola, where ski runs were contemplated. The state task force tried to promote cooperation on a joint state Environmental Impact Report and federal EIS. A local environmental group formed, demanding that a comprehensive EIS be prepared. Disney decided to quit its planning soon afterward for two reasons: the EIS process and potential legal resistance promised to stretch out for years, and the Forest Service would not trade its control of Mount Lola in a land swap.[59]

Disney's failed ventures in the Sierra ended any serious twentieth-century attempts to bring massive commercial recreational development to the range. The two areas were either too valuable in their primitive form or unsuited in other ways for such heavy development.

Clear-Cutting, the Spotted Owl, and a New Perspective

Like other western forests in the postwar era, those of the Sierra saw their share of clear-cutting, below-cost timber sales, roadbuilding, and wildlife problems. With the passage of NEPA and NFMA, Sierran national forests had to begin comprehensive planning, justify clear-cutting, and consider the environmental impact of their policies. Establishing balance in forest-management practices required that other Forest Service personnel (besides the silviculturalists) gain more influence. Public comment demanded a more evenhanded planning. Change proved to be hard for the Sierran national forests' leaders.[60]

Every national forest in the Sierra was required to create comprehensive plans to guide future actions. The planning process for each forest was lengthy because the plans now required public discussion. The Forest Service was literally learning as it went along. The road was uncharted and bumpy. In the Tahoe National Forest, for example, planning that began under NEPA and NFMA in the 1970s was not complete until 1990. During that time, two significant planning initiatives were produced: the one-volume, 1978–1979 *Final Environmental Statement and Timber Management Plan* and the six-volume, 1990 *Tahoe National Forest Land and Resources Management Plan and Environmental Impact Statement.* Beyond the difference in size, the two documents reflected changing attitudes among the staff professionals who prepared them.[61]

The 1978 document was primarily a timber-management plan, much like the previous plans when the TNF was gearing up for intensive management.

It paid little attention to the environmental effects of the proposed cutting and even less to the few respondents who commented on the draft version of the final plan.[62]

The plan stated that clear-cutting was the preferred method, with the goal of "regenerating" poorly stocked, uneven-age, and uneven-composition forest areas in the TNF. Selective cutting and brush clearing that left mixed-age and mixed-species trees to grow was judged to be too expensive and less productive. The emphasis was on maximizing timber output in the most efficient manner, and clear-cutting, the plan stated flatly, was "the most efficient volume producer." The vision of the forest for the future was of more "productive" species growing in the "regenerated" patches that would be cut and replanted under the plan. New methods of maximizing the amount of timber that could be cut, using new mathematical models for estimating harvest levels, were employed. A cut of 147 million board feet per year was the target set under the plan.[63]

It is interesting to examine the TNF response to public comment. Eleven organizations responded. Six were timber-production oriented. Four were environmental groups. Forty-three individuals responded—a significant number of them criticizing the clear-cutting emphasis in the proposed plan. In each case where groups such as the Sierra Club Mother Lode Chapter or individuals opposed clear-cutting, the response to these complaints was uniform: clear-cutting was productive, it was allowed in the law, it was part of a "preferred alternative" that produced more timber.[64]

When a new planning document became necessary a few years later, much had happened. Lawsuits were more common and environmental groups more organized. The internal culture of the Forest Service had also begun to change. As a result, the process that produced the 1990 plan was different from the previous effort. The new TNF plan, while still responding to the need to "get out the cut" that the Regional Forester's Office required, also reflected forces that were beginning to reshape Forest Service practices.[65]

In charge of formulating the new planning document was Geri Bergen, the new Tahoe National Forest supervisor. Trained as a forester and a botanist, she had entered the Forest Service in 1962 as a research forester at the Pacific Southwest Forest and Range Experiment Station. Between 1972 and 1978, she was involved in implementation and planning for NEPA issues in the California national forests. In 1978 she was assigned to the TNF as deputy forest supervisor—the first woman line officer in the Forest Service. In 1985 she was promoted to forest supervisor. She managed the forest and supervised the preparation of the 1990 Land and Management Plan for the TNF.[66]

Bergen began her work at the Tahoe generally accepting the idea that

clear-cutting and regeneration forestry were the keys to increasing forest productivity. While in the supervisor's position, she experienced firsthand the
challenges that came from the environmental community. She and the TNF
became party to a Natural Resources Defense Council lawsuit that concerned cutting too close to stream margins. After reviewing clear-cuts (one of
them near a present-day Forest Service nature trail site at Rock Creek, east of
Nevada City), she began working with staff to widen streamside margins in
sensitive locations.[67] She also experienced the tension that arose from planning for timber harvests while at the same time preserving from cutting areas
set aside for RARE II study. Bypassing these areas meant that if cut levels were
to remain at plan projections, more intensive cutting had to occur elsewhere.
Bergen worked with the regional forester to reduce the level of expected
cutting in the final TNF plan.[68]

The plan Bergen's TNF staff prepared differed in several ways from the one
that was in place when she assumed control of the Tahoe. It was intended to
be operative for ten to fifteen years before being modified and to cover all
major activities, including the controversial timber-harvest portion. But for
the first time, the document was more than just a timber plan. The public
response section was greatly expanded in comparison to its 1978 predecessor.
Over 12,000 letters on the draft EIS and land-management documents were
received in the comment period.[69]

A summary in the plan's introduction noted that the public wanted
greater emphasis on recreational opportunities, the maintenance of visual
qualities in the forest, protection of soil and water, less clear-cutting, more
roadless areas, and habitat protection, especially in the case of the spotted
owl. Bergen noted that as a result, the plan was modified to provide habitat,
soil, streamside, and visual-quality protections. She also promised fewer
clear-cuts and even-age management practices, with an increase in unevenen-
age and shelterwood provisions and retention of seed trees in timber sale
areas. Environmentalists, of course, did not agree with Bergen's assessment,
believing that it fell short of what a healthy Tahoe forest required.[70]

After completion of the plan, Bergen was promoted to a new post in
Washington, DC, as deputy director for environmental coordination. Acting
forest supervisor Frank Waldo, in a letter accompanying the Record of Decision for the plan, stated that the annual timber sale quantity for the plan had
been reduced from 142.3 to 129 million board feet.[71]

Forest planning in the TNF and other Sierra Nevada forests took place
over a period of roughly fifteen years, from 1976 to 1990. As an interim
operating procedure while the individual plans were being prepared, the
Forest Service established provisional land-management plans through the

1980s. Clear-cutting had been confirmed by NFMA as a procedure that could be used along with others to increase productivity. As a result, all Sierra Nevada interim land-management plans from the mid-1980s onward proposed increased use of clear-cutting.[72]

The Forest Service's rationale for this interpretation of NFMA intent was clear: managed forests gave more economic benefits than unmanaged forests, and "proper" harvest schedules maximized these benefits. Moreover, many of the range's forest stands were "mature" or "overmature" and thus past their peak growth periods. Accordingly, they should be harvested using even-aged methods. The cutover areas were to be replanted with conifers in "tree farms." This would replace mixed-conifer forests (which included undesirable white firs that had proliferated following cutting and fires) with more-productive conifer species. Many forest professionals supported these plans on the grounds that they would produce "regulated" forests consistent with preferred forestry practices of the time.[73]

Environmentalists, on the other hand, declared the plans just another excuse for continuing the intensive harvesting of past decades. In the southern Sierra Nevada, for example, Sequoia National Forest plans produced large-scale clear-cutting around sequoias, using the argument that this would aid regeneration of the sequoias. The immediate visual effect of such cutting brought fierce resistance from many environmentalists. Many also expressed concern about long-term problems for the sequoia, such as potential wind damage to the trees exposed by the clear-cutting.[74]

NFMA did not produce different forest practices as some of its supporters had intended. The Forest Service budgets for the 1980s still placed timber and roadbuilding levels well above all other noncommodity practices, including planning and (except for a brief time in the 1970s) soil and water activities. Ultimately the federal courts brought the issue to a head in 1989 with an injunction effectively shutting down most cutting of "old-growth" forests in Oregon and Washington because of the threat to the habitat of the northern spotted owl. Under intense pressure, in June 1990 the Fish and Wildlife Service listed the owl as threatened, and the Forest Service was ordered to come up with a plan for its survival.[75]

Although the ruling applied only to the northern forests, its impact reached to the Sierra Nevada as well. The range of the California spotted owl (*Strix occidentalis occidentalis*), closely related to its northern counterpart (*Strix occidentalis caurina*), included areas south of the Pit River into the Sierra Nevada and the Coast Range. Most of its surviving habitat was in Sierran national forest and Bureau of Land Management lands. In the late 1980s, the Forest Service sought to protect the species by preserving small

Spotted Owl Habitat Areas (SOHAS). Harvesting of trees in the SOHAS was allowed, except adjacent to nesting trees. The Fish and Wildlife Service research supporting the endangered listing of the northern spotted owl also suggested that SOHA policies might be inadequate to protect the California spotted owl, opening the Forest Service to litigation as had occurred in the Pacific Northwest. A Natural Resources Defense Council challenge to a series of timber sales in the Tahoe National Forest came in 1991. Rather than go to court to defend its intensive-management posture, the Forest Service decided to look for a different policy.[76]

In June 1991 several California and federal agencies, including the Forest Service, convened a California Spotted Owl Assessment and Planning Team. Environmental and timber interests and local government representatives were invited to observe the team's deliberations. Several alternative strategies for owl survival were considered. The team concluded that habitat protection for the owl was inadequate. Clear-cutting and harvesting large-diameter trees added to this problem. Fire-suppression policies of the past had also contributed to destruction of necessary tree stands because of destructive understory fires. The technical portion of the team's report recommended that only thinning and fuel-management activities continue.[77]

From 1989 to 1991, the Forest Service struggled to reconcile its operating practice of intensive management with growing scientific evidence, interagency strife, and public opinion that it was on the wrong track. Instead of managing the forests with an ecological focus as some of its own employees suggested, it was still committed to maximizing timber production. The owl crisis forced a public shift in policy. Between 1989 and 1992, Chief Forester Dale Robertson signaled that change was coming. He supported a "New Perspectives" initiative internally and with press releases, and in 1992 he officially announced that the new approach was adopted as policy. It was to be called "Ecosystem Management" and would constitute an ecological approach to managing Forest Service lands. Some critics in the service, as well as outside observers, expressed cynicism at the announcement, doubting that the "conversion" was real.[78]

Sierran Lakes and the Environmental Challenge

While much of the environmental controversy of the 1960s and 1970s in the Sierra focused on parks, forests, and rivers, two lakes in the range were also in trouble. One, Mono Lake, was the range's oldest, and the other, Tahoe, was the deepest. As with other environmental struggles in the Sierra, local and national environmental groups formed or organized on behalf of the two lakes, and municipal, state, and federal actions were involved in the conflict.

Mono Lake, on the eastern border of the Sierra Nevada, is a vestigial survivor of the ice age. Created from runoff from glaciers, it originally occupied some 316 square miles, covering not only the Mono Basin, but also Aurora Valley next door. As the ice age vanished, the lake retreated to a size of about 85 square miles, fluctuating in response to wet or dry weather cycles. Like most eastern Sierra lakes, it had no natural outlet. As a result, dissolved carbonates, sulfates, and chlorides turned it into a saline soup. It was not a dead lake, however. A form of brine shrimp and pupae of infusoria or alkali flies made it very rich in life and attracted wildfowl including California gulls, grebes, phalaropes, snowy plovers, avocets, ducks, and many other migratory birds to its shores and islands.[79]

Climate and precipitation variation either raised or lowered the lake level throughout the early historical period of the Sierra. That changed in 1941 with the completion of a diversion system. Water was taken from the principal streams that fed the lake, including Rush and Lee Vining Creeks, and shunted away in an aqueduct that connected to the Owens Valley diversion system supplying Los Angeles. After 1941, the lake level declined almost a foot a year. After 1970, when another diversion aqueduct—called the "Second Barrel"—was completed, the rate of decline increased to 1.6 feet annually. In drought years the lake fell even faster.[80]

As the lake declined, so did the wildfowl populations that depended heavily on its flies and shrimp before they journeyed on, or for feeding while nesting on the island breeding grounds. In 1940, a million ducks had used Mono's shorelines for feeding. In 1995 only 5,000 to 6,000 did so. Other migratory birds declined as well. In the 1980s the falling water level created a land bridge between the lake's shore and Negit Island, one of the chief nesting grounds for the California gull. Gull populations dropped catastrophically as coyotes crossed the land bridge and raided the now exposed nests.[81]

As the lake fell, the amount of exposed former lake floor naturally increased. Tufa formations (created when fresh water from springs in the lake encountered the complex chemical brew of its waters) were exposed or left high and dry. Fluctuations in the lake level and the lapping of waves at their base threatened the tufa with destruction. The shoreline with its exposed alkali residues was whipped by winds at times, creating dust storms as painful to Mono Lake's local citizens as similar storms were for residents in the Owens Valley to the south.[82]

This seeming destruction of Mono Lake and the streams that fed it could not go unnoticed. After all, the controversy over the fate of Owens Valley immediately to the south was legendary. The taking of the water in the Mono Basin was opposed almost from the beginning of Los Angeles's plan. Before the 1930s, some locals had hoped to turn Mono Lake into a desert resort, but the plan had little financial prospects. The depression crushed farmers in the area. At that time the city to the south began buying up water rights from ranchers and farmers as it had in Owens Valley. As Wallis McPherson, son of the erstwhile resort developer, said of the Los Angeles Water and Power Department purchasers, "They came very quietly, and with malice aforethought."[83]

Local resistance failed to stop the first damming and diversion. The construction of the second aqueduct immediately created new problems, drying up deep springs and giving rise to the dust storms. An attempt by Los Angeles to get permanent water license rights in the early 1970s was opposed by Inyo County. The case inspired a small group called Friends of Mono Lake, along with the Audubon Society and the Toiyabe Chapter of the Sierra Club, to mount a resistance. Failure followed in both cases as Los Angeles fought back with its superior economic resources. The Bureau of Land Management also protested the draining that was exposing the gull rookeries on Negit Island. It did not matter. How could anyone stand up to the powerful city water interests?[84]

In his moving account of the battle over Mono Lake, John Hart describes what it finally took to stop the megalopolis in its tracks. In the late 1970s, as the lake was perhaps on its way to ecological collapse, a group of graduate students studying the effects of the lake's decline on its life forms organized the Mono Lake Committee. They eventually convinced the Audubon Society to support them in a court challenge to Los Angeles's actions, based on their understanding of a vague legal principle called the "public trust doctrine." In 1983 they prevailed in the California Supreme Court, where the doctrine was accepted. This unlikely group of challengers brought the thirsty city's depredations to a halt, at least temporarily. The lake was not "saved," only given a stay of execution, as degradation from the effects of earlier diversions continued.[85]

Through the work of the Mono Lake Committee, Los Angeles's water diversions and other actions were forced into widespread public scrutiny. From this small beginning, the environmental group effectively put the issue before a national audience. Media coverage of the struggle was widespread. In 1979, for example, the committee drew the attention of the California government. A task force that studied the lake and its problems suggested that if the city would simply conserve and reclaim its wastewater, with some financial help to build facilities to treat that water, it could reduce the lake's decline.[86]

The task force was ignored. In 1983, some members of the California congressional delegation suggested that Mono Lake be designated a national monument. They promised that this action would not endanger Los Angeles's water claims. The city lobbied against the idea and commissioned scientific studies that questioned whether diversion had harmed gulls or, for that matter, threatened the lake at all. In 1984, Mono supporters got the lake included in the California Wilderness Act as a Forest Service National Forest Scenic Area. But the water diversion issue was still not resolved.[87]

The factor that finally brought the city's diversions to a halt, ironically, was natural. Heavy rains in 1982 and 1983 forced the Los Angeles Department of Water and Power to release water from its Mono diversion system because it was filled beyond capacity. The excess water was allowed to return to the long-dry Lee Vining and Rush Creeks. The floods carried with them brown and rainbow trout. The trout established themselves in the now flowing creeks. In effect, this re-created a fishery—there had been a popular and productive one before the diversions. A visiting fisherman persuaded California Trout (an advocate group dedicated to promoting the management of streams for wild fish populations) to take up the cause. Eventually that group joined with the Mono Lake Committee and the Audubon Society to launch legal action to save the newly established fishery. From 1984 to 1989, a series of California superior court and supreme court decisions decreed that Los Angeles had illegally diverted Mono Lake water and must cease its diversions from the streams.[88]

An ironic thing about the final decision was that although there indeed had been a fishery before Los Angeles dried up the creeks, it was not natural. The rainbows and browns there had been transplanted, non-native fish. In Mono Paiute precontact times there were probably no fish in the Mono drainage. Mono Paiute traveled across the Sierra to participate in spawning runs in the San Joaquin system, but on their side they had no native fish to capture. The life-sustaining alkali fly had been the group's dietary mainstay.[89]

The Public Trust and Cal Trout cases, as they were popularly known, forced the state government finally to address the issue of just what the lake's average level should be. When the Mono Lake Committee had taken up their battle to save the lake from destruction, they had settled on a 1970 lake-level minimum of 6,388 feet above sea level.[90] They scarcely believed that they could get the Department of Water and Power to accept even this low level. But a state Water Resources Control Board study and ruling established that a level of 6,391 feet could sustain the creeks and lake, restore some wildfowl habitat, and perhaps even draw some ducks back to the coves that had once supported their numerous presence. With everyone against them, the Department of Water and Power finally acquiesced, deciding not to appeal the board's decision. Mono this time was saved.[91]

In reflecting on the Mono struggle, John Hart credited the success of this impossible crusade to the tenacity and intelligent campaign of the individuals who constituted the Mono Lake Committee. Most notable were David and Sally Gaines and Martha Davis. Willingness to sacrifice and unwillingness to quit against great odds sustained them in their fight. Hart credits luck as playing a role as well.[92] It should be added, and not to take credit away from the Mono Lake Committee and the lawyers and environmental groups who supported the cause, that the times were also right. The struggle took place in the context of the environmental era. A sympathetic public, many of whom lived in Los Angeles itself, were prepared to accept limits on easy water and assume the costs of reclamation and restoration to keep the lake alive. Federal clean-air legislation provided a tool to force Los Angeles to cover the alkali-crusted shores and to protect the scenic qualities of the lake. Politicians in California and Washington, DC, responded to outpourings of support for Mono and broader environmental issues because they felt compelled to do so. But again, there should be a special place in paradise for the Mono Lake Committee heroes.

If Mono Lake had to be "discovered" and put on the environmental era's map, Tahoe was no stranger to trouble and environmental concern. From the 1860s to the turn of the century, there were those, including California state forestry officials, who wanted the lake and its forested shores put into a state park. This flurry of conservation activity was all to no avail. Between the first major cutting of its forests and on through the first three decades of the twentieth century, when recreation came to replace extractive industry, the lake underwent a healing process. The forest returned to the basin—albeit a forest simplified in species primarily to firs. The lake's waters, after a brief algal bloom late in the nineteenth century, cleared. As long as the shores and marsh areas were left relatively untouched, the in-flowing streams were cleansed of nutrients from the surrounding hillsides. Later scientific studies of the lake bottom showed surprisingly little effect from the early logging.[93]

But as we saw in the last chapter, the postwar economic boom created a new cycle of environmental problems. Development caused by downhill skiing and casino construction brought about rapid urbanization of the basin. There was now no "down season," as gambling and skiing created a new pattern of year-round use.[94] Population density in the Tahoe Basin exceeded that of any other area in the Sierra Nevada by 1980.[95]

The draining and filling of the lake's wetlands and marshes, as demonstrated at Tahoe Keys, removed the natural filtering structure that had prevented nutrients from flowing into the lake. Surrounding hillsides and lakeshore areas were modified with the building of houses, piers, roads, driveways, and parking areas. Between 1970 and 1978, a spurt of private land development on just 28,000 acres increased nutrient flows from erosion into the lake by 18 to 20 percent, according to a study by U.C.–Davis limnologist Charles Goldman. A 1979 study of the lake by the Western Federal Regional Council reported that 75 percent of the basin's marshes, 50 percent of its meadows, and 35 percent of its riparian zones were heavily damaged. Twenty-five percent of its marshes had been developed from 1969 to 1979 alone.[96]

The problems of the basin during this period cannot really be separated from one another. They formed a sort of deadly synergy. The Lake Tahoe Basin as described by scientists was a "nutrient sink." In other words, pollution created there by human or natural processes would make its way into the lake eventually if left alone. Fragmented governmental authority worsened this complex of problems, even as scientists began to come to grips with the causes of increasing air and water pollution.[97]

The first component of the problem was massive physical alteration of the basin through construction activities that disturbed basin soils, destroyed filtering marshland, and added nutrients to the lake. A second factor was that new development increased the production of sewage and air pollution, both of which produced still more nutrients that ended up in the lake. A third element involved the cycling of algae-producing nutrients already in the lake. This factor was not understood at first, but scientists eventually showed that the mixing of already-present nutrients with new sources from runoff and sewage significantly intensified algal growth. This effect compounded the problem of reducing the overall nutrient load. A fourth issue involved forest health. Drought and insect infestation destroyed much of the basin's forests in the 1980s, making them more fire-prone just as more people built into them. Together, these problems threatened the lake with certain degradation.[98]

So what was to be done? It would not be easy to forge a solution. There was limited scientific knowledge of lake processes. There was desire to profit from the lake by investors and basin landowners. There were fragmented and ineffective governing institutions that included towns in two states and two state governments with different ideas of what to do. There were more than sixty districts, agencies, and city and county jurisdictions alone. There were state and federal governmental agencies with different agendas and missions.[99]

Douglas Strong writes that the environmental movement at Tahoe began when local activists successfully resisted the attempt of casino and other lake business interests to get a new highway built to replace the old, winding road that connected Tahoe City and Tahoe Valley. The business interests wanted a faster, all-weather road cut through D. L. Bliss and Emerald Bay State Parks. The new route would include a bridge built across the mouth of Emerald Bay, an important feature of the lake. How convenient, but also how environmentally destructive. Not only would the highway and bridge deface and damage the bay, but the road also would cut through some of the small amount of remaining virgin forest on the lakeshore. Attempts were made to push the measure through the California legislature between 1958 and 1962.[100]

Resistance to the proposed desecration came from local residents, landowners, and Newton Drury, head of the California Division of Beaches and Parks. Eventually the local resisters adopted the title of Committee to Save the West Shore of Lake Tahoe. Their lobbying work against the project was aided by a rising concern about the building of inappropriate freeways elsewhere in the state, and the legislature ultimately shelved the project. The road and bridge were never built. Douglas Strong calls this action the "Catalyst for Conservation" at the lake because it awakened resistance to the problems created by growth advocates.[101]

The issue of uncontrolled growth in the basin helped provide the stimulus for another and much more effectively organized environmental group. The League to Save Lake Tahoe was created in 1965 and included some participants from the bridge-and-highway fight. The goal of the new group was to preserve environmental balance, scenic beauty, and recreational opportunity in the basin. The league became a force in resisting highway development. It also supported scientific research on water quality and promoted the creation of some form of regional government in the lake basin. As a result, it was an early supporter of the Tahoe Regional Planning Agency (TRPA) in the period from 1967 to 1969.[102]

When the TRPA proved ineffective in controlling the casino and other businesses' attempts to continue expansion in the 1970s, the League to Save Lake Tahoe removed its endorsement of the agency. It joined with other environmental groups such as the Sierra Club in litigation to compel observance of the bi-state agreement that had created the TRPA. The league and the club charged that when the agency bowed to pressure and approved a regional development plan that continued the destructive growth pattern, it had violated the federal mandate that created it. The league also joined in actions to strengthen the TRPA in 1980, reducing the power of local governments and Nevada interests. When the restructured agency produced a regional plan that still seemed geared to expansion, the league obtained an injunction that blocked nearly all construction in the basin. Eventually negotiation and collaboration between interests produced a plan closer to league ideals. The group was clearly a force to be reckoned with.[103]

Despite the TRPA's ups and downs, its emergence as an effective regional government was a major factor in bringing about environmental improvement in Tahoe Basin. Fragmentation of decision making had stood in the way of reducing or controlling the effects of growth. The need for a regional planning and management group that included county, city, and state agencies was generally accepted as early as the 1960s. How to establish such an entity was a different matter. The major problems of sewer effluent and the rapid expansion of housing and other developments led to scientific and engineering studies, and finally to legislation.

Between 1967 and 1969, the California and Nevada legislatures both created Tahoe regional planning groups. In 1969 federal legislation created the bi-state TRPA. But because of compromises in the legislation (largely driven by Nevada casino interests), the bi-state body was ineffective in limiting growth. An escape clause said that if no TRPA majority action was taken in sixty days on a development proposal, it was allowed to proceed on its own. This provision ensured delay from casino or housing interests. But even with its weaknesses, the TRPA represented a serious attempt to promote regional planning in the Tahoe Basin. It also conducted scientific studies that illuminated lake problems. In addition, in the 1970s both state legislatures also passed legislation mandating the transfer of sewage effluent outside the basin.[104]

In response to criticism in California and with growing pressure from the League to Save Lake Tahoe and the federal government, negotiations in 1979 and 1980 produced new legislation strengthening the TRPA. Under continuing environmentalist pressure, the agency eventually produced a new regional plan that significantly improved conditions in the basin. Most important was the effective establishment of "threshold standards" intended to limit further degradation of the lake's water quality. It was now understood that Tahoe's problems required long-term solutions. And because growth continued outside the areas of TRPA authority, the Tahoe-Donner area still faced serious environmental issues. The 1990s would see new initiatives to "save" the lake.[105]

A third major issue in the basin was forest health. We have already seen that there had been a nearly complete stand replacement of Tahoe Basin forests in the last decades of the nineteenth century. The simplified (primarily fir) forests that returned after the great clear-cut era were not as resistant to fire and disease as their predecessors. The new forests also were shaped by

Forest Service fire-suppression policies. The firs were simply allowed to multiply, without the thinning that would have occurred had fire been allowed to do its natural work. In the 1980s and 1990s, drought conditions and insect infestation devastated the basin's forests. In some areas, 80 percent of the trees in an area were dead or dying. In 1991 a Forest Service estimate stated that 300 million board feet of timber was dead or dying.[106]

As with other agency fragmentation, the Forest Service managed the basin as part of three national forests. In 1973, as part of general Tahoe Basin government consolidation, the Forest Service created the Lake Tahoe Basin Management Unit (LTBMU) out of parts of the Tahoe, Eldorado, and Toiyabe National Forests. In 1978 the unit produced a land management plan for basin forests that stressed forest health and lake-water purity over wood fiber production. Various federal land purchases over the years that followed put more land in the basin under Forest Service management, often taking lots that could not be built on without causing significant erosion. The Forest Service was joined by a California agency, the California Tahoe Conservancy, in these environmentally sensitive land purchases.[107]

Not all forest health questions, of course, have been answered. For example, the LTBMU instituted salvage logging to remove dead trees, but scientific study suggested that this activity might in fact make fire problems worse. A federal study showed the need for a carefully integrated plan that reduced surface fuel load and vertical and horizontal forest continuity in the basin forests at the same time. That would require thinning of forest stands, prescribed burning, and mechanical brush treatments. The LTBMU was pursuing studies on these lines as of 2002.[108]

The Environmental Impulse and the Sierra Nevada

In 1993, Philip Shabecoff, a journalist for the *New York Times,* summed up his understanding of the environmental impulse of the decades after 1960 in an influential history entitled *A Fierce Green Fire.* His account of the origins and spirit of the outpouring of environmental activism remains valuable today. His knowledge of the movement also inspired him to offer a hopeful look at what he called "the future of American environmentalism" in a successor book in 2000, *Earth Rising.*[109] In the new work he described the overall influence of the environmental impulse on the nation:

> As the 20th century drew to a close, it was clear that environmentalism
> had wrought profound changes in American life—to its landscape, its
> institutions, and its people. Since that first Earth Day, well more than

one hundred pieces of major federal legislation affecting the environment had become law. Every state and most major cities had some kind of environmental protection agency. Wary politicians and battle-scarred corporations grudgingly conceded that the environmental movement was here to stay and was a potent force to be reckoned with. . . .

Even more significant, perhaps, is that environmentalism has changed the way most Americans look at the world and the way we live our daily lives. Public opinion polls consistently show that a majority of Americans consider themselves to be environmentalists. Most of us now think of a healthy environment as a basic human right.[110]

As a stage on which a significant part of the environmental movement was played out, the Sierra Nevada was also profoundly affected through these years. Environmental legislation, federal and state court decisions, and other important federal and state agency actions continued to shape the range. Its national parks and national forests, its lakes, and many of its streams were in some way or another influenced by policies created during this time.

Perhaps the most significant force that wrought fundamental change upon reluctant agencies during this period was the growing perception that control over their power to act was being taken out of their grasp and was moving instead into the hands of federal or state courts. After the spotted owl decision in the Northwest was shown to have potential impact in the Sierra Nevada forests, all federal and state agencies began to realize that their policies were being more and more held hostage to the fate of a small owl whose habitat was rapidly disappearing.

The agencies recognized the near impossibility of trying to create public policy to manage their huge holdings to suit a single species. They also realized that boundaries between federal and state holdings were meaningless when it came to dealing with forestwide problems. Because of personnel changes that reflected the influence of new scientific ideas about the broader perspectives of what was coming to be called "ecosystem management," the agencies in the Sierra Nevada launched themselves onto a new path. The Age of Ecosystem Management emerged out of the Environmental Era, and the Sierra Nevada was about to be a testing ground for these new ideas.[111]

7: The Sierra in Peril and Ecosystem Politics

On Sunday morning, June 9, 1991, readers of the *Sacramento Bee* opened their paper to a front page dominated by images of the Sierra Nevada. Bold headlines proclaimed, "Majesty and Tragedy: The Sierra in Peril." At the top of page one, a color panel showed the starkly beautiful southeastern Sierra Nevada escarpment. Mount Whitney rose above the other snow-capped giants. This was certainly the "majesty" the headline promised. But below that image was another color photograph that overpowered the idyllic vision of those southern Sierran peaks. In it, a single male figure clad in a red parka and khaki trousers walked uphill through a landscape of desolation. Erosion gullies scarred the hillsides. The only trees were small, isolated, and skeletal. The solitary hiker trudged on into an area that looked as if it had been the target of a B-52 raid. He was the only thing alive. Here, then, was the "tragedy" announced in the headline.[1]

Over the next five days, the "Sierra in Peril" story dominated the *Bee*'s news coverage. The series became immensely influential. Not only did reporter Tom Knudson and the *Bee* receive a Pulitzer Prize, but their report also influenced how government agencies, environmental and resource groups, and the public looked at the Sierra Nevada. Instead of people thinking in terms of a number of separate problem areas—places where logging, air and water pollution, or wildlife destruction was to be fought over—now the whole damaged range stood revealed. The issues were Sierra-wide and were slowly killing John Muir's Range of Light. In Sierra Nevada environmental history, it was as if things were to be B.K. and A.K.—before and after Knudson. His articles spurred agency managers to take action and brought the debate over what to do about the myriad problems facing the range to the front burner of public attention. It put these issues out into the open where the public could see and understand what was at stake.[2]

Knudson's series is the ultimate "declension narrative," a term commonly used by environmental historians to describe a certain type of environmental history—an Eden-going-to-hell-in-a-handbasket story, an appeal to public consciousness intended to spur action. Labeling it as such does not diminish its value—it remains an important part of Sierra Nevada historical literature.[3]

"Sierra in Peril" was published June 9–13, 1991. The first article summarized the issues facing the Sierra: polluted air, dying forests, vanishing wildlife, eroding soil, and damage from economic development. This lead article emphasized that government was not doing much about the problems because of lack of funding for effective scientific research. But more than inaction was to blame. Knudson accused federal agencies, especially the Forest Service, of actively aiding the destruction.[4]

In the second article, Knudson presented an in-depth account of air pollution in the Sierra. The headline read, "Smog Fouls Crystal-Clear Mountain Air." The list of specific pollutants found in Sierran air included ozone, sulfur dioxide, polycyclic aromatic hydrocarbons, and carbon monoxide. All areas of the range were affected, although areas such as the Tahoe-Truckee and Mammoth urbanized zones and the western slopes of the southern Sierra were worse off. The *Bee* reporter introduced a German word—*Waldsterben,* or forest death—to describe the phenomenon that was claiming some six billion dead or dying trees in the Sierra. Ozone was singled out as one of the most important chemical killers at work. At Tahoe on the eastern side, 25 percent of trees in one study were claimed to have been injured by this pollutant.[5]

The third article focused on other causes of the death of Sierran forests. Most important was logging. Other factors, such as air pollution, drought, damage from insects, and fire-suppression policies, were named as contributors to the demise of Sierra Nevada forests. But it was logging by the Forest Service that was primarily to blame: cutting on ever-more-sensitive and unstable slopes, savaging wildlife habitat, using "salvage logging" as a justification for cutting more trees, and of course, increased clear-cutting. Forest Service announcements of concern for "biodiversity" and "new perspectives" did not mask the fact that "timber still runs the show" at the agency, Knudson said.[6]

On the fourth day, Knudson featured soil erosion. The most powerful support for the headline, "Flooded Land Choking Streams," was an in-depth story about one area—Last Chance Creek, a tributary of Indian Creek in Plumas National Forest. Knudson had used a photo of the area on the first day of the series—it was the image that showed what he described as "a moonscape of eroded land and denuded forest." The destruction was not blamed on a "random act of nature," but on actions and decisions of the Forest Service.[7]

After four days of unrelenting descriptions of the perils that threatened the Sierra, the fifth and last day of the series ran under the headline "Hopes for Reform Improve." Knudson reported that, all across the Sierra—in towns, on trails, and even in Forest Service circles—discussions of a hopeful nature were beginning to occur. The Forest Service regional office in San

Francisco said that a growing awareness of the range's vulnerability was beginning to take hold. As to how to approach the problems the series had exposed, a number of ideas by environmentalists and scientists were introduced. All of them were either regionally based or rangewide in focus—pointing away from the piecemeal approaches of agencies or conservation groups of the past. These proposals included the creation of a Sequoia National Preserve to protect the southern Sierra forests; a Range of Light National Park to combine Yosemite, Sequoia, and Kings Canyon under one management shield; a Sierra Biosphere Preserve that would function as a single "geographic and environmental entity" protecting the range from Lake Tahoe to Sequoia National Park; and a Sierra Nevada Commission that would control development along the lines of the California Coastal Commission. In addition to these proposals, reform of Sierra Nevada logging practices and state actions to strengthen air-pollution laws were mentioned.[8]

Much of the power of Knudson's investigation came from short case studies illustrating the problems he described. In one, he told the story of damage caused by heavy cutting in the Mill Creek area in the Tahoe National Forest in 1990. A timber sale was proposed. An environmental assessment was prepared. A clear-cut was approved. The environmental assessment claimed that clear-cutting would "improve bald eagle habitat, promote 'visual diversity,' even enhance recreation." Although the slopes of the timber sale area were steep and Mill Creek, "a clear, cold trout stream," cascaded through it, the logging proceeded with approval of the forest supervisor. Knudson quoted from the Forest Service assessment: "All practicable means to avoid or minimize environmental harm have been adopted"; and, "Soil and water resources will be protected." Then came Knudson's description of the effects of the clearcut: "That is not how things turned out. Today, the area is an open wound: a stump-scarred wasteland of barren slopes and eroding soil. Downhill, Mill Creek is clogged with mud and the trout are gone."[9]

The last section of the "Sierra in Peril" series, on hopes for reform, provided a break from the unrelenting jeremiad of Sierran woes that had gone before. But apparently Knudson could not allow himself a Hollywood, feel-good ending. The article closed with a case study entitled "Growth: Like Gold Rush of 49, People Pour into Hills." It was illustrated by a color photo of a house foundation being constructed on a ridgeline above the fast-growing Tahoe-Donner area and three smaller photographs that showed other examples of growth in the range. One of these focused on a foothill subdivision. Another showed a crowded main street in a gold rush–era town. The third depicted the construction of a shopping mall in Truckee—the caption read, "At the new Gateway shopping center in Truckee, a company called Trees to Go reintroduces coniferous trees into a parking lot where a forest once stood." Knudson said six of the ten fastest-growing California counties were in the Sierra. Service industries were rapidly replacing ranching, logging, and mining as the new economy. And new urban roads and power lines were affecting wildlife habitat and air quality. In Truckee, population had jumped 62 percent since 1980, weekend traffic and population had mushroomed well beyond that as tourists poured in, and air-quality problems had become severe.[10]

With that sour note, the series came to an end. But the Sierra Nevada would not be looked at in the same way after it was written. Within days, responses to the series, especially in the agencies that had been singled out for criticism, began to take shape. And not only in defensive ways, either. Agencies and the public got the point. It was the Sierra as an ecosystem that was in trouble. Knudson deserved the Pulitzer Prize he received for publicizing the idea of a rangewide crisis. A boundary line of historic consciousness had been crossed in the Sierra Nevada. For the next decade, ecosystem management and rangewide political actions would be the order of the day. Whether this viewpoint would provide successful strategies to get the Sierra out of peril was another matter.

The Politics of Ecosystem Management in the Sierra, 1990–1996

In August of 1992, I conducted an interview with Tom Knudson. By that time, "Sierra in Peril" had become a historic document, playing an important role in shaping Sierran resource policy. Public agencies with jurisdiction in the range were adjusting to the new perspective, forging alliances to coordinate activities, and thinking and acting in terms of the range as a single threatened ecosystem. Environmentalists and some business groups were also creating Sierra-wide alliances. I asked him why he thought the series had such an impact. He said that the articles apparently "struck a chord" or "hit a nerve." The public was clearly ready to respond to the main point—that Sierran issues could not be handled piecemeal. Knudson believed that his articles had awakened people to consider the range as a whole. He noted that he felt humbled by the response and, at the same time, was pleased by the power of the press to influence actions and bring change.[11]

Knudson had not defined the term *ecosystem* in the "Sierra in Peril" series, nor had he explained a related concept called "ecosystem management." But by 1990, in state and federal resource agencies, scientific communities, environmental groups, and to a lesser degree the public mind, ecological science and public policy were beginning to come together. This blending would have direct impact on how agencies managed public land and natural spaces in the future. As a journalist, Knudson had hit upon the exact center of a debate emerging within federal and state resource agencies on the escalating environmental problems facing the range.[12]

The age of ecosystem management was dawning in the Sierra. Controversies that focused on logging, owls, or places such as Yosemite or Tahoe continued, of course. But now they were more likely to be seen in a new context by state and federal resource agencies—ecosystem-oriented and Sierra-wide. Environmental and economic interest groups also responded to the new ideas and actions that the agencies proposed. Together, public and private groups and government actions forged a new approach to the range's management and use.

Without doubt, the most important factor that forced federal and state resource agencies to begin thinking in terms of managing resources on an ecosystem scale was the spotted owl controversy. It had the potential of disrupting all agency actions and severely affecting not only the forest product industry, but the economy of the state of California as well.[13]

Northern spotted owl litigation concerned the California Resources Agency as well as the U.S. Forest Service. Fish and Wildlife personnel in the Northwest had indicated that similar issues were likely to arise regarding the California spotted owl in the Sierra and the Coast Range. The potential for disruption in the California economy was real. Newly appointed state resources secretary Douglas Wheeler turned to the new idea of ecosystem management with hope that it could resolve the problems facing the state's public land management. Fresh from a post in the World Wildlife Fund, Wheeler was familiar with the bioregional concept and saw it as an alternative to single-species management—such as was occurring in the spotted owl issue. Working with the Inter-Agency Natural Areas Council and the Timberland Task Force created in 1989 to study forest issues, Wheeler and Governor Pete Wilson decided to develop a formal bioregional approach for California. In September of 1991, Wheeler negotiated a "Memorandum of Understanding on California's Coordinated Regional Strategy to Conserve Biological Diversity" among ten member groups—federal and state resource agencies, the University of California, and some local governments—to promote cooperation across jurisdiction lines.[14]

As Wheeler and his staff were contemplating their maiden voyage into bioregional management for the Klamath Bioregion, Knudson's articles appeared. Because of the publicity and high degree of interest that "Sierra in Peril" stimulated, Wheeler decided to focus on the Sierra ecosystem instead. In November of 1991 he convened a "Sierra Summit," inviting some 200 individuals. About 150 attended—heads of various federal and state resource agencies, scientists, local political leaders, businesspeople, and environmentalists. One journalist, Tom Knudson, was allowed to attend. The meeting, closed to all except those invited, was held at Fallen Leaf Lake at Tahoe in the middle of an early snowstorm.[15]

One of the more prominent speakers to address the group was Ronald Stewart, regional forester for the Pacific Southwest Region, which included the Sierra. Stewart's remarks in some particulars mirrored those of Tom Knudson. He cited population growth, commercial development, air pollution, and mounting threats to wildlife. Recreation use was expanding exponentially. Demands for water from the Sierra were increasing as well, even as drought was stretching the limits of the range's ability to produce it. In the national forests and in the Sierra Nevada, Stewart said, "Too many people are demanding too much from a shrinking land and resource base."[16]

After the "Summit," some critics contended that it had been elitist and unrepresentative. To try to dispel that idea, five regional meetings were held in Sierran communities over the following months. Some of these meetings (at Quincy, for example) produced agreement over problems in the range, but others generated anger and confrontation (in Placerville, a United Forest Families group assailed the panel). In all, 1,500 people attended the five regional conferences. Typically, in the most commodity-oriented areas, suspicion of the "Summit " initiative ran high.[17]

A Sierra Summit Steering Committee was created to evaluate the conference and the regional workshops and to suggest an agenda for future actions. Several months later, the committee issued a report. It suggested that agencies consider three main directions: cooperating across agency lines in the range's interest, developing more information and research about the range and its problems, and promoting activities that implemented sustainable economic growth.[18] In the months that followed the Sierra Summit, two developments appeared to move toward the report's stated goals. First came the creation of a "Sierra Nevada Research Planning" initiative to coordinate scientific research on the range, and second, a "California Environmental Resources and Evaluation System" was to be established to build an online database and geographic information system. The third goal, fostering sustainable economic growth, proved to be more controversial and led environmentalists and commodity-producing interests to form separate Sierra-wide bodies to promote their views.[19]

In the immediate aftermath of the Sierra Summit, further publicity reinforced the idea of an imperiled Sierra. In May of 1992 *Sunset* magazine published a profusely illustrated article entitled "Treasures and Troubles of the

Sierra Nevada." It followed the formula established by the "Peril" series—uncontrolled growth in the foothills, overstressed forests, trampled mountain meadows, polluted air, obstructed scenic views, and endangered animal and fish life. The author, Jeff Phillips, was shown in a photograph with Douglas Wheeler reviewing the page proofs of the article. Not surprisingly, Phillips lauded Wheeler's Sierra Summit. Phillips also noted that environmentalists were scheduling a conference in August to promote rangewide cooperation in developing a conservation strategy.[20]

Not all those attending the Sierra Summit shared consensus on its recommendations. Environmentalists were concerned about too much stress on economic development. Dissatisfied Sierra Nevada county politicians, commodity interests, and residents of timber-dependent counties feared further government "meddling" and limitations on logging. As a result of these different visions, both sides planned organizational meetings, hoping to build effective political coalitions. Interestingly, the two groups did agree with one major point made by the Sierra Summit and "Sierra in Peril"—namely, that any organization created from their actions had to deal with the range as a whole.[21]

Environmentalists acted first. With funding supplied by a group called Environment Now, a conference was held in Sacramento in August 1992. Its central theme was "Sierra Now." Those attending included representatives of environmental organizations and "amenity-oriented" (as opposed to commodity production) business interests, as well as scientists and local politicians. Tom Knudson was there and was applauded by the audience. Secretary Wheeler addressed the group and received a mixed response. Sequoia activist Martin Litton gave the keynote address and was enthusiastically received. After consideration of the range's environmental problems by panels of experts and scientists, a "Vision for the Sierra" was announced. One element of this "Vision" was a new organization to be called the Sierra Nevada Alliance. Its goal was to promote public policy that would protect, restore, and maintain ecological health in the Sierra Nevada. Intended to act as a federation representing environmental groups based in the range, in practice it has promoted collaborative action rather than going to court to challenge agencies or timber companies. It has also sponsored watershed organizing, using funds from federal and state sources to assist such activities. Since 1994 it has held annual conferences bringing together diverse environmental groups and other interests to discuss and act upon Sierran issues.[22]

In June of 1993, commodity-production and timber-dependent community interests, some Sierra Nevada county politicians, and Sierra-based chambers of commerce and business alliances organized the Sierra Economic

Summit. Concerned about further reduction of timber cutting and more government regulation, they announced resistance to new government entities such as those proposed at the Sierra Summit. They also feared new environmental organizations such as the Sierra Nevada Alliance. Tom Knudson was not invited to attend the conference. His "Sierra In Peril" series was denounced as biased and inaccurate by a conference spokesman. Resources Secretary Wheeler spoke and received a polite but chilly response. Representatives from the Sierra Nevada Alliance addressed the group, but their message was not welcomed. Alston Chase, author of *Playing God in Yellowstone,* gave a luncheon speech and heard his anti–federal management views applauded. There were various panels of experts and appearances by some local government representatives. The Sierra Economic Summit organizers called for the creation of an umbrella organization to represent business interests in the range. Several subsequent organizational meetings failed to produce results and no such umbrella group has materialized.[23]

In 1994 another business initiative led to the creation of the Sierra Business Council. This group, while not excluding agricultural or timber interests, primarily represented businesses serving the recreational and "amenity-oriented" economic expansion and population growth that had occurred in the Sierra since the 1950s. Its membership was Sierra-wide. The organization reflected economic changes going on in many portions of the range. A new population and new economic development were overlaying or replacing the commodity and timber interests that had traditionally dominated the region.[24] Environmental quality was seen as an important economic asset that traditional extractive industries could damage or destroy. Rapid population growth created new issues and calls to slow or control it.[25]

It was because of these issues that the Sierra Business Council was founded. In 1997 the group issued a report called *Planning for Prosperity.* It proposed that successful communities in the Sierra should plan for economic growth in a way that would preserve the amenities that had drawn businesses and people into the region in the first place. These included clean air, rural lifestyle, lack of crowding and urban sprawl, good schools, low crime rates, and natural beauty. *Planning for Prosperity* was intended to influence political leaders.[26]

As awareness of the new perspective on the Sierra spread in the wake of Knudson's articles, it was inevitable that the Sierra Club would respond. In May of 1992 the club's journal, *Sierra,* published an article by Joan Hamilton entitled "Visions of the Range of Light." It was a "State of the Sierra" piece that acknowledged reliance on Tom Knudson. There were four sidebars, all based on "Sierra in Peril," collectively entitled "Policies to Pursue." They focused on wildlife, forests, air pollution, and water quality. All four suggested strategies to cope with problems. The article recommended ecosystem approaches to the Sierra, as Wheeler had advocated at the Sierra Summit. Hamilton saw Wheeler's and similar actions as positive signs of coming changes in management in the range.[27]

In 1994 the Sierra Club defined a broad "Critical Ecoregions Program" that encompassed all of North America, defining twenty-one regional ecosystems, including the Sierra Nevada. The introduction to the program stated that task forces were being organized in each of these areas.[28] The Sierran program called for building on gains in existing protected areas but said that new actions to protect oak woodlands and chaparral zones were needed as well. The goal of the Sierran task force was defined: "The Club's objective is a Sierra Nevada wild enough to permit native species to migrate, recolonize after local extinctions, and adapt to long-term climate change." To accomplish such a program, the club and the public had to adopt a strategy that replaced older conservation activities with "organic, ecosystem efforts." The new initiative aimed for protection of "entire landscapes, habitats, and watersheds"; coordination with all environmental groups to develop an effective strategy; and cooperation with federal agencies. In particular, the club focused on programs to protect ancient forests, including banning logging and roads from such areas and providing more critical wildlife habitat throughout the Sierra. The overall goal in the "Sierra Nevada Ecoregion" was to return more-natural conditions to the range.[29]

The Wilderness Society's first published response to the idea of the Sierra Nevada as a threatened ecosystem occurred in the winter of 1993 with an article in its membership magazine, *Wilderness.* In "Dimming the Range of Light," George Wuerthner provided a description of the range's "superlatives," followed by a summary of its problems. This account of the troubled Sierra Nevada followed the by-now well-worn trail blazed by Knudson.[30] In 1994, another *Wilderness* article, Robert Divine's "Management and the Uncertainty Principle," provided a good description of the difficulty of defining "ecosystem management." The writer applied the lesson to the Pacific Northwest forests and did not mention the Sierra.[31]

The Wilderness Society launched a "Range of Light" program to be based on the information available in the newly published Sierra Nevada Ecosystem Project report. The SNEP report was based on a Forest Service–funded study conducted between 1993 and 1996. Its origins and recommendations will be discussed in more detail later. The Wilderness Society delayed its "Range of Light" project until SNEP was completed, introducing its ecosystem goals in a profusely illustrated pamphlet entitled *The Sierra Nevada:*

Renewing the Glow of the Range of Light. The pamphlet asked readers to play a role in helping the range at a time when it was at a crucial "crossroad."[32]

The Wilderness Society's project was to be based on information contained in its larger publication entitled *The Federal Forest Lands of the Sierra Nevada: A Citizens Guide to the Sierra Nevada Ecosystem Project Report.* This guide included several maps and transparencies and was tailored for use in facilitated workshops to be held in several locations in the Sierra Nevada in the months following its publication. The purpose of *Federal Forest Lands of the Sierra Nevada* was to summarize SNEP's four volumes and several thousand pages so that local forest activists could come to see the range as an interconnected ecosystem. But the workshops were also intended to give participants clear, science-based strategies to apply to their own watersheds or national forests. Immediate goals included instruction in developing letters to write to the regional forester, California senators, and Department of Agriculture officials. The Wilderness Society strategy was to create an educated populace conversant with the best information available on the Sierran ecosystem.[33]

Forest Issues and the Era of Ecosystems

The changing legal and political climate of the late 1980s and early 1990s found the Forest Service caught in a dilemma partly of its own making. Forest Service actions in the intensive-management era had resulted in forest policy often being made in the courts following challenges to timber sales, forest plans, or wildlife policies by environmental groups. Attempting to break free from what amounted to outside control, the service scrambled to reconsider its philosophy and commodity-production emphasis. The process of change began publicly in 1989 with Chief Forester Dale Robertson announcing that henceforth the Forest Service would be experimenting with a new set of principles. Robertson first labeled his initiative "New Perspectives" but later opted for the phrase *ecosystem management* to describe the new direction he hoped to take. Included in this policy would be ecosystem and ecological values, as well as sustained-yield practices.[34]

For the area covering the Sierra, Regional Forester Paul Barker issued a press release announcing a new environmental agenda in February of 1990:

"1990 begins the Decade of the Environment"
The ENVIRONMENTAL AGENDA for the National Forests in California has three major objectives—PRESERVATION, BIODIVERSITY, and SUSTAINABLE DEVELOPMENT FOR PEOPLE[35]

Barker's announcement of this new ecological perspective was somewhat inaccurate. Its timing reflected the fact that the Forest Service, like many public and private conservation and environmental groups, was commemorating the twentieth anniversary of Earth Day.[36] The new ecosystem orientation actually was only being explored by agency leadership in principle and had not been put into practice. No formal policy shifting the service to science-based ecosystem management had been formulated. And as of 1990, emphasis on timber production continued. As a consequence, many important timber-related issues still bedeviled the agency.[37] Because of pressing litigation and widespread public discontent, some in the leadership believed that there was a need to move toward bioregional perspectives. The Forest Service did begin to address some of the serious issues facing it, but certainly not consistently or with a clear idea of where it was going.[38] It is useful here to consider how and why national Forest Service and Region 5 (Pacific Southwest) leaders adopted "ecosystem management" as their chief management strategy for the Sierra—especially considering what happened to the idea as the agency's political strategies and priorities changed over the ensuing decade.

For the public record, Robertson on June 4, 1992, issued a press release stating that the New Perspectives initiative had made good progress. The goal of that initiative had been for the Forest Service to experiment "with more environmentally sensitive [ways] to manage the National Forests and Grasslands under its control." Because of the success of this experiment, he said, the Forest Service was ready to adopt a "new management philosophy" called "ecosystem management." It was the "right way" because forests were "dynamic and complex ecosystems," and it was time to put the management of national forests "on an ecological basis." The New Perspectives project had shown him that it was necessary to increase public involvement in forest planning. It was also necessary to establish effective partnerships with groups with shared interests, such as state and local governments, conservation groups, universities, and those in the private sector. He wrote that effective land management required significant scientific cooperation as well.[39]

This new ecosystem management idea had in fact already been introduced by James C. Overbay, deputy chief of the Forest Service, at a national workshop on "Taking an Ecological Approach to Management" in Salt Lake City on April 27, 1992. His speech to that meeting stressed the need for more public involvement, more scientific information, and greater interaction between scientists and resource managers in future agency actions.[40] On May 29, 1992, Hal Salwasser, director of the New Perspectives initiative, spoke to the Blue Mountains Biodiversity Conference in Walla Walla, Washington.

He said that for the past two years, his group had been exploring "new perspectives in the ecological dimensions of our management and research. This [was] happening in cooperation with universities, forest user groups, and professional societies through hundreds of projects across the country." He explained that all national forests had been directed to conduct "at least one project" to explore new scientific thinking. He added that New Perspectives and other resource initiatives had "furthered the shift to an ecosystem perspective in the 1980's and 1990's. Now, ecosystem management has been adopted as a fundamental concept for stewardship of the National Forests and national grasslands."[41] The Forest Service was obviously signaling that it was embarking on a new policy path.

On June 25, 1992, Chief Robertson informed all regional offices and stations that he was pleased with the responses he had received to his ecosystem-management directive. He said it was time to implement the new policy and that it would include changes in the agency's reliance on clearcutting that had so angered the public. He characterized it as the most important policy change since the 1960s. He told all regions and stations to begin the task of reorganization. New planning should include promoting significant public involvement, developing conservation partnerships, meshing ecosystem management with forest planning, providing for effective monitoring and evaluation, beginning appropriate training and recruiting of staff to make the new policy work, and creating effective methods to measure implementation of future actions.[42]

The Pacific Southwest Region and the Pacific Southwest Station submitted a joint draft of their plans to Robertson on September 4, 1992. In a cover letter, Regional Forester Ron Stewart noted: "The Strategy for implementing Ecosystem Management and Research does not directly address clearcutting since clearcutting is a specific management practice rather than an overall strategy. Instead, the analysis of appropriate use of clearcutting is addressed through the Planning Inventory, and Evaluation element." The chief was informed that the draft incorporated ecosystem management concepts for inclusion in forest plans and new projects.[43]

On October 29, Jerry Sesco and Jim Overbay at the national headquarters sent a reply stating that Chief Robertson was supportive of the region's work, noting that "Dale took $5 million out of the roads budget to OMB for scientific consultation for implementation of the policy on-the-ground." They closed by saying that, in the public's mind, reduction of clearcutting was "the most important sign of our shift in philosophy. It will be implemented over time to prevent disruption of [the] program. Line officers need to be personally involved to assure we remain productive and to keep our employees and our public involved. We have been poking the public in the eye with our clear-cutting of their National Forests."[44]

Upon receiving approval from Washington, in December of 1992 Regional Forester Stewart informed supervisors, staff directors, and the director of the PSW Station of the chief's acceptance of the "Strategy for Implementing Ecosystem Management and Research." The strategy was complex and is too long even to summarize here, but a selective sampling is useful. One interesting part said that the strategy was based on nineteen ecological principles. These were broad-ranging and philosophical, including such ideas as that humans are dependent on the biosphere, and that human needs and their impacts on sustainability of forest systems must be considered. Some generalized about interactions among organisms in ecological systems (natural selection occurs at all scales, and competition can create both diversity and natural extinctions). Others restated basic laws of natural systems ("The larger and more complex things become, the more energy required to maintain order") or of ecological economics ("Major changes in ecosystems, as in human systems, are costly to implement").[45] Heady stuff for an agency that had been primarily cutting trees and establishing single-species plantations for three decades.

Stewart's message also asserted the need to create a "Framework for Adopting New Approaches to Ecosystem Management and Research." He said there were three parts to this framework. The first was the need to create partnerships among the PSW Region and Station, the public, and Forest Service employees. The second involved planning, inventorying, and evaluation of scientific and technical information, data gathering, and technical support for ecosystem management and research. The third element concerned internal issues such as organization and training.[46] At several points in the strategy, Stewart emphasized the importance of public involvement in any future action.

Five elements of the strategy specifically mentioned "ecological" issues. One was the need to make a standard ecological classification system. The second was the need to create maps and inventories of resources using a consistent geographic information system protocol. The final three elements called for assessing existing, potential, and desired future conditions of the region's forest ecosystems.[47]

Obviously such an endeavor would be challenging to Region 5 and other forests facing the same fundamental shift in philosophy. At best, Stewart's ecosystem strategy was only an outline of possible actions. One humorous comment on the radical change it represented came from a district biologist in the Walker Ranger District of the Chippewah National Forest in Minnesota who headed an open letter to his fellow Forest Service employees with the words "There's No Such Thing As An Ecosystem." The biologist stated that he was not certain what an ecosystem was, although he could see lots of plants and rocks and trees that reacted over time to such things as fire or floods and then settled down with some sort of order prevailing again. He was not certain that firm boundaries for ecosystems existed: "This is a real problem, folks. I'm supposed to be doing ecosystem management and I can't even find one of the suckers. Hell, I'm tempted to go back and start working with good old stands and compartments. They were the edge of the area we clearcut or the edge of the disked area in a new permanent opening." He closed by asserting that the new rules lacked clear guidelines for policy or management. He said he might quit and begin managing his own small piece of land by mowing and cutting, and call his friends over to visit "my ecosystem."[48]

During the decade that followed the decision to adopt ecosystem management, several important challenges faced leaders and forest supervisors trying to operate under that policy in Region 5. First of all, it became clear that district officials would have to gather scientific information upon which to base any ecosystem policy for the Sierra. Next, the term *ecosystem management* needed to be more carefully defined. Meanwhile, the troublesome California spotted owl problem remained to be resolved, and a community-based logging plan in Quincy, California, potentially threatened actions being considered by the owl scientists in the Sierra. Proposals to increase salvage logging in western forests, including the Sierra, also looked as if they might disrupt ecosystem planning. To top off this list of confusing but interrelated issues, the regional leadership took on the task of amending the plans of the Sierran national forests and two others close by, in what was being called the "Sierran province." All of these things complicated any attempt by Region 5 officials to regain control of the agency's destiny and together constituted what can be called the politics of ecosystem management in the Sierra Nevada.

The need for a science-based study of the Sierra as an ecosystem resulted in the Forest Service's Sierra Nevada Ecosystem Project. SNEP began with two legislative actions in the U.S. House of Representatives in 1992. HR 5503 authorized Congress to appropriate $150,000 for an assessment of old-growth forests in the Sierra Nevada—essentially for some mapping and initial planning. HR 6013 called for the creation of a full-scale Sierra Nevada ecosystem study. HR 5503 passed and went on to a conference committee, where the $150,000 appropriation was authorized in January of 1993. The second bill did not get voted on because time in the session ran out. But two letters from congressmen to the chief of the Forest Service, Dale Robertson, made it clear that Congress wanted a complete ecosystem assessment of the range. The two letters acknowledged that $150,000 was not enough to complete such an assessment but promised further appropriations. Both letters stressed that the study must be conducted by an independent and interdisciplinary group of scientists. Under pressure to begin the large-scale assessment desired by Congress, the Forest Service added to the paltry congressional appropriation by committing some $6,500,000 more to fund the project.[49]

The legislation mandated the creation of a steering committee consisting of Forest Service personnel, several University of California scientists, and "a scientist of eminent standing from the National Academy of Sciences." U.C. professor Don Erman was chosen to head the science team that organized the study. The steering committee made clear in its "charge" to the science team that its goal was to carry out "a science based assessment." The study was to "incorporate the results of the review of the remaining old-growth as well as the other elements of this ecosystem." It was "not intended to be an *old-growth* or Sierra Nevada *forest* study, rather it [was] intended to be an *ecosystem* study for the Sierra Nevada range." Land ownership and agency boundaries were not to be factors in limiting its scope.[50]

SNEP was to provide a scientific baseline for ecosystem management in the Sierra Nevada. It was also intended to address how past and present patterns of use had affected the range. It was specifically charged with identifying trends and risks for the range as a whole under current policies. It was to consider policy choices that could produce ecological stability and social well-being at the same time. The investigation was to be structured into two major parts. The first would focus on an "initial assessment of the status of late-successional forests, key watersheds, and significant natural areas on the federally owned lands of the Sierra Nevada ecoregion." In the second part the science team would "evaluate various methodologies for simulating the implications of alternative management strategies for the Sierra Nevada ecoregion."[51]

The date for completion was set for 1995, a requirement that forced participants to meet strict timelines. Their studies were supposed to synthesize existing information. New research was not the goal of the project. Most of the peer-reviewed studies that were commissioned to form the scientific, economic, and historical basis for management options appeared in volume 2 of the project's final report. That volume contained six major sections, focusing on "Past Sierran Landscapes, Human Components of the Sierra

Ecosystem, Biological and Physical Elements of the Sierra Nevada, Agents of Change in the Sierra Nevada, SNEP Case Studies, and Building Strategies for the Sierra Nevada." (Some peer-reviewed studies submitted too late for initial editing were placed in volume 3 along with other commissioned studies.)[52]

SNEP technically met its 1995 deadline, although the actual printed study did not appear until June of 1996. A meeting in Sacramento in September of 1995 previewed some of the study's main elements. These included preliminary reports on fire, air quality, aquatic life, population, and economy.[53] Draft information on the SNEP study was presented to the press in March and again in early June of 1996. At a formal meeting in Placerville, science team members and contributors presented their findings to a large group that included local and state politicians. Secretary Wheeler was present, continuing his involvement in Sierra-wide issues. Also attending were small numbers of anti-SNEP activists. One group calling itself the American Land Rights Association (headquartered in Battleground, Wisconsin) issued dollar-bill facsimiles as handouts with Interior Secretary Bruce Babbitt's face printed on them. The "bill" was a "pink slip" intended for "all rural and resource community workers." Printed on the phony dollar bill also were the catch phrases "One Less Job SNEP is Here," and "URLANDSNEP controlled."[54]

The final SNEP report identified nine key points regarding management in the Sierra:

1. Climate change must be considered in future planning.

2. Accelerating population growth must be considered in future planning.

3. Agencies and jurisdictions must coordinate their activities to assist endangered natural systems.

4. Agency fire-suppression policies must be reconsidered.

5. Land managers must respond to threats to animal and plant diversity.

6. Because of the simplification and reduction of late successional old-growth forests by human actions, land managers must give immediate attention to restoring healthy forest conditions and promoting structural diversity.

7. Land managers must provide for sustainable ecological functions in rangelands and restore damaged uplands, meadows, and riparian systems, due to past and present impacts.

8. Land managers must take effective action to increase water quality

and reestablish and/or maintain populations of anadromous fish, amphibians, and aquatic invertebrates, due to the altered and impaired
habitats of aquatic and riparian systems.

9. Land managers must address areas of the Sierra Nevada severely
impacted by air pollution.[55]

The SNEP report will have long-term significance in Sierra Nevada environmental history. Its impact on environmental groups has already been
noted. As to its immediate influence on forest policy, it soon affected the
attempt by the Forest Service to create a California spotted owl policy.

A second significant issue involved the actual formulation of a Forest Service ecosystem policy for the Sierra Nevada. The idea predated "Sierra in
Peril," as noted. An ecosystem-management commitment by the Forest Service began in 1989 and was established formally in 1992 under Dale
Robertson. But like Moses, although Robertson could lead his people toward the promised land, he did not enter it as head of the Forest Service.
Because of constant criticism by environmentalists for policies they claimed
had supported excessive logging, President Bill Clinton replaced him in
1993.[56] The work to formulate an ecosystem-management framework had
already been assigned to an Ecosystem Management Steering Committee for
Region 5 in March of 1993. The team assembled to develop policy had to
define clear objectives for ecosystem management, delineate the major ecosystems in the region, and develop a process for incorporating the group's
ideas into planning for individual projects, as well as for larger forest-level
and multiforest-level activities.[57]

In April of 1995, the Pacific Southwest Region published *Sustaining Ecosystems: A Conceptual Framework.* It was to be the guide for implementing
ecosystem management in the region's national forests. It said that the new
policy combined current ecosystem theory with already existing efforts
within the Service to describe and classify ecosystems. As to ecosystem management, the report called it a "term created to distinguish that the ecosystem itself is the context for management rather than just its individual
parts." Moreover, "*Ecosystem Management* is the central theme for the future
of the Forest Service." The "Conceptual Framework" section of the new
policy stated that the purpose of ecosystem management was "Sustaining
Ecosystems in Region 5." Sustainability was defined as "conserving *biological
and cultural/social diversity.*" The "conceptual framework" was intended to
supply a "rationale and process" for doing this through the implementation
of Region 5's land and resource management plans. Ecosystem management
would not just affect the information upon which management decisions in

the region would be made. It required that collaborative decision-making (involving the public, Indian tribes, other government agencies, and communities) be an ongoing process—not just "input" at some point in the planning as had occurred in the past.[58]

The new policy was an answer to the broader criticism aimed at the service for its past timber policies. The "Conceptual Framework" asked Forest Service employees to accept that change was coming and asked all to support the new initiative as "a building block for the Region's future." The report's "Executive Summary" carried the following caveat: "In Application, we must recognize that ecosystem management will not work unless resulting actions are scientifically credible, legally defensible, and socially acceptable."[59] Obviously, the new planning direction for Region 5 was intended in part to put the Forest Service back into the good graces of scientists and public alike.

Ecosystem management did begin to permeate the agency's thinking and actions to a significant degree—even if political pressure and some internal resistance continued. Two new leaders of the Forest Service, Jack Ward Thomas and Mike Dombeck, early on supported a more important role for science in planning. In 1993, Thomas, as the agency's new chief, signaled clearly the road he expected the service to take: "It is time to consider land use in a broader context than a series of single-use allocations to address specific problems or pacify the most vocal constituencies. We cannot continue along our present path of dealing with the assured welfare of individual species as constraints and outputs of goods and services as objectives. The questions are bigger and more complex."[60]

The third important response to ecosystem thinking was the Forest Service's attempt to resolve the California spotted owl problem. The "assured welfare of individual species" was precisely the opposite direction from the one the service intended to take under ecosystem management. The agency was stuck with it in the Northwest, where the northern spotted owl was the subject of swirling legal controversy. But in California it was to be a different matter. At least the California Resources Agency and the Forest Service hoped so.

The California spotted owl was becoming part of a growing conflict over forest policy issues in the Sierra Nevada after 1990. California and federal forest and wildlife agencies were very concerned that legal challenges over spotted owl habitat conditions might bring all logging to a halt in the Sierra Nevada as it had in the Pacific Northwest. Something had to be done. In 1991, the Forest Service and the state of California created a California Spotted Owl Steering Committee to focus attention on the issue. It divided the problem in two, creating separate task forces to address policy review and policy formation. A technical-assessment team of federal and state scientists went to work studying the status of the owl in the Sierra. In late 1992, after comment and evaluation of the technical group's report, the team issued *The California Spotted Owl: A Technical Assessment of Its Current Status,* the so-called CASPO Report. The report concluded that the existing Forest Service owl-habitat management strategy based on so-called Spotted Owl Habitat Areas or SOHAS would likely lead to the extinction of the California spotted owl. It said that logging of large-diameter trees and fire-suppression policies had created forest conditions that could lead to the destruction of old-growth stands—primary habitat for the owl. The CASPO assessment recommended no more logging of large, old-growth forest stands, placing greater emphasis on thinning and fuel management in or near owl habitat. And, of course, the policy called for more research on the owl.[61]

In January 1993, the Forest Service adopted the technical-assessment team's formula and imposed rangewide limits on logging for the ten national forests of the Sierra Nevada Province. These limits were meant as part of an interim policy until a longer-term strategy could be created. Meanwhile, an environmental impact assessment study went forward.[62]

In January of 1995, the Forest Service issued a draft environmental impact statement (DEIS) for managing owl habitat in the Sierra Nevada. Subtitled "An Ecosystem Approach," it listed seven alternatives. The primary objective of most alternatives was to protect owl habitat as well as that of several other species listed as at risk while providing for sustainable levels of renewable resources production. The agency's preferred alternative (alternative C) proposed managing lower-slope old-growth late-successional forests and riparian zones to maximize owl habitat, creating a more open but still continuous forest cover for the mid-slope zone and providing for an open upper-slope/ridge zone where trees would be widely spaced. The mid-zone allowed moderate timber harvest and salvage activities.[63]

The DEIS drew criticism from environmentalists and the timber industry alike. Environmentalists complained that the proposed plan would open up more of the remaining old-growth areas of the Sierra Nevada to logging and roads. The California Forestry Association complained that the slightly over 400 million board feet of timber to be harvested fell far short of the over 700 million board feet it said was needed to sustain timber-dependent communities and the industry.[64]

After public review, the Forest Service prepared a revised draft environmental impact statement (RDEIS) that reportedly raised cut levels closer to those desired by the timber industry. In addition, the agency had eased restrictions on the interim policy that had protected larger trees as part of the owl plan. It was also reported that the Forest Service had concluded that increased logging would bring more jobs to Sierran towns and lessen the risk of wildfire, all without harm to declining plant and animal species. Predictably, the timber industry was jubilant and the environmental community furious. But the RDEIS was dead on arrival. Under intense pressure, the Clinton administration decided to withdraw the proposed draft before it had a chance to be reviewed widely. With the tables now turned, the California Forestry Association accused President Clinton of choosing "politics over the forest." Criticism from either the timber or the environmental lobby was expected, of course. But apparently the weight of scientific criticism from the Sierra Nevada Ecosystem Project may have had more influence on the decision by the Department of Agriculture to yank the RDEIS. Former California congressman Leon Panetta, now a close Clinton adviser, had been instrumental in getting SNEP created. He was the author of the 1991 House bill (HR 6013) that had proposed creating a comprehensive Sierra study. Panetta was reported to have influenced the decision to withdraw the RDEIS. Owl policy was in disarray as the full impact of the withdrawal became clear to Forest Service planners.[65]

Faced with spotted owl chaos, the secretary of agriculture created an independent science advisory team to evaluate the RDEIS and report to him. Obviously the public, the Congress, and the administration had no confidence that the Forest Service could be trusted to formulate "owl" policy. The advisory committee consisted of several distinguished scientists and experts drawn from the academic world to evaluate the content and methodology of the RDEIS, including how well it integrated information from the newly published SNEP report.[66]

After several meetings, the committee issued its report. Its conclusions were highly critical of the whole Forest Service direction. Because of confusion it found in the RDEIS, the committee stated, it had to divide its evaluation into two parts. One was called *"OWL"* and one entitled *"ECOSYSTEM."* The division resulted, it claimed, because the RDEIS had mixed policy issues together without adequately defining what its goals were. Was it a policy designed to save owls or one intended to manage the ten forests of the Sierran Province as an ecosystem? The committee judged both approaches by the Forest Service as "inadequate." It is worth quoting this double damnation here. Regarding the "OWL CONTEXT," the report stated: "As an EIS focused on maintenance of California spotted owl habitat. . . . , the RDEIS is inadequate. This inadequacy must be addressed in a revised or amended document. The Committee recommends that USDA consult with their legal counsel and the U.S. Fish and Wildlife Service, if it considers proceeding with the RDEIS without further revisions." Its view of the RDEIS in an ecosystem context was even more contemptuous:

> As an integrated EIS intended to address conservation strategies for national forests in the Sierra Nevada, the existing RDEIS is inadequate. The Committee believes it unlikely that an ecosystem strategy for the Sierra Nevada can be achieved by modifying the RDEIS. Based on the definition of an ecosystem strategy used by this Committee there are simply too many basic components missing or inadequately developed. When the Forest Service decides where on the spectrum, between the two contexts the RDEIS belongs, the shortcomings identified under the ECOSYSTEM context should be carefully examined. The route to a Sierra Nevada ecosystem strategy may be significantly different than the one followed by the RDEIS.[67]

As to the relationship of the RDEIS to the SNEP report, the committee said that the report bore none for obvious reasons: The RDEIS was issued before SNEP was completed. The spotted owl planning was not carried out in an ecosystem context. But the committee added that some recommendations in the SNEP report could be useful for the Forest Service to consider. Besides the general data and strategies that SNEP had advanced, recommendations the committee deemed especially valuable included "fire and stand modeling tools" and analysis "of the character and distribution of [late-successional old-growth] forests."[68]

The Republican-dominated Congress was not willing to accept the scientific advisory committee's assessment of the RDEIS. The House Committee on Forests and Forest Health sponsored the creation of another committee, led by U.C.–Berkeley professor Bill McKillop. Significant internal dissent arose during the preparation of what eventually was to be a more favorable assessment by McKillop of the RDEIS. Unlike the advisory committee's report, which has gained broad acceptance in the scientific community, the McKillop report had little influence.[69]

Obviously, after the advisory committee's critical report, the Forest Service did not dare to pursue an "owl" course and face the public scrutiny required under federal law. Probably no court would have supported it if it had tried to push the RDEIS forward on such a track. And as an "ecosystem approach," the RDEIS had so many shortcomings that this door was shut as well. As of 2003, no "revised" RDEIS on the California spotted own had surfaced. Instead, the Forest Service opted for a different tactic—amending the forest plans of the ten Sierran forests. That approach will be examined later in the chapter.

A fourth major Sierran forest issue arose with the creation of a local logging initiative in the Plumas National Forest area. In October of 1998, Congress enacted the Herger-Feinstein Quincy Library Group Forest Recovery Act. The legislation prescribed a specific type of management for a large portion of the Lassen, all of the Plumas, and the Sierraville Ranger District of the Tahoe National Forests. The act affected a very large landscape, it involved local public participation to a high degree, and it proposed an aggressive plan to reduce fire danger in a complex forest system. It also promised to promote the economic well-being of the timber-dependent communities of the area. While some heralded it as a way to end environmental battles in public forests, others saw it as a fatal blow to national forest policy development and a threat to the California spotted owl.[70] The Quincy Library Group story is one of the most important sagas of the age of ecosystem management in the Sierra.[71]

As noted, national forest policies of the 1980s and 1990s involved ecosystemwide controversies. While the "big players" (national environmental groups and timber-production interests) struggled on these enlarged landscape planes, local activists tended to address environmental issues as they had in the past, piece by piece. But in one case in the northern Sierra Nevada, in Plumas County, California, a take-no-prisoners battle erupted that came to have much broader implications. There, a small environmental group called the Friends of the Plumas Wilderness, Forest Service officers, county government officials, and the giant Sierra Pacific Industries began a struggle that reshaped policy formation in the northern Sierra Nevada.[72]

The Friends of the Plumas Wilderness, with help from the Wilderness Society, the Natural Resources Defense Council, and Sierra Club lawyers, devised a plan in the late 1980s to protect the last of the roadless and old-growth forest areas in the Plumas National Forest. They intended to direct future logging activities into already logged and roaded areas, and they initiated a lawsuit to force an end to relentless cutting in remote areas. The group's litigation got the attention of local politicians and the industry. This local threat coincided with a downturn in Forest Service timber sales and the drastic cutback that accompanied the spotted owl controversy in the Pacific Northwest and California. By 1992, the "Friends" plan that had been unacceptable to the politicians and timber executives earlier had become more interesting. Neutral ground was chosen—the public library in the town of Quincy (a venue where, the joke went, no voice could be raised). Out of the dialogue between these extremes came the Quincy Library Group (QLG) and a local community-oriented logging plan. National environmental group representatives from Sacramento and San Francisco found attending meetings inconvenient because of Quincy's isolated location and trusted the "Friends" to act in the broader interests of the environmental community, but later they rejected the QLG agreement. Some local environmentalists who did not agree with the direction the discussions took were also not included in the process later complained as well.[73]

The plan of the "Friends" formed the basis for hammering out a new proposal for forest management in the Plumas and nearby forest areas in the Lassen and Tahoe National Forests. Variations of the plan were incorporated in the alternatives offered in the DEIS and RDEIS of the Forest Service's California spotted owl plan.[74] The local environmentalists hoped to get protection for the wilderness-quality lands they most desired, the timber company was to get a large volume of wood from previously managed lands, and locals were to get jobs out of the deal. A proposal along these lines to require all timber cut under the plan to be processed in local mills was removed, however, under prompting from Sierra Pacific Industries, which had mills outside the region.[75]

In the meantime, a huge fire occurred near Loyalton. In the Tahoe National Forest but close to the Plumas area, this fire intensified fears about the danger present in local forests, giving further support to the new idea. However, the QLG prescription was not accepted by the Forest Service in the final owl EIS. The service's unwillingness was attributed to the concerns of newly appointed Forest Service chief Jack Ward Thomas, who was troubled by the prominent involvement of Sierra Pacific Industries in drawing up the QLG plan.[76]

Growing impatient with the Forest Service, in 1996 the Quincy group turned directly to Congress, thus ending the collaborative process. With the influence of a local Republican congressman, the QLG idea was taken under consideration in committee, and legislation was quickly drawn up. That draft included orders to the supervisors of the Lassen, Plumas, and Tahoe National Forests to apply the new cutting plan to 2.5 million acres of forestland under their jurisdiction. If enacted, the legislation would require the Forest Service to initiate a five-year pilot project that would include logging at the rate of 9,000 acres of roaded, second-growth lands per year, with thinning of another 40,000 to 60,000 roaded acres annually. For the duration of the project, some 150,000 acres of old-growth land was not to be logged, and all trees above 30 inches in diameter were to be protected. Wider buffer zones along streams were proposed.[77] As a comparison with this proposed logging level, the original 1995 draft EIS of the California spotted owl plan called for fuel treatment and cutting to be limited to 54,000 acres per year on all ten of the national forests of the Sierra Nevada Province.[78]

This draft legislation, called the Forest Recovery and Economic Stability Act, differed from the original Quincy Library Group proposal. Watershed protection contemplated in the QLG plan was downplayed, and the 2.5 million acres to be logged were exempted from forest-management legislation requirements and the Endangered Species Act.[79] One of the principal QLG environmentalists reportedly was "horrified" when she saw the original draft.[80] Intervention by a California congressman who opposed the legislation, but feared its passage with the suspension of environmental legislation included, led to an amendment to the draft. It required an EIS, public comment (which would have been blocked in the original), and the observation of all environmental laws—including those that involved spotted owls. In that form the House of Representatives passed the bill with only one dissenting vote.[81] In the Senate the bill sped along after being introduced by both California senators.[82]

But at that point resistance from over one hundred environmental groups succeeded in halting the Senate bill's progress. California senator Barbara Boxer played a key role when she changed her mind and withdrew support.[83] She did so when presented with information from local and national environmental groups who claimed that the bill would leave unprotected thousands of acres of old-growth forests mapped during the SNEP study.[84] The Sierra Club, Natural Resources Defense Council, Wilderness Society, and other opponents of the Quincy legislation were accused by its defenders of using false information in their attack on the Senate bill.[85] The national environmental organizations contended that the proposed law would put forest planning into the hands of local interests. In their view, the Quincy process had effectively excluded outside participation. The precedent that would be set by such local initiatives was frightening to the environmental community.[86]

Eventually, the Republican majority in Congress attached the Quincy legislation to a necessary appropriation bill that President Clinton signed. In December of 1998, the Forest Service gave notice of its intent to begin EIS planning under the provisions of NEPA.[87] In August of 1999, the final EIS actions were completed. The language of the Herger-Feinstein QLG Forest Recovery Act, as it was now called, was selected as the preferred alternative. It included a provision that proposed to reduce forest fuels through the development of "defensible fuel profile zones combined with area-wide treatments."[88] This statement reflected the growing awareness of the Forest Service and the public that fire was reemerging as a significant issue. The Forest

Service was to mount an aggressive fuel-reduction program that would combine timber harvesting and prescribed burning to reduce high fuel levels created by the logging and fire-suppression policies of the past.[89] In the future, logging industry and related political interests would point to the need to increase logging as a means of reducing danger to forests and communities threatened by wildfire. They ignored the fact that heavy logging had been a major contributor to increasing fire danger.

At that point, an interesting twist occurred concerning the actual implementation of the QLG cutting and fire-reduction plan. As of December 2000, no economic windfall for Sierra Pacific Industries and the region's timber-dependent communities existed, simply because no trees were being cut. As a part of the final EIS required for the law's implementation, the Forest Service said that provisions to protect the spotted owl had to be included. The service had not completed that study; therefore, only a small area of the total covered under the QLG plan was actually being considered for cutting. Quincy Group members blamed the Forest Service for delays. The Forest Service countered that it was not purposely trying to resist implementation. Congress had sent only a small amount of the money needed to put the plan into effect, they said. Besides, the QLG law required observance of existing environmental law. The frustrated QLG threatened a lawsuit.[90]

On January 18, 2001, the regional forester for the Pacific Southwest Region issued a Record of Decision (ROD) on another forest issue—the Sierra Nevada Framework, a plan revision for the national forests that made up what the Forest Service had begun to call the Sierran "Province." That ROD needs to be quoted here, because it illustrates the significance of the QLG-legislated forest planning in the Sierra Nevada: "For each national forest affected by this decision, a revised Allowable Sale Quantity (ASQ) will be established at the time of their Forest Plan Revision. Until these revisions are complete, the total annual Probable Sale Quantities (PSQ) green volume for the 11 national forests is estimated to be approximately 191 million board feet (mmbf) for the first five years, which includes approximately 137 mmbf from the pilot project for the Herger-Feinstein Quincy Library Group."[91] The Quincy plan remained controversial, especially as the fate of the larger Sierra Nevada Framework came under review by a new presidential administration.[92]

After assuming the presidency, George W. Bush and his resource advisers began to reverse or change many elements of federal resource policy.[93] Among other things, the Sierra Nevada Framework was significantly revised over the next two years. This revision increased levels of logging in the Sierra, notably including the QLG area.[94] When regional officials released their plan for public review, a *Sacramento Bee* reporter commented: "Putting some flesh on a proposal that has triggered months of rhetoric but few hard details, the U.S. Forest Service on Thursday released a 372-page management plan for the Sierra Nevada that would nearly triple logging, with most of it coming in the Plumas and Lassen national forests near Quincy." Of the 448-million-board-foot annual cut in the new proposal, he observed: "Nearly two-thirds of that logging would occur in the Plumas, Lassen, and Tahoe forests. The Plumas is the location of the disputed and stalled Quincy Library Group project, a pilot program that aimed to help local sawmills and reduce fire threats."[95]

Environmentalists expressed disbelief about the attempt to fully implement the QLG plan proposed in the Framework revision. For example, Craig Thomas of the Sierra Nevada Forest Protection Campaign said: "The Forest Service said in 1999 they couldn't do it and protect species. . . . It's a huge increase in logging." Steve Eubanks, forest supervisor for the Tahoe National Forest, explained this reversal by saying that Congress had called for full implementation of the Quincy plan and that new assessments on the owl and its habitat showed that the bird would not be harmed.[96]

The issue of the California spotted owl and the Quincy plan had been a serious concern of Forest Service officials when the logging group first advanced its proposal. Reluctance to adopt the experiment was traceable in part to the belief of scientists who conducted the owl EIS studies that the Quincy plan was a threat to owl habitat. As a result, the Forest Service had limited the amount of cutting of "fuelbreaks" that the original QLG plan had called for. The Forest Service had resisted full implementation, and the revisions in the QLG Herger-Feinstein legislation had required that all environmental requirements be respected.[97] Full implementation of the QLG in the new Bush administration plan caused concern among scientists such as Jared Verner (who had worked on the original owl study) and Barry Noon of Colorado State University. Both questioned the evidence that the Forest Service used to claim that owl populations were not threatened.[98]

Because the dust on the QLG implementation issue was not settled as this book went to press, it is impossible to predict an outcome. But it seems clear that the issue could end up in the courts.

A fifth issue affecting Sierra Nevada forests came from a national source—the decision of forest policy planners to expand salvage logging in the National Forests. In September of 1992, Tom Knudson returned to a theme that had been a part of his renowned "Sierra in Peril" articles—Forest Service logging practices. At issue was a "treatment" program that was expanding in the Sierra Nevada and all across the West. Knudson wrote: "Not long ago the issue was over clear-cutting. Today another kind of timber cutting is stirring controversy and concern: salvage logging." As he had before, Knudson hit the bull's-eye. His summary of the mounting controversy was clear and concise—as Forest Service "green timber sales" declined, salvage sales by the agency increased. That much was not at issue. What was at issue was the reason for the increased salvage cutting.[99]

Years of drought, disease, and insect infestation had damaged millions of trees in forests across the West. The Forest Service claimed it was promoting forest health and reducing fire danger through heavier salvage cutting. Timber interests and western politicians supported increased logging to reduce fire danger in the forests and near population centers, and to salvage dead or dying trees before they lost all commercial value. President George H. W. Bush had responded. Just four days before a campaign swing to the West Coast, he suspended several environmental rules so as to increase salvage cutting. Environmentalists were angry, and some scientists disagreed with the changes. They claimed that salvage logging would not solve the fire problem or that the salvage excuse was being misused to justify forcing timber sales back up to the unsustainable 1980s logging levels.[100]

By the time Knudson wrote about salvage logging, it had spent several years developing into a full-blown controversy. In fact, it could be traced back to 1976, when the Forest Service asked Congress to establish a revised policy to govern salvage logging in the national forests. The salvage definition covered removal of dead or dying trees as a way to encourage forest health and reduce fire danger. Revenues gained by the sale of salvage trees under this law went directly into Forest Service coffers and were not tied to annual budget appropriations. In 1976, salvage sales accounted for 762 million board feet, or 7 percent of the Forest Service's timber program. In 1990, salvage timber constituted 26 percent of timber sales with 2.8 billion board feet. In 1993, after two years of owl-related slowdowns in cutting of green timber, salvage cutting made up 43 percent of the timber program. Obviously, something had happened between 1976 and 1990 to change the way the Forest Service was operating. From the service's perspective, the reason for increased cutting under the 1976 law was clear: A succession of droughts from the mid-1980s had weakened many trees, and insect infestation in these trees had led to a great die-off in western forests, increasing the danger of catastrophic fires and loss of valuable timber. Forest Service personnel, according to an internal memo obtained by the Associated Press in 1992, were instructed to attach the word *salvage* to virtually all timber sales in order to expedite their approval.[101]

An example from the Tahoe National Forest brings the issue home to the

Sierra Nevada. In June of 1990, the *Reno Gazette-Journal* published an article based on information supplied to it by TNF officers. Drought and disease had left an estimated 2,000,000 dead or dying trees in the TNF. As a result, the agency had decided to focus its cutting away from green timber (average annual harvest of about 3,000 to 4,000 acres) and instead encourage its timber contractors to concentrate on 155,000 acres of dead or diseased trees under salvage provisions.[102]

In another case, an environmentalist complaining about overuse of the salvage provision in the Eldorado National Forest in 1993 cited Forest Service figures to show that there had not been a green timber sale on that forest since 1989. An Environmental Protection Agency official had complained to the forest supervisor there in 1988 that, under current policies, cutting in the Eldorado had exceeded sustainable levels.[103]

Between 1990 and 1995, pressure to increase "salvage" cutting mounted. In 1995 congressional representatives from western and southern areas where timber was an important interest pushed for salvage timber action. Legislation was drafted with Forest Service help to suspend environmental laws and allow for increased salvage cutting as an emergency measure. President Clinton vetoed the legislation, but by later attaching it as a rider to an essential appropriation bill, proponents of salvage cutting succeeded in getting the measure enacted into law. The salvage rider was intended not only to achieve suspension of environmental protections, but also to prevent citizen complaints from generating court actions and delays. No public comment or litigation on proposed salvage sales was allowed. The measure also ordered salvage sales to proceed even if net economic losses resulted from them. The rider carried a life span of two years—all timber sales under it had to be approved by the end of December 1996.[104]

Increased use of salvage sales and then the "salvage rider" drew howls of protest from environmentalists. These objections began in 1989 when it became clear that such sales were intensifying. Most environmental protest claimed that the salvage argument was only a cover to allow a timber-sale-committed Forest Service bureaucracy in Washington to increase timber cutting once again, after environmental challenges and "owls" had forced significant reduction in output. National deficit problems that forced other revenue cutbacks made salvage sales more attractive, it was charged, because the revenue from them went directly to the Forest Service and did not require appropriations in a time of tight budgets. Damage to forest health, valuable habitat loss, and cutting into owl territory were all problems laid at the feet of salvage sales. And all for profit alone, environmental groups asserted. Because the legislation precluded lawsuits, immediate actions to stop the cutting were impossible. Instead, pressure was directed at the White House.[105]

In California, environmentalists were especially concerned about eleven timber sales approved under the salvage rider. The sales included forest areas on the Klamath, Six Rivers, Toiyabe, and the Tahoe. One of the TNF sales was particularly troubling because ten miles of new road had been cut into an area where logging and roads had already caused significant disturbance.[106]

In 1996, under mounting protest, the Clinton administration ordered the creation of an interagency science panel to investigate the charges that the Forest Service was including too much green timber in salvage sales and that serious habitat damage was possibly resulting. The panel consisted of Forest Service, Bureau of Land Management, Fish and Wildlife Service, Federal Marine Fisheries Service, and Environmental Protection Agency personnel. It reviewed a number of sales. One approved sale on the Lassen included cutting on land set aside for the spotted owl. Although the committee's report said that most activities on the few sales they had investigated were appropriate under the legislation, it expressed serious concerns about how the law was working in practice. Problems were noted in several areas having to do with the very broad definition used by the Forest Service as to what actually constituted dead or dying trees. Much green timber had been included in salvage sales. Another problem was the unwillingness of the Forest Service and Bureau of Land Management to cooperate with other federal agencies working to enforce the Endangered Species Act. And finally, the Forest Service budgeting system that rewarded high levels of salvage logging was criticized. Salvage sales, the panel said, were often selected over other appropriate activities.[107]

As a result of the report, the Department of Agriculture ordered the cutoff date for ending of salvage sales under the salvage rider law to be bumped back to December 13, 1996, rather than the end of the month, when the law ceased to be operative. On January 1, 1997—the first possible day for filing suit after the rider law expired—the Sierra Club Legal Defense Fund, acting for four environmental organizations, challenged several timber sales. Four sales in northern California that had been approved under the revised deadline, including the 2,400-plus-acre "Bullshead" sale along the Truckee River, were part of the legal action.[108]

The salvage fight ended at that point, but it raised serious questions about the commitment of the Forest Service leaders to ecosystem management. The documented abuses revealed in the review of the policy by the interagency panel showed that a science-based approach to forest management was obviously not a deeply held commitment for agency leadership as a whole. Was their stance the last gasp of the timber-production elements in the service or a revelation of how the service would act if environmental restraints were removed? Clearly, the initiative for planning and operation of the Forest Service lay with the conservative and resource-production-oriented interests of Congress and the agency. What of the new staff at forest, region, and national levels who were committed to the new ecosystem approach? Could they gain influence in agency planning? What of the public and its view of an agency that flew in the face of clearly expressed desires for a more sustainable resource policy? Would trust of the agency ever be possible again? In the Sierra, many of these questions quickly surfaced—especially as the Forest Service, in the aftermath of the owl issue, struggled with amending the forest plans of what was now called the Sierra Nevada Province.

Without too much of a stretch, it seemed that the United States Forest Service at the end of the twentieth century was suffering a split-personality crisis—Jekyll and Hyde, as it were. In the salvage instance, the agency helped formulate and enforce a policy that actively discouraged public participation in its rush to log western forests. No scientific evaluation or NEPA process was used to guide salvage cutting. Mister Hyde was unrestrained. But in the creation and development of what came to be called the "Framework," science and public involvement were central in amending the forest plans of the Sierra Nevada. Kindly Dr. Jekyll was in his office at the Pacific Southwest Region headquarters and seemed to be successfully resisting drinking the noxious potion of earlier times.

A brief review of history is useful here to explain the Framework's origin. Wording to that noted at the opening of this section on ecosystem management had already been introduced by agency planners in 1992. As the 1990s came to a close, the Forest Service continued to draw intense criticism over its management of America's federal forests. It is in that troubled time that the origins of the Framework lie. The strongest criticism of the agency came from divergent ends of the political spectrum. First were industry interests allied with western politicians (especially Republicans) in Congress who passed salvage rider legislation to force an increase in cutting from the low owl-imposed levels. Criticism also came from environmental groups that increasingly relied on the courts (and sometimes the Clinton administration) to resist and shape forest policy in another desired direction.[109]

Amid this swirling controversy, a newly appointed Forest Service chief, Mike Dombeck, assumed control of the beleaguered agency when Jack Ward Thomas left. In his early policy statements, the Dombeck offered the principle of "collaborative stewardship" as a watchword for the direction he intended to take the agency. He also called for a change in its social focus, saying that multiple resource uses espoused during the 1950s and 1960s had to be reconsidered in light of changing needs in the 1990s. He emphasized recreation as a forest use that was growing increasingly important in Forest Service planning. Dombeck's rhetoric signaled a new emphasis for the agency within the ecosystem context.[110]

In the Sierra Nevada, the idea of collaborative stewardship was soon put to the test. In January 1998, Region 5 announced a new initiative, the Sierra Nevada Framework for Conservation and Collaboration (SNFCC).[111] Its purpose was to create a process for public involvement in amending the forest plans in eleven Sierran Province national forests. In addition to the national forests of the Sierra and the Lake Tahoe Basin Management Unit, the Modoc and Klamath forests were to be included. The new approach was to "incorporate the latest scientific information and broad public and intergovernmental participation in watershed and ecosystem planning."[112]

So here was yet another new initiative by the Forest Service. Was it to be casually disregarded, as the ecosystem approach was by the Mr. Hydes in the agency who had guided salvage logging? Or was it to be taken seriously and implemented by the Dr. Jekylls? Perhaps to ensure that the latter was to prevail, Regional Forester Lynn Sprague sent a memo to the heads of the Modoc, Klamath, Lassen, Plumas, Tahoe, Eldorado, Stanislaus, Sierra, Inyo, and Sequoia National Forests and the Lake Tahoe Basin Management Unit on May 1, 1998. It is worth quoting for its summary of the forces that compelled the agency to turn toward the lighter side of its personality:

> We have discussed with you the approach to the Sierra Nevada Conservation Framework (SNCF). The need and urgency for taking action are identified in SNEP, and other scientific sources, the CASPO RDEIS and the CASPO FAC [Federal Advisory Committee] Report. We are now moving forward in collaboration with state agencies, other federal agencies and numerous other partners, on all four tasks we outlined for this effort. This approach conforms with the Forest Service Natural Resource Agenda, specifically the two themes of watershed health and sustainable forest management and the principles of partnerships, science based decision making, collaborative stewardship and accountability. It also conforms with recommendations made in the CASPO FAC Report. PSW scientists are working in partnership with us to develop a strong scientific basis for all work required to assemble this framework.[113]

As a part of SNFCC, the service's Pacific Southwest Research Station issued a Sierra Nevada Science Review in July of 1998. The review provided a summary of "new information from recent science studies" about the range. It identified several high-priority items that needed immediate consideration: cultural, demographic, and socioeconomic changes; fire and fuels; old-forest ecosystems involving California spotted owls and certain forest carnivores; aquatic, riparian, and meadow systems, including habitat issues for several animal species; lower west-side conifer and hardwood zone issues; roads; and bighorn sheep. When the Forest Service formally announced its planning effort to begin the EIS process for the Federal Register in November 1998, it reduced the list of priority issues to five. Four were taken from the Science Review's list: old-forest ecosystems; aquatic, riparian, and meadow systems; fire and fuels; and lower west-side hardwoods. A fifth problem, with invading noxious weeds, was added at the urging of agency botanists and resource specialists.[114]

Thus it would seem the good doctor was in charge again. The agency was paying attention to SNEP, collaborating with other agencies, encouraging public involvement, and giving new emphasis to science. But was the doctor really assuming the dominant position in SNFCC? Some critics claimed to see the darker Hyde visage behind the kindly face presented to the public. For example, a *San Francisco Chronicle* editorial written near the end of the process complained that it was hard for the general public to understand the new plan amendment for the Sierra Nevada forests. The Forest Service promised to replace timber cutting as an agency priority, to consolidate management activity for Sierran forests, and to advance ecological health as a goal. Yet, the editorial claimed, the Forest Service actually favored the opposite position. Of the two preferred alternatives in the Framework draft, one projected an actual increase in timber cutting. As the editorial writer observed: "One, said to have the greater support in the agency, would permit cutting 351 million board feet of timber for the next five years—an increase from the 337 million board feet cut in 1998." The other preferred alternative would reduce the cut to 141 million feet annually—still too much for some critics. The justification for the cutting was fire danger. Both alternatives failed in effectively protecting wildlife and streamside areas, in the editorial writer's opinion.[115]

After the EIS process was launched, the Forest Service began the "Collaboration" part of the Framework. Numerous regional public meetings followed—nearly fifty of them as of July 29, 2000, when the last was held, in Sacramento. The DEIS considered at these meetings included eight alternatives. Environmental groups overwhelmingly chose alternative five. Its primary goal was active management of Sierra forests to maintain healthy ecosystems, stressing the need to place more old forest and hardwood lands into protected reserves. At the Sacramento meeting in July of 2000, the California Wilderness Coalition delivered 30,000 printed comment cards, sent from fifty-one countries and all fifty states, that supported this alternative. The Sierra Club, the Sierra Nevada Forest Protection Campaign, and most of those attending the San Francisco and Los Angeles meetings also supported alternative five. The agency indicated that it preferred alternatives six and eight. These two strategies stressed that integration of fuel-reduction and fire strategies must accompany old forest and hardwood protection. Each proposed more mechanical fuel reduction and herbicide use than alternative 5, which called for more prescribed burning and for caution on herbicide use.[116]

Alternative three in the EIS was the work of the Forest Service Employees for Environmental Ethics. Based on a study of the Sierra Nevada that FSEEE had prepared with the help of outside experts, it reflected the position of those Forest Service professionals who were troubled by the postwar emphasis on timber cutting at the expense of other values. It was similar to alternative five but stressed the need for local analysis and collaboration in watersheds in the restoration of Sierran forests. Many participants from the SNEP study had contributed to or reviewed the FSEEE study. It was titled *Restoring Our Forest Legacy: Blue Print for Sierra Nevada National Forests.*[117]

In January of 2001, Pacific Southwest regional forester Bradley Powell issued the Record of Decision on the Framework. He said that he had accepted a modified version of alternative eight as the "Environmentally Preferable Alternative." He gave specific reasons for choosing it over alternative five—the environmentalists' choice. He lauded alternative five as being best in the "short term," but deficient in the long run in protecting the key old-growth habitats of the spotted owl and other threatened species. Modified alternative eight had less immediate impact, he noted, but in the long run was more effective in ensuring the survival of old-growth and sensitive habitats. Fire issues played a major factor in his choice.[118]

But following Powell's decision to sign off on the Framework, the newly proposed policy took a ride on a political roller-coaster. George W. Bush became president, and hopes among forest-industry representatives for a reversal of the Record of Decision soared. Mike Dombeck resigned as chief forester. Bradley Powell was reassigned to another region. Environmentalist hopes declined further when Anne Veneman, no friend of environmental interests in the Sierra, was appointed secretary of agriculture. But soon she recused herself from decisions on the Sierra because as a lawyer she had taken

on clients who opposed some Clinton-era Sierran environmental decisions—notably those regarding roadless area and national monument designations. A new assistant secretary of agriculture, Mark Rey, long associated
with timber interests, eventually announced that while he would not throw
out the Framework, he would open new investigations into its possible
effects and consider other alternatives. The new regional forester, Jack Blackwell, announced that he was going to revisit certain elements of the Framework, including the possibility of allowing more logging. Environmentalists
and some newspapers that had generally come to accept the Framework expressed concern but waited for a clearer picture of agency plans, although
some threats of legal action were made.[119]

In November, newly appointed Forest Service chief Dale Bosworth indicated he would accept the Framework plan, but he also expressed his concern about it. He directed California regional forest officials to address wildfire issues more aggressively, make the plan more consistent with the
National Fire Plan funded by Congress to address local community protection, and link the plan more effectively with the Herger-Feinstein Quincy
Library Group Forest Recovery Act fire initiatives. In December, the new
assistant secretary of agriculture affirmed Bosworth's acceptance of the
Framework plan but indicated that he would also direct the Forest Service to
modify it to address concerns of loggers, ski resort operators, and four-
wheel-drive interests, all of whom generally disapproved of the Framework
that had emerged under President Clinton.[120]

It was not clear through most of 2002 whether the Forest Service could
actually reverse or cripple the policy. It had withstood widespread public
scrutiny. It had gained acceptance by many conservation and environmental
groups, and many believed that it was the key to resolving the Forest
Service's longstanding forest-management and owl-policy problems. Jack
Blackwell indicated in March of 2002 that he was uncertain about a plan like
the Framework that covered all actions for the eleven forests that made up
the Sierra region. He noted that "it is a long way across 11 national forests
from north to south. There is a tremendous change in elevation gradients
and climates." This remark seemed to signal the end for the "ecosystem management" concept in the Sierra. But at the same time, Jay Watson of the
Wilderness Society expressed a different perspective. He said that by reviewing and potentially dismantling the Framework and moving on a forest-by-
forest approach in league with the timber interests, the Forest Service was
facing failure. As he put it, "The Sierra is one mountain range."[121]

Environmentalists such as Watson and Craig Thomas of the Sierra Nevada Forest Protection Campaign expressed doubts that the Bush adminis-

tration could reverse the Framework's science-based policies and move more toward Rey's economic orientation. But they indicated that if Rey pushed too far, the courts might be brought in again. Chad Hanson of the John Muir Project stated that the suggested increases in commercial cutting levels threatened the protections put in place for threatened species such as the fisher and spotted owl. The new levels proposed by the regional forester also focused on cutting larger trees and not just underbrush and small trees, thus running counter to recommendations of the National Fire Plan. Challenges to Forest Service policy, few in number but important in content, began to make their way into the courts.[122]

As the year progressed, the Forest Service's Region 5 began modifying the Framework so as to focus on economic impacts and fire issues. A public meeting was organized to consider these issues, as well as the plan's relationship with tribal governments. Chief Bosworth and Regional Forester Blackwell said they were responding to 234 appeals to the Framework related to these concerns. It should be remembered that the agency had received some 30,000 public comments in support of alternative five, the one preferred by most environmentalists. At the completion of this economic review in 2003, the Framework as modified was expected to undergo public scrutiny under NEPA requirements.[123] Jay Watson of the Wilderness Society, in an interview conducted in November of 2002, noted that economic and fire issues had come to dominate Forest Service actions in the Sierra; he feared that ecosystem protection was being reduced to a secondary element and was being downplayed.[124]

As noted earlier, the new management plan for the Sierra Nevada was announced in June of 2003. Cutting levels were increased threefold over the initial levels proposed in the Framework as accepted by Regional Forester Powell. More latitude was given to district rangers in dealing with fire-damaged trees, and more grazing was allowed in meadow areas. Cutting of potentially dangerous small trees was promised to fire-threatened areas. The timber industry and agriculturists expressed support for the agency revision. As expected, complaints from environmentalists were strong.[125]

The issue of the fate of the spotted owl obviously did not disappear with the Forest Service release of its new plan. Forest Service personnel had cited new studies and had claimed that there was no danger to the owl with the full implementation of the QLG program as part of the revised Framework. As noted, environmentalists and some scientists challenged this claim. Another powerful player also voiced concern about the effects of increased cutting on the owl—the California Resources Agency. The first effective government support for an ecosystem approach to Sierran problems had begun with this agency under Douglas Wheeler. His successor, Mary Nichols, joined in protesting the increased cutting in the revised Framework. She offered to work with federal forest officials in formulating better owl and local fire-reduction projects. In a press release on March 17, 2003, she stated that not only would the new federal policy reduce public input and lessen agency accountability, but it would also "weaken existing protections by allowing more aggressive cutting of larger trees solely for the purposes of funding fuels management. . . . This degrades habitat for owls and [other] sensitive species. If the Forest Service proceeds on its present course without any changes, it's a recipe for listing of the owl, resulting in renewed conflict, litigation, and gridlock."[126]

Secretary Nichols was expressing the same concerns as her predecessor about possible economic and environmental effects should the California spotted owl end up being listed as endangered. Nichols based her protest on an opinion given by the Resources Agency's deputy assistant secretary and science adviser, Greg Greenwood. In commenting on Jack Blackwell's announcement of his plan to revise the Framework, Greenwood wrote: "The Forest Service proposal is the wrong answer for California. It prescribes the wrong dosage, treats the wrong disease—and is likely to make the patient sicker."[127]

As to the supposedly scientific basis for the revision, Greenwood said that Blackwell had relied upon very limited, and certainly not scientific, information:

What are the problems with the Framework? A usfs Review Team based its year-long assessment on two sources—a set of letters from District Rangers, and a computer simulation of management in one 54,000 acre watershed in El Dorado County.

The letters show how little effort has gone into actually implementing projects under the Framework. Out of 18 ranger districts on national forests south of Plumas County, covering the heart of the Sierra, only a half dozen actually implemented projects. Many letters simply reiterate old arguments with little real new information. As one Ranger wrote, "Although we have not yet implemented a Framework project, my experience crafting alternatives to address fuels, forest health and wildlife habitats (pre-Framework) tell me that . . . we will have difficulty meeting the intent of more old forest."

"Difficulty" hardly compels one to conclude that the Framework cannot be implemented, as the Review Team simply assumed throughout its work.

The letters show a diversity of opinions and a desire for local solutions. While limits on cutting are frequent topics, so are post-fire salvage rules, analysis requirements, and restrictions on herbicide use. Moreover, many Rangers are wistful in their desire for authority to specify local solutions. "The people at the local level should be trusted to know how to do the right thing and to make the right decision."

Few would contest the important need for local knowledge in making sound forest management decisions. Unfortunately, unfettered unilateral authority is a root cause of, and not a solution to, the controversy over forest policy in the Sierra. A nuanced approach to the sustainable management of ecosystems must allow flexibility but not license.[128]

Greenwood added that the revision "considers science as an expensive burden rather than the route to a new forest management and a foundation for stakeholder participation. It elevates harvesting larger trees as the primary source of funding when the technology and policies for biomass use and small log mills provide new opportunities for real economic gain."[129]

As this book goes to press, Governor Gray Davis was removed from office. His successor, Republican Arnold Schwarzenegger, replaced Mary Nichols are resources secretary.

The Forest Service had hoped to build public trust and regain control over its destiny when it instituted the ecosystem-management initiative.[130] After repeated challenges to its owl and other wildlife and logging policies in the Sierra, the Framework apparently had begun to satisfy some critics. Although not completely happy with the alternative selected by the agency, many environmentalists agreed that it could be worked with.[131] As it became clear that the revised Framework's fire-reduction plan emphasized more cutting of large trees, and further modification to promote more economic activity was being promoted by the agency, environmentalist support began to fall away. Court challenges seemed certain to replace collaboration, marking a return to pre-ecosystem-management days.[132] Mr. Hyde seemed to be back in the office at Region 5, this time wearing a firefighter's costume.

Ecosystems, Science, Monuments, and Sierran National Parks

Spotted owls and *Sacramento Bee* reporters had profound impact on the shaping of national forest policy in the 1990s. But other journalists who wrote of problems facing the national parks of the range did not have Tom Knudson's impact. In his "Sierra in Peril" series and other pieces, Knudson wrote on environmental issues at Yosemite, listing air pollution and acid rain as serious problems facing the park. Reporter Jeff Phillips, in *Sunset,* featured air pollution as both a visual and a biological problem in Sequoia National Park.[133] Why didn't his comments generate as much public response as Knudson's? There are two reasons. The first was that air pollution in Sequoia was primarily created outside the park. Central Valley agriculture, automobiles, and trucks provided most of the pollutants affecting the park's air and trees. This was a huge social and economic issue that neither park planners nor politicians were able or willing to take on. It would take a massive commitment from the state of California and the federal government to solve Sequoia's air problems. Perhaps not impossible, but certainly very difficult to achieve.

The second reason there was no sudden burst of energy to right obvious wrongs in park policy was traceable to the fact that as of 1980, general management plans for Yosemite, Sequoia, and Kings Canyon National Parks had just been formulated. These plans had been shaped through NEPA processes. They looked to a future where problems that resulted from automobiles, lack of commitment to effective scientific study of park resources, inappropriate tourist facility construction, and overuse and endangerment of the scenic and natural resources of the parks were supposed to receive greater park consideration. There was hope.

In Sequoia and Kings Canyon, in particular, the direction park management was taking was encouraging. Natural management was the watchword. Attention to the reintroduction of fire as part of the ecosystem was well established and had strong scientific backing.[134] National park environmental historian Richard Sellars listed Sequoia and Kings Canyon along with Yellowstone, the Channel Islands, and Shenandoah as Park Service success stories when it came to effective integration of scientific research into park planning and operation.[135] Progress was being made in moving employee and concession housing and other structures away from Cedar Grove and the Giant Forest. The completion of tourist service centers at Wuksachi and Lodgepole Villages was part of the decongesting of Sequoia that the general management plan had envisioned. Old visitor housing and other facilities were being torn out. In addition, in the 1990s Sequoia and Kings Canyon began planning to address other park issues that fell into the "natural" category. These included the thorny problem of what to do with cabins in Mineral King (their presence had been "grandfathered" temporarily into the park when Mineral King was taken over from the Forest Service), how to reduce the impact of pack animals on alpine meadows, and means of including the Kaweah River in the Wild and Scenic Rivers System. All of these issues reflected the natural management direction chosen in the 1970s and 1980s planning actions.[136]

But in Yosemite, the direction that park management was taking was more often contrary to natural management, at least when it came to the Valley. The General Management Plan of 1980 provided the basis for the park's immediate future. Park officials still promoted Valley visitor comfort as their primary mission. The tradition of serving more visitors and making them comfortable was deeply ingrained in park culture. Most of the 60,000 members of the public who, through their comments and workshop attendance in the late 1970s, had contributed to the plan's creation had stated that stricter preservation or limited access was preferable to more development. Some changes were initiated. Outside the Valley, wilderness designation was expanded, bighorn sheep were reintroduced,[137] and fire was returned as park policy. In the Valley, a few roads were closed to autos and a limited shuttle service was initiated. But this fell far short of the 1980 goal of banning automobiles from the park.[138]

As a result, more cars came to the Valley, circulating and recirculating trying to find parking places, and on some especially crowded summer days the park had to shut off auto entry to prevent gridlock.[139] If natural management was a goal, it apparently had little direct impact on day-to-day realities in the Valley. In 1992, park planners revised the contract with the commercial interests that provided visitor services, but this was hardly an action to reduce Valley crowding.[140] As Richard Sellars has noted, science and natural-management values were emerging as new ideas in the National Park Service. But the legislative mandate for providing enjoyment to the public, and the Park Service employee culture that rewarded development over other aspects of the park mission, pointed to less rather than more natural conditions in the Valley.[141]

Late in 1991, Park Service personnel began circulating a plan to redesign visitor housing in the Valley, reducing the number of old tent cabins and adding new motel units in their place. Overall, the total number of units was to be reduced. Public comment was solicited in the Valley, Los Angeles, Fresno, and San Francisco. Most responses were hostile—too much development, too little preservation of the natural. But the Park Service said its plan was in line with visitor surveys it had conducted—more comfort and newer facilities were what the public wanted. Some environmental groups threatened to go to court.[142]

After further work, a "Yosemite Valley Implementation Plan and Supplemental Environmental Statement" was announced in January of 1992, and official public comment began. While not specifically included in the announcement, it was clear from the planners' statements that some kind of large parking structure was on the agenda. It would act as a collecting station for car-driving visitors, planners said, transferring them to public transport. Presumably this action would meet the 1980 General Management Plan goal of reducing automobile use. Environmentalists, such as long-time Valley activist Dean Malley, reiterated their promise of a big fight if a structure of that type was built anywhere in the Valley. The sides were clearly drawn as public discussion began.[143]

By 1995, the Valley plan had evolved from the vague ideas of its beginnings, but the positions of the participants were little changed. The Park Service was even more committed to a large (20 acres), $9 million parking garage in the park. It opposed building a facility outside the Valley, saying it would cost twice that of the proposed location. But Wilderness Society and Sierra Club advocates were just as firmly committed to a facility or facilities outside the park. Some local business interests suggested an alternative that they said represented a better idea than one large structure anywhere. Why not small parking facilities outside the park at its several entrances, with shuttle service?[144] The debate and plan-formulation process continued without much change in either park or environmentalist perspectives in the two years that followed. Several alternatives for action were finally developed as required for the EIS. Park Service planners' preferred choices promised less noise and crowding, fewer buildings, and fewer vehicles in the Valley. And a big parking structure. While praising some parts of the plan, the Wilderness Society still held that a parking structure in the Valley was not the way to proceed.[145] At that juncture the issue drifted for a time. Undoubtedly court challenges from the environmentalists lay ahead.

But then nature intervened, and planning stopped dead in its tracks. Remember those forces that shaped the Sierra Nevada—faulting, uplifting, volcanism, glaciation, erosion, and humans? In January of 1997, two of them—erosion and human activities—combined to rearrange the terrain in Yosemite Valley. In late December of 1996, heavy snow fell in the northern and central Sierra. Then, from the first to the third of January, heavy rain fell on top of the snowpack, and the Merced and many other rivers in the Sierra became raging torrents. The Merced reached the flood stage of 8 1/2 feet and then soared past it to a record of 16 feet. In the Valley, the heavy stone bridges built cross the river caught and collected debris, making the flooding damage even worse. Campgrounds, tent cabins, employee housing, and motel and cabin facilities were washed away or damaged. Silt and debris clogged the Valley sewer system. Highways 41 and 120 that connected to the park were damaged, and even worse, a massive rockfall closed the important

El Portal route (Highway 140) completely. The park was closed indefinitely to allow emergency repairs to the sewer and electrical systems. In all, park officials estimated the cost of the flood at nearly 180 million dollars. Local congressmen, fearing further damage to the area's tourist economy, pushed for early reopening of the Valley. They drafted legislation to fund rebuilding the Valley infrastructure.[146]

In the floodplain, the slate was clean—or would be when the cement parking barriers and other debris from destroyed campgrounds and buildings were carted off. Money for recovery was on its way thanks to a generous Congress. The old excuse that significant changes in the Valley would have to wait upon increased funding was no longer appropriate. The reconstruction process could now go forward. Park superintendent B. J. Griffin spoke of the opportunity to learn "from mistakes of the past. Buildings and campgrounds constructed in the flood area will be replaced in scale, scope and function but relocated away from the flood zone." Adam Werbach, president of the Sierra Club, said, "This is an opportunity to improve access so more people can see Yosemite in a more natural state." Jay Watson, regional director of the Wilderness Society, concurred with Werbach's view of the need for natural reconstruction, saying, "Now is the time to do it."[147]

But for all the temperate and hopeful rhetoric, this was still Yosemite Valley they were talking about—one mile wide, seven miles long. What with rockfall zones and now a floodplain where no campgrounds, employee housing, or visitor housing would be replaced, the debate could obviously escalate, not diminish. What about cars and parking structures, Yosemite Lodge reconstruction, and road repairs? After the shock of the flood wore off, the fight was likely to begin again in earnest.

Between February and November 1997, planners worked to revise the proposed Valley implementation plan, incorporating new public comment. In November they announced a new draft. It proposed a temporary parking lot at Taft Toe to collect auto visitors, who would be put onto shuttle buses. A phased-in regional bus system to get more park visitors out of their cars was also proposed. Three bridges over the Merced were to be taken out. Four campgrounds were to be removed and two more reduced in size. Although environmentalists were still concerned over the Valley parking issue, positive comment on the proposal was forthcoming. The *Sacramento Bee* pointed out a change in perspective in national park operation—namely, a growing commitment to reducing car use in the park system. Examples of this policy shift included not only the new Valley plan, but changes at Grand Canyon, Crater Lake, Mount Rainier, Sequoia, and Zion National Parks.[148]

In May of 1998, a new Yosemite superintendent, Stan Albright, wrote an open letter to the public updating them about flood recovery plans and a planned redesign of Yosemite Lodge. He promised lodge improvements that were "better for the resources and better for the visitor experience." Plans for rebuilding employee housing were conjoined with the lodge redesign for a more comprehensive approach after public concern over their separation was voiced. The letter's closing paragraph showed Albright's focus: "I feel very strongly that we must proceed with the construction of guest lodging. We have a commitment to the public through the 1980 *General Management Plan* and the *Concession Services Plan* to provide lodging in Yosemite Valley. We have a commitment to Congress to rebuild flood damaged facilities wisely and efficiently." As in the past, development was safe but "resources" seemed open for modification.

In August of 1998, a separate plan for dealing with the transportation issue was advanced. A regional consortium had been working on the idea of several satellite parking and bus-ride facilities. Yosemite officials and representatives from five adjoining counties voted to consider a regional transportation system that would slowly phase in a voluntary park-and-ride program over several years, aiming to get 800,000 people on buses by the end of the decade. Jay Watson voiced his approval. Park officials did not drop their parking facility idea, however.[149] In October the regional committee working on parking issues reversed itself, asking for a delay of at least a year in implementing the plan. The Park Service indicated that it would proceed anyway with its plans, one of which involved a potential vehicle day-reservation system for daily visitors. No easy solution for the car issue was at hand.[150]

As things began to pile up in the recovery and Valley plan process, the long-threatened legal actions by environmentalists finally surfaced. The Sierra Club and a local group called Mariposans for Environmentally Responsible Growth challenged the Park Service's attempt to expedite reconstruction of the El Portal route, the most-used route into the park. In an attempt to speed the park's reopening, no environmental review of the project had been implemented. Charging that the widening and straightening of the old road posed serious potential impacts on the river (a Wild and Scenic River), the opponents of the new road project sued.[151] In another case, in November of 1998, a federal judge ordered a halt to plans to alter Yosemite Lodge and build an employee dormitory near Camp 4 (called Sunnyside, or the "climber's camp"). The issue was not only the crowding of the camp with a multistory dormitory, but the cumulative effects of proposed development—something the judge said the Park Service had not considered in their haste to rebuild.[152]

Faced with the chilling prospect of lengthy legal delays, the Park Service reacted swiftly. Part of the mounting pressure on the park officials came from the Secretary of the Interior Bruce Babbitt. From his office in Washington in December of 1998, surrounded by leaders from several environmental groups (National Parks and Conservation Association, Wilderness Society, and Natural Resources Defense Council), he ordered that all the various Valley plans be combined in a single comprehensive plan. All the issues could be considered together.[153] The next day, Stan Albright issued his response to Babbitt's announcement, saying that a new Valley plan was on its way that combined all the earlier plans into one. Compare his words with those of his May 1998 open letter that had stressed visitor comfort, spending congressional money to rebuild facilities, and concession contract compliance. Things had changed: "This process, which has been forged under the leadership of Secretary of the Interior Bruce Babbitt, will result in the best possible plan to move the Valley into the 21st Century. As with all projects, the park's General Management Plan (GMP) will be our guide for this ambitious effort. The GMP's overall goals, as you may remember, are to reclaim priceless natural beauty, reduce cars, congestion and crowding, and promote visitor understanding and enjoyment. These goals are valid today."[154]

After herculean labor, two draft EIS plans were produced. The first, a separate plan for the Merced necessitated by requirements of the Wild and Scenic River Act, was issued in January of 2000. The second, issued in April 2000, was the plan that combined all the separate Valley issues into one effort. Public hearings began on both. The Merced River plan was deliberately vague, park planners said, to allow for specific implementation elements to be included in the more comprehensive Valley plan.[155]

Two positions emerged as dominant at this stage of the ongoing conflict, generally reflecting the two camps in the Valley debate. The preferred alternative for the park planners in both documents was the second, which claimed to try to balance development and visitor use with river restoration and Valley protection. Included in it were a day-visitor-and-transit facility that would be constructed at Yosemite Lodge and more visitor-related development in the Merced corridor. Alternative four was more restrictive in both plans. The Merced River plan under this alternative pointedly sought to leave out any parking structure or lot in the Valley. It expanded the area of Merced streamside that would not be developed for heavy visitor use, thus increasing the amount of contiguous streamside, meadow, and black oak woodland. Overall, the park planners preferred alternatives under both plans provided for more in-Valley parking at various facilities. Both alternatives proposed quarter-mile riverside protection zones for the river, although the fourth alternative of the river plan protected more. Both sets of Valley alternatives promised voluntary out-of-Valley parking and transit centers at Badger Pass, South Landing, and El Portal. Both documents included provisions to reduce accommodations and Valley traffic, eliminate or relocate camping facilities from the floodplain, and remove some or all of the stone bridges that had intensified the flood effects.[156]

As of December 2000, numerous hearings and workshops had been held in California, as well as hearings in Seattle, Denver, Chicago, and Washington, D.C. For the Merced River plan, a Record of Decision was signed on August 9, 2000. It accepted the preferred alternative with some revisions, the most notable being the widening of the quarter-mile riverside protection boundary, making it closer to the proposals in alternative four of the draft.[157] On August 11, 2000, I met a protester preparing to embark on a rafting run down the Middle Fork of the American River. He wore a T-shirt that had a circle with a slash through it. Inside the slashed circle were the words *Merced River Plan*. He had just returned from a political demonstration in the Valley. It had been organized to protest what he said would be increased development in the river corridor if the plan were to be implemented.

In November of 2000, Interior Secretary Babbitt announced the final revised EIS for the Valley implementation plan. Predictably, environmental activists complained that too much development, especially in the sensitive river corridor, was still being encouraged. Air pollution issues from diesel buses was not effectively addressed. Commercial interests protested that the plan would deny access because of limitations on motel rooms. The EIS promised fewer cars in the Valley, with three outside parking areas proposed. Some development in sensitive meadow areas was slated for removal.[158]

By the end of the year 2000, most issues raised in the public discussion period had been settled. Besides the three out-of-Valley visitor centers and parking transfer sites envisioned in the plan, three other parking and transfer sites, at Badger Pass, El Portal, and either Hazel Green or Foresta, were being considered. These areas were expected to be most heavily used during the peak summer period for the park. In the Valley, a new visitor center was planned close to Yosemite Village, and changes in use of Northside and Southside Drives were envisioned. The systemwide trend toward reduction of auto travel in the national parks was coming to Yosemite. Other changes associated with the Merced River floodplain included removal of the existing stables and rebuilding the Lower Yosemite Falls area to make it more natural. Lodging in the floodplain generally was scheduled for removal, with natural restoration to follow. Camping facilities were slated to increase slightly, but with older campgrounds in the flooded areas replaced and rebuilt in different locations, and with greater variety in camp types. Obviously the flood, and the flood of money provided by Congress, would bring significant changes to Yosemite National Park.[159]

Beyond Yosemite, changes also were appearing in the southern part of the range. On the last day of Tom Knudson's "Sierra in Peril" series, he wrote of several proposals being considered that offered some hope for the embattled Sierra Nevada. One of these was a preserve to protect giant sequoia in Sequoia National Forest. A group of dedicated environmentalists was drumming up support for legislation to set aside some 400,000 acres that held the last remaining unprotected sequoia at the southern border of the range.[160]

What? Giant sequoia that were not protected? How could that be? From a modern perspective it was almost unbelievable that such an oversight could occur. Sequoia were clearly the most unique inhabitants of the Range of Light. For as long as European Americans have had contact with the *Sequoia gigantea,* they have expressed wonder at the size of the big trees. The sequoia grows naturally only in the Sierra Nevada. Groves of the tree can be found in a line stretching some 260 miles down the western flank of the Sierra, in a band extending between 4,000 to 7,500 feet in elevation. Altogether there are some seventy-five remaining sequoia groves.[161]

The northernmost outpost of the trees is in an out-of-the-way area of the American River drainage and is protected by Tahoe National Forest management regulations. Because of the cutting of the "Mother of the Forest" at Calaveras in the 1850s, as well as an additional 8,000 mature sequoia in Converse Basin in the last part of the nineteenth century, efforts to protect the trees have become part of the range's environmental history. Most of the central and southern sequoia groves were included in Calaveras State Park or Sequoia National Park. Only the southernmost groves in the Sequoia National Forest were still threatened by logging activities in the last two decades of the twentieth century.[162]

Environmental historian Rebecca Solnit has provided an excellent brief account of the movement to protect these southernmost giants. In the 1980s, because of clearcutting and intensive management by the Sequoia National Forest, activists such as Carla Cloer, Charlene Little, Martin Litton, and Joe Fontaine began efforts to shield the threatened southern groves. The Sequoia National Forest was cutting the larger commercial species of trees around and in the groves, as well as smaller sequoia. This action left only the largest remaining specimen sequoia standing in isolated small clumps. The logging was justified as clearing space so that sequoia seed could grow in the cleared areas. The plan was to replant "plantations" of commercial species in the logged zones as well, taking advantage of the higher-quality soil that the groves inhabited. The remaining sequoia were to be allowed to reseed themselves naturally in the spaces cleared by the heavy logging. Presumably this planning would produce natural regrowth of the sequoia and get out the cut for the Sequoia National Forest at the same time. Interesting thinking. Log a species that you say you want to propagate in order to promote its propagation.[163]

In 1990, under pressure from the local activists and the Sierra Club, the Sequoia National Forest agreed to leave larger buffer zones around sequoias while continuing logging in adjacent areas. But because the action was only supported by regulations that depended on undemonstrated compliance by the Forest Service, the activists sought federal legislation to create a sequoia reserve. It was this measure that Knudson had referred to. The Sierra Club created a special Sequoia Task Force. The Natural Resources Defense Council also took up the cause. In 1992 a bill was introduced in Congress to create a sequoia reserve out of portions of the Sequoia National Forest, but it languished because of strong conservative opposition. By the end of the century it became clear that legislation would not be forthcoming, and President Clinton created the Giant Sequoia National Monument by executive order. A 327,760-acre monument (smaller than the legislative proposal) was carved out of the Sequoia National Forest. It included some cutover areas such as the ill-fated Converse Basin, as well as some 13,000 acres of higher-elevation old-growth sequoia groves.[164]

Surprisingly, many in the environmental community were furious at the action. The main reason for their anger was that the presidential proclamation allowed timber sales in the area of the monument to continue if they had been approved before the monument was designated. If allowed to stand, these sales could actually increase cutting in the very areas presumably set aside to protect the sequoia and the forest ecosystem that surrounded them. This continued logging was justified by President Clinton strictly on economic terms and was allowed in order to gain local political support for the measure. The argument for cutting was that local mills might close if the timber sales were vacated. Supporters of the monument proposal said in its defense that all of the sales in question would be challenged in court. In their view, the fight for the monument had not ended with the executive order but only marked the beginning of an effort to expand protection to the areas included in an imperfect executive order.[165]

The end of the Clinton administration and the coming to office of George W. Bush changed the political dynamics of the debate over the Sequoia National Monument. In February of 2000, Interior Secretary Gale Norton said that President Bush would not seek to overturn the creation of the new Sequoia and other national monuments, but would work with western politicians and landowners to adjust boundaries instead. In October of 2001, a federal district court dismissed a lawsuit filed by Tulare County politicians, timber interests, and off-road-vehicle users who had sought to challenge Clinton's designation of the Sequoia Monument in the hope of reducing its size by removing non-sequoia buffer zones from around the big tree groves. A combination of environmental-group challenges and public outrage over some of the new administration's early proclamations in environmental matters made President Bush more cautious.[166] As with other Bush-administration environmental initiatives, bold reversals of policy were not attempted. Instead, regulation changes and actions taken at lower levels were used to accomplish resource-extraction goals.

Public expectations that the big trees and the surrounding ecosystem would truly be treated as a national monument (with a deemphasis on commercial activities) were quickly dashed. The key problem was that the monument was to be administered by the Forest Service and not the National Park Service. The same people who had been supporting policies to cut heavily in the surrounding forest and cut smaller sequoia were the ones preparing the Draft Environmental Impact Statement. Most of the work on the DEIS was conducted before the Scientific Advisory Board that was required by the presidential order creating the monument had met. That board later played only a limited role in the formulation of the six alternatives produced by the Sequoia National Forest personnel. Five of the six alternatives stressed continued logging, with the preferred alternative allowing the greatest amount of cutting. Only one of the alternatives suggested using fire management, similar to practices in the adjoining Sequoia National Park, and limited cutting for protection of structures or forest health. It was as if the eras of environmental influence and ecosystem management had never occurred. This book went to press before the final Record of Decision was announced.[167]

Epilogue: Perspective from Martis Valley

June 29, 2003—I am sitting inside the mouth of a prehistoric rock shelter looking out onto Martis Valley, just south of the sprawling community of Truckee, California. The rock shelter is located off the valley floor in a volcanic outcropping. I am talking with some members of the Nevada County Land Trust, explaining how the area has changed since its first occupants used it for refuge. This is not John Muir's shining "Range of Light" country. It's the lower northern and eastern edge of the Sierra, where volcanic rock still covers much of the granite heart of the range. Above me, the smoke-blackened roof attests to campfires that burned thousands of years ago. From this vantage point at the rock shelter's lip, I can look out and reflect upon the changes that have made this portion of the Sierra Nevada what it is today. And in its way, this Martis Valley site speaks to the future of the Sierra as well. It is part of a range heavily used by admirers and commercial interests alike.

Ancient people from what archeologists have called the Tahoe Reach, Martis, and Kings Beach archeological complexes used this area seasonally from about 8000 B.C. to around A.D. 1000 The valley and adjoining areas were then used until early historic times by the Washoe people. That means that this valley has been in continuous use for all of the Sierra's human history. The valley, creek tributaries, and creekside environment of the prehistoric days provided seeds and other vegetal resources, fish in spawning season, and waterfowl. The hillsides, ridges, and valley floor provided habitat for deer and rabbits. Basalt formations nearby provided raw material for tools used in hunting and other activities. The long occupation by a relatively small number of native people left little in the way of large-scale transformation of the environment. Smoke-blackened rock and the scattering of basalt flakes and projectile points do not represent big impacts on the surrounding landscape. Even the use of fire as a tool for altering the landscape was not as important on this eastern, lee side of the range, with its more-open and less-dense forests.[168]

To the north and south are historic pathways created by explorers and emigrants from the United States during the early opening phase of the Sierra's history. The greatest early impact in this area came between the 1860s and the 1880s from loggers, grazers, and sheepherders. The Washoe were driven away. The western Nevada silver strike at the Comstock and the building of the Central Pacific Railroad brought significant change to the Martis Valley and throughout the surrounding area. The hillsides were used for production of wood, beef, mutton, and wool. Those activities still leave their mark. The heavy logging in particular reduced the forests, and the arid climate has not been kind to reforestation. In the drainage system to the south of the shelter can still be found traces of the railroad logging operation of the Richardson brothers. A collapsed log trestle remains, built for a huge three-cylinder steam locomotive that used log rails for its flanged wheels. The locomotive dragged logs out of the drainage to the northeast to an impound dam, built from volcanic rock, at the mill site. Across the valley was another large logging operation, known as Schaffer's Mill. On that hillside can also be found remnants of V-flumes used to transfer cut timber. As the hillsides were logged, Basque and other sheepherders used both sides of the valley for free pasture. Carvings left on the bark of the oldest surviving aspens in some undeveloped areas provide us with names, dates, and even the very personal ideas of these herders. The Basque, employed by American sheep ranchers, continued to use Martis Valley rangeland until after the Second World War. The valley floor itself, in the heavy logging era, also had a working ranch—the Joerger Ranch—where dairy cattle provided milk and butter for the lumberjacks laboring nearby.[169]

Logging continued in the various drainages of the Truckee River, of which the forks of Martis Creek are a part, but declined in significance. Most of the basin's virgin forests were cut by the time of the Great Depression. The last big mill in Truckee closed a few years ago. But even as timber and the railroad gave Truckee an industrial base to rely on, Lake Tahoe, Donner Lake, and Independence Lake close by to the west drew tourists. Truckee was a gateway city served by the Central and Southern Pacific Railroads. Highway 40 and later Interstate 80 continued that function, giving the area a reliable and mixed economy. The Army Corps of Engineers, because of possible flood danger to the city of Reno, built a dam to contain the pitiable amount of water that came from Martis Creek. The rock-and-earth-fill structure sits almost directly below the escarpment that contains our rock shelter. Although various level lines show that the water in wet weather can rise significantly, it does not amount to much of a reservoir. "Martis Lake" originally was included into a Lahontan cutthroat trout recovery program. In the nineteenth century, the cutthroat were fished nearly to extinction by commercial and sports fishermen. The recovery of these native fish has not gone well, and non-native species dominate in the lake environs. Anglers are ordered to practice catch-and-release fishing, using only artificial lures and barbless hooks.

After the building of the Interstate, Truckee became a destination tourist site. The Northstar Resort was constructed on the western valley hillside across from where I sit. Included in that development were a golf course and various businesses, among them a restaurant called "Schaffer's Mill," named for the historic logging operation. A modern ski facility was the center of what was intended to be a year-round resort. From the rock shelter, the ski runs show prominently, condominiums peek through the sparse timber stands, and the golf course is also visible. Below the line of the golf course, between it and Highway 267 to Tahoe, is a natural area preserved as a wildlife refuge stretching up into the hillside north of Northstar.

By the 1980s and 1990s, the valley was included in a general burst of construction and growth in the Truckee area. Development occurred on the road to Squaw Valley and the old Highway 40 "Gateway" area as Tom Knudson attested to in the last article in his series. Because development was slowed in the nearby Lake Tahoe area, it made its way into the Martis Valley corridor instead. It was the largest flat area in the vicinity. Road improvement brought more traffic. Three golf courses (including Northstar's) are there now, as are a regional park, business and professional offices, apartment complexes, private home developments, an expanding Truckee-Tahoe regional airport, a new motel, and several real-estate broker's signs touting valuable commercial property appear on both sides of the highway. By the airport is a Truckee Sanitation District facility to serve the growing population. Next to it is a huge aggregate plant that provides, in less than a day, more "lithic resources" than the Martis's prehistoric users consumed in thousands of years. The plant contributes to the construction boom in the basin. The only area not slated for immediate development is the reservoir site and the small wildlife preserve.

In January of 2002, Placer County released a draft plan update reflecting the interest of the Northstar and East/West Partners in creating another large residential resort. That would require the expansion of Highway 267 to four lanes, provide 5,500 housing units for 19,000 expected residents, and entail the building of three new golf courses and the expansion of ski facilities. In addition, Sierra Pacific Industries has indicated that it wants to convert some of the lands it acquired as timber reserves in the area into houses and more golf facilities.

Visiting the Martis Valley rock shelter helped me find a graceful way to end this book. And especially to end it at a place that helped provide a retrospective on the range's human story. Martis Valley has an unbroken line of human use for nearly 10,000 years. No single culture lasted that long, of course. But I believe that there are few places where so many things come together in the Sierra Nevada. I realize that I could have chosen other locations that we have met in this history. On the eastern side, the communities around Lake Tahoe are facing development pressures like those we see here near Truckee. Mammoth Lakes, farther still to the south, is also experiencing rapid growth and significant expansion of year-round residential development. Western-flank foothill communities, while not developing for the same commercial-recreation reasons as the eastern locales, are also burgeoning. Urbanization has a long history in the range, even if the reasons for it have changed with time.[170]

Martis Valley is only a piece of the urbanizing portion of the Sierra Nevada. It is not necessarily the future for all of the range. But it does represent in microcosm the forces at work rangewide. The reality of the Sierra Nevada today is that too many people and interests want too much from it. The Sierra is huge. It is one of the great mountain ranges of the world. But it is finite. The publicly held oak woodlands of the lower west side and the mixed-conifer forests of the mid-elevation western flank are the subject of continuing struggle over how they are to be managed. This is also true in the few roadless areas left higher in the range. The rare and unique monumental areas such as Yosemite, Sequoia and Kings Canyon, and Lake Tahoe are increasingly visited. The preserved wilderness areas of the alpine portions of the range have too many demands being made on them as well.

The same is true of the watersheds of the range on both sides. No city authority, state project, federal agency, or agribusiness consortium that I know of has willingly given up its claim to any of the water of the range. None has ever seriously considered lessening its demands by setting limits on its use of Sierran water. Too many people with too many demands, whether it is Martis Valley or anywhere else. That is the reality today.

This environmental history of the Sierra Nevada has a purpose. It is intended to provide a rangewide summation of the role that humans have played in shaping the Sierra—to help give perspective and fill in some blanks. But most of all, I wanted to use history as a way to help readers to "see" the range as a whole. Along with faulting, uplifting, erosion, volcanism, glaciation, and fire, humans have shaped the range into what it is today. All of these forces can be expected, in varying degrees, to continue to do so. Nature is, after all, a big player. But the human element has been the primary focus of this book.

What people did in the Sierra Nevada in the past involved choices. At various times, native people chose to burn the land they occupied. Conservationists, environmentalists, and logging corporations struggled over what was to be done with the range's forests. The national forests are what they are today because the Forest Service chose to practice fire suppression and logging based on intensive-management practices. Lake Tahoe is neither a state park nor a national monument because of choices made in the past. Through the Wilderness Act, Congress made it possible for the longest contiguous wilderness area outside of Alaska to exist on the Sierra's spine. Because of an earthquake near the dam at Oroville, political decisions were made not to dam the American River at Auburn. The Sierra Nevada Ecosystem Project was created by the action of the Forest Service and Congress to provide a scientific baseline for choices to be made about the Sierra's future.

Choices for the future will continue to be made. These could include managing the private and public lands of the range so as to lessen environmental damage, contribute to a sustainable economy, and support the amenities that draw people into its foothill and other communities. Sprawl is, after all, a choice made by poor planning. The activities of the Sierra

Business Council and the research of environmental planners offer ways for people to consider how to shape a sustainable human society in the range's developing areas.[171]

Choices about whether to manage the forests of the Sierra Nevada for their health, restoration, and sustainable use can also be made. Fire in these forests must be addressed as part of an expanded view of Sierran forest policy—especially now that our actions have transformed them into "artifacts" through logging and fire suppression. Visions for such a sustainable forest policy are available in the Forest Service Employees for Environmental Ethics study *Restoring Our Forest Legacy,* various portions of the Sierra Nevada Ecosystem Project report, and parts of the original Sierra Nevada Framework.

National Parks and wilderness areas in the Sierra and elsewhere in the West can be managed to balance visitor use with scientific stewardship that preserves habitat for natural occupants.[172] President Clinton, just before leaving office, announced an initiative to begin planning to place millions of acres of national forest land, a large portion of it in the Sierra, into a roadless preserve.[173] Revision of management plans for Sierran National Parks continues also as part of an ongoing process, thanks to NEPA. And in the case of Yosemite Valley, the door to change is always open, as we have seen. Choices in the range's most pristine areas are still being made.

Lake Tahoe can possibly be prevented from turning green if we make choices to alter the way it is being used. There is some sign that the inexorable greening of the lake has slowed, and the Supreme Court has upheld the right of the Tahoe Regional Planning Agency to work effectively even if its plans inconvenience some private land owners.[174] The SNEP case study of the Tahoe area contains valuable information for anyone interested in the lake's future. In 1997, President Clinton and Vice-President Al Gore participated in a "summit" meeting concerning Tahoe. They promised funding to try to address ongoing problems of overdevelopment, and Congress has made an effort to go along some of the way. Hope for the lake continues.[175]

And while we are at it, let's consider a past choice of some significance. I'll put it in the form of a question. Does Hetch Hetchy have to remain a reservoir? We could rethink the decision made back in 1913. All it would take would be a choice to remove some concrete, then allow some time for natural processes to work alongside necessary remedial human actions. National parks are for perpetuity, are they not? San Francisco has never used all of the water it got from damming this portion of the Grand Canyon of the Tuolumne. California needs to rethink its electrical power needs. San Francisco could be included in the planning required for both water and power issues. Some might argue that the drowned valley would be imperfect. But so is Yosemite, even without a dam to worry about. While time may not heal all wounds perfectly, I would be willing to bet that a healing Hetch Hetchy Valley would have more to offer to humans and nonhumans alike than the reservoir that is there now. How realistic is it to think of such a feat of restoration, especially with the assured resistance of San Francisco? Do you remember the Mono Lake Committee? Did anyone believe that it could win against Los Angeles?[176]

It would take a long time for Hetch Hetchy to heal. But things could be learned from such a huge endeavor at working with natural processes in the Sierra. What was learned there could be usefully applied elsewhere in the range where human use has overpowered natural processes. It pleases me to think that my grandchildren and their children could someday walk on a Hetch Hetchy Valley floor pathway, reading signs that "interpret" the recovery project, as they gaze at the waterfalls above them. I suspect John Muir might also be pleased at such a prospect, however long a shot it might be.

PREFACE

1. Muir used and reused the quoted phrases often in articles and books he wrote over a long career. See John Muir, *The Mountains of California* (1894; reprint, Garden City, NY: Doubleday, 1961); John Muir, *My First Summer in the Sierra* (1911; reprint, Boston: Houghton Mifflin, 1976); John Muir, *The Yosemite* (1914; reprint, San Francisco: Sierra Club Books, 1988); John Muir, "Peaks and Glaciers of the High Sierra," in *West of the Rocky Mountains,* ed. John Muir (Philadelphia: Running Press, 1976). Many fine current books take the Sierra Nevada as their subject, but most focus on particular aspects of the range such as its geology (Mary Hill, *Geology of the Sierra Nevada* [Berkeley: University of California Press, 1975]) or its natural history (Verna R. Johnston, *Sierra Nevada: The Naturalist's Companion* [Berkeley: University of California Press, 1998]). There is a classic history of the Sierra Nevada by the late Francis Farquhar, *History of the Sierra Nevada* (Berkeley: University of California Press, 1965), but it is not really an environmental history and does not cover the years after 1960. It is worthwhile for any lover of the Sierra Nevada to read it, however. Three good contemporary environmental histories of parts of the range are: Lary M. Dilsaver and William C. Tweed, *Challenge of the Big Trees: A Resource History of Sequoia and Kings Canyon National Parks* (Three Rivers, CA: Sequoia Natural History Association, 1990); Douglas H. Strong, *Tahoe: An Environmental History* (Lincoln: University of Nebraska Press, 1984); and Alfred Runte, *Yosemite: The Embattled Wilderness* (Lincoln: University of Nebraska Press, 1990).

2. See the epigraph to this book for a brief version of the story, which can be found in Robert F. Heizer and Albert B. Elsasser, *The Natural World of the California Indians* (Berkeley: University of California Press, 1980), 217–18.

3. See Scott Stine, "Climate, 1650–1850," in Sierra Nevada Ecosystem Project, *Final Report to Congress,* vol. 2, *Assessments and Scientific Basis for Management Options* (Davis: University of California, Centers for Water and Wildland Resources, 1996) [hereafter cited as *SNEP,* vol. 2], 25–30.

4. An interesting account of Basque sheepherders and the aspen-tree-carving tradition that they developed to record their time in the Sierra and elsewhere—including the Pole Creek site—is discussed in J. Mallea-Olaetxe, *Speaking through the Aspens: Basque Tree Carvings in California and Nevada* (Reno: University of Nevada Press, 2000), 33.

5. Farquhar, *History of the Sierra Nevada;* Strong, *Tahoe;* Dilsaver and Tweed, *Challenge of the Big Trees;* Runte, *Yosemite;* Tim Palmer, *The Sierra Nevada: A Mountain Journey* (Washington, DC: Island Press, 1988); John Walton, *Western Times and Water Wars: State Culture and Rebellion in California* (Berkeley: University of California Press, 1992).

6. Dan Flores, *The Natural West: Environmental History in the Great Plains and Rocky Mountains* (Norman: University of Oklahoma Press, 2001), 101.

INTRODUCTION: MAJOR FORCES THAT HAVE SHAPED
THE SIERRA NEVADA

1. James G. Moore, *Exploring the Highest Sierra* (Stanford, CA: Stanford University Press, 2000), 6–7; Hill, *Geology of the Sierra Nevada*, 38–49; Paul Webster, *The Mighty Sierra: Portrait of a Mountain World* (New York: Weathervane Books, 1972), 24; Jeffrey P. Schaffer, *The Geomorphic Evolution of the Yosemite Valley and the Sierra Nevada Landscapes* (Berkeley: Wilderness Press, 1997), 6–8, 322, 332; Sierra Nevada Ecosystem Project, *Final Report to Congress,* vol. 1, *Assessment Summaries and Management Strategies* (Davis: University of California, Centers for Water and Wildland Resources, 1996) [hereafter cited as *SNEP,* vol. 1], 8; Stine, "Climate, 1650–1850," 25: Allan A. Schoenherr, *A Natural History of California* (Berkeley: University of California Press, 1992), 69–166; M. Kat Anderson and Michael J. Moratto, "Native American Land-Use Practices and Ecological Impacts," in *SNEP,* vol. 2, 187; Carolyn Merchant, ed., *Major Problems in American Environmental History* (Lexington, MA: D. C. Heath, 1993), viii; J. R. McBride, W. Russell, and S. Kloss, "Impact of Human Settlement," in *SNEP,* vol. 2, 1193.

2. Gary Snyder, *Mountains and Rivers without End* (Washington, DC: Counterpoint, 1996), 143.

3. Wallace B. Wolfenden, "Quaternary Vegetation History," in *SNEP,* vol. 2, 47; Schaffer, *Geomorphic Evolution of the Yosemite Valley and the Sierra Nevada Landscapes,* 106.

4. Stine, "Climate, 1650–1850," 25.

5. "California Volcano Starts to Stir," *Science News,* December 20, 1997, 396; USGS Volcano Hazards Program, Recent Earthquakes in California and Nevada, Long Valley Special Map, April 26, 1998, Internet source; Jennifer Bowles, "Ski Town's Wish," *Sacramento Bee,* November 26, 1997, B3 and following.

6. "California Volcano Starts to Stir," 396; Sandra Blakeslee, "Volcano in California Springs Unusual Carbon Dioxide Leak," *New York Times,* July 23, 1996, C4.

7. Hill, *Geology of the Sierra Nevada,* 1–5; Schaffer, *Geomorphic Evolution of the Yosemite Valley and Sierra Nevada Landscapes,* 277, 301, 332.

8. Farquhar, *History of the Sierra Nevada,* 1–70; Anderson and Moratto, "Native American Land-Use Practices and Ecological Impacts," 187; *SNEP,* vol. 1, 14.

9. Catherine S. Fowler and Sven Liljeblad, "Northern Paiute," in *Handbook of North American Indians,* vol. 11, *Great Basin,* ed. Warren L. D'Azevedo (Washington, DC: Smithsonian Institution, 1986), 435–38; John Hart, *Storm over Mono: The Mono Lake Basin and the California Water Future* (Berkeley: University of California Press, 1996), 14.

10. Hill, *Geology of the Sierra Nevada,* 42.

11. Verna Johnston, *Sierra Nevada* (Boston: Houghton Mifflin, 1970), 2; Norman Hinds, *Evolution of the California Landscape* (San Francisco: State of California, Divi-

sion of Mines, Department of Natural Resources, December 1952), 13; *SNEP,* vol. 1, 6; Muir, *Mountains of California,* 2–3, 4–5, 7–8.

12. *SNEP,* vol. 1, 6.

13. Hinds, *Evolution of the California Landscape,* 11–13; Johnston, *Sierra Nevada,* 2; *SNEP,* vol. 1, 8; Schoenherr, *Natural History of California,* 69; Norris Hundley Jr., *The Great Thirst: Californians and Water, 1770s–1990s* (Berkeley: University of California Press, 1992), 406–22.

14. Schoenherr, *Natural History of California,* 69, 73–92.

15. Hinds, *Evolution of the California Landscape,* 13; Johnston, *Sierra Nevada,* 2–3; Farquhar, *History of the Sierra Nevada,* 1–2, 23–50.

16. Carrie Peyton, "Tahoe's Depth Ranking Secure," *Sacramento Bee,* August 30, 1998 B1. According to a survey carried out by the U.S. Geological Survey in the summer of 1998 and reported in the *Sacramento Bee,* the currently accepted depth of Lake Tahoe is 1,590 feet, making it the second-deepest lake in North America.

17. Two newspapers near Tahoe also ran stories on the earthquake activity at the lake in November of 1998. See *Grass Valley Union,* November 12, 1998, A1, A11, and *Sacramento Bee,* November 12, 1998, B3.

18. Dilsaver and Tweed, *Challenge of the Big Trees,* 1–3; Strong, *Tahoe,* 1–4; Palmer, *Sierra Nevada,* ix, 250; Hill, *Geology of the Sierra Nevada,* 42; George Wuerthner, *California's Sierra Nevada* (Helena, MT: American and World Geographic, 1993), 6–8.

19. Timothy P. Duane, "Human Settlement, 1850–2040," in *SNEP,* vol. 2, 235–36.

20. John James, "Lake Tahoe and the Sierra Nevada," in *The Mountainous West: Explorations in Historical Geography,* ed. William Wyckoff and Lary Dilsaver (Lincoln: University of Nebraska Press, 1995), 335; Hinds, *Evolution of the California Landscape,* 13; Schoenherr, *Natural History of California,* 92; M. Barbour et al., *California's Changing Landscapes* (Sacramento: California Native Plant Society, 1993), 99; Muir, "Peaks and Glaciers of the High Sierra," 1; *SNEP,* vol. 1, 5.

21. Schoenherr, *Natural History of California,* 92–94; Barbour et al., *California's Changing Landscapes,* 99–121; Johnston, *Sierra Nevada,* 4–57, 243.

22. *SNEP,* vol. 1, 10–12.

23. Ibid., 13.

24. Muir, *Mountains of California,* 3–4.

25. Elna S. Bakker, *An Island Called California: An Ecological Introduction to Its Natural Communities,* 2d ed. (Berkeley: University of California Press, 1984), 195.

26. Samuel G. Houghton, *A Trace of Desert Waters: The Great Basin Story* (Salt Lake City: Howe Brothers, 1986), 51–71, 85–108.

27. David Beesley, "Reconstructing the Landscape: An Environmental History, 1820–1960," in *SNEP,* vol. 2, 5–8; Forest Service Employees for Environmental Ethics [hereafter cited as FSEEE], *Restoring Our Forest Legacy: Blueprint for Sierra Nevada National Forests* (Eugene, OR: FSEEE, 2000), 7–21; "Late Successional Old-Growth Forest Conditions," in *SNEP,* vol. 1, 92–111.

28. François Matthes, *The Incomparable Valley: A Geologic Interpretation of the Yosemite,* ed. Fritiof Fryxell (Berkeley: University of California Press, 1956), 80.

29. Mark Twain, *Roughing It*, vol. 2 of *The Works of Mark Twain* (Berkeley: University of California Press, 1972), 163.

30. John Walton, in his useful study of the Owens Valley, noted that the Owens Valley Paiute had developed a "self-sufficient agrarian society" that the early historic American settlers of the valley later built on. See Walton, *Western Times and Water Wars*, 15–16.

31. Elizabeth Hogan, ed., *Rivers of the West* (Menlo Park, CA: Lane, 1974), 17, 180; Diana Jacobs et al., *California Rivers: A Public Trust Report* (Sacramento: California State Lands Commission, 1993), 1–2, 6; Jeffrey Mount, *California Rivers and Streams: The Conflict between Fluvial Process and Land Use* (Berkeley: University of California Press, 1995), 4–6; Sierra Nevada Forest Protection Campaign, "New Sierra Management Plan Needs to Address Many Important Issues," *Stand* 2, no. 3 (summer/fall 1998): 1, 12–13.

32. Mount, *California Rivers and Streams*, 178, 180, 182; Houghton, *Trace of Desert Waters*, 51, 127.

33. Mount, *California Rivers and Streams*, 4–5; Bakker, *Island Called California*, 144–45; Hinds, *Evolution of the California Landscape*, 15; Palmer, *Sierra Nevada*, 306; Dilsaver and Tweed, *Challenge of Big Trees*, i.

34. Palmer, *Sierra Nevada*, 306; Mount, *California Rivers and Streams*, 5; Hart, *Storm over Mono*, 7.

35. George Hinkle and Bliss Hinkle, *Sierra Nevada Lakes* (Indianapolis: Bobbs-Merrill, 1949), 19–20; Hinds, *Evolution of the California Landscape*, 21; Strong, *Tahoe*, xiii.

36. Carl N. Skinner and Chi-Ru Chang, "Fire Regimes, Past and Present," in *SNEP*, vol. 2, 1041.

37. Johnston, *Sierra Nevada: The Naturalist's Companion*, 75.

38. Kat Anderson, *Indian Fire-Based Management in the Sequoia–Mixed Conifer Forests of the Central and Southern Sierra Nevada* (Yosemite National Park: Yosemite Research Center, July 15, 1993), 1–30; Kevin S. McKelvey et al., "An Overview of Fire in the Sierra Nevada," in *SNEP*, vol. 2, 1033; Skinner and Chang, "Fire Regimes," 1041.

39. Skinner and Chang, "Fire Regimes," 1047.

40. George R. Stewart, *Fire* (Boston: Houghton Mifflin, 1948), 137.

41. Skinner and Chang, "Fire Regimes," 1042; Johnston, *Sierra Nevada: The Naturalist's Companion*, 73–74.

42. Beesley, "Reconstructing the Landscape," 5–9; McKelvey et al., "Overview of Fire in the Sierra," 1034; Skinner and Chang, "Fire Regimes," 1057–58.

43. Beesley, "Reconstructing the Landscape," 9–17; Skinner and Chang, "Fire Regimes," 1041, 1059–62; Johnston, *Sierra Nevada: The Naturalist's Companion*, 80–85; Harold Biswell, *Prescribed Burning in California Wildlands Vegetation Management* (Berkeley: University of California Press, 1989), 1–3, 43–45, 49–50, 53–55; USDA, Forest Service, *Sierra Nevada Forest Plan Amendment: Draft Environmental Impact Statement* (Pacific Southwest Region: U.S. Forest Service, April 2000), 15.

44. Heizer and Elsasser, *Natural World of the California Indians*, 202, define world view as "a people's vision of the world they live in and how they relate to the environ-

ment, to others, and to the cosmos. Thus does world view form a people's pattern of day-to-day living."

I: A SIERRA SHAPED BY NATIVE PEOPLE

1. Beginning in 1851 with the so-called Mariposa Indian War, the Ahwahnichi people have tried to maintain use and ownership claims to the Yosemite Valley. Attempts to drive them out gave way to reluctant acceptance of their presence as laborers and users of the traditional resources of the area from that day to the present. See, e.g., Edward Castillo, "Petition to Congress on Behalf of the Yosemite Indians," *Journal of California Archeology* 5, no. 2 (winter 1978): 273–75, which contains a petition from the group to Congress pressing their claims. For recent accounts of the role of the Ahwahnichi and other culturally related groups' involvement in the revision of a major plan for Yosemite Valley development and the creation of an Indian Cultural Center there, see National Park Service, *Draft Yosemite Valley Plan: Supplemental Environmental Impact Statement* (Yosemite, CA: Yosemite National Park, 2000), chap. 4–40, chap. 5–4. Miwok basket weavers play an important role in Forest Service planning as well; see Jennifer Bates, "Progress Reports," *California Indian Basket Weavers Association Newsletter* 25 (December 1998): 8, where Bates discusses a "Consultation Day" during which the Tuolumne Tribal Council met with Stanislaus National Park district rangers and staff about logging, burning, and spraying activities that affected resources and areas of interest to the group. See also Rebecca Solnit, *Savage Dreams: A Journey into the Landscape Wars of the American West* (New York: Vintage Books, 1994), 272–85; R. H. Keller and M. F. Turek, *American Indians and National Parks* (Tucson: University of Arizona Press, 1998), 20–27, 233–35; and Mark David Spence, *Dispossessing the Wilderness: Indian Removal and the Making of the National Parks* (New York: Oxford University Press, 2000), 4–6, 101–32.

2. Quoted in C. R. Bates and M. J. Lee, *Tradition and Innovation: A Basket History of the Indians of the Yosemite–Mono Lake Area* (Yosemite National Park, CA: Yosemite Association, 1990), 15.

3. Ibid., 21; Ralph L. Beals, *Indian Occupancy, Subsistence, and Land Use Patterns in California, VI* (New York: Garland, 1974), 214.

4. Constance Knowles, "Vegetation Burning by California Indians As Shown in Early Records," typescript, Prepared for U.S. Forest Service in the 1930s under Contract to California Forest and Range Information Station, Copy from Forestry Library, University of California, Berkeley, 7, 9.

5. See Linda A. Reynolds, "The Role of Indian Tribal Governments and Communities in Regional Land Management," in *SNEP,* vol. 2, 207–23.

6. There is an ongoing and lively debate among social scientists on the role of natives as a force in shaping Sierran environments. See Anderson and Moratto, "Native American Land-Use Practices and Ecological Impacts," 187–89, and Albert J. Parker, "Fire in Sierra Nevada Forests: Evaluating the Ecological Impact of Burning by Native Americans," in *Fire, Native Peoples, and the Natural Landscape,* ed. Thomas R. Vale (Washington, DC: Island Press, 2002), 233–37, 258–62.

7. S. A. Barrett and E. W. Gifford, "Indian Life of the Yosemite Region: Miwok Material Culture," *Bulletin of the Milwaukee Public Museum* 2, no. 4 (March 1933): 127.

8. Stephen Powers, *Tribes of California* (1875; reprint, Berkeley: University of California Press, 1976); C. H. Merriam, "Indian Village and Camp Sites in Yosemite Valley," in *A Collection of Ethnographical Articles on the California Indians,* ed. Robert F. Heizer (1917; reprint, Ramona, CA: Ballena Press, 1976), 47–53; A. L. Kroeber, *Basic Report on California Indian Land Holdings, VI* (New York: Garland, 1974), 23, 40, 61–62; Beals, *Indian Occupancy, Subsistence, and Land Use Patterns in California,* 2–3, 33–35, 191–97, 213–15; Richard Levy, "Eastern Miwok," in *Handbook of North American Indians,* vol. 8, *California,* ed. Robert F. Heizer (Washington, DC: Smithsonian Institution, 1978), 398–413. See also Lafayette H. Bunnell, *Discovery of the Yosemite and the Indian War of 1851 Which Led to That Event* (1880; reprint, Yosemite Park, CA: Yosemite Association, 1990); and Jean-Nicolas Perlot, *Gold Seeker: Adventures of a Belgian Argonaut during the Gold Rush Years,* trans., ed., and with an introduction by Howard R. Lamar (New Haven: Yale University Press, 1985).

9. Barrett and Gifford, "Indian Life of the Yosemite Region," 129; Levy, "Eastern Miwok," 398–400; Powers, *Tribes of California,* 346; William L. Kahrl, ed., *The California Water Atlas* (Sacramento: Department of Water Resources, 1979), 70–71.

10. Beals, *Indian Occupancy, Subsistence, and Land Use Patterns in California,* 191–94; Merriam, "Indian Village and Camp Sites in Yosemite Valley," 47–53.

11. Levy, "Eastern Miwok," 402.

12. Besides showing long occupancy of the area, the changed relationship of native people with state and federal agencies means that the local Miwok community will have major influence on the road-planning activities. See Matthew Barrows, "Road Project Unearths Ancient Miwok Site," *Sacramento Bee,* September 6, 2001, A1, A18.

13. Barrett and Gifford, "Indian Life of the Yosemite Region," 134–36; Kahrl, ed., *California Water Atlas,* 17.

14. Beals, *Indian Occupancy, Subsistence, and Land Use Patterns in California,* 194, 195–98; "Coyote and Falcon Create People," Miwok creation story in Malcolm Margolin, ed., *The Way We Lived: California Indian Reminiscences, Stories, and Song* (Berkeley: Heyday, 1981), 155.

15. Anderson, *Indian Fire-Based Management,* 1–9.

16. Ibid., 4.

17. Barrett and Gifford, "Indian Life of the Yosemite Region," 136–76, 165–76.

18. Martin Baumhoff, "Environmental Background," in *Handbook of North American Indians,* vol. 8, *California,* ed. Heizer, 22–24; Anderson, *Indian Fire-Based Management,* 7, 152–55, 181–84.

19. "Coyote Steals Fire," Miwok creation story in *The Way We Lived,* ed. Margolin, 154.

20. Anderson, *Indian Fire-Based Management,* 33–34.

21. Anderson and Moratto, "Native American Land-Use Practices and Ecological Impacts," 187–206.

22. M. J. Moratto, T. F. King, and W. B. Wolfenden, "Archaeology and California's Climate," *Journal of California Archeology* 5, no. 2 (winter 1978): 157; Michael J. Moratto, *California Archeology* (Orlando: Academic Press, 1984), 70–71; Anderson and Moratto, "Native American Land-Use Practices and Ecological Impacts," 187–206.

23. Robert Elston, "Prehistory of the Western Area," in *Handbook of North American Indians*, vol. 11, *Great Basin,* ed. D'Azevedo (Washington, DC: Smithsonian Institution, 1986), 135; Moratto, *California Archeology,* 294–95; Joseph L. Chartkoff and Kerry Kona Chartkoff, *The Archaeology of California* (Stanford, CA: Stanford University Press, 1984), 74–75; Sven Liljeblad and Catherine S. Fowler, "Owens Valley Paiute," in *Handbook of North American Indians,* vol. 11, *Great Basin,* ed. D'Azevedo, 412.

24. Chartkoff and Chartkoff, *Archaeology of California,* 128; Moratto, *California Archeology,* 335–36.

25. Moratto, King, and Wolfenden, "Archeology and California's Climate," 153–54; Moratto, *California Archeology,* 336–37; Chartkoff and Chartkoff, *Archaeology of California,* 172; Albert B. Elsasser, "Development of Regional Prehistoric Cultures," in *Handbook of North American Indians,* vol. 8, *California,* ed. Heizer, 52–54; Anderson *Indian Fire-Based Management,* 154–55.

26. Moratto, *California Archeology,* 288–89; Heizer and Elsasser, *Natural World of the California Indians,* 59, 66; Anderson and Moratto, "Native American Land-Use Practices and Ecological Impacts," 187.

27. Anderson and Moratto, "Native American Land-Use Practices and Ecological Impacts," 191.

28. Ibid., 189–91; Heizer and Elsasser, *Natural World of the California Indians,* 19, 37–38.

29. Hundley, *The Great Thirst,* 14; Francis A. Riddell, "Maidu and Konkow," in *Handbook of North American Indians,* vol. 8, *California,* ed. Heizer, 370–86; Norman L. Wilson and Arlean H. Towne, "Nisenan," *Handbook of North American Indians,* vol. 8, *California,* ed. Heizer, 387–97; Levy, "Eastern Miwok," 398–413; Robert F. Spier, "Foothill Yokuts," in *Handbook of North American Indians,* vol. 8, *California,* ed. Heizer, 471–84; Robert F. Spier, "Monache," in *Handbook of North American Indians,* vol. 8, *California,* ed. Heizer, 426–36; Charles R. Smith, "Tubatulabl," in *Handbook of North American Indians,* vol. 8, *California,* ed. Heizer, 437–45; Maurice L. Zigmond, "Kawaiisu," in *Handbook of North American Indians,* vol. 8, *California,* ed. Heizer, 398–411; Moratto, *California Archeology,* 288–90; Anderson and Moratto, "Native American Land-Use Practices and Ecological Impacts," 189–91.

30. As with the Ahwahnichi and other Miwok groups, the Washoe have been fortunate in being closely involved in government planning that has affected Lake Tahoe in recent years. In 1997 the Washoe received notification that they would regain control of a portion of their ancestral homeland at and around Meeks Bay. They would also be allowed to build a cultural center there and to gather traditional plant materials. See Jon Christenson, "At Tahoe Forum, a Tribe Wins a Deal," *High Country News,* August 18, 1997, 4. Cooperation of the Washoe with federal authorities in cleanup of mining waste in areas in their territory in the Sierra is discussed in Chris

Bowman, "Washoe Indians Take Lead in Mine Cleanup," *Sacramento Bee,* June 7, 2000, A1, A14.

31. Warren L. D'Azevedo, "Washoe," in *Handbook of North American Indians,* vol. 11, *Great Basin,* ed. D'Azevedo, 466–98; Fowler and Liljeblad, "Northern Paiute," ibid., 435–65; Liljeblad and Fowler, "Owens Valley Paiute," ibid., 412–34; H. W. Lawton et al., "Agriculture among the Paiute of Owens Valley," in *Before the Wilderness: Environmental Management by Native Americans,* ed. Thomas Blackburn and Kat Anderson (Menlo Park, CA: Ballena Press, 1993), 329–77; David H. Thomas, Lorann S. Pendleton, and Stephen C. Cappannari, "Western Shoshone," in *Handbook of North American Indians,* vol. 11, *Great Basin,* ed. D'Azevedo, 262–82; Moratto, *California Archeology,* 343–45; Anderson and Moratto, "Native American Land-Use Practices and Ecological Impacts," 189–91; Hundley, *The Great Thirst,* 16–17.

32. Heizer and Elsasser, *Natural World of the California Indians,* 212.

33. Gary Snyder, *The Practice of the Wild* (New York: North Point Press, 1990), 11–12.

34. Beals, *Indian Occupancy, Subsistence, and Land Use Patterns in California,* 191–94.

35. Heizer and Elsasser, *Natural World of the California Indians,* 82–113; Anderson and Moratto, "Native American Land-Use Practices and Ecological Impacts," 187.

36. Anderson and Moratto, "Native American Land-Use Practices and Ecological Impacts," 187–91.

37. R. F. Heizer, "Natural Forces and Native World View," in *Handbook of North American Indians,* vol. 8, *California,* ed. Heizer, 649–50; Heizer and Elsasser, *Natural World of the California Indians,* 217–19; Sean L. Swezey and Robert F. Heizer, "Ritual Management of Salmonid Fish Resources in California," in *Before the Wilderness,* ed. Blackburn and Anderson, 299–327.

38. Moratto, *California Archeology,* 287, 290, 337; Heizer and Elsasser, *Natural World of the California Indians,* 9–10; George H. Phillips, *The Enduring Struggle: Indians in California History* (San Francisco: Boyd and Fraser, 1981), 9–12; Anderson and Moratto; "Native American Land-Use Practices and Ecological Impacts," 191.

39. Heizer and Elsasser, *Natural World of the California Indians,* 10, 72–73; Anderson and Moratto, "Native American Land-Use Practices and Ecological Impacts," 189–91.

40. Anderson and Moratto, "Native American Land-Use Practices and Ecological Impacts," 187–91; Anderson, *Indian Fire-Based Management,* 1–5. Albert J. Parker, a geographer, takes the view that the "key ecological issue is whether aboriginal burning produced novel vegetation compositions, forest structures, or physical environments—whether it pushed the Sierra Nevada landscape outside the bounds of variability imposed by non-human forces." Parker takes the position, based on his reading of Thomas R. Vale, another geographer, that pristine or natural conditions exist "*if these conditions would exist whether or not humans were present.*" Parker accepts the well-established view that Sierran natives used fire as a technology, and that there is significant ethnographic evidence that fire use was important in plant food production, hunting, and in production of fiber for baskets. But he argues that the "spatial extent and ecological impacts of such burning remains unclear." See Parker, "Fire in Sierra Nevada Forests," 235–36, 241–42.

41. Phillips, *Enduring Struggle,* 10–11; Baumhoff, "Environmental Background," 16–24; Dilsaver and Tweed, *Challenge of Big Trees,* 22–23; Henry T. Lewis, "In Retrospect," in *Before the Wilderness,* ed. Blackburn and Anderson, 389–400; Blackburn and Anderson, "Introduction: Managing the Domesticated Environment," in *Before the Wilderness,* 15–25, Anderson, *Indian Fire-Based Management,* 1–5, 51–57, 80.

42. Max Oelschlaeger, *The Idea of Wilderness: From Prehistory to the Age of Ecology* (New Haven: Yale University Press), 1–30, 172–204; Anderson, *Indian Fire-Based Management,* 1–2.

43. Anderson and Moratto, "Native American Land-Use Practices and Ecological Impacts," 193.

44. William Wallace, "Post-Pleistocene Archeology, 9000–2000 B.C.," in *Handbook of North American Indians,* vol. 8, *California,* ed. Heizer, 25; Bates and Lee, *Tradition and Innovation,* 16.

45. Anderson, *Indian Fire-Based Management,* 1–36; Lawton et al., "Agriculture among the Paiute of Owens Valley," 329–77.

46. Anderson and Moratto, "Native American Land-Use Practices and Ecological Impacts," 187–88, 195, 196–97; Charles D. Zeier, "Environmental and Cultural Setting," in *Changes in Washoe Land Use Patterns,* ed. Charles D. Zeier and Robert Elston (Madison, WI: Pre-History Press, 1992), 9–10; Anderson, *Indian Fire-Based Management,* 6–23; Hundley, *The Great Thirst,* 16–24.

47. Anderson, *Indian Fire-Based Management,* 1–7.

48. Ibid., 30.

49. John B. Leiberg, *Forest Conditions in the Northern Sierra Nevada, California,* Professional Paper # 8, Series H, Forestry, 5 (Washington, DC: Government Printing Office, 1902), 40.

50. Henry T. Lewis, "Patterns of Indian Burning in California: Ecology and Ethnohistory [1973]," in *Before the Wilderness,* ed. Blackburn and Anderson, 55–58.

51. Ibid., 55–57, 79–80.

52. Ibid., 85–86, 113.

53. Albert J. Parker argues that "structural heterogeneity of Sierran Forests" could have been the result of native actions as Lewis and Anderson state, but it could just as well have been the result of climate and natural fire disturbances. See Parker, "Fire in Sierra Nevada Forests," 251–52.

54. Lewis, "Patterns of Indian Burning in California," 113.

55. Anderson and Moratto, "Native American Land-Use Practices and Ecological Impacts," 194–97.

56. Anderson, *Indian Fire-Based Management.*

57. Rosalie Bethel quoted ibid., 296.

58. McKelvey et al., "Overview of Fire in the Sierra Nevada," 1033–34. Further evidence that Indian-caused fires reduced fire-return intervals well below the fifty-year levels of lightning-caused fires in sequoia groves in the southern Sierra is cited by Anderson, *Indian Fire-Based Management,* 268–69. Parker, in his "Fire in Sierra Nevada Forests," 253–57, argues that frequent fires are more likely a product of climate and lightning and, to a lesser extent, human causes.

59. Muir, *Mountains of California,* 113–14.

60. Anderson, *Indian Fire-Based Management,* 51–58, 152–55, 178, 182–206, 254–78, 279–80; Lewis, "Patterns of Indian Burning in California," 55–116; Runte, *Yosemite,* 9, Helen McCarthy, "Managing Oaks and the Acorn Crop," in *Before the Wilderness,* ed. Blackburn and Anderson, 220.

61. Anderson, *Indian Fire-Based Management,* 186–210; Anderson and Moratto, "Native American Land-Use Practices and Ecological Impacts," 193; Schoenherr, *Natural History of California,* 94, 119–20; McCarthy, "Managing Oaks and the Acorn Crop," 213–28; Glenn Farris, "Quality Food: The Quest for Pine Nuts in Northern California," in *Before the Wilderness,* ed. Blackburn and Anderson, 229–40; Heizer and Elsasser, *Natural World of the California Indians,* 73.

62. Skinner and Chang, "Fire Regimes," 1041, 1047, 1057; Lewis, "Patterns of Indian Burning in California," 85–86.

63. Maureen Gilmer, *California Wildfire Landscaping* (Dallas: Taylor, 1994), 1–4.

64. William Preston, "Serpent in the Garden: Environmental Change in Colonial California," in *Contested Eden: California before the Gold Rush,* ed. Ramón Gutiérrez and Richard J. Orsi (San Francisco: University of California and the California Historical Society, 1998), 266–67.

65. Sherburne F. Cook, *The Conflict between the California Indian and White Civilization* (Berkeley: University of California Press, 1976), 287–89; Beesley, "Reconstructing the Landscape," 4–5; Anderson and Moratto, "Native American Land-Use Practices and Ecological Impacts," 187–88, 199–200.

66. George H. Phillips, *Indians and Intruders in Central California, 1769–1849* (Norman: University of Oklahoma Press, 1993), 32–40; Edward Castillo, "The Impact of Euro-American Exploration and Settlement," in *Handbook of North American Indians,* vol. 8, California, ed. Heizer, 99–110; Robert Jackson, *Indian Population Decline: The Missions of Northwestern New Spain* (Albuquerque: University of New Mexico Press, 1994), 37–38; Albert Hurtado, *Indian Survival on the California Frontier* (New Haven: Yale University Press, 1988), 12–26; George H. Phillips, *Indians and Indian Agents: The Origins of the Reservation System in California, 1849–1852* (Norman: University of Oklahoma Press, 1997), 37; Randall Milliken, *A Time of Little Choice: The Disintegration of Tribal Culture in the San Francisco Bay Area, 1769–1810* (Menlo Park, CA: Ballena Press, 1995), 1–12; Sherburne F. Cook, "Historical Demography," in *Handbook of North American Indians,* vol. 8, *California,* ed. Heizer, 91–98.

67. Beesley, "Reconstructing the Landscape," 4–5.

68. Castillo, "Impact of Euro-American Exploration and Settlement," 99–110.

69. Bates and Lee, *Tradition and Innovation,* 25.

70. Milliken, *Time of Little Choice,* 31–60; Phillips, *Indians and Intruders,* 3–11, 32–33, 40–46.

71. Phillips, *Indians and Intruders,* 8–11, 32–33, 40–46; Jackson, *Indian Population Decline,* 37–38; Hurtado, *Indian Survival on the California Frontier,* 12–26; Dilsaver and Tweed, *Challenge of the Big Trees,* 26; Bates and Lee, *Tradition and Innovation,* 25.

72. Castillo, "Impact of Euro-American Exploration and Settlement," 104–7.

73. Jack D. Forbes, *Native Americans of California and Nevada: A Handbook* (Healds-burg, CA: Naturegraph Press, 1969), 38–43; Phillips, *Indians and Intruders,* 65–71.

74. Castillo, "Impact of Euro-American Exploration and Settlement," 106.

75. Phillips, *Indians and Intruders,* 65–71, 73–82, 83–89, 92–98; Hurtado, *Indian Survival on the California Frontier,* 70–76; Jedediah S. Smith, *The Southwest Expedition of Jedediah S. Smith: His Personal Account of the Journey to California, 1826–1827,* ed. G. R. Brooks (Lincoln: University of Nebraska Press, 1977), 128–70; Zenas Leonard, *Adventures of a Mountain Man: The Narrative of Zenas Leonard* (Lincoln: University of Nebraska Press, 1978), 189–200; Dana E. Supernowicz, "Historical Overview of the Eldorado National Forest" (M.A. thesis, California State University, Sacramento, 1983), 50–51; Paul F. Starrs, "The Public As Agents of Policy," *SNEP,* vol. 2, 128.

76. John Bidwell is quoted in Carlo Defarrari, "North District Ecosystem Man-agement Analysis Areas, Stanislaus National Forest, Sonora California: Historic Overview," typescript, Stanislaus National Forest Archive,1995.

77. Phillips, *Indians and Indian Agents,* 37; Runte, *Yosemite,* 9.

78. Hurtado, *Indian Survival on the California Frontier,* 88–95; Phillips, *Indians and Intruders,* 97–105, 135–36.

79. George R. Stewart, *The California Trail: An Epic with Many Heroes* (New York: McGraw-Hill, 1962), 319; David Beesley, "The Opening of the Sierra Nevada and the Beginnings of Conservation in California, 1827–1900," in *California History,* 75, no. 4 (winter 1996–97): 322–24.

80. Malcolm J. Rohrbough, *Days of Gold: The California Gold Rush and the Ameri-can Nation* (Berkeley: University of California Press, 1997), 1–6, 295–308; Thomas F. Howard, *Sierra Crossing: First Roads to California* (Berkeley: University of California Press, 1998), 1–52.

81. Beesley, "Opening of the Sierra Nevada," 322–25; Phillips, *Indians and Indian Agents,* 189–90.

82. Ronald N. Satz, *American Indian Policy in the Jacksonian Era* (Lincoln: Univer-sity of Nebraska Press, 1975), 126–27, 151–52, 293; Robert M. Utley, *The Indian Fron-tier of the American West, 1846–1890* (Albuquerque: University of New Mexico Press, 1984), 31–63; Phillips, *Indians and Indian Agents,* 3–15.

83. J. Ross Browne, *Crusoe's Island: A Ramble in the Footsteps of Alexander Selkirk, with Sketches of Adventure in California and Washoe* (New York: Harper and Brothers, 1872), 286. See also anthropologists Robert Heizer and Alan Almquist's use of Browne's views in *The Other Californians: Prejudice and Discrimination under Spain and the United States to 1820* (Berkeley: University of California Press, 1971), 85–89.

84. Accounts of the conflict between miners and settlers and Sierra Nevada Indi-ans include: Castillo, "Impact of Euro-American Exploration and Settlement," 107–10; Forbes, *Native Americans of California and Nevada,* 52–63; Hurtado, *Indian Sur-vival on the California Frontier,* 91–95; Phillips, *Indians and Indian Agents,* 38–73, 81–87, 189–90; Heizer and Almquist, *The Other Californians,* 65–85; Robert F. Heizer,

The Destruction of California Indians (Lincoln: University of Nebraska Press, 1974), 4–44; Walton, *Western Times and Water Wars,* 11–54.

85. Beesley, "Reconstructing the Landscape," 4–5.

86. Cook, *Conflict between the California Indian and White Civilization,* 278–82; Castillo, "Impact of Euro-American Exploration and Settlement," 108–10.

87. Cook, "Historical Demography," 91–98; Anderson and Moratto, "Native American Land-Use Practices and Ecological Impacts," 187; Heizer, *Destruction of California Indians,* 17–19, 29–30.

88. Riddell, "Maidu and Konkow," 385; Wilson and Towne, "Nisenan," 396; Robert M. Peterson, *A Case Study of a Northern California Indian Tribe* (San Francisco: R and E Research Associates, 1977), 12–21; Levy, "Eastern Miwok," 400–1; Bunnell, *Discovery of the Yosemite,* 49–52, 54, 81–83, 146–58, 167–70, 176–78; Thomas Jefferson Mayfield, *Indian Summer: Traditional Life among the Choinumne Indians of California's San Joaquin Valley* (Berkeley: Heyday Press–California Historical Society, 1993), 37–111.

89. Bates and Lee, *Tradition and Innovation,* 27.

90. Forbes, *Native Americans of California and Nevada,* 59–68.

91. D'Azevedo, "Washoe," 493; Strong, *Tahoe,* 10–11; James F. Downs, *Two Worlds of the Washoe* (New York: Holt, Rinehart, and Winston, 1966), 73–82; W. Troy Tucker, Charles D. Zeier, and Shelly Raven, "Perspectives on the Ethnohistoric Period," in *Changes in Washoe Land Use Patterns,* ed. Zeier and Elston, 189–90.

92. Fowler and Liljeblad, "Northern Paiute," 437–38, 455–59.

93. Liljeblad and Fowler, "Owens Valley Paiute," 429–30; Walton, *Western Times and Water Wars,* 11–54.

94. Cook, *Conflict between the California Indian and White Civilization,* 278–81.

95. Forbes, *Native Americans of California and Nevada,* 59.

96. Bates and Lee, *Tradition and Innovation,* 26.

97. Cook, *Conflict between the California Indian and White Civilization,* 287–91; Heizer, *Destruction of California Indians,* 15–19, 29–30; Fowler and Liljeblad, "Northern Paiute," 455–59; Beesley, "Reconstructing the Landscape," 4–5; Downs, *Two Worlds of the Washoe,* 76.

98. E. A. Stevenson to Thomas J. Henley, December 31, 1853, quoted in Heizer, *Destruction of California Indians,* 15–16.

99. Bunnell, *Discovery of the Yosemite,* 75–79, 109, 120–21. Continued reliance on the bow and arrow and traditional stalking methods using deerskin-and-antler disguises reveals that the use of firearms had not become widespread among Sierran natives at the time of contact. See Perlot, *Gold Seeker,* 260. See also Castillo, "Impact of Euro-American Exploration and Settlement," 108–9; Phillips, *Indians and Indian Agents,* 51–67.

100. Heizer, ed., *Destruction of California Indians,* 101.

101. Phillips, *Indians and Indian Agents,* 51–90, 97–98, 183–90; Downs, *Two Worlds of the Washoe,* 76–82; Beesley, "Reconstructing the Landscape," 4–5; Fowler and Liljeblad, "Northern Paiute," 457–59; Heizer, *Destruction of California Indians,* 4–6, 11, 17–19, 29–30; Phillips, *Enduring Struggle,* 43–44.

102. Quoted in Anderson, *Indian Fire-Based Management,* 298.

103. Planning to reintroduce fire on a large scale in the Sierra Nevada figures importantly in the major revision of forest plans for the Sierra Nevada Province in the so-called "Sierra Nevada Framework" of 2000–2001 and will be discussed in chapter 7. See Bradley E. Powell, *Record of Decision, Sierra Nevada Forest Plan Amendment, Environmental Impact Statement* (Vallejo, CA: Forest Service, R5 Regional Office, January 2001), 20–21. See also Anderson and Moratto, "Native American Land-Use Practices and Ecological Impacts," 187–200; McKelvey et al., "Overview of Fire in the Sierra Nevada," 1033–40; Biswell, *Prescribed Burning,* 38–60, 79–115; and Stephen J. Pyne, *Fire in America: A Cultural History of Wildland and Rural Fire* (Princeton, NJ: Princeton University Press, 1982), 71–83, 100–22, 261–321.

104. For an interesting discussion of this issue in a broader western context, see Patricia Nelson Limerick, *Legacy of Conquest: The Unbroken Past of the American West* (New York: W. W. Norton, 1987), 179–221, 323.

105. Barrows, "Road Project Unearths Ancient Miwok Site," *Sacramento Bee,* September 6, 2001, A1, A18.

106. Bates and Lee, *Tradition and Innovation,* 91–110; Keller and Turek, *American Indians and National Parks,* 21, 233–235; Spence, *Dispossessing the Wilderness,* 4–6, 101–32; J. H. Engbeck Jr., *State Parks of California from 1864 to the Present* (Portland, OR: Graphic Arts, 1980), 120–22; Reynolds, "Role of Indian Tribal Governments and Communities in Regional Land Management," 207–33; Solnit, *Savage Dreams,* 272–85. See also National Park Service, *Draft Yosemite Valley Plan: Executive Summary* (Yosemite National Park, CA: National Park Service, April 2000), table B, 4-40.

107. Christenson, "At Tahoe Forum, a Tribe Wins a Deal," *High Country News,* August 18, 1997, 4; Bowman, "Washoe Indians Take Lead in Mine Cleanup," *Sacramento Bee,* June 7, 2000, A1, A14; "Redwood National Park Revising Management Plan," *California Indian Basketweavers Association Newsletter* 25 (December 1996): 6; Lee Lyle Williams, "Participatory Research: Science for the People," *Practitioner* (newsletter of the National Network of Forest Practitioners), August 1998, 1; Lorena Gorbet, "Maidu Cultural and Group Action Plan for the Living Village and Stewardship Area," March 1998, typescript, California Indian Basketweavers Association, Grass Valley, CA, no pagination.

2: THE SIERRA GOLD MADE

1. Tim Palmer and Ann Vileisis, *The South Yuba: A Wild and Scenic River Report by the South Yuba Citizens League* (Nevada City, CA: SYRCL, 1993), viii–ix, 42–50.

2. James Delavan, *Notes on California and the Placers; How to Get There, and What to Do Afterwards* (1850; reprint, Oakland, CA: Biobooks, 1956), 102–3.

3. Kahrl, ed., *California Water Atlas,* 1–14.

4. Hogan, ed., *Rivers of the West,* 174–88; J. S. Holliday, *Rush for Riches: Gold Fever and the Making of California* (Berkeley: University of California Press, 1999), 65.

5. The California gold rush was memorialized in hundreds of diaries and memoirs of its participants. It has been examined in many different ways by generations of

historians and, by the time of its sesquicentennial, had been comprehensively considered. See Rohrbough, *Days of Gold*, 1–6, 19. The California Historical Society completed three volumes of a four-part series containing numerous articles on the period that are very important as well. The three volumes are: Ramón Gutiérrez and Richard J. Orsi, eds., *Contested Eden: California before the Gold Rush;* James J. Rawls and Richard J. Orsi, eds., *A Golden State: Mining and Economic Development in Gold Rush California;* and Kevin Starr and Richard J. Orsi, eds., *Rooted in Barbarous Soil: People and Culture in Gold Rush California* (San Francisco: University of California Press and the California Historical Society, 1998, 1998–99, and 2000, respectively).

6. Beesley, "Reconstructing the Landscape," 5–7. Two classic accounts of the discovery and life in the Comstock area of Nevada are Dan De Quille, *A History of the Comstock Silver Lode and Mines; Nevada and the Great Basin; Lake Tahoe and the High Sierras* (1889; reprint, New York: Promontory Press, 1974), and E. Van Vick Tomes, *Rocket of the Comstock: The Life of John W. Mackay* (New York: Ballantine, 1973).

7. Beesley, "Reconstructing the Landscape," 5–6; Ronald H. Limbaugh, "Making Old Tools Work Better: Pragmatic Adaptation and Innovation in Gold-Rush Technology," in *Golden State,* ed. Rawls and Orsi, 27–29.

8. The classic study of the California gold rush is by Rodman Paul, *California Gold: The Beginning of Mining in the Far West* (Lincoln: University of Nebraska Press, 1947).

9. Hinds, *Evolution of the California Landscape,* 10–13; Mount, *California Rivers and Streams,* 190; Matthes, *Incomparable Valley,* ed. Fryxell, 64.

10. Kahrl, ed., *California Water Atlas,* 11.

11. Leiberg, *Forest Conditions in the Northern Sierra Nevada,* 17–18, 52–53, 65–66, 87, 96–97, 109, 119–21, 132–33, 138–39, 145–46.

12. Beesley, "Opening of the Sierra Nevada," 324–32. There is no comprehensive environmental history of the gold rush. This chapter will focus on direct effects of the rush on the Sierran environment through mining, logging, grazing, market hunting, and water development. Other significant effects of transportation, agriculture, and urbanization will not be covered here because of space limitations. Useful works to consult on these topics are Howard, *Sierra Crossing;* E. G. Gudde, *California Gold Camps* (Berkeley: University of California Press, 1975); Ralph Mann, *After the Gold Rush: Society in Grass Valley and Nevada City, California, 1849–1870* (Stanford, CA: Stanford University Press, 1982); Lary Dilsaver, "After the Gold Rush," *Geographical Review* 75, no. 1 (January 1985); Lary Dilsaver, "The Development of Agriculture in a Gold Rush Region," *Association of Pacific Coast Geographers Yearbook* 48 (1986): 67, 73; Duane, "Human Settlement, 1850–2040," 235–44.

13. Paul, *California Gold,* 115–19. See also Randall Rohe, "Mining's Impact on the Land," in *Green versus Gold: Sources in California's Environmental History,* ed. Carolyn Merchant (Washington, DC: Island Press, 1998), 125–35.

14. Paul, *California Gold,* 124–70, 284–333; Lary M. Dilsaver, "From Boom to Bust: Post–Gold Rush Patterns of Adjustment to a California Mining Region, Vol. 1" (Ph.D. diss., Louisiana State University, 1992), 29–106; Mann, *After the Gold Rush,* 2–15; Beesley, "Reconstructing the Landscape," 5–6.

15. E. A. Stevenson to Thomas J. Henley, December 31, 1853, quoted in Heizer, *Destruction of California Indians,* 16.

16. Joseph W. Booth, "Diary, 1852–1853, Northern Mines," Bancroft Library, CF-87, 51–52; William Brewer, *Up and Down California in 1860–1864: The Journal of William H. Brewer,* ed. F. P. Farquhar (Berkeley: University of California Press, 1966), 397, 400–402; S. W. Carnahan, "Three Letters Sent to John Ramage, March 17–September 13, 1849," California Historical Society Library, MS 325; Beesley, "Reconstructing the Landscape," 5–6. An interesting photographic study of the Sierra Nevada by George E. Gruell, *Fire in Sierra Nevada Forests: A Photographic Interpretation of Ecological Change since 1849* (Missoula, MT: Mountain Press, 2001), 11–53, although concerned primarily with the issue of fire and vegetation change in the Sierra Nevada, has a section called "Miner's World" that clearly illustrates the effects of mining and related development in the immediate gold rush years. Rohe, in "Mining's Impact on the Land," 127–29, also comments on revegetation after mining operations.

17. John Wallace, "Letters, 1851–1856," Columbia, July 18, 1853, California Historical Society Library, MS 2242, no pagination.

18. Hank Meals, "Mercury Use and Gold Mining, Yuba River Watershed, 1849–1941," typescript, Tahoe National Forest, 1995, 1–10; Sacramento Regional County Sanitation District, *Sacramento River Mercury Control Planning Project: Final Report* (Sacramento: SRCSD, March 1997), 1–3, 21–21.

19. Delavan, *Notes on California and the Placers,* 99.

20. In the summer of 2000, I had the opportunity to run the river with a group of California state park employees and to see the Horseshoe Bend area first hand. The land in the bend lying east of the tunnel was extensively mined once water was diverted. See "From Rapids to Rituals, River Interpretive Program, August 11–13, 2000," Auburn State Recreation Area, California State Parks: File, Auburn State Recreation Area, Auburn, CA.

21. Adolphus Windeler, *The California Gold Rush Diary of a German Sailor,* ed. with an introduction by W. Turrentine Jackson (Berkeley: Howell-North, 1969), 11–24.

22. Ibid., 11–12.

23. Ibid., 16–24, 114–48.

24. Ibid., 114–48.

25. J. D. Borthwick, *Three Years in California* (1857; reprint, Oakland, CA: Biobooks, 1948), 92–93.

26. Ibid., 151.

27. Mount, *California Rivers and Streams,* 190.

28. Phillip R. May, *Origins of Hydraulic Mining in California* (Oakland, CA: Holmes, 1970), 33–36.

29. Paul, *California Gold,* 149–51.

30. Rohe, "Mining's Impact on the Land," 134–35.

31. Mount, *California Rivers and Streams,* 7–12, 190–91; California Department of Fish and Game, *Report to the Fish and Game Commission: A Status Review of the Spring-Run Chinook Salmon in the Sacramento River Drainage* (Sacramento: Resources

Agency, State of California, June 1998), sec. V, I, 11–16, sec. VI, I, 20; C. F. Wilkinson, *Crossing the Next Meridian: Land, Water, and the Future of the West* (Washington, DC: Island Press, 1992), 190.

32. G. K. Gilbert, *Hydraulic-Mining Debris in the Sierra Nevada* (Washington, DC: Government Printing Office, 1917), 43.

33. Robert L. Kelley, *Gold vs. Grain: The Hydraulic Mining Controversy in California's Central Valley* (Glendale, CA: Arthur H. Clark, 1959), 34–35; Mount, *California River and Streams,* 204; D. J. Larson, "Historical Water-Use Priorities and Public Policies," in *SNEP,* vol. 2, 183. For an overview of the environmental issues involved with hydraulic mining in the Sierra, see David Beesley, "Beyond Gilbert: Environmental History and Hydraulic Mining in the Sierra Nevada," *Mining History Journal* 7 (2000).

34. May, *Origins of Hydraulic Mining in California,* 40–59.

35. Beesley, "Reconstructing the Landscape," 6; Beesley, "Opening of the Sierra Nevada," 326–27; J. J. Hagwood, *The California Debris Commission: A History of the Hydraulic Mining Industry in the Western Sierra Nevada . . .* (Sacramento: U.S. Army Corps of Engineers, 1981), 5–14.

36. For discussion of the San Francisco connections, see Gray Brechin, *Imperial San Francisco: Urban Power and Earthly Ruin* (Berkeley: University of California Press, 1999), 34–36, 48–61.

37. Limbaugh, "Making Old Tools Work Better," 32–36; Hagwood, *California Debris Commission,* 14–19.

38. Kelley, *Gold vs. Grain,* 52–55, 133–34; Brewer, *Up and Down California in 1860–1864,* 455; Marilyn Ziebarth, "California's First Environmental Battle," *California History* 63 (fall 1984): 274–79; Larson, "Historical Water-Use Priorities and Public Policies," 183; Gilbert, *Hydraulic-Mining Debris in the Sierra Nevada,* 38–43.

39. Leiberg, *Forest Conditions in the Northern Sierra Nevada,* 44.

40. Gilbert, *Hydraulic-Mining Debris in the Sierra Nevada,* 46–51; Kahrl, ed., *California Water Atlas,* 16–19.

41. Kelley, *Gold vs. Grain,* 56; Ziebarth, "California's First Environmental Battle," 274–79, Hagwood, *California Debris Commission,* 2–28.

42. Ziebarth, "California's First Environmental Battle," 274–79.

43. Beesley, "Reconstructing the Landscape," 9–11. See also Beesley, "Beyond Gilbert," for an overview of the issue in environmental terms.

44. Raymond F. Dasmann, "Environmental Changes before and after the Gold Rush," in *Golden State,* ed. Rawls and Orsi, 116–18, 120–21.

45. Gilbert, *Hydraulic-Mining Debris in the Sierra Nevada,* 43–46.

46. Ibid., 67–68.

47. Ibid., 31, 67–68.

48. Mount, *California Rivers and Streams,* 208–10, and Rohe, "Mining's Impact on the Land," 127–35.

49. Jennifer A. Curtis, "A Sediment Budget of Hydraulic Gold Mining Sediment, Steephollow Creek Basin, California, 1853–1997" (master's thesis, Humboldt State University, 1999), 71–72.

50. Hagwood, *California Debris Commission,* 65–80.

51. Leiberg, *Forest Conditions in the Northern Sierra Nevada,* 38, 44.

52. Ibid., 55, 65, 98, 121, 131, 140, 147.

53. California State Lands Commission, *California's Rivers: A Public Trust Report* (Sacramento: California State Lands Commission, 1993), 17–20.

54. California Department of Fish and Game, *Report to the Fish and Game Commission: A Status Review of the Spring-Run Chinook Salmon,* sec. V, 1, 11, 15; Wilkinson, *Crossing the Next Meridian,* 190–92; Western Water Policy Review Advisory Commission, *Water in the West: Challenge for the Next Century* (Denver: Western Water Policy Review Advisory Commission, 1998), CD, Sacramento–San Joaquin River Basin Study, 27.

55. Meals, "Mercury Use and Gold Mining," 2–4; Charles N. Alpers and Michael P. Hunerlach, "Mercury Contamination from Historic Gold Mining in California," USGS Fact Sheet FS-061-00, n.d., 6 pages, unpaginated.

56. Meals, "Mercury Use and Gold Mining," 2, 7.

57. Sacramento Regional County Sanitation District, *Sacramento River Mercury Control Planning Project,* 1–2. See also Jason T. May et al., *Mercury Bioaccumulation in Fish in a Region Affected by Historic Gold Mining: The South Yuba River, Deer Creek, and Bear River Watersheds, California, 1999* (Sacramento: USGS, 2000), 1–17.

58. Hagwood, *California Debris Commission,* 14–16; Mount, *California Rivers and Streams,* 228; Kahrl, ed., *California Water Atlas,* 16.

59. Hagwood, *California Debris Commission,* 14–16; Carmel Barry-Meisenbach, *Historic Mining Ditches of the Tahoe National Forest, Report # 28* (Nevada City, CA: Tahoe National Forest, 1989), 12, 15.

60. Even after the legal ending of hydraulic mining, some hydraulic mining continued. In particular, Chinese immigrants, as well as white miners who had small-scale operations, mined illegally. They conducted operations during the winter months when the so-called debris inspectors could not detect mining activity because the river was already muddy. Of course, their effects were very small when compared with the older giant operations that the Sawyer decision closed down. See David Beesley, "More Than People v. Hall: Chinese Immigrants and American Law in a Sierra Nevada County, 1850–1920," *Locus* 3, no. 2 (spring 1991): 135–36.

61. Barry-Meisenbach, *Historic Mining Ditches of the Tahoe National Forest,* 2, 39–40; Larson, "Historical Water-Use Priorities and Public Policies," 168–71.

62. Maureen Jung, "Capitalism Comes to the Diggings," in *Golden State,* ed. Rawls and Orsi, 62–74; Paul, *California Gold,* 130–44; Limbaugh, "Making Old Tools Work Better," 36–47.

63. Limbaugh, "Making Old Tools Work Better," 36–47; Paul, *California Gold,* 139; Duane Smith, "Mother Lode for the West: California Mining Men and Methods," in *Golden State,* ed. Rawls and Orsi, 152–57; Rodman Paul, *The Far West and Great Plains in Transition, 1859–1900* (New York: Harper and Row, 1988), 15, 26–27.

64. Brechin, *Imperial San Francisco,* 38–44.

65. Paul, *Far West and Great Plains in Transition,* 26–27, 37–42; David Beesley,

"The Cornish Pump," *Nevada County Historical Society Bulletin* 33, no. 2 (April 1979): 7–16; Limbaugh, "Making Old Tools Work Better," 43–47; A. C. W. Bethel, "The Golden Skein: California's Gold-Rush Transportation Network," in *Golden State,* ed. Rawls and Orsi, 262–63. A minor Sierran industry that developed in support of the Comstock was commercial ice production. In both natural and constructed lakes and ponds, men were employed on both sides of the northern Sierra summit to cut and process ice that was used to cool miners working deep in the Comstock mines, where temperatures as high as 140 degrees existed. With completion of the Central Pacific, ice was also shipped to urban centers as far away as San Francisco. See Tom Macauley, "Truckee and the Ice Harvest," in *Fire and Ice: A Portrait of Truckee,* ed. Paul A. Lord Jr. (Truckee, CA: Truckee Donner Historical Society, 1981), 33–35, and Joanne Meschery, *Truckee: An Illustrated History of the Town and Its Surroundings* (Truckee, CA: Rocking Stone Press, 1978), 48.

66. David St. Clair, "The Gold Rush and the Beginnings of California Industry," in *Golden State,* ed. Rawls and Orsi, 193–202; Paul, *California Gold,* 50–66, 124–70, 284–333; W. A. Chalifant, *The Story of Inyo,* rev. ed. (Bishop, CA: Pinyon Book Store, 1933), 277–301; Frank S. Wedertz, *Bodie: 1859–1900* (Bishop, CA: Sierra Media, 1969), 1–18; Walton, *Western Times and Water Wars,* 75–84.

67. Paul, *California Gold,* 258–59.

68. Information from Gilbert's study of mining debris cited earlier is included along with other useful information on stream effects in Larson, "Historical Water-Use Priorities and Public Policies," 183.

69. Meals, "Mercury Use and Gold Mining," 1–10.

70. Chris Bowman, "No One Tracked the Cost in Environmental Damage," *Sacramento Bee,* January 18, 1998, sec. 4, 3; Grace Karpa, "Mercury Rises over Logging," *Sacramento Bee,* November 21, 1999, Neighbors sec., 1, 5; Tim Omarzu, "Mercury Study to Be Discussed," *Grass Valley Union,* June 24, 2000, AI, AII; California Biodiversity Council, "Interagency Team Studying Mercury Contamination in California Watersheds," *California Biodiversity News* 7, no. 2 (fall/winter 2000): 9; Sacramento Regional County Sanitation District, *Sacramento River Mercury Control Planning Project,* 1–2.

71. Mount, *California Rivers and Streams,* 198, 210–11; Denny Walsh, "High Court Denies Mokelumne Toxic Review," *Sacramento Bee,* October 5, 1994, sec. B, no page number. The article reported the refusal of the U.S. Supreme Court to reconsider a lower court ruling that had denied an appeal by the Central Valley Regional Water Quality Control Board and the East Bay Municipal Utility District to be released from their responsibilities for cleaning up discharges of sulfuric acid from the historic Penn Mine into the water agencies' system.

72. David Beesley, "Communists and Vigilantes in the Northern Mines," *California History* 64, no. 2 (spring 1985): 142–51.

73. The most complete account of forestry in California is C. Raymond Clar, *California Government and Forestry from Spanish Days until the Creation of the Department of Natural Resources in 1927* (Sacramento: Division of Forestry, Dept. of Natural

Resources, State of California, 1959), 65–160. See also R. W. Ayres, *History of Timber Management in the California National Forests, 1850–1937* (Washington, DC: Forest Service, Department of Agriculture, 1958), 3–11, and E. R. Stanford, "A Short History of California Lumbering" (M.A. thesis, University of California, 1924), 11–87. Contemporary accounts of cutting the sequoia include H. S. Anable,"Journals, 1852–1854," Bancroft Library, CF-137, 111–16, and Aubrey Drury, "The Livermore Family: Pioneers in California," typescript, Bancroft Library, C-D 5096, 37–38.

74. Ayres, *History of Timber Management*, 3; Stanford, "Short History of California Lumbering," 54–60; Beesley, "Reconstructing the Landscape," 6–7; David Beesley, "Whistle Punks and Steam Donkeys: Logging in Nevada County and the Northern Sierra during the Age of Animal and Steam Power," *Nevada County Historical Society Bulletin* 38, no. 4 (October 1984): 27.

75. Stanford, "Short History of California Lumbering," 67; Beesley, "Whistle Punks and Steam Donkeys," 26–27.

76. Drury, "Livermore Family," 34–35; Windeler, *Diary of a German Sailor*, 143; Wallace, "Letters 1851–1856," 6–8; William Higby, "Correspondence," Bancroft Library, C-B 627, Dec. 10, 1854.

77. Beesley, "Whistle Punks and Steam Donkeys," 26–28; Constance Darrow Knowles, "A History of Lumbering in the Truckee Basin from 1856 to 1936," Office Report, WPA Project # 9512373 for Forest Survey Division, California Forest and Range Experiment Station, Forestry Library, University of California, Berkeley, 2–3; Clar, *California Government and Forestry,* 44.

78. John Muir, *John of the Mountains: The Unpublished Journals of John Muir,* ed. Linnie Marsh Wolfe (Madison: University of Wisconsin Press, 1938), 229, 322–23, 429, 430–31. Dilsaver and Tweed, *Challenge of the Big Trees,* 59.

79. Clar, *California Government and Forestry,* 70–71, quotes from the First Biennial Report of the Board of Forestry. See also *First Biennial Report of the California State Board of Forestry for the Years 1886–1887* (Sacramento: State Office, 1887).

80. G. B. Sudworth, "Stanislaus and Lake Tahoe Forest Reserves, California and Adjacent Territory," in *Twenty-First Annual Report of the USGS, Part V, Forest Reserves* (Washington, DC: Government Printing Office, 1900), 512–513, 544, 547, 551, 566; Leiberg, *Forest Conditions in the Northern Sierra Nevada,* 18, 38–40, 48, 52–65, 71–78, 91–92, 114, 142, 151.

81. Clar, *California Government and Forestry,* 71–72; Strong, *Tahoe,* 21–22; Dick Wilson, *Sawdust Trails in the Truckee Basin: A History of Lumbering Operations, 1856–1936* (Nevada City, CA: Nevada County Historical Society, 1992), 57.

82. Drury, "Livermore Family," 30; Windeler, *Diary of a German Sailor,* 129; Beesley, "Whistle Punks and Steam Donkeys," 29–30.

83. *Reno Gazette,* September 14, 1881; Wilson, *Sawdust Trails,* ix, 1–8; Knowles, "Lumbering in the Truckee Basin," 1–30. Dick Wilson, historian of the basin's lumber industry, illustrated the total cut amount graphically: "Enough wood if all of it had been converted to planks and slabs four inches thick, to build a boardwalk thirty feet wide around the earth." See Wilson, *Sawdust Trails,* ix.

84. Knowles, "Lumbering in the Truckee Basin," 1–23. In reconnaissance conducted in many areas of the Tahoe-Truckee drainage, I have encountered numerous examples of abandoned V-flumes and chutes.

85. "Tahoe National Forest Splash Dam Study," typescript, Tahoe National Forest Archives, n.d.; Beesley, "Whistle Punks and Steam Donkeys," 28–29.

86. Donald J. Pisani, "The Polluted Truckee: A Study in Interstate Water Quality, 1870–1934," *Nevada Historical Society Quarterly* 20, no. 3 (fall 1977): 151–56.

87. Sandra Cherub, "Death of Tahoe's Forests Has Roots in Logging 150 Years Ago, Official Says," *Sacramento Bee,* September 22, 1994, section B, no page number.

88. Brechin, *Imperial San Francisco,* 44–49.

89. Beesley, "Opening of the Sierra Nevada," 327–28; Knowles, "Lumbering in the Truckee Basin, 1–23; Wilson, *"Sawdust Trails,* 25–30.

90. Knowles, "Lumbering in the Truckee Basin," 1–30; Wilson, *Sawdust Trails,* 25–30.

91. Beesley, "Reconstructing the Landscape," 7; Leiberg, *Forest Conditions in the Northern Sierra Nevada,* 179.

92. Leiberg, *Forest Conditions in the Northern Sierra Nevada,* 178–79; Strong, *Tahoe,* 30–33; Knowles, "Lumbering in the Truckee Basin," 12–23.

93. Beesley, "Reconstructing the Landscape," 7–8.

94. Charles Nordhoff, *Northern California, Oregon, and the Sandwich Islands* (1874; reprint, Berkeley: Ten Speed Press, 1974), 138.

95. Chas. D. Irons, ed. and comp., *W. F. Edwards' Tourists' Guide and Directory of the Truckee Basin* (Truckee, CA: "Republican" Job Print, 1883), 69–77; Beesley, "Reconstructing the Landscape," 7; Leiberg, *Forest Conditions in the Northern Sierra Nevada,* 44, 69–70, 117, 118, 122, 134, 140, 161, 176, 186; Sudworth, "Stanislaus and Lake Tahoe Forest Reserves," 508, 522, 510–11, 546, 552, 553, 554–56.

96. Clarence King, *Mountaineering in the Kings River Country of Sequoia and the Kings Canyon National Parks, 1864* (Silverthorne, CO: Vista Books, 1996), 18.

97. Leiberg, *Forest Conditions in the Northern Sierra Nevada,* 44–45; Sudworth, "Stanislaus and Lake Tahoe Forest Reserves," 522, 510–11, 554–55; Beesley, "Opening of the Sierra Nevada," 329, 331.

98. Muir, *Mountains of California,* 93; Muir, *My First Summer in the Sierra,* 3–31; Wilkinson, *Crossing the Next Meridian,* 96–97; William Kinney, "Conditions of Rangelands before 1905," in *SNEP,* vol. 2, 31–45.

99. Kinney, "Conditions of Rangelands before 1905," 31–45.

100. Michael Claytor and David Beesley; "Aspen Art and the Sheep Industry of Nevada and Adjoining Counties," *Nevada County Historical Society Bulletin* 33, no. 4 (October 1979): 25–27; Paul F. Starrs, "The Public As Agents of Policy," in *SNEP,* vol. 2, 129–31.

101. Muir, *Mountains of California,* 93; Muir, *John of the Mountains,* 173–74, 351; William A. Douglass and Jon Bilbao, *Amerikanuak: Basques in the New World* (Reno: University of Nevada Press, 1975), 233–46; William D. Rowley, *U.S. Forest Service Grazing and Rangelands: A History* (College Station: Texas A&M Press, 1985), 55–96;

David Beesley, "Changing Land Use Patterns and Sheep Transhumance in the North-eastern Sierra Nevada, 1870–1980," in *Forum for the Association of Arid Lands Studies,* ed. O. Templar (Lubbock: Texas Tech University, International Center for Arid and Semi-Arid Land Use Study, 1985), 3–5; Dilsaver and Tweed, *Challenge of the Big Trees,* 59–60.

102. Muir, *John of the Mountains,* 173–74, 351.

103. Leiberg, *Forest Conditions in the Northern Sierra Nevada,* 44–45; Sudworth, "Stanislaus and Lake Tahoe Forest Reserves," 522, 510–11, 554–55; Luther Wagoner, "Report on the Forests of the Counties of Amador, Calaveras, Tuolumne, and Mariposa," in *First Biennial Report of the California State Board of Forestry for the Years 1885–1886* (Sacramento: State Office, 1886), 43.

104. Jeronima Echeverria, "Basque 'Tramp Herders' on Forbidden Ground: Early Grazing Controversies in California's National Reserves," *Locus* 4, no. 1 (fall 1991): 52–53. See also Mary Austin's classic work on sheepherding in California, *The Flock* (1906; reprint, Reno: University of Nevada Press, 2001), 191–212, especially her account of gypsy herders in the Sierra and her estimates of damage caused by them.

105. Beesley, "Reconstructing the Landscape," 8. Henry T. Lewis, in his "Patterns of Indian Burning in California," 111, noted that although both Indians and whites burned in the Sierra, often at the same season, the reasons for sheepmen's and cattlemen's burning, and the areas they burned, were often different from those of the natives.

106. SNEP Science Team, *Summary of the Sierra Nevada Ecosystem Project* (Davis: University of California, Centers for Water and Wildland Resources, 1996), 5.

107. Ibid., 5–6.

108. Kinney, "Condition of Rangelands before 1905," 40–41.

109. Tracy I. Storer and Robert L. Usinger, *Sierra Nevada Natural History: An Illustrated Handbook* (Berkeley: University of California Press, 1963), 35–39; Raymond F. Dasmann, *California's Changing Environment* (Reno: Materials for Today's Learning, 1988), 9–14; Dasmann, "Environmental Changes before and after the Gold Rush," 107–13; Beesley, "Opening of the Sierra Nevada," 329–31.

110. Storer and Usinger, *Sierra Nevada Natural History,* 38–39; Schoenherr, *Natural History of California,* 381–84; Windeler, *Diary of a German Sailor,* 133.

111. Storer and Usinger, *Sierra Nevada Natural History,* 353–55.

112. Perlot, *Gold Seeker.*

113. Ibid., 266–67.

114. Ibid., 268.

115. Ibid., 287.

116. Ibid., 288–89.

117. Beesley, "Reconstructing the Landscape," 8–9.

118. King, *Mountaineering in the Kings River Country,* 18.

119. Borthwick, *Three Years in California,* 149, 234–35; William H. Brewer, *Such a Landscape: A Narrative of the 1864 California Geological Survey of the Sequoia and*

Kings Canyon from the Field Notes, Letters, and Reports of William Brewer (Yosemite National Park: Yosemite Association, 1989), 28–36.

120. Johnston, *Sierra Nevada,* 57–58; Schoenherr, *Natural History of California,* 134–35; Beesley, "Reconstructing the Landscape," 8–9.

121. Storer and Usinger, *Sierra Nevada Natural History,* 38–39.

122. D. Elliott-Fisk et al., "Lake Tahoe Case Study," in *Sierra Nevada Ecosystem Project, Final Report to Congress, Addendum* (Davis: University of California, Centers for Water and Wildlands Resources, 1997), 234–35; Pisani, "Polluted Truckee," 153, 165; Meschery, *Truckee,* 48; Don Thompson, "Halt to Fish Stocking Has Anglers Angry," *San Francisco Chronicle,* January 21, 2001, A20; Beesley, "Reconstructing the Landscape," 8–9.

123. Dasmann, "Environmental Changes before and after the Gold Rush," 108–18.

124. Ibid.; Tracy I. Storer and Lloyd P. Tevis Jr., *California Grizzly* (1955; reprint, Lincoln: University of Nebraska Press, 1978), 170–218; Borthwick, *Three Years in California,* 235–43.

125. Borthwick, *Three Years in California,* 130–31, 247.

126. Dasmann can be said to have begun serious historical study of the California environment with his *Destruction of California* (New York: Collier, 1966) and *California's Changing Environment* (Sacramento: Boyd and Fraser, 1981). Dasmann's article in the California Historical Society's first volume on the gold rush acknowledges significant effects on wildlife, grassland, forests, and gives special attention to hydraulic mining in California. See Dasmann, "Environmental Changes before and after the Gold Rush," 107–21. It is not my intent to set up a straw man for the sake of an argument, but to acknowledge that in terms of environmental impact, the gold rush in California may have no equal for the reasons noted in this chapter.

127. Dasmann, "Environmental Changes before and after the Gold Rush," 105–6.

128. J. S. Holliday, *The World Rushed In: The California Gold Rush Experience* (New York: Simon and Schuster, 1981).

129. An excellent discussion of the development of American resource law is that of Donald J. Pisani, "'I am resolved not to interfere, but to permit all to work freely': The Gold Rush and American Resource Law," in *Golden State,* ed. Rawls and Orsi, 123–45.

130. David Beesley, "Opening of the Sierra Nevada," 322–37.

3: CONSERVATION SHAPES THE SIERRA NEVADA, 1864–1900

1. See Bates and Lee, *Tradition and Innovation,* 15, and Delavan, *Notes on California and the Placers,* 103.

2. James M. Hutchings, *In the Heart of the Sierras: The Yo Semite Valley . . .* (Oakland: Pacific Press, 1886), 79–80.

3. Shirley Sargent, *Yosemite and Its Innkeepers: The Story of a Great Park and Its Chief Concessionaires,* foreword by Horace M. Albright (Yosemite, CA: Flying Spur Press, 1975), 1–3. Sargent's account of the various concessionaires covers the time to

the 1960s and is a valuable source for considering the roles both of the private promoters of the Valley and of the National Park Service. See also Stanford E. Demars, *The Tourist in Yosemite, 1855–1985* (Salt Lake City: University of Utah Press, 1991), 10, 24–26.

4. Smith, *Southwest Expedition of Jedediah S. Smith,* 169–70.

5. Ibid., 149–70; Leonard, *Adventures of a Mountain Man,* 120–39; Ferol Egan, *Frémont: Explorer for a Restless Nation* (Reno: University of Nevada Press, 1984), 197–222; William H. Goetzmann, *Army Exploration in the American West, 1803–1863* (Lincoln: University of Nebraska Press, 1979), 97–104; John Charles Frémont, *Report of the Exploring Expedition to the Rocky Mountains in the Year 1842, and to Oregon and North California in the Years 1843–44* (Ann Arbor: University Microfilms, 1966), 220–55.

6. Franklin Langworthy, *Scenery of the Plains, Mountains, and Mines,* ed. Paul C. Phelps from the 1855 edition (Princeton, NJ: Princeton University Press, 1932), 139; Vincent Geiger and Wakeman Bryarly, *Trail to California: The Overland Journal of Vincent Geiger and Wakeman Bryarly,* ed. David Potter (New Haven: Yale University Press, 1945), 200–4.

7. Charles Graydon, *Trail of the First Wagons over the Sierra Nevada* (St. Louis: Patrice Press, 1986), 19–78; David R. Lewis, "Argonauts on the Oregon Trail," in *New Directions in California History,* ed. James Rawls (New York: McGraw-Hill, 1988), 101–15; Nicholas Carriger, "Journal of an Orrigon Trip and Overland Journey to California, 1846," September 9–26, 1846, Bancroft Library, CF-III. Wayman is quoted in Herbert Eaton, *The Overland Trail to California in 1852* (New York: G. P. Putnam's Sons, 1974), 297.

8. Margaret A. Thompson, "Overland Travel and the Central Sierra Nevada, 1827–1849" (M.A. thesis, University of California, Berkeley, 1932), 1–140; Lewis, "Argonauts on the Overland Trail," 101–15; Olive Newell, *Tail of the Elephant: The Emigrant Experience on the Truckee Route of the California Trail, 1844–1852* (Nevada City, CA: Nevada County Historical Society, 1997), 172–243.

9. Geiger and Bryarly, *Trail to California,* 197–202; Eaton, *Overland Trail to California,* 276–77, 279, 305–6.

10. Frémont, *Report of the Exploring Expedition,* 233; Eaton, *Overland Trail to California,* 272, 275, 295; David Cosad, "Diary," California Historical Society Library, MS 453, July 16–23, 1849. Leonard, *Adventures of a Mountain Man,* 132.

11. Beesley, "Opening of the Sierra Nevada," 332–36. In this chapter the terms *conservation* or *conservationist* will generally be used to describe both the activities of conservation of resources, such as forests for practical uses, and the protection of beautiful landscape features from private economic development. Sometimes the term *preservationist* will be used in a general context as well, but such use is not intended to suggest distinct differences between viewpoints of the early conservation advocates. Many readers are probably familiar with the division that arose between conservationists such as Gifford Pinchot, first head of the U.S. Forest Service, and John Muir and other conservationists of his type. This latter group have been dubbed "preservationists," although in the early years of the movement both factions often worked

with each other and shared common goals. The major split that developed between the two has clouded the common sense of unity that bound the various types of conservationists in the early years before 1905. See Douglas H. Strong, *Dreamers and Defenders: American Conservationists* (Lincoln: University of Nebraska Press), 61–84, 85–110.

12. For a discussion of the meaning of preservation and conservation, see Char Miller, *Gifford Pinchot and the Making of Modern Environmentalism* (Washington, DC: Island Press, 2001), 1–12. See also Michael P. Cohen, *The Pathless Way: John Muir and American Wilderness* (Madison: University of Wisconsin Press, 1984), 294–97. For other examples of the rise of conservation and preservation in American thought and politics at the end of the nineteenth and beginning of the twentieth century, see Peter J. Schmidt, *Back to Nature: The Arcadian Myth in Urban America* (Baltimore: Johns Hopkins University Press, 1969), xii–xvi, 1–5; Thomas R. Dunlap, *Saving America's Wildlife: Ecology and the American Mind, 1850–1890* (Princeton, NJ: Princeton University Press, 1988), 3–6; Stephen Fox, *John Muir and His Legacy: The American Conservation Movement* (Boston: Little, Brown, 1981), 104–10; Samuel P. Hayes, *Conservation and the Gospel of Efficiency: The Progressive Conservation Movement, 1890–1920* (New York: Athenaeum, 1969), 1–17; Hans Huth, *Nature and the American: Three Centuries of Changing Attitudes* (Berkeley: University of California Press, 1957); Harold K. Steen, *The U.S. Forest Service: A History* (Seattle: University of Washington Press, 1976), 3–102; Alfred Runte, *National Parks: The American Experience,* 2d ed. (Lincoln: University of Nebraska Press, 1987), 1–81; Michael Williams, *Americans and Their Forests* (Cambridge, U.K.: Cambridge University Press, 1989), 395–424; Strong, *Dreamers and Defenders,* 1–7. A new perspective on the beginnings of conservation and preservation thought which brings the tools of deconstruction to the issue of wilderness and some of its early proponents is that of Kevin DeLuca and Anne Demo, "Imagining Nature and Erasing Class and Race: Carleton Watkins, John Muir, and the Construction of Wilderness," *Environmental History* 6, no. 4 (October 2001): 541–60.

13. In their interesting article "Imagining Nature and Erasing Class and Race," 541–56, DeLuca and Demo attempt the "deconstruction of wilderness" as a "social construction" represented by two of the many important contributors to the complex social and political movement of the late nineteenth century that is referred to as conservation and preservation by most historians. DeLuca and Demo's article is certainly useful in its examination of some of the cultural origins of Watkins's and Muir's thought, although their view is not particularly new. The idea about the limited social and cultural outlooks of early conservationists and preservationists has been clearly stated already by Stephen Fox, *John Muir and His Legacy,* and Michael P. Cohen, *The History of the Sierra Club, 1892–1970* (San Francisco: Sierra Club Books, 1988).

14. A full citation of these works is useful here: Alfred Runte, *Yosemite: The Embattled Wilderness* (Lincoln: University of Nebraska Press, 1990); Douglas H. Strong, *Tahoe: An Environmental History* (Lincoln: University of Nebraska Press, 1984); Lary M. Dilsaver and William C. Tweed, *Challenge of the Big Trees: A Resource History of Sequoia and Kings Canyon National Parks* (Three Rivers, CA: Sequoia Natural History Association, 1990); C. Raymond Clar, *California Government and Forestry from Span-*

ish Days until the Creation of the Department of Natural Resources in 1927 (Sacramento: Division of Forestry, Department of Natural Resources, State of California, 1959).

15. Clar, *California Government and Forestry,* 44, 60.

16. Hagwood, *California Debris Commission,* 19; Beesley, "Opening of the Sierra Nevada," 332–33.

17. Clar, *California Government and Forestry,* 56–70; Beesley, "Opening of the Sierra Nevada," 333–34; Farquhar, *History of the Sierra Nevada,* 129.

18. Assemblyman Crabb's initiative is quoted in Clar, *California Government and Forestry,* 68.

19. Ayres, *History of Timber Management,* 9–12.

20. Clar, *California Government and Forestry,* 59–60. Harold K. Steen in his valuable *U.S. Forest Service: A History,* 8–9, credits California for leading the nation's states in trying early to deal with the numerous problems of the federal forest lands.

21. "An Act Authorizing a Grant to the State of California of the 'Yo-Semite Valley,' and the Land Embracing the 'Mariposa Big Tree Grove,'" June 30, 1864 (13 Stat. 325), in *America's National Park System: The Critical Documents,* ed. Lary Dilsaver (Lanham, MD: Rowman and Littlefield, 1997), 11.

22. Samuel Bowles, *Across the Continent: A Summer's Journey to the Rocky Mountains, the Mormons, and the Pacific States with Speaker Colfax* (Springfield, MA: Bowles, 1866), 223.

23. Runte, *National Park,* 1–13; Beesley, "Opening of the Sierra Nevada," 332.

24. Lary Dilsaver, "The Early Years, 1864–1918," in *America's National Park System,* ed. Dilsaver, 7–9.

25. Bunnell, *Discovery of the Yosemite,* 56.

26. Runte, *National Parks,* 19–21; Carl Russell, *One Hundred Years in Yosemite: The Story of a Great Park and Its Friends* (Berkeley: University of California Press, 1947). Russell, as chief naturalist for the U.S. Park Service, provides a very useful chronology of the Valley, 179–93.

27. A good summary of early contact with the Valley is presented by Howard R. Lamar as editor of Jean-Nicolas Perlot, *Gold Seeker,* 239–42.

28. Runte, *Yosemite,* 13–16; Russell, *One Hundred Years in Yosemite,* 180–81; James M. Hutchings, *Scenes of Wonder and Curiosity, from Hutchings' California Magazine, 1856–1861,* ed. R. R. Olmstead (Berkeley: Howell-North, 1962), 272–286.

29. Demars, *Tourist in Yosemite,* 9–17, 20–23; Kevin Starr, *Americans and the California Dream: 1850–1915* (New York: Oxford University Press, 1973), 174–75, 181–83.

30. Horace Greeley, *An Overland Journey from New York to San Francisco in the Summer of 1859* (New York: H. H. Bancroft, 1860), 308; Thomas Starr King, *A Vacation among the Sierras: Yosemite in 1860* (San Francisco: Book Club of California, 1962), 43. See also the account of Samuel Bowles, *Across the Continent,* 223–37.

31. James M. Hutchings, *Scenes of Wonder and Curiosity in California* (San Francisco: Hutchings and Rosenfield, 1861), 61–131; Charles L. Brace, *The New West; or, California in 1876–78* (New York: G. P. Putnam and Son, 1869), 84–120; J. H. Beadle, *The Undeveloped West* (Philadelphia: National, 1873), 264–89; James B. Thayer, *A*

Western Journey with Mr. Emerson, ed. Shirley Sargent (Van Nuys, CA: Book Club of California, 1884, 1980), 67–86. See also Runte, *Yosemite,* 13–27.

32. Russell, *One Hundred Years in Yosemite,* 180–81; Bunnell, *Discovery of the Yosemite,* 280–85; Perlot, *Gold Seeker,* 292–300.

33. Demars, *Tourist in Yosemite,* 22–23, Starr, *Americans and the California Dream,* 182–83; R. F. Putnam, "Diary, April 18, 1862–June 18, 1876," reference to Hutchings, July 8, 1862, MS 1734, California Historical Society Library; Hutchings, *Scenes of Wonder and Curiosity in California,* 61–136; Schmidt, *Back to Nature,* xi–xvi, 3–5.

34. Runte, *Yosemite,* 16–18.

35. Frederick Law Olmsted to Virgil Williams, Thomas Hill, and Carleton Watkins, Yo Semite, August 9, 1865, in *The Papers of Frederick Law Olmsted,* ed. V. P. Ranney, vol. 5, *The California Frontier, 1863–1865* (Baltimore: Johns Hopkins University Press, 1990), 433.

36. Russell, *One Hundred Years in Yosemite,* 182–83; Runte, *Yosemite,* 32–35, 40, 47; Demars, *Tourist in Yosemite,* 26–29.

37. Earl Pomeroy, *In Search of the Golden West: The Tourist in Western America* (New York: Alfred Knopf, 1957), 46, 52, 59; Demars, *Tourist in Yosemite,* 15–22, 40–49; Peter J. Blodgett, "Visiting 'The Realm of Wonder': Yosemite and the Business of Tourism, 1855–1916," in *Yosemite and Sequoia: A Century of California National Parks,* ed. Richard J. Orsi, Alfred Runte, and Marlene Smith-Baranzini (Berkeley: University of California Press and the California Historical Society, 1990), 33–47; Starr, *Americans and the California Dream,* 174–75, 181–83.

38. Brace, *New West,* 85–120; Beadle, *Undeveloped West,* 264–89; Thayer, *Western Journey with Mr. Emerson,* 67–86; Grace Greenwood [Sara Jane Lippincott], *New Life in New Lands: Notes of Travel* (New York: J. B. Ford, 1873), 303–69. See also Runte, *Yosemite,* 13–27, 28–56.

39. Demars, *Tourist in Yosemite,* 40–49; Russell, *One Hundred Years in Yosemite,* 182–86; Runte, *Yosemite,* 38–41.

40. Russell, *One Hundred Years in Yosemite,* 184–86; Demars, *Tourist in Yosemite,* 62, 64–65; Blodgett, "Visiting 'The Realm of Wonder,'" 46.

41. Sargent, *Yosemite and Its Innkeepers,* 12.

42. Greenwood [Lippincott], *New Life in New Lands,* 327, 358–59.

43. Robert P. Gibbens and Harold F. Heady, *The Influence of Modern Man on the Vegetation of Yosemite Valley* (Berkeley: U.C. Division of Agricultural Sciences, 1964), 1–2; Runte, *Yosemite,* 9.

44. Both accounts are based on recollections written or given to others some thirty years after their first visits and therefore must be considered with caution. Bunnell, *Discovery of the Yosemite,* 75–81, 218, 218–20; Gustavus Pierson, "Recollection: Trip to Yosemite in 1855, Given to Bancroft Library in 1880," Bancroft Library C-D-136, 3–5; Gibbens and Heady, *Influence of Modern Man on Vegetation of Yosemite,* 2–5. Jean-Nicolas Perlot, in his account of the attempt to build a road to Yosemite Valley from Coulterville, gives some information on the roadbuilding but none on the vegetation of the Valley: Perlot, *Gold Seeker,* 292–300.

45. Benjamin Taylor, *Beyond the Gates* (Chicago: S. C. Griggs, n.d. [Taylor's account of his visit to Yosemite was published during the 1870s while the park was in state control]), 192–239; Russell, *One Hundred Years in Yosemite*, 131–34; Theodore A. Gobbert, "The Yosemite Valley Commission: The Development of Park Management Policies, 1864–1905" (M.A. thesis, California State College, Hayward, 1972), 1–23; Runte, *Yosemite*, 28–44.

46. Greenwood [Lippincott], *New Life in New Lands*, 327, 358–59; Russell, *One Hundred Years in Yosemite*, 181–84; Runte, *Yosemite*, 28–44, 37–38; Demars, *Tourist in Yosemite*, 36, 52; Gobbert, "Yosemite Valley Commission," 33–37.

47. Frederick Law Olmsted, "Preliminary Report upon the Yosemite and Big Tree Grove, August 1865," in *Papers of Frederick Law Olmsted*, ed. Ranney, vol. 5, *California Frontier*, 507–8.

48. John Todd, *Sunset Land* (Boston: Lee and Shepard, 1870), 76–120; Runte, *Yosemite*, 36–37.

49. Olmsted, "Preliminary Report upon the Yosemite and Big Tree Grove," 507. Olmsted's concern over Indian burning effects is interesting. Possibly he shared the views of many at the time that fire was an enemy to be excluded from the Valley. It might also be that in the ten or so years since Indian burning had been halted, brush and small trees had been growing and therefore fire did present a danger to the trees Olmsted mentioned. It should be remembered that Indian burning in the past was generally on a one-, two-, or three-year cycle and thus Indian burning in 1864 might cause more damage to trees after the park began to function.

50. "Yosemite Park," *Overland Monthly* 12, no. 1 (January 1874): 90.

51. Anne F. Hyde, "From Stage Coach to Packard Twin Six: Yosemite and the Changing Face of Tourism, 1880–1930," in *Yosemite and Sequoia*, ed. Orsi, Runte, and Smith-Baranzini, 69–70; Runte, *Yosemite*, 46–50; Russell, *One Hundred Years in Yosemite*, 184–85; Gobbert, "Yosemite Valley Commission," 33–38.

52. Gobbert, "Yosemite Valley Commission," 39–51; Runte, *Yosemite*, 46–53.

53. Runte, *Yosemite*, 45–56.

54. The following analysis is influenced by the numerous travelers' accounts of the Valley previously cited, and also by the comments of Runte, Gobbert, Hyde, Demars, Russell, Starr, and Blodgett.

55. John Muir, "By-ways of Yosemite Travel," *Overland* 13 (September 1874): 267.

56. Beesley, "Opening of the Sierra Nevada," 329; James W. Hulse, "The California-Nevada Boundary: History of a Conflict," pt. 1, *Nevada Historical Society* 23, no. 2 (summer 1980): 87–109; Michael Smith, *Pacific Visions: California Scientists and the Environment, 1850–1915* (New Haven: Yale University Press, 1987), 4–8, 29–30.

57. Smith, *Pacific Visions*, 28–30.

58. Farquhar, *History of the Sierra Nevada*, 129.

59. J. D. Whitney, *Geological Survey of California, Geology,* vol. 1, *Report of Progress and Synopsis of the Field Work from 1860 to 1864* (Philadelphia: Caxton Press of Sherman and Co., Published by the Authority of the Legislature of California, 1865), 212–363; Farquhar, *History of the Sierra Nevada*, 129–32.

60. Brewer, *Such a Landscape,* 46.

61. Whitney, *Geological Survey of California,* 364–93. One of the most accessible accounts of the expedition is that of Francis Farquhar's edition of William Brewer's journal, *Up and Down California in 1860–1864.* See also Farquhar, *History of the Sierra Nevada,* 134–41, and Moore, *Exploring the Highest Sierra,* 365, 370.

62. Runte, *Yosemite,* 29, 32; Farquhar, *History of the Sierra Nevada,* 138.

63. Olmsted, "Preliminary Report upon the Yosemite and Big Tree Grove," 202, 510; Runte, *Yosemite,* 29; Farquhar, *History of the Sierra Nevada,* 138.

64. Whitney, *Geological Survey of California,* 212–363; Moore, *Exploring the Highest Sierra,* 66.

65. Moore, *Exploring the Highest Sierra,* 65–67. Other useful estimates of the significance of the Whitney Survey are in Smith, *Pacific Visions,* 65–70, and Dilsaver and Tweed, *Challenge of the Big Trees,* 42–43.

66. Farquhar, *History of the Sierra Nevada,* 141–42; Moore, *Exploring the Highest Sierra,* 68.

67. Runte, *Yosemite,* 31–33, Smith, *Pacific Visions,* 65–70.

68. See Joseph Le Conte, *A Journal of Rambling through the High Sierra of California by the University Excursion Company* (1875; reprint, San Francisco: Sierra Club, 1930), and Smith, *Pacific Visions,* 42.

69. Hinkle and Hinkle, *Sierra Nevada Lakes,* 327.

70. Joseph Le Conte's article is excerpted in George W. James, *The Lake of the Sky: Lake Tahoe, in the High Sierras of California and Nevada . . .* (New York: J. F. Tapley, 1915), 86–101.

71. John Le Conte's articles are excerpted in James, *Lake of the Sky,* 63–77.

72. Donald Jackson and Mary Lee Spence, eds., *The Expeditions of John Charles Frémont,* vol. 1, *Travels from 1838 to 1844* (Urbana: University of Illinois Press, 1970), 635.

73. Twain, *Roughing It,* 163.

74. Strong, *Tahoe,* 13–15; Howard, *Sierra Crossing,* 97–98, 139–59.

75. David Beesley, "Independence Lake: A Brief Investigation of Its Uses over the Years," *Nevada County Historical Society Bulletin* 22, no. 2 (April 1978): 7–8; Hinkle and Hinkle, *Sierra Nevada Lakes,* 213–32.

76. Elliot-Fisk et al., "Lake Tahoe Case Study," 219–25.

77. Irons, ed. and comp., *Edwards' Tourists' Guide,* 21–29, 80–99; Strong, *Tahoe,* 15–19.

78. James, *Lake of the Sky,* vi–xii, 200–4, 381–85. An excellent account that provides information on the various communities that developed around the Lake Tahoe area is Barbara Lekisch, *Tahoe Place Names: The Origin and History of Names in the Lake Tahoe Basin* (Lafayette, CA: Great West, 1988).

79. W. B. Lardner and M. J. Brock, *History of Placer and Nevada Counties, California* (Los Angeles: Historic Record Co., 1924), 221–23.

80. Ibid., 221.

81. D. W. Cole, U.S. Reclamation Service, is quoted in James, *Lake of the Sky,* 353–54. James also notes the Floriston operation, ibid., 344.

82. James, *Lake of the Sky,* 114–15. See also Strong, *Tahoe,* 95–98.

83. Strong, *Tahoe,* 26; D. W. Cole quoted in James, *Lake of the Sky,* 353.

84. Lardner and Brock, *History of Placer and Nevada Counties,* 223; James, *Lake of the Sky,* 357–58; James W. Hulse, *The Silver State,* 2d ed. (Reno: University of Nevada Press, 1998), 230–31, 316–17.

85. Lardner and Brock, *History of Placer and Nevada Counties,* 223; James, *Lake of the Sky,* 353–58.

86. *Truckee Tribune* of Sept. 7, 1878, quoted by Strong, *Tahoe,* 57 (see also 56–57); Beesley, "Opening of the Sierra Nevada," 333; Donald J. Pisani, *Water, Land, and Law in the West: The Limits of Public Policy, 1850–1920* (Lawrence: University Press of Kansas, 1996), 136–42.

87. John Ise, *United States Forest Policy* (New Haven: Yale University Press, 1920), 62–109; Clar, *California Government and Forestry,* 85–87.

88. Strong, *Tahoe,* 57–59; Donald Pisani, "Lost Parkland: Lumbering and Park Proposals in the Tahoe-Truckee Basin," *Journal of Forest History* 21 (January 1977): 10–11.

89. Lake Bigler Forestry Commission Report quoted in Clar, *California Government and Forestry,* 88.

90. Clar, *California Government and Forestry,* 88–91; Pisani, "Lost Parkland," 11–12.

91. James, *Lake of the Sky,* 354.

92. Strong, *Tahoe,* 59; Beesley, "Opening of the Sierra Nevada," 333–34.

93. Strong, *Tahoe,* 59; Clar, *California Government and Forestry,* 88–90; Pisani, "Lost Parkland," 12–13.

94. Pisani, "Polluted Truckee," 151–54; James, *Lake of the Sky,* 113.

95. Pisani, "Polluted Truckee," 153–56.

96. Ibid., 155–56.

97. Clar, *California Government and Forestry,* 61–75, 88–91, 96–97.

98. Quoted in Clar, *California Government and Forestry,* 119–20.

99. Beesley, "Reconstructing the Landscape," 10; Clar, *California Government and Forestry,* 61–75, 88–91, 96–97.

100. Abbott Kinney, "Our Forests," *Overland Monthly* 7 (2d ser.), no. 48 (December 1886): 615–21.

101. Wagoner, "Report on the Forests," 39–44; Clar, *California Government and Forestry,* 144–48.

102. J. G. Lemmon, "Report of the State Botanist," and H. S. Davidson, "Report of the State Engineer," both in *Second Biennial Report of the California State Board of Forestry for the Years 1887–1888* (Sacramento: State Office, 1888), 53–41, 153–56.

103. California State Board of Forestry, *Third Biennial Report of the California State Board of Forestry for the Years 1889–1890* (Sacramento: State Office, 1890), 3–6. The fourth report is generally considered meaningless because the federal government had taken action to create forest reserves, achieving—or so it was hoped—effective control of most forest land in the state of California.

104. The most complete study of the politics of the controversy is that of Kelley, *Gold vs. Grain*. See also Ziebarth, "California's First Environmental Battle," 274–79, and Hagwood, *California Debris Commission*, 2–81. As part of a larger struggle to deal with reclamation issues in the Central Valley, see Robert Kelley, *Battling the Inland Sea: Floods, Public Policy, and the Sacramento Valley* (Berkeley: University of California Press, 1989), 199–219. See also Brechin, *Imperial San Francisco*, 13–70. An account of the environmental effects of hydraulic mining on the Sierra Nevada itself is in Beesley, "Beyond Gilbert.."

105. Gilbert, *Hydraulic-Mining Debris in the Sierra Nevada*, 43; Larson, "Historical Water-Use Priorities and Public Policies," 183.

106. Kelley, *Gold vs. Grain*, 34–42; Larson, "Historical Water-Use Priorities and Public Policies," 164–66; Hagwood, *California Debris Commission*, 6–8.

107. H. H. Bancroft, *The History of California*, vol. 7, *1860–1890* (San Francisco: The History Co. 1890), 646–48 n.

108. Leiberg, *Forest Conditions in the Northern Sierra Nevada*, 55, 98, 121, 161.

109. William H. Hall, "Nine Letters to Governor Pardee on the Drainage and Debris Work of 1878–1881," MS-913-10, California Historical Society Library; Kelley, *Gold vs. Grain*, 14–15; Larson, "Historical Water-Use Priorities and Public Policies," 164–65.

110. Hagwood, *California Debris Commission*, 26–31.

111. Ibid., 32–33; Beesley, "More Than *People v. Hall*," 136.

112. See Alpers and Hunerlach, "Mercury Contamination from Historic Gold Mining in California." Besides mercury contamination, this pamphlet also lists other hazards, including acidic water in hydraulic mine pits and physical hazards such as high walls and unstable slopes and mineshafts associated with the historic mining sites. See also May et al., *Mercury Bioaccumulation in Fish in a Region Affected by Historic Gold Mining*, 1–4, 917. See Mount, *California Rivers and Streams*, 207–10.

113. Mentioned earlier in the context of forest changes caused during the gold rush years, George Gruell's *Fire in Sierra Nevada Forests: A Photographic Interpretation of Ecological Change since 1849* provides useful visual images of forest composition change in many areas of the Sierra: lower-elevation oak woodlands and pine forests, mixed-conifer forests of the mid-elevation level, and the red fir–lodgepole forests of the higher-elevation west slopes, as well as the drier forests of the eastern Sierra from Mammoth to Tahoe. Gruell's emphasis is on fire issues, but he does include brief analysis of other change-causing agents.

114. Alfred Runte, "Introduction: The California National Parks Centennial," in *Yosemite and Sequoia*, ed. Orsi, Runte, and Smith-Baranzini, 1–5. For an effective introduction to the origins of the "National Forest Idea," see Alfred Runte, *Public Lands, Public Heritage: The National Forest Idea* (Niwot, CO: Roberts Rinehart, 1991), 1–58. The map on page 56 shows the location of the forest reserves created by actions of Presidents Harrison and Cleveland by 1898.

115. Dilsaver and Tweed, *Challenge of the Big Trees*, 59–62; Runte, *Yosemite*, 45–47; Douglas H. Strong, "A History of Sequoia National Park," (Ph.D. diss., Syracuse University, 1964), 57–92; Richard J. Orsi, "'Wilderness Saint' and 'Robber Baron':

The Anomalous Partnership of John Muir and the Southern Pacific Co. for the Protection of Yosemite National Park," *Pacific Historian* 29, nos. 2 & 3 (summer/fall 1985): 136–37.

116. Dilsaver and Tweed, *Challenge of the Big Trees,* 62–68; Runte, *Yosemite,* 47–55.

117. Williams, *Americans and Their Forests,* 393–99.

118. Moore, *Exploring the Highest Sierra,* 6, 142–45; Farquhar, *History of the Sierra Nevada,* 195–96.

119. Farquhar, *History of the Sierra Nevada,* 190–92.

120. Ibid., 189–90.

121. Macomb is quoted ibid., 191.

122. Steen, *U.S. Forest Service,* 17, 26–36.

123. Williams, *Americans and Their Forests,* 409–11.

124. Harold K. Steen, "The Origins and Purposes of the National Forests," in Runte, *Public Lands, Public Heritage,* 69–77.

125. Steen, *U.S. Forest Service,* 34–37, 53: Strong, *Dreamers and Defenders,* 66–67. Bernhard Fernow's famous report on forest conditions in the United States, published as he left as head of the Division of Forestry, is in B. E. Fernow, *Report upon the Forestry Investigations of the U.S. Department of Agriculture, 1877–1898,* House of Representatives, 55th Cong., 3d sess., Doc. 181 (Washington, DC: Government Printing Office, 1899).

126. The date for the creation of the Sierra Forest Reserve of 6,400 square miles was February 14, 1893; the Stanislaus Forest Reserve of 1,080 square miles was February 22, 1897; and the Lake Tahoe Forest Reserve of 213 square miles was April 13, 1899. See Henry Gannett, "Summary of Forest Work in 1899–1900," in *Twenty-First Annual Report of the United States Geological Survey to the Secretary of the Interior, 1899–1900, Part V—Forest Reserves* (Washington, DC: Government Printing Office, 1900), 13–14; Beesley, "Reconstructing the Landscape," 11.

127. Sudworth, "Stanislaus and Lake Tahoe Forest Reserves"; Leiberg, *Forest Conditions in the Northern Sierra Nevada.* See also Steen, *U.S. Forest Service,* 26.

128. Gannett, "Summary of Forest Work in 1899–1900," 15, 19.

129. Ibid., 20–21.

130. Leiberg, *Forest Conditions in the Northern Sierra Nevada,* 29, 52–159.

131. Ibid., 29.

132. Ibid., 32.

133. Sudworth, "Stanislaus and Lake Tahoe Forest Reserves," 508–14, 551–60; Leiberg, *Forest Conditions in the Northern Sierra Nevada,* 38–44; Steen, *U.S. Forest Service,* 26–46.

134. Steen, *U.S. Forest Service,* 37, 39–40, 42; Strong, "History of Sequoia National Park," 144–45, 150–51; Farquhar, *History of the Sierra Nevada,* 213–14; Beesley, "Reconstructing the Landscape," 11. An example of the high quality of George Sudworth's research interests and abilities is his *Forest Trees of the Pacific Slope* (Washington, DC: Government Printing Office, 1908).

135. Steen, *U.S. Forest Service,* 35, 40, 44, 50; Sudworth, "Stanislaus and Lake Tahoe Forest Reserves," 499–561. A selection from the manuscript diary of Sudworth for his 1900 survey was compiled by A. M. Avakian, "Excerpts [from the Field Notes of George B. Sudworth] on Fire, Lumbering, Range, and Soil and Water Conditions," Berkeley, CA, USFS California Forest and Range Experiment Station, December 1930. Avakian arranged Sudworth's notes and supplied his own pagination. Sudworth's notes contained photographs that were not included in the Avakian typescript.

136. Avakian, "Excerpts [from the Field Notes of George B. Sudworth]" 5–38.

137. Ibid., 31, 37.

138. John Muir, "The New Sequoia Forests of California" [*Harper's,* 1873], in *The Coniferous Forests and Big Trees of the Sierra Nevada by John Muir, 1878–1881,* ed. William Jones (Olympic Valley, CA: Outbooks, 1977), 26–40.

139. Lary Dilsaver and Douglas Strong, "Sequoia and Kings Canyon National Parks: One Hundred Years of Preservation and Resource Management," *California History* 69, no. 2 (summer 1990): 101; Dilsaver and Tweed, *Challenge of the Big Trees,* 61–62; John R. White and Samuel J. Pusateri, *Sequoia and Kings Canyon National Parks* (Stanford, CA: Stanford University Press, 1949), 30, 40; Strong, "History of Sequoia National Park," 104–10.

140. Dilsaver and Tweed, *Challenge of the Big Trees,* 54, 62–63.

141. William Tweed, *Kaweah Remembered: The Story of the Kaweah Colony and the Founding of Sequoia National Park* (Sequoia National Park: Sequoia Natural History Association, 1986), unpaginated [1–15]; Robert V. Hine, *California Utopianism: Contemplations of Eden* (San Francisco: Boyd and Fraser, 1981), 51–55; Strong, "History of Sequoia National Park," 81, 90, 104.

142. Dilsaver and Tweed, *Challenge of the Big Trees,* 64–67; Dilsaver and Strong, "Sequoia and Kings Canyon National Parks," 100–102; Strong, "History of Sequoia National Park," 130–37.

143. Dilsaver and Tweed, *Challenge of the Big Trees,* 67–68; Strong, "History of Sequoia National Park," 122.

144. Strong, *Dreamers and Defenders,* 96; Cohen, *History of the Sierra Club,* 6.

145. Orsi, "'Wilderness Saint' and 'Robber Baron,'" 136–37; Runte, *Yosemite,* 45.

146. Runte, *Yosemite,* 137.

147. Orsi, "'Wilderness Saint' and 'Robber Baron,'" 145–47; Runte, *Yosemite,* 50–54, Cohen, *History of the Sierra Club,* 14.

148. Runte, *Yosemite,* 54–55; Orsi, "'Wilderness Saint' and 'Robber Baron,'" 147–48; Dilsaver and Strong, "Sequoia and Kings Canyon National Parks," 16–17.

149. Dilsaver and Strong, "Sequoia and Kings Canyon National Parks," 17.

150. Orsi, "'Wilderness Saint' and 'Robber Baron,'" 148; Runte, *Yosemite,* 55–56; Dilsaver and Tweed, *Challenge of the Big Trees,* 70–72.

151. Steen, *U.S. Forest Service,* 37–46; Runte, *National Parks,* 58–64. A valuable summary of the ideas that led to the creation of national parks is given by Hans Huth, *Yosemite: The Story of an Idea* (1948; reprint, Yosemite, CA: Yosemite Natural History Association 1984), 3–40.

152. Cohen, *History of the Sierra Club,* 5–14; Fox, *John Muir and His Legacy,* 106–7.

153. Cohen, *History of the Sierra Club,* x–xiii, 13–16; Farquhar, *History of the Sierra Nevada,* 217–28.

154. Runte, *Yosemite,* 57–66; Cohen, *History of the Sierra Club,* 15–16; Dilsaver and Tweed, *Challenge of the Big Trees,* 76–83; H. Duane Hampton, *How the U.S. Cavalry Saved Our National Parks* (Bloomington: Indiana University Press, 1971), 130–63; Strong, "History of Sequoia National Park," 153–54.

155. John Muir, "Address on the Sierra Forest Reservation," Proceedings of the Meeting of the Sierra Club, November 23, 1895, *Sierra Club Bulletin* 1 (1896): 284.

156. William Russell Dudley, "Forest Reservations: With a Report on the Sierra Reservation, California," *Sierra Club Bulletin* 1, no. 7 (January 1896) (reprint, San Francisco: Sierra Club, 1950): 254–67.

157. Ibid., 267.

158. Marsden Manson, "Observations on the Denudation of Vegetation—A Suggested Remedy for California," *Sierra Club Bulletin* 2, no. 6 (June 1899) (reprint, San Francisco: Sierra Club, 1950), 295–311.

159. Cohen, *History of the Sierra Club,* 16.

4: ESTABLISHING RESOURCE MANAGEMENT, 1905–1945

1. Runte, *Public Lands, Public Heritage,* 32–35, 43–44; Runte; *National Parks,* xii–xiii; Beesley, "Reconstructing the Landscape," 11–17.

2. The quotation is in Muir, "Address on the Sierra Forest Reservation." See also Steen, "Origins and Purposes of the National Forests," 70, and Fox, *John Muir and His Legacy,* 106–7, 109.

3. Beesley, "Reconstructing the Landscape," 9–17.

4. Fox, *John Muir and His Legacy,* 114–15; Runte, *Public Lands, Public Heritage,* 48–52; Strong, *Dreamers and Defenders,* 98–102; Steen, *U.S. Forest Service,* 114–15; Cohen, *History of the Sierra Club,* 22–29; Miller, *Gifford Pinchot,* 119–24, 138–44.

5. Paul W. Gates, *History of Public Land Law Development* (Washington, DC: Government Printing Office, 1968), 462, 568–69; Steen, *U.S. Forest Service,* 28–31, 34–37.

6. Gates, *History of Public Land Law Development,* 571; Steen, *U.S. Forest Service,* 36.

7. Steen, *U.S. Forest Service,* 71–75.

8. Strong, *Dreamers and Defenders,* 9–38, 85–110.

9. Gifford Pinchot, *The Use of the National Forests* (Washington, DC: USDA, Forest Service, 1907), 5.

10. Fernow, *Report upon the Forestry Investigations of the U.S. Department of Agriculture,* 8, 18; Steen, *U.S. Forest Service,* 75.

11. Palmer, *Sierra Nevada,* 294–95; Beesley, "Reconstructing the Landscape," 11; W. T. Jackson, R. Herbert, and S. Wee, *History of the Tahoe National Forest* (Davis, CA: Jackson Research Projects and Tahoe National Forest, 1982), 130.

12. Steen, *U.S. Forest Service,* 78–89.

13. C. F. Wilkinson and H. Anderson, *Land and Resource Planning in the National Forests* (Washington, DC: Island Press, 1987), 1–3; Steen, *U.S. Forest Service,* 52–60. An

excellent environmental study of another western "dry forest"—or a forest similar to the Sierra where rainfall is limited primarily to one major season—is that of Nancy Langston, *Forest Dreams, Forest Nightmares: The Paradox of Old Growth in the Inland West* (Seattle: University of Washington Press, 1995), 21–41.

14. *SNEP*, vol. 1, 62; Beesley, "Reconstructing the Landscape," 15–16.

15. The Forest Service scientists who most influenced the new policies were George Sudworth, Coert Du Bois, S. B. Show, and E. I. Kotok. Their roles will be discussed later in this chapter.

16. Andrew D. Rodgers, *Bernhard Eduard Fernow: A Story of American Forestry* (Durham, NC: Forest History Society, 1991), 347, 531, 533.

17. Sudworth, *Forest Trees of the Pacific Slope*, 14–16.

18. Ibid., 15.

19. See Langston, *Forest Dreams, Forest Nightmares*, 3–10, for a comparable example of forest silviculturalists' actions in the Blue Mountains of eastern Oregon and Washington in the same period.

20. Steen, *U.S. Forest Service*, 135–36.

21. Joseph Grinnell and Tracy Irwin Storer, *Animal Life in the Yosemite* (Berkeley: University of California Press, 1924), 393–96; Steen, *U.S. Forest Service*, 136.

22. Two key works of the Forest Service shaped Sierran fire policy and influenced other federal and California state agencies' thinking about fire in the Sierra Nevada: S. B. Show and E. I. Kotok, *Forest Fires in California, 1911–1920: An Analytical Study* (Washington, DC: USDA Circular 243, Government Printing Office, February 1923), and S. B. Show and E. I. Kotok, *The Role of Fire in the California Pine Forests* (Washington, DC: USDA, Department Bulletin no. 1924, December 1924). For an effective discussion of the establishment of the Forest Service's fire-suppression policy, see David Carle, *Burning Questions: America's Fight with Nature's Fires* (Westport, CT: Praeger, 2002), 11–27.

23. Show and Kotok, *Role of Fire in the California Pine Forests*, 1.

24. The area of the study included sites in the Shasta, Klamath, Lassen, Plumas, Tahoe, Eldorado, Stanislaus, and Sierra National Forests.

25. Show and Kotok, *Role of Fire in the California Pine Forests*, 4.

26. Ibid., 4–5.

27. Ibid., 5–6, 70.

28. Ibid., 29–33, 50.

29. Ibid., 29, 34–35, 38–39, 40–41.

30. Beesley, "Reconstructing the Landscape," 15–16; Jackson, Herbert, and Wee, *History of the Tahoe National Forest*, 130–74; Steen, *U.S. Forest Service*, 173–95; Langston, *Forest Dreams, Forest Nightmares*, 247–63.

31. Beesley, "Reconstructing the Landscape," 15.

32. Ibid.

33. Pyne, *Fire in America*, 104–9, 264–68; Biswell, *Prescribed Burning*, 43–55.

34. Show and Kotok, *Forest Fires in California*, 1–3.

35. Ibid., 29–30, 39, 60. See also Pyne, *Fire in America,* 470–71, for his estimate of the significance of Show and Kotok on fire suppression in the National Forests.

36. Show and Kotok, *Role of Fire in the California Pine Forests,* 1–3, 22–24.

37. Ibid., 45–46.

38. Ibid., 24–44.

39. Biswell, *Prescribed Burning,* 43; Pyne, *Fire in America,* 470.

40. Show and Kotok, *Role of Fire in the California Pine Forests,* 47.

41. Ibid., 24.

42. Pyne, *Fire in America,* 104–9; Clar, *California Government and Forestry,* 488–94; Beesley, "Reconstructing the Landscape," 15–16.

43. In September 1923, as part of a campaign to promote congressional support for cooperative firefighting, three U.S. senators, including Senator Charles McNary; secretary of the Senate Select Committee on Reforestation; joined W. B. Lewis (the superintendent of Yosemite), Paul Redington (Pacific Region district forester), and representatives of the National Lumber Manufacturers Association, the California Fruit Growers Supply Company (a big user of Sierran timber to make shipping boxes) and the Yosemite Lumber Company on a tour of the California pine region in the Central Sierra. A photo album that chronicles their trip is in the Library of Congress. It is entitled "Illustrating the Lumber Industry in the California Pine Region," LC #2485, n.d. (inside the album is a date for the visit—September 4, 1923). See also Pyne, *Fire in America,* 104–9; Beesley, "Reconstructing the Landscape," 15–16.

44. For a discussion of the development of fire-exclusion practices into "dogma" by the Forest Service's leaders, including the creation of Smokey Bear as its symbol, see Carle, *Burning Questions,* 11–96.

45. Richard L. P. Bigelow, "History of Forest Supervisor R. L. P. Bigelow, Taken from His Diary from May 23, 1902, to April 30, 1936," typescript, Tahoe National Forest, Nevada City, California, 145–311; Jackson, Herbert, and Wee, *History of the Tahoe National Forest,* 132; Beesley, "Reconstructing the Landscape," 11–12.

46. Bigelow, "History of Forest Supervisor R. L. P. Bigelow," 145–311; Beesley, "Reconstructing the Landscape," 14–15. Jackson, Herbert, and Wee, in *History of Tahoe National Forest,* 130–74, list the following categories of important activities for the period of agency management in the Tahoe National Forest between 1900 and 1940: administration of Tahoe National Forest Lands, logging, mining, water development, grazing, and recreation. Some of these activities are not reflected in Bigelow's daily record, presumably because they took place out of his sight or concern.

47. Bigelow, "History of Forest Supervisor R. L. P. Bigelow," 418–19.

48. Ibid., 582–656.

49. Ibid., 375–584.

50. Ibid., 409, 414.

51. Runte, *Yosemite,* 103–4; Freeman Tilden, *The National Parks,* rev. and expanded by Paul Schullery (New York: Alfred A. Knopf, 1986), 22, 24–25; William Everhart, *The National Park Service* (Boulder, CO: Westview Press, 1983), 12–13.

52. "Auto Use in the National Parks: Proceedings of the Conference Held at the Yosemite National Park, October 14–16, 1912," in *America's National Park System,* ed. Dilsaver, 42–45. Both John Muir and William Colby of the Sierra Club attended the conference. See also Richard W. Sellars, *Preserving Nature in the National Parks* (New Haven: Yale University Press, 1997), 28–32.

53. Sellars, *Preserving Nature in the National Parks,* 37; Fox, *John Muir and His Legacy,* 139–40; Horace M. Albright as told to Robert Cahn, *The Birth of the National Park Service: The Founding Years, 1913–1933* (Salt Lake City: Howe Brothers, 1985), 34–35.

54. Sellars, *Preserving Nature in the National Parks,* 39–45; Cohen, *History of the Sierra Club,* 38–39.

55. "An Act to Establish a National Park Service, and for Other Purposes," 39 Stat. 535, in *America's National Park System,* ed. Dilsaver, 46–47.

56. Sellars, *Preserving Nature in the National Parks,* 43.

57. Farquhar, *History of the Sierra Nevada,* 203–4.

58. Hampton, *How the U.S. Cavalry Saved Our National Parks,* 3–5, 130, 147.

59. The quotation is in Farquhar, *History of the Sierra Nevada,* 204–5.

60. Hampton, *How the U.S. Cavalry Saved Our National Parks,* 150–51; Strong, "History of Sequoia National Park," 147–51.

61. Bigelow, "History of Forest Supervisor R. L. P. Bigelow," 46.

62. Beesley, "Reconstructing the Landscape," 7–8, 12.

63. Dilsaver and Tweed, *Challenge of the Big Trees,* 106–7; Farquhar, *History of the Sierra Nevada,* 205; "Fire Prevention Plan for the National Parks, 10th National Park Conference, February 15–21, 1928," in *America's National Park System,* ed. Dilsaver, 81–86.

64. Dilsaver, ed., *America's National Park System,* 9; Sellars, *Preserving Nature in the National Parks,* 15.

65. See Dilsaver and Tweed, *Challenge of the Big Trees,* 57–58, 69, 76–83, for a discussion of the various skirmishes that involved the Department of the Interior, the U.S. Cavalry, and the socialist community called the Kaweah Colony. In the legal battle, the colony lost its claims to the Giant Forest but won its claim to log in other areas desired by Sequoia park officials.

66. Runte, *Yosemite,* 72–76; Hampton, *How the U.S. Cavalry Saved Our National Parks,* 154–55.

67. Farquhar, *History of the Sierra Nevada,* 207; Russell, *One Hundred Years in Yosemite,* 187; Runte, *Yosemite,* 73–76.

68. Farquhar, *History of the Sierra Nevada,* 206–7; Fox, *John Muir and His Legacy,* 125–29.

69. Sellars, *Preserving Nature in the National Parks,* 15–16; Runte, *Yosemite,* 76.

70. Pamela A. Conners, "Influence of the Forest Service on Water Development Patterns in the West," in *The Origins of the National Forests,* ed. Harold K. Steen (Durham, NC: Forest History Society, 1992), 154–64. See also James C. Williams, *Energy and the Making of Modern California* (Akron: University of Akron Press, 1997), 168–78.

71. Dilsaver and Tweed, *Challenge of the Big Trees,* 95–96.

72. Sellars, *Preserving Nature in the National Parks,* 16, 138, 178; Runte, *Yosemite,* 80–82; Brechin, *Imperial San Francisco,* 101–2, 108–10.

73. Muir, *The Yosemite,* 187–91.

74. See the Joseph Le Conte photographs in Holway R. Jones, *John Muir and the Sierra Club: The Battle for Yosemite* (San Francisco: Sierra Club, 1965), "Requiem for Hetch Hetchy Valley," between pages 128 and 129. Photos prepared for San Francisco to show the potential for scenic vistas with a dam and the actual result of damming appear in the section "Hetch Hetchy the Promise," between pages 112 and 113.

75. Jones, *John Muir and the Sierra Club,* 94–117. See also Elmo R. Richardson, "The Struggle for the Valley: California's Hetch Hetchy Controversy, 1905–1913," *California Historical Society Quarterly* 38, no. 3 (September 1959): 249–58. Richardson's *Politics of Conservation: Crusades and Controversies, 1897–1913* (Berkeley: University of California Press, 1962), 43–44, 72, 110, 123, 125, 132, 137, 154, places the issue in a broader context. For San Francisco's view of the need to dam Hetch Hetchy, see Ray W. Taylor, *Hetch Hetchy: The Story of San Francisco's Struggle to Provide a Water Supply for Her Future* (San Francisco: Richard J. Orozco, 1926).

76. Runte, *National Parks,* 77–81.

77. Kendrick A. Clements, "Engineers and Conservationists in the Progressive Era," *California History* 58, no. 4 (winter 1979–80): 282–303; Richard Lowett, "The Hetch Hetchy Controversy, Phase II: The 1913 Senate Debate," *California History* 74, no. 2 (summer 1995): 193–96, 200–1.

78. H. M. Chittenden, *Report on the Water Supply System of the Spring Valley Water Company, San Francisco, California* (N.p.: n.p., 1912), 22.

79. John R. Freeman, *On the Proposed Use of a Portion of the Hetch Hetchy, Eleanor, and Cherry Valleys within and near to the Boundaries of the Stanislaus U.S. Forest Reserve and the Yosemite National Park as Reservoirs for Impounding Tuolumne River Flood Waters* (San Francisco: Board of Supervisors and Rincon Publishing, 1912).

80. Ibid., 303–9, 311–14, 327–56, 365–72.

81. Ibid., 9–13, 35, 49, 60.

82. Albright and Cahn, *Birth of the National Park Service,* 220, 269; "California National Parks Chronology," in *Yosemite and Sequoia,* ed. Orsi, Runte, and Smith-Baranzini, 8; Runte, *Yosemite,* 82; Brechin, *Imperial San Francisco,* 99–117

83. Farquhar, *History of the Sierra Nevada,* 240–41.

84. Albright and Cahn, *Birth of the National Park Service,* 4–5.

85. Everhart, *National Park Service,* 13–14; Horace M. Albright and Marian A. Schenck, *The Mather Mountain Party of 1915: A Full Account of the Adventures of Stephen T. Mather and His Friends in the High Sierra of California* (Three Rivers, CA: Sequoia Natural History Association, n.d.), 3–4.

86. Albright and Schenck, *Mather Mountain Party,* 5–6, 18, 22.

87. Franklin K. Lane to Stephen T. Mather, Director, National Park Service, May 13, 1918, and Hubert Work, Secretary of the Interior, "Memorandum for the Director, National Park Service, March 11, 1925," both in *America's National Park System,* ed. Dilsaver, 48–49, 62–63.

88. Beesley, "Reconstructing the Landscape," 12; Dilsaver and Tweed, *Challenge of the Big Trees,* 119–20.

89. Grinnell and Storer, *Animal Life in the Yosemite,* v–vii. See also Runte, *Yosemite,* 102–11, for his view of Grinnell's promotion of the vertebrate survey in Yosemite. Runte stresses Grinnell's scientific interest, noting that he had to be very careful and persistent in asking for Mather's support. Mather, according to Runte, gave only luke-warm support to the idea of a thorough science-based survey. Yet Mather was given a generous acknowledgment by Grinnell, demonstrating the deft political skills of the museum director.

90. Grinnell and Storer, *Animal Life in the Yosemite,* 1, 5–7, 10–12, 15–21. The specific zones (all based on Merriam) are illustrated in fig. 1 on page 7. The study area includes both flanks, but the zones were most clearly delineated on the western side, according to Grinnell and Storer. The zones were "Lower Sonoran," "Upper Sonoran," "Transition," "Canadian," "Hudsonian," and "Arctic Alpine," following Merriam's model.

91. Ibid., 1–3, 5–7, 231–32.

92. Ibid., 239.

93. Ibid., 95–98.

94. Ibid., 231–39.

95. Ibid., 239–40.

96. "Auto Use in the National Parks," in Dilsaver, *America's National Park System,* 42–45; Sellars, *Preserving Nature in the National Parks,* 61–63; Dilsaver and Tweed, *Challenge of the Big Trees,* 126–28.

97. Russell, *One Hundred Years in Yosemite,* 186; Sellars, *Preserving Nature in the National Parks,* 58–61; "California National Parks Chronology," 8–9.

98. Sellars, *Preserving Nature in the National Parks,* 63; Beesley, "Reconstructing the Landscape," 16.

99. Runte, *Yosemite,* 79–80.

100. Sellars, *Preserving Nature in the National Parks,* 71–81.

101. G. M. Wright, J. S. Dixon, and B. H. Thompson, *Fauna of the National Parks of the United States: A Preliminary Survey of Faunal Relations in the National Parks* (Washington, DC: Government Printing Office, 1933), quoted in *America's National Park System,* ed. Dilsaver, 105–7; Sellars, *Preserving Nature in the National Parks,* 91–93.

102. G. M. Wright, J. S. Dixon, and B. H. Thompson, *Fauna of the National Parks of the United States: Contribution of Wild Life Survey, Fauna Series No. 1, May, 1932* (Washington, DC: Government Printing Office, 1933), 131–34.

103. Ibid., 130.

104. Horace M. Albright, "Research in the National Parks," *Scientific Monthly* 36 (June 1933), in *America's National Park System,* ed. Dilsaver, 122–23, 130.

105. Frederick Clements to Yosemite National Park Superintendent Charles Thompson, June 7, 1933, File # 601-15, Yosemite National Park Research Library.

106. Yosemite National Park Superintendent Charles Thomson to T. C. Vindt, Chief Landscape Architect, National Park Service, December 1, 1931, File # 601-15, Yosemite National Park Research Library.

107. John Muir, "A Rival of the Yosemite: The Cañon of the South Fork of Kings River, California," in John Muir, *Picturesque California* (1888; reprinted, Golden, CO: Outbooks, 1978), 3.

108. Lary M. Dilsaver, "Conservation Conflict and the Founding of Kings Canyon National Park," in *Yosemite and Sequoia,* ed. Orsi, Runte, and Smith-Baranzini, 111.

109. Lary M. Dilsaver, "Resource Conflict in the High Sierra," in *Mountainous West,* ed. Wyckoff and Dilsaver, 281–90.

110. Dilsaver, "Conservation Conflict and the Founding of Kings Canyon National Park," 112–19.

111. Clar, *California Government and Forestry,* 218, 220, 225–30, 262–64, 280–81, 297–99, 322–24, 328–30, 332–35, 398–99, 443–48, 598–603.

112. Ibid., 488–90.

113. Ibid., 491–92.

114. Ibid., 491–92, 563–65; Steen, *U.S. Forest Service,* 185–95; Pyne, *Fire in America,* 352–53.

115. Beesley, "Reconstructing the Landscape," 14. Information for this analysis of railroad logging as part of my contribution to the Sierra Nevada Ecosystem Project comes from P. A. Conners, "West Side Lumber Company Contextual History," typescript, 1990, Stanislaus National Forest Archives, Sonora, CA; M. R. Brown and C. M. Elling, *An Historical Overview of Redwood Logging in the Hume Ranger District, Sequoia National Forest* (Porterville, CA: U.S. Forest Service, 1981); Supernowicz, "Historical Overview of the Eldorado National Forest"; R. Markley and C. Meisenbach, "Historical Summary: Tahoe National Forest Environmental History," typescript, 1995, Tahoe National Forest Archives, Nevada City, CA. A useful account of the development of railroad logging in northern California is W. H. Hutchinson, *California Heritage: A History of Northern California Lumbering* (Santa Cruz, CA: Forest History Society, 1974).

116. Beesley, "Reconstructing the Landscape," 14. See also Ted Wurm, *Hetch Hetchy and Its Dam Railroad* (Glendale, CA: Trans-Anglo Books, 1990), map in Legend, 79, 82, 145–47; Dorothy Deane, *Sierra Railway* (Berkeley: Howell-North, 1960), map of Sierra Railroad and Other Railroads, 6, 95–96.

117. David Myrick, *Railroads of Nevada and Eastern California,* vol. 1 (Berkeley: Howell-North, 1962), 398–442; Beesley, "Reconstructing the Landscape," 14–15.

118. Beesley, "Reconstructing the Landscape," 14.

119. There were significant differences between the large and heavily capitalized rail logging companies of this period and smaller mills that operated sporadically when lumber prices were high. A photo album created to promote passage of federal legislation supporting cooperative fire-suppression policy is located at the Library of Congress. It illustrates the differences between the two types of operations. One photo shows a fully modern and huge mill (possibly Madera Sugar Pine Company), while an accompanying photo shows a contemporary small mill representing any number of small mills that operating after the 1890s. While the scale of operation is significant, both types of operations generally faced the same chal-

lenge—namely, how to stay in business after all the "virgin" timber in the lower-elevation "pine region" of the Sierra was cut over. See "Illustrating the Lumber Industry in the California Pine Region," LC #2485, n.d. [probably September 4, 1923]. See also Beesley, "Reconstructing the Landscape," 14–15.

120. Beesley, "Reconstructing the Landscape," 14–15.

121. Donald Pisani, *Water, Land, and Law in the West*, 136: Hundley, *The Great Thirst*, 139–49, 170–92; Conners, "Influence of the Forest Service on Water Development Patterns in the West,"154–66; Beesley, "Reconstructing the Landscape," 12–13.

122. Clar, *California Government and Forestry*, 329–30, 334–35, 348, 412.

123. Pisani, *Water, Land, and Law in the West*, 41; Hulse, *Silver State*, 225–33.

124. Hundley, *The Great Thirst*, 234–43, 275–77; Pisani, *Water, Land, and Law in the West*, 48.

125. Hulse, *Silver State*, 227–33; Strong, *Tahoe*, 98–103; Pisani, *Water, Land, and Law in the West*, 48.

126. Strong, *Tahoe*, 103–6.

127. An effective study of the Owens River issue from the perspective of the Owens Valley residents is in Walton, *Western Times and Water Wars*, 131–97; see also Beesley, "Reconstructing the Landscape," 13. The East Bay cities turned to the Mokelumne drainage after its two larger competitor cities had made their choices; Hundley, *The Great Thirst*, 119–200.

128. Hundley, *The Great Thirst*, 141–53, 164–65; Walton, *Western Times and Water Wars*, 154–82.

129. Hundley, *The Great Thirst*, 160–61; William L. Kahrl, *Water and Power* (Berkeley: University of California Press, 1982), vii–x.

130. Hundley, *The Great Thirst*, 141–49, 161–65, 332–33; Walton, *Western Times and Water Wars*, 131–97, 264–65; 230–317; Kahrl, *Water and Power*, 330–50.

131. Mary DeDecker, "Owens Valley, Then and Now," in *Mountains to Desert: Selected Inyo Readings* (Independence, CA: Friends of the Eastern California Museum, 1988), 12–15.

132. Mary Austin, *The Land of Little Rain* (1903; reprint, New York: Dover, 1996), 61–66; DeDecker, "Owens Valley, Then and Now," 8–12.

133. Austin, *Land of Little Rain*, 64.

134. DeDecker, "Owens Valley, Then and Now," 9–10, 12, 14.

135. Conners, "Influence of the Forest Service on Water Development in the West," 164–66; Beesley, "Reconstructing the Landscape," 13.

136. Williams, *Energy and the Making of Modern California*, 98–99, 171–78; Conners, "Influence of the Forest Service on Water Development Patterns in the West," 159–64.

137. Strong, *Tahoe*, 98–101; Williams, *Energy and the Making of Modern California*, 180–85; Charles M. Coleman, *P.G. and E. of California: The Centennial Story of Pacific Gas and Electric Company, 1852–1952* (New York: McGraw-Hill, 1952), 102–35, 229, 282.

138. Jessica Teisch, "The Drowning of Big Meadows: Nature's Managers in Progressive-Era California," *Environmental History* 4, no. 1 (January 1999): 32–43.

139. Beesley, "Beyond Gilbert," Abstract of Paper in *Proceedings of the American Association for the Advancement of Science, Pacific Division* 18, no. 1 (June 19, 1999): 42.

140. Teisch, "Drowning of Big Meadows," 42.

141. Williams, *Energy and the Making of Modern California,* 183, 195.

142. John A. Britton, "Editorial," in *Pacific Service Magazine* 6 (November 1913): 208–9.

143. Frederick S. Myrtle, "Our Spaulding-Drum Development Recognized as a World Feature," *Pacific Service Magazine* 6 (November 1913), 195–96.

144. Strong, *Dreamers and Defenders,* 61–84, 111–33.

145. Beesley, "Reconstructing the Landscape," 11–17.

5: THE PHILOSOPHY OF "MORE," 1940–1970

1. R. B. Rice, W. A. Bullough, and R. J. Orsi, *The Elusive Eden: A New History of California,* 2d ed. (New York: McGraw-Hill, 1996), 488; Michael P. Malone and Richard W. Etulain, *The American West: A Twentieth-Century History* (Lincoln: University of Nebraska Press, 1989), 109, 118–19; Hulse, *Silver State,* 264–69; Strong, *Tahoe,* 46–50.

2. Paul Hirt, *A Conspiracy of Optimism: Management of the National Forests since World War Two* (Lincoln: University of Nebraska Press, 1994), xxi–xliii; David Beesley, "Sierra Nevada National Forests: An Environmental History," in FSEEE, *Restoring Our Forest Legacy,* 25–26; Beesley, "Reconstructing the Landscape," 17.

3. Timothy P. Duane, *Shaping the Sierra: Nature, Culture, and Conflict in the Changing West* (Berkeley: University of California Press, 1999), 73–121, provides current information on Sierra Nevada population growth patterns; see also Rice, Bullough, and Orsi, *Elusive Eden,* 490, for California.

4. Beesley, "Reconstructing the Landscape," 17.

5. Runte, *Yosemite,* 189–200; Dilsaver and Tweed, *Challenge of the Big Trees,* 227–30; Beesley, "Reconstructing the Landscape," 18.

6. Timothy P. Duane, "Recreation in the Sierra," *SNEP,* vol. 2, 558, 562.

7. Duane, "Human Settlement, 1850–2040," 239–40; Paul Smith, "Highway Planning in California's Mother Lode: The Changing Townscape of Auburn and Nevada City," *California History* 59, no. 3 (fall 1980): 208; Beesley, "Reconstructing the Landscape," 20.

8. Rice, Bullough, and Orsi, *Elusive Eden,* 530–31; Pisani, *Water, Land, and Law in the West,* 164–65; Houghton, *Trace of Desert Waters,* 61, 67, 70; Beesley, "Reconstructing the Landscape," 19–20.

9. Steen, *U.S. Forest Service,* 247, 251; Roger A. Sedjo, "Forest Resources: Resilient and Serviceable," in *America's Renewable Resources: Historical Trends and Current Challenges,* ed. K. D. Frederick and R. A. Sedjo (Washington, DC: Resources for the Future, 1991), 99; Hirt, *Conspiracy of Optimism,* 131.

10. Steen, *U.S. Forest Service,* 314.

11. Hirt, *Conspiracy of Optimism,* 45, 50, 91, 316 n. 10.

12. Ibid., 55–57, 137, 140–46; Steen, *U.S. Forest Service,* 313–15; Sedjo, "Forest Resources," 99–105; John A. Helms and John C. Tappeiner, "Silviculture in the Sierra," *SNEP,* vol. 2, 442.

13. Steen, *U.S. Forest Service,* 283–84, 314; Hirt, *Conspiracy of Optimism,* 113–15, 198, 241.

14. Hirt, *Conspiracy of Optimism,* 131, 180–81, 199; Steen, *U.S. Forest Service,* 313–16.

15. Pyne, *Fire in America,* 176–79, 286–90. For a discussion of this changing view, and especially the role played by University of California scientist Harold Biswell, see Carle, *Burning Questions,* 57–131.

16. Marion Clawson and Winston Harrington, "The Growing Role of Outdoor Recreation," in *America's Renewable Resources,* ed. Frederick and Sedjo, 262–65; Hirt, *Conspiracy of Optimism,* 57–58, 85, 160–62; Steen, *U.S. Forest Service,* 297, 301–2; Beesley, "Reconstructing the Landscape," 20.

17. James Johnston, "The Effects of Humans on the Sierra Nevada Mixed Conifer Forest," typescript, Lassen National Forest, n.d., 11; Beesley, "Sierra Nevada National Forests," 25.

18. The AFA call for increased production is quoted in S. T. Dana and M. Krueger, *California Lands: Ownership, Use, and Management* (Washington, DC: American Forestry Association, 1958), v.

19. Ibid., v, vii, ix–x, xvii, xx.

20. Ibid., xix–xx, 98–99, 138–40, 228.

21. Ibid., xx.

22. Ibid., 118, 152, 207–8.

23. Johnston, "Effects of Humans on the Sierra Nevada Mixed Conifer Forest," 11; Kevin McKelvey and James Johnston, "Historical Perspectives on Forests of the Sierra Nevada and the Transverse Ranges of Southern California," chap. 11 in J. Verner et al., technical coordinators, *The California Spotted Owl: A Technical Assessment of Its Current Status* (Albany, CA: Pacific Southwest Research Station, July 1992), 240–41.

24. Supernowicz, "Historical Overview of the Eldorado National Forest," 163.

25. "Tahoe National Forest Timber Management Policy Statement, May 15, 1949," typescript, S, Plans, R-5, Tahoe, Timber Management Policy Statement, Tahoe National Forest, Nevada City, CA, 7.

26. Harold E. Basey, *Sierra Nevada Textbook: A Comprehensive Reference,* 5th ed. (Groveland, CA: Robin Works, 1995), 66, 110.

27. Dana and Krueger, *California Lands,* 147.

28. Basey, *Sierra Nevada Textbook,* 66.

29. Dana and Krueger, *California Lands,* 147–48.

30. Ibid., 151–54.

31. Helms and Tappeiner, "Silviculture in the Sierra," 442.

32. Gary Snyder, "Ancient Forests of the Far West," in *Practice of the Wild: Essays by Gary Snyder* (New York: North Point Press, 1990), 135–36.

33. "Timber Survey Report, Foresthill Project, TNF, December 21, 1940," typescript, S, Plans, Timber Surveys–Tahoe, Foresthill Project, Tahoe National Forest, Ne-

vada City, CA, 1,3; "Appraisal Report, Brandy City Unit, April 30, 1943," typescript, S, Sales-Tahoe, Brandy City Unit, Proposed, TNF, Nevada City, CA, 2, 3; "Appraisal Report, Brandy City Unit, North Yuba Working Circle, April 5, 1947," typescript, Sales-Tahoe, Brandy City Unit, TNF, Nevada City, CA, 1–3.

34. "Tahoe National Forest Timber Management Policy Statement, May 15, 1949," 1, 5–6.

35. Ibid., 7–11.

36. Ibid., 6, 6a.

37. "Tahoe National Forest, Timber Management Plan for the Auburn Working Circle, CY 1959–1968," typescript, S, Plans-Tahoe, Timber Management 1959–1968, TNF, Nevada City, CA; "Timber Management Plan for the North Yuba Working Circle, Proposed Feb. 27, 1962, Approved July 1, 1963," typescript, 2410, Plans, North Yuba Working Circle, 1960–1969, TNF, Nevada City, CA.

38. The Timber Resources Review was instituted under Chief Richard McArdle between 1952 and 1958 as an attempt to project timber uses in America to the year 2000 and compare them with an inventory of the available timber supply. In the final published report, McArdle predicted no "timber famine" but maintained that timber resources would have to be managed more intensively—the origins of the phrase *intensive management*. The Tahoe plans reflected the chief's concern for more output from the forest. See Steen, *U.S. Forest Service,* for a discussion of the development of the Timber Resources Review, 285–90.

39. "Tahoe National Forest, Timber Management Plan for the Auburn Working Circle," 1, 26–27.

40. Unpaginated cover letter for "Timber Management Plan for the North Yuba Working Circle, TNF, 1960–1969."

41. "Timber Management Plan for the North Yuba Working Circle," 2–3.

42. Ibid., 23.

43. "TNF Timber Management Plan," May 15, 1949, 11; "Tahoe National Forest, Timber Management Plan for the Auburn Working Circle," 26; Steen, *U.S. Forest Service,* 301–2.

44. Susan R. Schrepfer, "Establishing Administrative 'Standing': The Sierra Club and the Forest Service, 1897–1956," in *American Forests: Nature, Culture, and Politics,* ed. Char Miller (Lawrence: University Press of Kansas, 1997), 125, 132; Cohen, *History of the Sierra Club,* 199.

45. Schrepfer, "Establishing Administrative 'Standing,'" 132–33; Cohen, *History of the Sierra Club,* 200–202.

46. Schrepfer, "Establishing Administrative 'Standing,'" 133–34; Cohen, *History of the Sierra Club,* 200.

47. Schrepfer, "Establishing Administrative 'Standing,'" 125–34; Cohen, *History of the Sierra Club,* 201–11; Steen, *U.S. Forest Service,* 303.

48. Donald Fairclough, "An Administrative History of Squaw Valley, 1949–1971" (M.A. thesis, Sacramento State College, 1971), 1–3.

49. Ibid., 2–3.

50. Donald Fairclough, "A History of Modern Skiing in the Tahoe National Forest," typescript in possession of author, May 1970, 1–9, 24–26; Fairclough, "Administrative History of Squaw Valley," 21–22; Duane, "Recreation," 570.

51. John L. Harper, *Mineral King: Public Concern with Government Policy* (Arcata, CA: Pacifica, 1982), 280–81.

52. Ibid., 61–116; Dilsaver and Tweed, *Challenge of the Big Trees*, 278–81; Dilsaver and Strong, "Sequoia and Kings Canyon National Parks," 106.

53. Duane, "Recreation," 576–80.

54. Sellars, *Preserving Nature in the National Parks*, 149.

55. Everhart, *National Park Service*, 166.

56. Sellars, *Preserving Nature in the National Parks*, 151–55; Dilsaver, ed., *America's National Park System*, 166.

57. Everhart, *National Park Service*, 25–26.

58. Bernard DeVoto, "Let's Close the National Parks," in *America's National Park System*, ed. Dilsaver, 188–89.

59. Conrad Wirth, "Mission 66: Special Presentation to President Eisenhower and the Cabinet," in *America's National Park System*, ed. Dilsaver, 193.

60. Runte, *National Parks*, 173; Sellars, *Preserving Nature in the National Parks*, 149.

61. Wirth, "Mission 66," 194–96.

62. Everhart, *National Park Service*, 26–27.

63. Runte, *National Parks*, 173; Sellars, *Preserving Nature in the National Parks*, 188–90; Stanley Cain, "Ecological Islands as Natural Laboratories," in *America's National Park System*, ed. Dilsaver, 202–7.

64. A. Starker Leopold, "Wildlife Management in the National Parks," in *America's National Park System*, ed. Dilsaver, 237–51.

65. Sellars, *Preserving Nature in the National Parks*, 200–217.

66. Beesley, "Reconstructing the Landscape," 17–19; Runte, *Yosemite*, 180; Dilsaver and Tweed, *Challenge of the Big Trees*, 236, 240–41.

67. Runte, *Yosemite*, 185; Runte, *National Parks*, 176, Sellars, *Preserving Nature in the National Parks*, 208; Demars, *Tourist in Yosemite*, 130.

68. Runte, *Yosemite*, 189–91; Demars, *Tourist in Yosemite*, 138.

69. Hilmer Oehlmann is quoted in Runte, *Yosemite*, 192–93.

70. Elizabeth S. O'Neill, *Meadow in the Sky: A History of Yosemite's Tuolumne Meadows Region* (Groveland, CA: Albicaulis Press, 1984), 142; Cohen, *History of the Sierra Club*, 134–42; Runte, *Yosemite*, 193–96.

71. O'Neill, *Meadow in the Sky*, 142.

72. Runte, *Yosemite*, 196; Sellars, *Preserving Nature in the National Parks*, 189; O'Neill, *Meadow in the Sky*, 138–39, 146.

73. Runte, *Yosemite*, 93, 140, 202–3; Demars, *Tourist in Yosemite*, 141.

74. Runte, *Yosemite*, 177–78; Sellars, *Preserving Nature in the National Parks*, 162; Johnston, *Sierra Nevada: The Naturalist's Companion*, 116–18.

75. Dilsaver and Tweed, *Challenge of the Big Trees*, 249.

76. Dilsaver, ed., *America's National Park System*, 166.

77. O'Neill, *Meadow in the Sky*, 137.

78. Demars, *Tourist in Yosemite*, 130–31; Runte, *Yosemite*, 192–203; Beesley, "Reconstructing the Landscape," 19.

79. Beesley, "Reconstructing the Landscape," 19; Dilsaver and Tweed, *Challenge of the Big Trees*, 255; William Tweed, "Summary for Sequoia and Kings Canyon National Park," typescript, Sequoia and Kings Canyon National Parks Archives, Three Rivers, CA.

80. John White and Samuel J. Pusateri, "Atmosphere in the National Parks," in White and Pusateri, *Sequoia and Kings Canyon National Parks*, 197–99; Sellars, *Preserving Nature in the National Parks*, 178.

81. Dilsaver and Tweed, *Challenge of the Big Trees*, 229.

82. Ibid., 242–44, 246.

83. Ibid., 233–37, 248–51.

84. In all, Richard Hartesveldt contributed six studies on sequoia between 1959 and 1967. See D. Parsons and V. King, *Scientific Research in Sequoia and Kings Canyon National Parks: An Annotated Bibliography* (Three Rivers, CA: Sequoia Natural History Association, April 1980), 17, 43–44. See also Dilsaver and Tweed, *Challenge of the Big Trees*, 181, 249–50, and Dilsaver and Strong, "Sequoia and Kings Canyon National Parks," 28.

85. Dilsaver and Tweed, *Challenge of the Big Trees*, 249–50.

86. Ibid., 251–52.

87. Ibid., 252–55.

88. Ibid., 246–48, 253–54.

89. "A Back Country Management Plan for Sequoia and Kings Canyon National Parks," issued 1963, in *America's National Park System*, ed. Dilsaver, 211–13. See also Dilsaver and Strong, "Sequoia and Kings Canyon National Parks," 29.

90. Between 1962 and 1971, annual backcountry use in the parks rose from 8,000 to 44,000. See Dilsaver and Strong, "Sequoia and Kings Canyon National Parks," 29.

91. "Back Country Management Plan," 213.

92. Ibid., 213–14.

93. Ibid., 214–15.

94. Dilsaver and Strong, "Sequoia and Kings Canyon National Parks," 29.

95. Leopold, "Wildlife Management in the National Parks," 240–41.

96. Ibid., 239–40.

97. Ibid., 238–39.

98. Ibid., 241.

99. Ibid., 248–49.

100. Ibid., 244–46; Johnston, *Sierra Nevada: The Naturalist's Companion*, 50–53, 173–74.

101. Strong, *Tahoe: An Environmental History* [hereafter cited as "*Tahoe* (1984)"], 116–17; Douglas Strong, *Tahoe: From Timber Barons to Ecologists* (Lincoln: University of Nebraska Press, 1999) [hereafter cited as "*Tahoe* (1999)"], 29–30. See also Elliott-Fisk et al., "Lake Tahoe Case Study," 228–29.

102. Strong, *Tahoe* (1984), 41–42; Strong, *Tahoe* (1999), 31; Elliott-Fisk et al., "Lake Tahoe Case Study,"237–39; Beesley, "Reconstructing the Landscape," 18–19.

103. Strong, *Tahoe* (1999), 26–28, 31; Elliott-Fisk et al., "Lake Tahoe Case Study," 238.

104. Strong, *Tahoe* (1999), 28–30; Elliott-Fisk et al., "Lake Tahoe Case Study," 237–38.

105. Strong, *Tahoe* (1984), 116–18; Strong, *Tahoe* (1999), 32; Elliott-Fisk et al., "Lake Tahoe Case Study," 228–29, 238.

106. Strong, *Tahoe* (1999), 32; Elliott-Fisk et al.,"Lake Tahoe Case Study," 223, 229.

107. Strong, *Tahoe* (1999), 57–58; Elliott-Fisk et al., "Lake Tahoe Case Study," 228–29.

108. Strong, *Tahoe* (1999), 57–59, 63; Elliott-Fisk et al., "Lake Tahoe Case Study," 225–28.

109. Strong, *Tahoe* (1999), 33.

110. Dana and Krueger, *California Lands,* 32–33.

111. William Stewart, "Economic Assessment of the Ecosystem," in Sierra Nevada Ecosystem Project, *Final Report to Congress,* vol. 3, *Assessments, Commissioned Reports, and Background Information* [hereafter cited as *SNEP,* vol. 3], 974.

112. Houghton, *Trace of Desert Waters,* 61–71, 85–108; Hulse, *Silver State,* 230–33; Pisani, *Water, Land, and Law in the West,* 164.

113. Hundley, *The Great Thirst,* 201–10, 232–98; Beesley, "Reconstructing the Landscape," 19.

114. Hundley, *The Great Thirst,* 232–72; Larson, "Historical Water-Use Priorities and Public Policies," 175–76.

115. Hundley, *The Great Thirst,* 272–98; Larson, "Historical Water-Use Priorities and Public Policies," 176; Beesley, "Reconstructing the Landscape," 19–20.

116. Strong, *Tahoe* (1984), 105–6; Houghton, *Trace of Desert Waters,* 67, 70; Beesley, "Reconstructing the Landscape," 20.

117. Strong, *Tahoe* (1984), 108–11; Pisani, *Water, Land, and Law in the West,* 164–65; Houghton, *Trace of Desert Waters,* 71, 98; Beesley, "Reconstructing the Landscape," 20.

118. Hundley, *The Great Thirst,* 164–65, 168, 229, 303, 332–35; Walton, *Western Times and Water Wars,* 264–65.

119. Dilsaver and Tweed, *Challenge of the Big Trees,* 201, 207, 237–38.

120. Stewart, "Economic Assessment of the Ecosystem," 995–98.

121. Ibid., 996–97.

122. Hirt, *Conspiracy of Optimism,* xxv.

123. Sellars, *Preserving Nature in the National Parks,* 213–14.

6: THE ENVIRONMENTAL CHALLENGE, 1960–1999

1. A number of historians and philosophers place the postwar environmental movement in the context of social and economic changes after World War II and the wave of reforms associated with the 1960s and 1970s. Many see it as being different in character from the earlier conservation movement. See Samuel P. Hays, *A History of Environmental Politics since 1945* (Pittsburgh: University of Pittsburgh Press, 2000), 1–5, 94–103 ; Philip Shabecoff, *A Fierce Green Fire: The American Environmental Movement* (New York: Hill and Wang, 1993), 91–99, 101–4, 110, 111–17, 129–47; Roderick

Nash, *American Environmentalism,* 3d ed. (New York: McGraw-Hill, 1990), 187–189; John Opie, *Nature's Nation: An Environmental History of the United States* (Fort Worth: Harcourt Brace College Publishers, 1998), 391, 491; Zachary Smith, *The Environmental Policy Paradox,* 2d ed. (Englewood Cliffs, NJ: Prentice Hall, 1995, 15–16; Hal K. Rothman, *The Greening of a Nation? Environmentalism in the United States since 1945* (Fort Worth: Harcourt Brace College Publishers, 1998), 83–134; Oelschlaeger, *Idea of Wilderness,* 281–319; Donald Worster, *Nature's Economy: A History of Ecological Ideas* (Cambridge, U.K.: Cambridge University Press, 1994), 342–87.

2. Nash, *American Environmentalism,* 9–11, 69–71, 113–15, 187–89; Rothman, *Greening of a Nation?* 3–5.

3. William O. Douglas, minority position in *Sierra Club v. Morton,* Supreme Court of the United States, quoted in Nash, *American Environmentalism,* 244.

4. Cohen, *History of the Sierra Club,* 451–52. For another discussion of the Mineral King case and *Sierra Club v. Morton* and the idea of environmental lawyer Christopher Stone's influence on Justice Douglas through his law review article and later his book *Should Trees Have Standing? Toward Legal Rights for Natural Objects* (Los Altos, CA: William Kaufman, 1972), see Harper, *Mineral King,* 172–80.

5. Hays, *History of Environmental Politics since 1945,* 22–26, 29–35, 54–58; Shabecoff, *Fierce Green Fire,* 107–10; Nash, *American Environmentalism,* 188; Worster, *Nature's Economy,* 350–51, Rothman, *Greening of a Nation?* 83–107.

6. Shabecoff, *Fierce Green Fire,* 111–19; Smith, *Environmental Policy Paradox,* 15–16; Opie, *Nature's Nation,* 438; Rothman, *Greening of a Nation?* 121–24; Hirt, *Conspiracy of Optimism,* 217–19.

7. Shabecoff, *Fierce Green Fire,* 129–32; Nash, *American Environmentalism,* xvi–xix; Worster, *Nature's Economy,* 350–59; J. Clarence Davies, *The Politics of Pollution* (New York: Pegasus, 1970), 37–58; Nash, *American Environmentalism,* xvi–xviii.

8. Hirt, *Conspiracy of Optimism,* 233–37; Wilkinson and Anderson, *Land and Resource Planning in the National Forests,* 31, 33, 173, 199, Larry Ruth, "Conservation and Controversy," *SNEP,* vol. 2, 148–56.

9. Wilkinson and Anderson, *Land and Resource Planning in the National Forests,* 335–45; Williams, *Americans and Their Forests,* 458–59; Sellars, *Preserving Nature in the National Parks,* 193; Ruth, "Conservation and Controversy," 153–54.

10. Wilkinson and Anderson, *Land and Resource Planning in the National Forests,* 345–52; Ruth, "Conservation and Controversy," 153–54; Palmer, *Sierra Nevada,* 297.

11. Dunlap, *Saving America's Wildlife,* 142, 151–55.

12. Wilkinson and Anderson, *Land and Resource Planning in the National Forests,* 322; Opie, *Nature's Nation,* 323.

13. Shabecoff, *Fierce Green Fire,* 133–34. Samuel Hays has pointed out that although litigation was an important tool for environmental activists, the courts have primarily used it to compel procedural, rather than substantive, responses from agencies or to provide more information to an interested public. See Hays, *History of Environmental Politics since 1945,* 132–34.

14. Wilkinson and Anderson, *Land and Resource Planning in the National Forests*, 40–41, 72–74; Hirt, *Conspiracy of Optimism*, 246–47; Ruth, "Conservation and Controversy," 151–52.

15. Wilkinson and Anderson, *Land and Resource Planning in the National Forests*, 347–49.

16. Steven Yafee, *The Wisdom of the Spotted Owl: Policy Lessons for a New Century* (Washington, DC: Island Press, 1994), 131–36; Ruth, "Conservation and Controversy," 157–58.

17. Sellars, *Preserving Nature in the National Parks*, 201, 214–17; Runte, *Yosemite*, 207–9.

18. Runte, *Yosemite*, 216; Sellars, *Preserving Nature in the National Parks*, 254–57; Biswell, *Prescribed Burning*, 110–11.

19. Johnston, *Sierra Nevada: The Naturalist's Companion*, 171–72; Runte, *Yosemite*, 206–9, 216–17.

20. Demars, *Tourist in Yosemite*, 130–31.

21. Ibid., 130–32; Runte, *Yosemite*, 202; Sellars, *Preserving Nature in the National Parks*, 208–9.

22. Demars, *Tourist in Yosemite*, 137–39; Runte, *Yosemite*, 205–6.

23. Demars, *Tourist in Yosemite*, 138; Runte, *Yosemite*, 205–6; Alfred Runte, "Planning Yosemite's Future: A Historic Perspective," in *Yosemite and Sequoia*, ed. Orsi, Runte, and Smith-Baranzini, 124–26; Harold Gilliam, "The Next Yosemite," *San Francisco Chronicle*, December 9, 1990.

24. Associated Press, "Yosemite Vendor's Fee to U.S. Revealed," *Grass Valley Union*, January 20, 1990; Carrie Dolan, "Golden Valley: MCA's Yosemite Unit Pays Little, Gains a Lot Running Concessions," *Wall Street Journal*, March 27, 1990, A1, A6; Associated Press, "Use Yosemite Concession Profits to Preserve Beauty, " *Grass Valley Union*, May 15, 1990; Associated Press, "Coalition Forms to Bid on Yosemite Concessions," *Grass Valley Union*, September 20, 1990; Associated Press, "Environmentalists Want to Operate Park Concessions," *Grass Valley Union*, September 25, 1990; Richard Turner and Laura Landro, "MCA Officials and Matsushita Plan Sale Talk," *Wall Street Journal*, September 28, 1990, A1, A10; Geraldine Fabricant, "MCA Expected to OK Buyout from Matsushita," *Sacramento Bee*, November 25, 1990.

25. Dilsaver and Tweed, *Challenge of the Big Trees*, 255.

26. Ibid., 287; Dilsaver and Strong, "Sequoia and Kings Canyon National Parks," 28–29.

27. Dilsaver and Tweed, *Challenge of the Big Trees*, 287–293; Dilsaver and Strong, "Sequoia and Kings Canyon National Parks," 30–31.

28. Dilsaver and Tweed, *Challenge of the Big Trees*, 295–298.

29. Ibid., 266–278; Dilsaver, "Resource Conflict in the High Sierra," 294–98.

30. Sellars, *Preserving Nature in the National Parks*, 233, 239, 242.

31. Dilsaver and Tweed, *Challenge of the Big Trees*, 262–63, Dilsaver and Strong, "Sequoia and Kings Canyon National Parks," 30. See also David Parsons and Patricia

Haggerty, *Scientific Research in Sequoia and Kings Canyon National Parks: An Annotated Bibliography, Update: 1980–1986* (San Francisco: U.S. Department of the Interior, NPS, Western Regional Office, n1986), 1.

32. Dilsaver, ed., *America's National Park System,* 270–71, Parsons and King, *Scientific Research in Sequoia and Kings Canyon National Parks,* 17, 43–44; Carle, *Burning Questions,* 97–173.

33. J. S. McLaughlin, "A Plan for Use of Fire in Ecosystem Management. Middle Fork of Kings River, February 29, 1968," in *America's National Park System,* ed. Dilsaver, 360–63; Dilsaver and Tweed, *Challenge of the Big Trees,* 263–65; Parsons and King, *Scientific Research in Sequoia and Kings Canyon National Parks,* 15.

34. Anderson, *Indian Fire-Based Management,* 1–30.

35. Cohen, *History of the Sierra Club,* 435–46.

36. Ruth, "Conservation and Controversy," 148–49.

37. Ibid., 149; Palmer, *Sierra Nevada,* 296.

38. Wilkinson and Anderson, *Land and Resource Planning in the National Forests,* 346–48; John B. Flippen, "The Nixon Administration, Timber, and the Call of the Wild," *Environmental History Review* 19, no. 2 (summer 1995): 37–38, 46–47, 52.

39. Ruth, "Conservation and Controversy," 153–54; Palmer, *Sierra Nevada,* 296.

40. Dilsaver, "Resource Conflict in the High Sierra," 294.

41. H. T. Harvey, R. J. Hartesveldt, and J. T. Stanley, *Wilderness Impact Study Report: An Interim Report of the Sierra Club Outing Committee on the Effects of Human Recreation Activities on Wilderness Ecosystems* (San Francisco: Sierra Club Outing Committee, 1972), 3–4, 15, 26, 49, 75–84.

42. John Englelenner, "Crowds Strain Wilderness Area near Casinos," *Sacramento Bee,* August 15, 1992, B1, B4.

43. Palmer, *Endangered Rivers,* 80, 94.

44. Ibid., 94, 125–28, 138, 145–46; Larson, "Historical Water-Use Priorities and Public Policies," 176–77.

45. Tim Palmer, *Stanislaus: The Struggle for a River* (Berkeley: University of California Press, 1982), 46, 50–56, 61–139.

46. A valuable chronology on the Auburn Dam issue was prepared by a student group, "Ecostudents," at Sierra College in 1996. It covers the time between 1949 and 1996 and includes articles and other documents discussing the issue. It is also a good example of student activism during the Age of Ecology. See "Sierra College Ecostudents," *The Auburn Dam Reader,* vols. 1 and 2 (Rocklin, CA: Ecostudents of Sierra College, Sewall Hall, April 1996), A1–5.

47. Bill Cassady quoted in Michael Rosenberg, "Dam Talk in Auburn," *Western Slope Connection* 2, no. 7 (April 26–May 9, 1977): 15.

48. Palmer, *Endangered Rivers,* 115–18; Mount, *California Rivers and Streams,* 281–86, discusses Auburn Dam in a broader flood control context.

49. John Krist, "Dam Builders Win Symbolic Victory," *High Country News,* September 30, 2002, 11.

50. Palmer, *Endangered Rivers*, 128–31.

51. Friends of the River, "National Wild and Scenic Rivers in California: A Status Report," pamphlet, Sacramento, 1999.

52. Opie, *Nature's Nation*, 393.

53. Dilsaver and Tweed, *Challenge of the Big Trees*, 280–281; Louise Jackson, *Beulah: A Biography of Mineral King Valley* (Tucson: Westernlore Press, 1988), 137–41, 145–47, 149–54. The Mineral King issue is an important case to consider in the transformation of the Sierra Club to an activist environmental organization. See Cohen, *History of the Sierra Club*, 67, 88, 340–45, 392–93, 395–96, 450–51, and Susan Schrepfer, "Perspectives on Conservation: Sierra Club Strategies in Mineral King," *Journal of Forest History* 20 (October 1976): 176–90.

54. Dilsaver and Tweed, *Challenge of the Big Trees*, 281–83, Opie, *Nature's Nation*, 393; Harper, *Mineral King*, 54–55, 71, 74, 76–79, 81–87, 91–95, 107–10, 169–81; Cohen, *History of the Sierra Club*, 340–45; 392–93.

55. Harper, *Mineral King*, 165–81, 202–3; Ruth, "Conservation and Controversy," 150; Dilsaver and Tweed, *Challenge of the Big Trees*, 299–307. See also Stephen Whitney, "Impact at Mineral King: 'A Conclusionary Document,'" *Sierra Club Bulletin*, May 1975, 9–10; "Final Mineral King EIS Released by Forest Service," *Sierra Club Bulletin*, April 1976, 35; "Final Mineral King EIS Indicated Severe Damage," in *Sierra Club Bulletin*, May 1976, 36.

56. Harper, *Mineral King*, 117–25, 129–30, 186–88; Whitney, "Impact at Mineral King," 10.

57. Dilsaver and Tweed, *Challenge of the Big Trees*, 301–2; Ruth, "Conservation and Controversy," 149–50; Jackson, *Beulah*, 161–70.

58. Harper, *Mineral King*, 194–95; Beesley, "Independence Lake," 7–10.

59. Douglas Strong, "Disney's Independence Lake Project: A Case Study in California's Environmental Review Process," *California History* 61, no. 2 (summer 1982): 100–19; Michael Rosenberg, "State to Expedite Disney Permit Process," *Western Slope Connection* 2, no. 4 (March 15–28, 1977): 3; Michael Rosenberg, "Disney Lobbies Supervisors: 'Total Commitment to Project,'" *Western Slope Connection* 2, no. 7 (April 26–May 9, 1977): 3, 24.

60. Ruth, "Conservation and Controversy," 154–56.

61. *Final Environmental Statement and Timber Management Plan, Tahoe National Forest* (Nevada City, CA: USDA, Tahoe National Forest, 1978); *Tahoe National Forest Land and Resources Management and Environmental Impact Statement* (Nevada City, CA: USDA, Tahoe National Forest, 1990).

62. *Final Environmental Statement and Timber Management Plan, TNF,* 1978.

63. Ibid., i, 42–46.

64. Ibid., iv–v, 45–46, 101–10, 126.

65. Interview with former Tahoe National Forest Supervisor Geri Bergen, May 27, 2000.

66. Ibid.

67. A photograph of the cutting near the stream edge at Rock Creek that generated

protest is in "The Fate of Our Forests," tabloid newspaper prepared by Sierra Nevada Group, Sierra Club, 1978, in collection of author.

68. Interview with Geri Bergen, May 27, 2000.

69. The campaign organized by environmentalists was more sophisticated, and had more local and national groups involved than in the earlier case. Similar campaigns existed for the other Sierran forests as well. See "Save the Tahoe National Forest," tabloid newspaper prepared by the Sierra Nevada Group of the Sierra Club, Protect American River Canyons, and South Yuba River Citizens League, 1986, in collection of author; "Fifty Year Plan Endangers Stanislaus National Forest," *Sierra Bonanza,* Mother Lode Chapter of the Sierra Club, 48, no. 1 (February 1986), no page number; Charles Gallardo, "22 Appeals Filed to Tahoe Management Plan," *Grass Valley Union,* October 25, 1990, 1, 3; "Disaster Strikes the Tahoe National Forest," in *Sierra Uplift,* Sierra Nevada Group, Sierra Club (September–October 1990): 1–2.

70. Geri Bergen, "Letter of Intent Accompanying *Tahoe National Forest Land and Resource Management Plan*" (Nevada City, CA: USDA FS TNF, 1990), no page number; TNFLRMP, Appendix A (Public Participation, Issues, Concerns and Opportunities, Forest Service Response to Comments), A1–A371.

71. Interview with Geri Bergen, May 27, 2000; TNFLRMP Record of Decision, 1990, 1–7, and unpaginated insert which states, "NOTICE, THE ASQ OF 2.3 MILLION BOARD FEET (MMBF) REFERRED TO IN THE PREFERRED ALTERNATIVE, HAS BEEN CHANGED BY THE REGIONAL FORESTER TO 129 MMBF. SEE THE RECORD OF DECISION FOR DETAILS."

72. Ruth, "Conservation and Controversy," 156.

73. Interview with William Baker (planner and NEPA coordinator, TNF), September 27, 1994. Baker was summarizing what were prevailing views of most Forest Service planners for the 1980s. He noted also that those views changed in the decade that followed.

74. Hirt, *Conspiracy of Optimism,* 23; Ruth, "Conservation and Controversy," 156–57.

75. Hirt, *Conspiracy of Optimism,* 267–69; Yafee, *Wisdom of the Spotted Owl,* ix–xvii, 115–32; Richard Freeman, "The EcoFactory: The United States Forest Service and the Political Construction of Ecosystem Management," *Environmental History* 7, no. 4 (October 2002): 633–37.

76. Ruth, "Conservation and Controversy," 157–58; David Beesley, "Sierra in Peril: Ecosystem Politics and Sierra Nevada Environmental History," *Wild Duck Review* 2, no. 6 (December 1996): 22.

77. Ruth, "Conservation and Controversy," 158–59; Beesley, "Sierra in Peril," 22.

78. Hirt, *Conspiracy of Optimism,* 23, 25, 287–89; Beesley, "Sierra Nevada National Forests," 26–28.

79. Hill, *Geology of the Sierra Nevada,* 136; Kahrl, *Water and Power,* 429–30; Hart, *Storm over Mono,* 264.

80. Kahrl, *Water and Power,* 430; Hart, *Storm over Mono,* 56–58, Walton, *Western Times and Water Wars,* 265; Norris Hundley, Jr., *The Great Thirst: Californians and Water: A History,* rev. ed. (Berkeley: University of California Press, 2001), 336–39.

81. Lisa Strong-Aufhauser, "The Mono Lake Water War," *Earth* 4, no. 5 (October 1995): 50–58; Hart, *Storm over Mono*, 16–20; Walton, *Western Times and Water Wars*, 265.

82. Hart, *Storm over Mono*, 20–21, 52–54; Walton, *Western Times and Water Wars*, 264–65; Hundley, *The Great Thirst* (rev. ed.), 338.

83. Wallis McPherson is quoted in Jim Mayer and Patrick Hoge, "The Struggle for Mono Lake," *Sacramento Bee*, July 10, 1994, A1, A14. See also Walton, *Western Times and Water Wars*, 264–65.

84. Hart, *Storm over Mono*, 59–60; Kahrl, *Water and Power*, 431–32.

85. Hundley, *The Great Thirst* (rev. ed.), 339–42; Hart, *Storm over Mono*, 61–101; Walton, *Western Times and Water Wars*, 265–67.

86. Kahrl, *Water and Power*, 433.

87. Hart, *Storm over Mono*, 103–4; 106–7; Walton, *Western Times and Water Wars*, 266–67. See also Los Angeles Department of Water and Power, "DWP Operations in the Mono Basin" and "Bird Studies Research Findings," both in *Mono Lake Background*, pamphlet in possession of author, n.d.; and Mono Lake Committee, "The Destruction of Mono Lake is Right on Schedule," newsprint tabloid in possession of author, n.d.

88. "Rush Creek Lawsuit Still Holds Water: Court Asked to Stabilize Mono Lake," *Mono Lake Newsletter* 8, no. 1 (summer 1985): 4–5; Hart, *Storm over Mono*, 108–13, 128–29; Walton, *Western Times and Water Wars*, 267–68; Hundley, *The Great Thirst* (rev. ed.), 342–44.

89. Liljeblad and Fowler, "Owens Valley Paiute," 415–16; Fowler and Liljeblad, "Northern Paiute," 437–38.

90. Mono Lake Committee, "6388 or Fight" in "The Destruction of Mono Lake is right on Schedule," 2.

91. Hart, *Storm over Mono*, 74–76, 174; Ann Bancroft, "Campaign to Save Mono Lake in Final Stretch," *San Francisco Chronicle*, September 31, 1994, A17; Hundley, *The Great Thirst* (rev. ed.), 345–47.

92. Hart, *Storm over Mono*, 65–66, 105–6, 175.

93. Elliot-Fisk et al., "Lake Tahoe Case Study," 218, 227; Hal Rubin, "Lake Tahoe: A Tale of Two States," *Sierra* 66, no. 6 (November–December 1981): 43; Beesley, "Reconstructing the Landscape," 7, 10.

94. Rubin, "Lake Tahoe," 43.

95. Duane, *Shaping the Sierra*, 91.

96. Elliott-Fisk et al., "Lake Tahoe Case Study," 223; Rubin, "Lake Tahoe," 44, 46.

97. Elliott-Fisk et al., "Lake Tahoe Case Study," 217, 226–27.

98. Ibid., 223–38; Strong, *Tahoe* (1999), 60–92.

99. Elliott-Fisk et al., "Lake Tahoe Case Study," 217–18; Rubin, "Lake Tahoe," 44.

100. Strong, *Tahoe* (1999), 60–61.

101. Ibid., 61; Elliott-Fisk et al., "Lake Tahoe Case Study," 239.

102. Strong, *Tahoe* (1999), 67–68; Elliott-Fisk et al., "Lake Tahoe Case Study," 218, 239.

103. Strong, *Tahoe* (1999), 85–88; Rubin, "Lake Tahoe," 44, 46.

104. Strong, *Tahoe* (1999), 67–71; Elliott-Fisk et al., "Lake Tahoe Case Study," 218, 229–30; Rubin, "Lake Tahoe," 44, 46.

105. Elliott-Fisk et al., "Lake Tahoe Case Study," 230–231; Strong, *Tahoe* (1999), 75–79, 84–88; Duane, *Shaping the Sierra,* 90–93.

106. Elliott-Fisk et al., "Lake Tahoe Case Study," 223; Beesley, "Reconstructing the Landscape, " 8, 10; Cherub, "Death of Tahoe's Forests Has Roots in Logging 150 Years Ago, Official Says," no page number.

107. Strong, *Tahoe* (1999), 82–83, 90–94; Elliott-Fisk et al., "Lake Tahoe Case Study," 223–25; California Tahoe Conservancy, *Progress Report* (Sacramento: California Tahoe Conservancy, n.d.), 5–8.

108. Elliott-Fisk et al., "Lake Tahoe Case Study," 223–25.

109. Shabecoff, *Fierce Green Fire,* xi–xv; Philip Shabecoff, *Earth Rising: American Environmentalism in the 21st Century* (Washington, DC: Island Press, 2000, 2001), xi.

110. Shabecoff, *Earth Rising,* 9–10.

111. Beesley, "Sierra in Peril," 22–24.

7: THE SIERRA IN PERIL AND ECOSYSTEM POLITICS

1. Tom Knudson, "Majesty and Tragedy: The Sierra in Peril," *Sacramento Bee,* June 9, 1991, A1.

2. Beesley, "Sierra in Peril," 22.

3. Knudson's "Sierra in Peril" series has become "history." It is seen as such not only by this historian, but by others looking into the twentieth-century history of the state of California. See, for example, Stephanie S. Princetl, *Transforming California: A Political History of Land Use and Development* (Baltimore: Johns Hopkins University Press, 1999), 271–78.

4. Tom Knudson, "State's Citadel of Stone, Wind Is under Siege," *Sacramento Bee,* June 9, 1991, A1, A4–A 5.

5. Tom Knudson, "Smog Fouls Crystal-Clear Mountain Air," *Sacramento Bee,* June 10, 1991, A1, A8–A 9.

6. Tom Knudson, "Today, the Sierra Nevada Forest Is Dying," *Sacramento Bee,* June 11, 1991, a1, a10–a 12.

7. Tom Knudson, "Flooded Lands Choking Streams," *Sacramento Bee,* June 12, 1991, A1, A8–A9.

8. Tom Knudson, "Hopes for Reform Improve," *Sacramento Bee,* June 13, 1991, A14.

9. Tom Knudson, "Clear Cut, Then Disaster," *Sacramento Bee,* June 9, 1991, A4.

10. Tom Knudson, "Growth: Like Gold Rush of 49, People Pour into the Hills," *Sacramento Bee,* June 13, 1991, A15.

11. Telephone interview with Tom Knudson, August 11, 1992.

12. For a discussion of the fundamentals of ecosystem science and their relationship to politics, see Hanna Cortner and Margaret Moote, *The Politics of Ecosystem Management* (Washington, DC: Island Press, 1999), 16–26; Jerry Franklin, "Ecosystem Management: An Overview," in *Ecosystem Management: Applications for Sustainable Forest and Wildlife Resources,* ed. Mark Boyce and Alan Haney (New Haven: Yale University Press, 1997), 20–26, 29–32, 49.

13. Princetl, *Transforming California,* 270–71; Freeman, "EcoFactory," 632–33.

14. Telephone interview with Douglas Wheeler, August 21, 1992; Douglas Wheeler (chairperson), *The Report of the California Timberland Taskforce* (Sacramento: Resources Agency, December 15, 1993), 1.

15. Telephone interview with Douglas Wheeler, August 21, 1992; Chris Bowman, "Conference on Range's Future Opens Today," *Sacramento Bee,* November 18, 1991, A1, A12. See also Tom Knudson, "Sierra Is Facing a Wide Range of Threats, Panel Says," *Sacramento Bee,* November 19, 1991, A9. See also Princetl, *Transforming California,* 271–72, 277–78.

16. Ronald Stewart, "Speech at Sierra Summit," November 18, 1991, in Tahoe National Forest Archives, Nevada City, CA.

17. Duane, *Shaping the Sierra,* 24; David Sneed, "Bioregion Concept Worries Officials," *Grass Valley Union,* March 1, 1992, A1.

18. Sierra Nevada Summit Steering Committee, *The Sierra Nevada: Report of the Sierra Nevada Summit Steering Committee* (Sacramento: Resources Agency, July 1992), 3–9.

19. Duane, *Shaping the Sierra,* 26.

20. Jeff Phillips, "Treasures and Troubles of the Sierra Nevada," *Sunset,* May 1992, 6, 92–100, 101–9, 112, 114.

21. Beesley, "Sierra in Peril," 22.

22. Ibid., 22–23; "Sierra Now: A Vision for the Future," conference summary, 1993; Sierra Nevada Alliance Conference Summaries, 1994, 1995, 1996, 1997, 1998. I attended the Sierra Now conference and several of the Sierra Nevada Alliance conferences as well.

23. Beesley, "Sierra in Peril," 23; "The Sierra Economy, Sustainable Development in Harmony with Nature," Sierra Economic Summit Conference, Sacramento, June 16–17, 1993. I attended the conference.

24. Sierra Business Council, *Sierra Nevada Wealth Index* (Truckee, CA: Sierra Business Council, 1996); Timothy P. Duane, "Managing the Sierra," in *California Policy Issues* 8 (January 1993): 180–81; Duane, *Shaping the Sierra,* 27.

25. Duane, "Managing the Sierra," 181.

26. Sierra Business Council, *Planning for Prosperity* (Truckee, CA: Sierra Business Council, 1997), 7–50.

27. Joan Hamilton, "Visions of the Range of Light," *Sierra,* May–June 1992, 77–88.

28. Jane Elder, "The Big Picture," *Sierra,* March–April 1994, 52–56.

29. "At Work in the Range of Light," *Sierra,* March–April 1994, 127.

30. George Wuerthner, "Dimming the Range of Light," *Wilderness* 57, no. 203 (winter 1992): 10–23, 31.

31. Robert Divine, "Management and the Uncertainty Principle," *Wilderness* 58, no. 207 (winter 1994): 10–23.

32. Wilderness Society, *The Sierra Nevada: Renewing the Glow of the Range of Light* (San Francisco: Wilderness Society, n.d.).

33. Wilderness Society, *The Federal Forest Lands of the Sierra Nevada: A Citizens Guide to the Sierra Nevada Ecosystem Project* (San Francisco: Wilderness Society, 1997), 1–2, 60–63.

34. For a discussion of the political origins of ecosystem management in the aftermath of the spotted owl and the loss of Forest Service influence on its own destiny, see Freeman, "EcoFactory," 632–40.

35. Paul F. Barker, Regional Forester, PSW, "An Environmental Agenda for the National Forests in California," typescript announcement, Tahoe National Forest Archives, Nevada City, CA, February 8, 1990.

36. Shabecoff, *Fierce Green Fire*, 119, 189.

37. George Wuerthner, "Dimming the Range of Light," in *The World of Wilderness: Essays on the Power and Purpose of Wild Country*, ed. T. H. Watkins and P. Byrnes (Niwot, CO: Wilderness Society and Roberts Rinehart, 1995), 178–80; Paul Roberts, "The Federal Chain-Saw Massacre," *Sacramento Bee*, Forum, May 25, 1997, F1, F6.

38. Freeman, "EcoFactory," 642.

39. Dale Robertson, "Ecosystem Management of the National Forests and Grasslands," press release to all Regional Foresters and Station Directors, June 4, 1992, copy in Tahoe National Forest Archives, Nevada City, CA.

40. James C. Overbay, "An Ecosystem Approach to Multiple-Use, Sustained-Yield Management," address to "National Workshop on Taking an Ecological Approach to Management," April 27, 1992, copy in Tahoe National Forest Archives, Nevada City, CA.

41. Hal Salwasser, "An Ecosystem Perspective for Managing the National Forests and Grasslands," speech given to the Blue Mountain Biodiversity Conference, Walla Walla, WA, May 29, 1992, copy in Tahoe National Forest Archives, Nevada City, CA.

42. Dale Robertson, "Ecosystem Management, Public Involvement, and Clearcutting," directive to all Regional Foresters and Station Directors, June 25, 1992, in Tahoe National Forest Archives, Nevada City, CA.

43. Ronald E. Stewart, Regional Forester to Chief, USDA Forest Service, "Strategy for Implementing Ecosystem Management, Public Involvement, and Clearcutting," September 4, 1992, in Tahoe National Forest Archives, Nevada City, CA.

44. Letter from USDA Forest Service, Washington, DC, re: PSW Region/Station's Strategy for Implementing Ecosystem Management and Research to Forest Supervisors, Staff Directors and Director, PSW Station, October 29, 1992. In Tahoe National Forest Archives, Nevada City, CA.

45. Ronald E. Stewart, "Strategy for Implementing Ecosystem Management and Research, Ecological Principles," December 15, 1992, in Tahoe National Forest Archives, Nevada City, CA.

46. Ronald E. Stewart, "Strategy for Implementing Ecosystem Management and Research, Framework," December 15, 1992, in Tahoe National Forest Archives, Nevada City, California.

47. Ronald E. Stewart, "Strategy for Implementing Ecosystem Management and Research, Ecological Classification, Inventory, Existing Condition, Potential Condi-

328   Notes to Pages 232–238

tion, and Desired Condition," December 15, 1992, in Tahoe National Forest Archives, Nevada City, CA.

48. Internal communication to other employees of the USDA FS from Paul Strong, District Biologist, Walker RD, Chippewah National Forest, Walker, Minnesota, "There's No Such Thing As an Ecosystem," August [n.d.] 1992, in Tahoe National Forest Archives, Nevada City, CA.

49. Sierra Nevada Ecosystem Project Science Team, *Sierra Nevada Ecosystem Project: Progress Report* (Davis, CA: Sierra Nevada Ecosystem Project Center, May 1994) [hereafter cited as *SNEP Progress Report*], Appendix A, 48; Letter to the Chief of the Forest Service from Committee Chairpersons, Congress of the United States, January 19, 1993, *SNEP Progress Report*, Appendix B, 50–51; Letter to the Chief of the Forest Service from Four Congressmen, Congress of the United States, January 26, 1993, *SNEP Progress Report*, Appendix D, 55; Duane, *Shaping the Sierra*, 36.

50. SNEP Steering Committee, "Sierra Nevada Ecosystem Project Charge from the Steering Committee," *SNEP Progress Report*, Appendix E, 58–59.

51. *SNEP Progress Report*, Executive Summary, 1–2.

52. *SNEP,* vol. 2, vol. 3.

53. Associated Press, "Ecosystem Gets Mixed Review," *Grass Valley Union,* September 21, 1995, A1, A3.

54. Tom Knudson, "Sierra Nevada Hurting, Draft of Key Report Says," *Sacramento Bee,* March 3, 1996, A1, A20; Tom Knudson, "Sierra's Problem: Too Many People," *Sacramento Bee,* June 11, 1996, B1; "Divided States of America" dollar bill handout, ephemera in collection of author.

55. As a participant in a Forest Service Employees for Environmental Ethics study of the Sierra Nevada, I summarized the main SNEP findings listed above. See FSEEE, *Restoring Our Forest Legacy,* 30. The summary is based on an analysis of *SNEP,* vol. 1.

56. Associated Press, "U.S. Forest Service Chief Robertson Ousted," *Grass Valley Union,* October 29, 1993, sec. A, no page number.

57. S. Hazelhurst, F. Magary, and K. Hawk, eds., *Sustaining Ecosystems: A Conceptual Framework* (San Francisco: USDA Forest Service, Pacific Southwest Region, April 1995), vii.

58. Ibid., v, xi, 2–3. For a discussion of Robertson's role in beginning ecosystem management, see Freeman, "EcoFactory," 639–46.

59. Hazelhurst, Magary, and Hawk, eds., *Sustaining Ecosystems,* xii.

60. Jack Ward Thomas quoted ibid., v.

61. Ruth, "Conservation and Controversy," 158–59. See also Princetl, *Transforming California,* 286–91.

62. Beesley, "Sierra Nevada National Forests," 27–28. See also the history summary of California Spotted Owl Federal Advisory Committee, *Final Report of the California Spotted Owl Advisory Committee* (Washington, DC: Department of Agriculture, December 1, 1997), chap. 1, 1–2.

63. U.S. Forest Service, *Draft Environmental Impact Statement, Managing California Spotted Owl Habitat in Sierra Nevada Forests of California: An Ecosystem Report* (San Francisco: USFS, Pacific Southwest Region, January 1995), S1–S2, S5–S6.

64. "F.S. Proposes 60 Percent Cut in Timber Harvest to Save Owl," *Mountain Messenger,* February 9, 1995, 1–2; David Sneed, "Owl-Protection Plan Draws Fire," *Grass Valley Union,* March 4, 1995, B1, B4; David Sneed, "Supervisors Critical of Forest Service Owl Plans," *Grass Valley Union,* March 16, 1995, A1, A3; James Wood, "Supervisors Err on Owl Plan," *Grass Valley Union,* March 31, 1995, "Other Voices," sec. B, no page number.

65. Associated Press, "New Policy on Logging Considered," *Grass Valley Union,* August 20, 1996; Alex Barnum, "Sierra Logging Plan Goes Back to Square One; Clinton Administration Balks at Easing Limits," *San Francisco Chronicle,* August 24, 1996, beginning page A1; Michael Doyle, "Disputed Timber Proposal Shelved," *Sacramento Bee,* August 24, 1996, A1, A22.

66. USDA, Forest Service, "Departmental Regulation # 1043-41," California Spotted Owl Federal Advisory Committee, March 3, 1997, in California Spotted Owl Federal Advisory Committee, *Final Report of the California Spotted Owl Advisory Committee,* Appendix A, 1–2.

67. Federal Advisory Committee, *Final Report of the California Spotted Owl Federal Advisory Committee,* chap. 2, "Issues and Recommendations," 1–6, 7–8.

68. Ibid., 8–9.

69. FSEEE, *Restoring Our Forest Legacy,* 29.

70. USDA, Forest Service, Pacific Southwest Region, *Final Environmental Impact Statement, Herger-Feinstein Quincy Library Group Forest Recovery Act* (San Francisco: USDA Forest Service, August 1999), chap. 1, 2–3; Federal Advisory Committee, *Final Report of the California Spotted Owl Federal Advisory Committee,* chap. 1, 1–4.

71. An excellent historical account of the creation of the Quincy Library Group is contained in a policy study written by Cristine H. Colburn, "Forest Policy and the Quincy Library Group," in *Finding Common Ground: Governance and Natural Resources in the American West* (New Haven: Yale University Press, 2002), 159–76.

72. Ed Marston, "The Timber Wars Evolve into a Divisive Peace," *High Country News,* September 29, 1997, 1, 8–13. For another view of the issue, see Timothy Duane, "Community Participation in Ecosystem Management," *Ecology Law Quarterly* 24, no. 4 (1997): 771–97.

73. Marston, "Timber Wars Evolve into a Divisive Peace," 8–9; Daniel Sneider, "Forest Gumption: Blueprint for a Green Compromise," *Christian Science Monitor,* July 18, 1997, 1, 8.

74. Federal Advisory Committee, *Final Report of the California Spotted Owl Federal Advisory Committee,* chap. 1, 1–4.

75. Duane, "Community Participation in Ecosystem Management," 788.

76. Marston, "Timber Wars Evolve into a Divisive Peace," 10.

77. HR 858, 105th Cong., 1st sess.

78. Marston, "Timber Wars Evolve into a Divisive Peace," 1.

79. Jon Margolis, "How a Foe Saved the Quincy Library Group's Bacon," *High Country News,* September 29, 1997, 13.

80. Tom Philp, "Fallout from a Logging Consensus in the Sierra," *Sacramento Bee,* November 9, 1997, Forum 1–2.

81. Margolis, "How a Foe Saved the Quincy Library Group's Bacon," 13.

82. Associated Press, "Quincy's Trail-Blazing Logging Plan Clears Senate Hurdle," *Sacramento Bee,* October 23, 1997, A3.

83. "Boxer Caves: Switch on Logging Bill a Political Gesture," *Sacramento Bee,* December 19, 1997, Internet source, sec. B, Editorials, no page number.

84. "Sierra Nevada Forest Protection Campaign Releases New Analysis: S. 1028— The Quincy Logging Bill—Would Log More Acres of Ancient Forest Than Headwaters," *Business Wire, Electric Library,* February 17, 1998, 1–2.

85. Associated Press, "Opponents: Compromise Forest Bill Could Ruin Wild Lands with Logging," *Grass Valley Union,* February 19, 1998, A1.

86. Duane, "Community Participation in Ecosystem Management," 796–97.

87. USDA, Forest Service, "eis for the Herger-Feinstein Quincy Library Group Forest Recovery Act Pilot Project, Notice of Intent to Prepare an Environmental Impact Statement," December 21, 1998.

88. USDA, Forest Service, *Herger-Feinstein Quincy Library Group Forest Recovery Act Final Environmental Impact Statement,* chap. 2, 1.

89. Ibid., 23–24.

90. Jane Braxton Little, "A Year Later, Quincy Forest Plan Leaves Saws Mostly Quiet," *Sacramento Bee,* August 21, 2000, A1, A7.

91. Bradley E. Powell, *Sierra Nevada Forest Plan Amendment: Final Environmental Impact Statement, Record of Decision* (Vallejo, CA: Forest Service, R5 Regional Office, January 2001), 11.

92. Tom Philp, "Logging Directives for Sierra Don't Jibe," *Sacramento Bee,* January 29, 2001, B7.

93. For a typical comment on the resource policies of the Bush administration that also contains a summary of what the reporter labels as "Bush's Environmental Record," see Mark Hertsgard, "Bush's Other War: Environment in Cross Hairs," *Sacramento Bee,* February 16, 2003, Forum, E1–E6.

94. For a sampling of press and environmental-group concern about Bush's revisions, see: Stuart Leavenworth, "Battle for the Forest, Sweeping Plan May Bring More Logging," *Sacramento Bee,* January 30, 2003, A1–A10; Associated Press, "Bush Plan Leaves Forest Care to Timber Firms," *Grass Valley Union,* March 7, 2003, C5; Zachary Cole, "White House Plan Doubles Sierra Logging," *San Francisco Chronicle,* state edition, March 7, 2003, A1–A21; Jason Swartz, "Plumas and Lassen National Forests Slated for Devastating 'Administrative Study' Logging Plan," *Wilderness Record,* spring 2003, 14.

95. Stuart Leavenworth, "Sierra Plan Calls for More Logging," *Sacramento Bee,* June 6, 2003, A3–A4.

96. Thomas is quoted and Eubanks is cited in Dave Moeller, "Higher Cut Levels on Sierra Proposed," *Grass Valley Union,* June 7, 2003, A7.

97. Colburn, "Forest Policy and the Quincy Library Group," 174–75.

98. Jane Braxton Little, "New Forest Plan Leaves Owls in a Lurch," *High Country News,* May 12, 2003, 3.

99. Tom Knudson, "Furor Grows as Drought, Fires Boost Salvage Logging of Trees," *Sacramento Bee,* September 9, 1992, A1, A6.

100. Tom Knudson, "President OKs Hike in Salvage Logging," *Sacramento Bee,* September 10, 1992, no page number.

101. Paul Roberts, "The Federal Chain-Saw Massacre: Clinton's Forest Service and Clear-Cut Corruption," *Harper's,* June 1997, 37–45. See also Roberts, "Federal Chain-Saw Massacre," *Sacramento Bee,* Forum, May 25, 1997, F1, F6.

102. Courtney Breen, "Forest Colors Hold Darker Meaning as Sierra Drought Enters Fourth Year," *Reno Gazette-Journal,* July 18, 1990, no page number.

103. Wuerthner, "Dimming the Range of Light," in *World of Wilderness,* 179–80.

104. Alex Barnum, "Republicans Blast Clinton on Forest Fire Policies," *San Francisco Chronicle,* September 13, 1996, A2; Roberts, "Federal Chain-Saw Massacre," *Harper's,* 48–49.

105. Jeffrey St. Clair, "Salvage Dreams," *Wild Forest Review* 3, no. 1 (February 15, 1996): 8–21.

106. Jane Braxton Little and News Service assistance, "Salvage Tree Cutting Abuse Cited in Report: Some Sales Had Mostly Live Trees," *Sacramento Bee,* December 13, 1996, section B, no page number.

107. Ibid.

108. Barbara Barte Osborn, "Lawsuit Delays Salvage Logging Operations," *Sacramento Bee,* January 1, 1997, B1.

109. This evaluation of the origin of the Framework is based on chap. 2, "Sierra Nevada National Forests: An Environmental History," that I contributed to FSEEE, *Restoring Our Forest Legacy,* 23–32.

110. Beesley, "Sierra Nevada National Forests," 31.

111. USDA, Forest Service, "In Brief: Sierra Nevada Framework for Conservation and Collaboration," press release, January 22, 1999, Pacific Southwest Region.

112. U.S. Forest Service, *Sierra Nevada Framework for Conservation and Collaboration: Summary of Existing Management Direction, Executive Summary* (San Francisco: Pacific Southwest Region, August 11, 1998), 3.

113. G. Lynn Sprague, Regional Forester, "Improving Conservation Options for National Forests in the Sierra Nevada," USDA, Forest Service, Pacific Southwest Region, R5, May 1, 1998.

114. Beesley, "Sierra Nevada National Forests," 31–32; USDA, Forest Service, *Sierra Nevada Science Review: Report of the Science Review Team Charged to Synthesize New Information of Rangewide Urgency to the National Forests of the Sierra Nevada* (San Francisco: Pacific Southwest Research Station, July 24, 1998), 8–50.

115. Editorial, *San Francisco Chronicle,* May 4, 2000, A22. See also Tom Knudson, "Forest Draft Unveiled for Sierra Land," *Sacramento Bee,* May 3, 2000, A1, A14.

116. USDA, Forest Service, *Sierra Nevada Forest Plan Amendment: Draft Environmental Impact Statement, Summary* (Vallejo, CA: Pacific Southwest Region, April 2000), 1–40; USDA, Forest Service, "Sierra Nevada Forest Plan Amendment DEIS: Public Comment and Public Meeting Schedule," Pacific Southwest Region, Vallejo,

CA, [2000], 1–6; USDA, Forest Service, "Sierra Nevada Forest Plan Amendment DEIS: Summary of Alternatives and Comparison of Consequences," Pacific Southwest Region, Vallejo, CA [2000], 1–21.

117. FSEEE, *Restoring Our Forest Legacy,* Executive Summary, 7–16.

118. Bradley Powell, *Record of Decision: Sierra Nevada Forest Plan Amendment, Environmental Impact Statement,* 21–22.

119. Associated Press, "Forest Service Plan Limits Sierra Logging," *Grass Valley Union,* January 13, 2001, A1; Jane Braxton Little, "A New Plan Frames the Sierra Nevada," *High Country News,* February 12, 2001, 6; Associated Press, "Timber Industry Hopes Bush Changes Policies," *Grass Valley Union,* February 21, 2001, A8; Michael Doyle, "Ag Secretary Recuses Self," *Sacramento Bee,* February 17, 2001, A9; Glen Martin, "White House Approves Timber Management in the Sierra Nevada," *San Francisco Chronicle,* December 29, 2001, A6; David Bayles, Conservation Director, Pacific Rivers Council, and Kieran Suckling, Executive Director, Center for Biological Diversity, to Editor of the *High Country News,* October 8, 2001, 13; Glen Martin, "Forest Service Considers More Logging in Sierra: Agency May Amend Framework," *San Francisco Chronicle,* January 1, 2002, S.F. Chronicle Electronic Data Base Source, three pages; Editorial, "Don't Undercut Sierra Plan," *San Francisco Chronicle,* January 20, 2002, S.F. Chronicle Electronic Data Base Source, 2 pages; Rebecca Claren, "No Game Plan for the Public Lands," *High Country News,* February 4, 2002; Associated Press, "Forest Official: Is Sierra Plan Too Strict?" *Grass Valley Union,* March 16, 2002, A11. The consideration of lawsuits against the George W. Bush administration's forest policies were only beginning to take form as this book was being finished, and hence can not be effectively analyzed here. The consensus amongst environmentalists and other journalistic sources about the Bush policies was that the administration generally tried not to directly challenge environmental decisions, preferring to use regulation changes as in the case of NEPA. In other ways the administration was accused of not being aggressive about appealing pro–resource developers court decisions. The victory of the Republican Party in the off-year election of 2002 led to prodevelopment politicians taking control of congressional committees. See Matthew Daly, "Bush Team to Rethink Key Environmental Laws," *Sacramento Bee,* August 30, 2002, A11; Angie Wagner, "GOP's Gains Worry Environmentalists," *San Francisco Chronicle,* November 9, 2002, A3; Associated Press, "Pact May Expedite Forest," *Grass Valley Union,* October 4, 2002, A5; William McCall, "Southerners Now Hold Key Posts on Land-Use Panels," *San Francisco Chronicle,* November 22, 2002, J6; Zachary Coile, "New Rules May Clear Way for Logging," *San Francisco Chronicle,* November 27, 2002, A1, A19; "No Forest Fingerprints: Bush Team Chips Away at Wildlife Protections," Editorial, *Sacramento Bee,* December 4, 2002, B6; Les Blumenthal, "Bush Toppling Forest Safeguards, Critics Say," *Sacramento Bee,* December 30, 2002, A1, A14.

120. Michael McCabe, "Forest Chief Upholds Sierra Protections: New Management Plan Reduces Logging," *San Francisco Chronicle,* November 17, 2001, S.F. Chronicle Electronic Data Base Source, two pages, and Glen Martin, "Sierra Plan Protects Timber: Agriculture Dept. OKs Tough Rules for Forest Management," *San*

Francisco Chronicle, December 28, 2001, S.F. Chronicle Electronic Data Base Source, three pages.

121. Associated Press, "Forest Official: Is the Sierra Plan Too Strict?" *Grass Valley Union,* March 16, 2002, A11; Rebecca Claren, "No Game Plan for the Public Lands," 3.

122. Martin, "Sierra Plan Protects Timber"; Martin, "Forest Service Considers More Logging in Sierra," 2–3. Legal challenges to Bush policies began late in 2002. Even in 2001, environmentalists were voicing concern that the Bush White House was refusing to punish alleged violations of environmental laws in order to aid timber companies, snowmobile manufacturers and users, land developers, and energy producers. See Tom Turner, "The Government Takes a Hike," *San Francisco Chronicle,* June 24, 2001, S.F. Chronicle Electronic Data Base, three pages. In November of 2002 the 9th U.S. Circuit Court of Appeals issued a temporary order prohibiting any cutting of green timber in a proposed salvage sale associated with the Star Fire near Lake Tahoe. The challenge to the cut had been lodged by the John Muir Project associated with the Earth Island Institute. See Associated Press, "9th Circuit Curtails Salvage Logging near Tahoe," *Grass Valley Union,* November 9, 2002, A3. A significant legal challenge to President Clinton's so-called Roadless Rule was rejected by the U.S. court of appeals in San Francisco. A suit had been brought by Boise Cascade Corporation, the state of Idaho, the Kootenai Indian tribe, and some motorized recreational groups. The U.S. district court in Boise, Idaho, had originally ruled in favor of these plaintiffs. The Forest Service did not challenge the ruling. But a consortium of environmentalist groups that included Earthjustice, the Sierra Club. Natural Resources Defense Council, the Wilderness Society, and the Idaho Conservation League appealed the decision and won in the federal appeals court in San Francisco. The ruling affected several areas across the West, including land near Sequoia–Kings Canyon National Park in the Sierra. See Jane Kay, "'Roadless Rule' Upheld for National Forests: Court's Decision Allows Ban to Begin Immediately," *San Francisco Chronicle,* December 14, 2002, A3. Bush policies to revise NEPA rules governing public appeals threatened to ignite further lawsuits. See Matt Jenkins, "Forest Planning Gets a Facelift: Critics Say the New Look Will Turn National Forests into Lawsuit Magnets," *High Country News,* December 23, 2002, 3.

123. "Workshop Slated on Plan for Sierra Nevada Forest," *Grass Valley Union,* December 11, 2002, A3; USDA, Forest Service, Pacific Southwest Region, "Socioeconomic Considerations in National Forest Management, Public Comment on Socioeconomic Concerns about Implementation [for] the Sierra Nevada Forest Plan Amendment," December 13, 2002, Nevada City, California.

124. Telephone interview with Jay Watson (regional director for the Wilderness Society), November 8, 2002.

125. Leavenworth, "Sierra Plan Calls for More Logging," A1–A4; Moeller, "Higher Cut Levels on Sierra Proposed," A7. Kate Campbell, "Bush Administration Proposes Workable Sierra Forest Plan," *AG Alert: The Weekly Newspaper for California Agriculture,* March 12, 2003, 1, 31; USDA, Forest Service, *Sierra Nevada Forest Plan Amendment: Draft Supplemental Environmental Impact Statement, Summary,* 1–22.

126. Press release from Secretary Mary D. Nichols, State of California Resources Agency, March 17, 2003.

127. Greg Greenwood, "Why the Forest Service Proposal for the Sierra Nevada Is Wrong for California: Greenwood on Sierra Framework," State of California Resources Agency, typescript, 1.

128. Ibid.

129. Ibid., 2.

130. Freeman, "EcoFactory," 632–33, 646–48.

131. Martin, "Sierra Plan Protects Timber," 3.

132. Martin, "Forest Service Considers More Logging in Sierra," 2–3.

133. Phillips, "Treasures and Troubles of the Sierra Nevada," 92–114; Tom Knudson, "Yosemite: How Best to Love It," *Sacramento Bee,* November 6, 1991, B1, B2.

134. K. J. Dawson and E .S. Greco, *Special Management Area: Visual Resources Management Study for the Sequoia National Park Prescribed Fire Management Program* (Davis, CA: Department of Environmental Design, December 1987), 10–11, 91.

135. Sellars, *Preserving Nature in the National Parks,* 272. See also Patrick Hoge, "Preserving Yosemite Valley: Historic Plan to Eliminate Most Vehicles Is Unveiled," *Sacramento Bee,* November 6, 1997, A16.

136. Steven Krefting, "Sequoia and Kings Canyon National Park Planning: A Golden Opportunity for a Special Place," *Wilderness Record,* May 1998, 3.

137. As to the success of reintroduction of the bighorn sheep, major problems of habitat were an issue, but even more serious was predation by mountain lions. This problem arose from environmental policies that encouraged the sheep introduction and also provided greater protection of the lions—more lions were eating a declining sheep population. See Paul Rauber, "The Lion and the Lamb: What Happens When a Protected Predator Eats an Endangered Species?" *Sierra* (March–April, 2001), 32–39, 80–81.

138. Sellars, *Preserving Nature in the National Parks,* 278–80; Runte, *Yosemite,* 208–16.

139. Chris Bowman, "A Parking Garage? In Yosemite Park," *Modesto Bee,* June 18, 1991, A1, and last page, section A.

140. Yosemite National Park, "Implementing the General Management Plan at Yosemite Lodge" and "Yosemite into the 21st Century," May 1998, 3.

141. Sellars, *Preserving Nature in the National Parks,* 280–82.

142. Tom Philp, "Yosemite Plan Hits Heavy Resistance at Public Hearings," *Sacramento Bee,* February 2, 1992, B1, B9.

143. Tom Philp, "Will View from Half Dome Include a Parking Plaza?" *Sacramento Bee,* January 2, 1994, B1, B6.

144. Michael Doyle and Mark Grossi, "Yosemite Valley Garage Recommended by Study," *Sacramento Bee,* September, 1994, B1, B2.

145. Greg Campbell, "Natural Wonder at Risk," *Bakersfield Californian,* May 26, 1996, Reprinted in NewsBank NewsFile.

146. Michael McCabe, "Yosemite Closed Indefinitely," *San Francisco Chronicle,* January 9, 1997, A1, A15; Nancy Vogel, "Yosemite's Flood Damage Estimated at $178 Million," *Sacramento Bee,* February 1, 1997, A4.

147. Barbara DeLollis, "Yosemite Repairs to Aid Goals," *Sacramento Bee,* February 3, 1997, B2.

148. Hoge, "Preserving Yosemite Valley," A1, A16.

149. Frank Clifford, "Yosemite Bus Plan Receives Approval: Limited Service to Begin Next Year," *Sacramento Bee,* August 5, 1998, B4.

150. Ron DeLacy, "Yosemite Bus Project Put on Hold As Critics Assail Board," *Sacramento Bee,* October 6, 1998, B4.

151. Associated Press, "Suit Seeks to Halt Project to Widen Road at Yosemite," *Sacramento Bee,* February 20, 1999, A4.

152. Christene Hanley, "Climbers Fight Yosemite Development," *Sacramento Bee,* November 11, 1998, D1, D6.

153. Michael Doyle, "Yosemite Plans Will Be Coordinated," *Sacramento Bee,* December 7, 1998, A3; Wendy M. Clarke, "After the Flood," *National Parks,* March–April 1999, 22–25.

154. Stanley Albright, "Dear Friend of Yosemite," Yosemite National Park, December 8, 1998.

155. National Park Service, *Merced Wild and Scenic River: Draft Comprehensive Management Plan and Supplemental Impact Statement* (Yosemite, CA: National Park Service, January 2000); National Park Service, *Draft Yosemite Valley Plan: Supplemental Environmental Impact Statement* (Washington, DC: Government Printing Office, April 2000).

156. National Park Service, *Merced Wild and Scenic River,* ES-1, ES-8, chap. 2, figs. 11-10 and 11-17, chap. 2, 71–78, 100–103; National Park Service, *Draft Yosemite Valley Plan,* chap. 2, 27–28, 87–88.

157. Yosemite National Park, "Planning Update," August 2000, 2.

158. Associated Press, "Yosemite Traffic, Parking to Be Reduced," *Grass Valley Union,* November 15, 2000, A7; Vicki Lee, "Chapter Chair's Report," *Mother Lode Chapter Bonanza* 63, no. 1 (February–March 2001): 2.

159. CSERC, "Newsletter," *Central Sierra Environmental Resource Center,* Twain Harte, CA, December 2000, 1–3.

160. Knudson, "Hopes for Reform Improve," A14.

161. Nancy Vogel, "Sierra's Living Time Capsules: Giant Sequoias Offer Clues to Ancient Past," *Sacramento Bee,* May 24, 1999, A1, A10.

162. Vogel, "Sierra's Living Time Capsules," A10; Rebecca Solnit, "Among the Giants," *Sierra,* July–August 1997, 30+, reprinted in SIRS Researcher, fall 1998.

163. Solnit, "Among the Giants," 30+.

164. Hamilton, "Visions of the Range of Light," 85, 88; Solnit, "Among the Giants," 30+; Matthew Jaffe, "Big News for the Big Trees," *Sunset,* September 2000, 38.

165. Jaffe, "Big News for the Big Trees," 40. I attended the California Wilderness Conference in May of 2000. One of the panel sessions focused on the Sequoia National Monument. Activists Martin Litton and Joe Fontaine took opposing sides on the issue. Litton attacked the proposal because of the existing sale provisions, and Fontaine defended it, saying that the fight over the sales was just beginning.

166. "Bush Won't Try to Undo Clinton Monument Orders," *Washington Post,* reprinted in *Sacramento Bee,* February 21, 2001, A6; Associated Press, "Judge: Let Monument Plan Stand," *Grass Valley Union,* October 3, 2001, A3; "Bush Vows Federal Help to Protect Ecosystems," *Chicago Tribune,* reprinted in *Sacramento Bee,* June 5, 2001, A6.

167. "More Logging to Save Trees," Editorial, *San Francisco Chronicle,* January 30, 2003, A18; Carla Cloer, "Chainsaws Sharpened for Giant Sequoia National Monument," in *Wilderness Record,* spring 2003, 12–13. The draft outline for the DEIS was consulted by me and was available at http:/www.r5.fs.fed.us/giant sequoia/.

168. Elston, "Prehistory of the Western Area," 135–48.

169. Irons, ed. and comp., *Edwards' Tourists' Guide,* 15, 20–27, 33–34, 69–70, 76–77, 78–79; Claytor and Beesley, "Aspen Art and the Sheep Industry of Nevada and Adjoining Counties," 25–31; United States Department of the Interior, United States Geological Survey Map, Martis Peak, California and Nevada, SE/4Truckee15' Quadrangle N 3915—W 12000/7.5, 1955, Photo Revised 1969.

170. The most useful account of present and projected growth in the Sierra Nevada is that of Timothy Duane, *Shaping the Sierra.*

171. Ibid., xiv–xxiii, 391–413.

172. Runte, *Yosemite,* 226–27.

173. Tom Kenworthy, "Initiative to Protect Forests Readied," *Sacramento Bee,* October 8, 1999, A10; *San Francisco Chronicle,* Editorial [Clinton Roadless Initiative], *San Francisco Chronicle,* November 15, 2000, A22.

174. Associated Press, "Annual Report: Tahoe at Its Clearest since 96," *Grass Valley Union,* April 25, 2002, A3; Associated Press, "High Court Backs Government in Tahoe Land Case," *Grass Valley Union,* April 24, 2002, A1, A10.

175. Elliott-Fisk et al., "Lake Tahoe Case Study," 217–64; *Christian Science Monitor,* Editorial, "Clear on Lake Tahoe," *Christian Science Monitor,* August 4, 1997, 20.

176. An organization exists that is seriously considering the restoration of Hetch Hetchy Valley and the removal of the O'Shaughnessy Dam. It is, unsurprisingly, named Restore Hetch Hetchy. I base some of my remarks on a pamphlet I obtained from the group.

This bibliography does not contain divisions (such as manuscripts, books, and articles) on the assumption that it is most useful to general as well as scholarly readers if a simple alphabetical division of sources is used. I chose this method based on a suggestion of *The Chicago Manual of Style, 14th Edition,* that the most useful method of identifying sources for readers should be adopted, and that "sometimes division merely makes finding a given item more difficult." For scholars, the physical location of a manuscript source is given in the notes.

"An Act Authorizing a Grant to the State of California of the 'Yo-Semite Valley,' and the Land Embracing the 'Mariposa Big Tree Grove.'" June 30, 1864 (13 Stat. 325). In *America's National Park System: The Critical Documents,* ed. Lary Dilsaver. Lanham, MD: Rowman and Littlefield, 1997.

"An Act to Establish a National Park Service, and for Other Purposes." 39 Stat. 535. In *America's National Park System: The Critical Documents,* ed. Lary Dilsaver. Lanham, MD: Rowman and Littlefield, 1997.

Albright, Horace M., as told to Robert Cahn. *The Birth of the National Park Service: The Founding Years, 1913–1933.* Salt Lake City: Howe Brothers, 1985.

Albright, Horace M., and Marian A. Schenck. *The Mather Mountain Party of 1915: A Full Account of the Adventures of Stephen T. Mather and His Friends in the High Sierra of California.* Three Rivers, CA: Sequoia Natural History Association, n.d.

Albright, Stanley. "Dear Friend of Yosemite." Yosemite National Park, December 8, 1998.

Alpers, Charles N., and Michael P. Hunerlach "Mercury Contamination from Historic Gold Mining in California." USGS Fact Sheet FS-061-00, n.d.

Anable, H. S. "Journals, 1852–1854." Bancroft Library, CF-137.

Anderson, M. Kat. *Indian Fire-Based Management in the Sequoia–Mixed Conifer Forests of the Central and Southern Sierra Nevada.* Yosemite National Park: Yosemite Research Center, July 15, 1993.

Anderson, M. Kat, and Michael J. Moratto. "Native American Land-Use Practices and Ecological Impacts." In Sierra Nevada Ecosystem Project, *Final Report to Congress.* Vol. 2, *Assessments and Scientific Basis for Management Options.* Davis, CA: University of California, Centers for Water and Wildland Resources, 1996.

Associated Press. "Annual Report: Tahoe at Its Clearest since '96." *Grass Valley Union,* April 25, 2002.

———. "Bush Plan Leaves Forest Care to Timber Firms." *Grass Valley Union,* March 7, 2003.

———. "Coalition Forms to Bid on Yosemite Concessions." *Grass Valley Union,* September 20, 1990.

———. "Ecosystem Gets Mixed Review." *Grass Valley Union,* September 21, 1995.

———. "Environmentalists Want to Operate Park Concessions." *Grass Valley Union,* September 25, 1990.

———. "Forest Official: Is Sierra Plan Too Strict?" *Grass Valley Union,* March 16, 2002.

———. "Forest Service Plan Limits Sierra Logging." *Grass Valley Union,* January 13, 2001.

———. "High Court Backs Government in Tahoe Land Case." *Grass Valley Union,* April 24, 2002.

———. "Judge: Let Monument Plan Stand." *Grass Valley Union,* October 3, 2001.

———. "New Policy on Logging Considered." *Grass Valley Union,* August 20, 1996.

———. "9th Circuit Curtails Salvage Logging near Tahoe." *The Grass Valley Union,* November 9, 2002.

———. "Opponents: Compromise Forest Bill Could Ruin Wild Lands with Logging." *Grass Valley Union,* February 19, 1998.

———. "Pact May Expedite Forest." *Grass Valley Union,* October 4, 2002.

———. "Quincy's Trail-Blazing Logging Plan Clears Senate Hurdle." *Sacramento Bee,* October 23, 1997.

———. "Suit Seeks to Halt Project to Widen Road at Yosemite." *Sacramento Bee,* February 20, 1999.

———. "Timber Industry Hopes Bush Changes Policies." *Grass Valley Union,* February 21, 2001.

———. "Use Yosemite Concession Profits to Preserve Beauty." *Grass Valley Union,* May 15, 1990.

———. "U.S. Forest Service Chief Robertson Ousted." *Grass Valley Union,* October 29, 1993.

———. "Yosemite Traffic, Parking to Be Reduced." *Grass Valley Union,* November 15, 2000.

———. "Yosemite Vendor's Fee to U.S. Revealed." *Grass Valley Union,* January 20, 1990.

"At Work in the Range of Light." *Sierra,* March–April 1994.

Austin, Mary. *The Flock.* 1906. Reprint, Reno: University of Nevada Press, 2001.

———. *The Land of Little Rain.* 1903. Reprint, New York: Dover, 1996).

Auburn State Recreational Area. "From Rapids to Rituals, River Interpretive Program, August 11–13, 2000." California State Parks. File, Auburn State Recreation Area, Auburn, CA.

"Auto Use in the National Parks: Proceedings of the Conference Held at the Yosemite National Park." October 14–16, 1912. In *America's National Park System: The Critical Documents,* ed. Lary Dilsaver. Lanham, MD: Rowman and Littlefield, 1994.

Avakian, A. M. "Excerpts [from the Field Notes of George B. Sudworth] on Fire, Lumbering, Range, and Soil and Water Conditions." Berkeley, CA, USFS California Forest and Range Experiment Station, December 1930.

Ayres, R. W. *History of Timber Management in the California National Forests, 1850–1937*. Washington, DC: Forest Service, Department of Agriculture, 1958.

"A Back Country Management Plan for Sequoia and Kings Canyon National Parks." Issued 1963. In *America's National Park System: The Critical Documents*, ed. Lary M. Dilsaver. Lanham, MD: Rowman and Littlefield, 1997.

Bakker, Elna S. *An Island Called California: An Ecological Introduction to Its Natural Communities*. 2d ed. Berkeley: University of California Press, 1984.

Bancroft, Ann. "Campaign to Save Mono Lake in Final Stretch." *San Francisco Chronicle*, September 31, 1994.

Bancroft, H. H. *The History of California*. Vol. 7, *1860–1890*. San Francisco: The History Co., 1890.

Barbour, M., B. Pavlik, F. Drysdale, and S. Lindstrom. *California's Changing Landscapes*. Sacramento: California Native Plant Society, 1993.

Barker, Paul F. "An Environmental Agenda for the National Forests in California." Typescript announcement, Tahoe National Forest Archives, February 8, 1990.

Barnum, Alex. "Republicans Blast Clinton on Forest Fire Policies." *San Francisco Chronicle*, September 13, 1996.

———. "Sierra Logging Plan Goes Back to Square One; Clinton Administration Balks at Easing Limits." *San Francisco Chronicle*, August 24, 1996.

Barrett, S. A., and E. W. Gifford. "Indian Life of the Yosemite Region: Miwok Material Culture." *Bulletin of the Milwaukee Public Museum* 2, no. 4 (March 1933).

Barrows, Matthew. "Road Project Unearths Ancient Miwok Site." *Sacramento Bee*, September 6, 2001.

Barry-Meisenbach, Carmel. *Historic Mining Ditches of the Tahoe National Forest, Report # 28*. Nevada City, CA: Tahoe National Forest, 1989.

Basey, Harold E. *Sierra Nevada Textbook: A Comprehensive Reference*. 5th ed. Groveland, CA: Robin Works, 1995.

Bates, C. R., and M. J. Lee. *Tradition and Innovation: A Basket History of the Indians of the Yosemite–Mono Lake Area*. Yosemite National Park: Yosemite Association, 1990.

Bates, Jennifer. "Progress Reports." *California Indian Basket Weavers Association Newsletter* 25 (December 1998).

Baumhoff, Martin. "Environmental Background." In *Handbook of North American Indians*. Vol. 8, *California*, ed. Robert F. Heizer. Washington, DC: Smithsonian Institution, 1978.

Bayles, David, Conservation Director, Pacific Rivers Council, and Kieran Suckling, Executive Director, Center for Biological Diversity, Letter to Editor of the *High Country News*, October 8, 2001.

Beadle, J. H. *The Undeveloped West*. Philadelphia: National, 1873.

Beals, Ralph L. *Indian Occupancy, Subsistence, and Land Use Patterns in California, VI*. New York: Garland, 1974.

Beesley, David. "Beyond Gilbert: Environmental History and Hydraulic Mining in the Sierra Nevada." *Mining History Journal* 7 (2000).

————. "Beyond Gilbert: Environmental History and Hydraulic Mining in the Sierra Nevada." Abstract of Paper in *Proceedings of the American Association for the Advancement of Science, Pacific Division* 18, no. 1 (June 19, 1999).

————. "Changing Land Use Patterns and Sheep Transhumance in the Northeastern Sierra Nevada, 1870–1980." In *Forum for the Association of Arid Lands Studies,* ed. O. Templar. Lubbock: Texas Tech University, International Center for Arid and Semi-Arid Land Use Study, 1985.

————. "Communists and Vigilantes in the Northern Mines." *California History* 64, no. 2 (spring 1985).

————. "The Cornish Pump." *Nevada County Historical Society Bulletin* 33, no. 2 (April 1979).

————. "Independence Lake: A Brief Investigation of Its Uses over the Years." *Nevada County Historical Society Bulletin* 32, no. 2 (April 1978).

————. "More Than People v. Hall: Chinese Immigrants and American Law in a Sierra Nevada County, 1850–1920." *Locus* 3, no. 2 (spring 1991).

————. "The Opening of the Sierra Nevada and the Beginnings of Conservation in California, 1827–1900." *California History* 75, no. 4 (winter 1996–97).

————. "Reconstructing the Landscape: An Environmental History, 1820–1960." *Sierra Nevada Ecosystem Project, Final Report to Congress.* Vol. 2, *Assessments and Scientific Basis for Management Options.* Davis: University of California. Centers for Water and Wildland Resources, 1996.

————. "Sierra in Peril: Ecosystem Politics and Sierra Nevada Environmental History." *Wild Duck Review* 2, no. 6 (December 1996).

————. "Sierra Nevada National Forests: An Environmental History." Chap. 2 in Forest Service Employees for Environmental Ethics, *Restoring Our Forest Legacy: Blueprint for Sierra Nevada National Forests.* Eugene, OR: FSEEE, 2000.

————. "Whistle Punks and Steam Donkeys: Logging in Nevada County and the Northern Sierra during the Age of Animal and Steam Power." *Nevada County Historical Society Bulletin* 38, no. 4 (October 1984).

Bergen, Geri. "Letter of Intent Accompanying *Tahoe National Forest Land and Management Plan.*" Nevada City, CA: USDA FS TNF, 1990.

Bethel, A. C. W. "The Golden Skein: California's Gold-Rush Transportation Network." In *A Golden State: Mining and Economic Development in Gold Rush California,* ed. James J. Rawls and Richard J. Orsi. San Francisco: University of California Press and California Historical Society, 1998–99.

Bigelow, Richard L. P. "History of Forest Supervisor R. L. P. Bigelow, Taken from His Diary from May 23, 1902 to April 30, 1936." Typescript, Tahoe National Forest, Nevada City, CA.

Biswell, Harold. *Prescribed Burning in California Wildlands Vegetation Management.* Berkeley: University of California Press, 1989.

Blackburn, Thomas C., and Kat Anderson, eds. *Before the Wilderness: Environmental Management by Native Californians.* Menlo Park, CA: Ballena Press, 1993.

Blakeslee, Sandra. "Volcano in California Springs Unusual Carbon Dioxide Leak." *New York Times,* July 23, 1996.

Blodgett, Peter J. "Visiting 'The Realm of Wonder': Yosemite and the Business of Tourism, 1855–1916." In *Yosemite and Sequoia: A Century of California National Parks,* ed. Richard J. Orsi, Alfred Runte, and Marlene Smith-Baranzini. Berkeley: University of California Press and the California Historical Society, 1990.

Blumenthal, Les. "Bush Toppling Forest Safeguards, Critics Say." *Sacramento Bee,* December 30, 2002.

Booth, Joseph W. "Diary, 1852–1853, Northern Mines." Bancroft Library, CF-87.

Borthwick, J. D. *Three Years in California.* 1857. Reprint, Oakland, CA: Biobooks, 1948.

Bowles, Jennifer. "Ski Town's Wish." *Sacramento Bee,* November 26, 1997.

Bowles, Samuel. *Across the Continent: A Summer Journey to the Rocky Mountains, the Mormons, and the Pacific States with Speaker Colfax.* Springfield, MA: Bowles, 1866.

Bowman, Chris. "A Parking Garage? In Yosemite Park." *Modesto Bee,* June 18, 1991.

———. "Conference on Range's Future Opens Today." *Sacramento Bee,* November 18, 1991.

———. "No One Tracked the Cost in Environmental Damage." *Sacramento Bee,* January 18, 1998.

———. "Washoe Indians Take Lead in Mine Cleanup." *Sacramento Bee,* June 7, 2000.

"Boxer Caves: Switch on Logging Bill a Political Gesture." *Sacramento Bee,* December 19, 1997, Internet Source, section B, Editorial, no page number.

Boyce, Mark, and Alan Haney, eds. *Ecosystem Management: Applications for Sustainable Forest and Wildlife Resources.* New Haven: Yale University Press, 1997.

Brace, Charles L. *The New West; or, California in 1876–78.* New York: G. P. Putnam and Son, 1869.

Brechin, Gray. *Imperial San Francisco: Urban Power and Earthly Ruin.* Berkeley: University of California Press, 1999.

Breen, Courtney. "Forest Colors Hold Darker Meaning as Sierra Drought Enters Fourth Year." *Reno Gazette-Journal,* July 18, 1990, no page number.

Brewer, William H. *Such a Landscape: A Narrative of the 1864 California Geological Survey of the Sequoia and Kings Canyon from the Field Notes, Letters, and Reports of William Brewer.* Yosemite National Park: Yosemite Association, 1989.

———. *Up and Down California in 1860–1864: The Journal of William H. Brewer.* Ed. F. P. Farquhar. Berkeley: University of California Press, 1966.

Britton, John A. "Editorial." In *Pacific Service Magazine* 6 (November 1913).

Brown, M. R., and C. M. Elling. *An Historical Overview of Redwood Logging in the Hume Ranger District, Sequoia National Forest.* Porterville, CA: U.S. Forest Service, 1981.

Browne, J. Ross. *Crusoe's Island: A Ramble in the Footsteps of Alexander Selkirk, with Sketches of Adventure in California and Washoe.* New York: Harper and Brothers, 1872.

Bunnell, Lafayette H. *Discovery of the Yosemite and the Indian War of 1851 Which Led to That Event.* 1880. Reprint, Yosemite Park, CA: Yosemite Association, 1990.

"Bush Vows Federal Help to Protect Ecosystems." *Chicago Tribune,* reprinted in *Sacramento Bee,* June 5, 2001.

"Bush Won't Try to Undo Clinton Monument Orders." *Washington Post,* reprinted in *Sacramento Bee,* February 21, 2001.

Cain, Stanley. "Ecological Islands as Natural Laboratories." In *America's National Park System: The Critical Documents,* ed. Lary M. Dilsaver. Lanham, MD: Rowman and Littlefield, 1997.

California Biodiversity Council. "Interagency Team Studying Mercury Contamination in California Watersheds." *California Biodiversity News* 7, no. 2 (fall/winter 2000).

California Department of Fish and Game. *Report to the Fish and Game Commission: A Status Review of the Spring-Run Chinook Salmon in the Sacramento River Drainage.* Sacramento: Resources Agency, State of California, June 1998.

California State Board of Forestry. *First Biennial Report of the California State Board of Forestry for the Years 1886–1887.* Sacramento: State Office, 1887.

———. *Second Biennial Report of the California State Board of Forestry for the Years 1887–1888.* Sacramento: State Office, 1888.

———. *Third Biennial Report of the California State Board of Forestry for the Years 1889–1890.* Sacramento: State Office, 1890.

California State Lands Commission. *California's Rivers: A Public Trust Report.* Sacramento: California State Lands Commission, 1993.

"California National Parks Chronology." In *Yosemite and Sequoia: A Century of California National Parks,* ed. Richard J. Orsi, Alfred Runte, and Marlene Smith-Baranzini. Berkeley: University of California Press and the California Historical Society, 1990, 1993.

California Tahoe Conservancy. *Progress Report.* Sacramento: California Tahoe Conservancy, n.d.

"California Volcano Starts to Stir." *Science News,* December 20, 1997.

Campbell, Greg. "Natural Wonder at Risk." *Bakersfield Californian,* May 26, 1996, reprinted in NewsBank NewsFile.

Campbell, Kate. "Bush Administration Proposes Workable Sierra Forest Plan." *AG Alert: The Weekly Newspaper for California Agriculture,* March 12, 2003.

Carle, David. *Burning Questions: America's Fight with Nature's Fires.* Westport, CT: Praeger, 2002.

Carnahan, S. W. "Three Letters Sent to John Ramage, March 17–September 13, 1849." California Historical Society Library, MS 325.

Carriger, Nicholas. "Journal of an Orrigon Trip and Overland Journey to California, 1846." September 9–26, 1846, Bancroft Library, CF-III.

Castillo, Edward. "The Impact of Euro-American Exploration and Settlement." In *Handbook of North American Indians.* Vol. 8, *California,* ed. Robert F. Heizer. Washington, DC: Smithsonian Institution, 1978.

———. "Petition to Congress on Behalf of the Yosemite Indians." *Journal of California Archeology* 5, no. 2 (winter 1978).

cserc. "Newsletter." *Central Sierra Environmental Resource Center,* Twain Harte, CA, December 2000.

Chalifant, W. A. *The Story of Inyo.* Rev. ed. Bishop, CA: Pinyon Book Store, 1933.

Chartkoff, Joseph L., and Kerry Kona Chartkoff. *The Archaeology of California.* Stanford, CA: Stanford University Press, 1984.

Cherub, Sandra. "Death of Tahoe's Forests Has Roots in Logging 150 Years Ago, Official Says." *Sacramento Bee,* September 22, 1994.

Chittenden, H. M. *Report on the Water Supply System of the Spring Valley Water Company, San Francisco, California.* N.p.: n.p., 1912.

Christenson, Jon. "At Tahoe Forum, a Tribe Wins a Deal." *High Country News,* August 18, 1997.

Christian Science Monitor. Editorial, "Clear on Lake Tahoe." *Christian Science Monitor,* August 4, 1997.

Clar, C. Raymond. *California Government and Forestry from Spanish Days until the Creation of the Department of Natural Resources in 1927.* Sacramento: Division of Forestry, Department of Natural Resources, State of California, 1959 .

Clarke, Wendy M. "After the Flood." *National Parks,* March/April, 1999 .

Claren, Rebecca. "No Game Plan for the Public Lands." *High Country News,* February 4, 2002.

Clawson, Marion, and Winston Harrington. "The Growing Role of Outdoor Recreation." In *America's Renewable Resources: Historical Trends and Current Challenges,* ed. K. D. Frederick and R. A. Sedjo. Washington, DC: Resources for the Future, 1991.

Claytor, Michael, and David Beesley; "Aspen Art and the Sheep Industry of Nevada and Adjoining Counties." *Nevada County Historical Society Bulletin* 33, no. 4 (October 1979).

Clements, Kendrick A. "Engineers and Conservationists in the Progressive Era." *California History* 58, no. 4 (winter 1979/80).

Clifford, Frank. "Yosemite Bus Plan Receives Approval: Limited Service to Begin Next Year." *Sacramento Bee,* August 5, 1998.

Cloer, Carla. "Chainsaws Sharpened for Giant Sequoia National Monument." *Wilderness Record,* spring 2003.

Cohen, Michael P. *The History of the Sierra Club, 1892–1970.* San Francisco: Sierra Club Books, 1988.

———. *The Pathless Way: John Muir and American Wilderness.* Madison: University of Wisconsin Press, 1984.

Coile, Zachary. "New Rules May Clear Way for Logging." *San Francisco Chronicle,* November 27, 2002.

Colburn, Cristine H. "Forest Policy and the Quincy Library Group." In *Finding Common Ground: Governance and Natural Resources in the American West.* New Haven: Yale University Press, 2002.

Cole, Zachary. "White House Plan Doubles Sierra Logging." *San Francisco Chronicle,* state edition, March 7, 2003.

Coleman, Charles M. *P.G. and E. of California: The Centennial Story of Pacific Gas and Electric Company, 1852–1952*. New York: McGraw-Hill, 1952.

Conners, Pamela A. "Influence of the Forest Service on Water Development Patterns in the West." In *The Origins of the National Forests*, ed. Harold K. Steen. Durham, NC: Forest History Society, 1992.

———. "West Side Lumber Company Contextual History." Typescript, Stanislaus National Forest Archives, Sonora, CA, 1990.

Cook, Sherburne F. *The Conflict between the California Indian and White Civilization*. Berkeley and Los Angeles: University of California Press, 1976.

———. "Historical Demography." In *Handbook of North American Indians*. Vol. 8, *California*, ed. Robert F. Heizer. Washington, DC: Smithsonian Institution, 1978.

Cortner, Hanna, and Margaret Moote. *The Politics of Ecosystem Management*. Washington, DC: Island Press, 1999.

Cosad, David. "Diary." California Historical Society Library, MS 453, July 16–23, 1849.

"Coyote and Falcon Create People." In *The Way We Lived: California Indian Reminiscences, Stories, and Song*, ed. Malcolm Margolin. Berkeley: Heyday, 1981.

"Coyote Steals Fire." *In The Way We Lived: California Indian Reminiscences, Stories, and Song*, ed. Malcolm Margolin. Berkeley: Heyday, 1981.

Curtis, Jennifer A. "A Sediment Budget of Hydraulic Gold Mining Sediment, Steephollow Creek Basin, California, 1853–1997." Master's thesis, Humboldt State University, 1999.

Daly, Matthew. "Bush team to rethink key environmental laws." *Sacramento Bee*, August 30, 2002.

Dana, S. T., and M. Krueger. *California Lands: Ownership, Use, and Management*. Washington, DC: American Forestry Association, 1958.

Dasmann, Raymond F. *California's Changing Environment*. Reno: Materials for Today's Learning, 1988.

———. *The Destruction of California*. Pbk. New York: Collier, 1966.

———. "Environmental Changes before and after the Gold Rush." In *A Golden State: Mining and Economic Development in Gold Rush California*, ed. James J. Rawls and Richard J. Orsi. San Francisco: University of California Press and California Historical Society, 1998–99.

Davidson, H. S. "Report of the State Engineer." In *Second Biennial Report of the California State Board of Forestry for the Years 1887–1888*. Sacramento: State Office, 1888.

Davies, J. Clarence. *The Politics of Pollution*. New York: Pegasus, 1970.

Dawson, K. J., and E. S. Greco. *Special Management Area: Visual Resources Management Study for the Sequoia National Park Prescribed Fire Management Program*. Davis, CA: Department of Environmental Design, December 1987.

D'Azevedo, Warren L. "Washoe." In *Handbook of North American Indians*. Vol. 11, *Great Basin*, ed. Warren L. D'Azevedo. Washington, DC: Smithsonian Institution, 1986.

Deane, Dorothy. *Sierra Railway*. Berkeley: Howell-North, 1960.

DeDecker, Mary. "Owens Valley, Then and Now." In *Mountains to Desert: Selected Inyo Readings*. Independence, CA: Friends of the Eastern California Museum, 1988.

Defarrari, Carlo. "North District Ecosystem Management Analysis Ares, Stanislaus National Forest, Sonora California: Historic Overview." Typescript, Stanislaus National Forest Archive, 1995.

DeLacy, Ron. "Yosemite Bus Project Put on Hold as Critics Assail Board." *Sacramento Bee,* October 6, 1998.

Delavan, James. *Notes on California and the Placers; How to Get There, and What to Do Afterwards.* 1850. Oakland, CA: Biobooks, 1956.

DeLollis, Barbara. "Yosemite Repairs to Aid Goals." *Sacramento Bee,* February 3, 1997.

DeLuca, Kevin, and Anne Demo. "Imagining Nature and Erasing Class and Race: Carleton Watkins, John Muir, and the Construction of Wilderness." *Environmental History* 6, no. 4 (October 2001).

Demars, Stanford E. *The Tourist in Yosemite, 1855–1985.* Salt Lake City: University of Utah Press, 1991.

De Quille, Dan. *A History of the Comstock Silver Lode and Mines; Nevada and the Great Basin; Lake Tahoe and the High Sierras.* 1889. New York: Promontory Press, 1974.

DeVoto, Bernard. "Let's Close the National Parks." In *America's National Park System: The Critical Documents,* ed. Lary M. Dilsaver. Lanham, MD: Rowman and Littlefield, 1997.

Dilsaver, Lary M. "After the Gold Rush." *Geographical Review* 75, no. 1 (January 1985).

———. "The Development of Agriculture in a Gold Rush Region." *Association of Pacific Coast Geographers Yearbook* 48 (1986).

———. "The Early Years, 1864–1918." In *America's National Park System: The Critical Documents,* ed. Lary M. Dilsaver. Lanham, MD: Rowman and Littlefield, 1997.

———. "From Boom to Bust: Post–Gold Rush Patterns of Adjustment to a California Mining Region, Vol. 1." PH.D. diss., Louisiana State University, 1992.

———. "Resource Conflict in the High Sierra." In *The Mountainous West: Explorations in Historical Geography,* ed. William Wyckoff and Lary M. Dilsaver. Lincoln: University of Nebraska Press, 1995.

Dilsaver, Lary, and Douglas Strong. "Sequoia and Kings Canyon National Parks: One Hundred Years of Preservation and Resource Management." *California History* 69, no. 2 (summer 1990).

Dilsaver, Lary M., and William C. Tweed. *Challenge of the Big Trees: A Resource History of Sequoia and Kings Canyon National Parks.* Three Rivers, CA: Sequoia Natural History Association, 1990.

"Disaster Strikes the Tahoe National Forest." *Sierra Uplift,* Sierra Nevada Group, Sierra Club (September–October 1990).

Divine, Robert. "Management and the Uncertainty Principle." *Wilderness* 58, no. 207 (winter 1994).

Dolan, Carrie. "Golden Valley: MCA's Yosemite Unit Pays Little, Gains a Lot Running Concessions." *Wall Street Journal,* March 27, 1990.

Douglass, William A., and Jon Bilbao. *Amerikanuak: Basques in the New World.* Reno: University of Nevada Press, 1975.

Downs, James F. *Two Worlds of the Washoe: An Indian Tribe of California and Nevada.* New York: Holt, Rinehart, and Winston, 1966.

Doyle, Michael. "Ag Secretary Recuses Self." *Sacramento Bee,* February 17, 2001.

———. "Disputed Timber Proposal Shelved." *Sacramento Bee,* August 24, 1996.

———. "Yosemite Plans Will Be Coordinated." *Sacramento Bee,* December 7, 1998.

Doyle, Michael, and Mark Grossi. "Yosemite Valley Garage Recommended by Study." *Sacramento Bee,* September, 1994.

Drury, Aubrey. "The Livermore Family: Pioneers in California." Typescript, Bancroft Library, C-D-5096.

Duane, Timothy P. "Community Participation in Ecosystem Management." *Ecology Law Quarterly* 24, no. 4 (1997).

———. "Human Settlement, 1850–2040." *Sierra Nevada Ecosystem Project, Final Report to Congress.* Vol. 2. *Assessments and Scientific Basis for Management Options.* Davis, CA: University of California, Centers for Water and Wildlands Resources, 1996.

———. "Managing the Sierra." *California Policy Issues* 8 (January 1993).

———. "Recreation in the Sierra." *Sierra Nevada Ecosystem Project, Final Report to Congress.* Davis, CA: University of California, Centers for Water and Wildlands Resources, 1996.

———. *Shaping the Sierra: Nature, Culture, and Conflict in the Changing West.* Berkeley: University of California Press, 1999.

Dudley, William Russell. "Forest Reservations: With a Report on the Sierra Reservation, California." *Sierra Club Bulletin* 1, no. 7 (January 1896). San Francisco: Sierra Club, 1950.

Dunlap, Thomas R. *Saving America's Wildlife: Ecology and the American Mind, 1850–1890.* Princeton: Princeton University Press, 1988.

Eaton, Herbert. *The Overland Trail to California in 1852.* New York: G. P. Putnam's Sons, 1974.

Echeverria, Jeronima. "Basque 'Tramp Herders' on Forbidden Ground: Early Grazing Controversies in California's National Reserves." *Locus* 4, no. 1 (fall 1991).

Egan, Ferol. *Frémont: Explorer for a Restless Nation.* Reno: University of Nevada Press, 1984.

Elder, Jane. "The Big Picture." *Sierra,* March–April 1994.

Elliott-Fisk, D., et al. "Lake Tahoe Case Study." In *Sierra Nevada Ecosystem Project, Final Report to Congress, Addendum.* Davis: University of California, Centers for Water and Wildlands Resources, 1997.

Englelenner, John. "Crowds Strain Wilderness Area near Casinos." *Sacramento Bee,* August 15, 1992.

Elsasser, Albert B. "Development of Regional Prehistoric Cultures." In *Handbook of North American Indians*. Vol. 8, *California,* ed. Robert F. Heizer. Washington, DC: Smithsonian Institution, 1978.

Elston, Robert. "Prehistory of the Western Area." In *Handbook of North American Indians*. Vol. 11, *Great Basin,* ed. Warren L. D'Azevedo. Washington, DC: Smithsonian Institution, 1986.

Engbeck, J. H., Jr. *State Parks of California from 1864 to the Present.* Portland, OR: Graphic Arts, 1980.

Everhart, William. *The National Park Service.* Boulder, CO: Westview Press, 1983.

Fabricant, Geraldine. "MCA Expected to OK Buy-out from Matsushita." *Sacramento Bee,* November 25, 1990.

Fairclough, Donald. "An Administrative History of Squaw Valley, 1949–1971." M.A. thesis, Sacramento State College, 1971.

———. "A History of Modern Skiing in the Tahoe National Forest." Unpublished typescript in possession of author, May 1970.

Farquhar, Francis. *History of the Sierra Nevada.* Berkeley: University of California Press, 1965.

Farris, Glenn. "Quality Food: The Quest for Pine Nuts in Northern California." In *Before the Wilderness: Environmental Management by Native Californians,* ed. Thomas C. Blackburn and Kat Anderson. Menlo Park, CA: Ballena Press, 1993.

"The Fate of Our Forests." Tabloid newspaper prepared by Sierra Nevada Group, Sierra Club, 1978, in collection of author.

Fernow, Bernhard E. *Report upon the Forestry Investigations of the U.S. Department of Agriculture, 1877–1898.* House of Representatives, 55th Cong., 3d sess., Doc. 181. Washington, DC: Government Printing Office, 1899.

"Fifty Year Plan Endangers Stanislaus National Forest." *Sierra Bonanza,* Mother Lode Chapter of the Sierra Club, 48, no. 1 (February 1986).

"Final Mineral King EIS Indicated Severe Damage." *Sierra Club Bulletin,* May 1976.

"Final Mineral King EIS Released by Forest Service." *Sierra Club Bulletin,* April 1976.

"Fire Prevention Plan for the National Parks, 10th National Park Conference, February 15–21, 1928." In *America's National Park System: The Critical Documents,* ed. Lary Dilsaver. Lanham, MD: Rowman and Littlefield, 1994.

"F.S. Proposes 60 Percent Cut in Timber Harvest to Save Owl." *Mountain Messenger,* February 9, 1995.

Flippen, John B. "The Nixon Administration, Timber, and the Call of the Wild." *Environmental History Review* 19, no. 2 (summer 1995).

Flores, Dan. *The Natural West: Environmental History in the Great Plains and Rocky Mountains.* Norman: University of Oklahoma Press, 2001.

Forbes, Jack D. *Native Americans of California and Nevada: A Handbook.* Healdsburg, CA: Naturegraph Press, 1969.

Forest Service Employees for Environmental Ethics. *Restoring Our Forest Legacy: Blueprint for Sierra Nevada National Forests.* Eugene, OR: FSEEE, 2000.

Fowler, Catherine S., and Sven Liljeblad. "Northern Paiute." In *Handbook of North American Indians*. Vol. 11, *Great Basin,* ed. Warren L. D'Azevedo. Washington, DC: Smithsonian Institution, 1986.

Fox, Stephen. *John Muir and His Legacy: The American Conservation Movement.* Boston: Little, Brown, 1981.

Franklin, Jerry. "Ecosystem Management: An Overview." In *Ecosystem Management: Applications for Sustainable Forest and Wildlife Resources,* ed. Mark Boyce and Alan Haney. New Haven: Yale University Press, 1997.

Freeman, John R. *On the Proposed Use of a Portion of the Hetch Hetchy, Eleanor, and Cherry Valleys within and near to the Boundaries of the Stanislaus U.S. Forest Reserve and the Yosemite National Park as Reservoirs for Impounding Tuolumne River Flood Waters.* San Francisco: Board of Supervisors and Rincon Publishing, 1912.

Freeman, Richard. "The EcoFactory: The United States Forest Service and the Political Construction of Ecosystem Management." *Environmental History* 7, no. 4 (October 2002).

Friends of the River. "National Wild and Scenic Rivers in California: A Status Report." Pamphlet, Sacramento, 1999.

Frémont, John Charles. *Report of the Exploring Expedition to the Rocky Mountains in the Year 1842, and to Oregon and North California in the Years 1843–44.* Ann Arbor: University Microfilms, 1966.

Gallardo, Charles. "22 Appeals Filed to Tahoe Management Plan." *Grass Valley Union,* October 25, 1990.

Gannett, Henry. "Summary of Forest Work in 1899–1900." In *Twenty-First Annual Report of the United States Geological Survey to the Secretary of the Interior, 1899–1900, Part V—Forest Reserves.* Washington, DC: Government Printing Office, 1900.

Gates, Paul W. *History of Public Land Law Development.* Washington, DC: Government Printing Office, 1968.

Geiger, Vincent, and Wakeman Bryarly. *Trail to California: The Overland Journal of Vincent Geiger and Wakeman Bryarly.* Ed. David Potter. New Haven: Yale University Press, 1945.

Gibbens, Robert P., and Harold F. Heady. *The Influence of Modern Man on the Vegetation of Yosemite Valley.* Berkeley: U.C. Division of Agricultural Sciences, 1964.

Gilbert, G. K. *Hydraulic-Mining Debris in the Sierra Nevada.* Washington, DC: Government Printing Office, 1917.

Gilliam, Harold. "The Next Yosemite." *San Francisco Chronicle,* December 9, 1990.

Gilmer, Maureen. *California Wildfire Landscaping.* Dallas: Taylor, 1994.

Gobbert, Theodore A. "The Yosemite Valley Commission: The Development of Park Management Policies, 1864–1905." M.A. thesis, California State College, Hayward, 1972.

Goetzmann, William H. *Army Exploration in the American West, 1803–1863.* Lincoln: University of Nebraska Press, 1979.

Gorbet, Lorena. "Maidu Cultural and Group Action Plan for the Living Village and Stewardship Area." March 1998, typescript, no pagination.

Graydon, Charles. *Trail of the First Wagons over the Sierra Nevada.* St. Louis: Patrice Press, 1986.

Greeley, Horace. *An Overland Journey from New York to San Francisco in the Summer of 1859.* New York: H. H. Bancroft, 1860.'

Greenwood, Grace [Sara Jane Lippincott]. *New Life in New Lands: Notes of Travel.* New York: J. B. Ford, 1873.

Greenwood, Greg. "Why the Forest Service Proposal for the Sierra Nevada Is Wrong for California: Greenwood on Sierra Framework." Typescript. State of California Resources Agency. Sacramento.

Grinnell, Joseph, and Tracy Irwin Storer. *Animal Life in the Yosemite.* Berkeley: University of California Press, 1924.

Gruell, George E. *Fire in Sierra Nevada Forests: A Photographic Interpretation of Ecological Change since 1849.* Missoula, MT: Mountain Press, 2001.

Gudde, E. G. *California Gold Camps.* Berkeley: University of California Press, 1975.

Gutiérrez, Ramón, and Richard J. Orsi, eds. *Contested Eden: California before the Gold Rush.* San Francisco: University of California Press and the California Historical Society, 1998.

Hagwood, Joseph J. *The California Debris Commission: A History of the Hydraulic Mining Industry in the Western Sierra Nevada . . .* Sacramento: U.S. Army Corps of Engineers, 1981.

Hall, William H. "Nine Letters to Governor Pardee on the Drainage and Debris Work of 1878–1881." MS 913-10, California Historical Society Library.

Hamilton, Joan. "Visions of the Range of Light." *Sierra* (May–June 1992).

Hampton, H. Duane. *How the U.S. Cavalry Saved Our National Parks.* Bloomington: Indiana University Press, 1971.

Hanley, Christene. "Climbers Fight Yosemite Development." *Sacramento Bee,* November 11, 1998.

Harper, John L. *Mineral King: Public Concern with Government Policy.* Arcata, CA: Pacifica, 1982.

Hart, John. *Storm over Mono: The Mono Lake Battle and the California Water Future.* Berkeley: University of California Press, 1996.

Harvey, H. T., R. J. Hartesveldt, and J. T. Stanley. *Wilderness Impact Study Report: An Interim Report of the Sierra Club Outing Committee on the Effects of Human Recreation Activities on Wilderness Ecosystems.* San Francisco: Sierra Club Outing Committee, 1972.

Hays, Samuel P. *Conservation and the Gospel of Efficiency: The Progressive Conservation Movement, 1890–1920.* New York: Athenaeum Press, 1969.

———. *Environmental Politics since 1945.* Pittsburgh: University of Pittsburgh Press, 2000.

Hazelhurst, S., F. Magary, and K. Hawk, eds. *Sustaining Ecosystems: A Conceptual Framework.* San Francisco: USDA, Forest Service, Pacific Southwest Region, April 1995.

Heizer, Robert F. *The Destruction of California Indians.* Lincoln: University of Nebraska Press, 1974.

———. "Natural Forces and Native World View." In *Handbook of North American Indians*. Vol. 8, *California*, ed. Robert F. Heizer. Washington, DC: Smithsonian Institution, 1978.

Heizer, Robert, and Alan Almquist. *The Other Californians: Prejudice and Discrimination under Spain and the United States to 1820*. Berkeley: University of California Press, 1971.

Heizer, Robert F., and Albert B. Elsasser. *The Natural World of the California Indians*. Berkeley: University of California Press, 1980.

Helms, John A., and John C. Tappeiner. "Silviculture in the Sierra." In *Sierra Nevada Ecosystem Project, Final Report to Congress*. Vol. 2, *Assessments and Scientific Basis for Management Options*. Davis, CA: University of California, Centers for Water and Wildlands Resources, 1996.

Hertsgard, Mark. "Bush's Other War: Environment in Cross Hairs." *Sacramento Bee*, Forum, February 16, 2003.

Higby, William. "Correspondence." Bancroft Library, C-B 627, Dec. 10, 1854.

Hill, Mary. *Geology of the Sierra Nevada*. Berkeley: University of California Press, 1975.

Hinds, Norman. *Evolution of the California Landscape*. San Francisco: State of California, Division of Mines, Department of Natural Resources, December 1952.

Robert V. Hine. *California Utopianism: Contemplations of Eden*. San Francisco: Boyd and Fraser, 1981.

Hinkle, George, and Bliss Hinkle. *Sierra Nevada Lakes*. Indianapolis: Bobbs-Merrill, 1949

Hirt, Paul. *A Conspiracy of Optimism: Management of the National Forests since World War Two*. Lincoln: University of Nebraska Press, 1994.

Hogan, Elizabeth, ed. *Rivers of the West*. Menlo Park, CA: Lane, 1974.

Hoge, Patrick. "Preserving Yosemite Valley: Historic Plan to Eliminate Most Vehicles Is Unveiled." *Sacramento Bee*, November 6, 1997.

Holliday, J. S. *Rush for Riches: Gold Fever and the Making of California*. Berkeley: University of California Press, 1999.

———. *The World Rushed In: The California Gold Rush Experience*. New York: Simon and Schuster, 1981.

Houghton, Samuel G. *A Trace of Desert Waters: The Great Basin Story*. Salt Lake City: Howe Brothers, 1986.

hr 858, 105th Cong., 1st sess.

Howard, Thomas F. *Sierra Crossing: First Roads to California*. Berkeley: University of California Press, 1998.

Hulse, James W. "The California-Nevada Boundary: History of a Conflict." Part 1. *Nevada Historical Society* 23, no. 2 (summer 1980).

———. *The Silver State: Nevada's Heritage Reinterpreted*. 2d ed. Reno: University of Nevada Press, 1998.

Hundley, Norris, Jr. *The Great Thirst: Californians and Water, 1770s–1990s*. Berkeley: University of California Press, 1992.

———. *The Great Thirst: Californians and Water: A History.* Rev. ed. Berkeley: University of California Press, 2001.

Hurtado, Albert. *Indian Survival on the California Frontier.* New Haven: Yale University Press, 1988.

Hutchings, James M. *In the Heart of the Sierras: The Yo Semite Valley. . . .* Oakland: Pacific Press, 1886.

———. *Scenes of Wonder and Curiosity in California.* San Francisco: Hutchings and Rosenfield, 1861.

———. *Scenes of Wonder and Curiosity, from Hutchings' California Magazine, 1856–1861.* Ed. R. R. Olmstead. Berkeley: Howell-North, 1962.

Hutchinson, W. H. *California Heritage: A History of Northern California Lumbering.* Santa Cruz, CA: Forest History Society, 1974.

Huth, Hans. *Nature and the American: Three Centuries of Changing Attitudes.* Berkeley: University of California Press, 1957.

———. *Yosemite: The Story of an Idea.* 1948. Reprint, Yosemite, CA: Yosemite Natural History Association.

Hyde, Anne F. "From Stage Coach to Packard Twin Six: Yosemite and the Changing Face of Tourism, 1880–1930." In *Yosemite and Sequoia: A Century of California National Parks,* ed. Richard J. Orsi, Alfred Runte, and Marlene Smith-Baranzini. Berkeley: University of California Press and California Historical Society, 1993.

Irons, Chas. D., ed. and comp. *W. F. Edwards' Tourists' Guide and Directory of the Truckee Basin.* Truckee, CA: "Republican" Job Print, 1883.

Ise, John. *United States Forest Policy.* New Haven: Yale University Press, 1920.

Jackson, Donald, and Mary Lee Spence, eds. *The Expeditions of John Charles Frémont.* Vol. 1. *Travels from 1838 to 1844.* Urbana: University of Illinois Press, 1970.

Jackson, Louise. *Beulah: A Biography of Mineral King Valley.* Tucson: Westernlore Press, 1988.

Jackson, Robert. *Indian Population Decline: The Missions of Northwestern New Spain.* Albuquerque: University of New Mexico Press, 1994.

Jackson, W. T., R. Herbert, and S. Wee. *History of the Tahoe National Forest.* Davis, CA: Jackson Research Projects and Tahoe National Forest, 1982.

Jacobs, Diana, Ed Chatfield, Lisa Lloyd, and Dorothy Walker. *California Rivers: A Public Trust Report.* Sacramento: California State Lands Commission, 1993.

Jaffe, Matthew. "Big News for the Big Trees." *Sunset,* September 2000.

James, George W. *The Lake of the Sky: Lake Tahoe, in the High Sierras of California and Nevada . . .* New York: J. F. Tapley, 1915.

James, John. "Lake Tahoe and the Sierra Nevada." In *The Mountainous West: Explorations in Historical Geography,* ed. William Wyckoff and Lary Dilsaver. Lincoln: University of Nebraska Press, 1995.

Jenkins, Matt. "Forest Planning Gets a Facelift: Critics Say the New Look Will Turn National Forests into Lawsuit Magnets." *High Country News,* December 23, 2002.

Johnston, James. "The Effects of Humans on the Sierra Nevada Mixed Conifer Forest." Typescript, Lassen National Forest, n.d.

Johnston, Verna R. *Sierra Nevada*. Boston: Houghton Mifflin, 1970.

————. *Sierra Nevada: The Naturalist's Companion*. Berkeley: University of California Press, 1998.

Jones, Holway R. *John Muir and the Sierra Club: The Battle for Yosemite*. San Francisco: Sierra Club, 1965.

Jung, Maureen. "Capitalism Comes to the Diggings." In *A Golden State: Mining and Economic Development in Gold Rush California*, ed. James J. Rawls and Richard J. Orsi. San Francisco: University of California Press and California Historical Society, 1998–99.

Kahrl, William L. *Water and Power*. Berkeley: University of California Press, 1982.

Kahrl, William L., ed. *The California Water Atlas*. Sacramento: Department of Water Resources, 1979.

Karpa, Grace. "Mercury Rises over Logging." *Sacramento Bee*, November 21, 1999, Neighbors section, 1, 5.

Kay, Jane. "'Roadless Rule' Upheld for National Forests: Court's Decision Allows Ban to Begin Immediately." *San Francisco Chronicle*, December 14, 2002.

Keller, R. H., and M. F. Turek. *American Indians and National Parks*. Tucson: University of Arizona Press, 1998.

Kelley, Robert L. *Battling the Inland Sea: Floods, Public Policy, and the Sacramento Valley*. Berkeley: University of California Press, 1989.

————. *Gold vs. Grain: The Hydraulic Mining Controversy in California's Central Valley*. Glendale, CA: Arthur H. Clark, 1959.

Kenworthy, Tom. "Initiative to Protect Forests Readied." *Sacramento Bee*, October 8, 1999.

King, Clarence. *Mountaineering in the Kings River Country of Sequoia and the Kings Canyon National Parks, 1864*. Silverthorne, CO: Vista Books, 1996.

King, Thomas Starr. *A Vacation among the Sierras: Yosemite in 1860*. San Francisco: Book Club of California, 1962.

Kinney, Abbott. "Our Forests." *Overland Monthly* 7 (2nd series), no. 48 (December 1886).

Kinney, William. "Conditions of Rangelands before 1905." *Sierra Nevada Ecosystem Project, Final Report to Congress*. Vol. 2. *Assessments and Scientific Basis for Management Options*. Davis, CA: University of California, Centers for Water and Wildland Resources, 1996.

Knowles, Constance Darrow. "A History of Lumbering in the Truckee Basin from 1856 to 1936." Office Report, WPA Project # 9512373 for Forest Survey Division, California Forest and Range Experiment Station, Forestry Library, University of California, Berkeley.

————. "Vegetation Burning by California Indians As Shown in Early Records." Typescript, Prepared for U.S. Forest Service in the 1930s under Contract to California Forest and Range Information Station, Copy from Forestry Library, University of California, Berkeley.

Knudson, Tom. "Flooded Lands Choking Streams." *Sacramento Bee*, June 12, 1991.

————. "Forest Draft Unveiled for Sierra Land." *Sacramento Bee,* May 3, 2000.

————. "Furor Grows as Drought, Fires Boost Salvage Logging of Trees." *Sacramento Bee,* September 9, 1992.

————. "Hopes for Reform Improve." *Sacramento Bee,* June 13, 1991.

————. "Majesty and Tragedy: The Sierra in Peril." *Sacramento Bee,* June 9, 1991.

————. "President OKs Hike in Salvage Logging." *Sacramento Bee,* September 10, 1992.

————. "Sierra Is Facing a Wide Range of Threats, Panel Says." *Sacramento Bee,* November 19, 1991.

————. "Sierra Nevada Hurting, Draft of Key Report Says." *Sacramento Bee,* March 3, 1996.

————. "Sierra's Problem: Too Many People." *Sacramento Bee,* June 11, 1996.

————. "Smog Fouls Crystal-Clear Mountain Air." *Sacramento Bee,* June 10, 1991.

————. "Today, the Sierra Nevada Forest Is Dying." *Sacramento Bee,* June 11, 1991.

————. "Yosemite: How Best to Love It." *Sacramento Bee,* November 6, 1991.

Krefting, Steven. "Sequoia and Kings Canyon National Park Planning: A Golden Opportunity for a Special Place." *Wilderness Record,* May 1998.

Krist, John. "Dam Builders Win Symbolic Victory." *High Country News,* September 30, 2002.

Kroeber, A. L. *Basic Report on California Indian Land Holdings, VI.* New York: Garland, 1974.

Lane, Franklin. Secretary of the Interior, Letter to Stephen T. Mather, Director, National Park Service, May 13, 1918. In *America's National Park System: The Critical Documents.* ed. Lary Dilsaver. Lanham, MD: Rowman and Littlefield, 1994.

Langworthy, Franklin. *Scenery of the Plains, Mountains, and Mines.* Ed. Paul C. Phelps from the 1855 edition. Princeton, NJ: Princeton University Press, 1932.

Lardner, W. B., and M. J. Brock. *History of Placer and Nevada Counties, California.* Los Angeles: Historic Record Co., 1924.

Langston, Nancy. *Forest Dreams, Forest Nightmares: The Paradox of Old Growth in the Inland West.* Seattle: University of Washington Press, 1995.

Larson, D. J. "Historical Water-Use Priorities and Public Policies." *Sierra Nevada Ecosystem Project, Final Report to Congress.* Vol. 2. *Assessments and Scientific Basis for Management Options.* Davis, CA: University of California, Centers for Water and Wildland Management, 1996.

Lawton, H. W., P. J. Wilke, M. DeDecker, and W. M. Mason. "Agriculture among the Paiute of Owens Valley." In *Before the Wilderness: Environmental Management by Native Americans,* ed. Thomas Blackburn and Kat Anderson. Menlo Park, CA: Ballena Press, 1993.

Leavenworth, Stuart. "Battle for the Forest, Sweeping Plan May Bring More Logging." *Sacramento Bee,* January 30, 2003.

————. "Sierra Plan Calls for More Logging." *Sacramento Bee,* June 6, 2003.

Le Conte, Joseph. *A Journal of Rambling through the High Sierra of California by the University Excursion Company.* 1875. Reprint, San Francisco: Sierra Club, 1930.

Lee, Vicki. "Chapter Chair's Report." *Mother Lode Chapter Bonanza* 63, no. 1 (February–March, 2001).

Leiberg, John B. *Forest Conditions in the Northern Sierra Nevada, California.* Professional Paper # 8, Series H, Forestry, 5. Washington, DC: Government Printing Office, 1902.

Lekisch, Barbara. *Tahoe Place Names: The Origin and History of Names in the Lake Tahoe Basin.* Lafayette, CA: Great West, 1988.

Lemmon, J. G. "Report of the State Botanist." In *Second Biennial Report of the California State Board of Forestry for the Years 1887–1888.* Sacramento: State Office, 1888.

Leonard, Zenas. *Adventures of a Mountain Man: The Narrative of Zenas Leonard.* Lincoln: University of Nebraska Press, 1978.

Leopold, A. Starker. "Wildlife Management in the National Parks." In *America's National Park System: The Critical Documents,* ed. Lary M. Dilsaver. Lanham, MD: Rowman and Littlefield, 1997.

Letter to the Chief of the Forest Service from Committee Chairpersons, Congress of the United States, January 19, 1993, *Sierra Nevada Ecosystem Project: Progress Report,* Appendix.

Letter to the Chief of the Forest Service from Four Congressmen, Congress of the United States, January 26, 1993, *Sierra Nevada Ecosystem Project: Progress Report,* Appendix.

Levy, Richard. "Eastern Miwok." In *Handbook of North American Indians.* Vol. 8, *California,* ed. Robert F. Heizer. Washington, DC: Smithsonian Institution, 1978.

Lewis, David R. "Argonauts on the Oregon Trail." In *New Directions in California History,* ed. James Rawls. New York: McGraw-Hill, 1988.

Lewis, Henry T. "In Retrospect." In *Before the Wilderness: Environmental Management by Native Americans,* ed. Thomas Blackburn and Kat Anderson. Menlo Park, CA: Ballena Press, 1993.

———. "Patterns of Indian Burning in California: Ecology and Ethnohistory [1973]." In *Before the Wilderness: Environmental Management by Native Americans,* ed. Thomas Blackburn and Kat Anderson. Menlo Park, CA: Ballena Press, 1993.

Liljeblad, Sven, and Catherine S. Fowler. "Owens Valley Paiute." In *Handbook of North American Indians.* Vol. 11, *Great Basin,* ed. Warren L. D'Azevedo. Washington, DC: Smithsonian Institution, 1986.

Limbaugh, Ronald H. "Making Old Tools Work Better: Pragmatic Adaptation and Innovation in Gold-Rush Technology." In *A Golden State: Mining and Economic Development in Gold Rush California,* ed. James J. Rawls and Richard J. Orsi. Berkeley: University of California Press and California Historical Society, 1998–99.

Limerick, Patricia Nelson. *Legacy of Conquest: The Unbroken Past of the American West.* New York: W. W. Norton, 1987.

Little, Jane Braxton. "A New Plan Frames the Sierra Nevada." *High Country News,* February 12, 2001.

———. "A Year Later, Quincy Forest Plan Leaves Saws Mostly Quiet." *Sacramento Bee*, August 21, 2000.

———. "New Forest Plan Leaves Owls in a Lurch." *High Country News*, May 12, 2003.

Little, Jane Braxton, and News Service assistance. "Salvage Tree Cutting Abuse Cited in Report: Some Sales Had Mostly Live Trees." *Sacramento Bee*, December 13, 1996.

Los Angeles Department of Water and Power. "Bird Studies Research Findings" and "DWP Operations in the Mono Basin." In *Mono Lake Background*. Pamphlet in possession of author, n.d.

Lowett, Richard. "The Hetch Hetchy Controversy, Phase II: The 1913 Senate Debate." *California History* 74, no. 2 (summer 1995).

Macauley, Tom. "Truckee and the Ice Harvest." In *Fire and Ice: A Portrait of Truckee*, ed. Paul A. Lord. Truckee, CA: Truckee Donner Historical Society, 1981.

Mallea-Olaetxe, J. *Speaking through the Aspens: Basque Tree Carvings in California and Nevada*. Reno: University of Nevada Press, 2000.

Malone, Michael P., and Richard W. Etulain. *The American West: A Twentieth-Century History*. Lincoln: University of Nebraska Press, 1989.

Mann, Ralph. *After the Gold Rush: Society in Grass Valley and Nevada City, California, 1849–1870*. Stanford, California: Stanford University Press, 1982.

Manson, Marsden. "Observations on the Denudation of Vegetation—A Suggested Remedy for California." *Sierra Club Bulletin* 2, no. 6 (June 1899). San Francisco: Sierra Club, 1950.

Margolin, Malcolm, ed. *The Way We Lived: California Indian Reminiscences, Stories, and Song*. Berkeley: Heyday, 1981.

Margolis, Jon. "How a Foe Saved the Quincy Library Group's Bacon." *High Country News*, September 29, 1997.

Markley, R., and C. Meisenbach. "Historical Summary: Tahoe National Forest Environmental History." Typescript, Tahoe National Forest Archives, Nevada City, CA, 1995.

Marston, Ed. "The Timber Wars Evolve into a Divisive Peace." *High Country News*, September 29, 1997.

Martin, Glen. "Forest Service Considers More Logging in Sierra: Agency May Amend New Framework." *San Francisco Chronicle*, January 1, 2002. S.F. Chronicle Electronic Data Base, 2–3.

———. "Sierra Plan Protects Timber: Agriculture Dept. OKs Tough Rules for Forest Management." *San Francisco Chronicle*, December 28, 2001, S.F. Chronicle Electronic Data Base Source, three pages.

———. "White House Approves Timber Management in the Sierra Nevada." *San Francisco Chronicle*, December 29, 2001.

Matthes, François. *The Incomparable Valley: A Geologic Interpretation of the Yosemite*. Ed. Fritiof Fryxell. Berkeley: University of California Press, 1956.

May, J. T., Roger L. Hothem, Charles N. Alpers, and Matthew A. Law. *Mercury*

Bioaccumulation in Fish in a Region Affected by Historic Gold Mining: The South Yuba River, Deer Creek, and Bear River Watersheds, California, 1999. Sacramento: USGS, 2000.

May, Phillip R. *Origins of Hydraulic Mining in California.* Oakland, CA: Holmes, 1970.

Mayer, Jim, and Patrick Hoge. "The Struggle for Mono Lake." *Sacramento Bee,* July 10, 1994.

Mayfield, Thomas Jefferson. *Indian Summer: Traditional Life among the Choinumne Indians of California's San Joaquin Valley.* Berkeley: Heyday Press–California Historical Society, 1993.

McBride, J. R., W. Russell, and S. Kloss. "Impact of Human Settlement." Vol. 2. *Assessments and Scientific Basis for Management Options.* Davis, CA: University of California, Centers for Water and Wildland Resources, 1996.

McCabe, Michael. "Forest Chief Upholds Sierra Protections: New Management Plan Reduces Logging." *San Francisco Chronicle,* November 17, 2001, S.F. Chronicle Electronic Data Base Source, two pages.

———. "Yosemite Closed Indefinitely." *San Francisco Chronicle,* January 9, 1997.

McCall, William. "Southerners Now Hold Key Posts on Land-Use Panels." *San Francisco Chronicle,* November 22, 2002.

McCarthy, Helen. "Managing Oaks and the Acorn Crop." In *Before the Wilderness: Environmental Management by Native Californians,* ed. Thomas C. Blackburn and Kat Anderson. Menlo Park, CA: Ballena Press, 1993.

McKelvey, Kevin, and James Johnston. "Historical Perspectives on Forests of the Sierra Nevada and the Transverse Ranges of Southern California." Chapter 11 in J. Verner et al., technical coordinators, *The California Spotted Owl: A Technical Assessment of Its Current Status.* Albany, CA: Pacific Southwest Research Station, July 1992.

McKelvey, Kevin S., et al. "An Overview of Fire in the Sierra Nevada." *Sierra Nevada Ecosystem Project, Final Report to Congress.* Vol. 2. *Assessments and Scientific Basis for Management Options.* Davis, CA: University of California, Centers for Water and Wildlands Resources, 1996.

McLaughlin, J. S. "A Plan for Use of Fire in Ecosystem Management. Middle Fork of Kings River, February 29, 1968." In *America's National Park System: The Critical Documents,* ed. Lary M. Dilsaver. Lanham, MD: Rowman and Littlefield, 1997.

Meals, Hank. *Columbia Hill, Nevada County, California: An Interpretive History.* Nevada City, CA: Susan Lamela, November 1997.

———. "Mercury Use and Gold Mining, Yuba River Watershed, 1849–1941." Typescript, Tahoe National Forest, 1995.

Merchant, Carolyn, ed. *Green versus Gold: Sources in California's Environmental History.* Washington, DC: Island Press, 1998.

———. *Major Problems in American Environmental History.* Lexington, MA: D. C. Heath, 1993.

Merriam, C. H. "Indian Village and Camp Sites in Yosemite Valley." In *A Collection of Ethnographical Articles on the California Indians,* ed. Robert F. Heizer. Ramona, CA: Ballena Press, 1917, 1976.

Meschery, Joanne. *Truckee: An Illustrated History of the Town and Its Surroundings.* Truckee, CA: Rocking Stone Press, 1978.

Miller, Char. *Gifford Pinchot: Making of Modern Environmentalism.* Washington, DC: Island Press, 2001.

Milliken, Randall. *A Time of Little Choice: The Disintegration of Tribal Culture in the San Francisco Bay Area, 1769–1810.* Menlo Park, CA: Ballena Press, 1995.

Moeller, Dave. "Higher Cut Levels on Sierra Proposed." *Grass Valley Union,* June 7, 2003.

Mono Lake Committee. "The Destruction of Mono Lake Is Right on Schedule." Newsprint tabloid in possession of author, n.d.

Moore, James G. *Exploring the Highest Sierra.* Stanford: Stanford University Press, 2000.

Moratto, Michael J. *California Archeology.* Orlando: Academic Press, 1984.

Moratto, M. J., T. F. King, and W. B. Wolfenden. "Archaeology and California's Climate." *The Journal of California Archeology* 5, no. 2 (winter 1978).

"More Logging to Save Trees." Editorial. *San Francisco Chronicle,* January 30, 2003.

Mount, Jeffrey. *California Rivers and Streams: The Conflict between Fluvial Process and Land Use.* Berkeley: University of California Press, 1995.

Muir, John. "Address on the Sierra Forest Reservation." Proceedings of the Meeting of the Sierra Club, November 23, 1895. *Sierra Club Bulletin* 1 (1896).

———. "By-ways of Yosemite Travel." *Overland,* vol. 13, September 1874.

———. *John of the Mountains: The Unpublished Journals of John Muir.* Ed. Linnie Marsh Wolfe. Madison: University of Wisconsin Press, 1938.

———. *The Mountains of California.* Garden City, NY: Doubleday, 1894, 1961.

———. *My First Summer in the Sierra.* 1911. Reprint, Boston: Houghton Mifflin, 1976.

———. "The New Sequoia Forests of California." [*Harper's,* 1873]. In *The Coniferous Forests and Big Trees of the Sierra Nevada by John Muir, 1878–1881,* ed. William Jones. Olympic Valley, CA: Outbooks, 1977.

———. "Peaks and Glaciers of the High Sierra." In *West of the Rocky Mountains,* ed. John Muir. Philadelphia: Running Press, 1976.

———. *Picturesque California.* 1888. Reprinted, Golden, CO: Outbooks, 1978.

———. *The Yosemite.* San Francisco: Sierra Club Books, 1914, 1988.

Muir, John, ed. *West of the Rocky Mountains.* Philadelphia: Running Press, 1976.

Myrick, David. *Railroads of Nevada and Eastern California.* Vol. 1. Berkeley: Howell-North, 1962.

Myrtle, Frederick S. "Our Spaulding-Drum Development Recognized as a World Feature." *Pacific Service Magazine* 6 (November 1913).

Nash, Roderick. *American Environmentalism.* 3d ed. New York: McGraw-Hill, 1990.

National Park Service. *Draft Yosemite Valley Plan: Executive Summary.* Yosemite. National Park, CA: National Park Service, April 2000, table B, 4–40.

————. *Draft Yosemite Valley Plan: Supplemental Environmental Impact Statement.* Washington, DC: Government Printing Office, April 2000.

————. *Draft Yosemite Valley Plan: Supplemental Environmental Impact Statement.* Yosemite, CA: Yosemite National Park, 2000.

————. *Merced Wild and Scenic River: Draft Comprehensive Management Plan and Supplemental Impact Statement.* Yosemite, CA: National Park Service, January 2000.

Newell, Olive. *Tail of the Elephant: The Emigrant Experience on the Truckee Route of the California Trail, 1844–1852.* Nevada City, CA: Nevada County Historical Society.

Nichols, Mary D. Secretary, State of California Resources Agency. "Press Release," March 17, 2003.

"No Forest Fingerprints: Bush Team Chips Away at Wildlife Protections." Editorial. *Sacramento Bee,* December 4, 2002.

Nordhoff, Charles. *Northern California, Oregon, and the Sandwich Islands.* 1874. Reprint, Berkeley: Ten Speed Press, 1974.

Oelschlaeger, Max. *The Idea of Wilderness: From Prehistory to the Age of Ecology.* New Haven: Yale University Press.

Omarzu, Tim. "Mercury Study to Be Discussed." *Grass Valley Union,* June 24, 2000.

Olmsted, Frederick Law. Letter to Virgil Williams, Thomas Hill, and Carleton Watkins, Yo Semite, August 9, 1865. In *The Papers of Frederick Law Olmsted,* ed. V. P. Ranney. Vol. 5, *The California Frontier, 1863–1865.* Baltimore: Johns Hopkins University Press, 1990.

————. "Preliminary Report upon the Yosemite and Big Tree Grove, August 1865." In *The Papers of Frederick Law Olmsted,* ed. V. P. Ranney. Vol. 5, *The California Frontier, 1863–1865.* Baltimore: Johns Hopkins University Press, 1990.

O'Neill, Elizabeth S. *Meadow in the Sky: A History of Yosemite's Tuolumne Meadows Region.* Groveland, CA: Albicaulis Press, 1984.

Opie, John. *Nature's Nation: An Environmental History of the United States.* Fort Worth: Harcourt Brace College Publishers, 1998.

Osborn, Barbara Barte. "Lawsuit Delays Salvage Logging Operations." *Sacramento Bee,* January 1, 1997.

Orsi, Richard J. "'Wilderness Saint' and 'Robber Baron': The Anomalous Partnership of John Muir and the Southern Pacific Co. for the Protection of Yosemite National Park." *Pacific Historian* 29, nos. 2 & 3 (summer/fall 1985).

Overbay, James C. "An Ecosystem Approach to Multiple-Use, Sustained-Yield Management." Address to "National Workshop on Taking an Ecological Approach to Management." April 27, 1992. Copy in Tahoe National Forest Archives, Nevada City, CA.

Palmer, Tim. *Endangered Rivers and the Conservation Movement.* Berkeley: University of California Press, 1986.

————. *The Sierra Nevada: A Mountain Journey.* Washington, DC: Island Press, 1988.

————. *Stanislaus: The Struggle for a River.* Berkeley: University of California Press, 1982.

Palmer, Tim, and Ann Vileisis. *The South Yuba: A Wild and Scenic River Report by the South Yuba Citizens League.* Nevada City, CA: SYRCL, 1993.

Parker, Albert J. "Fire in Sierra Nevada Forests: Evaluating the Ecological Impact of Burning by Native Americans." In *Fire, Native Peoples, and the Natural Landscape,* ed. Thomas R. Vale. Washington, DC: Island Press, 2002.

Parsons, D., and V. King. *Scientific Research in Sequoia and Kings Canyon National Parks: An Annotated Bibliography.* Three Rivers, CA: Sequoia Natural History Association, April 1980.

Parsons, David, and Patricia Haggerty. *Scientific Research in Sequoia and Kings Canyon National Parks: An Annotated Bibliography, Update: 1980–1986.* San Francisco: U.S. Department of the Interior, NPS, Western Regional Office, n.d.

Paul, Rodman. *California Gold: The Beginning of Mining in the Far West.* Lincoln: University of Nebraska Press, 1947.

———. *The Far West and Great Plains in Transition, 1859–1900.* New York: Harper and Row, 1988.

Perlot, Jean-Nicolas. *Gold Seeker: Adventures of a Belgian Argonaut during the Gold Rush Years.* Trans. and ed. with an introduction by Howard R. Lamar. New Haven: Yale University Press, 1985.

Peterson, Robert M. *A Case Study of a Northern California Indian Tribe.* San Francisco: R and E Research Associates, 1977.

Peyton, Carrie. "Tahoe's Depth Ranking Secure." *Sacramento Bee,* August 30, 1998.

Phillips, George H. *The Enduring Struggle: Indians in California History.* San Francisco: Boyd and Fraser, 1981.

———. *Indians and Indian Agents: The Origins of the Reservation System in California, 1849–1852.* Norman: University of Oklahoma Press, 1997.

———. *Indians and Intruders in Central California, 1769–1849.* Norman: University of Oklahoma Press, 1993

Phillips, Jeff. "Treasures and Troubles of the Sierra Nevada." *Sunset,* May 1992.

Philp, Tom. "Fallout from a Logging Consensus in the Sierra." *Sacramento Bee,* November 9, 1997, Forum.

———. "Logging Directives for Sierra Don't Jibe." *Sacramento Bee,* January 29, 2001.

———. "Will View from Half Dome Include a Parking Plaza?" *Sacramento Bee,* January 2, 1994.

———. "Yosemite Plan Hits Heavy Resistance at Public Hearings." *Sacramento Bee,* February 2, 1992.

Pierson, Gustavus. "Recollection: Trip to Yosemite in 1855, Given to Bancroft Library in 1880." Bancroft Library, C-D 136.

Pinchot, Gifford. *The Use of the National Forests.* Washington, DC: USDA, Forest Service, 1907).

Pisani, Donald J. "'I am resolved not to interfere, but to permit all to work freely': The Gold Rush and American Resource Law." In *A Golden State: Mining and Economic Development in Gold Rush California,* ed. James J. Rawls and Richard J.

Orsi. San Francisco: University of California Press and California Historical Society, 1998–99.

———. "Lost Parkland: Lumbering and Park Proposals in the Tahoe-Truckee Basin." *Journal of Forest History* 21 (January 1977).

———. "The Polluted Truckee: A Study in Interstate Water Quality, 1870–1934." *Nevada Historical Society Quarterly* 20, no. 3 (fall 1977).

———. *Water, Land, and Law in the West: The Limits of Public Policy, 1850–1920.* Lawrence: University Press of Kansas, 1996.

Pomeroy, Earl. *In Search of the Golden West: The Tourist in Western America.* New York: Alfred Knopf, 1957.

Powell, Bradley E. *Record of Decision: Sierra Nevada Forest Plan Amendment, Environmental Impact Statement.* Vallejo, CA: Forest Service, R5 Regional Office, January 2001.

———. *Sierra Nevada Forest Plan Amendment: Final Environmental Impact Statement, Record of Decision.* Vallejo, CA: Forest Service, R5 Regional Office, January 2001.

Powers, Stephen. *Tribes of California.* 1875. Reprint, Berkeley: University of California Press, 1976.

Preston, William. "Serpent in the Garden: Environmental Change in Colonial California." In *Contested Eden: California before the Gold Rush,* ed. Ramón Gutiérrez and Richard J. Orsi. San Francisco: University of California and the California Historical Society, 1998.

Princetl, Stephanie S. *Transforming California: A Political History of Land Use and Development.* Baltimore: Johns Hopkins University Press, 1999.

Putnam, R. F. "Diary, April 18, 1862–June 18, 1876." MS 1734, California Historical Society Library.

Pyne, Stephen J. *Fire in America: A Cultural History of Wildland and Rural Fire.* Princeton, NJ: Princeton University Press, 1982.

Rauber, Paul. "The Lion and the Lamb: What Happens When a Protected Predator Eats an Endangered Species?" *Sierra* (March–April, 2001).

Rawls, James J., and Richard J. Orsi, eds. *A Golden State: Mining and Economic Development in Gold Rush California.* San Francisco: University of California Press and California Historical Society, 1998–99.

"Redwood National Park Revising Management Plan." *California Indian Basketweavers Association Newsletter,* 25 (December 1996).

Reynolds, Linda A. "The Role of Indian Tribal Governments and Communities in Regional Land Management." In *Sierra Nevada Ecosystem Project, Final Report to Congress.* Vol. 2. *Assessments and Scientific Basis for Management Options.* Davis, CA: University of California Centers for Water and Wildland Resources, 1996.

Rice, R. B., W. A. Bullough, and R. J. Orsi. *The Elusive Eden: A New History of California.* 2nd ed. New York: McGraw-Hill, 1996.

Richardson, Elmo R. *Politics of Conservation: Crusades and Controversies, 1897–1913.* Berkeley: University of California Press, 1962.

———. "The Struggle for the Valley: California's Hetch Hetchy Controversy, 1905–1913." in *California Historical Society Quarterly* 38 (3 September 1959).

Riddell, Francis A. "Maidu and Konkow." In *Handbook of North American Indians.* Vol. 8, *California,* ed. Robert F. Heizer. Washington, DC: Smithsonian Institution, 1978.

Roberts, Paul. "The Federal Chain-Saw Massacre: Clinton's Forest Service and Clear-Cut Corruption." *Harper's ,* June 1997.

———. "The Federal Chain-Saw Massacre." *Sacramento Bee,* Forum, May 25, 1997.

Robertson, Dale. "Ecosystem Management of the National Forests and Grasslands." Press release to all Regional Foresters and Station Directors, June 4, 1992. Copy in Tahoe National Forest Archives, Nevada City, CA.

———. "Ecosystem Management, Public Involvement, and Clearcutting." Directive to all Regional Foresters and Station Directors, June 25, 1992. In Tahoe National Forest Archives, Nevada City, CA.

Rodgers, Andrew D. *Bernhard Eduard Fernow: A Story of American Forestry.* Durham, NC: Forest History Society, 1991.

Rohe, Randall. "Mining's Impact on the Land." In *Green versus Gold: Sources in California's Environmental History,* ed. Carolyn Merchant. Washington, DC: Island Press, 1998.

Rohrbough, Malcolm J. *Days of Gold: The California Gold Rush and the American Nation.* Berkeley: University of California Press, 1997.

Rosenberg, Michael. "Dam Talk in Auburn" *Western Slope Connection* 2, no. 7 (April 26–May 9, 1977).

———. "Disney Lobbies Supervisors: 'Total Commitment to Project.'" *Western Slope Connection* 2, no. 7 (April 26–May 9, 1977).

———. "State to Expedite Disney Permit Process." *Western Slope Connection* 2, no. 4 (March 15–28, 1977).

Rothman, Hal K. *The Greening of a Nation? Environmentalism in the United States since 1945.* Fort Worth: Harcourt Brace College Publishers, 1998.

Rowley, William D. *U.S. Forest Service Grazing and Rangelands: A History.* College Station: Texas A&M Press, 1985.

Rubin, Hal. "Lake Tahoe: A Tale of Two States." *Sierra* 66, no. 6 (November/December 1981).

Runte, Alfred. "Introduction: The California National Parks Centennial." In *Yosemite and Sequoia: A Century of California National Parks,* ed. Richard J. Orsi, Alfred Runte, and Marlene Smith-Baranzini. Berkeley: University of California Press and California Historical Society, 1993.

———. *National Parks: The American Experience.* 2d ed. Lincoln: University of Nebraska Press, 1987.

———. "Planning Yosemite's Future: A Historic Perspective." In *Yosemite and Sequoia: A Century of California National Parks,* ed. Richard J. Orsi, Alfred Runte, and Marlene Smith-Baranzini. Berkeley: University of California Press and California Historical Society, 1993.

———. *Public Lands, Public Heritage: The National Forest Idea.* Niwot, CO: Roberts Rinehart, 1991.

―――. *Yosemite: The Embattled Wilderness.* Lincoln: University of Nebraska Press, 1990.

"Rush Creek Lawsuit Still Holds Water: Court Asked to Stabilize Mono Lake." *Mono Lake Newsletter* 8, no. 1 (summer 1985).

Russell, Carl. *One Hundred Years in Yosemite: The Story of a Great Park and Its Friends.* Berkeley: University of California Press, 1947.

Ruth, Larry. "Conservation and Controversy." *Sierra Nevada Ecosystem Project Final Report to Congress.* Vol. 2. *Assessments and Scientific Basis for Management Options.* Davis: University of California, Centers for Water and Wildland Resources, 1996.

Sacramento Regional County Sanitation District. *Sacramento River Mercury Control Planning Project: Final Report.* Sacramento: SRCSD, March 1997.

Salwasser, Hal. "An Ecosystem Perspective for Managing the National Forests and Grasslands." Speech given to the Blue Mountain Biodiversity Conference, Walla Walla, WA, May 29, 1992. Copy in Tahoe National Forest Archives, Nevada City, CA.

San Francisco Chronicle. Editorial [Clinton Roadless Initiative]. November 15, 2000.

San Francisco Chronicle. Editorial [Sierra Nevada Framework Problems]. *San Francisco Chronicle,* May 4, 2000.

San Francisco Chronicle. Electronic Data Base Source, Editorial, "Don't Undercut Sierra Plan." *San Francisco Chronicle,* January 20, 2002.

Sargent, Shirley. *Yosemite and Its Innkeepers: The Story of a Great Park and Its Chief Concessionaires.* Foreword by Horace M. Albright. Yosemite, CA: Flying Spur Press, 1975.

Satz, Ronald N. *American Indian Policy in the Jacksonian Era.* Lincoln: University of Nebraska Press, 1975.

Schaffer, Jeffrey P. *The Geomorphic Evolution of the Yosemite Valley and the Sierra Nevada Landscapes.* Berkeley, CA: Wilderness Press, 1997.

Schmidt, Peter J. *Back to Nature: The Arcadian Myth in Urban America.* Baltimore: Johns Hopkins University Press, 1969.

Schoenherr, Allan A. *A Natural History of California.* Berkeley: University of California Press, 1992.

Schrepfer, Susan R. "Establishing Administrative 'Standing': The Sierra Club and the Forest Service, 1897–1956." In *American Forests: Nature, Culture, and Politics.* Ed. Char Miller. Lawrence, Kansas: University Press of Kansas, 1997.

―――. "Perspectives on Conservation: Sierra Club Strategies in Mineral King." *Journal of Forest History* 20 (October 1976).

Sedjo, Roger A. "Forest Resources: Resilient and Serviceable." In *America's Renewable Resources: Historical Trends and Current Challenges,* ed. K. D. Frederick and R. A. Sedjo. Washington, DC: Resources for the Future, 1991.

Sellars, Richard W. *Preserving Nature in the National Parks.* New Haven: Yale University Press, 1997.

Senate Select Committee on Reforestation. "Illustrating the Lumber Industry in the California Pine Region." LC #2485, September, 4, 1923.

Shabecoff, Philip. *Earth Rising: American Environmentalism in the 21st Century.* Washington, DC: Island Press, 2000.

———. *A Fierce Green Fire: The American Environmental Movement.* New York: Hill and Wang, 1993.

Show, S. B., and E. I. Kotok. *Forest Fires in California, 1911–1920: An Analytical Study.* Washington, DC: USDA Circular 243, Government Printing Office, February 1923.

———. *The Role of Fire in the California Pine Forests.* Washington, DC: USDA, Department Bulletin No. 1924, December 1924.

Sierra Business Council. *Planning for Prosperity.* Truckee, CA: Sierra Business Council, 1997.

———. *Sierra Nevada Wealth Index.* Truckee, CA: Sierra Business Council, 1996.

"Sierra College Ecostudents." *The Auburn Dam Reader,* vols. 1 and 2 (Rocklin, CA: Ecostudents of Sierra College, Sewall Hall, April 1996).

Sierra Economic Summit. "The Sierra Economy, Sustainable Development in Harmony with Nature." Sierra Economic Summit Conference, Sacramento, June 16–17, 1993.

Sierra Nevada Ecosystem Project. *Sierra Nevada Ecosystem Project, Final Report to Congress.* Vol. 1, *Assessment Summaries and Management Strategies.* Davis: University of California, Centers for Water and Wildland Resources, 1996.

———. *Final Report to Congress.* Vol. 2, *Assessments and Scientific Basis for Management Options.* Davis: University of California, Centers for Water and Wildland Resources, 1996.

———. *Final Report to Congress.* Vol. 3, *Assessments, Commissioned Reports, and Background Information.* Davis, University of California, Centers for Water and Wildland Resources, 1996.

———. *Final Report to Congress, Addendum.* Davis: University of California, Centers for Water and Wildland Resources, 1997.

Sierra Nevada Ecosystem Project Science Team. *Sierra Nevada Ecosystem Project: Progress Report.* Davis, CA: Sierra Nevada Ecosystem Project Center, May 1994, Appendix A and Executive Summary.

———. *Summary of the Sierra Nevada Ecosystem Project.* Davis: University of California, Centers for Water and Wildland Resources, 1996.

Sierra Nevada Ecosystem Project Steering Committee. "Sierra Nevada Ecosystem Project Charge from the Steering Committee." In *Sierra Nevada Ecosystem Project: Progress Report,* Appendix E.

Sierra Nevada Forest Protection Campaign. "New Sierra Management Plan Needs to Address Many Important Issues." *Stand* 2, no. 3 (summer/fall 1998).

"Sierra Nevada Forest Protection Campaign Releases New Analysis: S. 1028—The Quincy Logging Bill—Would Log More Acres of Ancient Forest Than Headwaters." *Business Wire, Electric Library,* February 17, 1998.

Sierra Nevada Group, Sierra Club, and Others. "Save the Tahoe National Forest." Tabloid newspaper prepared by the Sierra Nevada Group of the Sierra Club, Protect American River Canyons, and South Yuba River Citizens League, 1986, in collection of author.

Sierra Nevada Summit Steering Committee. *The Sierra Nevada: Report of the Sierra Nevada Summit Steering Committee.* Sacramento: Resources Agency, July 1992.

Sierra Now. "Sierra Now: A Vision for the Future." Conference summary, 1993.

Skinner, Carl N., and Chi-Ru Chang. "Fire Regimes, Past and Present." *Sierra Nevada Ecosystem Project, Final Report to Congress, vol. II, Assessments and Scientific Basis for Management Options.* Davis, CA: University of California, Center for Water and Wildlands Resources, 1996.

Smith, Charles R. "Tubatulabl." In *Handbook of North American Indians.* Vol. 8, *California,* ed. Robert F. Heizer. Washington, DC: Smithsonian Institution, 1978.

Smith, Duane A. *Mining in America: The Industry and the Environment, 1800–1980.* Niwot, CO: University Press of Colorado, 1993.

———. "Mother Lode for the West: California Mining Men and Methods." In *A Golden State: Mining and Economic Development in Gold Rush California,* ed. James J. Rawls and Richard J. Orsi. San Francisco: University of California Press and California Historical Society, 1998–99.

Smith, Jedediah S. *The Southwest Expedition of Jedediah S. Smith: His Personal Account of the Journey to California, 1826–1827.* Ed. G. R. Brooks. Lincoln: University of Nebraska Press, 1977.

Smith, Michael. *Pacific Visions: California Scientists and the Environment, 1850–1915.* New Haven: Yale University Press, 1987.

Smith, Paul. "Highway Planning in California's Mother Lode: The Changing Townscape of Auburn and Nevada City." *California History* 59, no. 3 (fall 1980).

Smith, Zachary. *The Environmental Policy Paradox.* 2d ed. (Englewood Cliffs, NJ: Prentice Hall, 1995.

Sneed, David. "Bioregion Concept Worries Officials." *Grass Valley Union,* March 1, 1992.

———. "Owl-Protection Plan Draws Fire." *Grass Valley Union,* March 4, 1995.

———. "Supervisors Critical of Forest Service Owl Plans." *Grass Valley Union,* March 16, 1995.

Sneider, Daniel. "Forest Gumption: Blueprint for a Green Compromise." *Christian Science Monitor,* July 18, 1997.

Snyder, Gary. "Ancient Forests of the Far West." In *The Practice of the Wild: Essays by Gary Snyder.* New York: North Point Press, 1990.

———. *Mountains and Rivers without End.* Washington, DC: Counterpoint, 1996.

———. *The Practice of the Wild: Essays by Gary Snyder.* New York: North Point Press, 1990.

Solnit, Rebecca. "Among the Giants." *Sierra,* July/August, 1997, 30+, reprinted in SIRS Researcher, fall 1998.

———. *Savage Dreams: A Journey into the Landscape Wars of the American West.* New York: Vintage Books, 1994).

Spence, Mark David. *Dispossessing the Wilderness: Indian Removal and the Making of the National Parks.* New York: Oxford University Press, 2000.

Spier, Robert F. "Foothill Yokuts." In *Handbook of North American Indians.* Vol. 8, *California,* ed. Robert F. Heizer. Washington, DC: Smithsonian Institution, 1978.

——. "Monache." In *Handbook of North American Indians.* Vol. 8, *California,* ed. Robert F. Heizer. Washington, DC: Smithsonian Institution, 1978.

Spotted Owl Federal Advisory Committee. *Final Report of the California Spotted Owl Advisory Committee.* Washington, DC: Department of Agriculture, December 1, 1997.

Sprague, G. Lynn. Regional Forester. "Improving Conservation Options for National Forests in the Sierra Nevada." USDA Forest Service, Pacific Southwest Region, R5, May 1, 1998

Stanford, E. R. "A Short History of California Lumbering." M.A. thesis, University of California, Berkeley, 1924.

Starr, Kevin. *Americans and the California Dream: 1850–1915.* New York: Oxford University Press, 1973.

Starr, Kevin, and Richard J. Orsi, eds. *Rooted in Barbarous Soil: People and Culture in Gold Rush California.* San Francisco: University of California Press and the California Historical Society, 2000.

Starrs, Paul F. "The Public As Agents of Policy." In *Sierra Nevada Ecosystem Project, Final Report to Congress,* Vol. 2. *Assessments and Scientific Basis for Management Options.* Davis, CA: University of California, Centers for Water and Wildland Resources, 1996.

St. Clair, David. "The Gold Rush and the Beginnings of California Industry." In *A Golden State: Mining and Economic Development in Gold Rush California,* ed. James J. Rawls and Richard J. Orsi. San Francisco: University of California Press and California Historical Society, 1998–99.

St. Clair, Jeffrey. "Salvage Dreams." *Wild Forest Review* 3, no. 1 (February 15, 1996).

Steen, Harold K. "The Origins and Purposes of the National Forests." In *Public Lands, Public Heritage: The National Forest Idea,* by Alfred Runte. Niwot, CO: Roberts Rinehart, 1991.

——. *The U.S. Forest Service: A History.* Seattle: University of Washington Press, 1976.

Stewart, George R. *The California Trail: An Epic with Many Heroes.* New York: McGraw-Hill, 1962.

——. *Fire.* Boston: Houghton Mifflin, 1948.

Stewart, Ronald E. "Speech at Sierra Summit." November 18, 1991, in Tahoe National Forest Archives, Nevada City, CA.

——. Regional Forester to Chief, USDA Forest Service, "Strategy for Implementing Ecosystem Management, Public Involvement, and Clearcutting." September 4, 1992. In Tahoe National Forest Archives, Nevada City, CA.

——. "Strategy for Implementing Ecosystem Management and Research, Ecological Classification, Inventory, Existing Condition, Potential Condition, and Desired Condition." December 15, 1992, no pagination. In Tahoe National Forest Archives, Nevada City, CA.

——. "Strategy for Implementing Ecosystem Management and Research, Ecological Principles." December 15, 1992, no pagination. In Tahoe National Forest Archives, Nevada City, CA.

———. "Strategy for Implementing Ecosystem Management and Research, Framework." December 15, 1992, no pagination. In Tahoe National Forest Archives, Nevada City, CA.

Stewart, William. "Economic Assessment of the Ecosystem." in *Sierra Nevada Ecosystem Project, Final Report to Congress.* Vol. 3. *Assessments, Commissioned Reports, and Background Information.* Davis: University of California, Centers for Water and Wildland Resources, 1996.

Stine, Scott. "Climate, 1650–1850." In *Sierra Nevada Ecosystem Project, Final Report to Congress.* Vol. 2. *Assessments and Scientific Basis for Management Options.* Davis, CA: University of California, Centers for Water and Wildland Resources, 1996.

Stone, Christopher. *Should Trees Have Standing? Toward Legal Rights for Natural Objects.* Los Altos, CA: William Kaufman, 1972.

Storer, Tracy I., and Lloyd P. Tevis Jr. *California Grizzly.* 1955. Reprint, Lincoln: University of Nebraska Press, 1955, 1978.

Storer, Tracy I., and Robert L. Usinger. *Sierra Nevada Natural History: An Illustrated Handbook.* Berkeley: University of California Press, 1963.

Strong, Douglas H. "Disney's Independence Lake Project: A Case Study in California's Environmental Review Process." *California History* 61, no. 2 (Summer 1982).

———. *Dreamers and Defenders: American Conservationists.* Lincoln: University of Nebraska Press.

———. "A History of Sequoia National Park." PH.D. diss., Syracuse University, 1964.

———. *Tahoe: An Environmental History* Lincoln: University of Nebraska Press, 1984.

———. *Tahoe: From Timber Barons to Ecologists.* Lincoln: University of Nebraska Press, 1999.

Strong-Aufhauser, Lisa. "The Mono Lake Water War." *Earth* 4, no. 5 (October 1995).

Sudworth, George B. *Forest Trees of the Pacific Slope.* Washington, DC: Government Printing Office, 1908.

———. "Stanislaus and Lake Tahoe Forest Reserves, California and Adjacent Territory." In *Twenty-First Annual Report of the USGS, Part V, Forest Reserves.* Washington, DC: Government Printing Office, 1900.

Supernowicz, Dana E. "Historical Overview of the Eldorado National Forest." M.A. thesis, California State University, Sacramento, 1983.

Swartz, Jason. "Plumas and Lassen National Forests Slated for Devastating 'Administrative Study' Logging Plan." *Wilderness Record,* spring 2003.

Swezey, Sean L., and Robert F. Heizer. "Ritual Management of Salmonid Fish Resources in California." In *Before the Wilderness: Environmental Management by Native Californians,* ed. Thomas C. Blackburn and Kat Anderson. Menlo Park, CA: Ballena Press, 1993.

Tahoe National Forest. "Appraisal Report, Brandy City Unit, April 30, 1943." Typescript, S, Sales-Tahoe, Brandy City Unit, Proposed, TNF, Nevada City, CA.

———. "Appraisal Report, Brandy City Unit, North Yuba Working Circle, April 5, 1947." Typescript, Sales-Tahoe, Brandy City Unit, TNF, Nevada City, California.

————. *Final Environmental Statement and Timber Management Plan, Tahoe National Forest.* Nevada City, CA: USDA, Tahoe National Forest, 1978.

————. *Tahoe National Forest Land and Resources Management and Environmental Impact Statement.* Nevada City, CA: USDA, Tahoe National Forest, 1990.

————. Tahoe National Forest Land and Resources Management Plan, Appendix A (Public Participation, Issues, Concerns and Opportunities, Forest Service Response to Comments

————. Tahoe National Forest Land and Resources Management Plan, Record of Decision, 1990.

————. "Tahoe National Forest Splash Dam Study." Typescript, Tahoe National Forest Archives, Nevada City, CA, n.d.

————. "Tahoe National Forest Timber Management Policy Statement, May 15, 1949." Typescript, S, Plans, R-5, Tahoe, Timber Management Policy Statement, Tahoe National Forest, Nevada City, CA.

————. "Tahoe National Forest, Timber Management Plan for the Auburn Working Circle, CY 1959–1968." Typescript, S, Plans-Tahoe, Timber Management 1959–1968, TNF, Nevada City, CA.

————. "Timber Management Plan for the North Yuba Working Circle, Proposed Feb. 27, 1962, Approved July 1, 1963." Typescript, 2410, Plans, North Yuba Working Circle, 1960–1969, TNF, Nevada City CA.

————. "Timber Survey Report, Foresthill Project, TNF, December 21, 1940." Typescript, S, Plans, Timber Surveys-Tahoe, Foresthill Project, Tahoe National Forest, Nevada City, CA.

————. Cover Letter for Timber Management Plan for the North Yuba Working Circle, TNF, 1960–1969.

Taylor, Benjamin. *Beyond the Gates.* Chicago: S. C. Griggs n.d. [ca. 1870s].

Taylor, Ray W. *Hetch Hetchy: The Story of San Francisco's Struggle to Provide a Water Supply for Her Future.* San Francisco: Richard J. Orozco, 1926.

Teisch, Jessica. "The Drowning of Big Meadows: Nature's Managers in Progressive-Era California." *Environmental History* 4, no. 1 (January 1999).

Thayer, James B. *A Western Journey with Mr. Emerson.* Ed. Shirley Sargent. 1884. Reprint, Van Nuys, CA: Book Club of California, 1980.

Thomas, David H., Lorann S. Pendleton, and Stephen C. Cappannari. "Western Shoshone." In *Handbook of North American Indians.* Vol. 11, *Great Basin,* ed. Warren L. D'Azevedo. Washington, DC: Smithsonian Institution, 1986.

Thompson, Don. "Halt to Fish Stocking Has Anglers Angry." *San Francisco Chronicle,* A20, January 21, 2001

Thompson, Margaret A. "Overland Travel and the Central Sierra Nevada, 1827–1849." M.A. thesis, University of California, Berkeley, 1932.

Tilden, Freeman. *The National Parks.* Revised and expanded by Paul Schullery. New York: Alfred A. Knopf, 1986.

Todd, John. *Sunset Land.* Boston: Lee and Shepard, 1870.

Tomes, E. Van Vick. *Rocket of the Comstock: The Life of John W. Mackay.* New York: Ballantine, 1973.

"Truckee Timber." *Reno Gazette,* September 14, 1881.

Tucker, W. T., C. D. Zeier, and S. Raven. "Perspectives on the Ethnohistoric Period." In *Changes in Washoe Land Use Patterns,* ed. Charles D. Zeier and Robert Elston. Madison, WI: Pre-History Press, 1992.

Turner, Richard, and Laura Landro. "MCA Officials and Matsushita Plan Sale Talk." *Wall Street Journal,* September 28, 1990.

Turner, Tom. "The Government Takes a Hike." *San Francisco Chronicle,* June 24, 2001, S.F. Chronicle Electronic Data Base, 3 pp.

Twain, Mark. *Roughing It.* Vol. 2 of *The Works of Mark Twain.* Berkeley: University of California Press, 1972.

Tweed, William. *Kaweah Remembered: The Story of the Kaweah Colony and the Founding of Sequoia National Park.* Sequoia National Park: Sequoia Natural History Association, 1986.

———. "Summary for Sequoia and Kings Canyon National Park." Typescript, Sequoia and Kings Canyon National Parks Archives, Three Rivers, CA.

U.S. Department of Agriculture, Forest Service. "Departmental Regulation # 1043-41." California Spotted Owl Federal Advisory Committee. March 3, 1997. In California Spotted Owl Federal Advisory Committee, *Final Report of the California Spotted Owl Advisory Committee.* Washington, DC: Department of Agriculture, December 1, 1997).

———. *Draft Environmental Impact Statement, Managing California Spotted Owl Habitat in Sierra Nevada Forests of California: An Ecosystem Report.* San Francisco: USFS, Pacific Southwest Region, January 1995.

———. "EIS for the Herger-Feinstein Quincy Library Group Forest Recovery Act Pilot Project, Notice of Intent to Prepare an Environmental Impact Statement." December 21, 1998.

———. "EIS for the Herger-Feinstein Quincy Library Group Forest Recovery Act Pilot Project: Notice of Intent to Prepare an Environmental Impact Statement." December 21, 1998.

———. *Herger-Feinstein Quincy Library Group Forest Recovery Act Final Environmental Impact Statement.* San Francisco, USDA Forest Service, August 1999.

———. "In Brief: Sierra Nevada Framework for Conservation and Collaboration." Press release, January 22, 1999, Pacific Southwest Region.

———. Internal Communication to other Employees of the USDA FS from Paul Strong, District Biologist, Walker RD, Chippewah National Forest, Walker, Minnesota. "There's No Such Thing As an Ecosystem." August [n.d.], 1992. In Tahoe National Forest Archives, Nevada City, CA.

———. Letter from USDA, Forest Service, Washington, DC, re: PSW Region/Station's Strategy for Implementing Ecosystem Management and Research to Forest Supervisors, Staff Directors and Director, PSW Station, October 29, 1992. In Tahoe National Forest Archives, Nevada City, CA.

———. *Sierra Nevada Forest Plan Amendment: Draft Environmental Impact Statement.* Pacific Southwest Region: U.S. Forest Service, April 2000.

———. *Sierra Nevada Forest Plan Amendment: Draft Environmental Impact State-ment, Summary.* Vallejo, CA: Pacific Southwest Region, April 2000.

———. "Sierra Nevada Forest Plan Amendment DEIS: Public Comment and Public Meeting Schedule." Pacific Southwest Region, Vallejo, CA, [2000].

———. "Sierra Nevada Forest Plan Amendment DEIS: Summary of Alternatives and Comparison of Consequences." Pacific Southwest Region, Vallejo, CA, [2000].

———. *Sierra Nevada Framework for Conservation and Collaboration: Summary of Existing Management Direction, Executive Summary.* San Francisco: Pacific South-west Region, August 11, 1998).

———. "Socioeconomic Considerations in National Forest Management, Public Comment on Socioeconomic concerns about Implementation [for] the Sierra Nevada Forest Plan Amendment." December 13, 2002, Nevada City, CA.

———. *Sierra Nevada Science Review: Report of the Science Review Team Charged to Synthesize New Information of Rangewide Urgency to the National Forests of the Si-erra Nevada.* San Francisco: Pacific Southwest Research Station, July 24, 1998.

U.S. Geological Survey. "Volcano Hazards Program, Recent Earthquakes in Califor-nia and Nevada, Long Valley Special Map, April 26, 1998." Internet source.

U.S. Department of the Interior. U.S. Geological Survey Map, Martis Peak, Califor-nia and Nevada, SE/4Truckee15' Quadrangle N 3915—W 12000/7.5, 1955, Photo Revised 1969.

Utley, Robert M. *The Indian Frontier of the American West, 1846–1890.* Albuquerque: University of New Mexico Press, 1984.

Vogel, Nancy. "Sierra's Living Time Capsules: Giant Sequoias Offer Clues to Ancient Past." *Sacramento Bee,* May 24, 1999.

———. "Yosemite's Flood Damage Estimated at $178 Million." *Sacramento Bee,* Feb-ruary 1, 1997.

Wagner, Angie. "GOP's Gains Worry Environmentalists." *San Francisco Chronicle,* November 9, 2002.

Wagoner, Luther. "Report on the Forests of the Counties of Amador, Calaveras, Tuolumne, and Mariposa." *First Biennial Report of the California State Board of Forestry for the Years 1885–1886.* Sacramento: State Office, 1886.

Wallace, John. "Letters, 1851–1856." Columbia, CA, July 18, 1853. California Historical Society Library, MS 2242.

Wallace, William. "Post-Pleistocene Archeology, 9000–2000 B.C." In *Handbook of North American Indians.* Vol. 8, *California,* ed. Robert F. Heizer. Washington, DC: Smithsonian Institution, 1978.

Walsh, Denny. "High Court Denies Mokelumne Toxic Review." *Sacramento Bee,* October 5, 1994.

Walton, John. *Western Times and Water Wars: State Culture and Rebellion in Califor-nia.* Berkeley: University of California Press, 1992.

Webster, Paul. *The Mighty Sierra: Portrait of a Mountain World.* New York: Weather-vane Books, 1972.

Wedertz, Frank S. *Bodie: 1859–1900.* Bishop, CA: Sierra Media, 1969.

Western Water Policy Review Advisory Commission. *Water in the West: Challenge for the Next Century.* Denver: Western Water Policy Review Advisory Commission, 1998), CD, Sacramento–San Joaquin River Basin Study.

Wheeler, Douglas. Chairperson. *The Report of the California Timberland Taskforce.* Sacramento: Resources Agency, December 15, 1993.

White, John R., and Samuel J. Pusateri. "Atmosphere in the National Parks." In White and Pusateri, *Sequoia and Kings Canyon National Parks.* Stanford, CA: Stanford University Press, 1949.

———. *Sequoia and Kings Canyon National Parks.* Stanford, CA: Stanford University Press, 1949.

Whitney, J. D. *Geological Survey of California, Geology.* Vol. 1. *Report of Progress and Synopsis of the Field Work from 1860 to 1864.* Philadelphia: Caxton Press of Sherman and Co., Published by the Authority of the Legislature of California, 1865.

Whitney, Stephen. "Impact at Mineral King: 'A Conclusionary Document.'" *Sierra Club Bulletin,* May 1975.

Wilderness Society. *The Federal Forest Lands of the Sierra Nevada: A Citizens Guide to the Sierra Nevada Ecosystem Project.* San Francisco: Wilderness Society, October 1997.

———. *The Sierra Nevada: Renewing the Glow of the Range of Light.* San Francisco: Wilderness Society, n.d.

Wilkinson, C. F. *Crossing the Next Meridian: Land, Water, and the Future of the West.* Washington, DC: Island Press, 1992.

Wilkinson, C. F., and H. Anderson. *Land and Resource Planning in the National Forests.* Washington, DC: Island Press, 1987.

Williams, James C. *Energy and the Making of Modern California.* Akron: University of Akron Press, 1997.

Williams, Lee Lyle. "Participatory Research: Science for the People." *Practitioner* [newsletter of the National Network of Forest Practitioners], August 1998.

Williams, Michael. *Americans and Their Forests.* Cambridge, U.K.: Cambridge University Press, 1989.

Wilson, Dick. *Sawdust Trails in the Truckee Basin: A History of Lumbering Operations, 1856–1936.* Nevada City, CA: Nevada County Historical Society, 1992.

Wilson, Norman L., and Arlean H. Towne. "Nisenan." In *Handbook of North American Indians.* Vol. 8, *California,* ed. Robert F. Heizer. Washington, DC: Smithsonian Institution, 1978.

Windeler, Adolphus. *The California Gold Rush Diary of a German Sailor.* Ed. with an introduction by W. Turrentine Jackson. Berkeley: Howell-North Books, 1969.

Wirth, Conrad. "Mission 66: Special Presentation to President Eisenhower and the Cabinet." In *America's National Park System: The Critical Documents,* ed. Lary M. Dilsaver. Lanham, MD: Rowman and Littlefield, 1994.

Wolfenden, Wallace B. "Quaternary Vegetation History." *Sierra Nevada Ecosystem Project, Final Report to Congress.* Vol. 2. *Assessments and Scientific Basis for Management Options.* Davis, CA: University of California, Centers for Water and Wildland Resources, 1996.

Wood, James. "Supervisors Err on Owl Plan." *Grass Valley Union,* "Other Voices," March 31, 1995.

Work, Hubert. Secretary of the Interior. "Memorandum for the Director, National Park Service [Stephen T. Mather], March 11, 1925." In *America's National Park System: The Critical Documents,* ed. Lary M. Dilsaver. Lanham, MD: Rowman and Littlefield, 1997.

"Workshop Slated on Plan for Sierra Nevada Forest." *Grass Valley Union,* December 11, 2002.

Worster, Donald. *Nature's Economy: A History of Ecological Ideas.* Cambridge, U.K.: Cambridge University Press, 1994.

G. M. Wright, J. S. Dixon, and B. H. Thompson. *Fauna of the National Parks of the United States: Contribution of Wild Life Survey, Fauna Series No. 1, May, 1932.* Washington, DC: Government Printing Office, 1933.

———. *Fauna of the National Parks of the United States: A Preliminary Survey of Faunal Relations in the National Parks.* Washington, DC: Government Printing Office, 1933.

Wuerthner, George. *California's Sierra Nevada.* Helena, MT: American and World Geographic, 1993.

———. "Dimming the Range of Light." *Wilderness* 57, no. 203 (winter 1992).

———. "Dimming the Range of Light." In *The World of Wilderness: Essays on the Power and Purpose of Wild Country,* ed. T. H. Watkins and P. Byrnes. Niwot, CO: Wilderness Society and Roberts Rinehart, 1995.

Wurm, Ted. *Hetch Hetchy and Its Dam Railroad.* Glendale, CA: Trans-Anglo Books, 1990.

Wyckoff, William, and Lary M. Dilsaver, eds. *The Mountainous West: Explorations in Historical Geography.* Lincoln: University of Nebraska Press, 1995.

Yafee, Steven. *The Wisdom of the Spotted Owl: Policy Lessons for a New Century.* Washington, DC: Island Press, 1994.

Yosemite National Park. "Implementing the General Management Plan at Yosemite Lodge." May 1998.

———. "Planning Update." August 2000.

———. "Yosemite into the 21st Century." May 1998.

"Yosemite Park." *Overland Monthly* 12, no. 1 (January 1874).

Zeier, Charles D. "Environmental and Cultural Setting." In *Changes in Washoe Land Use Patterns,* ed. Charles D. Zeier and Robert Elston. Madison, WI: Pre-History Press, 1992.

Ziebarth, Marilyn. "California's First Environmental Battle." *California History* 63, no. 4 (fall 1984).

Zigmond, Maurice L. "Kawaiisu." In *Handbook of North American Indians.* Vol. 8, *California,* ed. Robert F. Heizer. Washington, DC: Smithsonian Institution, 1978.